THE DIARY OF
JOHN QUINCY ADAMS
1794—1845

LONGMANS, GREEN AND CO.
55 FIFTH AVENUE, NEW YORK
221 EAST 20TH STREET, CHICAGO
TREMONT TEMPLE, BOSTON
210 VICTORIA STREET, TORONTO

LONGMANS, GREEN AND CO. LTD.
39 PATERNOSTER ROW, E C 4, LONDON
53 NICOL ROAD, BOMBAY
6 OLD COURT HOUSE STREET, CALCUTTA
167 MOUNT ROAD, MADRAS

THE DIARY OF
JOHN QUINCY ADAMS

1794–1845

*American Political, Social
and Intellectual Life
from Washington to Polk*

EDITED BY
ALLAN NEVINS

LONGMANS, GREEN AND CO.
NEW YORK · LONDON · TORONTO
1928

E
377
A2

Apr. '37   3.33   Stechert (Carnegie)

25907

PREFACE

THIS volume is a selection from " The Memoirs of John
Quincy Adams, Comprising Portions of his Diary from
1795 to 1848," published by Charles Francis Adams in twelve
large volumes between 1874 and 1877. The work, an unrivalled treasury for the social and political history of the time, has
long been out of print and is now rather rare and extremely
costly. Its ponderous bulk, moreover, makes it forbidding to
the general reader, and difficult of use by the ordinary student.
The editor has selected from it those passages which seem of
the greatest permanent worth, giving emphasis to the materials which throw light on the social background of the period,
on J. Q. Adams's character, and on the more dramatic political
and diplomatic events of the time. He has hoped thus to
present in six hundred pages all that the general reader and
ordinary student will desire of the diary. The research
worker will of course always have to consult the entire set.
The editor wishes to thank the original publishers, Messrs.
J. B. Lippincott & Company, for their kind permission to make
use of these materials.

CONTENTS

PAGE

CHAPTER I: 1794–1797 1

George Washington — Minister to Holland — Jay
and His Treaty — Special Ministry to Great Britain —
Presentation to George III — Mrs. Siddons — Marriage.

CHAPTER II: 1803–1809 17

Elected to the Senate — Aaron Burr — President
Jefferson — The Chase Impeachment — Harvard
Chair of Oratory — The Slave Trade — The Embargo
— Madison's Election.

CHAPTER III: 1809–1813 60

Minister to Russia — The Czar Alexander I — Life
in St. Petersburg — America and England at War —
Napoleon Invades Russia — His Retreat and Defeat
— Gallatin and Bayard Arrive.

CHAPTER IV: 1813–1815 110

The Battle of Leipsic — A Peace Conference With
England — The Meeting at Ghent — The British Demands Rejected — Relations With Clay and Gallatin — Satisfactory Terms Arranged

CHAPTER V: 1815–1817 156

Napoleon's Return from Elba — Paris in the Hundred
Days — Special Mission to England — Castlereagh
and the Prince Regent — News of Waterloo — The
Duke of Wellington.

PAGE

CHAPTER VI: 1817–1820 184

Secretary of State — President James Monroe — Defence of Jackson's Acts in Florida — Intrigues of Henry Clay and W. H. Crawford — The Florida Treaty — The Missouri Compromise.

CHAPTER VII: 1820–1821 230

Second Election of James Monroe — W. H. Crawford's Machinations — Conversations With Calhoun — Quarrel with Stratford Canning.

CHAPTER VIII: 1821–1825 260

Internal Revenue — Quarrel With Jonathan Russell — The Holy Alliance — The Monroe Doctrine — Election Intrigues — Tour of Lafayette — Election Goes to the House — Chosen President.

CHAPTER IX: 1825–1829 343

Labor as President — Death of John Adams — Jackson's Enmity — Chesapeake & Ohio Canal Opened — Relations With Henry Clay — Jackson Chosen President.

CHAPTER X: 1829–1831 391

Retirement and Study — Jefferson's Memoirs — Quarrels of the Jackson Administration — Death of Monroe — Election to Congress.

CHAPTER XI: 1831–1835 425

Service in the Twenty-second Congress — Nullification — Jackson's Stand Approbated — Frances Kemble — Twenty-third Congress — Death of William Wirt — Harvard Affairs.

PAGE

CHAPTER XII: 1835–1838 457
Twenty-fourth and Twenty-fifth Congresses — Death
of Marshall — Benjamin Lundy — The Slavery
Question — Election of Van Buren — The Storm Over
Anti-Slavery Petitions.

CHAPTER XIII: 1839–1841 497
The Twenty-sixth Congress — Webster and Whittier
— Shoulder Dislocated — William Henry Harrison
Elected — His Inauguration and Death — Accession
of Tyler.

CHAPTER XIV: 1841–1843 523
Quarrels of the Tyler Administration — Resignation
of the Cabinet — The Bunker Hill Celebration — Tour
in the West — Ovations in New York and Ohio —
Return to Washington.

CHAPTER XV: 1843–1845. 560
The Jackson Fine Bill — Stephen A. Douglas — Ex-
plosion on the "Princeton" — The Petition Fight
Renewed — Victory Won at Last — Death.

INDEX 577

INTRODUCTION

I T was one of the remarkable Adams line — the late Brooks
Adams — who wrote that " John Quincy Adams appears
to me to be the most interesting and suggestive personage of
the early nineteenth century." A certain excessive family pride
appears in this verdict; yet we may unhesitatingly pronounce
the second Adams to be one of the most picturesque, salient,
and provocative figures in all American history. Few of our
great statesmen have had an individuality so marked; perhaps
no other has combined so many anfractuosities, humors, and
prejudices with so much ability, liberality, and high rectitude
of character. Through a long lifetime he remained outlined
with singular constancy and prominence in the public eye. He
was only eleven when he accompanied his father on the special
mission of 1778 to France. He was very young when he embarked on his own diplomatic career, in which he was to serve at
the courts of Russia, Prussia, Holland, Sweden, France, and
Great Britain. He was Senator for a decade; he was Secretary
of State for eight busy years; he was President of the United
States for four. On the raw February day when, in 1848,
death seized him as he sat industriously writing at his desk in
the House of Representatives, he had spent nearly twenty
years of unremitting battle and toil in the lower chamber of
Congress. In whatever position he was placed, he made his
peculiarities of temperament, his strong views, and his intense
determination all felt. He stamped himself with the sharpest
imprint upon his time.

John Quincy Adams obviously fell short of such success in
statesmanship as men like Thomas Jefferson and Andrew Jackson in his own time achieved; and he did so because of certain
obvious faults. He was by his experience, his natural gifts,
and his spotlesss integrity apparently one of the best-equipped
men who ever entered the Presidency. Yet his Administration
was marked by failure. It was a period when the quarrels of

factions and the jealousies of sections were peculiarly keen, and Adams's stiff, unyielding temper was quite unfit to cope with either. It was the period also of a mounting tide of rough Western democracy, and intellectually and morally (though not at all socially) Adams was an aristocrat. He did not understand the crude masses, he had no arts to win their favor, and they did not understand him. His defects of organization — his irritability, his censoriousness, his pugnacity, his chilliness — crippled him in diplomacy and in Congress, and filled his pillow with thorns. Yet it is these very flaws which make him and his careful record of his acts so picturesque, so full of savor, and so absorbingly interesting to later students. He never wrote a word, made a speech, or embarked upon a measure which did not reflect his belligerent, sensitive, independent Puritanism. The fibre of the man, gnarled, tough, indurated, yet somehow after all attractive, is always evident.

To his contemporaries he was a frigid and icy New Englander; but we who have his diary can perceive that at heart he was really of a hot and passionate nature, volcanic in his hates, intense in his loves, compact of fervent feelings, and sometimes wrought up to the most extreme emotional pitch. The emotionalism of the diary is indeed one of its most appealing qualities. With what heartfelt joy does he record how, driving through the streets of London on his first mission, he providentially heard his trunk of confidential dispatches, cut way by a thief, fall to the street, and thereby saved it and his own reputation! How frankly he describes the explosions of temper between himself and Henry Clay during the discussions at Ghent, and gives credit to the suave Albert Gallatin for interposing to calm the squalls! To what a pitch of fervent religious ecstasy or despair a sermon again and again raises or lowers him, he shedding tears as he prays! How intemperately he blurts out his ill-natured resentment when his alma mater Harvard grants an honorary degree to President Jackson on the latter's visit to Cambridge, and how vehemently he justifies his refusal to attend the ceremonies! With what disgust he comments on the visit of John Tyler to Boston to dedicate the Bunker Hill Monument, comparing the shadow of the long Presidential nose with that of the shaft! How vividly he pictures his extremity of agitation during the Congressional gag-rule debates, when after a day of battle he would return home too excited to do anything but pace the chamber! With what tenderness he exclaims over the death of his humble coachman, killed by accident at the Capitol, or over the tale of some poor negro, come to beg his help in raising money to save a wife or child from sale!

No other American diarist touched life at quite so many points, over quite so long a period, as John Quincy Adams. He walked with the Czar Alexander I on the boulevards of St. Petersburg; he had audience with George III, who wanted to know if all the Adamses came from Massachusetts; he dined with Wellington; he saw Napoleon return to Paris from Elba; and he exchanged views with Mme. de Staël and Jeremy Bentham and Talleyrand. He saw George Washington receive the Creek chiefs; he dined repeatedly at the new White House with Jefferson, listening to his " staring " stories; and he lived to witness with disgust James K. Polk received to the Presidency amid the cheers of Democrats and slaveholders. He sat in the trial of Samuel Chase, and heard Aaron Burr make his farewell address; he was Senator from Massachusetts when the news of the *Chesapeake* outrage aroused Boston; and he was one of the grim band who voted against the resolution for the annexation of Texas — a resolution with which, he wrote, perished the liberties of mankind. He commented on the transcendentalism of Emerson and the novels of Bulwer; he shook the hand of Dickens; and he superintended the erection of the sculptures on the portico of the Capitol. He took an intense interest in science, laboring over his report on weights and measures till he suffered acutely from insomnia, and making it a classic of American metrology. To him more than any other American we owe the preservation of the Smithson bequest and the establishment of the Smithsonian Museum on a sound foundation. He taught oratory in Harvard University. He published original poetry, and versified Horace and La Fontaine; he read Bancroft and Byron; he expounded Shakespeare, and was proud when James H. Hackett circulated his disquisition on *Hamlet* in England; he appeared before the Supreme Court as counsel in the famous *Amistad* case. He was the chief author of the Monroe Doctrine.

As a diarist Adams had certain evident limitations. He was self-centered, he was pedantic, and he was singularly humorless; it was hard for him to make human contacts, as he recognized when he wrote on returning from a brilliant dinner at Holland House that he was " altogether stiff and dull beyond my usual measure." He never saw the funny side of such an episode as that of the first months of his Presidency, when the boat in which he was crossing to the far bank of the Potomac for a bath sank in mid-stream, and he had to swim back clothed in his shirt and hat, which latter he soon gave to the servant with him, Antoine. We grow a little tired of the frequent waspishness of his record, which results in such lists of enemies as that of Nov. 23, 1835, where he names thirteen men — among them Clay, Calhoun, Crawford, Jackson, Webster, and John Randolph — as having " used up their faculties in base and dirty tricks to thwart my progress in life."

But he did have a keen eye for much that was picturesque in mankind and interesting in the events and changes of the day. It was a shrewd observer who noted for us that the Princess Galitzin was " venerable by the length and thickness of her beard "; that the French Minister displeased Jefferson by his profuse gold lace; that " Mr. Jefferson tells large stories "; that the Prince Regent was " a Falstaff without the wit "; that Clay, in both public and private life, was " essentially a gamester "; that President Harrison's inauguration was a " showy shabby affair "; and that Crawford under Monroe was " a worm preying upon the vitals of the Administration." There are some striking vignettes drawn for us here — Benjamin Constant contradicting Mme. de Staël; the French and British Ministers in Washington engaged in fisticuffs; Aaron Burr brazenly entering the Senate after killing Hamilton; Crawford threatening President Monroe with his cane and calling him " You damned infernal old scoundrel! "; Van Buren receiving Clay's ironic congratulations on the joys of the Presidency; Clay cracking " greasy jokes " with Count Bodisco on the latter's marriage with a young Washington girl; Vice-President Calhoun permitting John Randolph in 1826 " in speeches of ten hours long to drink himself drunk with bottled porter, and in raving balderdash of the meridian of Wapping to revile the absent and the present, the living and the dead." We see Washington in that strange day when carriages stuck in mudholes on Pennsylvania Ave., when cold weather sent most of the members of Congress to stand "all the day .at the firesides in the lobby"; when Edward Everett's orations lasted three hours; when duelling was common, and W. Cost Johnson used to address the House half-tipsy, yet John Wentworth felt it necessary to explain that he had not said "By God" profanely, but "My God" reverently; and when mendacious journalists declared that J. Q. Adams himself went about without a waistcoat or stock, and barefoot.

The Diary is at its very best when it exhibits John Quincy Adams in the full course of some of his great struggles, championing his cause with dauntless disregard of the personal consequences. Probably nowhere else in the whole library of memoirs is there so full a picture of peace negotiations as that he gives of the discussions at Ghent which closed the War of 1812. His sketch of the English commissioner Goulburn in a transport of rage over Passamaquoddy Bay; of Henry Clay just sneaking off to bed after a wine-flushed night at cards as Adams rises to begin his day's work; of Bayard stubbornly insisting upon rewriting everything that Adams drafts — this is full of life and color. Hardly elsewhere in the literature of American politics is there such a study of intrigue and jealous ambition as in his day-to-day record of the great battle for the Presidency in 1824–25, when W. H. Crawford, just seizing the prize, was stricken with paralysis, and Henry Clay was left between Jackson and Adams, uncertain for a time to which he should give his decisive support. Adams admits that he himself thrilled with ambition for the honor; and he prudently remains silent in his diary as to just what passed between him and Clay in the momentous interview which decided Clay to turn to him. Though the diary is regrettably scanty for the years 1825–1829, no other President save Polk has yet offered us so clear an insight into his feelings and impressions in the anxious routine of the Presidency; from the day he decided to make Henry Clay his Secretary of State and let the wolves howl on, to the day when he stole away from the White House at nine in the evening to Meridian Hill in order to avoid seeing Jackson triumphantly inaugurated on the morrow. Intrigue, hatred, and slander surrounded him, yet he pursued his undeviating course in the serene consciousness of high motives. But the most dramatic record of all is that of how, as an old man, he met the forces of slavery in the gate, fought the

Southern advocates of the gag-rule from session to session, and, often beaten but never despairing, after a decade of unremitting conflict won an ever-memorable victory for the great Anglo-Saxon rights of free petition and of free speech.

It was the happiest feature of Adams's public life that he lived to taste the full sweets of this victory over those whom in his acrid way he calls the slave-mongers, and to hear abolition petitions again referred to committees in the House. It was a happy fact also that he lived to make a tour of the West, in which he was able to see how warm a place his brave fight for freedom had won him in the hearts of the people of New York and Ohio. There is nothing upon which it is pleasanter to dwell than the picture of Adams upon that memorable autumn journey of 1843 to Cincinnati, whither he had been invited by Professor Mitchell to lay the cornerstone of a new observatory. " It is an arduous, hazardous, and expensive undertaking," wrote the aged statesman as he contemplated it, " the successful performance of which is more than problematical, and of the event of which it is impossible for me to foresee anything but disappointment. Yet there is a motive pure and elevated, and a purpose benevolent and generous, mingling with the impulses which in this case I obey." He was then seventy-seven, shaken by a bad catarrhal cough, and with other ailments of age; yet he intrepidly faced a journey full of frontier hardship, in a season when he would feel the worst inclemency of winter. He toiled for weeks at an oration upon astronomy, the history of which he wished to illuminate in such a way as to kindle a permanent enthusiasm for science in the West; and he drew upon every library within miles of Quincy for material. " The hand of God himself has furnished me this opportunity to do good," wrote the old man. " But oh, how much will depend upon my manner of performing that task! And with what agony of soul must I implore the aid of Almighty Wisdom for powers of conception, energy of exertion, and unconquerable will to accomplish my design! "

The reception that was given the ex-President more than repaid him for hardships which left him seriously enfeebled. The weather was freezing; crossing the Hudson, he felt " as if I were incrusted in a bed of snow," and a little later the wheels of his car froze to the rails and could not be freed for an hour. On Lake Erie he was storm-bound for a day and a

half, and found it " as cold as Nova Zembla." From Cleveland
(where he was recognized in a barber-shop) to Columbus he
had to take a packet boat for two hundred miles on the Ohio
Canal, and found it crowded with humanity. With cabin
windows closed against the driving snow, and with wood-
burning stoves making the interior excessively hot, he was glad
at last to creep into his berth, suffering from " a headache,
feverish chills, hoarseness, and a sore throat, and my tussis
senilis in full force." His boat-mates wondered at the application with which he bent to his writing in the succeeding days
as the vessel stumbled along, at two and a half miles an hour,
like a blind nag; and some of them taught him euchre, of which
he had never before heard. But at Columbus the whole town
was out to welcome him, and the remainder of his journey
southward — during which the weather happily moderated
— was one continuous ovation. At Lebanon a famous politician
of the day, Thomas Corwin, welcomed him; at Cincinnati there
were processions, crowds, music, cheers, and an open-air address. The great day of the laying of the cornerstone was
spoiled by rain; but when the postponed oration was finally
delivered, the effect was all that he wished. Then he ascended
the Ohio, with more receptions and cheering crowds at every
landing, the last of them greeting him at Pittsburgh. The aged
ex-President found something " inexpressibly irksome " in
" these massmeetings, where the most fulsome adulation is
addressed to me face to face in the presence of thousands;"
but he doubtless found something very gratifying also. Nor
can there be any doubt that this prolonged Western ovation
helped to break down the already crumbling support behind
the gag-rule.

Begun in his boyhood, and continued until just before his
death, Adams's diary enables us to trace his intellectual and
spiritual development from stage to stage of a long life. There
is more of ardor in the early pages; there is more of philosophy in the later chapters. Throughout the long record the
great salient traits of industry, of conscientiousness, of high
independence, and of patriotism are always in evidence. His
courage to do what he thought right never wavered; his love
of effort and of achievement never for a moment sank into
indolence. Throughout the diary, too, we are struck by the
Roman simplicity and dignity of the man, unaffected by changes

in place or rank. Even when President, he pursued the same plain regimen; rising at four or five, building his own fire, reading his Bible with the aid of a commentary, and accomplishing many hours of work before most men would have been out of bed; devoting his days to public affairs; laboring again in the evenings, or lamenting the pressure of society when it intruded too much upon his nightly pursuits. It is interesting to note his love of books, and particularly of political works. His attention to exercise of body was as constant as to that of mind; he delighted to take long walks, for a great part of his later life he rode daily on horseback, and his summer swims in the Potomac have always been famous. Of his devotion to his family — his parents, his wife, his children — there are many touching evidences. In his last years we see a little more of moderation and tolerance than in his younger manhood, and his attention to religion manifestly increases. Yet to the end he remained a hard fighter, and he died with his armor on, still aggressively busy in the service of his country.

In all American political literature, there is no record of the kind which approaches this in interest and value. It may safely be said that it, as much as remembrance of any specific public act of John Quincy Adams's, will keep fresh to remote ages the memory of the rotund, short, bald little man, with piercing eyes and the high shrill voice that broke sharply in moments of excitement, who played so varied, so constant, and so noble a rôle on the national stage for a long half-century and more.

THE DIARY OF
JOHN QUINCY ADAMS
1794–1845

The Diary of
JOHN QUINCY ADAMS

CHAPTER I

1794–1797

GEORGE WASHINGTON — MINISTER TO HOLLAND — JAY AND HIS
TREATY — SPECIAL MINISTRY TO GREAT BRITAIN — PRESENTATION
TO GEORGE III — MRS. SIDDONS — MARRIAGE.

Boston, June 3, 1794.[1] — When I returned to my lodgings
at the close of the evening, upon opening a letter from my
father, which I had just before taken from the postoffice I
found that it contained information that Edmund Randolph,
Secretary of State of the United States, had, on the morning
of the day when the letter was dated, called on the writer, and
told him that the President of the United States had determined to nominate me to go to the Hague as Resident Minister
from the United States. This intelligence was very unexpected,
and indeed surprising. I had laid down as a principle, that I
never would solicit for any public office whatever, and from
this determination no necessity has hitherto compelled me to
swerve.

June 10. — On Sunday the 8th, my father arrived at Quincy
from Philadelphia, and on Tuesday the 10th I went from
Boston to Quincy to see him. I found that my nomination
had been as unexpected to him as to myself, and that he had
never uttered a word upon which a wish on his part could be
presumed that a public office should be conferred upon me.

[1] Some scattered earlier pages of John Quincy Adams's Diary, which are
not thought worth reprinting here, contain his very juvenile impressions of
Paris in 1785. He was in the French capital when the Queen Marie Antoinette's second son was born, and saw him christened before the Parliament, the
Diplomatic Corps, and the Bishops, at Notre Dame. "The King and all the
Court," he writes, "were dressed in clothes vastly rich, but in no peculiar
form."

His opinion upon the subject agreed with my own; but his satisfaction at the appointment is much greater than mine.

June 12. — I received a letter from the Secretary of State giving me notice of my appointment, and requesting me to go to Philadelphia.[2]

July 7. — I remained at New York, in order to get a little recruited and refreshed. I lodged at my brother-in-law, Col. W. S. Smith's. At dinner this day at his house, I met M. Talleyrand, the ci-devant bishop of Autun . . . now here in banishment. . . Talleyrand is reserved and distant.

Philadelphia, July 10. — I waited on Mr. Randolph, who immediately accompanied me and introduced me to the President of the United States. He said little or nothing to me upon the subject of the business on which I am to be sent. All his directions and intentions on this head I am to receive through the medium of his ministers. I dined with him, General, and Mrs. Knox.

July 11. — The day upon which I entered upon my twenty-eighth of age, I received my commission from the Secretary of State. At the same time I began the reading of six large folio volumes, containing the despatches from my father during his negotiations in Europe. By the invitation of the President, I attended the reception he gave to Piomingo and a number of other Chickasaw Indians.[3] Five chiefs, seven warriors, four boys, and an interpreter constituted the company. As soon as the whole were seated, the ceremony of smoking began. A large East Indian pipe was placed in the middle of the hall. The tube, which appeared to be of leather, was twelve or fifteen feet in length. The President began, and after two or three whiffs, passed the tube to Piomingo; he to the next chief, and so all round. Whether this ceremony be really of Indian origin, as is generally supposed, I confess I have some doubt. At least these Indians appeared to be quite unused to it, and from their manner of going through it, looked as if they were submitting to a process in compliance

[2] Adams, a young lawyer of Boston, probably owed his appointment to his journalistic activity. During the Genet excitement he published in the *Columbian Centinel* a series of Federalist papers signed Marcellus, Columbus, or Barneveld, which attracted much attention. Despite what he says in the Diary, the restlessly ambitious Adams was delighted by his promotion.

[3] The Chickasaws had just given valuable assistance in the campaign against the Creeks; and Washington was always eager to cultivate Indian friendship.

with *our* custom. Some of them, I thought, smiled with such an expression of countenance as denoted a sense of *novelty* and of *frivolity* too; as if the ceremony struck them not only as new, but also as ridiculous. When it was finished, the President addressed them in a speech which he read, stopping at the close of every sentence for the interpreter to translate it. Observed that the interpreter, at the close of every sentence, concluded by repeating the same word twice over. The sound was something like this, " Tshkyer! Tshkyer! " . . .

We accompanied Mrs. Knox to the theatre, which is spacious and elegant, and supplied with a very good company of performers. Part of the entertainment, however, we left, to go and pay the customary visit to Mrs. Washington. As this was merely a mark of respect, we retired as early as we could, and returned to the play. The remainder of the evening I was seated next to Mr. Fauchet, the Minister Plenipotentiary of the French Republic. I found him tolerably conversable, but reserved. He appears to be not much beyond thirty. He spoke of the Abbé Raynal, whom he knew; but said he had seldom seen him in later times, and without conversing on the subject of the Revolution.

July 12. — Dined with Mr. Hammond, the British Minister Plenipotentiary. There was no other company, and we were tolerably sociable. It was the renewal of an old acquaintance, but I felt it necessary to be peculiarly cautious with the Minister of a foreign nation, with whom the United States are now engaged in a controversy which bears a very serious aspect. He spoke of the late speech of the governor of Massachusetts (Samuel Adams), which appears to have given him much offence. He seemed to wish me to speak of that gentleman, and to expect that I should express not much respect for his character. I did not choose to gratify him; but spoke of the Governor in general terms, and with respect.

Boston, Sept. 17. — I went on board the ship *Alfred,* Stephen Macey commander, for London; together with my brother and a servant. Dr. Welsh and Dr. W. S. Smith accompanied us on board the ship, and returned on shore as soon as we were fairly under weigh. My friends, Daniel Sargent, Jr., and Nathan Frazier, Jr., went with us down as far as the lighthouse. At ten a.m. we weighed; and just at noon were abreast of the light. My friends then left us to return home.

" The name of your ship," said Frazier, " is auspicious," and alluding to the new French calendar, " You depart," said he, " on the day of Virtue, I hope you will return upon the day of Rewards." The pain of separation from my friends and country was felt as poignantly by me, at the moment when these two young men left the ship, as it ever has been at any period of my life. It was like severing the last string from the heart.

Oct. 14. — Discovered the lighthouse at Dungeness at about 11, passed it between 12 and 1 — soon came abreast of the White Cliffs, so celebrated in song, and just after 3 were opposite Dover. A signal was made for a pilot, who came immediately on board in a small boat. The men in the boat then proposed to carry on shore the passengers, and after a little chaffering whether their extortion should amount to a guinea, or only half a guinea, for each passenger, they came to the latter price, and took us on board.

Oct. 15. — We breakfasted at Canterbury, at the most indifferent house we found upon the road. At Dartford we dined; and arrived at the Virginia coffee-house, just below the Royal Exchange, at about half past seven in the evening. Just before we got to the London Bridge, we heard a rattling before us, and immediately after, a sound as of a trunk falling from the carriage. I instantly looked forward, and saw that both our trunks were gone. One of them contained all the public dispatches which I brought for the American Minister here, and which was my principal inducement for coming here. For a moment, I felt sensations of the severest distress. But my brother immediately alighted, and found the trunk of dispatches immediately under the carriage. The other trunk was a few rods behind, and in half a minute more must have been crushed to pieces by the horse's hoofs of a carriage which followed hard upon us. We secured them both inside our chaise for the rest of the way, and our driver assured us that the trunks could not have fallen unless the straps had been cut away. On reaching our lodgings, and bringing our trunks to a light, we found the conjecture of our postilion was well founded; but whether his sagacity arose from his being privy to the villainy, and concerned in it, or not, we had no means of determining; and as our things were saved, was of little consequence to us to know.

But for myself, I felt the most exquisite satisfaction at this hairbreadth escape from a misfortune which to my mind, as it respected myself personally, would have reduced me to the condition of regretting my other escape from the dangers of the seas.[4] Entrusted with dispatches of the highest importance, with numerous original documents relative to the depredations upon the American commerce, now a subject of negotiation between the two countries, with papers particularly committed to my care, *because* they were highly confidential, and the ground upon which I was directed by the President of the United States to take my passage first to London, in preference to an immediate opportunity to Amsterdam, with what a face could I have presented myself to the Minister for whom they were intended, to tell him that I had lost them on the way? How could I have informed the Secretary of State of the fate of his papers? What would have been my feelings on the reflection that they would probably all be put in the possession of the Ministry here? And how could I have supported the idea that the story, with a thousand alterations and exaggerations, would be resounded from one end of the United States to the other? What a field for the aspersions of malice!

Oct. 16. — Before we rose this morning, Tilly arrived in the coach from Deal. We indulged ourselves, indeed, beyond the usual hour, and made it late before we went to breakfast with Mr. Jay. We found there a Mr. Pierpont, who has just arrived from France, and who gave us some account of the state of things in Paris, where the moderate party now prevails. Indeed, nothing ever was more surprising to me than when Mr. Jay last evening asked me whether the death of Robespierre was known in America before I sailed. I repeated with utter astonishment, " Robespierre dead! " more times than was perfectly decent; and could scarcely believe I had heard right, until he assured me very seriously that about six weeks or two months since, Robespierre, with a considerable number of his partisans, were accused, tried, condemned, and executed, in less than twenty-four hours, by a party of *moderates* who had succeeded to his power, and from that day to this have loaded his memory with every possible execration, calling him by scarce any other name than *the Tyrant,* and imputing to

---

[4] Adams's ship had proved leaky and his voyage one of real peril.

him and his system all the horrible cruelties which have deso-
lated the country for the last two years.

Oct. 18. — Went to Drury Lane Theatre to see *Henry the
Eighth,* with a farce called *The Glorious First of June.* The
house itself has undergone a thorough alteration since I was
here before, and has been lately repaired at the expense, it is
said, of a hundred thousand pounds. The house was thin,
notwithstanding Mrs. Siddons appeared in the character of
Queen Catherine. She is as much as ever, and as deservedly,
the favorite of the public, but the enthusiasm of novelty is
past, and her appearance alone no longer crowds the houses,
as it was wont in the autumn of 1783. She performed the
part of Catherine to great perfection; much beyond the excellence of Mrs. Yates, whom I once saw and admired in the same
character.

Oct. 20. — I spent most of the forenoon at Mr. Jay's, in
company with Mr. Pinckney, in conversation upon the subject
of the negotiation now on foot between the former of these
gentlemen and the Ministry here. The plan of a treaty now
in discussion was read, and then taken up, and considered
article by article. The business, however, was not finished,
and we adjourned over the subject for a further meeting till
to-morrow. We dined with Mr. Jay, and afterwards I went
with Col. Trumbull, and Mr. Peter Jay, son to the Minister,
to Covent Garden Theatre. The performance of the night
was *Romeo and Juliet,* with a pantomime called *Oscar and
Malvina,* the subject of which is taken from Ossian.

Oct. 22. — We passed this forenoon like the two former,
and at length got through the discussion of the treaty. It is
far from being satisfactory to those gentlemen; it is much below
the standard which I think would be advantageous to the
country; but, with some alterations which are marked down,
and to which it seems there is a probability they will consent,
it is, in the opinion of the two plenipotentiaries, preferable
to a war. And when Mr. Jay asked me my opinion, I answered
that I could only acquiesce in that idea.

Oct. 27. — Mr. W. Vaughan called on us this morning, and
engaged us to dine with his father at Hackney to-morrow.
Dined at Mr. Copley's — with Mr. Erving and his son, whom
I knew last year in America, Mr. Clarke, Mrs. Copley's
father, their son, and two daughters. The eldest daughter may

be called handsome, if not beautiful, and is very pleasing in her manners. There is something so fascinating in the women I meet with in this country, that it is well for me I am obliged immediately to leave it.

Oct. 28. — I called early this morning upon Mr. Jay. In the first place, having received no answer to a letter I wrote the American bankers at Amsterdam on my arrival, for a draught to give me a pecuniary supply here, I found myself rather short in the necessary article of cash. I knew of no person upon whom I could more confidently venture to call than Mr. Jay, and found myself not disappointed in my idea. He very readily gave me the draught I requested, and offered to extend his goodness. I thought best, however, to take only a supply for my immediate occasion, feeling highly obliged to him for this additional instance of his friendship.

I then requested him to favor me with his advice respecting the conduct which in my public character it would be proper to hold during the crisis in which that country now stands. He was equally indulgent on that head, and I believe I shall derive much benefit from his counsel. He said that I should stand in a situation extremely delicate; that the parties which so unhappily divide that country, to which I am sent, might very possibly press me hard on either side to show some preference or partiality; that I ought very cautiously to avoid it, and take no part whatever in their internal dissensions.

Oct. 30. — A fresh wind sprang up in the night, and carried us over with such rapidity that soon after daybreak we made the land on the coast of Holland — but, though not more than four leagues distant from the shore, it was not till afternoon that we reached it.

Jan. 18, 1795. — To Amsterdam with the Post Waggon at nine in the morning. Arrived at Amsterdam about 4 p.m. — found it a moment of crisis. Saw Mr. Bourne several times in the evening. Mr. Willink, Mr. McEvers, Mr. Hubbard, Mr. Plenti, who appears very much embarrassed how to get away, and afraid of being stopped. Some symptons of agitation among the people. General Golofkin, Commander of the garrison here, received this morning from General Daandels, Commander of the Batavian Corps, an *order* to surrender, and lay down their arms. A Batavian, by the name of Krayenhoff, who fled lately from this City, and is cited to appear on Tuesday next before the Court of Schepens, came this afternoon; exhibited to the Regency a commission constituting him commander of this city. He demands of the magistrates to abdicate their authority. In the evening, the three-colored cockade began to make its appearance in the streets; they were noisy through the night. The Carmagnole song, and the Marseillaise hymn, were everywhere singing.

Jan. 20. — The day perfectly tranquil. Everything hitherto has passed without the smallest disorder. General Pichegru, and about two or three thousand of the French troops, entered the city this afternoon.[5] The General is lodged at the house of Mr. Hope, which was vacant.

Jan. 31. — Took passage in the Post Waggon at nine this morning, for the Hague. We had two companions in the carriage, Germans, speaking no other language than their own. Of course we had not much conversation. Arrived at the Hague between four and five p.m.

London, Nov. 11. — [Returning from Holland.] At about eight in the morning I descended from the stage coach and went to Osborne's Hotel, Adelphi Buildings, in the Strand. After breakfasting, went immediately to Great Cumberland Place, No. 1, to see Mr. Deas; but found he was not at home. Went from thence to Mr. Johnson's, the Consul, and delivered him my letters. Found Col. Trumbull with him. Sent my letters that were to be transmitted.

Nov. 16. — Meeting of the inhabitants of Westminster in the Palace Yard before Westminster Hall. Attended it. Saw, but did not hear, Mr. Charles Fox, the Duke of Bedford, and Mr. Grey speak to the people. There appeared to me to be about ten thousand people present. Few of them could hear their orators, but they waved their hats and shouted with as much fervor as if they really knew what they applauded.

Nov. 19. — Mr. W. Vaughan breakfasted with me. Conversation with him on the subject of commercial principles. . . Mr. Deas and Mr. Bayard called at about twelve. Went with them and Mr. Vaughan to see Mr. Ireland, and saw several of his manuscripts which, he assures us, have been lately discovered, and are original from the hand of Shakespear. They are deeds, billets, a love-letter to Anna Hatherwaye with

---

[5] Pichegru hoisted the tri-color in Holland and established the "Batavian Republic" as the ally of revolutionary France.

a lock of hair, designs done with a pen, a fair copy of *Lear,* three or four sheets of a *Hamlet,* and a tragedy, hitherto unknown, of *Vortigern and Rowena.* The last we did not see, as unfortunately some company came, to which Mr. Ireland was obliged to attend, and we accordingly took our leave. The marks of authenticity borne by the manuscripts are very considerable, but this matter will be likely to occasion as great a literary controversy as the supposed poems of Rowley and those of Ossian have done. They will be published in the course of a few weeks; and the play of *Vortigern* is to appear upon the Drury Lane stage. Sheridan has given five hundred pounds for it.

Nov. 20. — . . . At Drury Lane Theatre again, to see *Lear,* which was followed by the *Village Lawyer,* taken from the French *Avocat Patelin.* Kemble did tolerable justice to the part of the old King, and Mrs. Siddons could not do otherwise to that of Cordelia. But in this instance, as in several others, I have found that the stage does not support the merit of Shakespear in the closet. The acted play is very different from the printed one. An amour between Edgar, the illegitimate son of Gloster, and Cordelia, is introduced. And the catastrophe closes with their marriage, and with the gift of the kingdom to them by Lear, to whom it is restored for that purpose. If this termination be less pathetic than that of the original, it is more pleasing to those who are fond of poetical retribution.

Nov. 24. — Called on Dr. Edwards, by agreement, between twelve and one, to go with him and visit Mr. West. He proposed to me to take the same opportunity to visit Mr. Gouverneur Morris at the York Hotel, Covent Garden, which we did accordingly.[6] This is the first time I ever saw that gentleman, who conversed with as much freedom as from his character I expected. . . Mr. Morris, by his own account, must be a very able negotiator, for he gave us to understand that while he was our Minister in France, he knew everything that was going forward. It was his business to know it, he said, and he told us a number of curious anecdotes connected with the history of

---

[6] Gouverneur Morris had been appointed American Minister to France in 1792, and had remained at his post during the Reign of Terror; but he was hostile to the revolution, and the French Government had now just demanded his recall, partly in return for the American demand for Genet's recall. He had been close to the King while in Paris.

the Revolution in France — of the papers he had seen before the 10th of August, 1792, handed to him by the King,
and which contained the whole plan of the insurrection that
took place on that day. " It was," he says, " planned by the
Brissotine party of the Jacobins, but they were cowards, and
would have shrunk back from the execution, but for Wester-
mann, whom they had employed to command their Marseillese.
He was the greatest *mauvais sujet* in France, and when he had
once got fairly engaged in that business not only refused to
retreat, but threatened the others to denounce them if they
flinched. And yet," says Mr. Morris, " those people were
not ashamed of declaring the King guilty of an insurrection
against the people on that same 10th of August. If, however,
he had at the time of his trial put himself into the hands of
the other party, they would have spared his life." Chabot
himself said so to a person who told it to Mr. Morris. They
would not have suffered the trial, by asserting the principle
that the Convention had no right to try him. But, as he committed himself to the Brissotines, Chabot said that he must
die, that being the only way to get at them.

From this account of a first conversation it appears that
Mr. Morris is sufficiently communicative for a man of such
extraordinary diplomatic penetration. The time of secrecy
as to these affairs is indeed passed. But this parade of
sagacity, these lessons in the theory and practice of negotiation so freely given and so liberally tendered — what do they
mean?

Nov. 27. — Called, as requested, at Mr. Hammond's office,
and he introduced me to Lord Grenville. My conversation
with him will be related in my letters to the Secretary of
State. Some conversation afterwards with Mr. Hammond.
He told me he wished Mr. Pinckney would go home, and that
I might be placed here in his stead. Enquired whether I
should not like it as well as being at the Hague. Answered
him that this was a pleasant country, and that personally
I thought the residence here would be very agreeable. He
asked if I had any news from America. I answered, none.
He said he heard *the democrats* were quite *cock-a-whoop* —
talked very high of impeaching the President, etc. " There
always will be in all countries," said I, " people that will talk
very high. You find that in this country, as well as elsewhere."

" Ay," said he, " the best way is to let them talk." " Your
Government seem to think otherwise," I might have said; but
I prefered saying nothing, not choosing to imitate his conduct.
He suggested that the place of ordinary Minister here would
be very agreeable to me, because it would be succeeding to
the station my father had held. " That may do very well
for you," said I. " You may be an aristocrat with propriety;
but in my country, you know, there is nothing hereditary in
public offices."

This foolish talk of his is very intelligible. " I do see to the
bottom of this Justice Shallow;" but he knows not me. If I
stay here any time, he will learn to be not quite so fond, nor yet
quite so impertinent.

Dec. 1. — Called on Mr. Hammond at noon, as by appointment, and had considerable conversation with him. But his
tone with me begins already to be different from what it
was at first. His conversation was still such as if he thought
my personal feelings or sentiments upon political subjects would
have a tendency to make me complaisant. Asked if I had heard
anything of the President's intending to resign. Told him no.
He said he had heard such was his determination at the expiration of his present term, in case there should be no troubles in
the country. What sort of a soul does this man suppose I
have? He talked about the Virginians, the Southern people,
the Democrats; but I let him know that I consider them all
in no other light than as Americans. They never shall be
considered by me in any other light in treating with foreigners.
He spoke again of Mr. Randolph's resignation.[7] I told him
I had seen an account from which, if true, it appeared clearly
that there was nothing like bribery in the case. He said that
the President, Mr. Wolcott, Mr. Pickering, and Mr. Bradford were all fully convinced that Randolph was guilty. I
replied that, not having seen the papers, I could not be a competent judge of the facts; that the public officers he mentioned
might think there had been improper conduct without believing there was any corruption. He said he had not the smallest
doubt but Randolph was bribed by the French; and added, he
had better be quiet on that score; for if he presumed to deny

[7] Secretary of State Edmund Randolph had been guilty of improper relations with the French Minister in America, Fauchet, and had been forced from
Washington's Cabinet.

it, other proof, amounting to demonstration, would be produced. He said he would show me the next time I should see him the intercepted dispatches of Fauchet.

Dec. 8. — Received this morning a card from Lord Grenville, informing me that I am to have to-morrow, after the Levée, the audience I *solicited* of the King. This card was addressed to me as Minister Plenipotentiary from the United States of America. This circumstance struck me as singular, considering that I have no sort of pretension to that character. Dined with Mr. Hammond, and mentioned to him the mistake, presuming he would take proper notice of it.[8]

Dec. 9. — . . . After the Levée was over I was introduced into the private closet of the King by Lord Grenville, and, presenting my credential Letter, said, " Sir, to testify to your Majesty the sincerity of the United States of America in their negotiations, their President has directed me to take the necessary measures connected with the ratifications of the treaty of amity, commerce, and navigation concluded between your Majesty and the United States. He has authorized me to deliver to your Majesty this letter, and I ask your Majesty's permission to add, on their part, the assurance of the sincerity of their intentions." He then said, " To give you my answer, Sir, I am very happy to have the assurances of their sincerity, for without that, you know, there would be no such thing as dealings among men." He afterwards asked to which of the States I belonged, and on my answering, Massachusetts, he turned to Lord Grenville and said, " All the Adamses belong to Massachusetts? " To which Lord Grenville answered, they did. He enquired whether my father was now Governor of Massachuetts. I answered, " No, Sir; he is Vice President of the United States." " Ay," said he, " and he cannot hold both offices at the same time? " " No, Sir." He asked where my father is now. " At Philadelphia, Sir, I presume, the Congress being now in session." " When do they meet? " " The first week in December, Sir." " And where did you come from last? " " From Holland, Sir." " You have been employed there? " " Yes, Sir, about a year." " Have you been employed before, and anywhere else? " " No, Sir."

I then withdrew. Mr. Cottrell invited me to go and witness

---

[8] The British, disliking the temporary American representative, Deas, would gladly have thrust Adams into the position of the regularly accredited minister.

the ceremony of an address presented by the Bishop and Clergy of London, which was received upon the throne.

Dec. 28. — Frazier breakfasted with me; after which we went to see the Shakespear Gallery of Paintings. I was very highly gratified during three or four hours that we spent in looking them over. There is, indeed, a mixture of good and of indifferent things, but there was only one really disgusting to me. It was a scene in *The Midsummer Night's Dream.* Instead of the fine frenzy of the Poet, it gave nothing but a combination of madness and idiotism; instead of the sportive excursions of a sublime imagination, nothing but the darkling errors of a sick man's dreams. Among the paintings that struck me as the works of most special excellence were, a Death of Cardinal Beaufort, by Reynolds; an Ophelia Mad, by West; a Cassandra, by Ranney; a Hubert and Arthur, by Northcote; and some others. But one of the most pleasing reflections on this occasion arises from the idea of such a combination of talents and wealth concurring to pay their tribute to the greatest genius of their country.

The Hague, June 6, 1796. — Dined with M. d'Araujo. Bielfeld, Levsen, a physician whose name I knew not, Mr. Manoël, a Portuguese gentleman of a singular character, and my brother were of the company. We talked something of literature, a subject in which M. d'Araujo delights. He says the Dauphin editions of the Classics are contemptible.

June 30. — *Day.* On my return from England I determined to resume a life of application to business and study, which, during the principal part of my residence there, I found altogether impossible. It has not yet settled into a course perfectly regular, but it is hitherto equal to my expectations. Rise and dress at six. Read works of *instruction* from thence till nine. Breakfast. Read the papers and translate from the Dutch till eleven or twelve. Then dress for the day. Write letters or attend to other business that occurs till between two and three. Walk till half-past three. Dine and sit till five. Read works of *amusement* till between eight and nine. Walk again about an hour. Then take a very slight supper and my segar, and retire to bed at eleven. The variations from this course are not considerable. Those that have taken place as yet are marked in the diary. I have, as before mentioned, now devoted an hour a day to the study of Italian, which

Bielfeld and I are learning together. Too much of this time
is devoted to reading, and too litttle to society. But I was not
formed to shine in company, nor to be delighted with it; and I
have now a considerable lapse of time to repair.

July 19. — Finished reading Rowe's translation of the
Pharsalia. Dr. Johnson says it is not esteemed so much as it
is worth, and it will please more the better it is known. I have
never read it before, and have been gratified in the perusal.
I have occasionally compared it with the original, and find that
the translation has added near an hundred lines at the end of
the tenth book to close the action. It is not an epic poem.
Nor is it a fair criticism to compare it with the Æneid. It
has certainly much more originality, and the characters are
much more striking than those of Virgil.

July 20. — Began to read the translation of Ovid's *Meta-
morphoses,* as published by Garth. The first book is by
Dryden. He calls the palace of the Gods the *Louvre*
of the sky, and tells of Phaëton's going to the *Levée* of his
father Phoebus; as Rowe in one of Cato's speeches makes him
tell the soldiers they are fit only to pass as *heirlooms* from
Pompey to Cæsar. Such expressions remind me of Anthony's
present to Cleopatra of a tompion gold watch, in Swift.

Aug. 13. — At the French play this evening — *Othello, ou
le More de Venise.* A wretched travesty by Ducis from
Shakespear's *Othello,* with most of his defects, and innumerable others, with scarce one of his beauties. It has the merit,
however, of containing sarcasms upon aristocracy, and abuse
upon the government of Venice.

Sept. 4. — Finished reading the *Paradise Lost,* the admiration of which increases in my mind upon every perusal. A
criticism upon it would take too much time, and would have
nothing original. I mention therefore only two observations
which occur to me upon censures expressed by eminent men
without justice. Pope, after noticing the quibbles of the
angels and archangels (an undoubted blemish to the poem),
adds that Milton makes "God the Father turn a school-
divine." This is epigrammatic; but if the subject of the poem,
Paradise Lost, and the object of the poet, to justify the ways
of God to men, be considered, it appears to be an absolute
necessity that the justice of the Divine proceedings should be
established upon the assertion of free election in man. This
could not be explained without metaphysical argument; with-

out the nice distinctions which appear in the passages that the sarcasm of Pope would condemn.

Sept. 29. — Answer at length from the Committee of External Relations upon the subject of my former memorials. It is, take it for all in all, as curious a piece of diplomatic composition as I have met with. From its defiance of fact and contempt of argument, I shall be tempted to suspect it to be the composition of Noël. It behooves me now to be cool. The provocation of such a piece is so strong, that it is probably designed as such, and may be a French perfidy.

Dec. 31. — . . . *Day*. Rise in the morning at about seven. Translate two pages of history from Tacitus. Breakfast at about ten. Afterwards till two, dressing, receiving or paying visits, or writing letters. Dine between three and four. After dinner read a few papers of the Rambler. Walk of three or four miles immediately before or after dinner. Evening generally in company and at cards. Seldom at home, and reading a few of Cicero's Letters. A profound anxiety has taken possession of my mind. The situation of two objects the nearest to my heart, my country and my father, press continually upon my reflections. They engross every thought, and almost every power, every faculty.

March 4, 1797. — The day upon which the new Administration of the United States commences, and I am still uncertain what the elections have decided.[9] Everything has contributed to accumulate anxiety upon this event in my mind. Futurity laughs at our foresight. I can only pray for the happiness and prosperity of my country. Wrote a letter to my father.

June 5. — . . . Passed the evening with Cutting, Mr. Vancouver, and Marshall the younger, and Lee. Mr. Vancouver's brother has made the last voyage round the world, which is soon to be published. He himself is a traveller, a man of information and understanding. Cutting told us of Mr. Jefferson's instructions to the traveller Ledyard when he intended to try the passage across from Kamschatka. He was to carry nothing with him, no instruments, no books, nothing that could possibly tempt the avidity of a savage. But he was to keep the journal of his travels by pricking it with thorns

---

[9] Adams's father was of course installed as President on this day. Both father and son felt embarrassment over this new relationship; but Washington before retiring urged that the young diplomat be kept in the service.

upon his skin. He had a scale of a foot marked out with Indian ink, in inches, and lines, upon his arm, between the elbow and the wrist.

If he met any remarkable mountain or other object, of which he wished to know the latitude, he was to cut him a stick of three feet long, and in the same spot mark the length of its shadow by the rising and setting sun, and then by the point of intersection drawn from the extremity of the two shadows, he would find the length of the shadow at noon, whence the latitude might be collected. If he came across a river, and wished to measure its width, he was to plant a stick at some station upon the bank, then, with another stick, horizontally level his eye at the opposite bank; after which, turning round his stick and preserving it at the same angle, take a sight with it at some object on the bank where he stood and measure the distance, which would, of course, give him that across the river. Cutting was in extasies while he told all this. Poor Ledyard was stopped on his travels at Tobolsk, and afterwards died at Grand Cairo, on another journey into Abyssinia. But had he pursued his northwest road, whatever benefit his success might have procured to mankind, his journal upon his skin would not, I think, have been worth much.

London, July 18. — As I was going out this morning I met Mr. King, who delivered me letters from the Secretary of State of 27th May and 1st June, and from my father of 2d June. They direct me not to proceed to Lisbon, but wait here for a commission and instructions to the Court of Berlin.

July 26. — At nine this morning I went, accompanied by my brother, to Mr. Johnson's, and thence to the Church of the parish of All Hallows Barking, where I was married to Louisa Catherine Johnson, the second daughter of Joshua and Catherine Johnson, by Mr. Hewlett.[10] Mr. Johnson's family, Mr. Brooks, my brother, and Mr. J. Hall were present. We were married before eleven in the morning, and immediately after went out to see Tilney House, one of the splendid country seats for which this country is distinguished.

[10] Louisa Johnson was daughter of the American consul in London, and niece of the Maryland " signer " Thomas Johnson. The union thus contracted was destined to be happy and lifelong. In November, 1797, Adams proceeded to Berlin, serving there till the close of his father's Administration, and negotiating a treaty of amity and commerce between Prussia and the United States. He returned to the United States in September, 1801.

CHAPTER II
1803–1809

ELECTED TO THE SENATE — AARON BURR — PRESIDENT JEFFERSON — THE CHASE IMPEACHMENT — HARVARD CHAIR OF ORATORY — THE SLAVE TRADE — THE EMBARGO — MADISON'S ELECTION

Boston, Feb. 2, 1803. — The House of Representatives last Saturday assigned tomorrow, two o'clock, to make choice of the Senator for six years, instead of Mr. Mason, whose term expires on the 4th of March. The *Centinel* and *Palladium* published that the time was next Saturday. Mr. Russell, of Boston, moved this day in the House to postpone the choice until next Tuesday. Mr. Otis argued in favor of the postponement. The vote passed, but was afterwards reconsidered, and the original time again assigned for tomorrow, at twelve o'clock. This hurrying on is occasioned by a coalition of the Jacobin party (so called) with the Junto, who expect to carry Mr. Pickering for the six years.

Feb. 3. — The business in Senate this forenoon was of little consequence — no bills of general interest being before them. About one o'clock Mr. Otis came up from the House with a message; that the House had proceeded to the choice of a Senator in the Congress of the United States, in the room of Jonathan Mason, whose time of service expires on the 4th of March next; and that, on the ballots being taken, it appeared that John Quincy Adams had a majority of the whole number. The Senate assigned next Tuesday, twelve o'clock, to act upon this choice, and a nomination list in the meantime to be put up.

Feb. 8. — The Senate was occupied in discussing several bills and motions until twelve o'clock — the time assigned for the choice of a Senator in Congress for six years after the 4th of March next. The number of votes was twenty-six

17

(of course I did not vote at all). There were nineteen votes for John Quincy Adams, and seven for Thompson J. Skinner. The federal side of the House, therefore, was unanimous to concur in the choice made by the House.[1]

Washington, Oct. 21. — At eleven this morning I took my seat in the Senate of the United States, after delivering my credential letter to Mr. Otis, the Secretary, and being sworn to support the constitution of the United States by Mr. John Brown, of Kentucky, who is the President *pro tempore,* Mr. Burr, the Vice-President, being absent. There was little business done, and the Senate adjourned soon after twelve. Mr. Otis is much alarmed at the prospect of being removed from his office. It has been signified to him this day, that in order to retain it he must have all the printing done by Duane. His compliance may possibly preserve him one session longer. After the Senate adjourned, I went in without the bar of the House of Representatives; but they adjourned immediately afterwards. As I returned home I called at the President's, and, not finding him at home, left a card.

Oct. 23. — There is no church of any denomination in this city; but religious service is usually performed on Sundays at the Treasury office and at the Capitol. I went both forenoon and afternoon to the Treasury, but found there was this day no preaching there, on account of the indisposition of Mr. Laurie.

Oct. 31. — In Senate. Mr. Breckinridge introduced a resolution to wear crape a month for the three illustrious patriots, Samuel Adams, Edmund Pendleton, and Stevens Thompson Mason. I asked for the constitutional authority of the Senate to enjoin upon its members this act; and he referred to the manual, that such a regulation was merely conventional and not binding upon the members. I then objected against it as improper in itself, tending to unsuitable discussions of character, and to an employment of the Senate's time in debates altogether foreign to the subjects which properly belong to them. This led to a debate of three hours, in the course of which the resolution was divided into two — one for Mason,

[1] Adams was at this time sitting in the State Senate for the city of Boston. His choice to the Federal Senate was remarkable because of his youth, and because the honor was sought by the veteran Timothy Pickering. Shortly afterward Pickering arrived in Washington to fill a vacancy in the other Senatorial seat, and proved a jealous and antagonistic colleague.

as a matter of form and of course, to a member of the Senate holding the office at the time of his decease; the other for the two other illustrious patriots. The first was unanimously agreed to; the last by a majority of twenty-one to ten. . .

Day. From the 1st to the 20th of this month we were upon our journey from Quincy to Washington, with the customary irregularity of travelling. Here my mode of life is more uniform. I rise at about seven; write in my own chamber until nine; breakfast; dress; and soon after ten begin my walk to the Capitol. The distance is two miles and a half, and takes me forty-five minutes. I get there soon after eleven, and usually find the Senate assembled. We sit until two or three, and when the adjournment is earlier I go in and hear the debates in the House of Representatives. Home at four; dine, and pass the evening idly with George in my chamber, or with the ladies. They sup between nine and ten. At eleven is the hour for bed. This great change in the arrangement of my daily occupations and manner of living has affected my health in some degree, and the interest with which my mind seizes hold of the public business is greater than suits my comfort or can answer any sort of public utility.

Nov. 7. — . . . No business of consequence was done in the Senate, and they adjourned early, until Thursday, to give time for the workmen to repair the ceiling, which is ruinous. Another motive, not mentioned, might be that the annual horse races of the city are held this week. After the adjournment, I called upon the Secretary of the Treasury, and consulted with him on the appropriation bill; upon which he gave me the information desired. I also conversed with him respecting the settlement of my accounts, in which I presume all the difficulties are now removed. I called at the Auditor's office, but he was not there. Dined, with my wife, at the President's. The company were seventeen in number: Mr. Madison, his lady, and her sister, Mr. Wright and his two daughters, and Miss Gray, Mr. Butler, and General McPherson of Philadelphia, were there; also Mr. Eppes and Mr. Randolph, Mr. Jefferson's two sons-in-law and both members of the House of Representatives. After dinner Mr. Macon, the Speaker of the House, and Mr. John Randolph and Mr. Venable, came in. We came home at about six.

Nov. 2. — In Senate from eleven this morning until almost

ten at night, when the question on the proposed amendment to the Constitution was taken and carried — twenty-two yeas and ten nays, among which was my vote. Several good speeches were made by the members in the minority. That by Mr. Tracy was peculiarly excellent. On the other hand, Mr. Taylor's was unquestionably the best. It was almost eleven when I got home, having fasted the whole day.

Dec. 7. — Mr. Burr, the Vice-President of the United States, attended, and took the chair, as President of the Senate. General Armstrong, appointed by the Governor of New York a Senator instead of De Witt Clinton, also took his seat. All the business before the Senate was postponed, and a very early adjournment took place.

Dec. 20. — Going to the Senate this morning, the Vice-President in his carriage overtook me, and offered me a seat, which I accepted. He inquired after my father, and spoke of his *social* intimacy with him when he was a Senator and my father Vice-President. The Senate had little business before them, and soon adjourned. Mr. and Mrs. Huger and Mr. Purviance, a member of Congress from North Carolina, passed the evening with us. Snow.

Dec. 28. — In the Senate, I finally made a report from the Committee on the Treaty with England, which was made the order for to-morrow. The Vice-President attended, and explained the occasion of his absence yesterday. He was returning from Annapolis, and was delayed by the swelling of the waters of the Patuxent. It was from thence that he sent by express the apology which was read yesterday. Nothing of consequence was transacted.

Dec. 31. — *Day.* Differs only from that of the last month by a greater frequency of dining and passing evenings abroad.

The year now closing has been made remarkable as a part of my life, by one very unfortunate occurrence, and by several events which call for gratitude to an overruling Providence.

The failure of a commercial house in London, with which I had deposited a considerable part of my father's property, brought upon him a loss which is more distressing to me than to himself. It put me to great inconvenience to make the provisions to supply the chasm created by this circumstance; but its effects in diminishing the comforts of my father's age have been among the most painful things that ever happened to me. I have in some degree shared in the loss, and have done all in my power to alleviate its evils to him. But it has been and remains a continual source of uneasiness to me; nor have I any prospect that it will ever be removed. In the disposal of my property, however, to meet the necessities which arose from the protest and return of the bills I had drawn on the house, I met with several facilities and advantages which I had no right to expect. The calamity has fallen the lighter for this, and my own property has remained nearly in its former state. In my family I have been highly favored by the birth of a second son, and the unusual degree of health which we have all enjoyed. The restoration of my mother, too, from the gates of death, and from a confinement of five months, has filled my heart with the purest of enjoyments. My election as a Senator of the United States, for six years, has been the only important incident of my political career. It has opened to me a scene in some sort though not altogether new, and will probably affect very materially my future situation in life. I have already had occasion to experience, what I had before the fullest reason to expect, the *danger* of adhering to my own principles.[2] The country is so totally given up to the spirit of party, that not to follow blindfold the one or the other is an inexpiable offence. The worst of these parties had the popular torrent in its favor, and uses its triumph with all the unprincipled fury of a faction; while the other gnashes its teeth, and is waiting with all the impatience of revenge for the time when its turn may come to oppress and punish by the people's favor. Between both, I see the impossibility of pursuing the dictates of my own conscience without sacrificing every prospect, not merely of advancement, but even of retaining that character and reputation I have enjoyed. Yet my choice is made, and, if I cannot hope to give satisfaction to my country, I am at least determined to have the approbation of my own reflections.

Jan. 7, 1804. — . . . Tea and spent the evening at Mr. Pichon's. Citizen Jerome Bonaparte and his wife there — also the Vice-President, Secretaries, and several Frenchmen. Played chess with one of them, who beat me one game and

---

[2] Adams was an unpopular member of the Senate, partly because he was the son of a most unpopular father, partly because of his peppery and tactless traits, and partly because of his invincible independence of speech and action.

gave me another. Pichon is profoundly mortified at the marriage of Jerome.[3] He says it is impossible the First Consul should put up with it — 'tis a marriage against many laws, many usages, many opinions, and many prejudices, personal, official, and national, of the First Consul. Jerome is not of age; he is an officer; he is the First Consul's brother. The marriage will undoubtedly be broken. But Pichon hopes it will not affect the national honor. He has given express warning of all these facts to the lady's parents. But they have such an *inconceivable infatuation,* they and the whole family of the Smiths, for the match, that make it they must; and it was really the young man who was seduced.

Jan. 14. — The Senate met, though on Saturday, to pass the Louisiana Revenue bill, which they did; yeas twenty-nine, nays three. Mr. Tracy, Mr. Hillhouse, and Mr. White were absent. Mr. Pickering voted for the bill, and enjoyed no small satisfaction in his vote. Before I presented my resolutions denying the *right* of the Senate to concur in a bill for taxing the people of Louisiana without their consent, I showed them to Mr. Timothy Pickering, and had a free conversation with him upon them, and he made no objection against them. On the day when they were discussed, he affectedly left his seat, went out of the Senate room, came in again, kept in a perpetual bustle round the floor and in the lobbies, and just before the vote on my resolutions was taken, took great care to come and take his seat again, so as to be there for the vote. When his name was called, he arose, and, with a tone of great delight at his expedient, desired to be *excused* from voting, as *not having heard the discussion.* He was accordingly excused; but yesterday and to-day he has voted for the bill against which my resolutions were specially pointed. His conduct, taken together, speaks this language: " See how kindly I spare the feelings of my colleague! Take notice! his resolutions are ridiculous; but please to observe with how much delicacy I forbear to vote against them." Thus much for Mr. Pickering.

Jan. 27. — The Senate met only to adjourn over till Monday — on account of the Louisiana feast. About seventy members of the two Houses of Congress dined together at

---

[3] Napoleon's younger brother Jerome, visiting the United States as a naval officer, fell in love with Miss Elizabeth Patterson of Baltimore and though a minor, married her. Pichon was correct in his prediction of Napoleon's wrath.

Stella's. The President and the heads of departments were there by invitation. Scarcely any of the federal members were there. The dinner was bad, and the toasts too numerous. I left about thirty of the company there at eight in the evening.

March 2. — This was the return day on the summons to John Pickering, Judge of the District of New Hampshire, to answer to the articles of impeachment against him. The Senate met at ten o'clock. I called up my motion, made on the 4th of January, to declare that " any member of the Senate having previously acted and voted on a question of impeachment as a member of the House of Representatives, is thereby disqualified to sit and act, *in the same case,* as a member of the Senate sitting as a Court of Impeachments." The resolution was negatived — yeas eight, nays twenty.

March 27. — The first session of the Eighth Congress is at length closed. The two Houses met at ten o'clock this morning. The House of Representatives had almost finished their business. The Senate had eight bills to pass.

New York, April 8. — Mr. King and Mr. Wolcott called to see me, and I had long conversations with them, principally on public affairs. I paid a visit to Mr. Burr at his lodgings in the city. He says if the election were to be a fortnight later he should probably succeed. Nothing could have induced him to let his name be held up as a candidate for the office of Governor of New York but the absolute necessity of interposing to save the country from ruin by these family combinations, etc., etc., etc. Dr. Eustis dined with us.

Quincy, Oct. 3. — Mr. Quincy was here this morning, and urged me to consent to stand as a candidate for the office of the President of the university.[4] Upon which I could only repeat the answer I gave him when he mentioned it to me last week. I then supposed him joking; but he was this day very serious. It will not answer. They are still to choose a member of the corporation and a Professor of Divinity. Quincy opened to me more fully the real causes of their former delays, and the personal and family views which enter into these elections.

Washington, Oct. 31. — Paid visits to the President and Mr. Madison, both of whom I found at home. The President

---

[4] President Samuel Willard of Harvard died in 1804, and the first man chosen as his successor, Fisher Ames, declined.

conversed with me respecting the impressments by the British frigates upon our coast, and respecting the trade carried on by some of the merchants with the blacks at St. Domingo. This he appears determined to suppress, and I presume a law will pass for the purpose at the approaching session.

Nov. 5. — This was the day to which the session of Congress was adjourned. I attended at the Capitol at eleven in the morning. Only thirteen Senators attended, with the Vice-President, and, not being a sufficient number to form a quorum, barely met and adjourned. Mr. Giles appeared and took his seat instead of Mr. Venable, who has resigned since the last session. The Vice-President also gave notice that he had received a letter from Mr. Wells, of Delaware, containing the resignation of his seat. After the adjournment I went into the Representatives' chamber, which is where the Library was formerly kept. . .

N. B. — The Vice-President, Mr. Burr, on the 11th of July last fought a duel with General Alexander Hamilton, and mortally wounded him, of which he died the next day. The coroner's inquest on his body found a verdict of wilful murder by Aaron Burr, Vice-President of the United States. The Grand Jury in the County of New York found an indictment against him, under the statute, for sending the challenge; and the Grand Jury of Bergen County, New Jersey, where the duel was fought, have recently found a bill against him for murder. Under all these circumstances Mr. Burr appears and takes his seat as President of the Senate of the United States.

Nov. 16. — The races at length are finished, and the Senate really met this day. Mr. Bradley moved to go into the consideration of executive business, merely for the sake of having on the *printed* Journals an *appearance* of doing business, though there was really none to do. This vote passed, for mine was the only voice heard against it.

Nov. 23. — . . . Dined with the President. Mrs. Adams did not go. The company were Mr. R. Smith, Secretary of the Navy, and his lady, Mr. and Mrs. Harrison, Miss Jenifer and Miss Mouchette, Mr. Brent, and the President's two sons-in-law, with Mr. Burwell, his private secretary. I had a good deal of conversation with the President. The French Minister just arrived had been this day first presented to him, and appears to have displeased him by the profusion of gold lace on his clothes. He says they must get him down to a plain frock coat, or the boys in the streets will run after him as a sight. I asked if he had brought his *Imperial* credentials, and was answered he had. Mr. Jefferson then turned the conversation towards the French Revolution, and remarked how *contrary to all expectation* this great *bouleversement* had turned out. It seemed as if every thing in that country for the last twelve or fifteen years had been a DREAM; and who could have imagined that such an *ébranlement* would have come to this? He thought it very much to be wished that they could now return to the Constitution of 1789, and call back *the Old Family*. For although by that Constitution the Government was much too weak, and although it was defective in having a Legislature in only one branch, yet even thus it was better than the present form, where it was impossible to perceive *any limits*. I have used as near as possible his very words; for this is one of the most unexpected phases in the waxing and waning opinions of this gentleman concerning the French Revolution. He also mentioned to me the extreme difficulty he had in finding fit characters for appointments in Louisiana, and said he would now give *the creation* for a young lawyer of good abilities, and who could speak the French language, to go to New Orleans as one of the Judges of the Superior Court in the Territory. The salary was about two thousand dollars. We had been very lucky in obtaining one such Judge in Mr. Prevost of New York, who had accepted the appointment, and was perfectly well qualified, and he was in extreme want of another. I could easily have named a character fully corresponding to the one he appeared so much to want. But if his observations were meant as a *consultation* or an intent to ask whether I knew any such person I could recommend, he was not sufficiently explicit. Though if they were not, I know not why he made them to me. He further observed that both French and Spanish ought to be made primary objects of acquisition in all the educations of our young men. As to Spanish, it was so easy that he had learned it, with the help of a Don Quixote lent him by Mr. Cabot, and a grammar, in the course of a passage to Europe, on which he was but nineteen days at sea. But Mr. Jefferson tells large stories. At table he told us that when he was at Marseilles he saw there a Mr. Bergasse, a famous manufacturer of wines,

who told him that he would make him any sort of wine he
would name, and in any quantities, at six or eight sols the
bottle. And though there should not be a drop of the genuine
wine required in his composition, yet it should so perfectly
imitate the taste that the most refined connoisseur should not
be able to tell which was which. You never can be an hour in
this man's company without something of the marvellous like
these stories. His genius is of the old French school. It con-
ceives better than it combines. He showed us, among other
things, a Natural History of Parrots, in French, with colored
plates very beautifully executed.

Nov. 29. — At last the signal of approaching business is
given. Mr. Giles this day moved the appointment of a committee to draw up and report rules of proceeding for the
Senate in cases of impeachment generally. We are now to
have another specimen of what impeachments are under our
Constitution. This Mr. Giles has long been one of the most
inveterate enemies of Judge Chase in the United States, and
while a member of the House of Representatives, two years
ago, declared he would himself impeach him were he not
compelled by the state of his health to relinquish his seat in
Congress. He has now become one of the judges to try him,
and what chance of impartiality is to be expected from him
may be easily imagined. But the issue of this prosecution, like
that of Judge Pickering last winter, must be settled *out of
doors*. And for this purpose, Mr. John Randolph, the prose-
cutor, and Mr. Giles, the judge, are in daily conference together. It is said they have been obliged to delay the subject for some time on account of the difficulty of managing
Dr. Mitchell, who has always been averse to the impeachment,
and who has now become a Senator. But when I recollect the
conduct of many Senators at the last impeachment, and especially that of Mr. Bradley, of Vermont, I have little faith
in any resistance of principle in this Senate against the resolute
violence of the leaders in the House of Representatives.

Dec. 7. — . . . Three resolutions of the inhabitants of
Alexandria against the cession of that county to the State of
Virginia were received by the Vice-President, enclosed in a
letter from the Mayor of that city. But they were not read.
The resolutions, though couched in the most respectful lan-
guage, deny in a spirited manner the right of Congress to cede

the territory and people to any State, and declare it would be
extremely injurious to their interests to be ceded to Virginia.
Our Vice-President therefore did not dare to have them read.
For Mr. John Randolph has been raving all this session in
favor of the measure against which the Alexandrians protest,
and Mr. Giles drew up and procured the subscriptions of the
party in the Senate to the address to Governor Bloomfield,
asking him to screen Mr. Burr from trial for murder, of which
he now stands indicted.

Dec. 31. — . . . The year which this day expires has been
distinguished in the course of my life by its barrenness of
events.   During its first three and last two months I was
here attending my duty as a Senator of the United States.
The seven intervening months were passed in travelling to and
from Quincy, and in residence at my father's house there.   The
six months spent at Quincy were not idle.   Indeed, I have
seldom in the whole course of my life been more busily engaged.   I gave some attention to agricultural pursuits, but
I soon found they lost their relish, and that they never would
repay the labor they require.   My studies were assiduous and
seldom interrupted.   I meant to give them such a direction as
should be useful in its tendency; yet on looking back, and comparing the time consumed with the knowledge acquired, I have
no occasion to take pride in the result of my application.   I
have been a severe student all the days of my life; but an immense proportion of the time I have dedicated to the search of
knowledge has been wasted upon subjects which can never
be profitable to myself or useful to others.   Another source of
useless toil, is the want of a method properly comprehensive
and minute, in the pursuit of my inquiries.   This method has
been to me a desideratum for many years; I have found none
in books; nor have I been able to contrive one for myself.
From these two causes I have derived so little use from my
labors that it has often brought me to the borders of discouragement, and I have been tempted to abandon my books
altogether.   This, however, is impossible; for the habit has so
long been fixed in me as to have become a passion, and when
once severed from my books I find little or nothing in life
to fill the vacancy of time.

Jan. 2, 1805. — This was the day appointed for the appearance of Judge Samuel Chase to answer the articles of im-

peachment against him.[5]   At twelve o'clock the Senate went
from the committee room into their hall, which has been
prepared for the occasion. Mr. Chase was called, and appeared. He requested and obtained the permission of a seat,
upon which he read a paper of some length, requesting time
to prepare his answer, and for trial, until the first day of the
next session. He was interrupted several times by the Vice-
President, but proceeded and read his paper through. The
Vice-President then required him to reduce his request to
writing in the form of a motion, which he did.

Jan. 11. — . . . Dined at the President's, with my wife.
General Smith and his brother, of the navy, Mr. William
Smith, formerly a member of Congress, from Baltimore,
Mr. Williams and his two daughters, Mrs. Hall and Mrs.
Hewes, were there. So was the Vice-President. The President appeared to have his mind absorbed by some other object, for he was less attentive to his company than usual. His
itch for telling prodigies, however, is unabated. Speaking of
the cold, he said he had seen Fahrenheit's thermometer, *in
Paris,* at twenty degrees below zero, and that, not for a single
day, but that for six weeks together it stood *thereabouts.*
" Never once in the whole time," said he, " so high as zero,
which is *fifty* degrees below the freezing point." These were
his own words. He knows better than all this; but he loves
to excite wonder. Fahrenheit's thermometer never since
Mr. Jefferson existed was at twenty degrees below zero in
Paris. It was never for six weeks together so low as twenty
degrees above zero. Nor is Fahrenheit's zero fifty degrees
below freezing point. I asked him upon what foundation he
had, in his *Notes on Virginia,* spoken of the river Potomac as
common to Viriginia and Maryland. He said that it was in
the compact between the States — that the charter of Maryland had included the bed of the river, but the compact had
made it common. It is singular, however, if this be the case,
that among the vouchers expressly given in the book this compact is not at all mentioned, though a compact with Penn-

[5] Samuel Chase, a justice of the Federal Supreme Court, had addressed a
Baltimore grand jury in May 1803, assailing universal suffrage, " mobocracy,"
and the doctrine " that all men in a state of society are entitled to enjoy equal
liberty and rights." President Jefferson had suggested the impeachment of this
troublesome Federalist justice, and the House carried it through on eight charges,
including his conduct in the trial of sedition cases.

sylvania is. He added, however, that as to all the arguments inferred from these facts in the debate of the House of Representatives (alluding to Mr. J. Randolph's arguments), he considered them as mere metaphysical subtleties, and that they ought to have no weight. This conversation was interrupted by the entrance of General Turreau and Captain Marin; immediately after which we took leave.

Jan. 15. — Mr. Anderson was chosen President pro tem.; and the usual orders passed to notify the House of Representatives, and the President, of the choice. Mr. Bayard appeared and took his seat. The Georgetown Dam bill was debated; and both the amendments proposed by Mr. Giles and reported by the committee were rejected. The bill passed to the third reading. Upon the first amendment, respecting the pretended compact between Maryland and Virginia, I took a large part in the debate, and indeed an exclusive one on the side I advocated, as to the question of right. There were not more than seven members (I think not more than six) who rose in favor of the amendment. On this occasion, as on almost every other, I felt most sensibly my deficiency as an extemporaneous speaker. In tracing this deficiency to its source, I find it arising from a cause that is irreparable. No efforts, no application on my part, can ever remove it. It is slowness of comprehension — an incapacity to grasp the whole compass of a subject in the mind at once with such an arrangement as leaves a proper impression of the detail — and incapacity to form ideas properly precise and definite with the rapidity necessary to give them uninterrupted utterance. My manner, therefore, is slow, hesitating, and often much confused. Sometimes, from inability to furnish the words to finish a thought commenced, I begin a sentence with propriety and end it with nonsense. Sometimes, after carrying through an idea of peculiar force to its last stage, the want of a proper word at the close drives me to use one which throws the whole into a burlesque. And sometimes the most important details of argument escape my mind at the moment when I want them, though ever ready to present them before and after.

Jan. 21. — In Senate Dr. Logan presented the petition of certain Quakers, requesting the interference of Congress as far as they have power to check the slave trade. A question was made, whether the petition should be received, and very warmly debated for about three hours; when it was taken by yeas and nays — yeas nineteen, nays nine.

Jan. 22. — The weather excessively cold. In Senate, Mr. Jackson made a long speech upon a treaty with the Creek Indians. But there was not much attention paid to it, or to any other business this day transacted; most of the members being almost all the day at the firesides in the lobby.

Feb. 1. — . . . I sat some time with Mr. Giles, waiting for General Dayton, with whom I had agreed to go to General Turreau the French Minister's, where we all were to dine; and Mr. Giles gave me his opinions very freely on various subjects of a public nature; with an evident view to draw from me my opinions. I hope I was sufficiently upon my guard. He talked about his own Lousiana bill . . . From this subject he passed to that of the Georgia Land claims, which for some days have been debated with great heat and violence in the House of Representatives, and are not yet decided. In this case his theory and his practice agree entirely with those of Mr. Randolph — vehemently opposed to the claims, and urging against them suspicions, jealousies, and menaces instead of arguments. He said if those claims were not totally and forever rejected, Congress would be bribed into the sale of the United States lands, as the Georgia Legislature was to that sale; that nothing since the Government existed had so deeply affected him as this subject; that the character of the Government itself was staked upon this event. In the State of Virginia there was but one voice of indignation relating to it; that not a man from that State, who should give any countenance to the proposed compromise, could obtain an election after it. Mr. Jefferson himself would lose an election in Virginia if he was known to favor it.

Feb. 4. — This being the day fixed for receiving Judge Chase's answer, at about one o'clock the Senate went into the hall, which had been fitted up for the occasion. The managers from the House appeared, as did Mr. Chase, with Luther Martin and R. G. Harper, of Baltimore, and F. Hopkinson, of Philadelphia, as his counsel. They read his answer, which took them about three hours and a half; it being very full and particular to each article. Mr. Randolph, as Chairman of the House, asked for a copy of the answer, and time to consult the House of Representatives and to put in their replication.

Feb. 10. — . . . I dined with Mr. Stoddert at Georgetown. The Judges John Marshall, Bushrod Washington, and Winchester were there; Colonel Washington, Mr. David M. Randolph, formerly Marshal, Mr. Hopkins, formerly Treasurer of Virginia, and Mr. Lewis, a member of the House of Representatives. This company was very agreeable, and the dinner remarkably pleasant, which made me too sociable, and I talked too much. About nine in the evening I came home, and found Mr. Tabbs below. I enquired of Judge Marshall whether he knew the writer of a Vindication of his first volume of Washington's Life, against an attack of certain British Reviewers, which was published in the *Gazette of the United States*. He said he did not. But he complained that, from having been forced to precipitate so much the publication, there were so many errors and imperfections in it that he was ashamed of it.

Feb. 13. — The business first transacted this day was the declaration of the elections of President and Vice-President. The House of Representatives concurred in the resolution which yesterday passed in Senate on the subject. Mr. Tracy moved a resolution for having the galleries closed while the votes should be counted and declared; but this giving rise to some debate, the motion was withdrawn. At the last election they were closed. Mr. Wright moved, and insisted upon, a resolution that they should be *open;* which was carried. Mr. Smith of Maryland was chosen the teller on the part of the Senate. At precisely twelve the two Houses met in convention. The Vice-President opened the duplicate returns, and the votes were read and minuted down by the tellers. There was some question on the accuracy of the returns from the State of Ohio; but they were finally received. The whole number of electors and of votes was one hundred and seventy-six, of which one hundred and sixty-two were for Thomas Jefferson as President and George Clinton as Vice-President, and fourteen for Charles Cotesworth Pinckney as President and Rufus King as Vice-President.

Feb. 23. — This morning, at the opening of the Court, Mr. Rodney, on the part of the managers, read several authorities, upon which he stated they would rely in closing the cause, and which he therefore read for Judge Chase's counsel to consider; and among the rest he cited the case of Judge Addison's impeachment and removal in Pennsylvania. Mr. Luther Martin then commenced an argument for Judge Chase; taking up first the question as to the powers of impeachment and their limitation under our Constitution, and next the articles in their order. To the three first articles he spoke until half-past two o'clock; and, after an interval of half an hour, for an hour and half more upon the fourth article. It was half-past four o'clock, when, after apologizing for the length of his argument, which he excused from the great importance of the cause to his client and his country, he said he was very much exhausted, having taken nothing this day, and requested to be indulged until Monday to proceed.

Feb. 28. — The Vice-President being absent, Mr. Anderson was chosen President *pro tem.* The bill to allow Mr. Burr the privilege of franking during life passed, after a long and extraordinary debate, in which Mr. Wright said he could justify duelling by the example of David and Goliath in the Scriptures, and that this bill was now opposed only because *our* David had slain the Goliath of federalism. The question upon the passage of the bill was taken by yeas and nays. . .

Day. Rise at seven in the morning. Reading public papers, and amusing myself with my children, until nine. Breakfast; walk to the Capitol. Meet in Senate at ten. In Court half an hour later. Sitting in Court until three. Retire for half an hour, and, with the other members, take a cold collation. Return to Court — sit until six or seven in the evening. Walk home, which I usually reach, much fatigued and exhausted, between eight and nine. Pass a couple of hours in conversation, or in reading public papers, and close the evening at about eleven. As a variation from this course, I have this month spent several evenings in company abroad.

March 1. — . . . At half-past twelve o'clock the Court met. The hall was crowded with spectators. Mr. Burr ordered the civil officers in the upper galleries to turn their faces towards the spectators, and to seize and commit to prison the first person who should make the smallest noise or disturbance. He then directed the Secretary to read the first article of impeachment, which being done, he called upon each Senator by name, and put the question as agreed upon. The same course was pursued with all the succeeding articles. . .

When the answers were all given, the Vice-President desired the Secretary to read over the names of the Senators, together with their respective answers upon each of the articles; so that if any mistake in taking down the answers had been made it might be corrected. Mr. Otis read them accordingly. He had made one mistake, for he had taken down Mr. Howland's answer to the sixth article " Guilty," whereas he had answered " Not Guilty." But Mr. Howland took no notice of the error, and it was not corrected; so that upon the records his name stands as having answered " Guilty " to the sixth article. Mr. Otis had taken down all the rest correctly. After a short pause, the Vice-President said . . . " there not being a constitutional majority who answer ' Guilty ' to any one charge, it becomes my duty to declare that Samuel Chase is acquitted upon all the articles of impeachment brought against him by the House of Representatives." The Court then immediately adjourned; and thus terminated this great and important trial.[6] The Senate returned to their legislative apartment, and, after half an hour of relaxation, resumed business, and sat until seven in the evening. . .

As I was coming home, I overtook Mr. Cocke, who walked with me part of the way and spoke with much severity of Mr. John Randolph and his conduct upon this impeachment, and various other subjects; charged him with excessive vanity, ambition, insolence, and even dishonesty, which he exemplified by the misrecital of the Virginia law referred to in the fifth article of the impeachment, which he said must have been intentional. He told me that he had always been very sorry that this impeachment was brought forward, and though, when compelled to vote, his judgment had been as unfavorable to Mr. Chase as that of any member of the Court, he was heartily glad of the acquittal, which it appeared to him would have a tendency to mitigate the irritation of party spirit. He said that Mr. Randolph had boasted with great exultation that this was *his* impeachment — that every article was drawn by *his* hand, and that *he* was to have the whole merit of it; though, if the facts were so, it was not a very glorious feat for a young man to plume himself upon; for the undertaking to ruin the reputation and fortune of an old public servant, who had long

[6] Twenty-three Senatorial votes were needed to convict Chase, but on only one charge did as many as nineteen Senators vote him guilty. The political future of John Randolph of Roanoke, who managed the trial, was wrecked, and John Marshall was placed firmly in judicial power.

15907

possessed the confidence of his country, might be excusable, but was no subject to boast of.

March 2. — . . . At about one o'clock this day Mr. Burr, the Vice-President, after clearing the galleries, stated that it had been his intention to go through his constitutional career without leaving the chair; but, as he felt an indisposition coming upon him, he had concluded now to take leave of the Senate. He then, in an address of about twenty minutes, recapitulated the principles by which his conduct in the chair had been governed during the whole period of his Presidency. He mentioned one or two of the rules which appeared to him to need a revisal, and recommended the abolition of that respecting the *previous question,* which he said had in the four years been only once taken, and that was upon an amendment. This was a proof that it could not be necessary, and all its purposes were certainly much better answered by the question of indefinite postponement. In reflecting upon the decisions he had been called to make, though he had doubtless sometimes been mistaken, he could recollect no instance which he should now feel justified in recalling. Gentlemen to whom at any time they had particularly applied would naturally have their feelings excited at the moment, but he had no doubt they would on deliberate consideration acquit him of any intentional disrespect to them, and he was not conscious of any one member to whom on this account he owed an apology. He had made it a general rule not to give any reasons for his decisions at the time when they were made, because in most questions of order that arise in such an assembly it was still more essential that they should be settled promptly and without hesitation, than that they should always be settled right. Yet he trusted that gentlemen would not infer that because there was no reason given there was therefore none to give; that they would readily perceive that an instantaneous was not necessarily a precipitate act, and that what had been done without delay had not been done without reflection. It had been his invariable and resolute purpose to preserve the dignity of the situation in which he stood; and he took great satisfaction in the certainty that he should transmit the *prerogatives* of the chair unimpaired to his successor.

March 3. — . . . When the business was finished, I moved the usual order for a committee, with such as the House should

join, to notify the President that we were ready to adjourn.
On this committee I was appointed, with General Smith of
Maryland. We called at the House for their committee,
who were Messrs. J. Randolph, Nelson, and Huger. We accordingly went to the President, who was in one of the
committee rooms, and gave him the information as we were
directed. He desired us to inform the two Houses that he
had no further communications to make to them; whereupon
we returned, and the Senate was, at half-past nine in the evening, adjourned without day. It was almost eleven at night
when I got home.

Thus has terminated the second session of the Eighth Congress; the most remarkable transaction of which has been the
trial of the impeachment against Samuel Chase. This is a
subject fruitful of reflections, but their place is not here.
I shall only remark that this was a party prosecution, and has
issued in the unexpected and total disappointment of those
by whom it was brought forward. It has exhibited the Senate
of the United States fulfilling the most important purpose of
its institution, by putting a check upon the impetuous violence
of the House of Representatives. It has proved that a sense
of justice is yet strong enough to overpower the furies of
faction; but it has, at the same time, shown the wisdom and
necessity of that provision in the Constitution which requires
the concurrence of two-thirds for conviction upon impeachments. The attack upon Mr. Chase was a systematic attempt
upon the independence and powers of the Judicial Department,
and at the same time an attempt to prostrate the authority of
the National Government before those of the individual States.
The principles first started in the case of John Pickering, at the
last session, have on the present occasion been widened and improved upon to an extent for which the spirit of party itself
was not prepared. Hence, besides the federal members, six
out of twenty-five devoted to the present administration voted
for the acquittal of Judge Chase on all the charges, and have
for a time arrested the career of political frenzy. . . The pro-
phetic and solemn words of Mr. Burr, that the dying agonies of
the Constitution will be witnessed on the floor of the Senate,
were uttered with a pointed allusion to what had just passed,
and they lead to an anxious consideration of the temper of
metal to be found in the body as now composed. The essential

characters which *ought* to belong to the Senate are *coolness* and *firmness*. I hope that when the occasion shall call they will be found to possess them; and it would be doing injustice to the body and its members not to acknowledge that in this memorable instance these qualities have been eminently displayed. It has, however, furnished several instances of weak compliance as well as of honorable resistance, and I have some reason to believe that more than one member voted for the conviction of the Judge who at the same time disapproved altogether of the prosecution.

March 4. — I called this morning at Stelle's Hotel, and paid a visit to our new Vice-President, Mr. George Clinton, and had some conversation with him, in which he contrasted the appearance of this part of the country with that of New England and New York, much to the advantage of the latter. I then called upon Mr. Tracy, who has been for the last ten days very dangerously sick of a peripneumony, and at no small hazard was brought out on the 1st instant to give his vote on the sentence to the impeachment. It was a good deed, and he suffered no injury from the effort it required. He is now on the recovery, and went with me to the Senate chamber, where we saw the President and Vice-President sworn into office. The President previously delivered an inaugural address, in so low a voice that not half of it was heard by any part of the crowded auditory.

Quincy, Aug. 1. — Mr. S. Dexter, Dr. Kirkland, Mr. Holmes, of Cambridge, Mr. Storer, and Judge Davis, as a committee of the Corporation and Overseers of the University, came this morning to give me notice to my being elected the Professor of Oratory, on the foundation of Nicholas Boylston. I mentioned to them the impossibility I should be under of performing all the duties assigned to the professor in the Rules and Statutes, and that I could neither bind myself to residence at Cambridge, nor to attendance more than a part of the year. They supposed that the Statutes might be so modified as to accommodate me in these particulars, and requested me to state my own wishes in this respect to the chairman of the committee, in a letter, to which I agreed.[7]

Philadelphia, Nov. 25. — I had engaged our passage in

---

[7] Adams was the first Boylston professor of rhetoric and oratory; his service was limited to a small number of lectures, and came to an end in 1810.

the Newcastle packet *Rising Sun,* the same in which we came from that place last spring. . . After returning to Mrs. Decharms's, Mr. John Vaughan called on me, as did Dr. Rush. The object of the latter was to inform me of a conversation which he had with Mr. Madison, the Secretary of State, in the course of the last summer, respecting me. Mr. Madison, he said, had expressed himself in very favorable terms of me, and had told him that the President's opinion of me was equally advantageous, and that it was his wish to employ me on some mission abroad, if I was desirous of it. The Doctor therefore intimated that I might govern myself accordingly, and take such measures to manifest my views as I should think expedient. I told him that I had heretofore received suggestions of a similar nature; that I was obliged to Mr. Jefferson and Mr. Madison for their good opinion; that I never had, and I hoped I never should ask for any office of any man, and certainly never should solicit Mr. Jefferson for any place whatsoever; that all I could say to him was, that if Mr. Jefferson should nominate me for any office abroad to which he thought me competent, I would not refuse it merely because the nomination should come from him. He said this assurance was entirely satisfactory, and that he believed the apprehension of a disdainful refusal was the only thing which could deter Mr. Jefferson from offering me an appointment. I assured him there was no office in the President's gift for which I had any wish, and that, without being rich, I possessed the means of maintaining my family without feeling the necessity of any public station. He then made some remarks on the obligation a citizen is under to serve the public in places for which he is qualified, and concluded in complimentary terms, which I need not repeat, and ought to forget.

Washington, Nov. 30. — Paid visits this morning to the President, whom I found at home, and the Secretaries of State and of the Navy, whom I did not see. Called also on Mr. Otis at his office, where I met Mr. Plumer. At the President's door I met Mr. Israel Smith and Mr. Gaillard, who were on the same visit as myself. The President mentioned a late act of hostility committed by a French privateer near Charleston, South Carolina, and said that we ought to assume as a principle that the neutrality of our territory should extend to the Gulf Stream, which was a natural boundary, and within which we ought not to suffer any hostility to be committed. Mr. Gaillard observed that on a former occasion in Mr. Jefferson's correspondence with Genet, and by an act of Congress at that period, we had seemed only to claim the usual distance of three miles from the coast; but the President replied that he had then assumed that principle because Genet by his intemperance forced us to fix on some point, and we were not then prepared to assert the claim of jurisdiction to the extent we are in reason entitled to; but he had then taken care expressly to reserve the subject for future consideration, with a view to this same doctrine for which he now contends. I observed that it might be well, before we ventured to assume a claim so broad, to wait for a time when we should have a force competent to maintain it.   But in the mean time, he said, it was advisable *to squint at it,* and to accustom the nations of Europe to the idea that we should claim it in future.

Dec. 9. — . . . I dined at the President's, in company with the Tunisian Ambassador and his two secretaries.   By the invitation, dinner was to have been on the table precisely at sunset — it being in the midst of Ramadan, during which the Turks fast while the sun is above the horizon.   He did not arrive until half an hour after sunset, and, immediately after greeting the President and the company, proposed to retire and smoke his pipe.   The President requested him to smoke it there, which he accordingly did, taking at the same time snuff deeply scented with otto of roses.   We then went to dinner, where he freely partook of the dishes on the table without enquiring into the cookery.   Mrs. Randolph the President's daughter, and her daughter, were the only ladies there, and immediately after they returned to the drawing-room after dinner the ambassador followed them to smoke his pipe again.   His secretaries remained after him just long enough to take each a glass of wine, which they did not venture to do in his presence.   His dress differed from that of the Turks.   He wears his beard long.   His secretaries only wear whiskers.   His manners are courteous, but we were all unable to converse with him, except through the medium of an interpreter.

Jan. 16, 1806. — Mr. Wright gave notice that he should move next Monday for leave to bring in a bill for the protection and indemnification of American seamen.   His project, with which he is so delighted that he cannot hold it to himself, is to confiscate British debts, and with the money pay heavy wages to the seamen impressed by the British, while they keep them.

Jan. 30. — Met the committee on part of the President's message. . . The chairman, Smith of Maryland, presented two resolutions of his own drawing — the first an abstract declaration that no belligerent nation has a right to forbid a neutral nation any trade with her enemies, on the pretext that such trade was not permitted in time of peace; the second proposing a non-importation law for several months. These were discussed for some time, and, without coming to any decision, we adjourned until tomorrow.

Feb. 1. — Attended the committee on the President's message at ten this morning. The chairman's second resolution was further discussed; and it soon appeared that Dr. Logan and Mr. Baldwin were against it. They are for doing nothing. Mr. Baldwin made one of his serpentine speeches in favor of temporizing policy. The war in Europe could not last long: the *good man at the head of the British Government* could not live much longer; his death would bring in an entire new set of men, with different principles; there was no appearance of anything permanent in the present state of things; it would be sufficient for us to pass general resolutions declaring our rights on this and the other subjects of complaint that we have, without taking any further measures, etc. Dr. Logan was for asking the President to send an Envoy Extraordinary to negotiate. Perhaps Mr. Monroe had irritated the British Government and aggravated their offences. Mr. Monroe was known not to be friendly to England; he wanted to try the effect of another Minister there. He had heard Mr. Merry tell Mr. Madison that, before we went to war, we ought to be very sure that no other measure of a conciliatory nature remained.

Feb. 13. — . . . In the evening I went with the ladies to a party at Mr. Madison's. There was a company of about seventy persons of both sexes. I had considerable conversation with Mr. Madison, on the subjects now most important to the public. His system of proceeding towards Great Britain is, to establish permanent commercial distinctions between her and other nations — a retaliating navigation act; and ag-

gravated duties on articles imported from her. This is doubtless the President's favorite policy. Mr. Madison expressed
his entire approbation of the bill I have brought in respecting
foreign Ministers; that is, of the principle. The bill itself
he has not seen.

Feb. 25. — I dined at the President's, with a company of
fifteen members of both Houses, all federalists, and consisting chiefly of the delegations from Massachusetts and Connecticut. Mr. White, of Delaware, was also there. I came
home early in the evening, and spent it in writing. Conversing
with the President on public affairs, he told me that he understood Mr. Gregg's proposition was to be abandoned, and that
the question would be between *Mr. Nicholson's* resolutions or
nothing. I said it seemed probable that *nothing* would eventually have the preference. He said that then we must abandon
our carrying trade, for that unless something were done in
aid of negotiation Great Britain would never yield on this
point. His own preference is manifestly for Nicholson's
resolution, which is indeed a renewal of his own project in
1794, then produced in Congress by Mr. Madison. He appeared not well pleased when I intimated the suspicion that
nothing would be done. So he probably counts on the success
of Nicholson's motion.[8]

March 14. — General Turreau told me that he had been this
day in the House of Representatives to hear the debates, but
that as Mr. John Randolph rose to speak, he was afraid of
hearing things disagreeable said of his Emperor, and therefore immediately retired. He thought that a degree of respect
for the chiefs of other governments ought to be observed by
every speaker in a legislative assembly. He also told me that
the claim of the heirs of Beaumarchais was a just claim, which
would be established in any court of justice upon earth; and it
was singular that in this country there was no court of justice

[8] In this month of February, 1806, Adams introduced and supported a set of
resolutions condemning the British aggressions upon neutral trade, and requesting
the President to demand restoration and indemnification with regard to confiscated
property. Both these propositions were carried. When the second vote was taken
he entered in his Diary (Feb. 14) that "Thus my two resolutions are disposed
of much more favorably than I expected." But it was Republican votes which
carried them, and Adams's step aligned against him most of the New England
Federalists. From this time on he was more and more estranged from his party.
He supported the Non-Importation Act of April, 1806, though the Federalists
vigorously assailed it. Upon this his Diary contains little.

where its merits could be tried. I note these things for future remembrance.

Mar. 17. — The most important business done this day in Senate was the appointment of Mr. Armstrong, which finally prevailed. There was nothing said this day in his favor. The speakers against him were Mr. Smith of Maryland, Mr. Pickering, Mr. Wright, and myself, who closed the debate. The votes were fifteen to fifteen, and the Vice-President decided in favor of the appointment. Mr. Adair, of Kentucky, left his seat to avoid voting. He was averse to the appointment, but had not the courage to vote against it; and by his weakness this shameful transaction was accomplished. Of the fifteen members who voted for this nomination two-thirds at least answered with faltering voices. I consider it as one of the most disgraceful acts of Mr. Jefferson's administration.

Boston, May 13. — In the evening I attended a caucus of federalists at Faneuil Hall, who met to agree upon their list. Mr. Harrison Gray Otis made them a very good speech. They agreed to choose twenty-seven Representatives, and adopted the names presented to them. Then a motion was made for five more, which, after some opposition was adopted. These names were also agreed upon, though preparation had not properly been made for this measure. I came home at about ten. They were then about to dissolve the meeting. This was the first time I was ever present at a public caucus. I once attended a private one, in 1793 or 1794. It may be a necessary, but appears to me a clumsy, way of transacting such business.

June 12. — Between twelve and one o'clock I went to Cambridge. I was in a chaise alone, but met Mr. Barrett, of Quincy, and took him in with me. My father and the family at Quincy came into town, and went also to Cambridge before dinner. I dined with my father, Mr. Boylston, and Professor Ware, at President Webber's. In the afternoon I was installed as Boylston Professor of Rhetoric and Oratory. The hour fixed for the purpose was half-past three, but just at that time there arose a violent thunder-gust and shower, which delayed the performances about two hours. From the Philosophy chamber, where there was a meeting of the corporation and overseers, we went in procession to the meeting house, about five in the afternoon. The president began by an introductory prayer. Next followed an anthem. Then an address by the president, in Latin. Mr. Ware read the regulations of the professorship. I read and subscribed the declaration, and delivered it to the governor as chairman of the overseers. The president then declared me a professor, and I delivered the discourse I had prepared for the occasion. It was well received; but the company present was very small. The business was concluded by a hymn sung. The procession returned to the Philosophy chamber, where I stopped only a few minutes.

July 11. — I enter this day upon my fortieth year. And I this day commenced my course of lectures on rhetoric and oratory, — an undertaking of magnitude and importance, for the proper accomplishment of which I pray for patience and perseverance, and the favor from above, without which no human industry can avail, but which, without persevering industry, it is presumption to ask. . . My lecture was well received, and could I hope that the issue of the whole course would but bear a *proportion* to the effect of this introduction, I should be fully satisfied. Few persons except the scholars (the three senior classes) attended.

Washington, Jan. 13, 1807. — The first debate we have had in the Senate this session, upon the bill to relieve George Little; which, however, passed the third reading by a considerable majority. I took part in this debate without being sufficiently prepared, and therefore with little effect.

Jan. 15. — The Slave bill, which originated in Senate, was discussed in committee of the whole, and occasioned a long debate. Mr. Clay the new member from Kentucky, made an ardent speech upon one of the sections. He is quite a young man — an orator — and a republican of the first fire. I took, and intend to take, no part in the debates on this subject.

Jan. 22. — Met the committee on the Internal Sedition bill — Messrs. Giles, Tracy, Stone, Mitchell, and myself — all present. We came to no final determination. Senate was engaged all day upon the Bridge bill, with an interval of half an hour to read a messsage from the President respecting Burr's conspiracy. Mr. Maclay and myself spoke in opposition to the bill — Mr. Clay in its favor.

Feb. 6. — I had some difficulty in getting to and from the Capitol, owing to the violence of the wind and the severity of the cold. Both Houses were obliged to adjourn at an early hour, their windows having been blown in. The Senate, however, had gone through all the business before them. The new funding system act passed. The resolution I offered yesterday was, at the request of Mr. Bradley, referred to a select committee — Mr. Bradley, Mr. Giles, and myself. I spent the evening in my chamber; but the cold was so great that I wasted the time in idleness.

Feb. 15. — Judge Livingston, Mr. Verplanck, and General Van Cortlandt spent the evening here. I finished this day the last fair copy of some stanzas entitled "A Winter's Day," containing in verse a very minute and exact account of my daily occupations. . .

1

Friend of my bosom! would'st thou know
    How, far from thee, the days I spend,
And how the passing moments flow,
    To this short, simple tale attend.
When first emerging from the East
    The sunbeam flashes on my curtain,
I start from slumber's ties releas'd,
    And make the weather's temper certain.

2

Next on the closet's shelf I seek
    My pocket Homer, and compel
The man of many wiles, in Greek
    Again his fabled woes to tell,
How true he paints the scenes of life!
    How sweet the poet's honest prattle!
Far sweeter than fierce Ilium's strife
    And never-ending fields of battle.

3

At nine, comes Moses to my door,
    And down stairs summons *me* with ease,
But on my neighbor calls before,
    And knocks, " Miss Kitty — breakfast — please."
Again he louder knocks and stronger,
    Till Kitty answers, "Coming, Moses,"
And then, in half an hour, or longer,
    Comes Kitty, just as breakfast closes.

4

Then forth I sally for the day,
    And, musing politics or rhyme,
Take to the Capitol my way,
    To join in colloquy sublime.
There with the fathers of the land
    I mix in sage deliberation,
And lend my feeble voice and hand
    With equal laws to bless the nation.

5

The labors of the Senate o'er,
    Again, with solitary pace,
Down to Potomac's glassy floor
    My morning footsteps I retrace,
And oft, dejected or elate
    With painful or with pleased reflection,
In thought renew the day's debate,
    And canvass votes by retrospection.

6

At home I find the table spread,
    And dinner's fragrant steams invite,
But first the twofold stairs I tread,
    My atmospheric tale to write.
Then, seated round the social board,
    We feast, till absent friends are toasted,
Though sometimes *my* delays afford
    The beef or mutton *over-roasted*.

Feb. 16. — The Vice-President did not attend in Senate this day, being indisposed, and having been up all night with his daughter, who is at the point of death. Senate adjourned immediately on the information from the Secretary that the Vice President would not appear. I wrote to Mrs. Adams, enclosing the stanzas, and attended in the Supreme Court, where I heard part of an argument by Mr. C. Lee and by Mr. F. V. Key, in behalf of Swartwout and Bollman, upon the return of the writ of habeas corpus issued by this Court. I was obliged to leave the Court before the argument was closed, being engaged to dine with the President. The company consisted altogether of federal members of Congress. The President was less cheerful in his manners than usual, but told some of his customary staring stories. Among the rest, he said that before he went from Virginia to France he had some ripe pears sewed up in tow bags, and that when he returned six years afterwards he found them in a perfect state of preservation — self-candied.

Mar. 3. — . . . The Senate sat until past five P.M., then adjourned to seven, and sat again until almost midnight. About ten o'clock the joint committee of the two Houses, Dr. Mitchell and myself from the Senate, Mr. Varnum, Mr. Allston, and Mr. Gregg from the House, were sent with the usual notification of the recess to the President. He was not, as usual at the closing of the sessions, in the committee room at the Capitol, being detained by indisposition at his own house. The joint committee, excepting Mr. Gregg, went in a carriage together, and carried eight or ten bills for his signature. After he had done this, he said he had expected to receive this evening the Treaty lately signed by our Ministers with the Commissioners of Great Britain, at London; but it had not arrived. He had, however, seen a copy received this afternoon by Mr. Erskine, which he had been so obliging as to lend him. Dr. Mitchell said we had been requested by several members of the Senate, who had heard of this copy received by Mr. Erskine, to enquire whether there would probably be a call of the Senate at an early day to consider the Treaty; as some of them would, in that case, prefer to remain here. The President replied, in emphatic tone, "Certainly not!" He then added, that there were two things, either of which would prevent him from troubling the Senate with the consideration of this Treaty. The one was, that it contained no satisfactory article respecting the impressment of men from our ships — not even what they had offered at a previous stage of the negotiation; and the other was a declaration delivered by the British Commissioners at the time when the Treaty was signed, purporting that the King reserved the right of retaliating against the decree of the French Emperor of 21st November last; unless the United States should resist it. This, the President said, would involve us in the war, and compel us to make a common cause with Great Britain; and the only way he could account for our Ministers' having signed such a Treaty, with such circumstances, was by supposing that in the first panic of the French Imperial decree they had concluded a war would be inevitable, and that we must make a common cause with England. He should, however, continue amicable negotiations with England, and continue the suspension of the Non-Importation Act; and instructions had been sent in January to our Ministers, which he supposed they had by this time received, to give notice, even if they should have signed the Treaty without the article to protect our seamen from impressment, that it should not be ratified, and to renew the negotiation.

Boston, Apr. 5. — Mr. Dexter called upon me this afternoon. I attended the federal meeting at Faneuil Hall this evening. The hall was nearly as full as it could hold. Mr. Quincy was speaking when I went in. Mr. Otis and Mr. Gore succeeded him. But there was no diversity of opinion. The vote was put for supporting Mr. Strong as Governor at the election to-morrow, and Mr. Robbins as Lieutenant Governor, with the last year's list of Senators. They were all unanimously carried.

July 10. — A meeting of the citizens of Boston and the neighboring towns had been called to meet at the State House to consider the late outrageous attack of the British ship *Leopard* upon our frigate *Chesapeake,* and to adopt resolutions concerning it. I had been desirous of a regular *town meeting,* but this was utterly discouraged by the federalists, and the other party were afraid of calling it. The meeting was not numerous, and consisted almost entirely of friends to the present Administration. Mr. Morton urged me to act as moderator, but I declined.[9]

Washington, Nov. 3. — . . . Dined at the President's, with a company consisting chiefly of members of Congress — Messrs. Mitchell, Van Cortlandt, Verplanck, Van Allen, Johnson, Key, Magruder, Taylor, Calhoun, Butler, Thompson, and Eppes. I mentioned to Mr. Jefferson that the publishing committee had a letter from him to the Earl of Buchan, sent by him to the Massachusetts Historical Society with a view to its publication. But the committee thought it most consistent

[9] Adams's blood had boiled when he heard the outrage of the *Leopard* " openly justified at noonday " by a prominent Federalist, John Lowell. He helped draw up some rather belligerent resolutions adopted by this State House meeting. The Federalists were incensed. This, he later wrote, was the episode " which alienated me from that day and forever from the councils of the Federal party."

at least with delicacy to ascertain whether the publication would be not disagreeable to him. He asked whether it did not contain some free sentiments respecting the British Government. I told him it did. He then desired that it might not be published, *at least while he remained in public office;* and said he could not conceive why Lord Buchan could have sent it for publication, unless it were because it contained some compliments to himself. At dinner there was much amusing conversation between him and Dr. Mitchell, though altogether desultory. There was, as usual, a dissertation upon wines; not very edifying. Mr. Jefferson said that the *Epicurean* philosophy came nearest to the truth, in his opinion, of any ancient system of philosophy, but that it had been misunderstood and misrepresented. He wished the work of Gassendi concerning it had been translated. It was the only accurate account of it extant. I mentioned Lucretius. He said that was only a part — only the *natural* philosophy. But the *moral* philosophy was only to be found in Gassendi. Dr. Mitchell mentioned Mr. Fulton's steamboat as an invention of great importance. To which Mr. Jefferson, assenting, added, " and I think his torpedoes a valuable invention too." He then enlarged upon the certainty of their effect, and adverted to some of the obvious objections against them, which he contended were not conclusive. Dr. Mitchell's conversation was very various, of chemistry, of geography, and of natural philosophy; of oils, grasses, beasts, birds, petrifactions, and incrustations; Pike and Humboldt, Lewis and Barlow, and a long train of et cetera — for the Doctor knows a little of everything, and is communicative of what he knows — which makes me delight in his company. Mr. Jefferson said that he had always been extremely fond of agriculture, and knew nothing about it, but the person who united with other sciences the greatest agricultural knowledge of any man he knew was Mr. Madison. He was the best farmer in the world. On the whole, it was one of the most agreeable dinners I have had at Mr. Jefferson's.

Nov. 14. — In the evening I received a letter from Governor Sullivan. From the intelligence this day received from Europe, the opinion I have entertained for some months, that this country cannot escape a war is very much confirmed. It is a prospect from which I would gladly turn my eyes — to my parents, to my children, to my country, full of danger if not of ruin — yet a prospect which there is scarce a hope left of avoiding. May I meet it as becomes a man.

Nov. 17. — I observe among the members great embarrassment, anxiety, alarm, and confusion of mind, but no preparation for any measure of vigor, and an obvious strong disposition to yield all that Great Britain may require, to preserve peace, under a thin external show of dignity and bravery.

Nov. 25. — . . . Dr. Mitchell's Gun-boat bill was taken up in committee of the whole, and warmly debated, until, at his own motion, it was postponed for further consideration until next Monday (30th). I moved a resolution to request of the President a statement of impressed seamen since the last report. It lies for consideration. Dined at the President's, with my wife. Mr. and Mrs. Erskine and Mr. Foster were there — as were Mr. and Mrs. Blount, Mr. Barlow, and M. Fulton. The President said to Mr. Erskine that, by the accounts in the English newspapers, it was alleged that their Government had determined to transfer the pending negotiation here; " and that," said he, " I suppose will take us all winter, and in the meantime your nation will make peace, and leave us nothing to dispute about — *that is all my hope.*" If there was any sincerity in these words, *procrastination* includes the whole compass of Mr. Jefferson's policy, which I believe to be really the case. Mr. Fulton was very anxious to make an experiment of his torpedoes before both Houses of Congress.

Dec. 14. — Mr. Quincy brought me a transcript of the petition from Boston for the modification, suspension, or repeal of the Non-Importation Act, signed by upwards of eight hundred names. I had told General Smith of Maryland that this petition was coming, and asked him what should be done with it. He said it would be best to let it lie on the table with the petition from Philadelphia. I have conversed lately several times with him and Dr. Mitchell and Mr. Anderson, and told them that I believed the best thing that could be done by the Administration would be to give up this law and repeal it at once; but that, as the Executive would finally be the responsible party, and as it had been passed for the purpose of aiding in negotiation, so long as the President believed it would assist him, I would not countenance anything that should attempt to weaken the Government by opposition.

Dec. 18. — . . . We attended the Senate about noon. A motion was made for considering my proposed amendment to the Bridge bill, when a message came from the President. There was a private letter to the Vice-President, stating that the message was to be confidential or not, as Congress should deem expedient, and a request that two papers, being letters between General Armstrong and Champagny, the French Minister of Foreign Affairs, should be returned. From these documents it appeared that the Emperor of France had determined to carry the decree of 21st November, 1806, into full execution, without regard to her Treaty with us. The message enclosed also the King of England's proclamation recalling his seamen and authorizing their impressment from merchant vessels. It likewise recommended in unequivocal terms an immediate embargo.

Dec. 22. — Committee of enquiry again. Mr. Smith brought us a number of additional papers, which were read. I also read my draft of a report, after some little effort for its further postponement. Some diversity of opinion rose upon it, and Mr. Pope took the paper with him to look over. In Senate, we closed and opened our doors several times, on the several stages of the Embargo bill. We agreed immediately to the amendments from the House; and the bill was approved and signed by the President in the course of the day.[10] It was finally, after much debate, agreed to print the papers, excepting the two letters which the President had requested might be returned. The Potomac Bridge bill was debated at the third reading, but the question upon its passage not taken.

Dec. 31. — . . . *Day.* The whole of this month I have been so much engaged upon committees and their business that I have been obliged entirely to forego the continuation of my lectures. I rise generally with the sun, or a little before. Read or write until nine. Breakfast, and walk to the Capitol, where I am very much occupied until four. Walk home. Dine, and pass the evening in my chamber reading public

[10] Adams boldly supported the Embargo Bill of Jefferson, which was received with rage and despair by the commercial States. The New England Federalists were aroused to a new pitch of anger against Adams when they learned that he had been a member of the committee which reported the bill. Henceforth he was the target of unmerciful abuse.

papers or writing until nine at night. Supper below; bed about eleven. Occasionally spending an evening abroad.

I have more than abundant reason to be thankful for the blessings of Providence during the past year, which has been perhaps the most prosperous year of my life, and the least checkered with unpropitious events. After passing its two earliest months here, in March I returned home, and resumed my residence in Boston. There I passed the summer, and was blessed in the birth of a third son, who has hitherto had health beyond the common portion of an infant. My other children, though of more slender constitutions, have also been preserved to us, as have my parents and other near relations. On the return of the Congressional meeting, with my wife and infant boy I came safely here, where we have since remained. My private affairs have been improving, though I have contracted a large debt, which it must be my constant and unwearied care to discharge. My own health, with some slight interruptions, has been greater than I had known for many years. My general consideration among my fellow-citizens, though not marked by any new public testimonial in the course of the year, has been to my observation apparently rising. During the present session of the Senate my standing in that body has been singular — apparently so distinguished as to have excited jealousies, with little more real influence than heretofore. The usual principal leading characters of the Senate have been absent altogether, or principally, this session. Tracy and Baldwin are no more. Giles and Bayard have not yet appeared. Smith of Maryland has been absent nearly half the time. The leading members have been Bradley, Anderson, and Mitchell, with whom in respect of the business of committees I have been much associated. On most of the great national questions now under discussion, my sense of duty leads me to support the Administration, and I find myself of course in opposition to the federalists in general. But I have no communication with the President other than that in the regular order of business in Senate. In this state of things my situation calls in a peculiar manner for prudence; my political prospects are declining, and as my term of service draws near its close, I am constantly approaching to the certainty of being restored to the situation of a private citizen. For this event, however, I hope to have my mind sufficiently prepared. In the meantime, I implore that Spirit from whom every good and perfect gift descends to enable me to render essential service to my country, and that I may never be governed in my public conduct by any consideration other than that of my duty.

Jan. 1, 1808. — At noon I went with the ladies to pay the customary visit to the President. There was a very numerous company of men, women, and children; but no Indians. Mr. Monroe and General Wilkinson were the strangers of principal note present. We stayed about an hour, and returned immediately home. I employed the day and evening as usual, but rather more remissly.

Jan. 7. — The amendments to the bill supplementary to the Embargo were considered, and, with some others, modified and adopted. The bill passed the third reading. The report upon John Smith's case was taken up, and upon a motion that he should be heard by counsel, which on the yeas and nays was unanimously agreed to. Mr. Hillhouse attacked the report, and Mr. Bayard both that and the reporter with unusual virulence. At this I was not surprised; but Bayard carried it farther than I expected. Though much provoked, I forbore answering as I might have done. It is indeed a fiery ordeal that I have to go through. God speed me through it! In the evening I went with the ladies to a tea-party at Georgetown, at Governor Lee's. I could not well spare the time, but I felt that I wanted some dissipation. The insidious and false imputations which Bayard had attempted to cast upon me, in two long speeches delivered in his highest tone of eloquence, had affected me more than they ought to do. For, after all, I know it is not in his power now essentially to injure my credit either with the Senate or with the public, and that his most violent attacks upon me can give him nothing more than a hard-bought triumph on the mere forms of debate.

Jan. 9. — Both Houses met this day and passed the bill supplementary to the Embargo.

Jan. 23. — I dined with Mr. Bradley at his lodgings, and in the evening attended the convention of members to nominate suitable persons as candidates for the offices of President and Vice-President. There has been much question as to Mr. Bradley's authority to call this convention, which it seems he contends was given him at a convention on the last presidential election, four years ago. The New York members especially are extremely averse to it. There were, however, about ninety members who assembled under Mr. Bradley's summons; upon which he stated the authority formerly given him, and his reasons for calling the meeting. But he said that, as exception had been taken to his exercise of that authority, it was now at an end, and the meeting must proceed at their own pleasure. He said that he had issued his circulars to every republican member of both Houses; indeed, to every member, excepting *five* of the Senate and twenty-two of the House of Representatives. Nor should I have omitted them, said he, but that they have never been in the habit of acting with us. Mr. Giles moved that Mr. Bradley should take the chair; which he accordingly did. It was agreed that the members present should be counted, and Mr. Milledge and Mr. Varnum were appointed tellers. The number present was found to be eighty-nine. Mr. Bradley proposed the appointment of a clerk. Mr. Burwell and Mr. G. W. Campbell were successively chosen, and excused themselves from serving. Mr. Johnson, of Kentucky, was then chosen, and accepted. After some question whether there should be a viva voce nomination and a subsequent ballot, it was at last agreed to vote by ballot without nomination. On taking the ballots for the office of President, there were eighty-three votes for James Madison, three for James Monroe, and three for George Clinton. Before the ballot for Vice-President, Mr. Pope made a speech recommending unanimity for the choice of this office. The votes were seventy-nine for George Clinton, five for Henry Dearborn, three for John Langdon, and one for J. Q. Adams. The chairman then declared James Madison duly nominated, by a great majority of votes, as a candidate for the office of President, and George Clinton for that of Vice-President. A committee of correspondence was then chosen, consisting of a member from each State; but Connecticut and Delaware, not being present, had no members chosen. A resolution was then offered by Mr. Giles, and adopted, for publication, stating this nomination, and the reasons which induced the meeting to make it, after which the meeting adjourned without day, and I came home. Many of the persons who attended this meeting thought it precipitately called. Many refused to attend. The number present was a bare majority of the whole number of members. Twenty-seven federalists were not invited; about sixty others were absent, among whom were all the Virginian, or Randolph minority.

Feb. 13. — There were at the Capitol several members of both Houses, and Mr. Giles appeared much exasperated at a threat which has appeared from Mr. Monroe, of publishing another book — an electioneering book, to defeat Madison's election and promote his own.   Giles says he told Mr. Jefferson it would end in that, long since, and that he would after his return home pursue a course of conduct which would lead to his own destruction or to that of the administration.

Mr. Cook, of the House of Representatives, asked me for some private conversation; and then told me that many of the Eastern members were disgusted at the state of degradation and oppression in which the interests of that part of the country were kept by these negro votes (as he called them).   He said that Mr. Story was here, and very much hurt at the refusal of the House yesterday to hear him as counsel for the *Yazoo* claimants.   And he asked me *what was to be done?*   I told him that before anything could be done by way of concerted operation for retrieving that weight in the national councils to which we were justly entitled, it would be necessary that we should understand one another, and be sure that we could harmonize among ourselves; that I had little intimacy with the members of his general political opinions; that our weakness was the necessary consequence of our divisions; that unless these could be healed it was idle to think of attempting anything; that if a disposition to that object existed, I should be glad to contribute my aid for effecting it, and I should readily converse with any gentleman who wished it on the subject.

March 2. — Mr. G. W. Campbell and Mr. Gardenier this morning fought their duel, in which the latter was badly, if not mortally wounded.   Mr. Campbell afterwards took his seat in the House of Representatives as if nothing had happened. Mr. White did not make his appearance in Senate, and Mr. Bayard, after attending a few minutes, went out to visit his unfortunate friend.

March 4. — The Senate adjourned early, and I know not upon what they were engaged, for Mr. Nicholas asked for some conversation with me in the committee room of the Senate; to which we accordingly retired.   He then expressed much anxiety respecting the present state of affairs, and particularly respecting the rumors of French influence as predominating in the Administration. He was very solicitous that they should be refuted; declared they were entirely destitute of truth, and requested me to ask the President himself, who would be pleased to give me a direct answer on the subject. I told him that the jealousies and suspicions among my friends and neighbors were founded on a variety of circumstances, which gave them color and which were not easily susceptible of refutation. I then told him of a letter I had seen early last summer from the Governor of Nova Scotia, asserting that the British Government were informed of a plan determined upon by France to conquer the British Provinces on this continent and form a monarchy of them under General Moreau, and at the same time to introduce a more monarchical government in these States; all which was to be effected by means of a war between this country and Great Britain. This story, combined with many recent occurrences, was a source of distrust which could not without difficulty be removed. He disclaimed all knowledge or belief of such a plan, and supposed its objects to be merely a British device to divide and distract us.

March 19. — I went into the House of Representatives, and heard them debating on the Army bill. They soon adjourned. Sloan, the Quaker member from New Jersey, came and said he was now for George Clinton as President, and James Monroe for Vice-President, though he had voted for Mr. Madison at the meeting. William Duane, he said, was coming out in the *Aurora* very strong for Madison; but Clinton and Monroe would be elected. I spent the evening at home writing. As I went to the Capitol this morning I met Mr. Quincy, who turned about and walked back with me. Mr. Livermore, after making yesterday a motion in the House of Representatives to raise the embargo and suspend intercourse with France and Spain, which was refused to be considered, eighty-two to twenty-four, went off home this morning without giving notice to anybody at his lodgings. Mr. Rose's negotiation closed.

March 22. — On my arrival in Senate I found the message from the President had been received, containing the copies of all the negotiations with France and England for two or three years. The papers are very voluminous. We read until nearly four o'clock, and adjourned without doing anything else.

March 29. — There was little business done in Senate. Since the reading of the dispaches there appears a great list-lessness upon subjects of minor importance. After the ad-journment I went for a short time into the House of Repre-sentatives. They were on the Post Office bill. It seems the President has given an extra-official hint that he does not much apprehend war, and that the number of troops the House were raising would not all be wanted. So they have already reduced it from ten to six thousand.

March 31. — I finished my letter to H. G. Otis for publica-tion, and, before I sent it away, showed it to Mr. Anderson for his opinion whether there was anything in it that ought to be struck out — in particular, whether it treated my colleague, Mr. Pickering, with sufficient delicacy. He returned it with commendation, and without suggesting any alteration. I enclosed it to W. S. Shaw, with a request that he would get it printed immediately. I also wrote a few lines to H. G. Otis, mentioning this letter to him, and my motives for sending it to Shaw for publication.

April 11. — I reached the Capitol this morning rather later than usual, and found the Senate in session. The Vice-President had been formally complaining of the President for a mistake which was really his own. The message of the twenty-six of February was read in public because the Vice-President on receiving it had not noticed the word "*confi-dential*" written on the outside cover. This has been told in the newspapers, and commented on as evidence of Mr. Clinton's *declining years*. He thinks it was designedly done by the President to ensnare him and expose him to derision. This morning he asked Mr. Otis for a certificate that the message was received in Senate without the word " confi-dential; " which Otis declining to do, he was much incensed with him, and spoke to the Senate in anger, concluding by say-ing that he thought the *Executive* would have had more magnanimity than to have treated him thus. This scene hap-pened before I took my seat.

April 13. — A variety of business was done in Senate, but none which occasioned much debate. The Court-Martial bill, after having once passed to a third reading, was again taken up as at the second, and amended; after which it passed to the third reading.

After the adjournment, Mr. Anderson's committee on the negotiation message met, and considered a proposition for authorizing the President to suspend the Embargo during the recess of Congress, if circumstances to justify the measure should occur. I submitted a proposition for prohibiting all intercourse with France, Spain, Holland, and Great Britain, and repealing the Embargo with respect to the dominions of all foreign States not having issued decrees in violation of the laws of nations against us. This was rejected. I then proposed that the President be authorized to suspend the Non-Importation Act as well as the Embargo. This was agreed to.

April 25. — This day closed the first session of the Tenth Congress, which has been sitting precisely six months. The day passed in the usual hurry and confusion of a closing day; but without the usual differences between the two Houses; and it is remarkable that this is the first session since the establishment of the Government during which there has not been one instance of a conference upon disagreeing votes.

Boston, May 10. — I called on Chief-Justice Parsons [11] and had some conversation with him on political subjects. I found him, as I expected, totally devoted to the British policy, and avowing the opinion that the British have a right to take their seamen from our ships — have a right to interdict our trade with her enemies, other than the peace trade — and a right, by way of retaliation, to cut off our trade with her enemies altogether. He also thinks the people of this country corrupted, already in a state of voluntary subjugation to France, and ready to join an army of Buonaparte, if he should send one here, to subdue themselves. The only protection of our liberties, he thinks, is the British navy.

June 1. — General Varnum called upon me this morning and had some conversation with me on the subject of public affairs. He read to me a part of a letter from Washington, which states that it was circulated there, and had been asserted by a federalist, with the offer of a bet, that Mr. Madison had made me the offer of a foreign embassy provided I would join his party. I told him there was no foundation in the report — that I had never had any conversation with Mr. Madison, either about

[11] Theophilus Parsons (1750–1813) was chief justice of the State Supreme Court, and a man of great learning and influence. Adams was now finding himself, in his anti-British stand, in direct conflict with dominant New England sentiment.

the next election or about political party — that Mr. Madison had never made me any promises, and I was never inclined to receive any promises from him had he been disposed to make me any.

June 3. — The appointment of Mr. Lloyd as a Senator of the United States in my stead, after the third of March next, was this day confirmed by the Senate — twenty-one votes for Mr. Lloyd and seventeen for me.

June 8. — I found, on going into State Street, that Mr. Wheaton's anti-embargo resolutions were yesterday adopted by the Senate. I therefore this day sent a letter to the two Houses with my resignation of my seat as a Senator of the United States; which I enclosed to Mr. H. G. Otis, and left at his house, he not being at home.[12]

July 11. — I enter this day upon my forty-second year. I employed it from early in the morning until the dusk of evening assiduously writing at my lecture and reading. The day was dull and rainy until towards night, when the sky cleared and the sun with " farewell sweet " made its appearance. I walked nearly an hour in the Mall. The return of my birthday is one of the seasons which call upon me for reflection. In the course of the last year I have been called by my duties as a citizen and man to act and to suffer more than at any former period of my life. To my duties I have steadfastly adhered. The course I pursued has drawn upon me much obloquy, and the change of parties in the State, with an accumulated personal malignity borne me, both on my father's and my own account, by those who rule the State, produced in the first instance the election of a Senator to fill my place after the third of March next. The election was precipitated for the sole purpose of specially marking me. For it ought, in regular order, not to have been made until the winter session of the Legislature. They also passed resolutions enjoining upon their Senators a course of conduct which neither my judgment could approve nor my spirit brook. I therefore resigned my seat. For my future prospects I have no reliance but on the Disposer of events.

[12] Adams's term as Senator was to expire March 4, 1809. By electing his successor so many months before it was necessary to do so, the Massachusetts legislature administered a stinging and insulting rebuke to him. The anti-Embargo resolves underlined this rebuke, and Adams's pride compelled him to resign forthwith. The son of John Adams lost his office for supporting Thomas Jefferson!

March 4. — Going up to the Capitol, I met Mr. Quincy, who was on his way to Georgetown to get a passage to Baltimore. The Court met at the usual hour, and sat until twelve. Mr. Martin continued his argument until that time, and then adjourned until two.

I went to the Capitol, and witnessed the inauguration of Mr. Madison as President of the United States. The House was very much crowded, and its appearance very magnificent. He made a very short speech, in a tone of voice so low that he could not be heard, after which the official oath was administered to him by the Chief-Justice of the United States, the four other Judges of the Supreme Court being present and in their robes. After the ceremony was over I went to pay the visit of custom. The company was received at Mr. Madison's house; he not having yet removed to the President's house. Mr. Jefferson was among the visitors. The Court had adjourned until two o'clock. I therefore returned to them at that hour. Mr. Martin closed the argument in the cause of Fletcher and Peck; after which the Court adjourned. I came home to dinner, and in the evening went with the ladies to a ball at Long's, in honor of the new President. The crowd was excessive — the heat oppressive, and the entertainment bad. Mr. Jefferson was there. About midnight the ball broke up.

March 6. — This morning, while at breakfast, I received a note from Mr. Madison, the new President, requesting me, as I go up to the Capitol Hill, to call on him at his late residence, or at the President's house; which I accordingly did. He there informed me that he proposed to nominate me to the Senate as Minister Plenipotentiary to Russia. Mr. Jefferson had sent Mr. Short there last summer, but on his nominating him the Senate rejected the nomination. Mr. Madison said he had been informed the objection was not to the mission, but to the man; that the Emperor of Russia had so frequently and so strongly urged a wish for an interchange of Ministers with this country, that he, Mr. Madison, was very desirous of complying with that inclination; that the commercial relations between the two countries were important, and that in this desposition of the Emperor, perhaps some valuable advantages might be obtained. He apologized for not having given me earlier notice of this proposition, from the extraordinary pressure of business which the recent occurrences had thrown upon him; and observed that the nominations must be sent in within the course of half an hour. . .

I told him that, upon the little consideration I was able to give the subject upon this sudden notice, I could see no sufficient reason for refusing the nomination; though, from the circumstances, the confirmation by the Senate might be uncertain.

He again apologized for the shortness of the time, and said if, upon further consideration, I should perceive any insuperable obstacle to my acceptance, or the confirmation of the appointment, I might still reserve the right of finally declining.[13]

On these grounds I consented that the nomination should be made. The report of the nomination was circulated within an hour of the time when I went into court.

[13] The Senate confirmed the nomination of Adams as our first Minister to Russia by a vote of 19 to 7, Timothy Pickering stubbornly opposing him. He was fortunate in obtaining such an appointment, for he could have no political future in New England until after the War of 1812.

CHAPTER III

1809–1813

MINISTER TO RUSSIA — THE CZAR ALEXANDER I — LIFE IN ST. PETERSBURG — AMERICA AND ENGLAND AT WAR — NAPOLEON INVADES RUSSIA — HIS RETREAT AND DEFEAT — GALLATIN AND BAYARD ARRIVE.

Saturday, Aug. 5, 1809. — At noon this day I left my house, at the corner of Boylston and Nassau Streets, in Boston, accompanied by my wife, my youngest child, Charles Francis, my wife's sister, Catherine Johnson, my nephew and private secretary, William Steuben Smith, Martha Godfrey, who attends my wife as her chambermaid, and a black man-servant named Nelson, to embark on a voyage to Russia,[1] charged with a commission as Minister Plenipotentiary from the United States of America to that Court. We went in a carriage over Charles River bridge to Mr. William Gray's wharf in Charlestown, and there went on board his ship *Horace,* Captain Beckford, fitted out on a voyage to St. Petersburg direct. We found already on the ship Mr. Alexander H. Everett and Mr. Francis C. Gray, who are going with me, as secretaries attached to the Legation, but at their own expense. Mr. and Mrs. Gray were also at the vessel, with two of their other sons. There were also a number of gentlemen there, who took leave of us at the wharf. We left it precisely as the Boston and Charlestown bells were ringing one o'clock.

At this commencement of an enterprise, perhaps the most important of any that I have ever in the course of my life been engaged in, it becomes me to close the day by imploring the

---

[1] At this time France and Russia were on good terms; after the war of 1805–07, they had patched up a temporary peace at Tilsit. Russia had just concluded her war with Sweden by the conquest of most of Finland, and was still at war with Turkey.

blessing of Providence upon it — that its result may prove beneficial to my country, prosperous to my family and myself, and advantageous to all who are concerned in the voyage.

Aug. 6. — On rising this morning we found ourselves out of sight of land. Weather cool and foggy. Winds light and rather scant — about south, with some east. All the ladies, Charles, and Mr. Everett, who had never before been to sea, are sick. Mr. Gray, who likewise is a new sailor, has not yet been so. Mr. Smith and I scarcely perceive that we are at sea.

This is the fourth time in the course of my life I have embarked from Boston for Europe. The first was 11th February, 1778, in the *Boston* frigate, Captain Tucker. The second 14th November, 1779, in the *Sensible,* French frigate, Captain Chevagnes. The third, 17th September, 1794, in the *Alfred,* merchant ship, Captain Macey. On the first and second of the voyages I accompanied my father, who was going abroad upon public missions. On the third I went in a similar character myself and was accompanied by my brother. The separation from my family and friends has always been painful; but never in the degree which I feel it now. The age of my parents awakens, both in them and me, *the hopes* of our meeting again, and I now leave two of my own infant children behind. My father and mother are also deeply affected by my departure, and I received yesterday from my mother a letter which would have melted the heart of a Stoic.

Aug. 13. — Head winds and fogs continually rising and dispersing through the day — saw nothing. I read over again Plutarch's life of Lycurgus, and made some minutes from it. In the afternoon also I read two sermons of Massillon — on the forgiveness of injuries, and on the word of God. The first of these is the best of this author's sermons that I have yet read. The subject is indeed most interesting and copious, and the manner in which he treats it is adapted peculiarly to his auditory — to men of the world and courtiers.

Aug. 31. — *Day.* I rise about six o'clock, often earlier. Read ten or fifteen chapters in the Bible. We breakfast about nine. Spent half an hour afterwards upon deck — at noon sometimes take the observation by the quadrant. Read or write in the cabin until two. Dine. After dinner read or write again; occasionally visiting the deck for a walk until seven in the evening. Sup. Read or play at cards till eleven or twelve, when we all retire to bed. There is much time for study and for meditation at sea; and when the weather is as moderate as we have generally had it hitherto upon this passage, a person capable of useful application may employ his time to as great advantage as on shore. The objects which excite attention are concentrated within the bounds of the vessel; the rest of mankind for the time seem to be inhabitants of another planet.

Off Norway, Sept. 19. — We had a calm and quiet night — and this morning about six, the captain called me, and told me there was a cruiser close on board of us. I rose immediately, and within a quarter of an hour a brig with English colors lay alongside of us. Without speaking, she sent a boat with an officer and four men to us. The officer came on board, and after examining the captain's papers, left us, saying, " I suppose you may proceed." He told me it was fortunate we had not met him last night, for he might have fired into us; having been yesterday all day in pursuit of two Danish men-of-war, which they chased into Christiansand. This was a brig of eighteen guns. He gave the captain some news — as that the French had defeated the Austrians in a battle, and there was now an armistice between them; that the English in Portugal had also been defeated, and Lord Wellesley obliged to make good his retreat.

Off Denmark, Sept. 25. — At sunrise this morning we were abreast of Koll Point, the wind having been light and favorable the whole night, but it now came ahead, and in the midst of the passage of the sound we saw a British line-of-battle-ship and a sloop of war at anchor, with several other vessels anchored near them.

St. Petersburg, Oct. 23. — It was as fair as possible coming up to St. Petersburg. Admiral Kolokoltzof, who with the governor of Cronstadt paid me this morning a visit, offered me the use of a Government boat, with a deck and cabin, but at the same time advised us to stay here until the weather should be more moderate. The admiral the next in command under him, Lomenne, also paid us a visit, and recommended to us to wait for fine weather. But we could procure no lodgings at any public house. We had been already too burdensome to Mr. Sparrow, and could not think of continuing longer at his house. An American gentleman, Mr. Martin, was coming up to Petersburg, and offered to bear us company; and by delay we might have lost the finest opportunity for completing in three or four hours of time the remainder of our voyage. . .

When we came to the land, Mr. Martin immediately went and procured a carriage, in which the ladies rode with the child, while we walked to his lodgings. A Mr. Richardson, whom we met upon the quay, and who undertook to look out lodgings for us, came in early in the evening, and with him I went to the Hôtel de Londres, in the street called Newsky Perspective, and engaged an apartment of five indifferent chambers, but said to be the best in the city.

Oct. 25. — This morning Mr. Harris sent a note to the High Chancellor of the Empire, Count Romanzoff, informing him of my arrival, and of my wish to visit him, enquiring at what time it would be agreeable to him to receive this visit. He appointed seven o'clock this evening. Mr. Harris dined with us, and, at seven this evening went with me to the Chancellor's. We went according to the customary style, in full dress. The Count received us with courtly state and politeness. He asked for a copy of my credential letter, which I gave him, with a French translation. He said that the Emperor was now indisposed with a inflammation in both his legs, which confined him to a seat on his sofa, but he would be up again in the course of a few days.

Nov. 2. — Mr. Harris called again, and passed a couple of hours with us in the evening. He also sent me a Russian and French dictionary and grammar, from which I began the attempt to learn the characters of the Russian alphabet. Among the peculiarities of this country with which it will be proper to become more conversant, are the stoves, the kitchens, the double windows, the construction of the houses generally, and the drosskys. These and other things will be the subjects of more particular future observation. I tried this day two of their most ordinary liquors — the quas, at two kopecks the bottle, and the chitslisky, at five. They have a taste of small beer, with an acid not unpalatable to me, though much so to all the rest of the family.

Nov. 5. — At ten minutes past one, according to the appointment of M. de Maisonneuve, I went to the Imperial Palace, and at about two was conducted by him to the entrance of the Emperor's cabinet, the door of which was opened, and at which he stopped. I entered, and found the Emperor Alexander I alone.[2]

As I stepped forward, he advanced to me near to the door, and said, in French, "Monsieur, je suis charmé d'avoir le plaisir de vous voir ici."

I then presented to him my credential letter, and, addressing him in French, said that in delivering it, I was charged to add that the President of the United States hoped his Imperial Majesty would consider the mission as a proof of the President's respect for his Majesty's person and character, of his desire to multiply and to strengthen the relations of friendships and commerce between his Majesty's provinces and the United States, and of grateful acknowledgment for the frequent testimonials of good will which his Majesty, on many occasions, had given towards the United States.

He replied by desiring me to assure the President of the United States that this new addition to the relations between the two countries gave him great pleasure; that in everything that depended upon him he should be happy to contribute towards increasing the friendly intercourse between them; that with regard to the political relations of Europe, and those unhappy disturbances which agitated its different states, the system of the United States was wise and just, and they might rely upon it he would do nothing to withdraw them from it; that the continent of Europe was now in a manner pacified, and that the only obstacle to a general pacification was the obstinate adherence of England to a system of maritime pretensions which was neither liberal nor just; that the only object now to be attained by the war was to bring England to reasonable terms on this subject, and that she could no longer flatter herself with any support for her system upon the Continent; . .

In the midst of this conversation he had taken me by the arm and walked from near the door to a window opening upon the river — a movement seemingly intended to avoid being

---

[2] The Czar Alexander I had ascended the throne in 1801, and ruled Russia for a quarter century. He was a man of broad and liberal education, and being now little past thirty, had much of the ardor of youth; though helping Napoleon uphold the Continental system, he was introducing internal reforms. Already dominant opinion in Russia, always suspicious of Napoleon, was beginning to turn away from France.

overheard. I occasionally answered his remarks, by observing to him that, as the political duty of the United States towards the powers of Europe was to forbear interference in their dissensions, it would be highly grateful to the President to learn that their system in this respect met the approbation of his Imperial Majesty; that being at once a great commercial and a pacific nation, they were greatly interested in the establishment of a system which should give security to the fair commerce of nations in time of war; that the United States, and the world of mankind, expected that this blessing to humanity would be accomplished by his Imperial Majesty himself, and that the United States, by all the means in their power, consistent with their peace and their separation from the political system of Europe, would contribute to the support of the liberal principles to which his Majesty had expressed so strong and so just an attachment.

Nov. 12. — Mr. Harris answered my note this morning, and called upon me just before eleven o'clock. I went with him to the palace and attended the celebration of the mass, and the Te Deum. Just as we were going out from the house, I received a note from Count Romanzoff superscribed "très-pressée," informing me that her Majesty the Empress-mother had changed the hour for the presentation of Mrs. Adams to half-past two o'clock. I gave notice accordingly to Mrs. Adams.

On arriving at the palace, we were introduced first to the antechamber, where all the foreign Ministers were assembled; and I was soon called out to have a private audience of the Empress-mother.[3] She is said to be very much attached to the punctilio of etiquette, which the reigning Empress is not; but her Imperial Majesty is all condescension and affability; full of conversation, and upon a variety of topics. She spoke about America, which, she said, was "un pays bien sage." I told her that we were much obliged to her Majesty for the good opinion she entertained of us. She asked whether there were not great numbers of emigrants arriving there from Europe. I told her not many of late years. "How so?" said she. "I thought there were even in these times more than ever." I said that the ports of Holland and other

[3] The Empress-mother was the widow of the half-demented Czar Paul, who had been assassinated in 1801.

countries from which they were wont to embark had been closed against our commerce, and they could not find opportunities to go; that our commerce was shut out from almost all Europe.

" But," said she, " it is freely admitted here." I said, yes; it was an advantage which we still enjoyed and very much cherished; that from the friendly dispositions which his Majesty the Emperor was pleased to manifest towards the United States, I hoped we should continue in the enjoyment of this advantage, which was important to the interests of both countries.

She said there were many very excellent articles of commerce brought here from America. And, said I, many sent from this country equally important to us. So that it is a commerce extremely beneficial to both parties. This, she said, was the best kind of commerce. She enquired after Mr. Smith and Mr. Poinsett, who were presented here two or three years since, and of whom she spoke in very favorable terms. She asked me about our voyage. Said she had heard I had been at Berlin. Had I ever before been in Russia? I said I had, at a time when her Majesty was absent, travelling on the Continent. She said it must have been in 1781 and 1782. Which I said it was.

On taking my leave she said she was happy to see me; and hoped I should find my residence at Petersburg agreeable; that she would have the pleasure of making the acquaintance of my lady this day.

Nov. 14. — We came home at about four o'clock, and Mr. Harris dined with us. Between eight and nine in the evening we went to a splendid ball, given by the Chancellor, Count Romanzoff, to the Empress-mother, and at which were also present the Emperor and Empress, the Grand Duke Constantine, and the Grand Duchess Ann, with a court of about two hundred and fifty persons. As almost total strangers, we found this ball somewhat tedious. But it resembled in every respect the parties of a similar kind which we often attended at Berlin, where the King and royal family of Prussia were present. At this, however, the dresses were more splendid, and the profusion of diamonds and other precious stones worn both by the men and women, as well as of ribbons, blue and red, was greater than I ever witnessed anywhere. There was

a fine supper, served at ten or fifteen tables, covering the
second story of the house, besides the Emperor's table below;
which I did not see, but which is said to have been very highly
ornamented. The crowd in the dancing-rooms was very great.
The principal dancing was in what they call Polish dances,
consisting simply in a number of couples walking up and down
in the room as in a procession. The Emperor and Empress-
mother spoke, I believe, to all the foreign Ministers. He
asked me some questions about my former visit to St. Petersburg.

Nov. 15. — At two I went to Count Romanzoff's, by appointment. He received me in his private cabinet, apologizing for it, as intending by it an invitation to call upon him
whenever it might be agreeable to me. I told him the circumstances of the information which I had received from Mr.
Harris respecting the questionable passport, and its bearer,
Graham. He expressed himself much obliged to me for the
notice, of which he said he would make such use as might be
proper, without any exercise of authority which might affect
the possible rights of the individual. He entered also into much
general conversation. He assured me of his great attachment to the system of friendly intercourse with the United
States, and his conviction of long standing that the interests of
Russia perfectly harmonized with theirs. He said, Je dois
vous prévenir que nous sommes ici des grands Anglomanes;
that the prejudices in favor of England were founded upon
old habits and long-established commercial intercourse; but
that the English exclusive maritime pretensions, and views of
usurpation upon the rights of other nations, made it essential
to them, and especially to Russia, that some great commercial
state should be supported as their rival; that the United States
of America were such a state, and the highest interest of Russia
was to support and favor them, as by their relative situation
the two powers could never be in any manner dangerous to each
other; that he had been many years inculcating this doctrine at
this Court; that the Emperor had always manifested a favorable opinion of it; and he had had the satisfaction of perceiving the sentiments of his Imperial Majesty daily becoming
more strongly confirmed in this system. . .

He said he should make no scruple to say to me that he did
not approve the present system of France in relation to com-

merce; that he had seen and conversed with the Emperor Napoleon; that he had found him in general of a sound judgment and a quick perception, but that " en fait de commerce ce n'est qu'un étourdi." At the same time, he said, he hoped I should not think he meant to give him a mauvaise réputation. But he wished to know whether in the application of this system there was anything which could accommodate the views of the United States, and if there was, requested that I would suggest it.

I told him that the great and only object desirable to the United States was that to which they were entitled by right, freedom to their commerce — freedom of admission and departure for ships — freedom of purchase and sale for goods; the more completely they could obtain this, the better; that in the restrictions upon them, I thought the proceedings both of France and England unjust and impolitic; and was persuaded that the more liberal system established under his auspices by Russia was not only of great advantage to both countries, but would very much increase the commerce already existing between them.

Dec. 17. — Mr. Delapré, the keeper of the house at the Ville de Bordeaux, was here. I engaged him to furnish us our dinners at a stated price — twenty roubles a day — and I shall dismiss my cook. When a family becomes large, there is no possibility of observing economy in it without the closest attention to minute details. Since we entered this house my monthly expense books amount to double what they were the first month. We have a maître-d'hôtel, or steward; a cook, who has under him two scullions — mujiks; a Swiss, or porter; two footmen; a mujik to make the fires; a coachman and postilion; and Thomas, the black man, to be my valet-de-chambre; Martha Godfrey, the maid we brought with us from America; a femme-de-chambre of Mrs. Adams, who is the wife of the steward; a house-maid, and a laundry-maid. The Swiss, the cook, and one of the footmen are married, and their wives all live in the house. The steward has two children, and the washerwoman a daughter, all of whom are kept in the house. I have baker's, milkman's, butcher's, greenman's, poulterer's, fishmonger's, and grocer's bills to pay monthly, besides purchases of tea, coffee, sugar, wax and tallow candles. The firewood is, luckily, included as part of my rent. On all these articles of consumption the cook and steward first make their profits on the purchase, and next make free pillage of the articles themselves. The steward takes the same liberty with my wines. In dismissing my cook I shall attempt to escape from a part of these depredations. To avoid a great part of them is impossible. It is, I believe, the law of nature between master and servant that the servant shall spoil or plunder the master. In this country at least it is universal usage. It requires the most constant and minute attention to keep his pilfering within tolerable bounds; and among the losses occasioned by it the most valuable is the loss of time swallowed up in the business of such drudgery.

Jan. 8, 1810. — At supper I sat next to Count Czericheff, a young officer about twenty-five years old, who has been repeatedly sent by the Emperor in special missions, about the person of the Emperor of Austria and of the Emperor of France. He has been during the whole of the last campaign with Napoleon, and in his immediate family — constantly the companion of his table, and sleeping in his tent. He told me he had been present at eight pitched battles, among which were those of Eylau, Friedland, Essling, and Wagram. That of Essling, he said, was totally lost, " mais grandement," by the French, and that it was entirely the fault of the Austrians that they did not take advantage of it. He said that the military reputation of the Archduke Charles was irretrievably lost, and that all the present misfortunes were imputable to him almost alone. He told me several particulars relating personally to Napoleon. I asked him if he was subject to the epilepsy. He hesitated about answering, but finally said, not to his knowledge. Then, casting his eyes on both sides, as if fearful anybody might hear, he said, " il a la galle rentrée." He added that he slept little, waked often in the night, and would rise in his bed, speak, give some order, and then go to sleep again. The Duke de Mondragone told me it was not certain whether he was to marry a Princess of Saxony or of this country.

Feb. 27. — Count Romanzoff made many enquiries whether I had any intelligence from South America, which appeared to be an object of peculiar interest at this moment; but I had none. On some allusion that I made to the rigor with which the French Government and its dependencies were proceeding towards America, which I told him would most powerfully negotiate in the United States in favor of their reconciliation with England, he asked me whether I knew that Colonel Burr had gone to Paris. I said I had heard he was arrived there. He said he did not know of his arrival; but that he knew from a certain source that he was gone there. He said Colonel Burr had written a letter to him requesting permission to come here; but that, not being desirous of encouraging people who had fled from the violated laws of their own country to come into this, he had not answered his letter. If he wanted to come here he must make his application through me, and, if I had desired it, no difficulty would have been made. He enquired what Burr's project had been; which I explained to him as well as its complicated nature would admit in the compass of a short conversation.

April 29. — Easter Sunday; the greatest holiday of the Russian calendar. It celebrates the resurrection of Christ. The ceremonies, as at Christmas, begin at midnight. Mr. Everett and Mr. Smith attended at the Church of St. Isaac, where a service of about two hours was performed, partly without the church, around which the priests went three times successively in procession, and partly within it, where was a representation of the sepulchre from which the Saviour arose. The crowd of people attending was excessive. At midnight the signal was given by the firing of a cannon at the fortress, followed by several others; and at two or three subsequent periods of the night a salvo of twenty-five or thirty guns was fired. The midnight service is performed at all the churches, and the Emperor and imperial family attend at their chapel. Among the customs of the country is that of embracing one another at this period, and all the people who attend at the Court Chapel are admitted to kiss the Emperor's sleeve and the Empress's hand. It is also the custom to make presents upon this day, and particularly of eggs. The mujiks present real eggs, hard boiled and dyed red with logwood; for which they receive roubles. Persons of higher standing present eggs of sugar, glass, gilt wood, porcelain, marble, and almost every other substance, and of various dimensions, many of them made into cups, or boxes filled with sugar-plums; others with painting and biscuit figures upon them, emblematical of the crucifixion and resurrection. Some of these eggs are made to cost a hundred roubles or upwards. Servants present these eggs to their masters, and receive presents in return, as at the new year.

May 23. — There is a custom of visiting annually the Fortress of St. Petersburg this day, the occasion of which I have not heard. I thought I had not the time to spare, and did not go. Mr. Harris called upon me this afternoon, and told me he was informed that General Armstrong had left Paris. The French Ambassador gave this evening a splendid ball, on occasion of the marriage of the Emperor Napoleon. It was attended by the Emperor and imperial family. The hôtel was elegantly illuminated, as were those of General Pardo, Count Bussche, Mr. Six, the Chevalier de Bray, and Mr. Brancia, the Chargé d'Affaires of Naples. As the imperial family were at the ball, it was necessary to go early. We went at nine o'clock, but it was daylight as at noon, so that the illumination made scarcely any show at all. It was past two in the morning when the Court retired, after which we immediately came home. It was then again broad daylight, and, by the time I got to bed, almost sunrise. At midnight it scarcely could be called dark. The Emperor was gracious to everybody, even beyond his usual custom, which is remarkable for affability. He asked Mr. Harris to show him where Mrs. Adams sat, and danced a polonaise with her; and afterwards one with Catherine Johnson, a circumstance the more noticed, as she has not been presented at Court. He enquired of me whether I had taken a walk this day, and on my answering that I had, he observed that he had not met me. He said that the difference of my looks in the street, without a wig, from that in which he had usually seen me, had been the cause that the first time he had met me he did not recognize me.

June 10. — Wrote to the Secretary of State, and read Massillon's sermon upon the Assumption day of the Virgin Mary.

June 25. — Mr. Montréal offered me any money for which I might have occasion, to be drawn for at my own convenience. Mr. Harris made me the same obliging offer immediately after my first arrival here. Under the circumstances in which I find myself here, it is difficult to resist the opportunities thus presented for anticipating upon my regular income; but I am determined to do it. The whole experience of my life has been one continual proof of the difficulty with which a man can adhere to the principle of living within his income — the first and most important principle of private economy. From the month of July, 1790, when I commenced my career as a man, until the close of 1793, I was enabled to accomplish this purpose only by the assistance of small supplies from my father. I had then acquired the means of maintaining myself. In 1794 I was sent to Europe, and until my marriage, in 1797, kept more easily within my bounds than at any preceding or subsequent period. Since I have had a family, I have kept steady to my principle, but at the price of uncommon sacrifices of consideration and a reputation which, in the spirit of this age, economy cannot escape. In this country beyond all others, and in my situation more than any other, the temptations to excess in expense amount almost to compulsion. I have withstood them hitherto, and hope for firmness of character to withstand them in future. I declined with thanks Mr. Montréal's kind offer, as I had that of Mr. Harris.

July 16. — I dined at Monsieur de Laval's, at his country-seat, with a company of about twenty persons. He has a similar company every Monday at dinner during the summer, to which he and Madame de Laval, according to the custom of the country, gave me a general invitation. Mrs. Adams did not go with me; being confined to her bed, and this evening very unwell. . . After dinner came some additional company; among whom Princess Woldemar Galitzin, venerable by the length and thickness of her beard. This is no uncommon thing among the ladies of this Slavonian breed. There is at the Academy of Sciences the portrait of a woman now dead, but with beard equal to that of Plato. But of living subjects, the Princess Woldemar Galitzin is in this respect, of all the females that I have seen, the one who most resembles a Grecian philosopher.

Aug. 8. — I was engaged unavoidably until the instant when by appointment I was to call upon Count Romanzoff. . . I told him that setting aside all official character and responsibility, and speaking merely as an individual speculating upon public affairs, the advice I should give to his Excellency was, as soon as possible to convince the French Government that the Continental system, as they called it, and as they managed it, was promoting to the utmost extent the views of England; was, instead of impairing her commerce, securing to her that

of the whole world; and was pouring into her lap the means
of continuing the war, just as long as her Ministers should
think is expedient.   But I said that I could hardly conceive
that the Emperor Napoleon was so blind as not to have made
this discovery already.   Three years' experience, with the effects
of it becoming every day more flagrant, had made the inference
too clear and unquestionable.   The Emperor Napoleon, with
all his power, could neither control the elements nor the passions of mankind.   He had found that his own brother could
not, and would not, carry his system into execution, and finally
had cast at his feet the crown he had given him, rather than continue to be his instrument there any longer.   That country was
now united to France; but the trade with England would be carried on as before, and the only difference would be an increase
of contribution to pay some more French custom-house officers.

Aug. 9. — The interruption of my systematic occupations
still continues.   Letters and packages from America always
engross the first hours, and not unfrequently days, after their
arrival.   From the moment of my rising from bed this morning
until nearly the hour of dinner I was incessantly engaged with
Mr. Gray's newspapers, which, coming down to the 13th of
June, contain much news, particularly respecting the new elections in the State of Massachusetts.   I wrote, however, an
official note to Count Romanzoff concerning the two American
vessels at Archangel.   I could not walk until the evening.
On my return home, I found Mr. Harris had spent a couple of
hours with us.

Sept. 12. — Mr. Montréal told me many circumstances respecting the capture of the Duke d'Enghien, which was done
by a French corps of troops under the command of M. de
Caulaincourt.   He was then Aid-de-camp General of the First
Consul Bonaparte.   He was of a noble family of Picardy, and
his father had owed his fortune to the protection and patronage
of the Prince de Condé.   He received an order to go to
Strassburg, there to assemble the commander of troops stationed at that place, the mayor of the city, and two or three
other officers, and in their presence to open the second sealed
order which was delivered to him.   On the performance of
this duty, he found it contained an order to take a column of
troops which were placed at his disposal, to cross the Rhine,
and enter upon the territory of the Grand Duke of Baden;

to seize the person of the Duke d'Enghien, who resided there in the country at a house of his own, and transport him to the prison Vincennes, near Paris. He was very much distressed at having such a commission intrusted to him, but he executed it; and it was for that service that he was rewarded with his Duchy, his embassy here, and other rewards and honors. The Duke d'Enghien was residing at that place with the knowledge and consent of Bonaparte. He used even occasionally to go to Strassburg to the play, with the consent of Bonaparte, who had been asked whether he had any objection to it, and had made none. The Duke had notice of the approach of the French troops, and was advised to make his escape, as it was supposed they could have no other object than to take him; but he had refused, on the idea that is was impossible there could be any design to seize him. He was carried to the prison of Vincennes, and, without any formality of process, shot at two o'clock the next morning. The examination and interrogations which were published the next morning in the *Moniteur* were sheer fabrications — no trial and no interrogatory was had; and the persons whose names were signed to these seeming judicial documents never saw them until they found them in the newspapers. The Duke was shot at two o'clock in the morning, and buried in a ditch which surrounds the prison.

Sept. 26. — I have made it a practice for several years to read the Bible through in the course of every year. I usually devote to this reading the first hour after I rise every morning. As, including the Apocrypha, it contains about fourteen hundred chapters, and as I meet with occasional interruptions, when this reading is for single days, and sometimes for weeks, or even months, suspended, my rule is to read five chapters each morning, which leaves an allowance of about one-fourth of the time for such interruptions. Extraordinary pressure of business seldom interrupts more than one day's reading at a time. Sickness has frequently occasioned longer suspensions, and travelling still more and longer. During the present year, having lost very few days, I have finished the perusal earlier than usual. I closed the book yesterday. As I do not wish to suspend the habit of allowing regularly this time to this purpose, I have this morning commenced it anew, and for the sake of endeavoring to understand the book better, as well as giving some variety to the study, I have begun this time with Ostervald's French translation, which has the advantage of a few short reflections upon each chapter.

Sept. 27. — I had some conversation with the French Ambassador, from which I understood that he has received new instructions relative to the commerce in what are called colonial articles. . .

He told me that, to be candid, there was a pretty strong sentiment against the colonial trade at Paris, because they considered it as all English.   For, says he, you, for instance, raise no sugar.   I told him that he was much mistaken; that a great deal of sugar was raised in the United States, and particularly in the country ceded to us by France — Louisiana. But cotton — indigo — we were perhaps the greatest raisers of these articles in the world — they were among our most valuable staple articles.   Besides, there were the Spanish Islands — South America.   These were not English, and the Emperor Napoleon could not consider them as such; for he had more than once officially declared his friendship to them, and his willingness for their independence.

With regard to that, he said, he could not give an opinion. But as to the certificates of origin said to be given by French Consuls in America, he was assured that they must be false, as the Consuls no longer gave any such certificates.

I assured him in the most earnest terms that this was a mistake; that, to my certain knowledge, vessels which had sailed from the United States as late as the month of June had brought genuine certificates of origin from the French Consuls.   I then added that if these were the sentiments prevailing still with the French Government, I could not but lament it; that as long as they prevailed, however strong the friendly dispositions towards the United States might be said to be, the course of policy pursued must be injurious to them in the highest degree.   "You will do us," said I, "immense injury; you will oppress the Continent of Europe and yourselves with it; but take my word for it, and I pray you three years hence to remember what I say, you will do England more good than harm; you will not cut off her communication with the Continent, you will not essentially distress her commerce, but you will lay the world under the most grievous contributions for her benefit and advantage."

Oct. 8. — On rising this morning, I found the ground and roofs of the houses covered with snow, which had fallen in the course of the night. This may be considered as the signal for the approach of winter. We have had, since the first of this month, our double windows put in. The external windows consist of two parts. There are six panes to each window. The panes are twenty-five inches long and nineteen inches wide. The two uppermost are in a sash and fastened to the walls of the house; the other four are in two corresponding door-sashes suspended on both sides of the wall, and closing together with bolts both upwards and downwards. The double windows are of six panes in one sash, of corresponding size with the external windows. In most of the chambers one of the windows has one of the lower parts in the form of a door, corresponding in the external and internal window, and which serves as a ventilator when occasion requires. Between the two windows a trough about an inch deep of sand closes the crack at the bottom of the external window. The cracks all round the internal window, between it and the wall, are stuffed with oakum, and a paper border is pasted over it. Thus the windows are hermetically sealed; and this is the occasion of the equable warmth which they so commonly have in this country.

Oct. 11. — As I was walking on the Mall in front of the Admiralty, I met the Emperor, who stopped and spoke to me. He said the autumn had been finer than the summer. " But as to summer," said he, " we have had none. You must have a terrible opinion of our climate." I said that as long as one enjoyed good health all climates might be rendered agreeable.

" You have a countryman arrived, I hear," said his Majesty. " Yes, Sire." " Mr. Jones," said he; " an acquaintance, I am told, of Mr. Poinsett's." " Yes, Sire; Mr. Poinsett carried home with him such agreeable ideas of his visit to Russia, that he inspired Mr. Jones with the desire of visiting the same country." " And where did Mr. Jones see Mr. Poinsett? " " They returned in company together from Europe to America." " What! has Mr. Jones been in Europe before? " " Yes, Sire; he has travelled in France, Italy, and England."

Nov. 13. — I walked to the foundry, and in returning upon the quay of the Neva met the Emperor, first on horseback, and the second time walking. He then stopped and spoke to me about the weather and the appearance of the river. He asked me what was my habitual walk. I told him commonly to the foundry. He asked where I lived. I told him in the new street, in a corner house, partly fronting on the Moika — the apartments where the Count Einsiedel had lived. He knew it by this description, and said the situation of the house was not good; on account of walking. I said its situation was not remarkably advantageous, but that the walks in every part of the city were so convenient that it rendered the situation of a house almost immaterial. And pointing to the quay on which we stood, I said it was one of the finest works ever made by men's hands. He said they had a great advantage in possessing so much of the material, the granite rock, of which in Finland there were immense masses; that the rock on which the statue of Peter the First was placed was one of the smallest of those rocks which could have been found; that it formed blocks of whole mountains, and that there were places where it was to be seen at once in both stages of its first formation and of its last decay. I told him that I was acquainted with this rock, and that my own country produced it in great plenty; that it was considered as hardening and becoming more solid by being exposed to the air. He said it did for a certain period of time, after which it decayed and crumbled into dust. But he added that it would last a long time, and then, looking at the wall bordering the quay, observed, with a smile, "There is no danger for this yet."

Nov. 30. — *Day.* The sun rises now about nine in the morning. It is scarcely daylight at eight, and I seldom rise from bed before ten. Read five chapters in the French Bible, with Ostervald's reflections. Breakfast. Noon has arrived. A visitor or two brings it easily to three o'clock — or I write a letter, long or short, or a day's record in this book, and the day is gone. It darkens soon after two o'clock, even in the few days when the sun is seen, which is, upon the average, about once a week. The six others there is a gloomy half-darkness through the day, so that from ten until two I can just see to write. From three to five I walk. Dine at five, sit usually until seven. Spend two or three hours after dinner in my cabinet, reading Levesque, or writing short-hand on anything that must not be postponed. From nine or ten at night until one or two in the morning I pass in company abroad, or at home at cards with the ladies. The difficulty of writing anything, and the disgust at the occupation, grows upon me in a distressing manner, and I feel more and more every day the importunity of miscellaneous company.

Dec. 30. — The year 1810 is past; and to all past time we are already dead. It has been to me rich with the blessings of Providence, for which I would be duly grateful to the Giver of all good. Having been employed in the service of my country, I am not conscious of its having witnessed any neglect in the performance of my official duties, nor can I charge myself with any intentional wrong in the private affairs of life. But I have indulged too much indolence and inactivity of mind, and have not turned my leisure time to good account. I have pursued no object steadily, and the year has left no advantageous trace of itself in the annals of my life. I have formed my domestic establishment here in a very exact proportion to my means, but upon such an establishment a public Minister here can enjoy very little consideration, and must be subject to great animadversion. It is with great difficulty that I have hitherto adhered to my principles, and having now a full year's experience, I think I shall be able to carry it through. I begin already to be sensible of the approaches of age. I cannot hope for any intellectual improvement upon my faculties from the present time. I pray for the power and the will to make a better improvement of them; and for the blessing of Heaven continually upon my parents and children, my wife, my brother, sister, and all connected with them; upon my native country, and, according to the will of the eternal Disposer of events, upon the world of my fellow-creature, man.

Jan. 13, 1811. — At twelve o'clock I attended with Mr. Smith at the palace. Between one and two the mass was finished, and the Emperor and Empresses came to the diplomatic circle. The fire of the last night occasioned the principal fund for conversation. The Empresses spoke to me, as usual, of my wife and children. The Emperor said to me, " J'apprends que vous ne quittez." I said, " J'espère, Sire, que je n'aurai pas encore ce malheur." He replied, " J'espère que cela ne sera pas de sitôt." Monsieur de Maisonneuve gave me the tickets of invitation to the supper at the Hermitage, for myself, Mrs. Adams, and Catherine Johnson. The Grand Marshal of the Court, Count Tolstoy, asked me if the ladies would come, and on my telling him that they so intended, he desired me to recommend to them the entrance at the Hermitage, where he would give orders that they should be admitted. This is considered as a very extraordinary distinction, which M. de Maisonneuve specially noticed.

Jan. 20. — Our footman Paul had a daughter born on the Russian New Year's day, of which, according to the custom the country, he immediately gave me notice. Paul himself is a Finlander, and a Lutheran; but, his wife being a Russian of the Greek Church, the child, which is a daughter, was to be christened after the fashion of the Greek Church. Paul asked Mrs. Adams and Martha to stand as godmother, and Mr. Gray as godfather, and the child was baptized in our parlor, this day, at eight o'clock P.M. There was a priest and an inferior attendant not in clerical habits, who chanted the Slavonian service, the priest from a mass-book. A plated vessel of the size of a small bathing-tub contained the water, which the priest consecrated at the commencement of the ceremony. Three tapers were at first fixed at the end most distant from the priest and at the two sides of the baptismal vase. The child was brought in and held by the nurse, until the priest took it naked and plunged it three times into the water. With a pencil-brush, before and after plunging, he marked a cross on its forehead and breast, and finally on its forehead, shoulders, and feet — repeating the same thing afterwards with a wet sponge. A shirt and cap, provided by the godmother, were then put upon the child, and a gold baptismal cross, furnished by the godfather. Tapers lighted were put into their hands, two of them from the sides of the vase, round which they marched three times, preceded by the priest. He then with a pair of scissors cut off three locks of the child's hair, which, with wax, he rolled up into a little ball, and threw into the water in which the child was baptized; and finally, after a little more chanting from the book, the ceremony was concluded.

Jan. 23. — . . . I mentioned to the Count [Romanzoff] that the President of the United States, in consideration of circumstances relating to my private affairs, had given me per-

mission to return to the United States, and that I had received
a letter to take leave of the Emperor, with a discretionary
power to deliver it when I should be ready for my departure.
I presumed it would be proper for me to keep it until that time.
He said certainly; or even to suppress it altogether, if I was
not under the necessity of going. And he could assure me,
when I should go, I should be much regretted here; that they
had a very great and sincere esteem for me, and would be
happy that my stay should be prolonged. I assured him that I
was strongly sensible of the kindness and friendly reception
that I had experienced here, and should be desirous of remaining as long as I could. At any rate, I could not take my leave
until the approach of summer; and perhaps I might stay until
the appointment of a successor.

Jan. 25. — Between twelve and one o'clock I attended with
Mr. Smith at the Winter Palace. Mr. Everett likewise attended. It was nearly two when the imperial family came in
to the circle. The Emperor told me that from what the Chancellor had told him he found it was verified, as he had mentioned to me before, that I expected to go away, and he was
sorry for it.

I told him that at least I hoped it would not yet be for
some time, probably for some months.

He said, " Je regretterai beaucoup votre départ, j'espère
que votre séjour ici se prolongera encore." The Empresses
spoke about my wife, as usual, and the Empress-mother asked
me whether I had seen the ceremony of the 6th instant, and
what I thought of it. She knew very well that I had seen
it, having spoken to me after her return from the procession,
and while upon the balcony; but in the necessity of making
conversation, and the desire to appear affable, this is one of
her common practices — to ask questions about what she very
well knows, and when she is sure that the person to whom
she speaks knows that she needs no answer. She reminds me
of the personage in Molière, who, upon being asked whether
he understands Latin, answers, " Oui, mais faites comme si
je ne le savois pas." General Pardo, a Spaniard, and Count
Maistre, a Savoyard, are the only two persons of the corps
diplomatique who have any interesting literary conversation,
and they are always amusing. The General had seen a new
opera, *Helena,* which he said was very different — the music

wretched, without force or color. . . Pardo was musing, I
suppose, upon his Greek translation of Horace's odes, for he
suddenly broke out, as we entered the Salle du Trône, where
the circle was to be held —

> " Et la palme d'Horace
>   Croît et fleurit toujours au sommet du Parnasse."

The General spoke it with enthusiasm, and in uttering
the second line flourished his hand upwards higher than his
head. The lines are from Piron's *Métromanie,* which he said
nothing but prejudice could prevent him from placing on a
par with Molière. After some commonplace observations
of comparison between the two poets, Count Maistre repeated
two other lines from *Métromanie,* about which he told us an
anecdote. The lines are spoken by the old man who suddenly
found himself a poet at fifty years of age —

> " Un beau jour ce talent en moi se trouva,
>   Et j'avois cinquante ans quand cela m'arriva."

He said the Empress-mother was one day in conversation with
Prince Kurakin, now the Russian Ambassador at Paris, and a
young officer, and upon some occasion repeated the first of
these lines, and then seemed to be trying to recollect the second.
The young officer looked as if he was going to assist her
memory, and Prince Kurakin trod two or three times on
his toes. When the Empress left them, the officer asked Prince
Kurakin why he trod upon his toes. " I was afraid," said the
Prince, " that you were going to help the Empress to the
second line of her quotation, and only meant to give you a
hint qu'il ne faut jamais parler de cinquante ans à la Cour."
" So! " said the officer. " Voilà ce que c'est que d'être courtisan.
It was lucky for me that I did not know what the second line
was, for I should certainly have repeated it, without thinking at
all of its application." The Count asked me if we had any theatres or dramatic poets in America; and we talked about
Shakspeare, and Milton, and Virgil, and l'Abbé Delille. It
was about two o'clock when the Court was over.

March 11. — In walking my usual round this morning, I
met the Emperor upon the Fontanka. He stopped and talked
about the weather — said it was very windy, and that I was
in the direction to have it shortly afterwards in the face. I told

him that as it was not cold, and I had already been walking long enough to quicken the circulation, I should scarcely perceive the wind. I asked him whether this very warm weather, which has now continued nearly a fortnight, would not break up the river. He said that it would be a very extraordinary instance if it did; that the river had never been known to break up before the middle of March, and sometimes not until May. I observed that the last year it had waited until the 30th of April; but I thought it could not stand so long this season. " But," said he, " we shall be paid for all this moderate weather before the winter ends. The spring never begins before its time without relapsing afterwards into winter. Even last year, on the 31st of May, our style — think of that, our style — I was going to Twer, and had on the road a very considerable flight of snow. We gain nothing by having mild weather too soon." While he was in the midst of these remarks, a carriage-and-four passed us in the street. He stepped aside from before me, put up his glass to see who was in the carriage, bowed, and took off his hat, and then stepped back to me, and finished the sentence which he had broken off in the middle.

March 18. — Lüxbourg told me that his letters from Count Montgelas, the Bavarian Minister of Foreign Affairs, informed him that all their advices from Paris concurred in stating that the coolness between France and Russia was becoming more and more notorious, but that hopes were entertained that it would not come to an absolute rupture this season. He says that the Emperor Napoleon scarcely speaks to Prince Kurakin, and that Monsieur de Champagny has had quite an angry conversation with Mr. Nesselrode at a public dinner and before a large company. Yesterday the Ambassador dined with the Emperor, who, after dinner, was in conference with him until ten o'clock, and this day the Ambassador has been engaged writing, and has admitted nobody. In the meantime both parties continue to arm and prepare for war. There are now at least two hundred thousand men stationed on the frontier from Riga to Kiev, and yesterday or the day before one hundred and eighty heavy cannon were sent off from this city, in addition to all those that had been sent before. On the other hand, France has just sent a large quantity of fire-arms to Dantzic and Warsaw; and the number of troops under arms in the duchy of Warsaw is from fifty to sixty thousand men.

May 24. — Mr. Krehmer sent me the London *Courier,* from 19th to 26th April, where I found articles which give me great concern upon the account of my country. They threaten war in the most unequivocal terms. I fear the British Ministry have made it unavoidable. They menace us with an "Iliad of woes," and already deny us every particle of compassion for our sufferings under them. Non nobis, Domine! If our trial is now to come, God of Justice and of Mercy! give us spirit to bear with fortitude and to derive ultimate power and virtue from all the evils that they can inflict, and spare us from that woe of woes, the *compassion* of Britons!

May 31. — I took my usual morning's walk. On the Fontanka, near the bridge through which the canal joins the river, I met the Emperor walking. As he approached me he said, "Monsieur Adams, il y a cent ans que je ne vous ai vu;" and coming up, took and shook me with great cordiality by the hand. After some common observations upon the weather, which has been very fine, but which this day was cold and autumnal, and which he thought would yet come to snow, before the end of this month, Russian style, he asked me whether I intended to take a house in the country this summer. I said, no; that I had for some time had such an intention, but had given it up. "And why so?" said he. I was hesitating upon an answer, when he relieved me from embarrassment by saying, "Peut-être sont-ce des considérations de finance?" As he said it in perfect good humor, and with a smile, I replied in the same manner. "Mais, sire, elles y sont pour une bonne part." "Fort bien," said he; "vous avez raison. Il faut toujours proportionner la dépense à la recette." A maxim worthy of an Emperor, though few Emperors practise upon it. He then asked me if I had received any late news from America. I said I had. He replied that he also had lately received some very interesting dispatches from Count Pahlen which had given him much pleasure. He asked how our affairs stood with England. I said they had a very hostile appearance, and that the English journals were threatening us with the last extremities, but that my own letters from America did not appear to expect that a war would ensue.

June 4. — . . . I had written yesterday a note to Count Romanzoff, requesting a conference with him, and this morning found on my table a note from him appointing this day at noon for that purpose. I went accordingly at that hour. . . I thanked the Count for the packets which he had sent me, brought by former couriers. He said he understood they were packets which he should be sorry for; as they were to occasion my return home. I told him that they contained notice of my appointment to an honorable office in my own country; but that there was some tie which attached me so strongly to this country that I should probably not go yet. I then mentioned the situation of my wife, which would make it impossible for me to embark for America certainly until very late in the season, and probably before the next year. He asked me if the office was of a nature which would admit of being long vacant. I answered that I considered it would not; that it ought to be filled as soon as possible; and I could not go immediately to assume the discharge of its duties. I had written to the President of the United States, requesting him to excuse me from accepting it, and to appoint another person. He then said that he should this evening ask the Emperor's permission to dispatch a courier to Paris, and should probably send him in the course of the day after to-morrow. If I wished to send any letter or packet to the Chargé d'Affaires of the United States, he would be happy to forward it for me. I accepted his offer; and I then observed that from the idea which since my residence here I had formed of the importance and mutual benefit of the commercial relations between the United States and Russia, from the signal manner in which Russia had distinguished herself from all the other belligerent powers of Europe . . . , and from a wish to increase and render still more advantageous the commerce between the two countries, the idea and desire had occurred to me of cementing still further their amity by a treaty of commerce. I had suggested this idea to the American Government, and was now authorized to propose the negotiation of such a treaty, if it should be agreeable to the Emperor. I had thought it most advisable to make to him at first this verbal communication, instead of sending him an official note upon the subject. I requested him to consider it as confidential, so that at least it should be made known only when he thought it advisable; as I had communicated the knowledge of it to no person whomsoever.

July 15. — I had some conversation with the French Ambassador. He asked me how our affairs stood with England. I told him I thought it probable that his Government would make our peace with England. " How ? " " By not keeping their word. They had promised to repeal the Berlin and Milan decrees, and had not kept their promise." " Oh! but you must seize two or three English vessels, and then I will promise you that you may come freely to France, and will never be troubled with the Berlin and Milan decrees. Only you must not bring English merchandise to us."

" Americans will not bring you any English merchandise, except when you insist upon having it. But you give so many licenses for trading with England, that there is no temptation of profit to carry any English goods to you." " No, no! we do not give any more licenses. Ay! ay! my spies " (he had said in a joke that his spies had not informed him that I had moved into his neighborhood), " my spies give me quite different information. Well, if we get English merchandise, it is only to burn it." " Yes; and you have burnt so much that now you are obliged to send for more for your own use."

All this was said on both sides in a sort of banter; half jest, half earnest.

July 26. — I have this day been married fourteen years, during which I have to bless God for the enjoyment of a portion of felicity, resulting from this relation in society, greater than falls to the generality of mankind, and far beyond anything that I have been conscious of deserving. Its greatest alloy has arisen from the delicacy of my wife's constitution, the ill health which has afflicted her much of the time, and the misfortunes she has suffered from it. Our union has not been without its trials, nor invariably without dissensions between us. There are many differences of sentiment, of tastes, and of opinions in regard to domestic economy, and to the education of children, between us. There are natural frailties of temper in both of us; both being quick and irascible, and mine being sometimes harsh. But she has always been a faithful and affectionate wife, and a careful, tender, indulgent, and watchful mother to our children, all of whom she nursed herself. I have found in this connection from decisive experience

the superior happiness of the marriage state over that of
celibacy, and a full conviction that my lot in marriage has been
highly favored.

July 30. — The whole morning was engrossed by one of
those occasional occupations which so often divert me from
business of more urgency. I found in an American newspaper
a return of the whole population of the United States by the
last census of 1810, and I engaged myself in calculations
resulting from a comparison of it with the returns of 1790
and 1800. The proportion of increase between the second and
third censuses is exactly the same as that between the first and
second. It is between thirty-six and thirty-seven per cent. in
ten years; rather more than three per cent., and very near
thirty-one per thousand. I do not think it possible that this
proportion should continue even for the next ten years. It is
a phenomenon which the world never witnessed before, and
which probably will never be seen again. The state in which
we have been the last twenty years is too happy a condition
for human nature long to endure. Blessed be God for it, and
may He still protract it, notwithstanding the . . . vices by
which we have forfeited almost the right to ask his favor!

Aug. 6. — [Count Lüxbourg] told me that he believed there
was very little religion in France. When he was last there
he had made it a particular object of his personal
observation. He had supposed before he went there
that the result of the horrible revolution through which they
had passed would have been to awaken religious ideas in the
people, and to have given their minds a peculiar direction that
way. He saw no such thing. He saw no disposition with
regard to religion but that of profound indifference. It was
not a fashion of infidelity such as had been known in France
thirty or forty years ago — not a sectarian atheism, courting
martyrdom; but total indifference — a total absence of all
thought concerning religion. He had mentioned it to the
Emperor Napoleon, and perceived that the remark had displeased him. He asked him on what he founded his opinion.
The Count answered that as he had before going to France
entertained the idea that he should find strong symptoms of
religious propensities, he had made it a point to observe, and
had repeatedly gone into the principal churches of Paris on
Sundays and holidays in service-time. They were all absolutely

deserted — scarcely a soul to be seen, except here and there an occasional straggler, who looked as if he had been sent on an errand and had come into the church and taken a chair to rest himself on the way. The Emperor had replied, " Perhaps it may be so, but I assure you it is not my fault. On the contrary, I know the importance of religious sentiments, and encourage the propagation of them as much as I can. There are even five or six popular writers to whom I give pensions for this purpose, and among them are Chateaubriand and Madame de Genlis." " Now," said the Count, " he considers these people as drugs of the Imperial Pharmacopoeia — ingredients to be mixed up in the chemical mass of an Emperor's government. His own idea is political, and not at all religious."

Aug. 16. — I received a note from Count Maistre, the Sardinian Minister, requesting me to return him his manuscript translation of Plutarch's treatise on the Delays of Divine Justice, which he lent me some weeks ago. I have read it, and been pleased with his preface and notes. The translation is too much dilated. The argument against Wittenbach, to prove that the Christian Scriptures were known to Plutarch, is weak. He commends Wittenbach's learning and ingenuity, but censures his infidelity. There are two points in the character of Plutarch's style which the French denominate *bonhomie* and *naïveté;* they are well represented in the old translation of Amyot, but I do not find them in that of Count Maistre. He has doubtless corrected some mistakes and elucidated some obscure passages. Plutarch reasons well, but leaves much of the mysterious veil over his subject which nothing but Christian doctrine can remove.

Oct. 17. — Walking afterwards upon the quay, I met Mr. E. Plummer and Mr. Smith, of Boston, who informed me of the arrival of several American vessels. Met the Emperor, who asked me if I had returned into the city, and where I lived now. I told him in a corner house of the Vosnesensky and Little Officer's Streets. He said he knew well where it was; and after living thirty-five years in a place he ought to be well acquainted with it. He enquired whether Madame was confined. I told him she had been. " When? " " More than two months ago." " What! in the country? " " In the country." He shrugged his shoulders and waved his hand, which is a fashion of gesture that he often uses to intimate that he did not know a thing you are telling him, without saying it. And he does not say it, because he cannot. I believe he knew my wife had been confined perfectly well. But he asked me the question for the sake of conversation, and to please me; and after asking it, he could not seem to know anything about it. His mother does the same thing more remarkably still. He pursued the enquiries. Had her confinement been fortunate? Entirely so. And what had she got? A daughter. He then said he believed I did not walk now so much as formerly. Just the same. "But," said he, "we have lived very near each other this summer, and I do not know how it has happened that we have never met." I said it was true, that it had been long since I had the honor of seeing him. "Not once, that I recollect," said he, "the whole summer. Yet I was often riding and walking." I said I believed the cause of it was that I had generally been walking at his Majesty's hour of dinner. He finished by making an observation upon the weather. He said nothing upon any political topic.

Oct. 25. — I met the Emperor upon the Fontanka. He observed I had no gloves on my hands, and asked me if I was not cold without them. I told him I had accustomed myself to going without gloves, and seldom wore any but in extreme cold weather. He appeared to be much surprised at this, for the wearing of gloves or mittens is so universal in this country that I suppose it struck him as oddly to see a man with bare hands as it would have been had he met one barefooted. In general, the Emperor is extremely quick and particular in observing slight peculiarities in dress.

Nov. 7. — I continued reading the first volume of Chateaubriand's *Itinéraire*. It is merely a journal — but the journal of a man of genius. He alleges the motives of his journal — to look for scenery for his Martyrs, to visit Greece for the sake of its antiquities, and a religious pilgrimage to *Jerusalem*. This book is a good *study* for a traveller who wishes to give himself or others an account of what he sees. The two introductory memoirs, and every page of the book, are full of *erudition* — book-learning. He thinks he has discovered the ruins of ancient Sparta. He mentions the trees and plants which he met on his way as a *botanist*. He paints with elegance and truth the manners of all the people with whom he converses — Turks, Greeks, Jews, Italians, janissaries, mariners, guides, etc. He reflects, perhaps, too much.

Nov. 13. — Mr. Fisher called on me and proposed paying a visit to Mr. Dubrowsky, the Librarian of the Imperial Library. While I was dressing to go with Mr. Fisher, Mr. Harris came in, and sat with me nearly an hour. It was thus past three o'clock before I went out with Mr. Fisher. I would have postponed the visit to Mr. Dubrowsky to another day, but Fisher was anxious to go this day, and I accompanied him. Mr. Dubrowsky received us in an obliging manner, and showed us a number of curious manuscripts — principally curious on account of the persons to whom they had belonged. Among them were a mass-book belonging to the unfortunate Mary Queen of Scots, which she used while in prison in England, with many things written with her own hand upon the margins and blank pages; an English Chronicle, and some other books, with the names of James [I], Charles [I] and O. Cromwell written on their first and last blank leaves. There was another name, which I took to be *Edvardus,* and supposed to be that of Edward the Sixth. But Mr. Dubrowsky said it was *Ricardus;* and upon my asking him which of the Richards, he answered, Richard *the Fourth* — which gave me no very high opinion of his antiquarian knowledge. There was a small Latin Bible, written upon a soft and beautiful kind of vellum, which he pretended was human skin.

Nov. 22. — Walked again, about an hour before dinner, upon the quay, and met a numerous company of walkers; among them was the Emperor, who told me that he had made the acquaintance of a countryman of mine, a Mr. Fisher. I told him that Mr. Fisher had mentioned to me having had the honor of seeing his Majesty. "So you know him, then?" said he. "Yes, Sire, intimately." "From what part of America does he come?" "From Philadelphia." "He speaks French very well." "Tolerably well, Sire." "Is the French language very common in your country?" "Not very common, and not at all so except in the commercial cities." "In England I have heard that the French is scarcely ever spoken, and in Germany it is extremely rare among the common people. But you, I suppose, have people of almost all nations mixed together." "Of most European nations, Sire. But chiefly Germans and Irish people; a few French, but altogether fewer than is generally supposed." "And do they all amalgamate well together?" "Very well, Sire, in a length of time." "And does it not sometimes produce difficulties or confusion at the elections for your assembly?" "None that are of material consequence." "And if they are elected, how do they express themselves?" "They sometimes make speeches in English, and often speak very well, only their pronunciation is a little laughed at. But one of our Ministers, for instance, was a German, and was many years a member of Congress, where he made speeches as well as any other member."

Feb. 4, 1812. — At noon I called upon Count Romanzoff, according to his appointment. He apologized to me for receiving me in his full dress, which he said was occasioned by his having just received a deputation of Cabardinians; and I excused myself for *not* being in full dress — at which he took no displeasure. I began by informing him, with my thanks to him for the packets which he had sent me, brought by the courier from Paris, that I had received in them dispatches from the Secretary of State, and a letter personally from the President of the United States; that the President, according to the request which my inability to return to the United States last summer had made necessary on my part, had nominated another person to the judicial office which had been previously designated for me, and had instructed me to remain here; a circumstance which I thought it proper to communicate to this Government; which was one of my motives in requesting the conference with him. . .

I said that as to negotiations between France and England, I did not much believe in them, or in their success, if really attempted; but that I had heard there were prospects of war between France and Russia, which I lamented. He had mentioned the Emperor Napoleon (the print of him, in all his imperial accoutrements as Napoléon le Grand, was hanging at the side of the wall, over the sofa upon which we were sitting), and how much was it to be wished that it were possible the *will* of peace and tranquillity could be inspired into his heart. The world might then be allowed to enjoy a little peace.

The Count shook his head, and said, "No; it is impossible. Tranquillity is not in his nature. I can tell you, in confidence, that he once told me so himself. I was speaking to him about Spain and Portugal, and he said to me, ' I must always be *going*. After the Peace of Tilsit, where could I go but to Spain? I went to Spain because I could not go anywhere else.' And this," said the Count, " was all that he had to say in justification of his having gone into Spain and Portugal. And now, as perhaps there is not quite satisfied with his going, he may intend to turn against us, from the same want of any other place where to go."

Feb. 23. — I consulted Borel's tables of the Russian weights, measures, and coins, to see how he states the metre. He has the arsheen right at 28 English inches, but he makes 71.19 metres = 100 arsheens, and 140.48 arsheens = 100 metres; the first of which makes the metre = 39.331 English inches, and the second, 39.334. This difference in the fraction is itself considerable, and would amount to five inches in a mile. But the metre, as I have found it, is 25/1000 or 1/40 of an inch longer than either of these measures gives it; and 1/25 of an inch added to the shortest of these would only make the measure as given by Webster. This would make a difference of at least five feet in a mile. I drew diagrams of the French demilitre and of the déci-litre, according to the dimensions prescribed by the French law. The capacity of the first is 30.509 cubic inches, and of the second, 6.1 cubic inches. I was then curious to compare them with the capacities of our glasses and bottles in common use. I measured the dimensions of a tumbler and calculated its contents, after which I adjourned this pursuit until to-morrow.

March 13. — This morning I finished the perusal of the German Bible, which I began 20th June last. There are many differences of translation from either the English or the French translation — some of which I have compared in the three versions. Many passages, obscure and even unintelligible to me in the English, are clear in the French and German. Of the three, the German, I think, has the fewest of these obscurities. But the eloquence of St. Paul strikes me as more elevated and sublime in the English than in either of the others. In the German New Testament there is a transposition in the arrangement of the books, the Epistle to the Hebrews being separated from the rest of St. Paul's, and placed after those of Peter and John.

March 19. — Walked upon the quay, and met the Emperor. He told me he had seen one of our Americans this morning who must have very strong military propensities, for he had gone out when there were at least fifteen degrees of frost to see one of the regiments march, which were leaving the city. He meant Mr. Fisher. I said perhaps he had some acquaintance among the officers. " No; not in that regiment. But he is acquainted with Mr. Fenshaw, who belongs to the regiment that will go next Saturday. And so it is," continued his Majesty, " after all, that war is coming which I have done so much to avoid — everything. I have done everything to prevent this struggle (cette lutte), but thus it ends." " But," said I, " are all hopes vanished of still preserving the peace ? " " At all events," said he, " we shall not begin the war; my will is yet to prevent it; but we expect to be attacked." " Then," said I, " as your Majesty has determined not to commence, I would fain hope it may still pass over without a war." " I wish it may," said he. " Mais tous les indices sont à la guerre. Et puis — il avance toujours. Il a commencé par prendre la Pomérainie Suédoise — voilà qu'à présent il vient d'occuper *la Prusse* — il ne peut pas beaucoup plus avancer sans nous attaquer." I said it was to be hoped he would stop somewhere. " Oh, oui — j'espère bien qu'il ne viendra pas jusqu'ici." Seven or eight regiments have already marched from St. Petersburg within the last three weeks for the frontiers, and others are following twice or three times each week.

March 20. — I took this morning a longer walk than usual, for the purpose of measuring by the number of my paces and by the time taken to walk it the difference between the first and second werst columns in the Czarskozelo road. I found it, as on a former occasion, thirteen hundred and sixty-six paces; but I walked it in eleven minutes, the cold having quickened my step. Paucton states the pace of a man five feet two and a half inches, French, tall, to be two and a third feet, or twenty-eight inches pied du Roi, and at the rate of one hundred and twenty-one in a minute. My own height is five feet seven inches, English — about half an inch higher than Paucton's standard; and I have found, by experiments frequently repeated, that my ordinary pace is two feet six inches and eighty-eight one-hundredths of an inch, or about twenty-nine French inches, and that in my ordinary pace I walk one hundred and twenty steps to a minute.

April 19. — I finished reading Watts's discourse on the education of children and youth. He gives a contrasted description of the excessive rigor and severity with which children had been usually brought up about a century before he wrote, and of the most profuse and unlimited liberty indulged to children in his age. Watts died before the middle of the last century, and this discourse must have been written some years before his death. The indulgence of fashionable education has become much more profuse and unlimited than it was when he complained of it as excessive, and it is much to be wished it were turned again towards rigor — not perhaps to the extreme of the seventeenth century, but to much more than I am able to practise. Watts himself inclines to the system of severity, and from my own experience I concur altogether in the opinion with him. The sections upon self-government, on collecting rules of prudence, and on the sports and diversions of children. He undervalues, I think, the languages, both ancient and modern. But the course of my life has probably led me to overrate them. He prohibits plays, masquerades, assemblies, and the gaming-table, all of which, except the last, have now acquired such an ascendency that no writer upon education would venture to proscribe them.

April 25. — When I finally found out Mr. Severin's, I spent about two hours with him, examining his collection of Russian coins. He has them from the time of Peter the Great's grandfather, and a great variety of them. He has also a large collection of foreign coins, which were packed up, as he is about to remove into another house. I therefore could not see them. He showed me, however, his Cromwell's guinea, which looks perfectly new, and has a head of the Protector extremely well executed and a great likeness. The greatest curiosities of his Russian coins are the roubles with the heads of Peter and Ivan on one side, and Sophia holding the sceptre on the other, and a rouble of Peter III, with a head of Catherine II struck over that of Peter, whose profile is still discernible upon it. He has a Bank of England dollar with similar remnants of the Spanish coinage upon it.

May 14. — In the morning I met and walked with the French Ambassador, and had much conversation with him. He still professes to hope that the war [between France and Russia] will not commence at present. But since the Emperor's departure he is in a manner left here with nothing to do. He says if Nesselrode had been sent to Paris there would have been no war this year. But I asked him whether the late trial at Paris, in which Nesselrode's name was a little involved, would not have hurt him. He said no; the matter would not have been made so public.[4]

June 28. — Mr. Rayneval, the Secretary of the French Embassy, called upon me this morning to take leave. He goes this night as a courier, with his wife, and is not unconcerned as to the safety of his passage out of the country. He told me that a courier had arrived last night from Wilna in forty-seven hours, with the news that hostilities had commenced — that the French had crossed the Niemen or Memel River at Kovno, which we found upon the great Russian map. On their passage the Russian troops there had retired. The two Empresses, it was expected, he said, would return to the City this evening, and would reside here. It was said to be customary in time of war — or at least in wars " un peu intéressantes." They have not been more than a week or ten days in the country. I received the letter from Mr. Russell brought by Mr. Proud. The French Ambassador paid us a visit in the evening. He is yet waiting for his passports from Wilna. He thinks the passage of the river at Kovno a very formidable manoeuvre, and says that it cuts off four divisions from the Russian line. " *Now*," he says, " they are quite astonished at it here, because they expected to be attacked on the side of Grodno; and *now* they begin to be sorry that passports were refused him for going to Wilna."

June 30. — The St. Petersburg *Gazette* of this morning contains the Emperor's rescript to Count Nicolas Soltykoff, the President of the Imperial Council, announcing the invasion

---

[4] War between Russia and France had by now become inevitable. The French alliance was intolerable to Russia because it conflicted with her national pride; because the Continental system was ruinous to her; and because Napoleon's Polish policy was thoroughly unfriendly to Russia. In this war the advantage of numbers was on the side of France. Napoleon could concentrate on the borders of Russia at least 500,000 men, whereas Alexander could not mobilize there more than 200,000. But Alexander rightly counted on space and time to win his victories for him.

of the Russian territories by the French, and his resolution never to make peace so long as an enemy remains in arms upon his territory.

July 9. — . . . Talking of the war, Count Bussche said he had been yesterday to purchase some fusees to make sport for his children; that he had seen a very large board painted with a Fame and trumpets and many military trophies, as a transparency for an illumination. He asked what it was, and was told it had been ordered by the Empress-mother. "Ay!" said the Ambassador, "they prepare for illumination beforehand. I know they will illuminate, let the event be what it will. But I shall look, the next day after, upon the map, to see where the headquarters are, and perhaps they will be at Smolensk." He mentioned, and Mr. Harris had told me the same thing before, that the Russians expected there would be a great battle to-day, because this was the anniversary of the battle of Pultowa.

July 11. — I am forty-five years old. Two-thirds of a long life are past, and I have done nothing to distinguish it by usefulness to my country or to mankind. I have always lived with, I hope, a suitable sense of my duties in society, and with a sincere desire to perform them. But passions, indolence, weakness, and infirmity have sometimes made me swerve from my better knowledge of right and almost constantly paralyzed my efforts of good. I have no heavy charge upon my conscience, for which I bless my Maker, as well as for all the enjoyments that He has liberally bestowed upon me. I pray for his gracious kindness in future. But it is time to cease forming fruitless resolutions.

July 26. — At ten this morning, the hour appointed for the celebration of the Te Deum for the peace concluded with the Ottoman Porte,[5] I went with Mr. Smith to the Kazan Church, and we were there waiting upwards of two hours before the Empresses, with the two Grand Dukes Nicholas and Michael, made their appearance. . . The commentaries upon the state of things were various. It was generally agreed that the French army is wedged in between the first and second Russian armies, and in an extremely dangerous position. Count Maistre said, if the Emperor Alexander was in such a position we could not sleep for anxiety. " Mais — voilà ce que c'est —

---

[5] Early in 1812 the new Russian commander, Kutuzov, defeated the Turks decisively, and in May signed in Bucharest a peace with them.

l'étoile de cet homme. And, what is strange, the private letters from the officers in the army are written in the finest spirits imaginable — gay as larks; wherever they go, the ladies and gentlemen of the vicinities go into the cities with them and make agreeable society; and they have charming music," etc. Mr. Bezerra could hardly believe that the Emperor should have gone to Moscow.

Aug. 5. — I met Don Francisco Colombi and Mr. Zea, who informed me that Count Wittgenstein had totally defeated Marshal Oudinot with great slaughter, and had taken his baggage, artillery, and three thousand prisoners. In Spain, too, he said, all was going on well, and Lord Wellington was as Salamanca. After dinner I had a visit from Claud Gabriel, the black man in the Emperor's service, who went to America last summer for his wife and children, and who is now come back with them. He complains of having been very ill treated in America, and that he was obliged to lay aside his superb dress and sabre, which he had been ordered to wear, but which occasioned people to insult and even beat him.

Aug. 6. — Mr. Proud dined with us, and brought with him the New York *Commercial Advertiser* of 22d June, containing the message from the President of the United States to Congress, communicating the sequel of the correspondence between Mr. Monroe and Mr. Foster, and recommending a declaration of war; the report of the Committee of Foreign Relations upon this message, also recommending an immediate appeal to arms; the act declaring war, approved 18th June; the proclamation of the President founded upon the act of Congress; and the yeas and nays in both Houses upon the act — seventy-nine to forty-nine in the House of Representatives, and nineteen to thirteen in the Senate; two Senators, Mr. Bradley and Mr. Whitesides, absent. Minturn and Champlin sent off a pilot-boat from New York to Gottenburg with this intelligence, for the purpose of securing their property there and here from British capture on this occasion. The vessel arrived at Gottenburg 23d July, and Mr. Proud, who is an agent of Minturn and Champlin, received the paper by express from that place.

Aug. 14. — Mrs. Adams and Catherine, the two children, Mrs. Helm, the infant's nurse, and Martha, went with me to Oranienbaum. We left home at half-past nine in the morning, and precisely at noon stopped at a house kept by an English-woman, Mrs. Tringham, where we dined.   The distance is thirty-five wersts, besides three to the werst-stone within the city, from which they begin their admeasurement — twenty-five English miles — which our horses ran without once stopping to rest or to drink.   We had four horses in a line, driven by the coachman, and two leaders by the postilion.   Seven persons, including the two children, in the coach.   At Oranien-baum we went to see the palace, with its gardens and adjacent buildings, which, though smaller and less magnificent than those of Peterhof, command a finer prospect and are kept in better condition.

Sept. 6. — I received this morning a note from Madame de Staël, requesting me to call upon her at the Hôtel de l'Europe, at four o'clock this afternoon, concerning something relative to America.   I found Lord Cathcart, the newly-arrived British Ambassador, with her; also Admiral Bentinck, a young man who appeared to be an attendant upon Lord Cathcart, Madame de Staël's son and daughter, a son of Admiral Bentinck, a boy, and two or three other men, whom I could not ascertain.   To every soul in the room I was a total stranger.   Madame de Staël was in very animated conversation with Lord Cathcart, and expressing in warm terms her admiration of the English nation as the preservers of social order and the saviors of Europe.   She also complimented his Lordship very highly upon his exploit at Copenhagen.   My Lord looked a little awkward at the size and rankness of the lady's applause; to the personal tribute offered to himself he made no answer, but to the besmearing of his nation, he answered that his nation was a nation which, as such, felt itself bound by moral obligations, which it would always fulfill, and to which it would never be false.

I thought of the moral obligations of the Copenhagen expedition, and of the American Revolutionary War.   Lord Cathcart had his share in both. . .

Madame de Staël had leisure for some conversation with me.   She has lands in the State of New York, upon Lake Ontario, and stocks in the United States funds, and she wished to enquire how she could continue to receive her interest in England while there is war between the United States and Great Britain.   This introduced a conversation upon the war, which appeared to be to her a topic far more interesting than the affairs upon which she had sent to consult me. But, as she was going out to dinner, she desired me to come again to-morrow morning, and asked me why I had not been to see her before, having known her father by reputation. She said she had read my father's book with great pleasure, and that her father had often spoken of it with great esteem.

Sept. 7. — I called again upon Madame de Staël this morning, and had a second long conversation with her upon politics. She is one of the highest enthusiasts for the English cause that I have ever seen; but her sentiments appear to be as much the result of personal resentment against Bonaparte as of general views of public affairs. She complains that he will not let her live in peace anywhere, merely because she had not praised him in her works. She left the city this day for Stockholm.

Sept. 15. — They are organizing the new armament for the defence of the country, and the nobility of the governments of St. Petersburg and Moscow have given one man in ten of their peasants for the army. I saw many of them this morning, just in from the country, with the one-horse wagons, and the families of the recruits taking leave of them. The number of volunteers is very great; and if they find it as easy to organize and discipline them as they find it to raise the men, there is little danger for the country to apprehend from the invasion under which it now suffers.

Sept. 21. — At seven this evening I called by appointment upon Count Romanzoff, who told me that he had asked to see me by the Emperor's command; that, having made peace and re-established the relations of amity and commerce with England, the Emperor was much concerned and disappointed to find the whole benefit which he expected his subjects would derive commercially from that event· defeated and lost by the new war that had arisen between the United States and England; that he had thought there were various indications that there was on both sides a reluctance at engaging and prosecuting this war, and it had occurred to the Emperor that perhaps an amicable arrangement of the differences between the parties might be accomplished more easily and speedily by indirect than by a direct negotiation; that his Majesty had directed him to see me and to enquire whether I was aware of any difficulty or obstacle on the part of the Government of the United

States if he should offer his mediation for the purpose of effecting a pacification.

I answered that it was obviously impossible for me to speak on this subject otherwise than from the general knowledge which I had of the sentiments of my Government; that I was so far from knowing what their ideas were with regard to the continuance of the war, that I had not to this day received any official communication of its declaration, but that I well knew it was with extreme reluctance they had engaged in the war; that I was very sure that whatever determination they might form upon the proposal of the Emperor's mediation, they would receive and consider it as new evidence of his Majesty's regard and friendship for the United States; and that I was not aware of any obstacle or difficulty which could occasion them to decline accepting it. For myself, I so deeply lamented the very existence of the war, that I should welcome any facility for bringing it to a just and honorable termination.

Sept. 24. — The reports that the French are in possession of Moscow continue to obtain credit, and it was said there was a formal capitulation, but nothing has yet been officially published by the Government respecting it.

Sept. 27. — Nothing is published respecting the late battles at or near Smolensk, of which there are now said to have been four.[6] The reports concerning them are exceedingly various. The letters from the officers assert the advantage to have been constantly on the Russian side, and wonder why the Commander-in-Chief, Barclay de Tolly, ordered the retreat. There is now an extraordinary clamor against that General.

Sept. 29. — . . . After dinner I had some conversation with Mr. Laval. He is going, with his family, and Princess Beloselsky and hers, to Sweden. He told me that since the loss of Moscow the very idea of negotiating for peace was offensive to the Emperor, and so it would continue, unless his army should be defeated, which it has not yet been. If they should be victorious, the perseverance in the war would follow of course. But in case of one or two defeats, and one would probably produce two, the change of sentiment and of policy might be very sudden and complete, and the desire for peace as strong as the aversion to it now.

[6] Heavy fighting at Smolensk ended in the French capture of the city only after Napoleon's cannon had reduced it to smouldering ruins. Napoleon gave up the idea of wintering there and pushed on with his fatal march to Moscow.

Sept. 30. — I called at one this afternoon upon Mr. Laval. I found Mr. Harris there. Madame de Laval talked much about going to England. . . I had some further conversation with Mr. Laval. He says there are dreadful accounts of the burning of Moscow since the French entered it. There were two attempts made to burn the houses next to that in which *he* (Napoleon) had taken his quarters, in consequence of which his troops set fire to the city in many places at once, and it is feared that the whole city may be destroyed. The Emperor Alexander, since the loss of Moscow, has said publicly at his own table, " Il n'y a qu'un coquin qui puisse prononcer actuellement le mot de paix." His spirit stiffens with adversity. The situation of the French army in the midst of their triumphs is considered as absolutely desperate; it is supposed that Napoleon wishes to negotiate, and this is the strongest reason for the determination not to negotiate here.

Oct. 27. — About noon this day the report of cannon from the fortress announced that important and pleasing intelligence from the armies had been received; about half an hour after, Mr. Harris, the Consul, came in. He had just come from Count Romanzoff's, where he had been with his nephew upon a visit of taking leave. The news was a great victory of Marshal Koutouzof over the King of Naples (Prince Murat), and the retaking of Moscow by General Wintzingerode's corps, though in achieving it Wintzingerode was himself taken prisoner.[7] In the evening I received from the Grand Master of the Ceremonies a notification to attend a Te Deum to-morrow morning at the Kazan Church, on account of these events. The city was illuminated by night. Mr. Harris lent me an English *Courier* of 6th October, which he had borrowed from Count Romanzoff, containing a confirmation of the capture of the *Guerrière* frigate; but with it an account of the surrender of General Hull and his army, and of the taking of Fort Detroit by the British. It would be useless, and the attempt would be vain, to express my sensations upon this event. There are scarcely any details of the affair given. The honor of my country — O God! suffer it not to go unredeemed!

Nov. 4. — Went out to Ochta, and dined at Mr. Krehmer's. Mr. Harris was there, Mrs. Pitt, the wife of the English clergyman, and two Mr. Gisbornes, sons of Dr. Gisborne

---

[7] Napoleon's retreat from Moscow began on Oct. 24.

the author, who live with Mr. Krehmer. There was much political conversation, characteristic as well of the present state of affairs as of the feelings of the speakers. The passions of almost all the politicians whom I now see and hear are concentrated upon the head of one man. It seems almost universally to be considered that the destinies of mankind hang upon Napoleon's life alone; and in proportion to the force of this sentiment is the ardor for his death. I know not how it has been with former conquerors during their lives, but I believe there never was a human being who united against himself such a mass of execration and abhorrence as this man has done. There is indeed, on the other hand, an admiration of him equally enthusiastic, as for every great conqueror there always must be; but I have never yet seen the person by whom he was regarded with affection.

Dec. 3. — I dined at Count Romanzoff's with a company of about forty persons; among whom were the ladies of the celebrated Generals who are now dispelling, as Count Litta remarked, like the fog before the sun, the immense armies of the Emperor Napoleon, and levelling with the dust his colossal military reputation, Princess Koutouzof Smolenski, Countess Wittgenstein, Baronesses Benningsen, Wintzingerode, and several others. The day was rendered peculiarly joyous to them by the news of a fresh, splendid victory over the corps of the French Marshals Victor and Oudinot, by Count Wittgenstein, which arrived this morning. Within the compass of ten days the Russian armies have taken between forty and fifty thousand prisoners, with cannons, baggage, and ammunition in proportion. There is nothing like it in history since the days of Xerxes.

Dec. 7. — On returning this morning from my walk I found a note from Count Romanzoff, proposing a change of the time and place which he had fixed for seeing me, and asking me to call upon him between one and two o'clock this afternoon at the Hotel of Foreign Affairs, which I accordingly did.

I told him that my motive for desiring this conversation with him was, that since I saw him last I had received from my Government official notice of the declaration of war by the United States against Great Britain, together with a letter from the Secretary of State, dated first July; that I had not received any instruction to make an official communication on the subject to this Government, but the Secretary of State had explicitly expressed the views of the Government at this juncture on several points, which I thought it important to communicate to him. The first was the desire of the United States that this war might be confined to them and Great Britain, that no other power might be involved in it; that the United States wished to preserve unimpaired their relations of amity with all other powers, and that this wish was declared in a particular manner in regard to Russia; that the war between Russia and France, though it could not then be known in America to have commenced, was anticipated as inevitable, and was a subject of great regret to the American Government; that the state of our affairs with France was said to be in an unsettled condition, and there was not much expectation of any speedy settlement of them satisfactory to us; but that, whatever course they might take, the American Government did not contemplate any more intimate connection with France; nor was it aware of any occurrence whatsoever which could induce it to enter into any such connection. This sentiment, I said, was expressed in terms as strong as language could employ, and the desire of the United States to maintain in their full extent the friendly and commercial relations with Russia was in terms of equal earnestness.

Dec. 9. — The news of the Emperor Napoleon's being killed is not authenticated; that of his having effected his escape becomes more credited; though, if true, his situation must still be extremely perilous, and almost desperate. The disappointment here at the belief of his escape is very great, and has given rise to various rumors, that one, and even two of the Russian armies have been defeated; of which there is probably no foundation.

Dec. 19. — The Emperor Alexander left this city early this morning to go to the army. There have been for some days rumors of his departure, but they were so much contradicted that it was finally quite unexpected.

Dec. 24. — The Emperor's birthday, which, for the first time since I have been here, passed over without any celebration and almost without notice. There was a petty illumination of the streets for about two hours in the evening, and nothing more. The country has suffered so much by the last summer's invasion, and there have perished such great multitudes of the people and armies, while other multitudes still greater are reduced to ruin and beggary, that the Emperor himself has determined there should be no expensive festivities this winter at his Court, and he particularly forbade the customary celebration of his birthday. I was playing at ombre with the ladies, when I received a note from Mr. Harris, with a London gazette extraordinary of 27th November, containing the official account (British) of the total defeat of the second American attempt to invade Upper Canada, and the surrender of General Wadsworth and nine hundred men. The symptoms disclosed by these repeated shameful terminations of impotent assaults are distressing to the feelings of one who loves his country. The reliance of man in all cases can only be upon Heaven. God grant that these disasters instead of sinking may rouse the spirit of the nation, and that they may learn, though from adversity, the skill and discipline which will be the pledges of their future prosperity!

Dec. 31. — I offer to a merciful God at the close of this year my humble tribute of gratitude for the blessings with which He has in the course of it favored me and those who are dear to me, and I pray for a continuance of his goodness. Above all, I pray that He who worketh in us both to will and to do, may grant to me and mine that temper of heart and that firmness of soul which are best adapted duly to receive all his dispensations, whether joyous or afflictive. It has pleased Him in the course of this year to lay his chastening hand upon me, and to try me with bitter sorrow. My endeavors to quell the rebellion of the heart have been sincere, and have been assisted with the blessing from above. As I advance in life its evils multiply, the instances of mortality become more frequent, and approach nearer to myself. The greater is the need of fortitude to encounter the woes that flesh is heir to, and of religion to support pains for which there is no other remedy. Religious sentiments become from day to day more constantly habitual to my mind.

Feb. 1, 1813. — . . . I said [to Count Romanzoff] I had heard that Count Lauriston was dead. There was such a report, he answered — that he had been found frozen to death in his carriage; and it was not improbable, as no mention was made of him among the Generals and Ministers who followed Napoleon upon his return to Paris. It was probable, too, that Lauriston's death might be hastened by chagrin at the idea of having contributed by his counsels to the ruin of the army. For it is said to have been by his advice, against the opinion of Caulaincourt and of all the other Generals, " qu'il fit la sottise de Moscou." It was Napoleon's own opinion, and Lauriston flattered him by concurring with it; not from base motives, but because it was his real opinion that by pushing on to Moscow we should be induced to negotiate, and, if terms of peace not too severe should be offered us, we should accept them. It is scarcely credible how complete the destruction of that immense army had been. And they could no longer disguise it. He had seen a letter from the Duke of Bassano, written at Berlin, to some of the French agents, in which were these identical words: " Il faut avouer que les circonstances ne nous sont pas favorables."

I observed that this was by no means disclosing a secret. The Count replied that it was not, but that it showed that their acknowledgment of the fact became every day more complete. The details surpassed everything that imagination could have anticipated. It was remarkable that at Dresden, the very spot which Napoleon had chosen for his point of departure, where in May last he had made such a pompous and ridiculous display of power, where he had assembled Emperors and Kings, and distributed their seats at the Elector's table, and published them in all his gazettes, as if he had been there a monarch surrounded by his vassals — that exactly there, on his return, he entered the city in a single sledge, without servants, without guards. His very Mameluke had been frozen to death, and he was obliged to borrow four thousand louis of the Elector to continue his journey, and six shirts from his Minister. At Weimar he had passed through without stopping, and left an apology behind to the Duke for not having visited him, that he was absolutely not in a presentable condition.

March 3. — Sir Francis d'Ivernois paid me a long visit, and in return for my Silesian letters gave me two of his own publications — *Les Trois Offrandes,* and *Napoléon Administrateur et Financier.* He found Mr. Harris with me, and we had a long conversation together upon political affairs. He has all the prejudices and all the passions of an English Ministerialist — which was to be expected; but he very stoutly contends that the British Ministers deplore the war with America. Mr.

Harris mentioned to him Sir Robert Wilson's assertion at Dr. Creighton's table, that Mr. Perceval had told him a very few days before his death that he was determined upon a war with America. Sir Francis said he did not believe that Mr. Perceval had ever said any such thing to Sir Robert Wilson; that Mr. Perceval was the only member of the British Cabinet deeply, strongly, inflexibly attached to the Orders in Council; that he probably would not have abandoned them to prevent a war with America, but he did not believe they would produce a war. Sir Francis said that he had been very intimately acquainted with Mr. Perceval, who had been with him and left him not five minutes before he was murdered; that he had often conversed with him on the subject of America; that Mr. Perceval always expressed himself averse to a war with America, but he did not believe it would come to a war. Sir Francis appeared to hope that the war between America and England would be short; he founded his hopes on the expectation that the war would become too unpopular in America to be pursued. On this point, as on almost every other, I found his opinions at the greatest possible variance from mine.

April 3. — The news had just been received of the taking of Hamburg by the Russians. Young Gourieff had carried the keys of the city to Count Wittgenstein, at Berlin. The whole city, seventy-five thousand people, came out to meet the Russians in triumph, and such transports of joy were never before known. The mayor of the city, Abendroth (a sinister name, as Baron Budberg observed), they had thrown out of the windows. The King of Prussia had written a letter to Prince Koutouzof, placing all his troops under his command, submitting to him without restriction the whole management of the war, and requesting him to take the Prince Royal of Prussia for his aid-de-camp. This, it was remarked, was the only way in which anything could be done to good purpose.

April 10. — Count Romanzoff asked me if I had seen Mr. Schlegel's pamphlet. I knew nothing even of the man. He said Mr. Schlegel [8] was a gentleman who had been here with Madame de Staël, and was still with her at Stockholm. A pamphlet had lately been published, ostensibly by him, though without his name. Madame de Staël, he supposed, was not

[8] August Schlegel, the German critic and poet, was tutor of Mme. de Staël's children for some years after 1804.

the author of it, but he believed she had given it quelques coups de brosse. . . He said with regard to its contents that he totally differed from the opinions it contained, and was much like Madame de Staël herself. She was a perfect sample of Frenchwomen. It was impossible for a human mind to have more wit and vivacity, but such was the extreme mobility of her imagination, and such the inconsistency of her ideas, that in the result of every conversation you have with her, it is the same thing as if you had been talking avec une folle.

April 17. — Mr. Lewis sent me a letter he received last evening from Gottenburg, with news from America to 23d February. Further disasters by land, and successses upon the sea. "In the day of prosperity be joyful, but in the day of adversity consider: God also hath set the one over against the other, to the end that man should *find nothing after him.*" (Instead of which read, "*not know what is to come.*") Ecclesiastes vii. 14. So it is translated in Luther's German Bible. One thousand more men, with a General Winchester, killed or taken in Canada, and the *Java* frigate sunk by the *Constitution,* Captain Bainbridge. I walked alone after dinner, and on returning home read the fifth Tusculan, translated by Bouhier.

May 11. — At dinner I was seated between Count Kotschubey and General Bétancourt, with both of whom I had some conversation. That with the Count was chiefly political, on our war with England. My feelings on this subject, and some remarks and questions of the Count, urged me to a degree of warmth bordering at least on indiscretion. Count Romanzoff, who was unusually marked in his attentions to me, said, in a tone of pleasantry, "How happens it that you are constantly beating at sea the English, who beat all the rest of the world, and that on land, where you ought to be the strongest, the English *do what they please?*" I answered him in the same manner, that I knew not how to account for it, unless by supposing that these times were reserved to keep the world in a continued state of wonder, and to prove that there is something new under the sun. He replied that there had once been a confusion of tongues, and now, he believed, was the time for a confusion of minds.

May 28. — There has been no official publication of military events since the battle at Lützen, and the consequence is, innumerable rumors of every description are in circulation, upon none of which any dependence is to be placed. A retreat of the Russian and Prussian armies followed immediately after the battle of Lützen, and the official silence observed since that time has occasioned some disappointment and uneasiness in the public mind. Vague and groundless reports of defeat and disaster have been whispered about, and other reports of success and victory have been spread abroad to counteract them. Mr. Lewis informed me of news from England that the United States sloop-of-war *Hornet* had sunk an English sloop-of-war of superior force, called the *Peacock*.

June 12. — There are a multitude of rumors about the city. An Austrian declaration of war against France. The retreat of the French army back to Dresden. The evacuation of Hamburg by the Swedes. Its occupation by a body of Russian troops. A declaration of war by Denmark against Sweden, Russia and Prussia. The battles of 19th, 20th, and 21st May, in and round Bautzen, were nearly as bloody and as indecisive as that of Lützen. The Russian semi-official accounts acknowledge a retreat on the 21st, and they claim a victory on the 26th, at Haynau, in Silesia, of their rear-guard over the French advanced guard. The subsequent retreat of the French was occasioned by the hostilities, commenced or declared, of Austria.

June 17. — The appointment of Messrs. Albert Gallatin and James A. Bayard to come to Russia upon the business of the mediation is announced in the *National Intelligencer*. They were to sail from Philadelphia about the first of May.[9]

June 22. — I received this morning a note from Count Romanzoff, requesting me to call upon him at one o'clock afternoon, which I did. I took with me the French translation of the two papers containing the manifesto on our declaration of war against Britain, which are to be published. . . I also showed him, and left with him, the *National Intelligencer* containing the article relative to the appointment of Messrs. Gallatin and Bayard, which I received yesterday, observing that he had judged more correctly than I had on the probability of this fact. He said that he was very sorry to say he had re-

[9] Romanzoff's suggestion in September of Russian mediation between America and England had been eagerly seized upon in Washington. Gallatin and Bayard were hurriedly dispatched to St. Petersburg to act with Adams in treating with England. England refused the mediation. But she shortly consented to send commissioners to Gothenburg (the place being immediately changed to Ghent) for direct negotiations with the American representatives.

ceived, since he had seen me, further dispatches from Count
Lieven, stating that the British Government, with many very
friendly and polite assurances that there was no mediation
which they should so readily and cheerfully accept as that of
the Emperor of Russia, had, however, stated that their differences with the United States of America, involving certain
principles of the internal government of England, were of a
nature which they did not think suitable to be settled by a
mediation.

I said this was no more than I had expected; that I much
regretted the failure of this new attempt at negotiation, but
that I was happy that the solemnity which the President had
given to the acceptance of the Emperor's offer, by the appointment of two persons so highly distinguished in our country,
would at least manifest the sense which he entertained of the
Emperor's friendly sentiments and proposal, as well as the
constant desire of the American Government for peace.

June 24. — After dinner Mrs. Adams and Charles went
with me to the Kazan Church, where we saw the preparations
for the funeral ceremony at the interment of Prince Koutouzof
Smolensky. The catafalque is in the centre of the church, immediately under the dome — a cubic basis, and about twelve
feet high, with steps to ascend at the four corners. There is
an arch in the middle of it, high enough for a man to pass
through; the coffin is placed at the summit, on bars, over a
cavity large enough to let it down by machinery. The
coffin is said to weigh sixty poods — about a ton avoirdupois.
It is surrounded by trophies — French eagles and standards,
and bashaws' horse-tails.

July 3. — I received a note from Count Romanzoff enclosing a letter from Messrs. Gallatin and Bayard, and one from
Mr. Speyer, at Stockholm. The first informs me of the appointment of these two gentlemen jointly with myself as En-
voys Extraordinary and Ministers Plenipotentiary to negotiate
a peace with Great Britain under the mediation of the Emperor
of Russia; of their arrival at Gottenburg, and their intention
to proceed as speedily as possible to St. Petersburg; also that
Mr. Harris is appointed Secretary to the Legation.

July 21. — Mr. Harris came in and told me that Mr. Gallatin and Mr. Bayard had just arrived. I immediately went to
see them at the lodgings he has taken for them. I invited them,
and Mr. Milligan, Mr. Dallas, and Mr. Gallatin, Jr., who

are with them, to go home with me and dine; but they excused themselves, being much fatigued, and having been three nights without sleep.   I sat with them about an hour, in which they gave us the latest information from America, and I communicated to them the general state of affairs here.   They gave me a large bundle of letters and dispatches from the United States, which, with the exception of an hour at dinner, I was employed in reading until ten at night.   I thank Almighty God for the favors communicated to me by these dispatches, and I pray for the gracious aid of his Spirit to discharge with zeal, integrity, and discretion the new duties required of me.

July 23. — At one I called, as by appointment, upon Count Romanzoff, and told him that I had received instruction from the American Government to remain here under the commission which I have hitherto held, and that I had been mistaken in supposing that my colleagues had other destinations, independent of the mission here.   My conjecture had been founded on the doubt whether the President would have appointed the mission solely upon the expectation that the mediation would be accepted by the British Government.   But I was now instructed that the President, considering the acceptance by the British as probable, though aware that if they should reject it this measure might wear the appearance of precipitation, thought it more advisable to incur that risk than the danger of prolonging unnecessarily the war for six or nine months, as might happen if the British should immediately have accepted the mediation and he should have delayed this step until he was informed of it.   And a great object with him was to manifest not only a cheerful acceptance on the part of the United States, but in a signal manner the sentiments of consideration and respect for the Emperor, and to do honor to the motives on which he offered his mediation.   Another gentleman, Mr. Crawford, was appointed Minister to France.

The Count said he regretted much that there was such reason to believe the British would decline the mediation; but on transmitting the copy of the credential letter to the Emperor, he would determine whether to renew the proposal; as the opposition in England might make it an embarrassing charge against the Ministry if they should under such circumstances reject it.

CHAPTER IV

1813–1815

THE BATTLE OF LEIPSIC — A PEACE CONFERENCE WITH ENGLAND
— THE MEETING AT GHENT — BRITISH DEMANDS REJECTED — RELA-
TIONS WITH CLAY AND GALLATIN — SATISFACTORY TERMS ARRANGED

St. Petersburg, August 3, 1813. — Mr. Gallatin and Mr.
Bayard came about one o'clock; we considered the answer we
had received from Count Romanzoff to our first official note,
and concluded that no reply to it would be necessary for the
present. We finally agreed upon the note to be sent relative
to the treaty of commerce with Russia. Mr. Harris's commission not extending to this object, I requested my colleagues
to take some order concerning it.

Aug. 5. — On returning home, I found an answer from Count
Romanzoff to our note yesterday sent in, and a note to me
requesting me to call upon him to-morrow evening, between six
and seven, in the country; also a letter from Mr. Speyer, and an
enclosure from Mr. Beasley, with the *Times* of 9th July, containing the account of the capture of the *Chesapeake*. I went
with what appetite I might to Mr. Pflug's, in the country, to
dinner, — the company, ladies and gentlemen, thirty-three or
thirty-four persons.

Aug. 17. — In the evening, Mr. Gallatin, Mr. Dallas, and
Mr. Harris were here. Mr. Gallatin had received a letter
from Mr. Alexander Baring, relating to our mission, which he
left with me to read, and requested me to call on him and Mr.
Bayard to-morrow morning. Mr. Baring writes that the
British Government have refused the mediation, but offer to
treat with us directly at London, or, if we prefer it, at Gottenburg.

Aug. 18. — Called this morning on Messieurs Gallatin and
Bayard, and returned the letter from Mr. Baring, upon which

we had a conversation of about two hours. We concluded that it was not a foundation upon which any measure could be taken by us. The letter is very well written, and shows the English feelings on the subject of mediation clearly enough. The wish to draw us to London is very freely avowed, but nothing, other than vague and general expressions, to encourage a hope that we should have any prospect of success there. My colleagues are anxious and uneasy under the responsibility of staying here with the knowledge that England has declined the mediation. They desired me, if I should see Count Romanzoff, to ask him for an official notification in writing of his intention to renew the proposal of mediation to England; and Mr. Bayard intimated his wish that in that notification the Count would invite him to stay here for an answer.

Sept. 13. — Early this morning I received a notification from the Department of the Ceremonies for a Te Deum at the Kazan Church at twelve o'clock. I attended it with Mr. Smith. All the mystery of the courier's having come from Töplitz was explained by Count Litta. The Russian, Austrian, and Prussian head-quarters were at Töplitz. The victory of the 30th August was complete — the divisions of Victor and Vandamme totally destroyed — Vandamme himself, and seven thousand men, eighty pieces of cannon, standards, eagles, and ammunition-wagons. The allies had commenced the siege of Dresden, and had taken one of the outworks. Gouvion St.-Cyr had thrown himself with thirty thousand men into Dresden; on the 27th Napoleon came with sixty thousand men and ten thousand cuirassiers, and attacked the allies before Dresden — they fought the whole day, and he made no impression. He renewed the attack the 28th, with no better success. The 29th he turned about, crossed the Elbe at Königstein, marched down the riverside, crossed it again, and entered Bohemia. The Russian army followed him down on the other side of the river. Kleist, with the Prussians, at the same time went down and crossed the mountains. Schwartzenberg and the Austrians came in a still different direction, and on the 30th, from all quarters at once, attacked the French army, which was entirely cut to pieces, and in a state of total dissolution.

Oct. 30. — I went to the lodgings of Mr. Gallatin and Mr. Bayard; while I was there, Mr. Todd came in with further reports contained in English newspapers of an action between the American and British fleets on Lake Ontario, in which the British were defeated. I had received the account in a letter from Mr. Speyer last Monday; but as it rested upon very remote and indirect authority, and there was then no other account of it received here, I had not indulged myself to give it credit. I may now hope it is not entirely without foundation.

Nov. 2. — Mr. Lewis gave me the first news of the great victory of the allies over Napoleon and his army near Leipsic — there had been a rumor of this battle yesterday. The report now comes from the Empress-mother — Leipsic taken by storm, four French Marshals, fourteen Generals, thirty-six thousand men, and one hundred and fifty pieces of cannon taken.

Nov. 20. — I had heard before that Lord Walpole had said the British Government had not been informed of the offer of Russia to mediate until last summer, which appeared extraordinary; and now, hearing him say so expressly, to be sure of not mistaking his meaning, I asked him if I had understood it correctly.

He said I had; repeated over again what he had said to Mr. Bayard, adding that they were the last words Castlereagh said to him when he left England. Lord Walpole has an apparent frankness and some coarseness in his manners. He said they kept Michaelmas in England the 29th September; that it was a universal and indispensable custom to dine upon goose; that it was called goose-day; that members of Parliament always dined that day with their constituents. He dined with the mayor of the place he represented. The constituents gave very good dinners, and " we do not get drunk — but something devilish near it." He told me that he had been two or three years in the Admiralty; that the Admiralty cost twenty millions a year; that he and the other members proposed in 1811 to reduce it two millions, but the First Lord would not consent, and his voice weighed more than all the others put together. He said that Vansittart was a devilish fine fellow; that Pitt had undoubtedly been one of the first men in the world for finance, but Vansittart, who had been only a Secretary of the Treasury under him, was a much bolder man, and had done things from which Pitt recoiled with horror.

Nov. 30. — *Day.* I rise, on the average, about six o'clock in the morning, and retire to bed between ten and eleven at night. The interval is filled up as it has been nearly two years, or, more particularly, as since I placed Charles at school. The four or five hours that I previously devoted to him I now employ in reading books of science. These studies I now pursue not only as the most delightful of occupations to myself, but with a special reference to the improvement and education of my children. I feel the sentiment with which Tycho Brahe died, perhaps as strongly as he did. His " ne frustra vixisse videar " was a noble feeling, and in him had produced its fruits. He had not lived in vain. He was a benefactor to his species. But the desire is not sufficient. The spark from heaven is given to few. It is not to be obtained by entreaty or by toil. To be profitable to my children seems to me within the compass of my powers. To that let me bound my wishes and my prayers. And may that be granted to them!

Jan. 24, 1814. — I called again upon Mr. Schubert, whom I found at home, and to whom I took the little volume published at Boston, by Judge Davis, upon comets. I had much conversation with him upon astronomical subjects, and he promised to lend me Bode's *Uranographia.* I mentioned to him Adam Smith's fragment on the *History of Astronomy,* of which he had never heard, and which I promised to send him. I asked him about Kepler's manuscripts which are in the library of the Academy of Sciences, and of which he told me he had made great use in composing his popular astronomy. He did not recollect among Kepler's manuscripts having seen the one against Calvin, but he had not paid much attention to the theological works. He would, however, look over them again, and see if he could find the one about which I enquired. There were twenty-four volumes of the manuscripts, among which was a collection of letters, but there were few of them that were interesting so as to deserve publication.

Feb. 4. — Mr. Harris called upon me this morning, and told me that he should postpone his departure until next Tuesday. He brought me my letter-book of the joint mission, to which some additions are still to be made. I told him that before he went away there were two subjects upon which I thought it best to have some explanation with him. The first was to enquire whether he had formed a commercial connection with Mr. Lawrence Brown, an English merchant in this place; and if he had, whether he considered it as compatible with the office of Secretary to a Legation for negotiating peace. He said he had not. . .

The second object of my enquiry was, whether Mr. Bayard had ever said anything to him with regard to my disposition towards him. He said Mr. Bayard had once said to him, "Mr. Harris, I have reason to believe that Mr. Adams is no friend of yours"; that he (Harris) had asked him upon what grounds he had formed such an opinion; that he had avoided particularizing, but had repeated he had very very good reason to believe I was not friendly to him, or that he was no favorite in my family. All he would say further was, that I did not like Harris's politics, and that my motive for being unfriendly to him was, that he was the Secretary to the extraordinary mission instead of my nephew. Harris said that these suggestions had given him great pain; that, excepting on one occasion, which he had hoped would be forgotten, he was conscious of never having given me occasion to be unfriendly to him; that as to his politics, he could have none but those which favored the interests of his country, and that he had taken no step whatsoever to obtain the office of Secretary to the Legation.

I told him that I would deal with him in perfect candor. It was possible that, in conversation with Bayard, I might at some time have lightly said, "Harris is more of a Russian, or takes more pleasure in the success of the allies, than I do"; but that I had certainly never said anything to him which could warrant him making the inference that I was unfriendly to him, and that his imputation of the motive was as false as the insinuation itself; that I had never wished that my nephew should have had the appointment of secretary to this mission; and if I had, I should never have been unfriendly to him (Harris) because he had been preferred. Mr. Bayard and I had formerly been in strong opposition to each other in the Senate of the United States. When he came here, one of my most earnest wishes was to harmonize with him. I had uniformly treated him with respect and attention. There had been no misunderstanding or variance between us; but he had repeatedly made attempts to injure Mr. Gallatin in my opinion, and I had now reason, since their departure, to believe that he had made similar attempts against me upon the mind of Mr. Gallatin. . . I observed to Harris that I hoped never again to be placed in relations which would make it necessary to associate with Mr. Bayard. . .

Feb. 27. — Three. I rose at this early hour to have the benefit of seeing a clear sky without moonlight. I was able just to discern two of the stars of the sixth magnitude in the Lion. I spent two full hours at the chamber-windows on both sides of the house, and, besides all my former celestial acquaintance, recognized the Crow, Hercules, and head of Ophiuchus, and the star of the second magnitude in the first claw of the Scorpion, from my own chamber, and the Dolphin and Antinoüs from the front side of the house.

March 8. — Dr. Galloway was here this morning, and prescribed for me a vial of Sacred Elixir. I am very unwell, and have strong symptoms of the jaundice; a lassitude which has almost, but not yet quite, suspended all my industry; a listlessness which, without extinguishing the love of life, affects the mind with the sentiment that life is nothing worth; an oppression at the heart, which, without being positive pain, is more distressing than pain itself. I still adhere, however, to my usual occupations. I feel nothing like the tediousness of time, suffer nothing like *ennui.* Time is too short for me, rather than too long. If the day were of forty-eight hours instead of twenty-four, I could employ them all, so I had but eyes and hands to read and write.

March 25. — Continued my Chronological Dissertation and reading Sully's *Memoirs,* also Crabbe's *Poems,* lent us by Dr. Beresford. Sully has taken such hold on me that I shall read him through if I have time. Crabbe's colors are gloomy, but his picture of human life is true. His *Parish Register* gives views of the village very different from those of Goldsmith. He says that since the flood Auburn and Eden can no more be found. But there is a bright and a dark side to almost everything in this world. Goldsmith's picture shows only the sunshine of the village. Crabbe shows scarcely anything but the shade. His characters are drawn with strong and distinct features. His satire is sometimes as caustic as that of Juvenal — especially in the stories of Sir Richard Monday and the Lady of the Manor. I have long doubted the soundness of the *morals* involved in these dismal pictures of human existence. Crabbe is not quite so melancholy as Dr. Johnson. Both of them are too much so. Life in all its forms, high and low, has great, oppressive cares, and sometimes overwhelming calamities.

March 29. — I read the fourth book of Sully's Memoirs, it introduces a new military personage and a great general, Alexander Farnese, Prince of Parma, opposed to Henry IV. This book, like the rest, is full of instruction for a general and a statesman; but the best book in the world is like the pipe that Hamlet offers to Rosenkrantz and Guildenstern: it will discourse excellent music only to those who know how to govern the ventages. Sully tells his story with candor, occasionally acknowledges his own faults, and even, though more gently, those of his master. One of Henry's faults was the rashness with which he exposed his person in action. . . His greatest, or rather his only, vice, was his passion for women; which was so excessive that, in my mind, it casts a foul and indelible stain upon his character. It is, indeed, one of those vices for which mankind always had, and ever will have, great indulgence. But to men in such stations and placed under such circumstances as his, it is one of the most pernicious and fatal of vices. Whether it is so constitutional in some men, and was in him, as to be uncontrollable, I cannot undertake to say. But I can never consider the disgrace of a goat as the honor of a man.

April 1. — Mr. Nathaniel H. Strong this morning brought me dispatches from the Secretary of State — one addressed to Mr. Bayard and myself, the other to me alone; letters from Mr. Gallatin and Mr. Bayard, at Amsterdam, and one from Mr. Bourne, enclosing one from Mr. Beasley.[1] The dispatch to Mr. Bayard and me, of which Mr. Bayard retained the original and enclosed to me a copy, directs us both to repair, immediately upon the receipt of it, to Gottenburg, there to enter upon a negotiation of peace with England, conformably

[1] The period between August, 1813, and April, 1814, Adams had passed in drearily waiting at St. Petersburg. Lord Castlereagh had refused for a second time to accept the Russian offer of mediation between Great Britain and America. But on Nov. 4, 1813, the British did write a note to the American Government offering to treat directly. The news of this proposal reached St. Petersburg in January, 1814. On the 25th of that month, Gallatin and Bayard left the Russian capital and travelled to Amsterdam, which they reached in March. Here they learned that President Madison had accepted Lord Castlereagh's offer with alacrity, and had appointed a new peace commission, comprising Adams, Bayard, Henry Clay, and Jonathan Russell; Gallatin being later added. Partial news of all this reached Adams on the date noted above. The road to peace was now opening.

to a proposal made by the British Government and accepted by that of the United States. Mr. Monroe intimates that there will be other American Commissioners; but his letter is dated 8th January, before the nominations were made. Mr. Henry Clay and Mr. Jonathan Russell were the persons ultimately appointed. Mr. Gallatin is not in the commission. Mr. Monroe directs me to leave the affairs of the United States here, in my absence, in the charge of Mr. Harris.

April 2. — I called upon Lord Walpole at one o'clock, the hour he had appointed, told him the order I had received to go to Gottenburg, and asked him if he could inform me whether commissioners on the part of Great Britain had been appointed. He said he could not; that he had received no dispatches from his Government of later date than 24th December. There are now twenty-two mails from England due. But, he said, by his last accounts from Stockholm, of the 23d of March, he learnt that some of the mails were landed; they might be expected every day. He had heard from private letters that George Hammond had been appointed, but there must be others; he did not know who.

April 11. — At twelve o'clock I went with Mr. Smith to the Winter Palace, and attended the Te Deum for Marshal Blücher's victory, and the taking of Rheims par assaut; and the Cercle Diplomatique afterwards held by the Empress-mother. It had been preceded by the mass, which we did not attend. . . Princess Woldemar Galitzin was at the Te Deum, not knowing that her grandson, young Count Strogonoff, has been killed, though it has been known all over the city these ten days. Count Maistre was informed only by accident of his son's being wounded, and that it was but slightly. He mentioned it to the Empress, who offered to transmit letters to or from him. "Vous savez," said she, " que j'ai d'excellens Commissionnaires à l'armée à présent. J'ai quatre fils à l'armée, and it gives me many a moment of heartache." As she went away, I said to the Count, " Bella matribus detestata." " Ay," said he, "but for her sons there is no great danger; though, to be sure, the ball that killed Moreau might have struck the Emperor."

April 23. — . . . We soon after met Count Litta, who told us there was this morning an estafette from the King of Würtemberg, further confirming the taking of Paris. It was a good, a great, and a happy piece of news; for everything had passed quietly, and the greatest of all was the declaration by the Emperor Alexander, alone, but speaking in the name of all the allies. This was very proper, because he was the one in whom the greatest confidence was to be placed. The courier was still expected, but at Berlin they had already had their firing of cannon and their illuminations. It was Count Schwerin that had carried the news there. Mr. Bardaxi told me his news from Spain, brought by a courier to him yesterday. It was the same Count Romanzoff had told me. Mr. Bardaxi said that Bonaparte's system was too violent; it could not stand. He had committed two great faults — the war with Spain, and the war with Russia. He had ruined Spain. But Spain would be indebted to him for her liberty and her happiness. Without him Spain would never have been free; and now within ten years Spain would astonish the world by the wisdom of her institutions. I thought these opinions all sufficiently correct, excepting the last.

April 27. — I was employed the whole day in packing up and preparing for my departure. Mr. Smith attended the Te Deum for Paris. I did not attend it, being the rule of etiquette not to appear in the presence of the Empress after having taken leave. The notice for the last preceding Te Deum was not even sent me. I supposed this one was sent for Mr. Smith. I was likewise so busy with my preparations that I could not conveniently spare the time. I went out, however, in the evening, to see the illuminations, which were universal, and some of them splendid. The most brilliant of all were those at the fortress. It was very cold, and the wind blew so strong that all the designs of illumination were baffled in the execution; for before any one of them was completely lighted, half the lamps were blown out. In many places where expensive preparations had been made they totally failed.

April 28. — I had finally fixed upon this day for my departure on the journey to Gottenburg, and was employed from the time of my rising until half-past one P.M. in finishing my preparations. I had visits during the morning from Mr. Hurd, Mr. Norman, and Mr. Montréal; the last of whom informed me that a courier had this morning arrived from the Emperor with the news that Napoleon Bonaparte, on having the decree of the French Senate notified to him, declaring that he was cashiered, had immediately abdicated the throne, and thus that the war is at an end. With this prospect of a general peace in Europe I commenced my journey to contribute, if possible, to the restoration of peace to my own country. The weight of the trust committed, though but in part, to me, the difficulties, to all human appearance insuperable, which forbid the hope of success, the universal gloom of the prospect before me, would depress a mind of more sanguine complexion than mine. On the providence of God alone is my reliance. The prayer for light and vigilance, and presence of mind and fortitude and resignation, in fine, for strength proportioned to my trial, is incessant upon my heart. The welfare of my family and country, with the interests of humanity, are staked upon the event. To Heaven alone it must be committed.

June 24. — St. John's Day, and the day of our arrival at Ghent. We came down to the ferry about nine in the morning, and were obliged to wait there an hour and a half before we could cross it. We saw several ships of the line on the river, with the white flag, and thirteen large ships on the stocks — eight of the line, and five frigates, all of which are to be demolished and half of the materials to be delivered up to the English. At the " Tête de Flandre," where we landed, there was a dispute between the postmaster and some collecting-officers, which of them should not receive our money for the turnpikes. The postmaster was at last obliged to receive it. We came through St. Nicholas and Lokeren to Ghent, where we arrived at four in the afternoon, and took lodgings at the Hôtel des Pays-Bas, on the Place d'Armes, the best public-house in the city. I dined in my chamber alone, Mr. Russell having been the whole day quite unwell. Towards evening I took a walk round the city, and wrote part of a letter. At an early hour I retired for the night. The distance from Antwerp here is six and one-half posts — about thirty English miles; the road a perfect level, and well-paved; the country a continual garden.

June 29. — Soon after I arose this morning I saw the troops again under arms in front of my chamber-windows, and an extraordinary activity among them indicated the approach of the Emperor of Russia. The bells and the carillon began soon afterward to ring. About eleven o'clock I went out and followed the crowd to one of the streets through which he was to pass. He passed just at noon, on horseback, with a suite of fifteen or twenty officers. He was distinguished from them only by the greater simplicity of his dress — a plain green uniform, without any decoration and even without facings. Very few of the crowd knew him as he passed. He stopped about ten minutes at one of the squares, while a Prussian regiment, drawn up there, defiled before him. He afterwards stopped again, while a French regiment of the garrison of Hamburg passed. But he went through the city and immediately proceeded on his journey to Antwerp. It rained almost the whole day, and there was a heavy shower while he rode through the city. He had entered it, however, in an open calèche, that everybody might have an opportunity of seeing him. His condescension and affability were, as usual, conspicuous. The bells and carillon rang several times in the course of the day. In the evening Messrs. Bayard, Clay, Shaler, Milligan, and myself went to the ball at the Hôtel de Ville. There were two or three hundred persons at the ball. The ladies not remarkable either for beauty or elegance. We stayed about two hours, and returned to our lodgings before midnight.

June 30. — At eleven o'clock this morning the American Commissioners now here had a meeting at my chamber. Mr. Bayard, Mr. Clay, and Mr. Russell attended it. The conversation was desultory, and came only to the result of determining to send the *John Adams* home as soon as may be convenient; and of writing to Mr. Beasley, to obtain a passport for her from the British Admiralty. We agreed also to order two English newspapers to be sent us, and several other articles of necessity. We proposed to have regular meetings, and to keep a journal of our proceedings, when we shall all be assembled. We received information that Mr. Gallatin had arrived in Paris.

July 8. — Prince Henry left this city about noon. I dined again at the table-d'hôte at one. The other gentlemen dined together, at four. They sit after dinner and drink bad wine and smoke cigars, which neither suits my habits nor my health, and absorbs time which I cannot spare. I find it impossible, even with the most rigorous economy of time, to do half the writing that I ought.

July 9. — The American Ministers had this day a meeting in my chamber, from twelve o'clock noon until four. All the members were present, and we had a general conversation upon a variety of objects relating to our own situation here, and to our present mission. We agreed to have in future daily meetings, and to meet again in my chamber at twelve o'clock on Monday. I proposed the question whether we should make an official communication to the British Government of our being here, waiting for their Commissioners. This was not agreed to; but it was determined that a letter to our own Government should be written, to inform the Secretary of State that we are here, and transmit copies of the correspondence relating to the removal of the seat of negotiation from Gottenburg to Ghent.

July 18. — I had promised Mr. Meulemeester to call upon him about two o'clock this afternoon, to go with him and see the public library belonging to the city; but, as the mission had its ordinary meeting at noon, with which we were occupied until nearly four o'clock, I could not go. I proposed that we should deliberate upon the subjects mentioned in our instructions, and endeavor to prepare something upon the principal points referred to in them, to have it ready upon the arrival of the British Commissioners. I instanced the article concerning impressment, and mentioned the difficulty which there would be in attempting to draw it up. Some essays to that end were made by Mr. Bayard and Mr. Gallatin. It was found we had not here a set of the laws and treaties of the United States, without which we cannot proceed. Mr. Bayard has, however, a set on board the *Neptune,* at Antwerp.

July 30. — I went with Mr. Clay to the Hôtel de Ville, which was formerly the imperial palace, and we saw the ceremony of the " mariage civil " performed by the adjoint Mayor of the city. There were about twenty couples to be married this day. We saw six or seven of them go through the ceremony, which was very short. It appeared to consist only in the calling over the names, ages, and characters of the parties and their witnesses, who were usually five or six.

Aug 7. — The British Commissioners arrived last evening, and are lodged at the Hôtel du Lion d'Or. Mr. Baker, the Secretary to the Commission, called this morning, first upon Colonel Milligan, who lodges at the Hôtel des Pays-Bas, and

where Mr. Baker supposed we were yet lodged.   He afterwards came and called on Mr. Bayard, and notified to him
the arrival of the British Commissioners, with a proposal from
them that we should meet them to-morrow at one o'clock,
afternoon, at their lodgings, an exchange our full powers, and
arrange the mode of proceeding between us for the future.
Mr. Bayard received this notification, which he agreed to communicate to his colleagues, and promised that we would send
an answer this evening.

We had a meeting at noon, and were all of opinion that this
first step of the British Commissioners was advancing, on their
part, an offensive pretension to superiority.   I referred my colleagues to Martens, book vii. chap. lv. section 3, of his Summary, where the course now taken by the British Commissioners
appears to be precisely that stated there to be the usage from
Ambassadors to Ministers of an inferior order.   I proposed
that Mr. Hughes should call in the evening on Mr. Baker, and
say that we should be happy to meet and confer with the Commissioners, and exchange full powers with them, at any time
which they would indicate, and at any place other than their
own lodgings.

Aug. 8. — We had a meeting of the mission at noon, in which
we had some deliberation concerning the manner in which it
would be proper to proceed with the British Commissioners.
At one o'clock we went, accompanied by Mr. Hughes, to the
Hôtel des Pays-Bas, and found the British Commissioners
already there.   They are James, Lord Gambier, Henry Goulburn, Esquire, a member of Parliament and Under-Secretary
of State, and William Adams, Esquire, a Doctor of Civil Laws.
The Secretary to the Commission is Anthony St. John Baker.
Mr. Russell was absent, not having yet returned from Dunkirk.
After the first ordinary civilities had passed, we produced, on
both sides, the originals and copies of our full powers.   The
copies, attested by the Secretary of each Commission respec-
tively, were exchanged.   Lord Gambier then addressed us,
with assurances on the part of the British Government of their
sincere and earnest desire that this negotiation might terminate in a successful issue, and the ardent hope of the British
Commissioners that we might all have the satisfaction of restoring the blessings of peace to our respective countries.

This I answered by making similar assurances on our

part. . . Mr. Goulburn, the second British Commissioner, then replied. He renewed the professions of the sincere desire of the British Government for peace, and added the most explicit declaration that nothing that had occurred since the first proposal for this negotiation would have the slightest effect on the disposition of Great Britain with regard to the terms upon which the pacification might be concluded. He proceeded to say that the British Government thought it would be most conducive to this end to discard all retrospective considerations with regard to anything that had taken place, and had instructed them in relation to certain points which they supposed would naturally arise for discussion upon this negotiation. These points he was charged by his colleagues to state; with a request to be informed whether they were such as by our instructions we were authorized to discuss, and that we would also on our part state any other points upon which we also might be instructed to propose for discussion. Those which he was directed to present were — 1. The forcible seizure of mariners on board of American merchant vessels, and, connected with that subject, the claim of the King of Great Britain to the allegiance of all the native-born subjects of Great Britain. 2. The including of the Indian allies of Great Britain; and, for the purpose of obtaining a permanent pacification, the drawing of a boundary line for the Indians; and it was necessary to observe that on both parts of this point Great Britain considered them as a *sine qua non* to the conclusion of a treaty. 3. The partial revision of the boundary line between the United States and the British possessions in North America — upon which, on a question asked by Mr. Bayard, he explained that in such revision Great Britain did not contemplate an acquisition of territory.

Aug. 9. — The British Commissioners came at eleven; and, in the name of the mission, I stated that we were instructed upon the first and third points presented by them, and that on the second and fourth points we were not. I then proceeded to state the points proposed on our part. 1. A definition of blockade, and, as far as may be mutually agreed, of other neutral and belligerent rights. 2. Certain claims of indemnity to individuals for captures and seizures preceding and subsequent to the war. 3. I added that we were instructed upon a variety of other points which might with propriety be subjects for discussion, either upon a negotiation for peace or upon that of a treaty of commerce, which, in the event of a propitious termination of this negotiation, we were also authorized to conclude; that in order to simplify and facilitate as much as possible the great object of peace, we had discarded every point which did not more peculiarly belong to that and was not immediately relevant to it. . .

Mr. Gallatin said that so far as respected the including of the Indians in the peace, the United States would have neither interest nor wish to continue the war with the Indians when that with Great Britain should be terminated; that Commissioners had already been appointed to treat of peace with the Indians, and very probably the peace might already be made. He said that the policy of the United States towards the Indians was the most liberal of that pursued by any nation; that our laws interdicted the purchase of lands from them by any individual, and that every precaution was used to prevent the frauds upon them which had heretofore been practised by others. He stated that this proposition to give them a distinct boundary, different from the boundary already existing, and by a treaty between the United States and Great Britain, was not only new, it was unexampled. No such treaty had been made by Great Britain, either before or since the American Revolution, and no such treaty had, to his knowledge, ever been made by any other European power.

Mr. Goulburn said that they were certainly treated as in some respects sovereigns, since treaties were made with them both by Great Britain and the United States.

Treaties with them Mr. Gallatin admitted, but treaties between European powers defining their boundaries there were, to his knowledge, none.

Mr. Bayard asked what was understood by Great Britain to be the effect and operation of the boundary line proposed. Was it to restrict the United States from making treaties with them hereafter as heretofore? from purchasing their lands, for instance? Was it to restrict the Indians from selling their lands? Was it to alter the condition of the Indians, such as it has hitherto existed?

Mr. Goulburn answered that it was intended as a barrier between the British possessions and the territories of the United States; that it was not to restrict the Indians from selling their lands, although it would restrict the United States from purchasing them.

Aug. 13. — Lord Gambier and Dr. Adams, Mr. Baker and Mr. Gambier, Mr. Shaler and Mr. Meulemeester, dined with us. Mr. Goulburn sent an excuse this morning; he is unwell and confined to the house, having burst a blood-vessel, as they say, in the throat, and having yesterday lost his voice, so that he could not speak. We had no meeting this day, my draft of a dispatch being still in the hands of my colleagues. Mr. Gallatin had it all day yesterday, and gave it to Mr. Bayard, who took it for a second time, and retained it until this evening, when he gave it to Mr. Russell.

After being employed great part of this day in writing, I was engaged two or three hours on looking over treaties for the articles respecting the Indians and the fisheries. Mr. Meulemeester spent the evening with us. I played a game of chess with Mr. Shaler.

Lord Gambier told me that he had been in Boston in the year 1770, with his uncle, who then had the naval command there; that he was then a boy of twelve years of age; that in 1778 he was at New York during our contest, and then commanded a frigate. He spoke to me of my father as having known him at that time, and also of the family of Mr. Bowdoin. He mentioned the English Bible Society, of which he said he had the happiness to be one of the vice-presidents, and of a correspondence they had with the Bible Society in Boston, of which I told him I was a member. He expressed great satisfaction at the liberality with which they had sent a sum of money to replace the loss of some Bibles which had been taken by a privateer as they were going to Halifax.

Mr. Bayard asked Lord Gambier, upon some remark that Jerome Bonaparte's son was born in England, how the doctrine of allegiance would apply to him. His Lordship laughed, and said, "We won't talk about that now." I asked Dr. Adams to what part of England his family belonged. He said that originally they came from Pembrokeshire, in Wales, but they had removed from thence four or five generations since, and of late had resided in Essex. Their arms were a plain red cross. They had heretofore been possessed of a considerable estate in Wales, no part of which, however, had descended to the present generation. I think we are not cousins.

Aug. 18. — We had a meeting of the mission at two o'clock, when we signed the dispatch to the Secretary of State, No. 2, containing the account of our first conferences with the British Commissioners. I was charged also to make the draft of another dispatch, accounting for the detention of the *John Adams,* and to serve as a justification for Captain Angus.

Aug. 19. — Mr. Baker had been here from the British Commissioners, requesting a conference at their house at three o'clock. We went as requested. On taking their seats at the table, Mr. Goulburn had a dispatch from their Government before him, which, he informed us, was the answer to that which they had sent by their messenger. He proceeded to state its contents. The British Government expressed some surprise that we had not been instructed on the points of an Indian pacification, and boundary, as it might naturally have been expected that Great Britain could not consent to make a peace and leave her allies at the mercy of a more powerful enemy. She might therefore justly have supposed that the American Government would have furnished us with instructions to agree to an article on this subject; but the least she can demand is, that the American Commissioners should sign a provisional article, subject to the ratification of their Government, so that if it should be ratified the treaty should take effect, and if not, that it should be null and void. And we were desired to understand that if unfortunately the conferences should be suspended by our refusal to agree to such an article, Great Britain would not consider herself bound, upon a renewal of the negotiations, to abide by the terms which she now offers. As we had requested to be explicitly informed of the views and intentions of Great Britain in proposing this article, we were to know that the Indian territories were to be interposed as a barrier between the British Dominions and the United States, to prevent them from being conterminous to each other, and that neither Great Britain nor the United States should acquire by any purchase any of these Indian lands. For the line Great Britain was willing to take the treaty of Greenville for the basis, with such modifications as might be agreed upon. With respect to the other boundary line, that of the British territories, Great Britain still adhered to the principle of asking for no conquests. But as Great Britain, on the side of Canada, was the weaker of the two nations. and

had no designs of conquest there, and as it had been stated
that the United States had, on their part, had the design
of conquering Canada, it was required by Great Britain that
the United States would stipulate to have no naval force
upon the Lakes, from Ontario to Superior; and neither to
build any forts in future, nor to preserve those already built
upon their borders.   It would also be necessary for Great
Britain to obtain a communication between the provinces of
New Brunswick and Canada, a mere road from Halifax to
Quebec, which would take off a small corner of the province of
Maine.   These propositions must be considered as proofs
of the moderation of Great Britain, since she might have
demanded a cession of all the borders of the Lakes to
herself.   She would also require a continuance of the right
of navigating the Mississippi, as secured to her by the former
treaties.

Mr. Gallatin asked what was proposed to be done with the
inhabitants, citizens of the United States, already settled
beyond the line of the Treaty of Greenville — the Territories
of Michigan, of Illinois, and part of the State of Ohio, amounting perhaps to one hundred thousand, many of whom had been
settled there with their ancestors one hundred years.

Mr. Goulburn said that their case had not been considered
by the British Government; that it might be a foundation for
the United States to claim a particular modification of the
line, and if that should not be agreed to they might remove.

Dr. Adams said that undoubtedly they must shift for themselves.

Mr. Bayard asked whether the proposition respecting the
Indian pacification and boundary was still presented as a *sine
qua non;* to which they answered that undoubtedly it was.

He asked whether that relating to the Lakes was of the
same character.

Dr. Adams answered, " One *sine qua non* at a time is enough.
It will be time enough to answer your question when you have
disposed of that we have given you."

I observed that, for my own part, I should not wish for another conference before we should have received from the
British Commissioners a written statement of their propositions.

This was agreed to on all sides, and they suggested that

they should also expect our written answer to their note prior to the next conference.

I observed there might be in their note itself some things susceptible of verbal explanation, which we might desire before we should send the answer; in which case, I presumed, they would have no objection to our asking another conference.

To this they assented, though not without some objection from Dr. Adams, which he finally gave up. They promised to furnish us the written note as soon as possible. Lord Castlereagh himself arrived in this city last night, and proceeds in a day or two to Brussels. Our conference lasted about an hour.

After dinner we had a meeting of the mission, and determined to write another dispatch to the Secretary of State, but not to wait for the written note of the British commissioners, nor to delay the departure of the *John Adams* an hour longer. Mr. Gallatin made minutes for this dispatch, and agreed to make the draft of it, to be ready to-morrow morning.

In my account of our conference with the British Commissioners this morning I omitted to state the following facts. Mr. Gallatin, adverting to the late account in the English newspapers of their having taken possession of Moose Island, in the Bay of Passamaquoddy, enquired whether the statement which had been published was correct, that they meant to keep it.

They said it was; that it was a part of the province of Nova Scotia; that they did not even consider it a subject for discussion.

Mr. Goulburn said he could demonstrate in the most unanswerable manner that it belonged to them, and Dr. Adams said we might as well contest their right to Northamptonshire.

Mr. Gallatin asked whether, in requiring us to keep no naval force on the Lakes and no forts on their shores, they intended to reserve the right of keeping them there themselves. They said they certainly did.

After the conference was finished, Mr. Bayard said to Mr. Goulburn, that if the conferences were suspended he supposed Goulburn would take a trip to England. Goulburn said, " Yes, and I suppose you will take a trip to America."

In general, their tone was more peremptory and their language more overbearing than at former conferences. Their deportment this day was peculiarly offensive to Mr. Bayard. Mr. Clay has an inconceivable idea, that they will finish by receding from the ground they have taken.

Aug. 21. — I began the first draft of an answer to the note of the British Commissioners, which gave me occupation for the day, and which I did not finish. Mr. Clay had written something on his part, and Mr. Gallatin, according to his custom of composition, had taken minutes of the subjects to be treated and the ideas to be contained in it. All these were read at our meeting at two o'clock this afternoon. I found, as usual, that the draft was not satisfactory to my colleagues. On the general view of the subject we are unanimous, but in my exposition of it, one objects to the form and another to the substance of almost every paragraph. Mr. Gallatin is for striking out every expression that may be offensive to the feelings of the adverse party. Mr. Clay is displeased with figurative language, which he thinks improper for a state paper. Mr. Russell, agreeing in the objections of the two other gentlemen, will be further for amending the construction of every sentence; and Mr. Bayard, even when agreeing to say precisely the same thing, chooses to say it only in his own language. It was considered by all the gentlemen that what I had written was too long, and with too much argument about the Indians. It is, however, my duty to make the draft of the dispatch, and they usually hold me to it. We received invitations to dine next Saturday with the British Commissioners: the chance is that before that time the whole negotiation will be at an end.

Aug. 22. — I finished this morning my draft of an answer to the note of the British Commissioners, and gave it before breakfast to Mr. Gallatin, who kept it for his amendments and additions the whole day.

Aug. 23. — We had this morning a meeting of the mission, when my draft of an answer to the note of the British Commissioners, with Mr. Gallatin's corrections and alterations, Mr. Clay's two or three paragraphs, and an attempt at a totally new draft begun and not finished by Mr. Bayard, were read and discussed; and Mr. Hughes was directed to make out a new draft from the shreds and patches of them all. About one-half of my draft was agreed to be struck out; a half of the remainder was left for consideration. We all dined at the Intendant's.

Aug. 25. — We had a meeting this morning, when the answer to the note of the British Plenipotentiaries was finally agreed to and signed. It was carried to them by Mr. Hughes, and will bring the negotiation very shortly to a close.

Aug. 28. — We had a short meeting at two o'clock, and concluded upon leaving this house at the expiration of our month, the day after to-morrow. As we shall certainly not have occasion to stay here more than a week or ten days at the utmost, we had proposed to Lanmeier to remain, paying the rent not for the whole month, but in proportion to the time we shall stay. But although his partner had yesterday agreed to this proposal, they sent us this morning a joint letter, stating that they paid their rent by the month, and had other contracts of the same kind, and making appeals to our generosity. We therefore determined not to enter upon the second month.

Aug. 31. — Mr. Baker, the Secretary of the British Plenipotentiaries, came this morning and enquired for Mr. Hughes, who not being here, he asked for Mr. Gallatin; he told him that in consideration of the great importance of their reply to our note, they had concluded to refer it to their Government for instructions. It would occasion only a delay of a few days.

Sept. 1. — This morning I paid a visit to the British Plenipotentiaries and to Mrs. Goulburn. I did not, however, see her, but only her husband. Lord Gambier and Dr. Adams, with Mr. Baker, went yesterday to Brussels, to return on Saturday. Mr. Goulburn told me that after having prepared their note in reply to ours, from the great importance of the subject, they had thought best to transmit it to their Government for approbation before they sent it in to us. He said he expected their messenger this evening; and I enquired whether he expected to receive by him the answer to their last reference. He said that would depend on the time which it took their dispatch to arrive in England, but he thought it more probable that the answer would come next Sunday — that their messengers came regularly twice a week, on Thursdays and Sundays. I told him I hoped his Government would reconsider some parts of their former propositions before they sent their final instructions. He did not think it probable, and I found the more I conversed with him the more the violence and bitterness of his passion against the United States disclosed itself. His great point in support of the Indian boundary was

its necessity for the security of Canada.   He said that the
United States had manifested the intention and the determination of conquering Canada; that, " excepting us," he believed it was the astonishment of the whole world that Canada
had not been conquered at the very outset of the war; that
nothing had saved it but the excellent dispositions and military
arrangements of the Governor who commanded there; that in
order to guard against the same thing in future, it was necessary to make a barrier against our settlements, upon which
neither party should encroach; that the Indians were but a
secondary object, but that as being the allies of Great Britain
she must include them, as she made peace with other powers,
including Portugal as her ally; that the proposition that we
should stipulate not to arm upon the Lakes was made with
the same purpose — the security of Canada.   He could not
see that there was anything humiliating in it; that the United
States could never be in any danger of invasion from Canada,
the disproportion of force was too great.   But Canada must
always be in the most imminent danger of invasion from the
United States, unless she was guarded by some such stipulation
as they now demanded; that it could be nothing to the United
States, to agree not to arm upon the Lakes, since they never
had actually done it before the present war.   Why should they
object to disarming there, where they had never before had a
gun floating?

I answered that the conquest of Canada had never been an
object of the war on the part of the United States; that
Canada had been invaded by us in consequence of the war, as
they themselves had invaded many parts of the United States
— it was an effect, and not a cause, of the war; that the
American Government never had declared the intention of
conquering Canada. . .

He insisted that the Indians must be considered as independent nations, and that we ourselves made treaties with them and
acknowledged boundaries of their territories.

I said that, wherever they would form settlements and
cultivate lands, their possessions were undoubtedly to be respected, and always were respected, by the United States; that
some of them had become civilized in a considerable degree —
the Cherokees, for example, who had permanent habitations,
and a state of property like our own.   But the greater part of

the Indians could never be prevailed upon to adopt this mode
of life; their habits and attachments and prejudices were so
averse to any settlement, that they could not reconcile themselves to any other condition than that of wandering hunters.
It was impossible for such people ever to be said to have
possessions. Their only right upon land was a right to use it
as hunting-grounds, and when those lands where they hunted
became necessary or convenient for the purposes of settlement,
the system adopted by the United States was, by amicable
arrangement with them, to compensate them for renouncing
the right of hunting upon them, and for removing to remoter
regions better suited to their purposes and mode of life. This
system of the United States was an improvement upon the
former practice of all European nations, including the British.
The original settlers of New England had set the first example
of this liberality towards the Indians, which was afterwards
followed by the founder of Pennsylvania. Between it and taking the lands for nothing, or exterminating the Indians who had
used them, there was no alternative. To condemn vast regions
of territory to perpetual barrenness and solitude that a few
hundred savages might find wild beasts to hunt upon it, was a
species of game law that a nation descended from Britons
would never endure. It was incompatible with the moral as
with the physical nature of things. If Great Britain meant
to preclude forever the people of the United States from settling and cultivating those territories, she must not think of
doing it by a treaty. She must formally undertake, and accomplish, their utter extermination. If the Government of
the United States should ever submit to such a stipulation,
which I hoped they would not, all its force, and that of Britain
combined with it, would not suffice to carry it long into execution. It was opposing a feather to a torrent. The population
of the United States in 1810 passed seven millions; at this
hour it undoubtedly passed eight. As it continued to increase
in such proportions, was it in human experience, or in human
power, to check its progress by a bond of paper purporting
to exclude posterity from the natural means of subsistence
which they would derive from the cultivation of the soil? Such
a treaty, instead of closing the old sources of discussion, would
only open new ones. A war thus finished would immediately
be followed by another, and Great Britain would ultimately find

that she must substitute the project of exterminating the whole American people for that of opposing against them her barrier of savages.

" What! " said Mr. Goulburn, " is it, then, in the inevitable nature of things that the United States must conquer Canada ? "

" No."

" But what security, then, can Great Britain have for her possession of it ? "

" If Great Britain does not think a liberal and amicable course of policy towards America would be the best security, as it certainly would, she must rely upon her general strength, upon the superiority of her power in other parts of her relations with America, upon the power which she has upon another element, to indemnify herself, by sudden impression upon American interests, more defenceless against her superiority, and in their amount far more valuable, than Canada ever was or ever will be."

Sept. 5. — I have been copying Mr. Clay's private journal of the conferences, which it may be useful hereafter to compare with my own. This morning the British Commissioners sent their reply to our last note, which was received by Mr. Gallatin and by him brought to me. We had shortly after a meeting of the mission, when it was read and considered. Mr. Bayard pronounced it a very stupid production. Mr. Clay was for answering it by a note of half a page. I neither thought it stupid nor proper to be answered in half a page. Each of the gentlemen wanted it for some hours, and Mr. Gallatin proposed to make an analysis of its contents, to minute what would deserve to be noticed in our answer, to which we all agreed. After dinner Mr. Meulemeester and Mr. Bentzon called upon us, and we went with them to the private theatre to see *La Rhetorique.*

Sept. 8, III. 45. — Just before rising, I heard Mr. Clay's company retiring from his chamber. I had left him with Mr. Russell, Mr. Bentzon, and Mr. Todd at cards. They parted as I was about to rise. I was up nearly half an hour before I had daylight to read or write. From that time until ten I was employed on the draft and minutes of Mr. Gallatin, Mr. Bayard, and Mr. Clay. I struck out the greatest part of my own previous draft, preferring that of Mr. Gallatin upon the

same points. On the main question, relative to the Indian
boundary, I made a new draft of several paragraphs, comprising the principal ideas of them all, and introducing an additional view of the subject of my own. I had also prepared
a paragraph concerning the employment of savages. I was
not a little gratified to find that Mr. Bayard in his draft had
taken the true and strong ground respecting Indian rights, and
had even quoted the very passage of Vattel which I had produced to him at our meeting on the 25th of last month, and
at which he had then appeared to be a little nettled. I read
my new draft to Mr. Gallatin in his chamber, and at eleven
o'clock gave the papers to Mr. Russell.

Sept. 20. — I was closing my copy of four pages, when the
third note from the British Plenipotentiaries was brought to
me, together with some late English newspapers that they had
sent us. After reading the note, and the two proclamations of
General Hull and General Smyth, enclosed with it, I took them
immediately in to Mr. Gallatin. They were shortly after read
by our other colleagues, and we had, at one o'clock, a meeting
of the mission. The British note is overbearing and insulting
in its tone, like the two former ones; but it abandons a great
part of the *sine qua non,* adhering at the same time inflexibly
to the remainder. The effect of these notes upon us when they
first come is to deject us all. We so fondly cling to the vain
hope of peace, that every new proof of its impossibility oper-
ates upon us as a disappointment. We had a desultory and
general conversation upon this note, in which I thought both
Mr. Gallatin and Mr. Bayard showed symptoms of despondency. In discussing with them I cannot always restrain the
irritability of my temper. Mr. Bayard meets it with more of
accommodation than heretofore, and sometimes with more
compliance than I expect. Mr. Gallatin, having more pliability
of character and more playfulness of disposition, throws off my
heat with a joke. Mr. Clay and Mr. Russell are perfectly
firm themselves, but sometimes partake of the staggers of the
two other gentlemen.

Mr. Gallatin said this day that the *sine qua non* now presented — that the Indians should be positively included in the
peace, and placed in the state they were in before the war —
would undoubtedly be rejected by our Government if it was
now presented to them, but that it was a bad point for us to

break off the negotiation upon; that the difficulty of carrying on the war might compel us to admit the principle at last, for now the British had so committed themselves with regard to the Indians that it was impossible for them further to retreat.

Mr. Bayard was of the same opinion, and recurred to the fundamental idea of breaking off upon some point which shall unite our own people in the support of the war.

In this sentiment we all concur. But, as its tendency is to produce compliance with the British claims, it is necessary to guard against its leading us in that career too far. I said it was not more clear to me that the British would not finally abandon their present *sine qua non,* than it had been that they would adhere to their first; that if the point of the Indians was a bad point to break upon, I was very sure we should never find a good one. If that would not unite our people, it was a hopeless pursuit.

Mr. Gallatin repeated, with a very earnest look, that it was a bad point to break upon.

"Then," said I, with a movement of impatience and an angry tone, "it is a good point to admit the British as the sovereigns and proctectors of our Indians."

Gallatin's countenance brightened, and he said, in a tone of perfect good humor, "That's a non-sequitur." This turned the edge of the argument into mere jocularity. I laughed, and insisted that it was a sequitur, and the conversation easily changed to another point.

Sept. 21, IV. 30. — Wrote about half an hour by candle-light this morning. This being the day of the autumnal equinox, I must henceforth, for half a year, rise by the light of the morning stars. I wrote again four pages of copying, and we had our mission meeting.

Mr. Gallatin produced his analysis of the last British note, and his minutes of the proposed answer, which he it to draft. The original of the British note was delivered to me. I found both Mr. Gallatin and Mr. Bayard this day as firm on the point we had yesterday discussed as any of us.

In the evening we all attended a tea- and card-party at Mr. Meulemeester's, where I played whist with him, Madame Canighem, and another lady, name unknown. As we came home, Mr. Clay mentioned to me his satisfaction at finding that Mr. Bayard was now so strong in sentiment with us. Of Mr. Gallatin he had always been sure. There was another card-party in Mr. Clay's chamber last night, and I heard Mr. Bentzon retiring from it after I had risen this morning.

Sept. 25. — We met at one o'clock, and sat until past five, debating the new draft of our answer to the British note. I had proposed to leave out a large part of Mr. Gallatin's draft, but he insisted upon retaining most of what he had written, and it was retained. In this debate I had continued evidence of two things. One, that if any one member objects to anything I have written, all the rest support him in it, and I never can get it through. The other, that if I object to anything written by Mr. Gallatin, unless he voluntarily abandons it every other member supports him, and my objection is utterly unavailing. They supported him thus this day in a paragraph respecting Florida, directly in the face of our instructions, which I produced and read. I was reduced to the necessity of declaring that I would not sign the paper with the paragraph as he had drawn it. He objected to mine because it said that the proceedings of the American Government could be completely justified with regard to Florida. Gallatin said he did not think they could; that he had opposed for a whole year what had been done, before he could succeed in stopping the course they had taken. Mr. Bayard said that he was very much committed on the subject of Florida, too; and Mr. Clay, though he thought the Government perfectly justifiable, did not perceive any necessity for saying so. Mr. Russell was of the same opinion. I had no alternative but to say I would not sign the paper with the paragraph as Mr. Gallatin had written it; for that pointedly said that we would not discuss the subject of Florida with the British Plenipotentiaries, though our instructions had expressly authorized us to bring it before them. Mr. Gallatin finally consented himself to take my paragraph with an alteration.

On the other hand, in repelling an insolent charge of the British Plenipotentiaries against the Government of the United States, of a system of perpetual encroachment upon the Indians under the pretence of purchases, I had taken the ground of the moral and religious duty of a nation to settle, cultivate, and improve their territory — a principle perfectly recognized by the laws of nations, and, in my own opinion, the only solid and

unanswerable defence against the charge in the British note.
Gallatin saw and admitted the weight of the argument, but
was afraid of ridicule. Bayard, too, since he has been reading Vattel, agreed in the argument, and was willing to say
it was a duty. But the terms God, and Providence, and Heaven,
Mr. Clay thought were canting, and Russell laughed at them.
I was obliged to give them up, and with them what I thought
the best argument we had. My proposal of the amnesty passed
more smoothly, and almost without alteration.

Sept. 29. — As I was sitting at my writing-table this morning, before eight o'clock, one of the servants of the house
opened my door, and my brother-in-law, Mr. George Boyd,
of Washington City, came in quite unexpectedly. He comes
as a messenger with dispatches from the Department of State
to the mission, and from the Treasury Department to Mr.
Crawford, Mr. Gallatin, and myself. He left Washington the
12th of last month, at twelve hours' notice, and sailed on the
16th, from New York, in the *Transit,* a fast-sailing Baltimore
schooner. . . In the evening we had our large tea- and card-
party, which became a ball. Invitations had been sent to about
one hundred and fifty persons, and there were about one hundred and thirty who came. None of the British Legation.
All the principal noblesse and merchants of the city were here.
The company began to assemble between seven and eight
o'clock. At eleven we had a supper; after which the dancing
recommenced, and the party broke up just before three in
the morning. I played whist with the Intendant's lady,
Madame Borlut de Lens, the Mayor's sister, and Prince
d'Aremberg, the Commander-in-Chief of all the Belgian troops.
I danced part of a Boulangère. Our garden was illuminated
with the variegated colored lamps, and there was an inscription of eight poor French verses over the central gate, between
the garden and back yard.

Oct. 9, V. — From which time until our meeting at two
in the afternoon I was engaged in copying the note yesterday
received from the British Plenipotentiaries. At the meeting
we had some desultory conversation on the subject of the
answer to be given to the British note. We came to no determination, but agreed to meet at eleven to-morrow morning.
Mr. Bayard suggested the propriety of asking for a conference
before we should answer the note. We thought we could not

break off on the refusal to accept the article proposed, but that we might demand, before we accepted it, their whole project of a treaty. Yet if they should eventually refuse to give their project until we should formally have admitted their article, he was still not for breaking off. Mr. Clay was for rejecting any proposition to disarm upon the Lakes, if we admitted the present article; because he considered that the two articles together would deliver the whole western country up to the mercy of the Indians. The inconvenience and danger of admitting any preliminary article thus dictated was distinctly perceived by us, but none of us were prepared to break off upon it.

Oct. 10. — We had our meeting of the mission at twelve, and had much further conversation concerning the answer to the last British note. Mr. Clay and Mr. Gallatin were very desirous it should be short — not more than four pages. I was of opinion it ought to be long — at least at long as the note itself. It was agreed, however, that Mr. Gallatin should prepare a draft, to be offered to the meeting to-morrow.

Oct. 12. — I made a draft of an answer to the last note from the British Plenipotentiaries, but had not finished it when the time of our meeting came. At the meeting, Mr. Gallatin produced his draft, and I read parts of mine. They differed much in the tone of the composition. The tone of all the British notes is arrogant, overbearing, and offensive. The tone of ours is neither so bold nor so spirited as I think it should be. It is too much on the defensive, and too excessive in the caution to say nothing irritating. I have seldom been able to prevail upon my colleagues to insert anything in the style of retort upon the harsh and reproachful matter which we receive. And they are now so resolved to make the present note short, that they appeared to reject everything I had written, and even much of Mr. Gallatin's draft. We agree to accept the article offered to us as an ultimatum. Mr. Gallatin's idea is to adopt it, as perfectly conformable to the views we ourselves had previously taken of the subject. Mine is to consider and represent it as a very great concession, made for the sake of securing the peace. But in this opinion I am alone. I also strongly urged the expediency of avowing as the sentiment of our Government that the cession of Canada would be for the interest of Great Britain as well as the United States. I had drawn up a paragraph upon the subject conformable to our instructions. My colleagues would not adopt it. . .

Mr. Clay took the two drafts, to shorten that of Mr. Gallatin and to adopt from mine anything that he might think proper to be taken. Mr. Bayard and myself sat after dinner until past ten o'clock, conversing upon subjects of American politics and of our present negotiation. He was extremely friendly and confidential in his manner, and spoke with an openheartedness which I very cordially returned. He appears very anxious for the acceptance of the article offered us by the British Plenipotentiaries, and dwells with the greatest earnestness on the project of accomplishing the peace, or of uniting our whole country in support of the war against our eternal and irreconcilable foe.

Oct. 13. — We had a meeting of the mission at two. Mr. Clay had a new draft of an answer to the last note of the British Plenipotentiaries. I disliked it very much in all its parts, but could obtain only that small parts of it should be struck out. It was finally settled as it is to be sent, and given to Mr. Hughes, to be prepared for our signatures at eleven o'clock to-morrow morning.

Oct. 14. — The British Ministers sent us the *Times* of the 10th and 11th, containing the official accounts of the taking of Machias and other towns in Passamaquoddy Bay, and the destruction of the frigate *Adams* by the expedition from Halifax, under Sir T. C. Sherbrooke, together with the failure of our attempt to take Michillimackinac, and the taking of Plattsburg by the British Canadian Army. At noon we met in Mr. Clay's chamber and signed our answer to the fourth note from the British Plenipotentiaries, which Mr. Hughes immediately took to them. Mr. Clay, who was determined to foresee no public misfortune in our affairs, bears them with less temper, now they have come, than any other of us. He rails at commerce and the people of Massachusetts, and tells what wonders the people of Kentucky would do if they should be attacked.

Oct. 18. — I had some conversation with Mr. Russell, who read me a letter he was writing to Mr. Crawford, and who now told me he was much dissatisfied with our last note to the British Plenipotentiaries. I reminded him that I had not only declared myself dissatisfied with it, but had offered another draft, and of a totally different character. I asked him why he had not supported me. He said he had expected Mr. Clay would have been the most stubborn of us all upon the point relative to the Indians, and, finding him give way, and being himself the youngest member of the mission, and being from a State that cared nothing about Indian affairs, he had not thought it was his business to be more stiff about it than others. I told him of the long conversation I had with Bayard, and how powerfully Bayard had operated upon me in it. I added that he had previously had a similar conversation with Clay, and I believed had worked still more forcibly upon him. Russell said that Bayard always talked about keeping a high tone, but when it came to the point he was always on the conceding side.

Oct. 22. — We received this day the fifth note from the British Plenipotentiaries. It has the same dilatory and insidious character as their preceding notes, but is shorter.

Oct. 26. — We all dined with the British Plenipotentiaries. No other company there than ourselves and Mr. Van Aken. It was a dull dinner. Lord Gambier complained of the incendiaries who were constantly employed in the English newspapers, blowing the flames of war. He spoke also of the sort of warfare now carried on between some of the London and Paris papers. He asked me if we had made any acquaintances here. I said we had. He replied that they knew nobody but the Intendant's family.

Oct. 27. — We all dined at the Intendant's, except Mr. Russell, and Todd, who was engaged in packing up for Mr. Connell. Prince d'Aremberg and some other general officers were there. We stayed the evening, when there was an additional party of ladies. Mr. Clay and myself played whist with the Intendant's lady and Madame de Crombrugge. The play was too low for Mr. Clay, who soon grew weary and impatient.

Oct. 29. — At two o'clock we had a meeting of the mission. Mr. Russell was not present. We had some further desultory conversation concerning the drawing up a project of a treaty. Mr. Gallatin had made some minutes, upon which we had much loose conversation. I urged the propriety of making out at once the project in the form of a treaty, both for the sake of saving time and of being fully prepared to deliver it immediately to the British Plenipotentiaries whenever they shall consent to the exchange of projects. This was at last agreed to. Mr. Gallatin undertook to draw up the articles respecting the boundaries and Indians, and I promised to prepare those respecting impressment, blockade, and indemnities.

Oct. 30. — I began making a draft for the project of a treaty. Mr. Gallatin was employed in the same manner. At two o'clock we had a meeting of the mission, but Mr. Clay was not present until the meeting was over, and Mr. Russell not at all. We looked over the articles drawn by Mr. Gallatin and myself, which being unfinished, we agreed to meet every day, at two o'clock, until the whole project shall be prepared. Mr. Gallatin proposes to renew the two articles of the Treaty of Peace of 1783, the stipulation for our right to fish, and dry and cure fish, within the waters of the British jurisdiction, and the right of the British to navigate the Mississippi. To this last article, however, Mr. Clay makes strong objections. He is willing to leave the matter of the fisheries as a nest-egg for another war, but to make the peace without saying anything about it; which, after the notice the British have given us, will be in fact an abandonment of our right. Mr. Clay considers this fishery as an object of trifling amount; and that a renewal of the right of the British to navigate the Mississippi would be giving them a privilege far more important than that we should secure in return. And as he finds, as yet, no member of the mission but himself taking this ground, he grows earnest in defence of it.

Oct. 31. — As I was beginning to read my draft of articles for the project of a treaty, a packet was brought to us from the British Plenipotentiaries, together with the *Times* newspapers to the 28th inclusive. The dispatch contained their sixth note, dilatory and evasive as heretofore, and also a short unsigned note, with an Admiralty passport for the *Transit*. It was agreed to send immediately Mr. Todd with a copy of this note to Ostend, to reach Mr. Connell before the sailing of the *Chauncey*. He went away immediately after dinner. We had little deliberation, and came to no result upon the contents of the sixth note, for we all fell to reading the newspapers until dinner-time. Mr. Clay is losing his temper and growing peevish and fractious. I, too, must not forget to keep a constant guard upon my temper, for the time is evidently approaching when it will be wanted.

Day. My usual rising hour is between five and six in the morning, but I find myself inclining too much to relax from these hours of industry, and to run later into the evening than I have been accustomed these three years. The morning hour very generally corresponds with the evening hour, and the time before breakfast is invariably that upon which I can most depend. I light my candle and my fire immediately on rising, and now read and write about an hour by candle-light every morning. On Tuesdays and Fridays I write to my wife, which employs me until breakfast-time, nine o'clock, and commonly an hour or two afterwards. Our usual hour for the meeting of the mission is two P.M. We have occasional extraordinary meetings at other hours. The ordinary meeting almost always lasts till four, when we dine. If finished sooner, I now take a short walk in the interval. We dine at four, and usually sit at table until six or seven. About once a week I go to the theatre, which finishes between ten and eleven. Sometimes we pass the evening in company, and at others I walk on the Place d'Armes and call to see Mrs. Smith. I seldom read or write after dark, and am in bed sometimes before ten, and almost always by eleven. I am hitherto not at all embarrassed with the length of the evenings, and seldom close them so soon as I would choose. My chief fault now is a great relaxation of my customary exercise. This must be corrected.

Nov. 10, VI. 30. — A second day belated. On examining the drafts for the note with the amendments of Messrs. Clay, Bayard, and Russell, I found more than three-fourths of what I had written erased. There was only one paragraph to which I attached importance, but that was struck out with the rest. It was the proposal to conclude the peace on the footing of the state before the war, applied to all the subjects of dispute between the two countries, leaving all the rest for the future and pacific negotiation. I abandoned everything else that was objected to in my draft, but wrote over that paragraph again, to propose its insertion in the note. I had gone through my examination of the papers at breakfast-time, and Mr. Gallatin took them. At eleven o'clock we had the meeting of the mission. Everything in the note, as amended, was agreed to without difficulty, excepting my proposed paragraph. Mr. Clay objected strongly against it, because we are forbidden by our instructions from renewing the article of the Treaty of 1794, allowing the British to trade with our Indians. Mr. Gallatin, who strenuously supported my proposition, thought it did not necessarily include the renewal of that article of the Treaty of 1794, because it only offers the state before the war with regard to the objects in dispute. The Indian trade never had been in dispute. He admitted, however, that if the British government should accept the principle and propose the renewal of the treaties, we could not after this offer refuse it.

I stated in candor that I considered my proposal as going that full length; that I was aware it would be a departure from our instructions as prepared in April, 1813. But the Government, for the purpose of obtaining peace, had revoked our instructions of that date upon a point much more important in its estimation, the very object of the war; and I have no doubt would have revoked them on the other point, had it occurred to them that they would prove an obstacle to the conclusion of peace. I felt so sure that they would now gladly take the state before the war as the general basis of the peace, that I was prepared to take on me the responsibility of trespassing upon their instructions thus far. Not only so, but I would at this moment cheerfully give my life for a peace on this basis. If peace was possible, it would be on no other. I had, indeed, no hope that the proposal would be accepted. But on the rupture it would make the strongest case possible in our favor, for the world both in Europe and America. It would put the continuance of the war entirely at the door of England, and force out her objects in continuing it. . .

Mr. Clay finally said that he would agree to the insertion of my proposal in the note, but reserving to himself the right of refusing to sign the treaty if the offer should be accepted and the principle extended beyond his approbation.

The draft was then taken by Mr. Hughes to be copied out fair, and Mr. Gallatin, Mr. Russell, and myself remained to compare the residue of the articles as they were prepared. A concluding article, providing for the ratifications and their exchange, was prepared by Mr. Gallatin and me; after which I went out and walked about an hour. Mr. Hughes was prepared with the note at his rooms, at the back of our house. I took the project to him, and he copied on it the concluding article. They were then brought back to our dining-room, and we signed the note — Mr. Clay still manifesting signs of reluctance. He objected to the formal concluding article, and thought it ridiculous, and he recurred again to the paragraph proposing the state before the war as the general basis of the treaty. He said the British Plenipotentiaries would laugh at us for it. They would say, " Ay, ay! pretty fellows you, to think of getting out of the war as well as you got into it! "

I think it very probable this commentary will be made on our proposal; but what would be the commentary on our refusing peace on those terms? Mr. Russell dined with us about five o'clock, and immediately after dinner Mr. Hughes took our note and project to the British Plenipotentiaries.

Nov. 27. — About eleven in the morning, Mr. Gallatin came into my chamber, with a note received from the British Plenipotentiaries. They have sent us back with this note the project of a treaty which we had sent them, with marginal notes and alterations proposed by them. They have rejected all the articles we had proposed on impressment, blockade, indemnities, amnesty, and Indians. They have definitively abandoned the Indian boundary, the exclusive military possession of the Lakes, and the uti possidetis; but with a protestation that they will not be bound to adhere to these terms hereafter, if the peace should not be made now. Within an hour after receiving these papers we had a meeting of the mission at my chamber, when the note and the alterations to our project proposed by the British Plenipotentiaries were read, and we had some desultory conversation upon the subject. All the difficulties to the conclusion of a peace appear to be now so nearly removed, that my colleagues all considered it as certain.[2] I think it myself probable. But unless we take it precisely as it is now offered, to which I strongly incline, I distrust so much the intentions of the British Government, that I still consider the conclusion as doubtful and precarious.

[2] So extreme had been the dissensions of the peace conference that the sudden turn toward concord was an astonishing event. It was due in the main to the action of the British Cabinet. Lord Liverpool had been pertinacious in demanding peace; Lord Castlereagh, who had at first opposed it, and had been responsible for the original intolerable terms of the British, had become alarmed by certain differences at the Congress of Vienna with the Emperor of Russia and King of Prussia. He had suddenly decided that it would be prudent to end the war, and had written home urging concessions — which were now at last made in Ghent.

Nov. 28. — At eleven o'clock we met, and continued in session until past four, when we adjourned to meet again at eleven to-morrow morning. Our principal discussion was on an article proposed by the British Government as a substitute for the eighth of our project. And they have added a clause securing to them the navigation of the Mississippi, and access to it with their goods and merchandise through our territories.

To this part of the article Mr. Clay positively objected. Mr. Gallatin proposed to agree to it, proposing an article to secure our right of fishing and curing fish within the British jurisdiction. Mr. Clay lost his temper, as he generally does whenever this right of the British to navigate the Mississippi is discussed. He was utterly averse to admitting it as an equivalent for a stipulation securing the contested part of the fisheries. He said the more he heard of this the more convinced he was that it was of little or no value. He should be glad to get it if he could, but he was sure the British would not ultimately grant it. That the navigation of the Mississippi, on the other hand, was an object of immense importance . . . Mr. Gallatin said that the fisheries were of great importance in the sentiment of the eastern section of the Union; that if we should sign a peace without securing them to the full extent in which they were enjoyed before the war, and especially if we should abandon any part of the territory, it would give a handle to the party there, now pushing for a separation from the Union and for a New England Confederacy, to say that the interests of New England were sacrificed, and to pretend that by a separate confederacy they could obtain what is refused to us.

Mr. Clay said that there was no use in attempting to conciliate people who never would be conciliated; that it was too much the practice of our Government to sacrifice the interests of its best friends for those of its bitterest enemies; that there might be a party for separation at some future day in the Western States, too.

I observed to him that he was now speaking under the impulse of passion, and that on such occasions I would wish not to answer anything; that assuredly the Government would be reproached, and the greatest advantage would be taken by the party opposed to it, if any of the rights of the Eastern States should be sacrificed by the peace; that the loss of any part of the fisheries would be a subject of triumph and exultation, both to the enemy and to those among us who had been opposed to the war; that if I should consent to give up even Moose Island, where there was a town which had been for many years regularly represented in the Legislature of the State of Massachusetts, I should be ashamed to show my face among my countrymen; that as to the British right of navigating the Mississippi, I considered it as nothing, considered as a grant from us. It was secured to them by the Peace of 1783, they had enjoyed it at the commencement of the war, it had never been injurious in the slightest degree to our own people, and it appeared to me that the British claim to it was just and equitable. The boundary fixed by the Peace of 1783 was a line due west from the Lake of the Woods to the Mississippi, and the navigation of the river was stipulated for both nations. It has been since that time discovered that a line due west from the Lake of the Woods will not touch the Mississippi, but goes north of it. The boundary, therefore, is annulled by the fact. Two things were contemplated by both parties in that compact — one, that the line should run west from the Lake of the Woods; the other, that it should touch the Mississippi. In attempting now to supply the defect, we ask for the line due west, and the British ask for the shortest line to the Mississippi. Both demands stand upon the same grounds — the intention of both parties at the Peace of 1783. If we grant the British demand, they touch the river and have a clear right to its navigation. If they grant our demand, they do not touch the river; but in conceding the territory they have a fair and substantial motive for reserving the right of navigating the river. I was not aware of any solid answer to this argument.

Dec. 1. — At half-past ten this morning we had our meeting, previous to proceeding to the conference with the British Plenipotentiaries. Mr. Gallatin had prepared a minute of the alterations and amendments which we wish to obtain to the British project, and an article for restoring the British rights to navigate the Mississippi, and our right to the fisheries within the British jurisdiction. This minute and article were to be left with the British Plenipotentiaries. We agreed upon the mode in which we should proceed in the conference, and at twelve o'clock went to their house. As soon as we were seated at the table, Lord Gambier said he was happy that we had now met again; that as we had left to them the option of the place of meeting, they had proposed their own house, supposing it equally agreeable to us. We had really thought it no mark of civility in them to name their own house, nor was it even conformable to our agreement at the commencement of the negotiation, which was, that we should meet alternately at the house of each other. Our last conference had been at their house, and, regularly, this should have been at ours.

Dec. 2. — When we received, last Sunday, the note from the British Plenipotentiaries, with their proposals and alterations of our project, it became probable that we should ultimately sign a treaty of peace. Mr. Russell then proposed that we should henceforth keep the state of the negotiation exclusively to ourselves, and communicate the papers to no person whatsoever, excepting our Secretary, Mr. Hughes. This was agreed to by us all. Nevertheless, Mr. Bentzon went off the next morning for London, and Mr. Howland for Havre. Bentzon called upon me about eight o'clock of the morning of his departure, and was as inquisitive about the state of the negotiation as he could indirectly be. With Mr. Gallatin he was more direct in his enquiries. Bentzon's father-in-law, John Jacob Astor, of New York, had before the war made a settlement at the mouth of Columbia River, on the Pacific Ocean. A British ship-of-war, the *Raccoon,* has, during the war, broken it up. Bentzon stated to Mr. Gallatin that Astor had a ship at Canton, in China; that if peace should be made, the instant it is signed Astor intends to dispatch an order from England, without waiting for the ratification in America, to the ship at Canton to proceed immediately to Columbia River and renew the settlement there before the British will have time to anticipate him. Bentzon supposed that there was a public interest connected with this project, important enough to induce us to communicate to him the state of the negotiation and the prospects of peace. Mr. Gallatin observed to him that he must in that case communicate his proposals in writing, and we would deliberate upon them. Bentzon drew up a paper, and gave it to Mr. Gallatin, with liberty to show it to me, and perhaps to Messrs. Bayard and Clay, but not to Mr. Russell. Of course we could neither deliberate upon it nor give Mr. Bentzon the information he desired.

Dec. 11. — The meeting was in my chamber, and it was near noon before we were all assembled. The questions were resumed. What should be done with the present British proposals, and in what manner; whether by another conference or by a written note? . . .

Mr. Gallatin said it was an extraordinary thing that the question of peace or war now depended solely upon two points, in which the people of the State of Massachusetts alone were interested — Moose Island, and the fisheries within British jurisdiction.

I said that was the very perfidious character of the British propositions. They wished to give us the appearance of having sacrificed the interests of the Eastern section of the Union to those of the Western, to enable the disaffected in Massachusetts to say, the Government of the United States has given up *our* territory and *our* fisheries merely to deprive the British of their right to navigate the Mississippi.

Mr. Russell said it was peculiarly unfortunate that the interests thus contested were those of a disaffected part of the country.

Mr. Clay said that he would do nothing to satisfy disaffection and treason; he would not yield anything for the sake of them.

" But," said I, " you would not give disaffection and treason the right to say to the people that their interests had been sacrificed? "

He said, No. But he was for a war three years longer. He had no doubt but three years more of war would make us a warlike people, and that then we should come out of the war with honor. Whereas at present, even upon the best terms we could possibly obtain, we shall have only a half-formed army, and half retrieve our military reputation. He was for playing *brag* with the British Plenipotentiaries; they had been playing *brag* with us throughout the whole negotiation; he thought it was time for us to begin to play *brag* with them. He asked me if I knew how to play *brag*. I had forgotten how. He said the art of it was to beat your adversary by holding your hand, with a solemn and confident phiz, and outbragging him. He appealed to Mr. Bayard if it was not.

" Ay," said Bayard: " but you may lose the game by bragging until the adversary sees the weakness of your hand."

And Bayard added to me, " Mr. Clay is for bragging a million against a cent."

I said the principle was the great thing which we could not concede; it was directly in the face of our instructions. We could not agree to it, and I was for saying so, positively, at once. Mr. Bayard said that there was *nothing* left in dispute but the principle. I did not think so.

" Mr. Clay," said I, " supposing Moose Island belonged to Kentucky and had been for many years represented as a district in your Legislature, would you give it up as nothing? Mr. Bayard, if it belonged to Delaware, would you? " Bayard laughed, and said Delaware could not afford to give up territory.

Mr. Gallatin said it made no difference to what State it belonged, it was to be defended precisely in the same manner, whether to one or to another.

It was agreed positively to object to the British proposals on both points — the first, as inconsistent with the admitted basis of the status ante bellum; and the second, as unnecessary, contrary to our instructions, and a new demand, since we had been told that they had brought forward *all* their demands.[3]

Dec. 14. — Began upon the journal of the day before yesterday, and wrote until eleven, the hour of our mission meeting, which was again held in my chamber. I had proposed several alterations, chiefly erasures from Mr. Gallatin's new draft of the note to the British Plenipotentiaries. The most important was one in which he expressed our willingness to agree to an article for negotiating hereafter concerning the Mississippi navigation and the American *liberties* in the fisheries, provided our claim to those liberties by our construction of the Treaty of 1783 should be in no wise considered as impaired thereby. Mr. Bayard had proposed an additional amendment, stating that we were forbidden by our instructions to enter upon a discussion respecting the fisheries. I had intended to propose the same amendment, but omitted it merely from an apprehension that it would not be adopted. I supported that proposed by Mr. Bayard, but he himself did not, and it was not admitted.

[3] Moose Island, Maine, having been left to arbitration, is now American territory.

The passage which I wished to be stricken out was also retained, and others inserted, expressly and explicitly with the view ultimately to give up the point if necessary. I contended for Mr. Bayard's amendment, and for erasing the passages which I thought objectionable, as long as argument could have any effect.

Dec. 22. — After returning home, I walked round the Coupure, and, as I was coming back, met in the street Mr. Bayard, who told me that the answer from the British Plenipotentiaries to our last note had been received; that it accepted our proposal to say nothing in the treaty about the fisheries or the navigation of the Mississippi, and, indeed, placed the remaining points of the controversy at our own disposal. As soon as I came into my chamber, Mr. Gallatin brought me the note. It agrees to be silent upon the navigation of the Mississippi and the fisheries, and to strike out the whole of the eighth article, marking the boundary from the Lake of the Woods westward. They also refer again to their declaration of the 8th of August, that Great Britain would not hereafter grant the liberty of fishing, and drying and curing fish, within the exclusive British jurisdiction, without an equivalent. They accepted our proposed paragraph respecting the islands in Passamaquoddy Bay, with the exception of a clause for their restitution if the contested title to them should not be settled within a limited time. Instead of which, they gave a declaration that no unnecessary delay of the settlement should be interposed by Great Britain. . .

Mr. Clay soon after came into my chamber, and, on reading the British note, manifested some chagrin. He still talked of breaking off the negotiation, but he did not exactly disclose the motive of his ill humor, which was, however, easily seen through. He would have much preferred the proposed eighth article, with the proposed British paragraph, formally admitting that the British right to navigate the Mississippi, and the American right to the fisheries within British jurisdiction, were both abrogated by the war.

Dec. 24. — I wrote letters to the Secretary of State and to my mother, to be prepared for Mr. Hughes, and took my last letter to the Secretary of State to Mr. Smith, for a duplicate to be made. Engaged much of the morning in preparing the copies of papers to be transmitted by Mr. Hughes. Mr. Clay

was not ready with his copy of the treaty at three o'clock, and
Mr. Hughes called upon the British Plenipotentiaries to postpone the meeting until four. At that hour we went to their
house, and after settling the protocol of yesterday's conference, Mr. Baker read one of the British copies of the treaty;
Mr. Gallatin and myself had the two other copies before us,
comparing them as he read. Lord Gambier, Mr. Goulburn,
and Dr. Adams had our three copies, comparing them in like
manner. There was a variation between the copies merely
verbal, which arose from the writing at full length, on both
sides, the dates, which in the drafts were in arithmetical figures.
All our copies had the Treaty of Peace of seventeen hundred
and eighty-three. All the British copies had it one thousand seven hundred and eighty-three. There was the same
difference in the date of the signature of this treaty. It was
not thought necessary to alter either of them. A few mistakes
in the copies were rectified, and then the six copies were signed
and sealed by the three British and the five American Plenipotentiaries. Lord Gambier delivered to me the three British
copies, and I delivered to him the three American copies, of the
treaty, which he said he hoped would be permanent; and I told
him I hoped it would be the last treaty of peace between Great
Britain and the United States. We left them at half-past six
o'clock.

Dec. 25. — *Christmas-day.* The day of all others in the
year most congenial to proclaiming peace on earth and good
will to men. We had a meeting of the mission at one o'clock.
My draft of a dispatch to the Secretary of State had passed
through the hands of all my colleagues, and had been altered
and amended by them all. I agreed to all the amendments excepting one by Mr. Clay, which, at the first reading, I had not
perceived.

Dec. 27. — We had a meeting of the mission in my chamber
at one o'clock. . . Mr. Gallatin had made a minute of the
objects still to be determined upon by the mission, and among
them was the disposal of the books, maps, and other effects,
and papers. Mr. Gallatin proposed that the books and other
articles, except the papers, should be packed up and sent to
Mr. Beasley, for the use of the mission to London hereafter.
Mr. Clay thought they ought to be sent by the *Neptune* to the
Department of State. Then came the question about the

papers. Mr. Clay was very earnest to have them with him in the *Neptune,* because he had no copies of them at all, and he thought they ought to be deposited in the Department of State, where he could have access to them hereafter. He said they might hereafter be interesting as historical records, and the Department of State was the proper place for them.

I said that according to the usage in similar cases, and the precedent in the case of the former mission, I considered that the custody of the papers would, at the termination of the mission, devolve upon me, subject to the orders of our Government, and I should take charge of them accordingly.

Mr. Clay immediately kindled into a flame, and said that he should, both physically and morally, revolt at any such pretension, that because I happened accidentally to be in possession of the papers I should assert a right to keep them.

I said it was not because I was in possession of the papers, for I would instantly, or at any other time, put every one of the papers into his possession, if he desired it; but I should still consider myself entitled to the keeping of them. Mr. Gallatin declared himself to be of the same opinion.

Jan. 5, 1815. — On rising this morning, instead of diplomatic papers and letters concerning the loan, of which I have a large file to copy; instead of the arrears with my correspondents, which I have to bring up, and the still more urgent arrears of this journal, which are increasing every day, the fancy struck me of answering the couplets yesterday sung by Mr. Meulemeester's daughter. So farewell for this day all grave and reverend occupation! I could think of nothing but my couplets. The banquet today was at the Hôtel de Ville, and was given by subscription by the principal gentlemen of the city. We sat down to table about five o'clock, in the largest hall of the building, fitted up for the occasion with white cotton hangings. The American and British flags were intertwined together under olive-trees, at the head of the hall. Mr. Goulburn and myself were seated between the Intendant and the Mayor, at the centre of the cross-piece of the table. There were about ninety persons seated at the table. As we went into the hall, " Hail Columbia " was performed by the band of music. It was followed by " God save the King," and these two airs were alternately repeated during the dinner-time, until Mr. Goulburn thought they became tiresome. I was of the same opinion. The Intendant and the Mayor alternately toasted " His Britannic Majesty," and " the United States," " the Allied Powers," and " the Sovereign Prince," " the Negotiators," and " the Peace." I then remarked to Mr. Goulburn that he must give the next toast, which he did. It was, " the Intendant and the Mayor; the City of Ghent, its prosperity; and our gratitude for their hospitality and the many acts of kindness that we had received from them." I gave the next and last toast, which was, " Ghent, the city of peace; may the gates of the temple of Janus, here closed, not be opened again for a century! "

Jan. 6. — We had at length the meeting of the mission, in Mr. Gallatin's chamber, at two o'clock. . . Mr. Clay then asked if I had come to a final determination concerning the papers; that if I had, and determined to keep them, it might be proper to transmit to the Secretary of State a copy of the letter from the three members to me, and of my answer.

I said, Certainly; it had always been my expectation and intention that copies of those letters should be transmitted to the Secretary of State; that I had not come to a final determination concerning the papers. I had wished to state at the meeting of the mission that the time was premature for a final disposal of them; that with a written demand from three members of the mission to have the papers packed up and sent away, I should be reluctant at keeping them; but unless the papers were specified, I knew not which to send away nor which to reserve, and unless the person were named to me, I knew not to whom to deliver them. I knew not where nor how to send them to the *Neptune*. The mission was not terminated. We had just communicated to the British Government that we were empowered to conclude a treaty of commerce. It was probable they would accept the proposal after the ratification of the peace. In that case the effects and papers would be wanted again. I considered myself entitled to the custody of the papers, and if they were to be taken out of my hands, the person must be named to whom I should give them, and must give me a receipt for them.

Mr. Clay said there was the principle and the modus. As to any right of mine to keep the papers, he could not reason about it. He could not think or speak of it with patience. There was nothing in the nature of our Government, nothing in the nature of the mission, that gave any color to it. If it had been asked as a matter of courtesy, he was willing to show all suitable respect to the first-named member of the mission. But a privilege! a prerogative! he could never acknowledge or submit to it; that as to specifying the papers, that could not have been done by him, because they were in my possession; that there was no necessity for naming the person to whom I should deliver them. I might take them on with me to Paris, and give them to any other member of the mission who would return by the *Neptune,* or I might send them by Mr. Smith, who would probably go to the *Neptune* from hence. He was desirous of parting in friendship with everybody; we had here transacted our business together, he hoped to the satisfaction of our country, and he did not wish to go away with any heartburnings between any of us.

All this was said in an acrimonious and menacing tone. I said it was not improbable I should return to the United States in the *Neptune* myself. I had brought a list of all the books and other effects, except the papers, which was on the table. I should pack them up, and leave them here, to be sent where and how the mission should direct. The copying-press and the papers I intended to take with me to Paris, and would deliver them ultimately to any person named and authorized to receive them, according as I had offered, by a majority of the mission. The paper I had received was not an act of the majority, it was the act of three members.

"And although," said Mr. Clay, "those three members form a majority."

"Certainly," said I; "an act of the greater number without consulting the other members is not an act of the majority."

Clay now lost all the remnant of his temper, and broke out with, "You *dare* not, you *cannot,* you SHALL not insinuate that there has been a cabal of three members against you; no person shall impute anything of the kind to me with impunity. It is not unexampled that a paper should be drawn up and signed without consulting the whole mission. You gave me to sign, the very day when I took this paper to you, the answer to a letter from the Prussian Minister at the Hague. It was already signed by two members of the mission, and I had never seen it — nay, I did not know there was such a letter to answer. The letter I presented to you was shown to

Mr. Gallatin; he was consulted upon it, and might have signed it if he had pleased. As it was addressed to you, and known to be against your opinion, it was not necessary to consult you."

I replied, "What I *dare* say, I have dared to say in writing. Gentlemen may draw from it what inferences they please; I am not answerable for them. I am perfectly satisfied that your letter and my answer should be transmitted to our Government, and I assure you that if you do not transmit them, I shall."

CHAPTER V
1815–1817

NAPOLEON'S RETURN FROM ELBA — PARIS IN THE HUNDRED DAYS
— SPECIAL MISSION TO ENGLAND — CASTLEREAGH AND THE PRINCE
REGENT — NEWS OF WATERLOO — THE DUKE OF WELLINGTON.

Brussels, January 26, 1815. — I had ordered my horses
at ten o'clock this moring having yet partly to pack my trunks.
Antoine came to my chamber just after I had kindled my fire,
and we were both busied until eleven in finishing the preparations. I had intended to call yesterday upon Mr. Nuytens to
take leave, but had not found a moment for the purpose. . .
At a quarter past eleven o'clock I entered my carriage, and
left the Hôtel des Pays-Bas and the city of Ghent, probably
never to see them again. My residence in the city has been
of seven months and two days, and it has been the most memorable period of my life.

Paris, Feb. 4. — At a quarter-past four in the morning I
took my departure from Gournay-sur-Aronde, and reached
Pont Sainte Mayence, the second stage, just after daylight. On
the starting from this stage, I found a bridge over the river
Oise, which had been blown up last winter, and which they are
now rebuilding. This was the first and only trace of injury to
the country from the late war that I perceived on the road. The
bridge is already sufficiently restored for foot-passengers, but
not for carriages. I crossed it myself, and waited on the south
side of it for my carriage, which went over in a ferry-boat,
about two hundred yards below. I met on the Paris side of
the bridge a miller, who told me that the bridge had been blown
up to stop the Cossacks.

Feb. 7. — At half-past eleven o'clock I called at Mr. Crawford's house, where Mr. Russell, Mr. Clay, Mr. Jackson,
Colonel Milligan, and Mr. Todd soon after assembled, and we
all proceeded together, just at twelve, to the Tuileries. Most
of these gentlemen had already been presented a fortnight

ago, and now went again.   Mr. Bayard did not now attend.
We waited only a few minutes in the introductory hall, where
I found an old acquaintance of mine, the Chevalier Brito,
Chargé d'Affaires from Portugal, whom I had known at the
Hague.   I was introduced to General Waltersdorff, the Danish
Minister, who told me he had been in America, and had known
my father there; and I also was recognized by General Fagel,
whom I had known at Berlin, and who is now the Dutch
Minister here.   I was introduced to Mr. Dargainaratz, the
King's secretary, " à la conduite des Ambassadeurs," and to
Mr. Lalive, "introducteur des Ambassadeurs."   We were
presented first to the King, and then successively to the Duchess
and Duke d'Angoulême, and then to Monsieur, Comte
d'Artois, and lastly to the Duke de Berri.

Feb. 12. — The tendency to dissipation at Paris seems to
be irresistible.   There is a moral incapacity for industry and
application, a " mollesse," against which I am as ill guarded
as I was at the age of twenty.   I received on Friday a letter
from Mr. Smith, requesting me to look out for lodgings for
him, and Mr. Todd promised me yesterday to call upon me this
day at noon and go out with me for the purpose.

Feb. 15. — I had received on Monday a note from General
La Fayette, mentioning that he would come to the city this
day; and remained at home expecting him all the morning, until
Mr. de Tracy informed me that he would be at the dinner at
Madame de Staël's.   On returning to my lodgings, I waited
until half-past five for Mr. Clay, who was to have called to
take me up.   I then took a carriage, and, on arriving at
Madame de Staël's, found Mr. Clay there.   He had called for
me after I had left my lodgings.   General La Fayette, Mr.
Victor de Tracy, and Mr. Le Ray de Chaumont dined there,
with the Duke de Broglie, who is to marry Madame de
Staël's daughter, several other gentlemen, and one lady.   Mr.
Benjamin Constant was of the party.   There were seventeen
persons at the table.   The conversation was not very interesting — some conversation between the lady and Mr. Constant,
who seemed to consider it as a principle to contradict her.
At one time there were symptoms of a conversation arising
upon a subject of political economy, upon which she said,
" J'interdis tout discours sur l'économie politique.   Ah! je
crains l'économie politique — comme le feu."

March 2. — Zerah Colburn came this morning with his father and another man, whose name was not mentioned to me. The boy was born 1st September, 1804, and has, it would seem, a faculty for the composition and decomposition of numbers by inspiration. His father says he discovered it in him in August, 1810, when he was not quite six years old and had never learnt the first rules of arithmetic. Even now he cannot do a common sum in the rule of three, but he can by a mental operation of his own extract the roots of any power or number, and name the factors by which any given number is produced. I asked him what it was that had first turned his attention to the combination of numbers. He said he could not tell.

March 7. — I called to see Mr. Bayard at the Hôtel de l'Empire, and found him very ill, with a severe cough and some fever; his throat is much ulcerated. While I was there, Mr. Clay, Colonel Milligan, and Mr. Speyer came; also Mr. Gallatin and his son, who had just arrived from Geneva. They had stopped at the Hôtel du Nord, but there was no room there to receive them. Mr. Bayard first mentioned to me that Bonaparte was in France. The proclamation of the King, declaring him a a rebel and traitor, is in the *Moniteur* of this morning. In walking the streets afterwards, I found the hawkers had got it, and cried it as the " Ordonnance du Roi, concernant Napoléon Bonaparte." He landed on the first of this month, near Cannes, in the Department of the Var — they say with twelve hundred men and four pieces of cannon. In the evening I went to the opera, where they performed Quinault's *Armide* with the music of Gluck.[1]

March 11. — After dinner, just as I was going out, I met Mr. Erving, who told me he would call another day. He told me the British had been totally defeated before New Orleans, and forced to re-embark, with the loss of their General, Pakenham, and he says the game is up with these people.

March 12. — Evening at the Théâtre Français — *Ariane,* by Thomas Corneille, and Molière's *Georges Dandin.* The house very thin. . . On returning home, I found numerous patrols of soldiers, national guards, and sentinels at the corners of the streets; news placarded upon the pillars, and clusters of

---

[1] Napoleon slipped away from Elba on Feb. 26, 1815; landed in France on March 1; was joined by Marshal Ney on March 14; and on March 19 was in Paris. Adams was in Paris for approximately half of the Hundred Days.

people collecting and attempting to read them by the light of the lamps. I stopped a moment at one of these clusters, when a patrol came up, and the soldier at their head said, in a low voice, " Dispersez-vous, messieurs, dispersez-vous." Another patrol, meeting two soldiers in a red uniform, made them stop, and all cried, " Vive le Roi ! " A hand-bill of news, " très-satisfaisantes," from Monsieur, was circulating, promising the speedy deliverance of Lyons. The agitation in the city has much increased within these two days.

March 14. — Evening at the opera — *Tamerlan* and the ballet of *Télémaque*. The opera is the same fable as Voltaire's *Orphelin de la Chine*. I met the Baron Bielefeld, who concurred in the opinion prevailing, that the Government will be maintained. A strong spirit to support it has, yesterday and this day, appeared. The moment of consternation has passed away, and that of confidence and energy has succeeded. The number of volunteers who have offered themselves at Paris to march against Bonaparte is greater than the Government could accept. A corps of five hundred men has been formed of the students at law, who offered themselves in a body. I sat next to one of them at the opera, and heard him express all his feelings to his next neighbor on the other side. He would have said the same to me, but, as a stranger, I avoid all conversation upon the topics of the times with persons unknown to me. He appeared to be in great anxiety.

March 18. — I . . . called upon Mr. Gallatin, and found General Turreau with him. I did not immediately recognize the General. He offered us his congratulations upon the ratification of the treaty, and also upon the brilliant defence of New Orleans. He told us that he had been utterly ruined since he left America; that about a year ago he had been starved out of Würzburg; that since then he had been reduced to less than one-third of his pay; that he had lost his eldest son; that his second son was now eighteen years old, and had made already two campaigns; that now it had pleased his Majesty to replace him in full activity of service; that he was expecting his orders to march; that he had been to receive them, and was told they would be transmitted to him. Mr. Gallatin said he had heard that is was expected Bonaparte would be last night at Auxerres, and he supposed there would be a battle to-morrow. Turreau smiled, shrugged his shoulders, and said,

" Une bataille — allons donc," sufficiently indicating his opinion that there would be no battle.

March 19. — Beale is in much anxiety from the fear of events here. He says that Marshal Ney, with all his troops, has gone over to Napoleon, who will be here to-morrow, because it is the King of Rome's birthday. I went out half an hour before dinner, and walked round by the Tuileries and the Place du Carrousel, where a great concourse of people was assembled. The King was going out to review the troops, who are to march out to-morrow morning to meet Napoleon. No appearance of anything like defection to the royal cause was discernible, but the countenances of the attendants at the Tuileries marked dejection. Mr. Crawford told me yesterday that a person of our acquaintance assured him that when the officers of the garrison of Paris attempted to prevail upon the troops to cry, " Vive le Roi! " the soldiers would say, "Oh, yes! 'Vive le Roi!'" and laugh. They had not a hope that the soldiers would fight for the King.

March 20. — Mr. Beale came in and told me that the King and royal family were gone. They left the Palace of the Tuileries at one o'clock this morning, and took the road to Beauvais. It was but last Thursday that the King, at the Séance Royale, talked before the two legislative chambers of dying in defence of the country.

Between one and two o'clock I went out, first to Mr. Smith's. Most of the shops in the streets were shut, it being the Monday of Passion-week. There was a great crowd of people upon the Boulevards, but the cries of " Vive l'Empereur! " had already been substituted for those of " Vive le Roi! " I had received a letter from Mr. Beasley, with the account of the arrival in England of the ratification of our Ghent Treaty.

March 21. — About two o'clock I walked out on the Boulevards, and saw some of the troops entering the city. I had found by my newspaper, which was brought me this morning, with the title of *Journal de l'Empire,* that the Emperor had arrived between eight and nine o'clock last evening at the Palace of the Tuileries, at the head of the same troops which had been sent out in the morning to oppose him. I went around by the Place Vendôme, and through the garden of the Tuileries, to the Place du Carrousel, where there were several regiments of cavalry passing successively in review before the Emperor. I mixed with the crowd of people, heard their cries of " Vive l'Empereur ! " and heard their conversations among themselves. The troops were the same garrison of Paris which had been sent out against Napoleon, and who entered the city with him last evening. The front of their helmets and the clasps of their belts were still glowing with the arms of the Bourbons, the three flower de luces. There appeared to be much satisfaction among the soldiers, but among the people I saw scarcely any manifestation of sentiment, excepting in the cries of " Vive l'Empereur ! " in which a very small part of the people present joined their voices.

March 29. — The day was remarkably fine. The trees are putting fully forth their leaves. At noon I went to the Hôtel des Relations Extérieures, and had an interview of half an hour with Mr. de Caulaincourt, Duc de Vicence. . . He said that a revolution had been rendered unavoidable by the misconduct of the Bourbons; that with the exception of a handful of emigrants, who had been twenty years carrying on a war against their country, the dissatisfaction had been universal. If the Emperor had not returned there would have been in less than six months an insurrection of the people, the operation of which would have been dreadful; that by the Emperor's return it had been effected without a drop of blood shed. His government was now established throughout France, more completely and effectually than it was eighteen months ago. He (the Duke) had last evening enquired of Fouché (the new Minister of Police), who received reports from every part of the country. He had assured him that there was not one report made to him from any quarter of any act of violence or resistance. The return to the present order of things accomplished itself everywhere without an effort. It was inconceivable. Nothing like it was to be found in history.

April 9. — I paid visits to Mr. Crawford, Mr. Bayard, and Mr. Erving, but found neither of them at home; then went to the Place du Carrousel, where the Emperor was reviewing troops. It was impossible, from the concourse of people, to approach near enough to the court of the Tuileries to see anything of the review. Afterwards I walked in the garden of the Tuileries, which was throughout crowded with people. Under the Emperor's windows the throng was very great. He came and stood about five minutes at one of the windows, and was hailed with loud and general acclamations of " Vive l'Empereur ! " I had a more distant view of his face than when I had last seen him. On my return home, I purchased in one of the shops at the Palais Royal a volume just published, entitled " One Year of the Life of the Emperor Napoleon," with which I amused myself until dinner-time.

April 21. — Mr. Crawford told us that he heard the Emperor was going this evening to the French Theatre. I went with Mrs. Adams. The Emperor was there, but we could get seats only in a box on the same side of the theatre as he was seated, and we could not see him. The house was so crowded that the musicians of the orchestra were driven from their seats, and the music was heard only from behind the scenes. The airs of " La Victoire," " Veillons au Salut de l'Empire," and " La Marseillaise " were called for, and played repeatedly.

April 23. — We went to the mass at the chapel of the Tuileries. The tickets were marked for half-past ten, but we were obliged to walk in the garden near half an hour before we were admitted, and then waited an hour and a half longer before the Emperor came in. The mass then began, and lasted less than half an hour. The music was excellent. The opera-singers Lays, Nourrit, and Madame Albert assisted in the performance of the service. The lower part of the chapel, where we were, was full of company. The ladies only were seated on benches. I had a full and steady view of the Emperor's countenance.

May 2. — I sent Antoine to the Count de Tracy's to inform him and his family that I was going out to General La Fayette's, and offering to take anything they might have to send. At half-past eight we left the Hôtel du Nord, and came out of the city by the Porte St. Antoine, and through Charenton and Gros-Bois to Brie-Comte Robert, where we dined. We then proceeded through Guignes, Fontenay, and Rozoy to La Grange, the General's seat, where we arrived between six and seven in the evening. The distance from Paris is fourteen leagues, and Brie is the half-way station.

May 3. — A gentleman of the neighborhood, a Mr. de Meun, was here this morning at breakfast. The General took me out to see his flocks of merinos, of which he has a thousand, his cattle, and his horses. The house is an ancient castle, built of granite, has a centre and two wings, with four turrets, pointed in sugar-loaves. He says there is a tradition that it was built in the time of Louis le Gros. It was heretofore surrounded by a moat with a drawbridge, but he has changed the direction of the water into that of a winding canal. His park was laid out by a painter, in the English style, and is beautifully picturesque. He has surrounded the house with trees — poplars, willows, pines, firs, locusts, and the horse-chestnut and oak at further distance. One side of the wall at the front entrance to the house is covered from the ground to the roof with ivy, which he planted by the advice of Mr. Fox, who came to visit him when he was last in France. Mr. George La Fayette and Mr. Pillet went this day together to Paris.

May 4. — There was a continual rain the whole day, which confined us to the house. The General received the newspapers from Paris, and we had a variety of topics for political conversation. General Victor de la Tour Maubourg came on a visit, was here at dinner, and passes the night here.

May 11. — All the morning we were engaged in making preparations for our departure.

London, May 25, 1815. — The face of the country from Dover to London was quite familiar to me. I had travelled the whole way twice, and the greater part of it many times. Although eighteen years have elapsed since I was last in England, its outward appearance remains much the same, and the ride from Dover to London is one of those which present the country in its most favorable light.

We met on the road a regiment of soldiers, marching to Dover, to embark for Flanders; many beggars, and families of apparent paupers, wandering about the country, without shed or shelter. The cities have all the show of prosperity, but with an extraordinary proportion of cards upon the houses, advertising them for sale. We did not stop to dine on the road, but took at Dartford a sandwich and a glass of ale. We stopped at the "Green Man," Blackheath, at the six-mile stone, and found there Mr. Williams, one of Mr. Beasley's clerks with a letter from him, informing me that he had taken lodgings for me at No. 67 Harley Street, Cavendish Square.

May 29. — Lord Castlereagh had appointed eleven o'clock this morning for me to see him at his house in St. James's

Square. After waiting nearly an hour beyond that time for my carriage, I took a hackney coach, and went there. The Duke of Orleans was with him, and I waited about another half hour before he received me. I gave him a copy of my letter of credence to the Prince Regent, upon which he said he would take the orders of his Royal Highness as to the time when he would receive it. There was some general conversation upon the subject of the concerns mutually interesting to the two nations.[2]

June 1. — I dined at Earl Grey's. The invitation was for half-past six o'clock. I went at seven, and found Mr. Clay and Mr. Gallatin just there. We were the first of the company. Lord Rosslyn, Sir James and Lady Mackintosh, Sir John Newport, Mr. Horner, Mr. Kinnaird, and Mr. Clements were of the party. The ladies withdrew after dinner, but the men sat not more than half an hour after they were gone. The conversation was partly about Bonaparte and partly about the business before Parliament. Lord Grey said something to me about America, and strongly expressed his hopes that we should continue on terms of friendship with this country. But with regard to the impressment of seamen, he spoke like other English statesmen. It was between eleven and twelve o'clock when I came home.

June 6. — I received from Messrs. Robinson and Goulburn and Dr. Adams, the Commissioners appointed to negotiate with us for a treaty of commerce, a note requesting me to meet them at the Office for Trade at two o'clock to-morrow, and a note from Mr. Gallatin, asking me to return, with my observations, the sketch of a treaty which he had drawn up and put into my hands. After Mr. Clay and Mr. Gallatin had concluded, in consequence of their interviews with Lord Castlereagh and with Messrs. Robinson and Goulburn and Dr. Adams, that it was expedient for them to enter into a commercial negotiation, Mr. Gallatin made a draft of a treaty in two sets of articles, one relating to objects merely commercial, and the other to the belligerent and neutral collisions, which he gave me some days after my arrival here to examine. I had read them over

---

[2] Adams's business in Great Britain was to negotiate a treaty of commerce; and as the summer progressed he had many interviews with Castlereagh upon the fisheries, impressment, the slaves taken by the British navy, and other subjects. In the end he succeeded in relaxing somewhat the British restrictions upon American trade with the British West Indies.

in a cursory manner, but have not been able to give them the attention which the importance of the subject deserves.

June 8. — It was almost three when the Prince Regent began to give private audiences. The first was to Lord Grenville, who, as Chancellor of the University of Oxford, presented to him a book containing an account of the visit of the allied sovereigns there last summer. The second was to me. Lord Castlereagh, as the Minister of Foreign Affairs, introduced me into the Prince's closet, where he stood alone, and, as I approached him, speaking first, said, " Mr. Adams, I am happy to see you." I said, " Sir, I am directed by the President of the United States to deliver to your Royal Highness this letter, and in presenting it I fulfil the commands of my Government when I express the hope that it will be received as a token of the earnest desire of that Government not only faithfully and punctually to fulfil all its engagements contracted with that of Great Britain, but for the adoption of every other measure that may tend to consolidate the peace and friendship and to promote the harmony between the two nations."

The Prince took the letter, and, without opening it, delivered it immediately to Lord Castlereagh, and said, in answer to me, that the United States might rely, with the fullest assurance, upon his determination to fulfil on the part of Great Britain all the engagements with the United States.

He then asked me if I was related to Mr. Adams who had formerly been the Minister from the United States here. I said I was his son. He enquired whether I had ever been before in England. I had. With a public mission? Once, with a special mission, during the absence of the Minister then accredited here. He said he had known two of the former Ministers of the United States here, who were Mr. Pinckney and Mr. Rufus King — very gentlemanly men.' Mr. King was very much of a gentleman.

June 11. — At seven in the evening I went and took up Mr. Todd at his lodgings, at the Blenheim Hotel, and we went and dined at Lord Castlereagh's. . . Lord Castlereagh treated us with the politest attention. He seated me at his right hand, and Mr. Clay at his left. Lord Westmorland was at my right, Lord Liverpool between Mr. Clay and Mr. Gallatin. The conversation at table was here, as everywhere else, about Napoleon. Lord Castlereagh had a miniature picture of him on a snuff-box, which he said he had bought of Isabey, at Vienna. It was the general opinion of all the noble lords present that Napoleon would shortly take refuge in America; for as to another island of Elba, that was out of the question. That experiment would not be tried a second time.

Lord Castlereagh spoke of him with studious moderation; said he thought his speech to the Legislative Assembly, this day received, was a very good speech; that it noticed in moderate terms the capture of a French frigate in the Mediterranean, but *pretended* that it was hostility in time of peace.

June 22. — Shortly after rising this morning I received a note from Lord Castlereagh's office, announcing the splendid and complete victory of the Duke of Wellington and Marshal Blucher over the French army, commanded by Bonaparte in person, on Sunday last, the 18th. In the course of the day I received from the same office two copies of the *Gazette Extraordinary,* containing the Duke of Wellington's dispatch of the 19th.

June 23. — In the evening we all rode round the streets to see the illuminations for the great victory of the 18th. They were not general, nor very magnificent. The whole range of their variety was, "Wellington and Blucher," "Victory," "G. P. R.," and "G. R." The transparencies were very few, and very bad. We came home about midnight.

June 28. — I went with George to the House of Commons. We were admitted under the gallery. The debate was upon a grant of six thousand pounds sterling annually, in addition to eighteen thousand pounds, the present establishment of the Duke of Cumberland, on the occasion of his marriage with the Princess of Solms. The house was unusually full, and the debate animated, though temperate. The speakers in favor of the grant were Lord Castlereagh, Mr. Vansittart, the Chancellor of the Exchequer, and Mr. Bathurst; those against it were Mr. Keene, Sir M. W. Ridley, Mr. Bennett, Sir C. Burrell, and Mr. Wynne. The characters of both parties to the marriage were treated with very little respect on any side of the House.

July 1. — The draft copy names the British Government and Plenipotentiaries first in the preamble and throughout the treaty. I determined to have our counterpart with the alter-

native, and showed to Mr. Gallatin the passage in the instructions from the Secretary of State to me of 13th of March, on
the subject of the precedence and order of signatures in the
Ghent Treaty. Mr. Gallatin still thinks it a matter of no importance. He showed me his draft of a dispatch to the
Secretary of State, to be sent with the treaty.

July 2. — I postponed the usual writing of my journal to
prepare the draft for our copy of the treaty. The changes
in the order of the parties were, in the preamble, in the first,
second, and fifth articles. I made the draft of them myself,
and gave them to Mr. Grubb to be copied, with the draft received from the British Plenipotentiaries. . .

I then told Mr. Gallatin that I had given the treaty to be
copied, and had taken the alternative throughout the whole
instrument. Upon which he said, in a peremptory and somewhat petulant manner, " Oh, that is entirely wrong; it will
throw the whole business into confusion. Why, you yourself
said yesterday it was not necessary in the body of the treaty."
I said I had observed that *it was not so material* in the body of
the treaty, but if the British Plenipotentiaries gave up the
point in the preamble and ratifying clause, it was impossible
that they should object to the admission of the same principle
in the body of the treaty. I then showed him the copy of
the Treaty of Paris which I have, printed in French, and in
which the King of France is first named in the first article, as
well as in the preamble. He was yet, however, not satisfied, and asked me if I had told Mr. Clay of the directions
I had given for making out our fair copy, and what Mr. Clay
said to it. I told him that I had; that Mr. Clay disapproved
the directions that I had given as he did, and thought the whole
point of no importance.

Mr. Gallatin then said that I must give the transcriber orders
to make out the copy without any alteration in the body of the
treaty; which I peremptorily refused, and added, in a heated
and angry manner, " Mr. Gallatin, you and Mr. Clay may
do as you please, but I will not sign the treaty without the
alternative observed throughout." " Now, don't fly off in this
manner," said Mr. Gallatin. " Indeed, sir," said I, " I will
not sign the treaty in any other form. I am so far from thinking with Mr. Clay that it is of no importance, that I think it by
much the most important thing that we shall obtain by this

treaty. The treaty itself I very much dislike, and it is only out of deference to you and Mr. Clay that I consent to sign it at all. I should infinitely prefer to sign no treaty at all, being perfectly convinced that we obtain nothing by it but what we should obtain by the regulations of this Government without it."

July 3. — While we were waiting for Mr. Goulburn and Dr. Adams, I recollected that I had left home without taking my seal. I immediately went in Mr. Gallatin's carriage, and returned with my seal. I found on my return the British Plenipotentiaries assembled. We began by collating the copies. Mr. Robinson took our copy as made out by my direction. I took and read the British copy. Not a word of objection was made by the British Plenipotentiaries to any of the transpositions in our copy. There were in the British copy several errors. Mr. Ellis, the clerk who had made it out, was called in, and made the corrections as the errors were noticed. Our copy was correct, having been previously collated by Mr. Grubb and me this morning. The two copies were then signed and sealed by the Plenipotentiaries on both sides — the three signatures on each side in succession, and those of the two parties on a line, the American signatures and seals being first in our copy, and the British signatures and seals first in the British copy.

July 10. — Mr. Wilberforce paid me a visit, and expressed to me his high satisfaction at the restoration of peace between our two countries. He spoke about an abusive article in the *Quarterly Review* against America, concerning which he had received from America letters from two gentlemen, one of them enclosing an answer to it, which he had not had time to read. He found the article was ascribed to Mr. Canning, he thought erroneously, and he should write to Canning about it.

Aug. 26. — I paid a visit to General Dumouriez, who is almost my next-door neighbor, and returned to him the letters which were left with me about a fortnight since with several letters from the post-office. The letters had given me some insight into the views and present situation of the man, and I had now a long conversation with him, which gave me more. Dumouriez was at one time an important personage in the world. It is now more than twenty years since he was obliged to fly from the army which he had led to victory, and seek refuge among the enemies whom he had vanquished. He is now seventy-five years of age, burning with ambition to return to France and recommence a career in which, by a confession more true than sincere, in one of the letters, he said he had done nothing but " des brillantes sottises." The ineradicable vices of his character are vanity, levity, and insincerity. They are conspicuous in his writings, and were not less remarkable in his conversation with me. Like all vain people, his greatest delight is to talk of himself. He told me that he had been twelve years in the service of his country. That he had first been sent for to assist in a plan of defence for his country against a French invasion. He had made his bargain with the British Government; they had offered him terms which he had accepted, and he lived upon them comfortably, though not in opulence.

Dec. 18. — In our walk into the City this day I was struck with the gas-lights which are introduced in the streets and most of the shops in the neighborhood of the Mansion House. They are remarkably brilliant, and shed a light almost too dazzling for my eyes. They are also attended with an inconvenience of offensive smell, which I thought perceptible even in the streets, and they are thought to be unhealthy. For lighting streets, however, and open places, it is probable they will supersede the use of oil.

Jan. 12, 1816. — I first went to the counting-house of the brothers Baring & Co., and saw Mr. Alexander Baring. We had some conversation upon general topics. I mentioned the approaching session of Parliament. He said it would pass off in perfect quietness. There was no opposition. The Ministers were firm as *rocks*. I asked him whether something would not be said about the distress of the agricultural interest, of which we occasionally heard; how the revenue would stand, and whether they could give up the property tax. He said, laughing, that the agricultural interest was, to be sure, in a bad state, but the revenue of the year would exceed that of the last. There had been, however, a falling off in the last quarter — not of the excise, but of the customs.

March 13. — We went to the Oratorio, at Drury Lane, and heard *Israel in Egypt*. The principal singers were Braham, Bellamy, Pine, Wulfingh, Mrs. Salmon, Mrs. Dickons, Miss Burrell, and Barnett a boy about twelve years old. Braham, Mrs. Salmon, and Barnett were the best. *Israel in Egypt* was in two parts, to which was added a third part, consisting of several foolish ballads, and a grand battle symphony, composed by Beethoven, to show the triumph of the " Rule Britannia " and " God save the King " over " Malbrook." Bad music, but patriotic. The house was full; the entertainment, like that of all English oratories, dull.

April 15. — Easter Monday. Mrs. Adams came with Mr. and Mrs. King just at six o'clock. I had been doubtful whether to go in full Court dress, or in frock: an accident determined me to go in full dress, which I found was right. We reached the Mansion House at a quarter-past six, but it was too late. Six was the hour appointed, and the company were actually sitting down to table when we arrived. The seats at the Lord Mayor's table were therefore all occupied; and it was with the utmost difficulty that we obtained seats at the side-table, at the head of which sat the Sheriff, Mr. Bell. . .

As we rose from table, Mr. Lyttleton, whom I had seen at St. Petersburg, recognized and spoke to me. Lord Erskine asked me if I had ever seen his speech in the House of Lords upon the Orders in Council. I told him I had seen it only as it had appeared in the newspapers. He said it had been taken in short-hand by his friend Mr. Perry, and published in a pamphlet. He would give me one of them, and would come out and see me at my house. I asked him after his son, who had been Minister in America; he said he resided at Brighton, and his wife had just brought him her eleventh child. He said what a pity and a shame it was that they had refused to ratify his arrangement and recalled him. I said he had been one of the best friends to both countries that had ever been concerned in their affairs, and I was very sure if his bargain had been confirmed, and he not recalled, the war between the two countries would never have taken place.

" Damn them! " said he. " And now that Canning is coming back again — and coming into office again! "

I said he had a little too much wit for a Minister of State.

" Oh," said he, " he is utterly and totally unfit for the office."

May 2. — Marriage of the Princess Charlotte of Wales. The dissipation of yesterday and that of this day disqualified me for any serious occupation, and I could write nothing but an answer to the invitation from the Fishmongers' Company to dine with them at their Hall on the 23d of this month. At three in the afternoon I left home, and walked until the carriage, with Mrs. Adams, overtook me, a mile beyond Acton. Just at eight o'clock we went to Carlton House, which we reached without difficulty, although the streets from Piccadilly, and particularly Pall Mall, were thronged with immense crowds of people. The company to be present at the nuptial ceremony were collecting until about nine o'clock, in an apartment called " the crimson room." There were perhaps two hundred persons present — the Royal family, the Cabinet Ministers, the foreign Ambassadors and Ministers, the household officers and all their ladies, the Archbishops of Canterbury and York, and the Bishops of London and Salisbury. About nine the Queen and Princess came in, followed by the Prince Regent, and soon afterwards by the parties to be married. The service was read remarkably well by the Archbishop of Canterbury, and the responses were very distinctly and audibly made by the Prince and Princess. After the ceremony, they both kneeled to the Prince Regent and to the Queen.

June 2. — I dined with Lord Holland, at Holland House, his country-seat. It is about midway between the Brentford and Acton Roads, and the entrance-gate is at the side of the Kensington Turnpike. A very large brick house, built in the Gothic style, and four or five hundred years old. The library is in a central hall, which extends through the whole breadth of the house, nearly two hundred feet long, not more than thirty wide. The company were Count and Countess Lieven, with whom came a young English lady, Count Beroldingen, the Minister from the King of Wurtemberg, the Earl and the Countess of Jersey, the Earl of March, eldest son of the Duke of Richmond, Lord and Lady Grenville, Sir James Mactintosh, and some other gentlemen. Eighteen sat down to table. The dinner was elegant, the wines choice, the dessert excellent, and might have seemed to me better but that Madame Bourke, an accomplished epicure, had forewarned me that Lord Holland had the best confectioner in London. The tone of society was easy and agreeable. . . I sat between Count Lieven and Sir James Mackintosh at dinner, and had much conversation with the latter. I had much also with Lord Holland after dinner, and was pleased with every part of the conversation except my own. I offended Count and Countess Lieven by bluntly saying that I had never known such a thing as hot weather in Russia. I said two or three silly things to Sir James Mackintosh, and was altogether stiff and dull beyond my usual measure. I asked Sir James if he was engaged upon a history of England. He told me he was, from the revolution of 1688. He asked me if I thought Dr. Franklin had been sincere in the professions which he made here, that he lamented the Revolution which was to separate the colonies from Great Britain; which he said he did the day before he last left London, even to tears.

I told him I did not believe Dr. Franklin wished for the Revolution — nor Washington. He asked me if any the leading men had. I said, perhaps my father, Samuel Adams, and James Otis. He asked me if we had any popular writers in America. I said, none. Any good history of the Revolution? I mentioned Gordon, Ramsay, and Marshall's *Life of Washington*. He said he had met in India several masters of American merchant vessels, particularly from Salem, and found from them that America had two strong characters of English descent — a multitude of newspapers, and stage-coaches. He also told me that he had last year introduced Walter Scott to Mr. Clay, the first of his admirers that he had ever seen from Kentucky. He spoke of Scott's three novels as admirable delineations of Scottish manners, and of characters. The construction of the stories, to which I objected, he said was good for nothing. I thought there was in the last of the three no new picture of manners peculiarly Scottish; that is, nothing which had not already been painted in *Waverley* and *Guy Mannering*. He mentioned the Antiquary himself. I said the character was well drawn, but I did not perceive it to be peculiarly national. He said there was its pedantry, altogether Scotch; he was himself a Scotchman, and he understood that whatever contest there might be about other qualities, the palm of pedantry was universally awarded to his country.

July 3. — After employing the morning upon this journal and part of a letter, which I could not finish, I complied with a petition from my sons. We dined at three o'clock, and immediately afterwards all went to Covent Garden Theatre and saw *The Jealous Wife*.

July 29. — In the evening we went into London and attended Mrs. Wellesley Pole's rout. The Prince Regent was there, but none of the foreign Ministers, and very few persons whom we knew. There was much melancholy music on the harp and piano, and some singing. We were there nearly two hours, during which the Prince sat lolling on a sofa, between two old ladies dressed in black (a Court mourning for the Queen of Portugal), dropping now a word at the right hand, now a word at the left, and unapproachable to all the rest of the company. There was a Lady Caroline Lamb there, a very notorious character, authoress of a scandalous novel lately published, called *Glenarvon*.[3]

July 30. — I received letters from Mr. Grubb, and from Mr. Smith, who scruples to give a passport to William Temple Franklin as a citizen of the United States. His case is a very peculiar one. He was born in London, before the American Revolution. His father, Governor Franklin, was a refugee, and of course never ceased to be a British subject. But he was adopted when a child by his grandfather, Dr. Benjamin Franklin, was educated by him, and resided with him the whole time of his mission in France, from 1777 to 1785. He was the Doctor's secretary, and was also the Secretary to the American Commissioners who negotiated the preliminaries of 1782 and the definitive Treaty of 1783. I consider him, therefore, as having been then constituted a citizen of the United States. In 1785 he accompanied his grandfather to America, resided there five or six years, and the Doctor left him a principal part of his estate. Shortly after the old gentleman's death, Temple came to Europe, and has never since been in America. I wrote to Mr. Smith to give him a passport.

Aug. 8. — Dined at the Mansion House, with the Lord Mayor. It was a dinner to the Duke of Wellington, and for the purpose of presenting to him a resolution of thanks from the Common Council of London, voted shortly after the battle of Waterloo, and upon that occasion. The party was small — a single table of about thirty-six persons. The Duke of Cambridge and Prince Leopold had been invited, but sent excuses. . .

Before dinner, the Lord Mayor introduced me to the Duke of Wellington. I observed that I had already been introduced

[3] Lady Caroline Lamb, who had married Lord Melbourne in 1805, was " notorious " chiefly for her relations with Byron.

to him. " Oh, yes," said he; " at Paris." " No: at the Prince Regent's last levee at Carlton House, by your Grace's brother Mr. Wellesley Pole." " Oh! ay! yes! " said the Duke, who had obviously forgotten me and my introduction. This is one of the many incidents from which I can perceive how very small a space my person, or my station, occupies in the notice of these persons, and at these places. The Lord Mayor intimated to me that I was to take my place at table after Lord Darnley and Lord Erskine, and before Lord Clifton, who, he observed, was not a Peer. But as, in handing the ladies down, I took the Lord Mayor's eldest daughter, Miss Wood, it happened that I found myself at table next above Lord Darnley, with Miss Wood between us. There were no cards, as on former occasions, in the plates. Before we were seated, the Lord Mayor repeatedly told Lord Darnley that he was not high enough; but there was no higher place that he could have taken except mine, and I did not take the hint of offering it to him. We kept our seats, therefore, as we had taken them.

The Lord Mayor and Lady Mayoress sat, as usual, at the head of the table, side by side; the Duke of Kent at the right hand of the Lord Mayor, and the Duke of Wellington at the left hand of the Lady Mayoress. The dinner was of turtle and venison, and otherwise luxurious as usual. At the dessert the loving cups of champagne punch and the basins of rose-water went round. The steward, at the passing of the cups, and at the first toast, " The King," went through the nomenclature of the company, according to custom, naming the American Minister immediately after Lord Erskine. . . Every toast, excepting the first (" The King "), was drunk standing, with what they call three times three — hip! hip! hip! and nine huzzas — for the Lord Mayor observed that it was impossible to do anything in the City without noise. With all this, the dinner was inexpressibly dull. The company was obviously not well assorted. The Duke of Wellington yawned like L'Eveillé in the *Barbier de Seville,* and his aids occasionally laughed in the sardonic manner, as if it was at themselves for being in company with the City. Wellington has no lively flow of conversation, but he bore the daubing of flattery spread over him at every toast with moderate composure. The general aspect of his countenance is grave and stern, but sometimes it opens to a very pleasing smile. The City Resolutions, elegantly written and illuminated upon parchment, were read by a City officer and delivered to him in the drawing-room before dinner.[4]

Aug. 25. — . . . I went into London, and dined at the Marquis d'Osmond's, the French Ambassador. It was St. Louis's day, and a great diplomatic dinner. . . Mr. George Canning came late, after the company had sat down to table. He made acquaintance with me by asking me to help him to a dish that was before me, and to take a glass of wine with him. After dinner, at his request, the Earl of Liverpool formally introduced him to me. This gentleman, whose celebrity is great, and whose talents are perhaps greater than those of any other member of the Cabinet, has been invariably noted for the inveteracy of his bitterness against the United States, and I suppose considers it as a rule of personal courtesy to make up by an excess of civility for the rancor which he has so constantly manifested against us. Mr. Russell more than once mentioned to me that such had been his conduct towards him. He and Lord Liverpool both talked about the great and rapid increase of the population of the United States. They enquired when the next Presidential election would take place, and who would probably be elected. I told them Mr. Monroe. Lord Liverpool said he had heard Mr. Monroe's election might be opposed on account of his being a Virginian. I said that had been made a ground of objection to him, but would not avail.

Aug. 30. — The Duke of Sussex, Lord Erskine, the Lord Mayor, the Chevalier de Freire, Portuguese Minister, Sir Robert Wilson, Doctor Nicholas and his two eldest daughters,

---

[4] Adams's stay in England was being prolonged by the difficulties of negotiation. He saw nearly all the chief political leaders; he attended many dinner parties; and he made a number of friends. One of these was Jeremy Bentham, who was greatly interested in American politics and culture, and who took a number of long London walks with Adams, discussing contemporary affairs and ideas. Another was the tailor-reformer, Francis Place, whose control of the Westminster election struck Adams as remarkable. A third was William Wilberforce, who talked at length with Adams upon the suppression of the slave trade. During part of his stay in England Adams took a house at Ealing, which gave him a refuge from society and " table-cloth oratory." His limited means dictated this step. " One of the strongest reasons for my remaining out of town," he states, " is to escape the frequency of invitations at late hours, which consume so much precious time, and with the perpetually mortifying consciousness of inability to return the civility in the same manner."

dined with us. The Duke was unwell, but in good spirits. . .
Lord Erskine was quite entertaining, and amused the company
with many of his puns. He is much addicted to this practice.
He repeated to us an epigram which he had sent to the *Morn-ing Chronicle,* and which was published in that paper. It was
in four lines, and the idea was, that of all the people slain on
Waterloo's immortal field there was not one who fell half so
flat as Walter Scott. He insists positively that Scott is not
the author of *Waverley, Guy Mannering or the Astrologer,*
and *The Antiquary.* Lord Erskine says the country is ruined;
but as, after opposing the original wars against the French
Revolution for many years, he finished by supporting the wars
against Napoleon, he is a little puzzled and a little over-anxious to maintain his own consistency. He never once at-tended in Parliament the whole of the last session, and it will
probably be wise for him not to attend the next.

Sept. 16. — The newspapers of this morning contain the
official dispatches from Lord Exmouth, announcing the com-plete success of his expedition against Algiers. The attack
was on the 27th of August, and the whole Algerine fleet was
destroyed, with the arsenal, storehouses, and part of the bat-teries on the shore. He gives the loss of the Turks as between
six and seven thousand men. The returns of his own loss, in-cluding that of the Dutch squadron coöperating with him, are
one hundred and forty-one killed, and seven hundred and
forty-two wounded. The next morning the Dey submitted to
all the terms prescribed, delivered up all the Christian slaves
in and near Algiers, repaid all the money which had been paid
for the ransom of the Neapolitans and Sardinians under Lord
Exmouth's former treaties in April, and stipulated the formal
abolition of slavery in Algiers forever. This is a deed of real
glory.

Nov. 8. — The day was fine, and I walked to Ealing, Acton,
Gunnersbury, and Brentford. In the lane from Gunnersbury
down to the Brentford Road I saw a man, decently dressed,
lying stretched upon the ground by the side of the road, his
face downward, and apparently asleep, or dead. There was in
the adjoining field a man trimming the hedge, of whom I en-quired whether he knew anything of this person. He said he
found him lying there, had attempted to raise him up, but
could not get him to speak. I asked him if the man was in

liquor. He did not know. I requested him to come and repeat the attempt to raise him up. I then spoke to him, and he
answered; said he was not in liquor, but had a bad leg; had
walked from near Windsor, going to Lambeth, to try and get
into the hospital, for which he had a certificate from a physician. He had found himself faint, and laid down there. I
asked him if he was in want. He said he had eaten nothing
for two days. By this time two other persons had come up.
I gave him a shilling, and advised him to stop at the public
house at Turnham Green and take some nourishment. The
number of these wretched objects that I meet in my daily walks
is distressing. Many of them beg. They are often insolent,
and sometimes exhibit figures that seem prepared for anything.
It is not a month since a man was found dead, lying in a field
by the side of the road, between Dumouriez's house and Dr.
Goodenough's. Not a day passes but we have beggars come
to the house, each with a different hideous tale of misery. The
extremes of opulence and of want are more remarkable, and
more constantly obvious, in this country than in any other that
I ever saw.

Dec. 23. — By the second post, after twelve at noon, I received a note from Lord Castlereagh, dated on Saturday, and
requesting me to call on him at eleven o'clock this morning. I
immediately went into London, and at three o'clock, when I
reached his house, found him still at home. He told me that,
as he was going out of town for two or three days, he had sent
for me to tell me that he had not forgotten the promise that he
had made me before he went to Ireland; that the subject of my
note of 27th September, proposing the negotiation of a commercial treaty, should be taken up by this Government immediately after his return; that it had been taken up — two Cabinet Councils had already been held upon it; and as it embraced
a variety of important objects, as soon as they could be sufficiently matured for instructions to be given him under which
he could discuss them with me, I should hear from him
again. . .

From this topic he passed immediately to that of the slave-
trade, which he said was now carrying on to a very great extent, and in a shocking manner; that a great number of vessels
for it had been fitted out in our Southern States, and that the
barbarities of the trade were even more atrocious than they

had been before the abolition of it had been attempted. The vessels sailed under the flags of the nations which still allowed the trade, Spain and Portugal; they were very small, and sailed like lightning. One vessel of one hundred and twenty tons, taken by Sir James Yeo, had six hundred slaves on board. She had been out three days, and there were thirty of them already dead. These vessels escape capture by the rapidity of their operations. They have agents on the slave coast, who purchase and collect the slaves together on the shore. The vessels occasionally approach until they see on the shore the flag flying, which is the signal that the agents are ready with the slaves. Then they go and take them on board, and disappear again in the course of a very few hours. If on approaching the land they do not see the flag, they immediately go off again, and remain some time out of sight of land. The slaves, when taken, are carried to Brazil, the coast of South America, and the Havannah.

Dec. 24. — In September, 1815, I received a letter from H. G. Spofford, of the State of New York, dated 8th August, 1815, in which he says he had been the preceding winter at Washington, where the President had told him they were intending to reserve for me the best office in the gift of the administration, as long as possible without injury to the public service. As this referred to a period previous to my appointment for the mission to England, I did not understand what was meant by it, but supposed it was an intention contingent upon my return home immediately after the Peace of Ghent. After this, the first intimation that I had on this subject was from G. Boyd, who, when last here, told me there was a talk about the offices at Washington — that the place of Secretary of State would be offered to me by Mr. Monroe. The next was from Mr. John Winthrop, on the 5th of this month. Since then it has been announced in all the newspapers, as extracted from American newspapers, that it is settled I am to be recalled and to be Secretary of State. Lastly, my mother, in her letter of 26th November last, mentions a message from the President, by the Secretary of the Navy, that if Mr. Adams returned, that the office would be offered to him. Spofford's letter had entirely escaped my recollection until within these few days. I had no expectation, or belief, that the office would be offered to me, until the receipt of my mother's letter, and now I consider it still a matter of great uncertainty. The question whether I ought to accept the place, if it should be offered, is not without difficulties in my mind. A doubt of my competency for it is very sincerely entertained, and ought perhaps to be decisive. At all events, if I could be rationally justified in accepting it, if offered, I perceive no propriety in taking any step whatever to seek it. The person who is to nominate for the office will be Mr. Monroe, and from him I have received no such intimation; nor any from the present President, with an express authority to ask me for an answer.

Jan. 28, 1817. — Mr. Chester's note informed me that the Prince Regent would open the session of Parliament at two o'clock. . . I ordered the carriage at half-past one. . . We . . . moved slowly up Parliament Street, till the Prince passed by us on his return. As we turned round, we saw Viscount Hampden in his robes as a Peer, in his carriage next behind ours, and in like manner belated. The Prince passed us within ten minutes after we returned. A mixture of low but very audible hissing, of faint groaning, and still fainter attempts to raise a shout among the populace, contrasted with the heavy magnificence of the gilded but tasteless and clumsy State coach, the gorgeous splendor of the golden harness, and the sky-blue silk ribbons with which the eight cream-colored royal horses were bedizened. The populace manifested no symptoms of riot, but a troop of horsemen preceded the carriage with drawn swords, pressing back the crowd, preventing their approach to the carriage, and urged by a leader constantly repeating in a tone of extreme earnestness, "Keep them back! keep them back!" There were among the crowd great numbers of very wretched and ill-looking persons. They talked with more or less freedom. We heard one man say, "He is gone into a strong hysteric." Another said, "Throw mud at him." He has been so long accustomed to this sort of treatment from the populace, that he may perhaps have grown callous to it; but I did not envy him his feelings.

Jan. 29. — The humors of the populace yesterday were, it seems, not confined to the hissing, groaning, mocking, and evil speaking which we heard. The Prince Regent's carriage entered St. James's Park at the Horse Guards. He returned to St. James's Palace, and on his way thither, after passing by

Carlton House, the window at the left side was broken by bullets shot from an air-gun, or stones thrown by the rabble. The Duke of Montrose, Master of the Horse, and Lord James Murray, a Lord of the Bedchamber, were in the carriage with the Prince. Lord James Murray was examined before both Houses of Parliament, and declared that he had not the least doubt that the first fractures were made by two bullets shot from above — it might be from a tree — but no report was heard, no bullets found in the carriage, and the opposite window, though up, was not broken, and immediately after, a large stone was thrown, which shattered the glass to pieces.

Feb. 3. — . . . We went to Drury Lane, and saw *Richard the Third,* with the pantomime of *Harlequin Horner,* with a clown issuing from the Christmas pie. Kean performed Richard. The play is not exactly Shakespeare's. Colley Cibber brought it out improved and amended, and John Kemble has improved upon it again. More than half the original tragedy, including many of the finest scenes, is discarded. Two or three scenes from the third part of *Henry the Sixth* are transferred to this play. There are modern additions, not well adapted to Shakspeare's style, and his language itself is often altered, and seldom for the better. As it is, however, it has constantly been from Cibber's time one of the standing favorites of the public on the English stage, and the character of Richard is one of the trying tests of their greatest tragic actors. I never saw it performed but once before, and that was at Boston in 1794. It is by many of Kean's admirers considered as his greatest part; but his performance this night in some degree disappointed me.

April 16. — Soon after rising this morning, I received four letters. One from James Monroe, President of the United States, dated the 6th March last, informing me that he had, with the sanction of the Senate, committed to me the Department of State. He requests me in case of my acceptance of the office to return to the United States with the least possible delay to assume its duties, and mentions that he sends a special messenger with the letter, and copies by various conveyances. That which I received is a quadruplicate, and came by a vessel from Boston to Liverpool.

April 24. — The Duke of Wellington called in person, and

invited me and Mrs. Adams to the wedding at his house this evening. The Duchess afterwards called and left her card. Mrs. Adams also went and left cards for herself and me at the Duke's house. We were obliged to make a short dinner, and left the table at nine o'clock to go to Apsley House, at Hyde Park Corner, which is now the Duke of Wellington's. We were, however, very early. . . The service was read by Dr. Goodall, Provost of Eton School, who had been formerly the Colonel's tutor. The special license from the Archbishop of Canterbury for the marriage was on the table, and described the parties as Felton Bathurst Harvey, a Colonel in the army, and Louisa Caton, of Annapolis, in the province of Baltimore, spinster. I signed my name on the parish Register Book as one of the witnesses.

After the ceremony was over, the bride distributed her favors, roses of silver ribbon, to all the company. Mr. Wellesley Pole invited us all to go to his house. The servants had all white cockades distributed to them, which they put into their hats. We went to Mr. Pole's, and passed another hour there. We came home before supper, and between one and two in the morning.

April 30. — William Temple Franklin is now preparing for publication an octavo edition of Dr. Franklin's correspondence, the quarto edition of the volume published last December being already exhausted.

To get rid of my own reflections, I walked my rounds, and purchased Todd's Milton and other books.

May 6. — I was obliged to leave George Joy at St. Paul's Churchyard, to go and dine with Mr. Jeremy Bentham, in Queen Square Place, Westminster, St. James's Park, at the back of which his house stands; and I walked with him an hour, till dinner-time. The company were, Mr. and Mrs. Koe, who live with him, Mr. George Ensor, a Scotchman, and Mr. William Mill, an Irishman, both authors, and a boy of twelve or thirteen, whom Mr. Bentham is educating. Bentham had engaged to come for me at five o'clock, to my lodgings, which he did. Just before dinner he took me into his library, and there asked me if I would dine with him there and have a tête-à-tête conversation after dinner with him next Sunday, to which I readily agreed.

May 14. — The time appointed for my attendance at Carlton House was half-past two o'clock, at which time I was there. I found there Mr. Chester, the Assistant Master of the Ceremonies, and the Swedish Minister, Baron Rehausen. Half an hour later, Lord Castlereagh came, and we waited then an hour longer before it was announced to us that the Prince Regent was ready. Lord Castlereagh first went in with Baron Rehausen, who took leave upon a permission of absence. He is going to Sweden upon that profession, but does not expect to come back again. While he was with the Prince, Chester remarked, with a smile, that it was a singular kind of life that the Regent led — that we had waited so long because he had not risen when we came, and that he was scarcely ever out of his bed till three in the afternoon. Chester also enquired of me in what manner I should choose to receive the usual present given to foreign Ministers on the termination of their missions, which, he said, was for Ambassadors one thousand pounds, and for Ministers of the second order, five hundred. I told him that by the Constitution of the United States no person in their service was permitted to accept a present from any foreign sovereign. . .

The prohibition of the Constitution of the United States in this case has my hearty approbation, and I wish it may be inflexibly adhered to hereafter. The usage itself, as practised by all European Governments, is, in my judgment, absurd, indelicate, with at least very strong tendencies to corruption. On the part of the United States there is a peculiar reason for prohibiting their servants from taking such gifts, because, as they never make presents to the Ministers of foreign powers who have been accredited to them, there is not even the plea of reciprocity to allege for allowing it. For American Ministers to be receiving gifts from foreign powers whose diplomatic agents in America never receive anything in return, would exhibit them rather as beggars receiving alms from opulent princes, than as the independent representatives of a high-minded and virtuous republic. The governments of Europe are themselves becoming ashamed of this despicable custom. Count Romanzoff, since his resignation as Chancellor of the Russian Empire, has made up a fund from the value of all the presents of this kind that he had ever received, and made an appropriation of the whole, together with an additional sum from his own property, to the public service of the state, in aid of the pensions granted to invalid and wounded soldiers. I have a strong impression that the peculiar propriety of this patriotic sacrifice was suggested to him by the example of the principle established by this regulation in the Constitution of the United States. Lord Castlereagh, in the course of his negotiations at the Vienna Congress, and at Paris, received twenty-four snuff-boxes, each worth one thousand pounds sterling, besides other articles equally costly. . .

Immediately after Rehausen came out from the Prince Regent's cabinet, I went in, accompanied by Lord Castlereagh, and delivered the letter of recall. . . The character of this person is a composition of obtundity and of frivolity. He is a Falstaff without the wit, and a Prince Henry without the compunctions. His only talent is that of mimicry, which he exercises without regard to dignity or decorum, to the fitness of his own character, or to the feelings of others. His supreme delight is to expose persons dependent upon him to ridicule, and to enjoy their mortification. He seemed not to comprehend how it was possible to manage a Government where the members of the executive Government could not sit as members of the Legislature, and he thought the mode of communication between the Legislative and Executive Departments, by the means of committees, was a sucking of brains on both sides, which must encumber all public business and increase all its difficulties. He spoke, however, in perfect good humor, and dismissed me as graciously as he had received me.

May 15. — At nine o'clock this morning I called upon Mr. Jeremy Bentham, and took a walk of three hours with him before breakfast. We walked in a part of the town where I had not before been. We went and viewed the spot where Ranelagh had formerly stood. It was once a place of highly fashionable resort in the summer season, but was gradually deserted, and at last totally broken up.

CHAPTER VI

1817–1820

SECRETARY OF STATE — PRESIDENT JAMES MONROE — DEFENCE OF JACKSON'S ACTS IN FLORIDA — INTRIGUES OF HENRY CLAY AND W. H. CRAWFORD — THE FLORIDA TREATY — THE MISSOURI COMPROMISE.

New York, August 6, 1817. — Immediately after daylight this morning the ship was within three miles of the highlands of Neversink, and the new Sandy Hook light-house in full sight, as well as the two old ones. All the lights were still burning. The morning was fine, and almost all the passengers soon came upon deck. The sun rose clear, and Venus was visible more than a quarter of an hour after she had risen: air and water both at 67. There were a number of vessels in sight, and among the rest a pilot-boat schooner, from which a pilot, named Bird, came on board at six. We had a fair and light breeze, which took us up to the wharf at New York, where we landed at one in the afternoon, immediately from the ship. The approach to New York was slow, and the termination of the voyage as agreeable as could be wished. The sentiment with which, after an absence of eight full eventful years, I touched once more my native land were of a mingled nature: of the deepest gratitude to the Supreme Disposer for all the enjoyments and preservations of that long period, and particularly for the safe and happy close of the voyage just completed, together with an anxious forecast of the cares and perils of the new scene upon which I am about to enter.[1]

Aug. 11. — At four o'clock Mr. Astor and General Morris, Marshal of the district, came from the Committee of Arrangements, and I went with them to the public dinner at Tammany Hall. There were about one hundred persons pres-

[1] Monroe's appointment of Adams to the State Department — "a trust of weight and magnitude which I cannot contemplate without deep concern" — showed how much he was now identified with the Democratic-Republican party.

ent, most of whom were introduced to me — among them Governor De Witt Clinton.

Aug. 14. — Called on Mr. Trumbull, and found him with the frame for his picture of the Declaration of Independence, upon which he is just preparing to begin. He accompanied me, first to the City Hall, where I visited Governor Clinton, and afterwards to the Academy of Arts, the Historical Society, the Cabinet of Natural History, and the Museum.

Aug. 15, IV. — By some negligence of mine, which I should think inexcusable in another, I mistook the hour of the morning, as indicated by my watch, and after rising thus early, instead of rousing the rest of the family and packing up with all possible expedition, I sat down to write at this journal, and continued thus employed till the boys came knocking at the door, and announcing that it was close upon seven o'clock. We then made what dispatch we could, but the clock struck seven before we left Mrs. Bradish's house, and just as we came to Fulton Street, Captain Forman met us, and informed us that the steamboat had been about five minutes gone. For the next opportunity by the steamboat we must have waited until Monday. I therefore went immediately to Crane wharf, and found the packet *Fame,* Captain Gardiner, bound to Newport and Providence, and prepared to sail at five o'clock this afternoon.

Quincy, Aug. 18. — I had engaged the stage to come directly to this place, without going into Boston. We left Walpole at seven o'clock, and, after stopping at Dedham to change horses arrived here between ten and eleven, and had the inexpressible happiness of finding my dear and venerable father and mother in perfect health.

Boston, Aug. 22. — This morning I took a walk with Mr. Foster round the town, and witnessed with delight its great increase and improvements during the eight years of my absence from it. The Central Wharf, New Cornhill, and Common Street are three great masses of buildings erected within that time, and there are so many others of less extent, but contributing equally to the elegance and comfort of the place, that they compose scarcely less than half the town. The only alteration which I perceived with regret was the demolition of Beacon Hill.

Aug. 26. — My father accompanied me at three o'clock to

the Exchange Coffee House, where the public dinner was provided. It was attended by about two hundred persons, the greater part of them my old friends and acquaintance. Mr. William Gray presided: and Governors Brooks and Phillips, Chief-Justice Parker, and Judge Story, Generals Dearborn, father and son, and Humphreys, and Miller, President Kirkland, Dr. Freeman, Captain Hull, and some others, were present as guests.

Washington, Sept. 20. — We departed from the Indian Queen Tavern, Baltimore, at six o'clock this morning in the stage, with three fellow-travellers unknown to us. Breakfasted at McCoy's, formerly Supurrier's, twelve miles from Baltimore, and arrived in Washington City at four in the afternoon. I then went to Mr. Rush's lodgings at O'Neal's Tavern, but he was not there. Mr. Rush had already been to find me. He soon after came, and requested me to go with him to the President's, which I did. The President, James Monroe, returned last Wednesday from a tour of nearly four months to the eastern and western parts of the United States. He is in the President's House, which is so far restored from the effects of the British visit in 1814 that it is now for the first time again habitable.[2] But he is apprehensive of the effects of the fresh painting and plastering, and very desirous of visiting his family at his seat in Virginia. He is therefore going again to leave the city in two or three days, but said his absence would only be for a short time. He told me that Mr. Rush was to be my successor at the Court of Great Britain, and directed me to make out instructions for him. He also entered largely upon the motives of the mission which he had contemplated sending to South America, which has, however, failed for the present, and upon which, he said, he should converse further with me before his departure. After some general conversation upon the state of the public relations with Great Britain, Spain, and France, I left him.

[2] Madison, on returning to the city after the British capture, had used the beautiful Octagon House of Colonel Tayloe. When Monroe's Administration began Congress was still compelled to use the "Brick Capitol," a building of three stories which was erected by private enterprise as a temporary refuge. Many of the executive offices were in 1817 still of the most makeshift sort. A Representative from Massachusetts named Mills wrote of Washington in 1815 that it was "a miserable desert," and that "the first appearance of this seat of the national government has produced in me nothing but absolute loathing and disgust."

Sept. 22. — Mr. Rush called upon me this morning immediately after breakfast, and accompanied me to the office of the Department of State, where the official oath, faithfully to execute the trust committed to me, prescribed by the Act of Congress establishing the Department of Foreign Affairs, and the oath to support the Constitution of the United States, were administered to me by Robert Brent, a justice of the peace for the District of Columbia. . . I received from Mr. Rush and Mr. Brent some information with regard to the transaction of business at the office. Brent says it is much in arrear, but without any accumulation of it since Mr. Rush has been at the head of the Department. The office hours are from nine in the morning to three in the afternoon. Mr. Rush mentioned to me several affairs upon which the President, who has left town this morning for Virginia, desired me to proceed immediately to business.

Oct. 1. — In the evening I began to draw up the instructions for Richard Rush. Reflected upon a general principle for drafting instructions to Ministers going abroad. First idea — reference to the treaties between the two countries: began upon that. To consult Rush himself. Some particulars of instructions should be circular. What are they?

Oct. 3. — I had visits this morning from Mr. Levett Harris, Mr. Nourse, the Registrar of the Treasury, and Mr. Correa de Serra, the Portuguese Minister. Harris had just returned from visits to Mr. Jefferson, Mr. Madison, and President Monroe, and Correa was going to pay them. Correa says he calls them the Presidential Trinity, and that last year he called them the past, the present, and the future.

Oct. 24. — It was past three before I could call at the President's and I was with him upwards of an hour. I asked him at what time it would best suit his convenience that I should call upon him daily. He said he had given a general order to receive me at all times, but in a few days he would fix upon some regular hour to see me, as it would be necessary for him to take some part of the day for exercise.

Oct. 25. — At eleven o'clock I went to the office and immediately afterwards to the President's, where there was a Cabinet meeting. Mr. Crawford, Mr. Rush, and the acting Secretary at War, G. Graham, was there. The President proposed a series of questions, relating chiefly to Spain and the South

American insurgents. They were discussed until half-past three o'clock.

Oct. 30. — The Cabinet meeting at the President's was fixed for twelve o'clock, but it was half-past twelve before I got to the office, and the President sent a message to say he was waiting for me. I attended immediately, and the meeting sat till near four. . . The President said he had offered the office of Secretary of War to Mr. Calhoun, of South Carolina, and was daily expecting his answer. Mr. Crowninshield, the Secretary of the Navy, was on his way to the city, and expected here in a few days, and he (the President) had written this morning to Mr. Wirt, of Richmond, Virginia, offering him the office of Attorney-General: but it was very doubtful whether he would accept it. The President said that he should have been very desirous of having a Western gentleman in the Cabinet, but he could not see his way clear. He had taken great pains to inform himself, but he could not learn that there was any one lawyer in the Western country suitably qualified for the office. He had particularly enquired of Judge Todd, who had assured him there was no such suitably-qualified person. This, he said, was perfectly confidential. Graham said that he had enquired this morning of Mr. Clay, who had told him, also confidentially, the same thing — that there was no lawyer in that country fit for the office of Attorney-General.

Nov. 7. — At the President's I found Mr. Crawford, . . I spoke to the President of the approaching arrival of Mr. Greuhm, the new Prussian Minister Resident and Consul-General, and asked him if he would now fix a time for receiving him, or wait until after his arrival. The President preferred waiting till after his arrival, and said it was his desire to place the foreign Ministers here much upon the same footing as the American Ministers were placed at the European Courts, upon a footing of form and ceremony. They had heretofore visited the Presidents familiarly, and called to take tea at their houses, as among individuals. He thought that improper. The intercourse between the Chief Magistrate and foreign Ministers should be reserved and formal. He had given them notice of this intention soon after he entered upon his office. If they wished to ask for personal audiences, he would always grant them and receive them in form.

Nov. 17. — This morning I drafted an answer to Mr. Bagot's letter concerning Stewart and took it to the President's. . . He did not like the draft of a letter to Bagot, and desired me to write another. On my reading Aguirre's letter to me, and his statement of his conversation with Rush in July, the President desired me to send a copy of it immediately to Rush, and ask for a statement of the conversation. I spoke about Ebeling's library, and what I had done to purchase it, with a view to give Congress the option of having it for their library. He said that all books on the geography of America became obsolete in ten years, and that one hundred and fifty volumes would comprise everything worth having concerning America.

Nov. 21. — On calling at the President's this morning with the draft that I had made of an answer to Mr. Correa, according to his directions yesterday, I found it did not exactly suit his ideas and I was obliged to make an alteration of the draft. The President went again into the subject of the intercourse between him and the foreign Ministers, which he wishes to restore to the state in which it was under the administrations of President Washington and my father, and which has been departed from in those of Mr. Jefferson and Mr. Madison. But in this retrograde movement he is anxious to avoid everything that may run counter to the popular feeling, and everything that may displease the foreign Ministers themselves. The case of Mr. Correa is peculiarly embarrassing, because his intimacy with Mr. Jefferson and Mr. Madison was great, and had existed before his appointment as Portuguese Minister.

Dec. 6. — I called next at Mr. Nourse, the Registrar's, office, and conversed with him on the affairs of the Indians. Thence I went to the President's. Mr. Calhoun was there, and the President introduced him to me. Mr. Crawford came in. There was conversation upon various subjects. Mr. Clay had already mounted his South American great horse. Mr. Robertson, of Louisiana, follows him, "non passibus aequis." Clay's project is that in which John Randolph failed, to control or overthrow the Executive by swaying the House of Representatives. He intends to bring forward his motion to acknowledge the Government of Buenos Ayres, and perhaps Chili, and Mr. Crawford came with proposals from him to the Executive, professing a wish to harmonize with the Executive as to the manner of bringing it forward. Mr. Calhoun pronounced himself most decisively against the measure: I had done the same before, and the President now, after some little hesitation, did the same. I have no time to give the details.

Dec. 24. — The President gave me for perusal a statement from the Department of War of a question between that Department and General Andrew Jackson — a letter from the President to Jackson of 5th October, and Jackson's answer of the 22d. The Department issued an order to a subordinate engineer officer, within Jackson's division, directly to the officer, and not through Jackson as the Commander-in-Chief in the district. Jackson afterwards issued a general order throughout his district forbidding his officers to obey any order from the Department of War not sent through him. The President's is very kind and conciliatory, but urges Jackson that he was wrong. The answer is moderate in language, and acknowledges the conciliatory character of the President's letter, but adheres to the principle of Jackson's order, and proposes a compromise of withdrawing his order on condition that the order from the Department of War which occasioned his should be withdrawn first. . .

I dined with my wife at Mr. Crawford's. Mr. Gaillard, Mr. and Mrs. Clay, Mr. and Mrs. Calhoun, Mr. Macon, Mr. Troup, Mr. Roberts, and a Miss Vail were the company. Clay came out with great violence against the course pursued by the Executive upon South American affairs, and especially in relation to Amelia Island. Clay is as rancorously benevolent as John Randolph. He has taken his stand of opposition from the first day of the session, and his object is evidently to make grounds for it. There has been a strong expectation that he would hold this course, and he has not held the public or the Government in suspense concerning his intentions.

Jan. 6, 1818. — Attended at eleven o'clock the Cabinet meeting at the President's concerning Amelia Island. . . Mr. Crawford, Crowninshield, and Wirt are with the President, for withdrawing the troops. Calhoun and I are for keeping possession of the island, subject to negotiation for it with Spain. If I understand the characters of my colleagues, Crawford's point d'honneur is to differ from me, and to find no weight in any reason assigned by me. Wirt and Crowninshield will always be of the President's opinion. Calhoun thinks for himself, independently of all the rest, with sound judgment, quick discrimination, and keen observation. He supports his opinions, too, with powerful eloquence.

Jan. 9. — This question was again discussed with great earnestness till past four o'clock. Calhoun urged retaining it, with great force and effect. I repeated the arguments of the former day, and added new ones, as they occurred to me now.

The President, without giving up his opinion, was very apparently affected by the conflict of sentiment among his advisers. Crawford was staggered, and maintained his ground more feebly than the former day. Crowninshield candidly told me that the argument was decidedly with us, but that he thought the best policy would be to give the island up. Mr. Wirt, who came in very late, and heard little of the debate, was still of the President's opinion, and if he changes will, I believe, change with him. We parted, leaving the question yet undetermined and the President not a little embarrassed.

These Cabinet councils open upon me a new scene and new views of the political world. Here is a play of passions, opinions, and characters different in many respects from those in which I have been accustomed heretofore to move. There is slowness, want of decision, and a spirit of procrastination in the President, which perhaps arises more from his situation than his personal character.

Jan. 12. — At the President's I found Mr. Desha, member of Congress from Kentucky. Mr. Calhoun and Mr. West were also there. Mr. Calhoun soon went away, and Mr. Crowninshield came in. The message concerning Amelia Island was still under consideration, and the President had modified it to the purpose of retaining the possession of it for the present. It appeared from some remarks of the President's that Crawford had been there and agreed to this modification. Mr. Crowninshield was also satisfied with the change, and Mr. Wirt had some scruples, which were, however, soon removed.

Jan. 22. — My wife received this morning notes from Mrs. Monroe, requesting she would call upon her this day at one or two o'clock, and she went. It was to inform her that the ladies had taken offence at her not paying them the first visit. All ladies arriving here as strangers, it seems, expect to be visited by the wives of the heads of Departments, and even by the President's wife. Mrs. Madison subjected herself to this torture, which she felt very severely, but from which, having begun the practice, she never found an opportunity of receding. Mrs. Monroe neither pays nor returns any visits. My wife returns all visits, but adopts the principle of not visiting first any stranger who arrives, and this is what the ladies have taken in dudgeon. My wife informed Mrs. Monroe that she should adhere to her principle, but not any question of etiquette, as she did not exact of any lady that she should visit her.[3]

Feb. 13. — Mr. Bassett came as Chairman of a Committee of the House of Representatives on the Beaumarchais claim to examine papers. He said it had been reported at the Capitol that I had refused to see him, and sent him word that I was engaged: but he had contradicted the report. It shows that I have watchful enemies at the Capitol.

Feb. 27. — Morning visit at my house from Mr. Onis, the Spanish Minister. He came to ask for an answer to his late note concerning Don Diego Murphy, who, while acting as Spanish Vice-Consul at New Orleans, was assaulted and beaten by a Frenchman, whom the District Attorney here refuses to prosecute. Onis complained, also, that his own house had been of late repeatedly insulted — windows broken, lamps before the house broken, and one night a dead fowl tied to the bell-rope at his door. This, he said, was a gross insult to his sovereign and the Spanish monarchy, importing that they were of no more consequence than a dead old hen. But if Spain was weak, it was ungenerous to insult her weakness, which was owing to the unparalleled efforts she had made for the deliverance of all Europe from tyranny. I told him I hoped it was nothing more than the tricks of some mischievous boys. He

---

[3] The Adamses gave weekly parties on Tuesday evenings; and a good many Washingtonians stood in awe of Mr. and Mrs. Adams because of their long acquaintance with European society. This feeling may have heightened the sensitiveness revealed by this paragraph. Representative E. H. Mills wrote that Mrs. Adams was "on the whole, a very pleasant and agreeable woman; but the Secretary had no talent to entertain a mixed company, either by conversation or manners."

said he had long been willing to think so, but was now convinced they were deliberate outrages of the South Americans now here.

March 12. — I called upon Mr. Calhoun, the Secretary of War. He thinks the vote upon the South American independence question in the House of Representatives will be very strong in support of the course pursued by the Administration. I am not quite so confident.

March 17. — Found Mr. Crawford at the President's with Mr. Hay and Mr. J. J. Monroe. The President has a fever, and is confined to his chamber. We were again requested to postpone seeing him upon business till to-morrow.

March 18. — Lee came to give me a hint on a very ridiculous affair, but which shows how I am situated. My office of Secretary of State makes it the interest of all the partisans of the candidates for the next Presidency (to say no more) to decry me as much as possible in the public opinion. The most conspicuous of these candidates are Crawford, the Secretary of the Treasury, Clay, the Speaker of the House of Representatives, and De Witt Clinton, Governor of New York. Clay expected himself to have been Secretary of State, and he and all his creatures were disappointed by my appointment. He is therefore coming out as the head of a new opposition in Congress to Mr. Monroe's administration, and he makes no scruples of giving the tone to all his party in running me down. On the publication of the concluding part of my late letter to Onis, he went about the House of Representatives showing and sneering at a passage where it is said that the United States, after waiting thirteen years for Justice from Spain, could, without much effort, wait somewhat longer. . .

Of Crawford's rivalry I have yet had no other evidence than what has seemed to me a sort of effort to differ from me in opinions concerning the important measures to be pursued by the Administration, and a disposition to impress upon my mind every particular of Clay's operations against me.

When Everett was here, he asked me if it would not be advisable to expose Clay's conduct and motives in the newspapers, to which I answered very explicitly in the negative. He also asked me if I was determined to do nothing with a view to promote my future election to the Presidency as the successor of Mr. Monroe. I told him I should do absolutely nothing. He said that as others would not be so scrupulous, I should not stand upon equal footing with them. I told him that was not my fault — my business was to serve the public to the best of my abilities in the station assigned to me, and not to intrigue for further advancement. I never, by the most distant hint to any one, expressed a wish for any public office, and I should not now begin to ask for that which of all others ought to be most freely and spontaneously bestowed.

March 28. — At the President's this morning I had the voluminous dispatches from G. W. Erving, at Madrid, and from Worthington and Halsey, at Buenos Ayres, to read. But the President, though convalescent, is yet so weak that he declined hearing them wholly read, and asked me to state the substance of them to him. When I told him that Worthington, one of the informal agents sent to South America to collect information, had been concluding a treaty there, he said, with quick and irritated tone, " Dismiss him instantly. Recall him! Dismiss him! Now, to think what recommendations that man had! Dismiss him at once, and send him the notice of his dismission by every possible channel. Send it to Halsey, though Halsey himself is recalled. However, the Commissioners when they arrived there will have set all right."

But the subject which seems to absorb all the faculties of his mind is the violent systematic opposition that Clay is raising against his Administration. Clay appears to have made up his account to succeed Monroe in the Presidency, and supported his election in the expectation of being appointed Secretary of State.[4] In this he was disappointed, and though offered the War Department, declining accepting it, and from that moment formed the project of rising upon the ruin of the Administration. He therefore took opposition ground upon all the cardinal points of policy taken by the President, but most especially upon the constitutional question concerning internal improvement, and upon South American affairs.

April 4. — At the President's. . . The President spoke of his desire to appoint some person from the Western Country

---

[4] A series of precedents made the Secretary of State at this time the heir-apparent to the Presidency. Clay had hoped, as Adams says, for this post; he still hoped to succeed Monroe. So did William H. Crawford, who had come very near receiving the nomination in 1816, and who hoped his Secretaryship of the Treasury would prove a stepping-stone to a higher honor. So, a little later, did John C. Calhoun. The two former of these leaders at once, and Calhoun later, exhibited a lively political jealousy of Adams.

to one of the highest offices of the Government. He had informed Mr. Clay of his intention to appoint me Secretary of State, and had offered him the War Department, which he declined. He had also consulted him as to his disposition, whether he would accept the mission to England, which he had also repelled, observing that he was satisfied with the situation which he held, and could render more service to the public than in the other situations offered him. The War Department had then been offered to Governor Shelby, of Kentucky, at the urgent recommendation of Colonel R. M. Johnson, who had expressed the opinion he would accept it, but he declined on account of his age, his habits, and a determination that he had taken not to engage again in the public service. . .

We went and dined at Mr. Middleton's, at Georgetown. Mr. and Miss Crowninshield, Judge Johnson, of Louisiana, Mr. and Mrs. G. W. Campbell, General Dickerson, and General and Mrs. Ringgold were there. The weather having been foul, the roads were bad. Our carriage in coming for us in the evening was overset, the harness broken, and the boy Philip took a sprain in the side, so that we were obliged to take him home in the carriage. We got home with difficulty, being twice on the point of oversetting, and at the Treasury Office corner we were both obliged to get out of the carriage in the mud. I called out the guard of the Treasury Office and borrowed a lantern, with which we came home. We immediately sent for the surgeon nearest at hand, who came and bled Philip. It was a mercy that we all got home with whole bones.

April 8.— At the President's. He spoke to me again of the projected missions to Constantinople and to Russia. . . He said also, that when in Virginia last autumn, he had enquired of Mr. Jefferson how it would suit to appoint General Jackson to the Russian mission. His answer was, " Why, good God! he would breed you a quarrel before he had been there a month! " I told the President that as the other persons whom he had consulted personally knew all the characters much better than I did, I should press no further the objection to Mr. Campbell. The President said that there was another dificulty in the way of appointing Jackson. He was second in command, and such a distinction conferred upon him might seem an undue preference shown him over his superior officer, Brown.

April 10. — At the President's this morning I met Mr. Crawford and Mr. Wirt. There was some conversation upon the claim of Mr. Silsbee and others for the Algerine money. Crawford was for huffing the demand, and refusing to be teased about it. Crawford would not act so in his own Department: but such are the mazes of the human heart. This is not the first time I have seen the drift of Crawford's advice. While he is assiduously making friends to himself, he has no objection to my making as many enemies to myself as circumstances will admit.

April 28. — Mr. Wirt appears to think more about his salary, or what he called bread and meat for his children, than of any other subject. There was a bill before Congress at the close of the late session for increasing the salaries of all the heads of Departments. It passed through both Houses, but fell through by a disagreement between them upon the details. Mr. Wirt wrote some time since to the President, urging him to recommend to Congress an increase of salary for the Attorney-General, and a clerk to be allowed him, and an office, and various other comforts and conveniences. The President asked Mr. Crawford and me whether we thought he ought to make a recommendation by special message for this increase of salary, which he said must of course include all the heads of Departments. We both agreed that he ought not: that any measure of Congress for that purpose should be spontaneous on the part of Congress. Wirt, however, is much dissatisfied, and gave some hints of resigning. He has a large family, and cannot hold the office of Attorney-General without a sacrifice of private practice for which the salary cannot compensate. I think he will not hold the place long, and, although he has opinions and prejudices not very appropriate to an Attorney-General of the United States, the President would not easily fill his place. He has two faults which may have an influence in the affairs of this nation — an excessive leaning to State supremacy, and to popular humors.

May. 4. — The President sent me word this morning that he had returned from his short tour to Virginia. When I called at his house, I found there Mr. Calhoun and Mr. Crowninshield: Mr. Crawford came in shortly afterwards. The dispatches from General Jackson were just received, containing the account of his progress in the war against the

Seminole Indians, and his having taken the Spanish fort of St. Mark's, in Florida, where they had taken refuge. They hung some of the Indian prisoners, as it appears, without due regard to humanity. A Scotchman by the name of Arbuthnot was found among them, and Jackson appears half inclined to take his life. Crawford some time ago proposed to send Jackson an order to give no quarter to any white man found with the Indians. I objected to it then, and this day avowed that I was not prepared for such a mode of warfare.

May 21. — Prepared a dispatch for Jonathan Russell, Minister at Stockholm. . . On reading my draft to the President, he wished it to be made more explicitly in letting Mr. Russell know that his mission must terminate in the course of the present year, and that he must not expect at present any further employment by the Executive in Europe. And in doing this he wished me to express to him the satisfaction of the President with his conduct while he has been in the public service in Europe.

I suggested to the President that Mr. Russell was a man who would consider that such a conclusion should not flow from such premises: that he had a high opinion of his own merits and services, and was by no means disposed to quit his hold upon diplomatic employment: that, in short, he would not easily get rid of him.

He said, in a quick and sharp tone, that he could assure me he should very easily get rid of him.

I observed that Mr. Russell had <u>very</u> explicitly told me that he considered himself entitled to a better mission than that of Sweden.

" Entitled ! " said the President. " No man in this country is entitled to any appointment from the Executive."

May 24. — Forbes came in from Baltimore with the news that the houses of Smith and Buchanan, Hollins and McBlair, Didier and D'Arcy, four Williamses, and many others, this day failed. Smith and Buchanan have been for many years the greatest commercial house in Baltimore: the others have all been in immense business, but bank speculation is what has broken them down. They will undoubtedly drown numberless others with them. In truth, the commercial, manufacturing, and agricultural interests of the country are in a very distressed situation, and their prospects are still worse. The revenue, and even the tranquillity of the Union, will be most seriously affected by it, and, as always happens, the disorder of things will produce discord of opinions and bitterness of political opposition. The greatest danger is of the application of remedies worse than the disease — paper money and prohibitions. The political empirics are already as busy as spiders in weaving their tangles for Congress and the national Executive.

June 9. — We spent the evening at the French Minister Hyde de Neuville's, a small musical party. Mr. Bagot spoke to me of certain publications in the newspapers, mentioning the execution by sentences of court-martial, under the orders of General Jackson, of two Englishmen, named Arbuthnot and Ambrister, taken with the Seminole Indians in this war. These publications say that the evidence against them proved the greatest perfidy on the part of the British Government. Mr. Bagot was very much hurt by this charge of perfidy, for which he said there was not the slightest foundation.

June 18. — The President spoke of the taking of Pensacola by General Jackson, contrary to his orders, and, as it is now reported, by storm. This, and other events in this Indian war, makes many difficulties for the Administration.

June 26. — At the President's. He had concluded to go from the city this evening to his farm, in Loudoun County, Virginia, thirty-three miles distant from hence: and, though the moment is very critical, and a storm is rapidly thickening, he has not read many papers that I left with him, and he puts off everything for a future time.

July 10. — Had an interview at the office with Hyde de Neuville, the French Minister — all upon our affairs with Spain. He says that Spain will cede the Floridas to the United States, and let the lands go for the indemnities due to our citizens, and he urged that we should take the Sabine for the western boundary, which I told him was impossible. He urged this subject very strenuously for more than an hour. As to Onis's note of invective against General Jackson, which I told him as a good friend to Onis he should advise him to take back, he said I need not answer it for a month or two, perhaps not at all, if in the meantime we could come to an arrangement of the other differences.

July 15. — Attended the Cabinet meeting at the President's, from noon till five o'clock. The subject of deliberation was General Jackson's late transactions in Florida, particularly the taking of Pensacola.[5] The President and all the members of the Cabinet, except myself, are of opinion that Jackson acted not only without, but against, his instructions: that he has committed war upon Spain, which cannot be justified, and in which, if not disavowed by the Administration, they will be abandoned by the country. My opinion is that there was no real, though an apparent, violation of his instructions: that his proceedings were justified by the necessity of the case, and by the misconduct of the Spanish commanding officers in Florida. The question is embarrassing and complicated, not only as involving that of an actual war with Spain, but that of the Executive power to authorize hostilities without a declaration of war by Congress. There is no doubt that defensive acts of hostility may be authorized by the Executive; but Jackson was authorized to cross the Spanish line in pursuit of the Indian enemy. . .

Calhoun, the Secretary at War, generally of sound, judicious, and comprehensive mind, seems in this case to be personally offended with the idea that Jackson has set at nought the instructions of the Department. The President supposes there might be cases which would have justified Jackson's measures, but that he has not made out his case.

July 16. — Second cabinet meeting at the President's, and the question of the course to be pursued with relation to General Jackson's proceedings in Florida recurred. As the opinion is unanimously against Jackson excepting mine, my range of argument now is only upon the degree to which his acts are to be disavowed. It was urged that the public dissatisfaction at the taking of Pensacola is so great that the Administration must immediately and publicly disclaim having given any au-

[5] Adams's chief initial troubles as Secretary of State lay in handling the relations of the United States and Spain. The South American colonies of Spain were waging a struggle for independence, which threatened constantly to involve the United States. Adams labored at all times for a policy of reserve and caution, which Monroe approved; but Henry Clay in Congress demanded recognition of the new Latin-American republics. The boundaries of Louisiana were still hazy, and negotiation with Spain was required to define them. In Florida the Spanish title to territory was unquestionable; but Andrew Jackson's Indian campaigns led him directly into this territory, where he seized upon the Spanish town of Pensacola. Adams was prepared to defend Jackson's action, but it wounded the Spanish pride deeply, and caused great resentment.

thority for it, and publish all the instructions given to him to throw the blame entirely upon him.

July 17. — Cabinet meeting at the President's — the discussion continued upon the answer to be given to Onis, and the restoration of Florida to Spain. The weakness and palsy of my right hand make it impossible for me to report this discussion, in which I continue to oppose the unanimous opinions of the President, the Secretary of the Treasury Crawford, the Secretary of War Calhoun, and the Attorney-General Wirt. I have thought that the whole conduct of General Jackson was justifiable under his orders, although he certainly had none to take any Spanish fort. My principle is that everything he did was defensive; that as such it was neither war against Spain nor violation of the Constitution.

July 21. — A Cabinet meeting, at which the second draft of my letter to Mr. Onis was read and finally fixed. Mr. Wirt read what he called a second edition of his article for the *National Intelligencer*. I strenuously re-urged my objections, especially to a paragraph declaring that the President thought he had no constitutional power to have authorized General Jackson to take Pensacola. . . I finally gave up the debate, acquiescing in the determination which had been taken. The Administration were placed in a dilemma from which it is impossible for them to escape censure by some, and factious crimination by many. If they avow and approve Jackson's conduct, they incur the double responsibility of having commenced a war against Spain, and of warring in violation of the Constitution without the authority of Congress. If they disavow him, they must give offence to all his friends, encounter the shock of his popularity, and have the appearance of truckling to Spain. For all this I should be prepared. But the mischief of this determination lies deeper: 1. It is weakness, and confession of weakness. 2. The disclaimer of power in the Executive is of dangerous example and of evil consequences. 3. There is injustice to the officer in disavowing him, when in principle he is strictly justifiable. . .

Calhoun says he has heard that the court-martial at first acquitted the two Englishmen, but that Jackson sent the case back to them. He says, also, that last winter there was a company formed in Tennessee, who sent Jackson's nephew to Pensacola and purchased Florida lands, and that Jackson him-

self is reported to be interested in the speculation. I hope
not.

July 25. — The President two days ago very abruptly asked
me to see Mr. Bagot and propose through him to the British
Government an immediate coöperation between the United
States and Great Britain to promote the independence of
South America. I asked him what part of South America.
"All South America, and Mexico, and the islands included."
I told him I thought Great Britain was not yet prepared for
such a direct proposition: and, entering into details, I immediately found it was a crude idea, which he immediately abandoned. But I conjectured that either Rodney and Bracken-
ridge, or the Richmond *Enquirer,* had put it into his head.
For the Richmond *Enquirer,* which Clay's *Kentucky Reporter*
calls the President's domestic paper, is, on the contrary, the
paper by which Virginia works upon the President. Its influence is much more upon him than for him, and it is excessively impatient for the acknowledgment of Buenos Ayres.

Aug. 15. — I received a number of packages, and among
the rest James's *Naval and Military History of the Late War
between the United States and Great Britain.* Looking into
these volumes, I became so much engaged with them that
they absorbed all the office hours. They are written with
considerable ability, and with extreme and anxious labor to
exalt the naval and military character of Great Britain by
the events of the late war, and to depress that of the American people.

New York, Sept. 1. — Called about eleven o'clock at Mr.
Trumbull's house, and saw his picture of the Declaration of
Independence which is now nearly finished. I cannot say I
was disappointed in the execution of it, because my expectations were very low: but the picture is immeasurably below the
dignity of the subject. It may be said of Trumbull's talent as
the Spaniards say of heroes who were brave on a certain day:
he has painted good pictures. I think the old small picture far
superior to this large new one. He himself thinks otherwise.
He has some books on the President's table which the Abbé
Correa advised him to letter on the backs, Locke and Sidney.
I told him I thought that was not the place for them. They
were books for the members to read at home, but not to take
with them there. I advised him to letter them simply
"Journals."

Quincy, Sept. 9. — The storm continues night and day; it again prevented me from going to Boston, and again kept me confined to the house. It is but this moment that I have brought up my arrears at the approach of evening; for, having examined George in a passage of Plato's *Crito,* and then referred to the volume of the *Bibliothèque des Philosophes* containing Dacier's translation of it, I was allured by the *Phædo,* which immediately succeeds, and could not lay down the book until I had read it through. This delicious but unseasonable occupation consumed the morning, almost to the hour of dinner. If the study of Plato were my proper business, I should be wasting my time with something else. The reflections that have occurred to me upon this perusal of the *Phædo* might be useful to me hereafter if I had time to commit them to writing. The arguments of Socrates to prove the immortality of the soul are so weak that they hardly deserve the name of arguments. His principle, that all things are generated by their contraries, that heat and cold, greatness and littleness, life and death, produce each other, is an absurdity.

Washington, Oct. 24. — I met Mr. Calhoun, who asked me to enquire of Mr. Bagot whether he had any authority to agree to a temporary line between the British territories and ours to the northwest, and said he was establishing a line of posts in that direction to cover our frontier and prevent the British traders from crossing the line to trade with the Indians within our boundaries. I called afterwards at Calhoun's office, where he showed me upon the map the positions where the new posts are to be established.

Washington, Nov. 2. — The mail brought me too fatal a confirmation of my apprehensions in a letter from my son John, dated at Boston last Wednesday the 28th of October, informing me that between eleven and one o'clock of that day my mother, beloved and lamented more than language can express, yielded up her pure and gentle spirit to its Creator. She was born on the 11th of November, 1744, and had completed within less than a month of her seventy-fourth year. Had she lived to the age of the Patriarchs, every day of her life would have been filled with clouds of goodness and of love. There is not a virtue that can abide in the female heart but it was the ornament of hers. She had been fifty-four years the delight of my father's heart, the sweetener of all his

toils, the comforter of all his sorrows, the sharer and height-
ener of all his joys. It was but the last time when I saw my
father that he told me, with an ejaculation of gratitude to the
Giver of every good and every perfect gift, that in all the
vicissitudes of his fortunes, through all the good report and
evil report of the world, in all his struggles and in all his sorrows, the affectionate participation and cheering encouragement of his wife had been his never-failing support, without
which he was sure he should never have lived through them.
She was the daughter of William Smith, minister at Wey-
mouth, and of Elizabeth Quincy, his wife. Oh, God! may I
die the death of the righteous, and may my last end be like
hers! On receiving this deeply distressing intelligence, I immediately left my office and came home.

Nov. 8. — I began the draft of a dispatch to G. W. Erving,
in which I propose to give a succinct account of the late Seminole War from its origin, and to trace the connections between
Arbuthnot, Woodbine, Nicholls, and McGregor with that
war, in such a manner as completely to justify the measures of
this Government relating to it, and as far as possible the proceedings of General Jackson. The task is of the highest order: may I not be found inferior to it!

Nov. 19. — Major William Jackson, of Philadelphia,
called upon me: he is here as agent for the surviving officers of
the Revolutionary War who are applying to Congress for further remuneration for their services. He left with me a copy
of his memorial to Congress, and of a pamphlet that he has
lately printed on the subject. He says the President has
promised all his support to the memorial, and requested, if it
should be in my power, to give any assistance to it, which I
assured him I would. As he was the Secretary of the Convention of 1787, which formed the Constitution of the United
States, I asked him to call again at my office this day, to look
at the journals and papers deposited by President Washington
in the Department of State, 19th March, 1796, and, if he
could, to explain the condition in which they are. He did accordingly call, and looked over the papers, but he had no recollection of them which could remove the difficulties arising from
their disorderly state, nor any papers to supply the deficiency
of the missing papers. He told me that he had taken extensive minutes of the debates in the Convention, but, at the re-

quest of President Washington, had promised they should never be published during his own life, which he supposed had been a loss to him of many thousand dollars. He told me how he had been chosen Secretary to the Convention, for which place W. T. Franklin and Beckley were his competitors, and said that by far the most efficient member of the Convention was Mr. Madison; that Mr. Hamilton took no active part in it and made only one remarkable speech.

Dec. 10. — At the President's. I mentioned to him Mr. Hyde de Neuville's extreme desire to have him and Mrs. Monroe attend his ball next Monday.[6] The President was disposed to gratify him, if there had been an example since the existence of the present Constitution of a President's going to the house of a foreign Minister. He said he would send to ask Major Jackson, who had been President Washington's private Secretary, what his practice had been, and he would consult the gentlemen of the Administration concerning it, for which he appointed a meeting at one o'clock to-morrow. Mr. de Neuville came to the office in high anxiety concerning it, and I appointed to see him to-morrow at three o'clock.

December 11. — At the President's, where I met Mr. Crawford and Mr. Calhoun. The President found, upon enquiry of Jackson, that President Washington never had been at the house of any foreign Minister: nor had any other President. He determined, therefore, not to break through the established usage. Next came the question with regard to Mrs. Monroe, upon which we could have no deliberation, and which was therefore left to her own decision. The President went and consulted her, and she said she did not think it proper for her to go to any place where it was not proper for her husband to go. The President said he should request his daughter, Mrs. Hay, to go.

---

[6] Hyde de Neuville, the French Minister, offered this ball to celebrate the evacuation of French territory by the Allied troops. De Neuville's entertainments were known as the gayest in the little city. Americans marvelled at dinners where he served " turkeys without bones, and puddings in the form of fowls, fresh cod disguised like a salad, and celery like oysters." He gave dances on Saturday evenings, though New Englanders still considered the hours after sunset on Saturday as a holy season. Adams was by no means unaware of the social humors of Washington. He alludes in his Diary to the occasion when he accepted an invitation by the British Minister to the christening of his latest-born child. It was rumored by Adams's enemies that he had acted as proxy to the Prince Regent in the ceremony, and he was hotly denounced as " too damn friendly to England."

Dec. 12. — I called at Peale's and told him I could not sit this day; then called upon Mrs. Hay, with whom was her mother, Mrs. Monroe. Her object was to desire me to inform Mr. Hyde de Neuville that she would, at the request of her father, though she said it was much against her own inclination, go to the ball next Monday; but it was upon conditions: first, that it should leave her position with the ladies of the foreign Ministers precisely where it was: that she would afterwards neither visit them, nor receive visits from them nor accept of any invitation to their parties: second, that no rank or station should be assigned to her at the ball — no pretence of distinguishing her as the President's daughter: that at supper she would find her place somewhere among the Commodores' wives, but must have no particular distinction shown her: third, that Mr. De Neuville might write to his own Government whatever he pleased upon the subject, but that if an account of the ball was to be published in the newspapers here, her name should not be mentioned as having been present.

Dec. 17. — Mr Hopkinson called this morning, and I had a conversation of two hours with him upon the subject of the state of our affairs with Spain, the Seminole War, and General Jackson's proceedings in Florida. With all these concerns, political, personal and electioneering intrigues are intermingling themselves with increasing heat and violence. This Government is indeed assuming daily more and more a character of cabal, and preparation, not for the next Presidential election, but for the one after — that is, working and counterworking, with many of the worst features of elective monarchies. Jackson has made himself a multitude of friends, and still more enemies. The course pursued by the Administration has satisfied neither party, but neither can find much to attack in it.

Dec. 25. — The Seminole War and General Jackson's proceedings in Florida are subjects upon which there is much agitation, misapprehension, and conflict of opinion in the public mind: and in Congress parties are rallying round the questions involved in these transactions, and connecting themselves with the views of individuals upon the Presidency. There is a considerable party disposed to bring forward Jackson as a candidate, and the services of his late campaign would have given them great strength if he had not counteracted his own interest by several of his actions in it. But he wrote an inconsiderate letter to the Governor of Georgia, and by that and other imprudences turned the whole of that State against him. He had all Kentucky against him, upon something of a similar cause, before. He has also turned against him all the Governors of the States and the high sticklers for State rights. All Virginia is against him, for this and other causes.

Dec. 30. — During the cold weather I run almost insensibly into the practice of keeping later evening hours, which is followed, of course, by later rising in the morning. In the evening my room is warm and comfortable for writing; in the cold mornings it takes two or three hours before the fire warms it to a suitable temperature. This month, therefore, I have risen mostly after daylight, and have retired to bed between eleven and twelve. I have likewise been several times in company abroad, which absorbs every time an evening and a part of the next morning. The distribution of the day continues regular, but the month has been far less effective to industrious occupation than the last. My friends earnestly urge me to mingle more in society and to make myself more extensively known. But I am scarcely ever satisfied with myself after going into company, and always have the impression that my time at home is more usefully spent.

> Let not thine eyelids close at parting day
> Till, with thyself communing, thou shalt say,
> What deed of good or evil have I done
> Since the last radiance of the morning sun?
> In strict review the day before thee pass,
> And see thyself in truth's unerring glass.
> If, scorning self-delusion's fraudful ways,
> Her solemn voice reproving Conscience raise,
> With keen contrition, aid Divine implore
> Each error to redeem, and wrong no more.

Washington, Jan. 1, 1819. Friday — Began the year by commencing the draft of a dispatch to Richard Rush, London, and then finished the fifth volume of this diary, and the journal of the year that has just expired, by entering the transactions of yesterday. Went with Mrs. Adams to pay the New Year's visit at the President's. One of our horses was vicious, so that it was with difficulty we got there. The President's house was also more crowded that I ever saw it on a similar occasion.

January 5. — I had conversation with several members of Congress. Some of them gave me notice that a formidable and concerted attack upon my letter to Erving is to be brought forward in the House of Representatives next week. Clay has already commenced his attack upon it in convivial companies out-of-doors. Last winter Clay's principal attack was levelled against the President himself, but, finding that this only injured himself, he has this winter confined his hostilities to me. My letter to Erving has been so well received in Congress and by the public that it has redoubled his rancor against me, and among all the knots of intriguers in Congress, by the partisans of half a dozen candidates for the next Presidency (including General Jackson), there is one common object of decrying me. There is not in either House of Congress an individual member who would open his lips to defend me or move a finger to defeat any combination to injure me.

January 7, 1819. — Attended the Cabinet meeting at the President's. . . In the course of the discussion, Crawford betrayed his inveteracy against General Jackson more than he had ever done before, and even let out, as a justification for the very extraordinary proposal of abandoning Pensacola even if not re-demanded by Spain, that it would show to the world that it had been taken contrary to orders. That Crawford has been all along deeply inveterate against Jackson, as is asserted in a letter from Nashville lately published in the *Aurora,* I have not seen adequate proof. But since the publication of that letter, it is impossible to avoid perceiving that he is so. It happens, unfortunately, that Crawford's interest and stimulus of personal ambition, prematurely roused by his having been started as a candidate for the Presidency against Mr. Monroe at the late election, now pushes him not only to contribute in running down Jackson as a formidable rival, but even to counteract, as much as is in his power, the general success of the Administration, and particularly that of the Department of State.

January 18. — There was a highly panegyrical article upon me in the *National Register* of the day before yesterday, I know not by whom written: and the same day the Librarian of Congress, Watterston, sent me a volume of letters from

Washington, just published by him, in which he has depicted also a character of me among others. The rest had been published in the *National Register* last winter : mine had then been omitted. He now has me at full length, and quite as favorably as I deserve.

January 23. — As I was going to the President's, General Jackson and his suite were going out. The President called him and Colonel Butler back, and introduced them to me. The General arrived this morning from his residence at Nashville, Tennessee, and had already called at my office. Among the rumors which have been circulated by the cabal now intriguing in Congress against Jackson, it has been very industriously whispered that Mr. Jefferson and Mr. Madison had declared themselves in very strong terms against him. I had mentioned this report a few days since to the President, who told me that he was convinced there was no foundation for it. This morning he showed me in confidence a letter he had just received from Mr. Jefferson. It not only expresses full satisfaction with the course pursued by the Administration, but mentions my letters of 12th March last to Onis, and of 28th November to Erving, in terms which it would not become me to repeat. He advises that they, with others of my letters to Onis, should be translated into French and communicated to every Government in Europe, as a thorough vindication of the conduct and policy of this Government.

Jan. 25. — Robertson [7] brought a letter from Mr. John Pope to Mrs. Adams, and had some conversation with me upon the local politics of Kentucky. That State is divided between two parties, with Clay the head of one of them, and Pope of the other. Clay, by the superiority of his talents, by a more artful management of popular feelings, and by the chances of good fortune, notwithstanding the more correct moral character of his antagonist, has acquired a great ascendency over him, and not only keeps him depressed in public estimation, but uses every possible means of the most rancorous and malignant enmity to ruin him. Robertson thought some time since that Clay intended to offer himself at the next election of Governor of the State as a candidate, and it is well understood that his object is to organize and embody a systematic opposition of the whole Western country against the

[7] George Robertson, thrice elected to the House from Kentucky.

present Administration, the operation of which is to take effect at the end of Mr. Monroe's eight years.

February 3. — General Jackson came to my house this morning, and I showed him the boundary line which has been offered to the Spanish Minister, and that which we proposed to offer upon Melish's map. He said there were many individuals who would take exception to our receding so far from the boundary of the Rio del Norte, which we claim, as the Sabine, and the enemies of the Administration would certainly make a handle of it to assail them: but the possession of the Floridas was of so great importance to the southern frontier of the United States, and so essential even to their safety, that the vast majority of the nation would be satisfied with the western boundary as we propose, if we obtain the Floridas. He showed me on the map the operations of the British force during the late war, and remarked that while the mouths of the Florida rivers should be accessible to a foreign naval force there would be no security for the United States.

He also entered into conversation upon the subject of discussion now pending in the House of Representatives on his proceedings in the late Seminole War, upon that which is preparing in the Senate under the auspices of Mr. Forsyth, of Georgia, and upon the general order given by Jackson in 1817, which was considered as setting at defiance the War Department. He imputed the whole to Mr. Crawford's resentments against him on account of his having at the last Presidential election supported Mr. Monroe against him; said there was not a single officer in the army known to have been at that time in favor of Monroe whom Crawford had not since insulted: that Mr. Monroe was of an open, fair, unsuspecting character, amiable in the highest degree, and would not believe human nature capable of the baseness which Crawford, while holding a confidential office under him, was practising against him.

I told Jackson that Mr. Crawford had never in any of the discussions on the Seminole War said a word which led me to suppose he had any hostile feeling against him. He replied that, however that might be, Crawford was now setting the whole delegation of Georgia against him, and by intentional insult and the grossest violation of all military principle had compelled him to issue the order of 1817. Crawford, he said,

was a man restrained by no principle, and capable of any baseness. . . . Crawford was now canvassing for the next Presidential election, and actually wrote a letter to Clay proposing a
coalition with him to overthrow Mr. Monroe's Administration.

That Crawford has written such a letter to Clay as Jackson has informed, is to the last degree improbable. He has
too much discretion to have put himself so much in Clay's
power. But that all his conduct is governed by his views to
the Presidency, as the immediate successor to Mr. Monroe,
and that his hopes depend upon a result unfavorable to the
success, or at least to the popularity of the Administration, is
perfectly clear. The important and critical interests of the
country are those the management of which belongs to the
Department of State. Those incidental to the Treasury are
in a state which would give an able financier an opportunity to
display his talents: but Crawford has no talents as a financier.
He is just, and barely, equal to the current routine of the business of his office. His talent is intrigue. And as it is in the
foreign affairs that the success or failure of the Administration will be most conspicuous, and as their success would promote the reputation and influence, and their failure would lead
to the disgrace, of the Secretary of State, Crawford's personal
views centre in the ill success of the Administration in its foreign relations; and, perhaps unconscious of his own motives,
he will always be impelled to throw obstacles in its way, and to
bring upon the Department of State especially any feeling
of public dissatisfaction that he can.

The only possible chance for a head of Department to attain the Presidency is by ingratiating himself personally with
the members of Congress: and, as many of them have objects
of their own to obtain, the temptation is immense to corrupt
coalitions, and tends to make all the public offices objects of
bargain and sale. That there has been intercourse of this
kind, more or less explicit, between Crawford and Clay, can
scarcely be doubted. But a coalition between them would be
liable to many difficulties. They are both native Virginians.
Clay's ambition has been so pampered by success that he has
evidently formed hopes of coming in as the immediate successor of Mr. Monroe. He refused both the War Department
and the mission to England. Last winter he aimed at the un-

limited control of the House of Representatives, and at the formation of a Western party. His prospect of coalition then was with Governor Clinton, and it was positively, but I think erroneously, said to have been effected. It has this winter much more the appearance of being concluded with Crawford; but the Georgian attack upon Jackson has scarcely any support from the West, though an immense effort has been made to engage Virginia in the cause, and with partial success. Clay's opposition has hitherto been so unsuccessful that he sees, I believe, the necessity of contenting himself with a secondary station under the next Presidency, and this may bring him back to a coalition with Crawford or Clinton, as the chances may arise. His opposition to Jackson now is involuntary, and merely counteractive.

Feb. 6. — A shocking incident occurred this day, which occasioned a general sensation of horror and disgust. Armistead Thomson Mason, late a Senator in Congress from Virginia, son of Stevens Thomson Mason, also formerly a Senator, was this morning, at Bladensburg, shot through the heart, in a duel fought with muskets at six paces' distance by John McCarty, his cousin by blood, and nearly related to him by marriage. The muskets were loaded each with three balls, and McCarty escaped with life only because the balls struck the butt end of his musket, glanced off, and wounded him in the arm.

Feb. 22. — Mr. Onis came at eleven, with Mr. Stoughton, one of the persons attached to his Legation. The two copies of the treaty made out at his house were ready: none of ours were entirely finished. We exchanged the original full powers on both sides, which I believe to be the correct course on the conclusion of treaties, though at Ghent, and on the conclusion of the Convention of 3d July, 1815, the originals were only exhibited and copies exchanged. I had one of the copies of the treaty, and Mr. Onis the other. I read the English side, which he collated, and he the Spanish side, which I collated. We then signed and sealed both copies on both sides — I first on the English and he first on the Spanish side. . .

The acquisition of the Floridas has long been an object of earnest desire to this country. The acknowledgment of a definite line of boundary to the South Sea forms a great epoch in our history. The first proposal of it in this negotiation was my own, and I trust it is now secured beyond the reach of revocation. It was not even among our claims by the Treaty of Independence with Great Britain. It was not among our pretensions under the purchase of Louisiana — for that gave us only the range of the Mississippi and its waters. I first introduced it in the written proposal of 31st October last, after having discussed it verbally both with Onis and De Neuville. It is the only peculiar and appropriate right acquired by this treaty in the event of its ratification.[8]

Feb. 23. — In the Washington *City Gazette* of this day there was an article announcing that the President had yesterday communicated to the Senate a treaty concluded with the Spanish Minister; and then, noticing the western boundary line from the Sabine, says it is thought the Senate will not, without strong opposition, relinquish the territory between the Sabine and the Rio del Norte, and concludes, "We trust the Senate will not agree to it." This paragraph comes, directly or indirectly, from Mr. Clay.

March 12. — I told Senator Ninian Edwards that General Parker had said to me the other evening at Dr. Thornton's that he was afraid General Jackson had gone from this city to Virginia with the determination to challenge J. W. Eppes. I hoped it was not so. He said, No; that he had intended it; that some intimation of this intention had been given to the President, and J. J. Monroe had come with two earnest messages to him to interfere and restrain Jackson from this design. He had called upon him, and met Eaton, of Tennessee, coming from him. Eaton had been endeavoring to appease him, without success. When he (Edwards) went in, he found Jackson exasperated beyond anything that he ever witnessed in man. But Jackson was always willing to listen to the advice of those whom he knew to be his friends, and to give it all due weight. So he sat down with him and argued the case till two or three o'clock in the morning, and then left him per-

---

[8] Adams might well congratulate himself upon this treaty with Spain. It gave the United States the cession of Florida; we agreed in return to pay Spanish claims not exceeding five million dollars; and the boundaries of the Louisiana Purchase were defined in an exceedingly satisfactory manner. The United States did nothing more for its part than to concede the Sabine instead of the Rio Grande as the southwestern boundary; a concession which Henry Clay at once prepared to attack. The treaty also met heavy obstacles in Madrid.

fectly calm and good-humored, and rescued from his project of fighting Eppes.

March 13. — The President has determined to set out the last week of this month upon a tour of three or four months to the South and West. As the Ministers of France, Spain, and England are all going to Europe on leave of absence before he will return, and it is very doubtful whether either of them will ever come back, and as the Russian Minister, Daschkoff, is finally recalled, they were all desirous of some occasion upon which they might take leave of the President and of his lady. After some consideration whether it should be by an extra drawing-room or a dinner, he concluded upon the last, and invites the whole Corps Diplomatique to dine with him next Tuesday.

March 19. — Mr. Nicholas Biddle called here this morning. He came two or three days since to see the President, with whom he has a particular and confidential intimacy, and is about to return immediately to Philadelphia. Met Mr. Crawford at the President's.

April 3. — My wife had a large tea-party this evening, but as there was scarcely any music, and no other occupation, it was dull. Gales, the editor of the *National Intelligencer,* spoke of a pamphlet circulated by General Scott, containing his correspondence with General Jackson, which sprung from an anonymous letter received by Jackson, whence a quarrel has arisen between them. The day before the President went away, Calhoun had received a letter from Scott signifying to him his intention to effect the publishing this correspondence in a pamphlet, in defiance or by an evasion of an order from the War Department of 21st February, 1818, which prohibited newspaper publications of quarrels between officers of the army. Scott had some time before written to Calhoun manifesting the same intention, and complaining that it was provoked by Jackson, who had shown about among his friends incomplete copies of the correspondence, suppressing one of Scott's letters. Calhoun had answered dissuading the publication, and Scott had replied persevering in his determination.

April 14. — Mr. Bagot [9] is a younger brother of Lord Bagot, a Peer of Great Britain; and his wife, a very discreet, amiable, and lovely woman, is daughter of Mr. William Wel-

---

[9] Charles Bagot, the British Minister, was returning home.

lesley Pole, Master of the Mint, and brother of the Duke of
Wellington. Bagot is about thirty-five, tall, well proportioned,
and with a remarkably handsome face: perfectly well bred,
and of dignified and gentlemanly deportment. The principal
feature of his character is discretion, one of the most indispensable qualities of a good negotiator; but neither his intellectual
powers nor his acquisitions are in any degree striking. His
temper is serious, but cheerful. He has no depth of dissimulation, though enough to suppress his feelings when it is for
his interest to conceal them. He has resided here three years
and though coming immediately after a war in which the national feelings here were highly exasperated against his country, has made himself universally acceptable. No English
Minister has ever been so popular; and the mediocrity of his
talents has been one of the principal causes of his success.
This is so obvious that it has staggered my belief in the uni-
versality of the maxim that men of the greatest talents ought
to be sought out for diplomatic missions. Bagot has been a
better Minister than a much abler man would have been; better for the interest of England — better for the tranquillity
of this country — better for the harmony between the two
nations, for his own quiet, and for the comfort of those with
whom he has had official intercourse here. For a negotiation
that would require great energy of mind, activity of research,
or fertility of expedients, such a man would not be competent:
but to go through the ordinary routine of business and the
common intercourse of society, to neutralize fretful passions
and soothe prejudices, a man of good breeding, inoffensive
manners, and courteous deportment is nearer to the true diplomatic standard than one with the genius of Shakspeare, the
learning of Bentley, the philosophical penetration of Berkeley,
or the wit of Swift.

April 18. — The President of the Bank of the United
States, Langdon Cheves, arrived in the city the evening before
last and this day left it upon his return to Philadelphia. His
appearance here has given rise to various rumors and surmises.
Its real cause is the tottering situation of the bank, which will
very shortly be reduced to the alternative of calling in all its
notes and trading on those of other banks or of stopping
payment.

May 6. — De Witt Clinton's political fortunes have been

more marked with starts of good and evil fortune than those
of any other man in the Union. He has been taken up and
laid aside at least half a dozen times, and was never more low
and discredited in public opinion than immediately before he
was elected Governor of New York without opposition. He
is, in fact, a man of great talents, and has magnificent purposes
of public service. He has comprehensive views and great
designs. But with these high and honorable materials of ambition he employs those of a baser sort — the charlatanery of
popular enticement. He affects to be a man of universal science, and smatters in agriculture, the arts, manufactures, and
antiquities and everything that smacks of combination and
vote-making. He has been laboring all his life in combinations and coalitions and political intriguing with individuals
and with parties. He began his political life as a furious Republican, and rose with the downfall of the federal party in
New York. He then made common cause with Burr and his
partisans, afterwards quarrelled with them, and then coalesced
with them again. Till the commencement of the late war with
England he continued, however, through all his changes, an
ardent Republican; but no sooner was that war declared than
he veered about, thrust himself forward as head of a peace
party, negotiated for and obtained the support of the federalists as a candidate for the presidency, in opposition to the re-
election of Mr. Madison, in 1812, and had agents travelling
about the country and bargaining with individuals of influence
to obtain their support to secure his election. . . The chance
is against him for his own re-election the next year. But ups
and downs are the natural characters of such a man's history.
His ability ranks him among the first men in the Union; he is
the most eminent, though not the ablest, man in the State of
New York, and, as he is yet not more than fifty years old, another fall will by no means be decisive of his fate for life.
Crawford, however, obviously considers him now as a rival
removed, and evidently reckons upon the support of New
York for himself at the proper time.

May 10. — I received the package of books which I have
been expecting from Boston — the Cicero and Tacitus given
me by Wells and Lilly in return for the Ernesti edition of
mine, which they had to print their Cicero from. I cannot
indulge myself in the luxury of giving two hours a day to these

writers: but to live without having a Cicero and a Tacitus at hand seems to me as if it was a privation of one of my limbs. The edition of Wells and Lilly is a very handsome one.

May 27. — I had some conversation with Crawford on the present situation and prospects of the country, which are alarming. The banking bubbles are breaking. The staple productions of the soil, constituting our principal articles of export, are falling to half and less than half the prices which they have lately borne, the merchants are crumbling to ruin, the manufactures perishing, agriculture stagnating, and distress universal in every part of the country. The revenue has not yet been, but must very sensibly and very soon be affected by this state of things, for which there seems to be no remedy but time and patience, and the changes of events which time effects. Crawford showed me his last bank returns, which are as large as usual, and the condition of the Treasury is daily improving. But there will be a great falling off in the revenue of the next year.

June 4. — A man by the name of Jenkins, a writing-master, who said he originally came from Dorchester but belonged now to New York, came this morning with a printed sheet of texts of Scripture, prayers, verses, and pious admonitions against duelling, which he had the project of having reprinted. . . I declined signing it, and told him I made it a general rule not to give certificates of recommendation for anything which, if useful, must carry its recommendation with itself. . . My wife, who was present, thought I had treated him harshly, and no doubt he thought so still more himself. I thought the man's anti-duelling printed sheet of Bible texts and prayers a device worse than useless — liable to the derision of scoffers, and utterly inadequate ever to prevent a single duel. To have recommended it would, with my opinions, have been to countenance an imposition upon the public. I felt it an impertinence in a man, a total stranger to me, to come and ask my certificate of recommendation to such mummery, and still more to open upon me a lecture of half an hour upon the duty of a man in high office to patronize and recommend poor and ingenious persons like him. I bore all this with composure, answered his allegations on the duty of patronage, and said nothing passionate, or personally offensive to him: but my wife says that I looked all the ill temper that I suppressed in words. The result is that I am a man of reserved, cold, austere, and forbidding manners: my political adversaries say, a gloomy misanthropist, and my personal enemies, an unsocial savage. With a knowledge of the actual defect in my character, I have not the pliability to reform it.

June 10. — Crawford told me much of the information which he is receiving with respect to the operations of the Bank, and the gigantic frauds practising upon the people by means of those institutions. The banks are breaking all over the country; some in a sneaking and some in an impudent manner; some with sophisticating evasions and others with the front of highwaymen. Our greatest real evil is the question between debtor and creditor, into which the banks have plunged us deeper than would have been possible without them. The bank debtors are everywhere so numerous and powerful that they control the newspapers throughout the Union and give the discussion a turn extremely erroneous, and prostrate every principle of political economy. Crawford has labors and perils enough before him in the management of the finances for the three succeeding years.

Oct. 24. — Attended public worship at Mr. McCormick's church. He read the morning service for the twentieth Sunday after Trinity, and a sermon from Psalm cl. 6: " Let everything that hath breath praise the Lord. Praise ye the Lord." Since I have now resided at Washington I have not regularly attended at any church — partly because I have permitted the week to encroach too much upon the Sabbath, and have not been sufficiently attentive to the duties of the day, but chiefly because, although the churches here are numerous and diversified, not one of them is of the Independent Congregational class to which I belong, the church to which I was bred, and in which I will die.

Nov. 16. — At noon, after a mere call at the office, I attended at the President's, where Mr. Crawford and Mr. Wirt soon afterwards came. The President read to us the portion of his message that he has prepared. . . Crawford preferred the general expressions, and told a story about old Governor Telfair, of Georgia, who, having got into a sharp correspondence with some officer, and looking over a draft of a letter which his Secretary had prepared for him, to the officer, pointed to a paragraph which struck him as too high-toned, and told his Secretary he would thank him to make that passage " a little more mysterious." We all laughed very heartily at the joke — which so pleased Crawford that he told the story over again in detail; but it was good upon repetition.

Nov. 26. — At twelve o'clock I went to the President's, where I found Mr. Crawford. I read as well as I could from the Spanish the letter from the Duke of San Fernando to Mr. Forsyth, finally declaring the determination of the King of Spain to delay the ratification of the treaty, and to send a Minister to the United States to ask for explanations. I found that Mr. Crawford, who at the last meeting was wavering upon the policy of taking possession of Florida, was now very decided in favor of it, and urged all the considerations that recommend it very forcibly.

As the President has appeared to hesitate, and as the dispatches from Europe have produced in my own mind a disposition to pause and review before the decisive step is taken, I suggested all the reasons that occurred to me in favor of a recommendation to Congress to wait until this new Minister shall arrive, and demand his explanations. As I am still doubtful myself whether the boldest course is not also the safest, my argument was not very strong nor very ardent. . .

The President said it was an exceedingly difficult question, and he would think profoundly upon it before coming to his final determination. I told him that I had the more freely given him all my present impressions from a consideration that it was by our Constitution the President himself who was responsible for all the great national measures recommended by him. The heads of Departments are responsible only as his subalterns. The measure now to be adopted will be in itself an act of war. It may very probably involve us in a real and very formidable war. I would not have it said that by my advice we had crossed the Rubicon without looking before or behind us. And there are strange workings in the human mind. Until yesterday I had invariably thought and advised the President as Crawford did this day. Until this day Crawford, without directly advising otherwise, had constantly hinted doubts and thrown dampers in the way. Lately, and particularly yesterday, I saw that my advice had become irksome to the President — that he was verging to a suspicion that I was spurring him to rash and violent measures. I fell, therefore, entirely into his own views of the subject, and Crawford, having discovered this, immediately took the ground I had abandoned, and is for at once assuming the offensive with Spain. The enemies of Mr. Monroe's Administration, and my enemies, have been continually laboring with the industry and venom of spiders to excite in his mind a jealousy of me. They have so far succeeded that whatever I earnestly recommend, he distrusts.

Dec. 3. — I went to the President's at noon, where there was a Cabinet meeting. Crawford, Thompson, and Wirt were present. The President read the draft of his message, which is nearly prepared. It is less pleasing, and will, I think, be more criticised, than either of his former messages at the commencement of the sessions of Congress. It presents a situation of public affairs less auspicious, and a variety of topics upon which there will probably be vehement debates. The question with Spain is drawn out more into detail, and yet is not shown in so clear a light as I could have wished it might be. . .

When the rest of the message, a very long one, was gone through, the President said that was all, except one subject which as this was a new Congress, he thought it his duty to recommend to their consideration. He then produced a manuscript long enough itself for two moderate messages, recommending the proposal by Congress of an amendment to the Constitution, authorizing them to make internal improvements by roads and canals; with an elaborate argument to prove that the authority had not been given by the Constitution. It is a paper which he drew up last winter and was then anxious to communicate in some way to Congress. He then read it at a Cabinet meeting, but finally postponed producing it to the public at that time. After he had now read it through, a general silence ensued, until I remarked that when the message at the commencement of the first session of the last Congress was prepared, I had taken the liberty of suggesting some considerations upon which it had appeared to me desirable that the whole paragraph should be omitted. I now retained the same opinion, and the course pursued by Congress on that subject since the former message had, in my mind, added new motives for the omission of it at present. The debates in the House of Representatives on that part of the former message had been full of irritation, and not altogether respectful to the Executive. . .

However, the President had determined, I have no doubt upon long determination, to send it, and he has probably motives for this measure which he has not disclosed. It is to all apparent purposes so injudicious, that the President, who is a man of strong judgment and great discretion, would certainly not produce it without objects to answer, adequate to balance the ill effects which he cannot but see it will be attended with in Congress. He has been brought into mortifying dilemmas by his declaration of faith on the internal improvement question: for Congress have passed Acts to all appearance in the face of his opinions, which Acts he has with great reluctance approved. This has given the appearance of inconsistency between his doctrine and his conduct, which he has severely felt, and he draws nice distinctions to reconcile them together, which will be sharply sifted in Congress and by the public. The Cabinet meeting broke up between four and five o'clock.

Dec. 6. — I found Mr. Wirt with the President, who was discussing with him the question about the part of his proposed message to Congress recommending an amendment of the Constitution, giving Congress the power to make internal improvements by roads and canals. He said he had deliberately considered the objections which I had suggested the other day, and they had determined him to strike out all the argumentative part, and to retain, if anything, only the passage in which he enumerates all the advantages, which the Union would derive from the investment of such a power in Congress, and his opinion that the power is not given by the Constitution.

I renewed and repeated all the arguments which I had before used to prevail upon him to leave it out altogether. There was, as I had supposed, a motive which he had not mentioned till now, for saying something upon the subject in this message. When he was upon his tour last summer, and passed through Lexington, Kentucky, Clay, who lives there, was absent from home, at New Orleans, and was supposed to have absented himself on purpose. An attempt was made by some of his partisans to make the inhabitants of the town pass a slight upon the President, by omitting to show him attentions similar to those with which he had been received elsewhere.

The effect of it was that the respect shown him there was rather more strongly marked than in almost any other place. A committee from the town went out fifteen miles from it to meet him, and accompanied by a numerous cavalcade, escorted him in. They presented him a very respectful address, in which, however, they said something about internal improvements. He answered by declaring that he was deeply impressed with the importance and necessity of them: but, believing that the power to make them had not been granted to Congress by the Constitution, he was anxious that it should be given to them by an amendment. . .

After a long and earnest discussion, Wirt told the President that he believed it would be better to omit the whole paragraph, and the President determined that he would. This resolution, importing, as I know it does, a sacrifice both of opinion and of feeling, affords a very strong proof of his magnanimity and of his disposition to listen to counsel — a disposition which in so high a place is an infallible test of a great mind. The advice that I have given him on this occasion was dictated by a pure regard for himself, and a deep conviction that if he had introduced the subject into the message at all, it would have injured him and much increased the disquietude of his future public service. . .

The President told me that several members had come to him yesterday and asked him whether it would be advisable to displace Clay as Speaker. He had advised against it. First, because it would be giving Mr. Clay more consequence than belongs to him. Secondly, because Mr. Clay, in the course which he has pursued and is pursuing aginst the Administration, has injured his own influence more than theirs. If it should be necessary to put him down, let it be done by his constituents. Thirdly, because there is no member of the Administration from the Western country. It is gratifying to them to have one of their members Speaker of the House. There is no other person from the Western section sufficiently eminent to put in competition with him.

Dec. 10. — There was a Cabinet meeting at the President's at noon, Messrs. Crawford, Thompson, and Wirt present. The Act of Congress against the slave-trade of the last session, and the questions of construction arising from it, were under consideration. The Colonization Society are indefatigable in their efforts to get hold of the funds appropriated by that Act: and having got the ear of the President, and Crawford for purposes of his own being one of them, they have already got their fingers into the purse: the Government is to pay fifteen hundred dollars for half the freight of a vessel they are about sending to Africa. Their Colony is to be formed at the island of Sherbro on the Coast of Guinea, about five degrees north of the line, so perfect a desert that they are to send out even the timber to build the huts in which their colonists are to dwell. And with all the multitudes of their members, and auxiliary societies and newspaper puffs they have no funds, and they are ravenous as panthers for the appropriation of a hundred thousand dollars of the last session. Crawford's construction of the law would deliver up to them the whole of it without reserve, though he professes to be very much upon his guard against them, and to have no belief in their success.

Dec. 13. — I called at Mr. Calhoun's, to consult him. . . As Mr. Gallatin has asked to be recalled, and proposes to return to the United States next spring, I asked Calhoun whether he would accept the mission to France. He said it would suit him in every other respect but the expense. He could not afford it. I said it was not easy to reply to that objection, the salaries of our Ministers abroad being so excessively inadequate to their necessary expenses that they could not remain long in Europe without drawing upon their private resources. But, as I expected more from him than from any other man living, to the benefit of the public service of this nation, I wished from purely public motives that he could go and spend some time in Europe, because I was convinced it would much enlarge his sphere of usefulness, by familiarizing him with facts and a description of knowledge which could in no other way be acquired.

He said he was well aware that a long and familiar practical acquaintance with Europe was indispensable to complete the education of an American statesman, and regretted that his fortune would not bear the cost of it. We had not time to continue the discussion, but I told him I should speak to him about it again.

Dec. 16. — The President spoke to me on the subject of the etiquette of visits. It would seem that some of the Senators have been to complain that the Secretary of State refuses to pay them the first visit. He mentioned it with much delicacy, but observed that it occasioned uneasiness, heart-burnings, and severe criticism. He wished, therefore, that the heads of Departments would meet and agree upon some rule which they should all observe for visiting, as one of the great difficulties arose from different persons following different practices.

I told the President what my own practice had been, the deputation that came to me two years ago from the Senators, my answer to them then, and the rules since observed by myself and my wife. I said I would with pleasure consult the other heads of Departments, and abide by such rules as a majority of them should agree to. He desired it might be done as soon as possible.

December 21. — I dined at the President's with a company of twenty-five persons — ladies and gentlemen. The heads of Departments and their ladies, excepting Mr. and Mrs. Calhoun, were there; the President of the Senate, Barbour, the Speaker of the House, Clay, and several members of both Houses. Clay told over again his story of the bottle of Kentucky wine that he once brought as a present to Mr. Madison, and of Robert Smith's saying it tasted of whiskey: of his (Clay's) disposition at the time to cut off Smith's head for the remark, and of its afterwards turning out that there really was whiskey in the wine — identically the same story which I heard him tell at the President's table once before.

Jan. 8, 1820. — One of the most remarkable features of what I am witnessing every day is a perpetual struggle in both Houses of Congress to control the Executive — to make it dependent upon and subservient to them. They are continually attempting to encroach upon the powers and authorities of the President. As the old line of demarkation between parties has been broken down, personal has taken the place of principled opposition. The personal friends of the President in the House are neither so numerous, nor so active, nor so able as his opponents. Crawford's personal friends, instead of befriending the Administration, operate as powerfully as they can, without exposing or avowing their motives, against it. Every act and thought of Crawford looks to the next Presidency. All his springs of action work not upon the present, but upon the future, and yet his path in the Department is now beset with thorns, from which he shrinks, and which I think he will not ward off with success. In short, as the first Presidential term of Mr. Monroe's Administration has hith-

erto been the period of the greatest national tranquillity enjoyed by this nation at any portion of its history, so it appears
to me scarcely avoidable that the second term will be among
the most stormy and violent. I told him this day that I
thought the difficulties before him were thickening and becoming hourly more and more formidable. In our foreign relations, we stood upon terms with England as favorable as can
ever be expected, but with a state of things dissatisfactory for
the present, and problematical for the future, with regard to
our commercial intercourse with her American Colonies.
With France our situation was much less pleasing and more
unpromising. She is pressing absurd claims, and refusing satisfaction for the most just and unequivocal claims on our
part. . .

A prospect thus dark and unpropitious abroad is far more
gloomy and threatening when we turn our eyes homeward.
The bank, the national currency, the stagnation of commerce,
the depression of manufactures, the restless turbulence and
jealousies and insubordination of the State Legislatures, the
Missouri slave question, the deficiencies of the revenue to be
supplied, the rankling passions and ambitious projects of individuals, mingling with everything, presented a prospect
of the future which I freely acknowledged was to me appalling. I asked him whether these apprehensions were visionary, and, if not, whether he had contemplated any distinct
system of measures to be in preparation for the embarrassments which it was obvious to foresee as inevitable at no distant
day.

He said that, as to the Missouri question, he apprehended
no great danger from that. He believed a compromise would
be found and agreed to, which would be satisfactory to all
parties.

Jan. 18. — Colonel Richard M. Johnson, a Senator from
Kentucky, called at my office, and told me that the President
had referred him to me upon certain proposals made by Billy
Duane, who was a very foolish and unaccountable fellow,
who might have made twenty fortunes, but, having always
been the worst enemy to himself that lived, was now poor
and embarrassed, and involved in a lawsuit with the Government, and had written him two letters containing projects
in which he should be glad to assist him. His first project

was, that understanding this Government were about to furnish ten thousand stands of arms to the South Americans of Venezuela, Duane would be glad to have the agency of selling them, for which an allowance of five or six per cent should be made to him by way of commission. The other was, that he (Duane) should be sent as Agent for the Government to Venezuela and New Granada. . .

I called at the President's and reported to him what Colonel Johnson had said. The President said that Colonel Johnson might have been more worthily occupied than in becoming the medium of such proposals: that the project of furnishing ten thousand stands of arms to Venezuela for the sake of making a profitable job to Duane had something in it that was disgusting: and that it was to be secretly done made it worse. If we were to furnish arms to the South Americans, it should be done openly in the face of day. As to sending Duane as an Agent to South America, he had no confidence in him, and believed him to be as unprincipled a fellow as lived. There was not, and had not been for years, a day passed but his newspaper had been filled with abuse and slander upon the Administration: and if such a man should be sent off as a public agent it would give a general disgust to the people of this country who would universally consider it as buying off his opposition. He was not worth buying. His abuse was a recommendation. . . This Duane is an Irish adventurer, bred for a Roman Catholic priest, but who, after some years of turbulence in his own country, and then in India, finally settled here, and has been nearly twenty-five years editor of the *Aurora,* the most slanderous newspaper in the United States. But as his industry is indefatigable, and as he writes with facility, his editorial articles are interesting, and he has often had much influence, especially in the State of Pennsylvania. He is now poor, and growing old, and his present proposal is substantially to sell his silence. The President offers nothing for it but his contempt.

Jan. 24. — I walked with R. M. Johnson to the Senate chamber and heard Mr. Pinkney close his Missouri speech. There was a great crowd of auditors. Many ladies, among whom several seated on the floor of the Senate. His eloquence was said to be less overpowering than it had been last Friday. His language is good, his fluency without interruption or hesitation, his manner impressive, but his argument weak, from the inherent weakness of his cause.

Feb. 11. — I went up to the Capitol and heard Mr. King in the Senate, upon what is called the Missouri question. He had been speaking perhaps an hour before I went in, and I heard him about an hour. His manner is dignified, grave, earnest, but not rapid or vehement. There was nothing new in his argument, but he unravelled with ingenious and subtle analysis many of the sophistical tissues of the slave-holders. He laid down the position of the natural liberty of man, and its incompatibility with slavery in any shape. He also questioned the Constitutional right of the President and Senate to make the Louisiana Treaty; but he did not dwell upon those points, nor draw the consequences from them which I should think important in speaking to that subject. He spoke, however, with great power, and the great slave-holders in the House gnawed their lips and clenched their fists as they heard him. . . We attended an evening party at Mr. Calhoun's, and heard of nothing but the Missouri question and Mr. King's speeches. The slave-holders cannot hear of them without being seized with cramps. They call them seditious and inflammatory, when their greatest real defect is their timidity. Never since human sentiments and human conduct were influenced by human speech was there a theme for eloquence like the free side of this question now before Congress of this Union. By what fatality does it happen that all the most eloquent orators of the body are on its slavish side? There is a great mass of cool judgment and plain sense on the side of freedom and humanity, but the ardent spirits and passions are on the side of oppression. Oh, if but one man could arise with a genius capable of comprehending, a heart capable of supporting, and an utterance capable of communicating those eternal truths that belong to this question, to lay bare in all its nakedness that outrage upon the goodness of God, human slavery, now is the time, and this is the occasion, upon which such a man would perform the duties of an angel upon earth!

Feb. 13. — Attended the divine service at the Capitol, and heard Mr. Edward Everett, the Professor of the Greek language at Harvard University, a young man of shining talents and of illustrious promise. His text was from I Cor. vii. 29: "Brethren, the time is short," and it was without comparison the most splendid composition as a sermon that I ever heard delivered. He had preached it last Sunday evening, where my sons had heard him, and George had written to me that it was the finest sermon he had ever heard, and foretelling that he would preach it again here. Hackneyed as this subject, the shortness of time, is, I never before saw so forcibly exemplified the truth that nothing is stale or trite in the hands of genius. His composition is more rich, more varied, more copious, more magnificent, than was that of Buckminster. There were passages that reminded me perhaps too much of Massillon, but the whole sermon was equal to any of the best that Massillon ever wrote. It abounded in splendid imagery, in deep pathos, in cutting satire, in profound reflections of morals, in coruscations of wit, in thunder-bolts of feeling. His manner of speaking was slow, and his articulation distinct, perhaps to excess. There was some want of simplicity both in the matter and manner. . . Mr. Clay, with whom I walked, after the service, to call upon Chief-Justice Marshall, told me that although Everett had a fine fancy and a chaste style of composition, his manner was too theatrical, and he liked Mr. Holley's manner better.

Clay started, however, immediately to the Missouri question, yet in debate before both Houses of Congress, and, alluding to a strange scene at Richmond, Virginia, last Wednesday evening, said it was a shocking thing to think of, but he had not a doubt that within five years from this time the Union would be divided into three distinct confederacies. I did not incline to discuss the subject with him. We found Judges Livingston and Story with the Chief Justice.

Feb. 17. — Dr. Thornton came again to the office to re-urge his pretension for appointment as Agent of the United States to Venezuela or any other part of South America. Of all the official duties of my station, there is none that tries the temper so severely as that of conflicting with the stubborn perseverance of unsuccessful candidates for office. To persist in reiterated refusal without ever falling into harshness of manner is a labor more than herculean. An unprovokable temper is the first of qualities to be prayed for in the discharge of these duties.

February 23. — A. Livermore and W. Plumer, Junr, members of the House of Representatives from New Hampshire, called upon me, and, conversing on the Missouri slave question, which at this time agitates Congress and the Nation, asked my opinion of the propriety of agreeing to a compromise. The division in Congress and the nation is nearly equal on both sides. The argument on the free side is, the moral and political duty of preventing the extension of slavery in the immense country from the Mississippi River to the South Sea. The argument on the slave side is, that Congress have no power by the Constitution to prohibit slavery in any State, and, the zealots say, not in any Territory. The proposed compromise is to admit Missouri, and hereafter Arkansas, as States, without any restriction upon them regarding slavery, but to prohibit the future introduction of slaves in all Territories of the United States north of 36° 30' latitude. I told these gentlemen that my opinion was, the question could be settled no otherwise than by a compromise.

Feb. 24. — I had some conversation with Calhoun on the slave question pending in Congress. He said he did not think it would produce a dissolution of the Union, but, if it should, the South would be from necessity compelled to form an alliance, offensive and defensive, with Great Britain.

I said that would be returning to the colonial state.

He said, yes, pretty much, but it would be forced upon them. I asked him whether he thought, if by the effect of this alliance, offensive and defensive, the population of the North should be cut off from its natural outlet upon the ocean, it would fall back upon its rocks bound hand and foot, to starve, or whether it would not retain its powers of locomotion to move southward by land. Then, he said, they would find it necessary to make their communities all military. I pressed the conversation no further: but if the dissolution of the Union should result from the slave question, it is as obvious as anything that can be foreseen of futurity, that it must shortly afterwards be followed by the universal emancipation of the slaves. A more remote but perhaps not less certain consequence would be the extirpation of the African race on this continent, by the gradually bleaching process of intermixture, where the white portion is already so predominant, and by the destructive progress of emancipation, which, like all great religious and political reformations, is terrible in its means though happy and glorious in its end. Slavery is the great and foul stain upon the North

American Union, and it is a contemplation worthy of the most
exalted soul whether its total abolition is or is not practicable: if
practicable, by what it may be effected, and if a choice of means
be within the scope of the object, what means would accomplish
it at the smallest cost of human suffering. A dissolution, at
least temporary, of the Union, as now constituted, would be
certainly necessary. . . The Union might then be reorganized
on the fundamental principle of emancipation. This object
is vast in its compass, awful in its prospects, sublime and
beautiful in its issue.

Feb. 26. — I went into the hall where the Supreme Court
of the United States were in session. They were engaged
in a prize cause of no considerable interest, and I soon passed
into the House of Representatives, where John Randolph was
speaking upon one of the Missouri slave questions. I heard
him between three and four hours. His speech, as usual, had
neither beginning, middle, nor end. Egotism, Virginian aristocracy, slave-scourging liberty, religion, literature, science, wit,
fancy, generous feelings, and malignant passions constitute a
chaos in his mind, from which nothing orderly can ever flow.
. . Clay, the Speaker, twice called Randolph to order. . .
He disputed the call and the decision as long as he could, and
then, as if yielding, said he would try t'other tack. It was useless to try to call him to order; he can no more keep order than
he can keep silence.

Feb. 27. — Called upon Mr. R. King at his lodgings at
Crawford's Hotel, Georgtown. Found him still absorbed in
the Missouri slave question, upon which he has been the great
champion of freedom and the Northern interest. The partisans of slavery have spread abroad the idea that he has been
actuated in this affair by motives of personal ambition — that
he is making an effort to get up a new division of parties and to
put himself at the head of half the Union, despairing of ever
being able to obtain the highest powers and honors of the
whole. It is not easy to account for the course that King
has pursued throughout this affair without allowing something
for the instigations of personal expectancy.

CHAPTER VII

1820–1821

SECOND ELECTION OF JAMES MONROE — W. H. CRAWFORD'S MACHI-
NATIONS — CONVERSATIONS WITH CALHOUN — QUARREL WITH
STRATFORD CANNING.

Washington, March 2, 1820. — The compromise of the
slave question was this day completed in Congress. The Senate
have carried their whole point, barely consenting to the formality of separating the bill for the admission of the State
of Maine into the Union from that for authorizing the people
of the Territory of Missouri to form a State Government.
The condition that slavery should be prohibited by their Constitution, which the House of Representatives had inserted,
they have abandoned. Missouri and Arkansas will be slave
States, but to the Missouri bill a section is annexed, prohibiting slavery in the remaining part of the Louisiana cession north
of latitude 36° 30′. This compromise, as it is called, was
finally carried this evening by a vote of ninety to eighty-seven
in the House of Representatives, after successive days and
almost nights of stormy debate.

March 3. — When I came this day to my office, I found
there a note requesting me to call at one o'clock at the President's house. It was then one, and I immediately went over.
He expected that the two bills, for the admission of Maine,
and to enable Missouri to make a Constitution, would have
been brought to him for his signature, and he had summoned
all the members of the Administration to ask their opinions
in writing, to be deposited in the Department of State, upon
two questions: 1, Whether Congress had a Constitutional
right to prohibit slavery in a Territory: and 2, Whether the
eighth section of the Missouri bill (which interdicts slavery
forever in the Territory north of thirty-six and a half lati-

tude) was applicable only to the Territorial State, or could extend to it after it should become a State.

As to the first question, it was unanimously agreed that Congress have the power to prohibit slavery in the Territories. . . I had no doubt of the right of Congress to interdict slavery in the Territories, and urged that the power contained in the term " dispose of " included the authority to do everything that could be done with it as mere property, and that the additional words, authorizing needful rules and regulations respecting it, must have reference to persons connected with it, or could have no meaning at all. As to the force of the term needful, I observed, it was relative, and must always be supposed to have reference to some end. Needful to what end? Needful in the Constitution of the United States to any of the ends for which that compact was formed. Those ends are declared in its preamble: to establish justice, for example. What can be more needful for the establishment of justice than the interdiction of slavery where it does not exist? . .

After this meeting, I walked home with Calhoun, who said that the principles which I had avowed were just and noble: but that in the Southern country, whenever they were mentioned, they were always understood as applying only to white men. Domestic labor was confined to the blacks, and such was the prejudice, that if he, who was the most popular man in his district, were to keep a white servant in his house, his character and reputation would be irretrievably ruined.

I said that this confounding of the ideas of servitude and labor was one of the bad effects of slavery: but he thought it attended with many excellent consequences. It did not apply to all kinds of labor — not, for example, to farming. He himself had often held the plough: so had his father. Manufacturing and mechanical labor was not degrading. It was only manual labor — the proper work of slaves. No white person could descend to that. And it was the best guarantee to equality among the whites. It produced an unvarying level among them. It not only did not excite, but did not even admit of inequalities, by which one white man could domineer over another.

I told Calhoun I could not see things in the same light. It is, in truth, all perverted sentiment — mistaking labor for slavery and dominion for freedom. The discussion of this Missouri question has betrayed the secret of their souls. In the abstract they admit that slavery is an evil, they disclaim all participation in the introduction of it, and cast it all upon the shoulders of our old Grandam Britain. But when probed to the quick upon it, they show at the bottom of their souls pride and vainglory in their condition of masterdom. They fancy themselves more generous and noble-hearted than the plain freemen who labor for subsistence. They look down upon the simplicity of a Yankee's manners, because he has no habits of overbearing like theirs and cannot treat negroes like dogs. It is among the evils of slavery that it taints the very sources of moral principle. It establishes false estimates of virtue and vice: for what can be more false and heartless than this doctrine which makes the first and holiest rights of humanity to depend upon the color of the skin? . .

I have favored this Missouri compromise, believing it to be all that could be effected under the present Constitution, and from extreme unwillingness to put the Union at hazard. But perhaps it would have been a wiser as well as a bolder course to have persisted in the restriction upon Missouri, till it should have terminated in a convention of the States to revise and amend the Constitution. This would have produced a new Union of thirteen or fourteen States unpolluted with slavery, with a great and glorious object to effect, namely, that of rallying to their standard the other States by the universal emancipation of their slaves. If the Union must be dissolved, slavery is precisely the question upon which it ought to break. For the present, however, this contest it laid asleep.

March 4. — King apparently came to talk with me of the compromise and the Maine and Missouri bills. There were, however, so many persons present that he said but little. He is deeply mortified at the issue, and very naturally feels resentful at the imputations of the slave-holders, that his motives on this occasion have been merely of personal aggrandizement — " close ambition varnished o'er with zeal." This imputation of bad motives is one of the most envenomed weapons of political and indeed of every sort of controversy. It came originally from the devil: " Doth Job fear God for nought? " Many of our public men have principles too pliable to popular impulse, but few are deliberately dishonest and there is not a man in the Union of purer integrity than Rufus King.

March 5. — It was said that in the hottest paroxyms of the Missouri question in the Senate, James Barbour, one of the Virginian Senators, was going round to all the free-State members and proposing to them to call a convention of the States to dissolve the Union, and agree upon the terms of separation and the mode of disposing of the public debt of the lands, and make other necessary arrangements of disunion. Dana said he told him that he was not for calling a convention to separate, but he had no objection to a convention to form a more perfect union. I observed that I thought a convention might, in the course of a few years, be found necessary to remedy the great imperfections of the present system. . . I added that there were three subjects, each of which might produce a state of things issuing in such a necessity. One was, the regulation of the currency, banks, and paper money: another, the impotence of the National Government to make internal improvements by roads and canals: and the third was slavery.

March 9. — Samuel Lawrence Gouverneur, of New York, was this day married to Maria Hester Monroe, the President's youngest daughter. The parties are cousins by the mother's side, and Gouverneur has been nearly these two years in the President's family, acting as his private secretary.

March 14. — An account, preceding the mail from New York, announced the arrival there of a vessel from Liverpool bringing the intelligence of the death of the British King, George the Third, and of the Duke of Kent. It had first been known here yesterday. The papers this day received confirmed it. The Duke of Kent died on the 24th of January, and the King the 29th of the same month. George the Third had reigned sixteen years the sovereign of this country. I suppose there are about half a million of souls in this Union who were once his subjects: four-fifths of that number born his subjects — of whom I was one. The forty-fourth year is revolving since the people of North America cast off their allegiance to him and declared their independence. Of the fifty-six signers of that instrument, only four are at this day numbered among the living — John Adams, of Massachusetts, my father, Thomas Jefferson, of Virginia, William Floyd, of New York, and Charles Carroll, of Carrollton, Maryland. The last ten years of the life of George the Third he has been kept in confinement at Windsor, in a state of mental alienation, blind, and perhaps deaf. Imagination can scarcely conceive a state of existence more calamitous, or a contrast more awful of the extremes of human grandeur and debasement in one person.

March 18. — G. A. Otis was at the office. He is proceeding with his translation of Botta's *History of the American Revolution,* and borrows my French translation of it to take with him to Philadelphia. But his main object was to renew and urge his solicitation for a Consular appointment abroad, and particularly for that of Liverpool, from which he wished that Mr. Maury should be removed: not that he (Otis) would wish to supplant any man, but because Maury is an old man, and that the business of his office is, and for some time has been, transacted by his clerk, who is an Englishman. There is something so gross and so repugnant to my feelings in this cormorant appetite for office, this barefaced and repeated effort to get an old and meritorious public servant turned out of place for a bankrupt to get into it, that it needed all my sense of the allowances to be made for sharp want and of the tenderness due to misfortune to suppress my indignation. He asked me if I would advise him to press these considerations personally upon the President: to which I barely answered no.

March 22. — Before I left my house this morning to go to my office, W. S. Smith came in and told me that Commodore Decatur had just been brought in from Bladensburg, mortally wounded in a duel with Commodore James Barron, who was also wounded, but not dangerously. I went immediately to Decatur's house: on the way met Captains McDonough and Ballard, who were coming from it, and whose information was discouraging but not decisive. At the house I saw Generals Brown and Harper, Colonel Bomford, and E. Wyer. Brown and Harper were flattered by some uncertainties of Dr. Lovell the Surgeon-General, who, I suppose, thinks it humane to keep Mrs. Decatur and her father, who is with her, in suspense as long as possible. Wyer, who had seen Decatur, told me that he could not survive the day. He died between nine and ten o'clock this evening. The nation has lost in him one of its heroes — one who has illustrated its history and given grace and dignity to its character in the eyes of the world. . .

The sensation in the city and neighborhood produced by this catastrophe was unusually great. But the lamentations at the practice of duelling were, and will be, fruitless, as they always are. Forbes called at my house this evening: he had been sitting an hour with Barron, who is at Beale's Congress Hotel on Capitol Hill. He has a ball in his body, which spared his life by hitting and glancing from the hip-bone. The cause of the duel is said to have been Decatur's resistance, as one of the Commissioners of the Navy, to the restoration of Barron to the naval service. Barron had been suspended for five years, from 1807, by the sentence of a court-martial, of which Decatur was a member, for the unfortunate affair of the *Chesapeake* frigate with Berkeley's squadron. The five years expired during our late war with Great Britain. Barron was then in Europe, and did not return to the United States during our war with Great Britain: though he made application for a passage in the *John Adams,* from Gottenburg, in June, 1814. After the peace he came back, and claimed to be restored to active employment, which it is said Decatur prevented him from obtaining. He has also spoken of him in slighting and contemptuous terms. A correspondence of mutual crimination and defiance has been passing between them since last June, and is now to be published.

March 24. — I went to my office; and attended the funeral of Decatur. There were said to be ten thousand persons assembled. An order of procession had been announced in the newspapers, and was inverted at the house. The procession walked to Kalorama, where the body was deposited in the family vault of the Barlows. A very short prayer was made at the vault by Dr. Hunter, and a volley of musketry from a detachment of the Marine Corps closed the ceremony over the earthly remains of a spirit as kindly, as generous, and as dauntless as breathed in this nation, or on this earth. I walked with Mr. Crawford. John Randolph was there; first walking, then backing his horse, then calling for his phaeton, and lastly crowding up to the vault as the coffin was removed into it from the hearse — tricksy humors to make himself conspicuous.

March 25. — King talked much of the contested election now approaching in New York between De Witt Clinton, the present Governor, for re-election, and D. D. Tompkins, now Vice-President, who, it seems, prefers returning to the State Government. Both parties have been anxious to obtain the support of King, whose influence it is supposed would carry many federal votes. But he avoids taking a decided part in favor of either side. The objections against Clinton are political tergiversations, intrigues, caballing, and insatiable ambition. Those against Tompkins are that his accounts as formerly Governor of New York are unsettled, and that a large balance stands against him, for the expenditure of which he can produce no vouchers. They are both men of talents, and from early youth have been in a succession of important public offices; Clinton supported by an aristocratic name and hereditary family influence, and Tompkins by extreme popularity of manners and deportment.

March 29. — I attended at one o'clock the meeting at the President's. Messrs. Crawford, Calhoun, and Thompson, the Secretary of the Navy, were there, the latter having returned on the 23d from New York. He walked in the procession at Decatur's funeral. Wirt was not at the meeting this day, being confined, unwell at home. The President proposed for consideration the question, upon the proposal of Manuel Torres, that the Government should sell upon credit to the Republic of Colombia, any number short of twenty thousand stand of arms, to enable them to extend the South American Revolution into Peru and Mexico. By one of those backstair proceedings which I often feel without seeing, a report has been made from the Ordnance Department to the Secretary of War, just at the critical moment, that there are some thousand stand of English arms which might with advantage to the public service be sold. . . I said there was no hesitation in my mind. To supply the arms professedly for the purpose set forth in the memorial of Torres would be a direct departure from neutrality, and act of absolute hostility to Spain, for which the Executive was not competent, by the Constitution, without the authority of Congress. This was enough for me. But I would go further. It would, in my opinion, be not only an act of war, but of wrongful and dishonorable war, committed in the midst of professions of neutrality. . .   The decision was unanimous that the proposal could not be complied with, and I am to answer Mr. Torres accordingly.

A remark that I have occasion frequently to make is, that moral considerations seldom appear to have much weight in the minds of our statesmen, unless connected with popular feelings. The dishonorable feature of giving secret aid to the revolutionists, while openly professing neutrality, was barely not denied. The President admits it. No one else seems to think that it ought to stand in the way of measures otherwise expedient, especially if supported by popular prejudice. My own deliberate opinion is, that the more of pure moral principle is carried into the policy and conduct of a Government the wiser and more profound will that policy be.

March 31. — Clay's affairs, private and public, have been growing desperate ever since the commencement of Mr. Monroe's Administration. He then refused the War Department and the mission to London; nothing would satisfy him but the Department of State; and, failing to obtain that, he projected a new opposition, of which he should be the head, and which should in the course of two Presidential terms run down Monroe, so that he might come in as the opposition successor. His engines the first session were South America and internal improvement. Both then failed. The next session he took up the Seminole War, but of that mighty controversy he was no longer the primary leader. He had ranged himself under the Crawford banners. That struggle was more stubborn, but also failed. The great majority of the people took the other side. The Missouri question then arose, and disconcerted Clay's projects by presenting party combinations and divisions very unsuitable to them. It looked to a dissolution of the Union upon principles which could not serve his purposes. But that question having been for the present compromised, he recurs to South American and Spanish affairs for his main engine of opposition. The Florida Treaty, when concluded last winter, was universally considered as obtaining so much more for us than had ever been expected, that not a voice could be raised against it in either House of Congress. Now the public feeling is different. For while the King of Spain refuses to ratify because, he says, his Minister conceded too much, the people of our Western country have been instigated against the treaty as not having obtained enough. The Missouri question, too, has operated to indispose every part of the Union against the treaty; the North and East, because they do not wish even to have Florida as another slave State; and the South and West, because they wish to have all the territory to the Rio del Norte for more slave States.

April 6. — In the *National Intelligencer* of yesterday there was a notice signed by General Samuel Smith, a Representative in Congress from Baltimore, as Chairman of the caucus in 1816 which nominated candidates for the offices of President and Vice-President of the United States, at the election then ensuing. He states that he has been required by numbers of members from various parts of the Union to call a meeting for consultation whether a nomination shall now be made. He therefore summons a meeting of Republican and other members of Congress who may think proper to attend at the Representative Hall at the Capitol, next Saturday evening at half-past seven o'clock in the evening, to determine whether it be expedient that a nomination should now be made of candidates for the offices of President and Vice-President. This is the result of caballing. There is at present no ostensible intention to oppose the re-election of Mr. Monroe as President in any part of the Union. Every attempt to form a new fixed opposition party has hitherto failed. But the Vice-Presidency is, to call things by their proper names, in the market. . . Samuel Smith, in the midst of a stupendous ruin of reputation and fortune as a merchant, maintains yet his consideration and influence as a politician, or at least struggles hard to maintain it, and is now baited to this hook by the view of a vacant Speaker's chair, which he is told he has a clear pretension to occupy. So that the object of this caucus is to announce Clay as candidate for the Vice-Presidency, and to make way for Smith as the future Speaker. To prepare the minds of members for this, Clay has given out that he has met with a heavy loss by the failure of a person whose notes he had endorsed, and which he was last summer obliged to pay, to the amount of twenty-five thousand dollars; that his private affairs have thus become embarrassed; so that, having a family of children to support, he can no longer afford to come to Congress, and intends to resign his office as Speaker before the close of the present session. That his affairs are embarrassed, there is no doubt. According to the general rumor, he has more than once won and lost an affluent fortune at the gaming-table.[1] The last winter was an unlucky one for him, and before he left this city he was said to have met with embarrassing losses. In his Florida Treaty speech the other day,

---

[1] At one time Clay was reported to have lost $8,000 at the card-table.

he made an ingenuous confession that in his youth he had
sometimes indulged in a mode of amusement which years
and experience had determined him to abandon.   This resolution was doubtless formed under similar circumstances to those
in which Regnard's Hector concludes that Seneca must have
written his philosophical reflections.   I am, nevertheless, in-
credulous as to his resignation of the Speaker's office.   His
political prospects are not so entirely blasted as that measure
would indicate his own conviction that they are; and in this
country, politicians of desperate private fortunes always find
the means of keeping themselves above water as public men.
In politics, as in private life, Clay is essentially a gamester,
and, with a vigorous intellect, an ardent spirit, a handsome
elocution, though with a mind very defective in elementary
knowledge, and a very undigested system of ethics, he has
all the qualities which belong to that class of human characters.

May 2. — D. P. Cook, the Representative in Congress from
the State of Illinois, and T. Fuller, one of the members from
Massachusetts, successively called at my house this morning. . .   Fuller said it was apparent that preparations were
making for a violent canvass for the Presidential election of
1824.   I said there had been scarcely anything but such canvassing since 1816.   He said he hoped I did not intend to withhold myself from the contest.   I told him the principle of my
life had been never to ask the suffrage of my country, and never
to shrink from its call.   If life, and health, and private circumstances admitting of it, and a belief of competency to the
station, not inferior to others who may be competitors for it,
should be mine after the vicissitudes of the next four years,
I shall adhere to the principle upon which I have always acted.
Whether any portion of the country will think of calling for
my services will certainly depend upon the series of future
events.   I know the disadvantages on which I now stand, and
am conscious of my inability to make interest by caballing, bargaining, place-giving, or tampering with members of Congress.   I have been here three sessions, with a colleague in the
Executive Administration who at the caucus preceding the last
Presidential election was a candidate against Mr. Monroe, and
came very near out-voting him; who considers himself, therefore, as quite entitled to the succession; who, as a Virginian
born, is sure of the support of that State against any one not

of the same origin; as a slaveholder, has the first pledge of votes from the South and Southwest; and possesses an immense patronage throughout the Union, which he exercises to promote his purposes without scruple and without restraint.

May 10. — Clay this day gave notice that it was his intention shortly to retire from public life, and he has publicly notified the people of his district that he shall not offer himself as a candidate for Congress at the next election, in August. This is owing to the embarrassed state of his private affairs, which makes it necessary for him to return to the practice of the bar.

May 12. — Pennsylvania has been for about twenty years governed by two newspapers in succession: one, the *Aurora,* edited by Duane, an Irishman, and the other, the *Democratic Press,* edited by John Binns, an Englishman. Duane had been expelled from British India for sedition, and Binns had been tried in England for high treason. They are both men of considerable talents and profligate principles, always for sale to the highest bidder, and always insupportable burdens, by their insatiable rapacity, to the parties they support. With the triumph of Jefferson, in 1801, Duane, who had contributed to it, came in for his share, and more than his share, of emolument and patronage. With his printing establishment at Philadelphia he connected one in this city; obtained by extortion almost the whole of the public printing, but, being prodigal and reckless, never could emerge from poverty, and, always wanting more, soon encroached upon the powers of indulgence to his cravings which the heads of Departments possessed, and quarrelled both with Mr. Madison and Mr. Gallatin for staying his hand from public plunder. In Pennsylvania, too, he contributed to bring in McKean, and then labored for years to run him down — contributed to bring in Snyder, and soon turned against him. Binns in the meantime had come, after his trial, as a fugitive from England, and had commenced editor of a newspaper. Duane had been made by Mr. Madison a colonel in the army; and as Gibbon, the captain of Hampshire militia, says he was useful to Gibbon, the historian of the Roman Empire, so Duane, the colonel, was a useful auxiliary to Duane, the printer, for fleecing the public by palming upon the army, at extravagant prices, a worthless compilation upon military discipline that he had published.

May 17. — Ninian Edwards, the Senator from Illinois, and W. Lowndes, member of the House of Representatives from South Carolina, called this morning at my house to take leave. Edwards spoke of the state of parties and of public affairs. At the next session, he says, the great struggle will come on. Edwards is first cousin to the Popes of Kentucky and Illinois, and therefore not in the interest of Clay, of whom John Pope is the unsuccessful rival in Kentucky. But, as a Western man, Edwards feels himself to be rowing against the general current of Western feeling, and is uneasy under it. He remarks with anxiety the ascendency which Clay has been acquiring during the latter part of the session of Congress, and seems to dread that he will carry all before him. He supposes that he will resign his seat as Speaker, but not as member, of the House; that he will immediately engage extensively in the practice of the law, and will come next winter and attend at the same time the session of the Supreme Court and of Congress.

May 22. — I called upon Mr. Calhoun, and he went with me to Mr. Thomas Law's, in Prince George's County. On the ride we had much conversation upon various topics. I asked him whether he knew what was the occasion of the President's calling the cabinet meeting on Saturday. He said it was a letter that he had received from Mr. Jefferson, in which, though mentioning in terms of high commendation the Florida Treaty, he yet advises that its ratification should not now be accepted, but that we should look to the occupation of Texas. This explains to me what had been utterly unaccountable in the call of that meeting three days after my last note to Vivés and after the receipt of his answer. It reminded me of O'Brien's shrewd remark, that an old sea-captain never likes that his mate should make a better voyage than himself.

We conversed upon politics past, present, and future. Calhoun's anticipations are gloomy. He says there has been within these two years an immense revolution of fortunes in every part of the Union; enormous numbers of persons utterly ruined; multitudes in deep distress; and a general mass of disaffection to the Government, not concentrated in any particular direction, but ready to seize upon any event and looking out anywhere for a leader. The Missouri question and the debates on the tariff were merely incidental to this state of things. It

was a vague but wide-spread discontent, caused by the dis-
ordered circumstances of individuals, but resulting in a general
impression that there was something radically wrong in the
administration of the Government. These observations are
undoubtedly well-founded. The disease is apparent, the remedy not discernible. The primary cause is that which has been
the scourge of this country from its Colonial infancy — speculations in paper currency, now appearing in the shape of banks;
the great multiplication, followed by the sudden and severe
reduction, of fictitious capital; then the great falling off in the
prices of all our principal articles of exportation, the competition of foreign manufactures carried on by starving workmen,
with ours loaded with high wages, the diminution of commerce
and the carrying trade, and the accumulation of debt as long
as credit could be strained — all this, with ambitious and crafty
and disappointed men on the watch for every misfortune and
welcoming every disaster, together with the elated hopes, the
dazzling promise, and the mortifying reverses of the Florida
Treaty, accounts too well for the loss of popularity by the
Administration within the last year.

June 4. — Among the letters received this day was one from
Josiah Quincy, Corresponding Secretary to the American
Academy of Arts and Sciences, at Boston, announcing to me
that the Society had at their annual meeting, on the 30th of
last month, elected me their President. I answered the letter,
and accepted the office, because I thought there would be an
appearance of affectation in refusing it. The arts and sciences
have been the objects of my admiration through life. I would
it were in my power to say they have been objects of my successful cultivation! Honors like these produce in my mind humiliation as well as pride.

June 16. — Richard Forrest showed me this day a letter
from John Jacob Astor, dated at Rome in April. He wishes
that a hint may be given to the President that Albert Gallatin
may not be recalled from the mission to Paris, and says there
are many reasons for his being retained there, but does not
explain them. Forrest supposes Astor means that it is the
wish of Gallatin himself, and says he has a letter from another
gentleman, but who did not wish his name to be known, stating
explicitly that it is Gallatin's wish. The President therefore
understood very exactly the state of mind in which Gallatin

wrote the letter last winter requesting his recall. Gallatin has been twelve years Secretary of the Treasury, and seven years a Minister abroad. His foreign nativity was, at the opening of Mr. Madison's Administration, the insuperable bar to his obtaining the Department of State, and thereby cut off forever his prospects of coming to the Presidency. There is now no place at home which would be suitable for him and agreeable to him and he would live contented in France if the salary would defray his unavoidable expenses. But it will not; and, although he may remain there one or two years longer, he will be compelled to return by want of means to remain.

June 23. — The censorial power of the President of the United States over the moral and official conduct of the officers appointed and subject to removal by him, is one of those the exercise of which is of the most extreme delicacy. . . In the discharge of this most painful and ungracious duty the President seems to me more governed by momentary feelings, and less by steady and inflexible principle, than I think he ought. But his failing leans to virtue's side. He is universally indulgent, and scrupulously regardful of individual feelings. He is perhaps too reluctant to exercise this power at all. He rather turns his eyes from misconduct, and betrays a sensation of pain when it is presented directly to him. Whether this weakness, as it appears to me to be, is not better than its proximate energy, is perhaps doubtful. In the theory of a President's duties, with almost as much indulgence, and the same tenderness for the feelings of individuals, I should look for a little more vigilance to observe and a little more rigor to control the faults of executive officers. One of the consequences of this tendency to censorial laxity is the necessity under which I have often found myself, of presenting to the President cases requiring censure and, after having presented them, of bringing them again and again before him, until something is done, for whatever he consents to do, unless it is to be executed immediately, he never thinks of it afterwards.

July 15. — I went out this evening in search of conversation, an art of which I never had an adequate idea. Long as I have lived in the world, I never have thought of conversation as a school in which something was to be learned. I never knew how to make, to control, or to change it. I am by nature a silent animal, and my dear mother's constant lesson in childhood, that children in company should be seen and not heard, confirmed me irrevocably in what I now deem a bad habit. Conversation is an art of the highest importance, and a school in which, for the business of life, more may perhaps be learnt than from books. It is, indeed, and must be, desultory and superficial; and, as a school, consists more in making others talk than in talking. Therein has been, and ever will be, my deficiency — the talent of starting the game.

September 7. — W. Lee came with a letter from M. M. Noah, editor of the New York *Advocate,* a Jew, who was once Consul at Tunis, recalled for indiscretions, and who has published a book of travels against Mr. Madison and Mr. Monroe. He has great projects for colonizing Jews in this country, and wants to be sent as Chargé d'Affaires to Vienna for the promotion of them. He is an incorrect, and very ignorant, but sprightly writer, and as a partisan editor of a newspaper has considerable power. He urges with great earnestness his merits in supporting the Administration, as a title to the President's favor. He is, like all the editors of newspapers in this country who have any talent, an author to be let. There is not one of them whose friendship is worth buying, nor one whose enmity is not formidable. They are a sort of assassins who sit with loaded blunderbusses at the corner of streets and fire them off for hire or for sport at any passenger whom they select. They are principally foreigners; but Noah is a native.

Sept. 29. — I received this morning a letter from Mr. Stratford Canning, informing me that he had arrived late last evening in the city, with a credential letter as Envoy Extraordinary and Minister Plenipotentiary from the King of Great Britain, of which, together with the letter of recall of Sir Charles Bagot, he enclosed copies, and requesting me to appoint an hour to receive him.

Oct. 22. — Mr. R. Forrest called at my house this evening with a servant of Roth's, the French Chargé d'Affaires. A colored woman, who lives with Roth as his cook, has been taken up on suspicion of receiving stolen money, and committed to prison by Timms, who is doorkeeper to the Senate, and a magistrate and member of the City Council. A shopkeeper by the name of Holmead dropped yesterday from his pocket, in the street, a cheque upon one of the banks for a hundred dollars, and a hundred and fifty dollars in bank-bills. A mulatto boy of fourteen or fifteen years of age found the cheque, and not knowing how to read, took it to a shop to enquire what it was. He was then called upon for the bank-bills, and, denying that he had found them, was tortured, thumb-screwed, and hung by the neck (so this man says) to extort confession from him. He finally named several persons to whom he said he gave the bills, and among the rest the father of Roth's cook. He denied having received the bills, but his daughter was imprisoned on suspicion of having received them from him. This is a sample of the treatment of colored people under criminal charges or suspicions here.

Nov. 12. — I called upon Mr. Calhoun, the Secretary of War, and rode with him to the President's. As we were riding, Calhoun spoke to me with great concern at the reappearance of the question upon the admission of Missouri as a State into the Union. After all the difficulty with which it was compromised at the last session of Congress, the Convention which made their Constitution has raised a new obstacle by an article declaring it to be the duty of the Legislature to pass laws prohibiting negroes and persons of color from coming into the State; which is directly repugnant to the article in the Constitution of the United States which provides that the citizens of each State shall be entitled to all privileges and immunities of citizens in the several States. Calhoun said that he did not know how this difficulty could be surmounted, unless by considering the article in the Missouri Constitution as null and void upon the very principle of its repugnancy.

Nov. 18. — Members of Congress, visitors at the office, occupied again all the hours of business. This rapid and continual change of persons and of subjects calling for attention has such an effect upon the memory that the proverbial defect of that quality may be accounted for without supposing it intentional or pretended. Every man comes with a story, demand, or solicitation of his own; almost every one comes to ask favors. No sooner has one left the office than another enters. I have often attempted to keep a minute of the names of the persons who come from day to day, but without success. I have not time to write the name of one who retires before another comes in. Eight or ten thus succeed one another without leaving a moment's interval. When they are gone, often while some of them are here, comes in a mail of letters, dispatches, and newspapers. Pressing business of the office, suspended while the visitors are with me, admits of no further delay. The sun goes down upon business uncompleted.

Nov. 29. — I returned Mr. Baldwin's visit, and had a long conversation with him on the subject of the Missouri question of the present session. . . I told him if I were a member of the Legislature of one of the free States, I would move for a declaratory act, that so long as the article in the Constitution of Missouri depriving the colored citizens of the State, say of Massachusetts, of their rights as citizens of the United States within the State of Missouri, should subsist, so long the white citizens of the State of Missouri should be held as aliens within the Commonwealth of Massachusetts, not entitled to claim or enjoy within the same any right or privilege of a citizen of the United States. And I would go further, and declare that Congress having given sanction to the Missouri Constitution, by admitting that State into the Union without excepting against that article which disfranchised a portion of the citizens of Massachusetts, had violated the Constitution of the United States; wherefore, until that portion of the citizens of Massachusetts whose rights are violated by the article in the Missouri Constitution should be redintegrated in the full enjoyment and possession of those rights, no clause or article of the Constitution of the United States should, within the Commonwealth of Massachusetts, be so construed as to authorize any person whomsoever to claim the property or possession of a human being as a slave. And I would prohibit by the law the delivery of any fugitive slave upon the claim of his master. All which I would do, not to violate but to redeem from violation, the Constitution of the United States. . . If slavery be the destined sword in the hand of the destroying angel which is to sever the ties of this union, the same sword will cut in sunder the bonds of slavery itself. A dissolution of the Union for the cause of slavery would be followed by a servile war in the slave-holding States, combined with a war between the two severed portions of the Union. It seems to me that its result must be the extirpation of slavery from this whole continent; and, calamitous and desolating as this course of events in its progress must be, so glorious would be its final

issue, that, as God shall judge me, I dare not say that it is not
to be desired.

Dec. 18. — Mr. Sanderson came to the office. He has undertaken the publication of a biography of the Signers of the
Declaration of Independence. . . I asked him who was to
furnish the life of Samuel Chase. He said that application
had been made to his family for access to his papers, but he
had no papers that could be applied with any use to this purpose. I told him I considered Mr Chase as one of the men
whose life, conduct, and opinions had been of the most extensive influence upon the Constitution of this country. He not
only signed the Declaration of Independence, but was an active and distinguished member of the Congress during the
early and most critical period of the Revolution. He was a
man of ardent passions, of strong mind, of domineering temper. His life was consequently turbulent and boisterous. He
had for some years almost uncontrolled dominion over the
politics of the State of Maryland; at other times was unpopular in the extreme, and was more than once impeached. Appointed by President Washington one of the Judges of the
Supreme Court of the United States, he had continued in that
office upwards of twenty years, until his death. He was the
only Judge of that Court who had ever been impeached. His
impeachment had settled some principles and some practice
of our Constitutional law. But he himself, as a judge, had
settled others of the highest importance — one of them, in
my opinion, of very pernicious importance. He decided, as I
think, directly in the face of an amendatory article of the Constitution of the United States (the seventh), that this Union
in its federative capacity has no common law — a decision
which has crippled the powers not only of the judiciary, but
of all the Departments of the National Government.

Dec. 25. — Christmas Day. — No attendance at the office.
I gave the day to relaxation, and, with a view to make an experiment upon the taste of the younger part of our present
family, after breakfast I read aloud Pope's *Messiah,* a poem
suited to the day, and of which my own admiration was great
at an earlier age than that of my son Charles, the youngest person now in my family. Not one of them, excepting George, appeared to take the slightest interest in it; nor is there one of
them who has any relish for literature. Charles has a great

fondness for books, and a meditative mind, but neither disposition nor aptitude for public speaking or correct reading.
Charles must teach himself all that he learns. He will learn
nothing from others. Literature has been the charm of my
life, and, could I have carved out my own fortunes, to literature would my whole life have been devoted. I have been a
lawyer for bread, and a statesman at the call of my country.
In the practice of the law I never should have attained the
highest eminence, for the want of natural and spontaneous
eloquence. The operations of my mind are slow, my imagination sluggish, and my powers of extemporaneous speaking very
insufficient. But I have much capacity for, and love of, labor,
habits on the whole of industry and temperance, and a strong
and almost innate passion for literary pursuits. The business
and sometimes the dissipations of my life have in a great
measure withdrawn me from it. The summit of my ambition
would have been by some great work of literature to have
done honor to my age and country, and to have lived in the
gratitude of future ages. This consummation of happiness
has been denied me.

Dec. 27. — Attended the funeral of Mr. Burrill. . . After
the ceremony was over, Mr. Calhoun rode with me, and I left
him at the War Office. We were remarking upon the number
of members of Congress already mingling with the dust of
this region, among whom are two successive Vice-Presidents,
George Clinton and Elbridge Gerry. There are plain, modest,
and tasteless marble monuments over their remains, which the
lapse of a few short years will demolish. We were remarking
how exclusively by the nature and genius of our institutions we
confine all our thoughts and cares to present time. We have
neither forefathers nor posterity. This burying-ground is remote from any church. The funeral is a mere commitment of
earth to earth. There is nothing to soothe the afflicted, or to
rouse the thoughtless, by the promise and the warning which
a church would give of the connection between time and eter-
nity; nothing to remind the attendant at the funeral that death
is a transition from this to another world. There is a resolution of Congress, existing ever since the death of Washington, that a monument in honor of his memory should be
erected. I said to Calhoun that I thought, under that resolution, Congress ought to build a church of durable stone, equal

in dimensions to Westminster Abbey or the Panthéon at Paris; that sheltered under the roof and within the walls of this church should be the sepulchral monument of Washington, and around it, suitably disposed, those of the statesmen and legislators of this Union whose lives may from time to time honorably close during their attendance here in the service of their country.

Jan. 1, 1821. — At the drawing-room at the President's. It was more thronged with company than I ever saw it on any similar occasion. " Donec eris felix, multos numerabis amicos." Mr. Monroe, by a vote, with a single exception unanimous, of all the electoral colleges of this Union, has just been re-elected President of the United States for a second term of four years. No such state of things as the present has existed since the establishment of the present Constitution; for although the second election of Washington, like the first, was unanimous, yet the opposition to his Administration was more organized and more violent than it now is to that of Mr. Monroe.

Jan. 12. — Mr. Calhoun called this morning at my house, and apologized for having missed dining with us yesterday; he had forgotten the day of the invitation, and did not discover the mistake until last evening after having dined at home.

Jan. 17. — Mr. Canning called upon me at the office, to have what he called a little gossiping conversation with me, but he stayed with me at least three full hours, and at last, after it was nearly dark, drawing out his watch, he exclaimed, " God bless me! 'tis near six o'clock, and I have invited a large party to dine with me at five. I believe you must offend me." Our conversation had been upon a great variety of topics, political and literary, but not upon anything of business.

Jan. 26. — Mr. Canning, the British Minister, called at the office, and, intimating that he came to have some conversation with me in his official character, observed that, having been some days since present at a debate in the House of Representatives, he had heard some observations made by Mr. Nelson, of Virginia, importing a design in the Government of this country to form some new settlement on the South Sea; that he should not particularly have noticed this but that in the *National Intelligencer* of this morning, a paper generally considered as partaking in some sort of an official character, there was a publication signed by Mr. Eaton, a member of the Senate, which was a part of the Executive Government, and which disclosed an avowed project for such a settlement on the Pacific Ocean. He had, therefore, thought it his duty to call upon me and enquire what were the intentions of the Government in this respect.

The personal communications between Mr. Canning and me hitherto had all been of a character so conciliatory and friendly that, although much surprised both at the form and substance of this address, I answered him that I had not read the publication of Mr. Eaton, nor had I heard of the remark which he mentioned to have been made by Mr. Nelson; that I was not acquainted with the opinions of those members of Congress on this subject, but, from a prevailing disposition in the country, it was very probable that our settlement at the mouth of Columbia River would at no remote period be increased.

He immediately assumed an air widely different from that of the easy familiarity with which the conversation had commenced, and, with a tone more peremptory than I was disposed to endure, said he was greatly surprised at receiving this answer. With a corresponding change of tone, I told him he could not be more surprised than I was, both at the form and substance of his address on this occasion.

"And am I to understand this," said he, " as the determination of the American Government? "

"No sir," said I; "you are to understand nothing as the determination of the American Government that I say to you without consultation with and directions from the President. What I have now said to you is merely an opinion of my own."

He then repeated that he was greatly surprised to hear it, as he conceived such a settlement would be a direct violation of the article of the Convention of 20th October, 1818.

I immediately rose from my seat to look for the volume of the laws of the United States which contained the Convention. While I was looking for it, Mr. Canning said it was not his wish to take me upon this subject by surprise, and that, if it would be more agreeable to me, he would call upon me some other day.

Without replying to this remark, having found the book, I resumed my seat, and, after reading audibly the article of the Convention respecting the boundary, said, "Now, sir, if you have any charge to make against the American Government for a violation of this article, you will please to make the communication in writing."

He then said, with great vehemence, "And do you suppose, sir, that I am to be dictated to in the manner in which I may think proper to communicate with the American Government?"

I answered, "No, sir. We know very well what are the privileges of foreign Ministers, and mean to respect them. But you will give us leave to determine what communications we receive, and how we will receive them; and, you may be assured, we are as little disposed to submit to dictation as to exercise it."

He then, in a louder and more passionate tone of voice, said, "And am I to understand that I am to be refused henceforth any conference with you on the business of my mission?"

"Not at all, sir," said I; "my request is that if you have anything further to say to me upon this subject, you would say it in writing. And my motive is, to avoid what, both from the nature of the subject and from the manner in which you have thought proper to open it, I foresee will tend only to mutual irritation, and not to an amicable arrangement."

Jan. 27. — Mr. Canning again repeated his surprise at the tone and temper with which his application yesterday had been received. He said he had examined and re-examined himself, and had in vain enquired what could have been the cause of the asperity with which he had been treated by me.

"Sir," said I, "suppose Mr. Rush should be present at a debate in the House of Commons, and should hear a member in the course of a speech say something about the expediency of sending a regiment of troops to the Shetland Islands, or a new colony to New South Wales; suppose another member of Parliament should publish in a newspaper a letter recommending the same project; and suppose Mr. Rush should then go to Lord Castlereagh and formally allege those two facts as his motives for demanding whether the British Government had any such intentions; and, if answered that very probably they might, he should assume an imperious and tragical tone of surprise and talk about a violation of treaties: how do you think it would be received?"

He said that now he fully understood me, and could account for what had passed; this answer was perfectly explicit. But did I consider the cases as parallel?

"So far as any question of right is concerned," said I, "perfectly parallel."

"Have you," said Mr. Canning, "any claim to the Shetland Islands or New South Wales?"

"Have you any claim," said I, "to the mouth of Columbia River?"

"Why, do you not know," replied he, "that we have a claim?"

"I do not know," said I, "what you claim nor what you do not claim. You claim India; you claim Africa; you claim —— "

"Perhaps," said he, "a piece of the moon."

"No," said I; "I have not heard that you claim exclusively any part of the moon; but there is not a spot on this habitable globe that I could affirm you do not claim; and there is none which you may not claim with as much color of right as you can have to Columbia River or its mouth."

"And how far would you consider," said he, "this exclusion of right to extend?"

"To all the shores of the South Sea," said I. "We know of no right that you have there."

"Suppose," said he, "Great Britain should undertake to make a settlement there, would you object to it?"

"I have no doubt we should," said I.

Jan. 29. — I was at the President's, and made to him a full verbal report of my conference with Mr. Canning on Saturday. He said he did not think it probable that Mr. Canning would be countenanced by his Government; but he might perhaps make report to them of our conferences, tinctured with the temper which he had shown in them. It would therefore be advisable that I should make a written minute of what passed between us, and keep it for future occasion.

Feb. 6. — I went for a few minutes into the hall of the Senate, and, finding them occupied upon business of little public interest, passed into the House of Representatives, where they were debating upon the General Appropriation bill, and particularly upon a motion made by Mr. Clay for an appropriation of an outfit and salary for a minister to any independent Government of South America. This has been Clay's principal instrument of opposition to Mr. Monroe's Administration through the whole of his first Presidential term. He has not succeeded in any part of it; but, as there has always been a portion of popular sentiment in favor of his projects, and as the flouting canvassers in the House are of his side, he has kept the ball up at every one of the four sessions. Towards the close of the last session, he obtained a vote, by a majority of four or five, that such an appropriation ought to be made. He now moved that the appropriation should be made, as an amendment to the general bill. It was opposed principally by Mr. Lowndes.

Feb. 11. — We had a small party, consisting of C. J. Ingersoll, N. Biddle, J. Sergeant, and W. S. Smith, to dine with us, and much conversation upon the merits of Kean, the English tragedian, who is now performing at Philadelphia. He is the popular favorite of the day in England; but he is of that class of actors described by Hamlet as " tearing a passion to tatters." His vice is exaggeration; and it is the vice of almost all the literature of the age. I have never seen upon the English stage a male performer of the highest order; none to compare with what I conceive Garrick to have been; none to compare with what I have seen performed by Mrs. Siddons, Mrs. Jordan, and Miss Farren in female parts. I have seen no more powerful actor than Kean in England; yet in his delineations of character I cannot divest myself of the impression produced by the likeness of a caricature.

Feb. 14. — [Electoral votes counted.] Party conflict has performed its entire revolution, and that unanimity of choice which began with George Washington has come round again in the person of James Monroe. In the survey of our national history, this latter unanimity is much more remarkable than the first. To this last unanimity there is the exception of a single vote, given by William Plumer, of New Hampshire, and that vote to my surprise and mortification, was for me. If there was an electoral vote in the Union which I thought sure for Mr. Monroe, it was that of Mr. Plumer. I deeply regretted the loss of Mr. Plumer's vote, because it implied his disapprobation of the principles of the Administration, and although by giving the vote for me he obviously exempted my share in the Administration from any essential portion of the censure, I could take no pleasure in that approbation which, though bestowed on me, was denied to the whole Administration.[2]

Feb. 16. — William A. Burwell, a member of the House of Representatives from Virginia, died this morning. He had been once for a short time private Secretary to Mr. Jefferson during his Presidency, and soon after was elected member of Congress, when little beyond the age necessary for qualification. He was always re-elected, and has been fourteen years a member. He was a man of moderate talents and respectable private character, full of Virginian principles and prejudices, a mixture of wisdom and Quixotism, which has done some good and much mischief to the Union. Burwell took no lead in anything. He scarcely ever spoke; never originated a measure of any public utility, but fancied himself a guardian of the liberties of the people against Executive encroachments. His delight was the consciousness of his own independence, and he thought it heroic virtue to ask no favors.

Feb. 22. — Ratifications of the Florida Treaty exchanged. General Vivés came, according to appointment, at one o'clock, to the office of the Department of State, with Mr. Salmon, his Secretary of Legation. Our preparations were not entirely completed when he came, but were ready within half an hour. I then took the treaty with the King of Spain's ratification myself; the General took the treaty with the President's ratification. Mr. Ironside held one of the originals executed by me and Mr. Onis, and Mr. Salmon another. Mr. Brent held the printed copy with the President's proclamation. Mr. Salmon read, from the original in his hand, the treaty, all the rest comparing their respective copies as he proceeded. I read in like manner the English, from the treaty which we retain with the Spanish ratification. Both the ratifications were then examined and found correct. . . I sent at the same time, to both Houses, the report upon weights and measures, prepared conformably to a resolution of the Senate of 3d March,

---

[2] Plumer's vote was given to Adams because he thought that Monroe had shown a "want of foresight and economy;" not, as is often said, because he wished Washington alone to have the honor of a unanimous vote for the Presidency.

1817, and one of the House of Representatives of the 14th of December, 1819.

And thus have terminated, blessed be God, two of the most memorable transactions of my life. This day, two years have elapsed since the Florida Treaty was signed. Let my sons, if they ever consult this record of their father's life, turn back to the reflections of the journal of that day. Let them meditate upon all the vicissitudes which have befallen the treaty, and of which this diary bears witness, in the interval between that day and this. Let them remark the workings of private interests, of perfidious fraud, of sordid intrigues, of royal treachery, of malignant rivalry, and of envy masked with patriotism, playing to and fro across the Atlantic into each other's hands, all combined to destroy this treaty between the signature and the ratification, and let them learn to put their trust in the overruling providence of God. I considered the signature of the treaty as the most important event of my life. It was an event of magnitude in the history of this Union. The apparent conclusion of the negotiation had been greatly and unexpectedly advantageous to this country. It had at once disconcerted and stimulated my personal antagonists and rivals. It promised well for my reputation in the public opinion. Under the petals of this garland of roses the Scapin, Onis, had hidden a viper. His mock sickness, his use of De Neuville as a tool to perpetrate a fraud which he did not dare attempt to carry through himself, his double dealing before and after the signature, his fraudulent declarations to me, and his shuffling equivocations here and in Spain, to acquire the reputation of having duped the President and me, were but materials in the hands of my enemies to dose me with poison extracted from the laurels of the treaty itself. An ambiguity of date, which I had suffered to escape my notice at the signature of the treaty, amply guarded against by the phraseology of the article, but leaving room to chicanery from a mere colorable question, was the handle upon which the King of Spain, his rapacious favorites, and American swindling land-jobbers in conjunction with them, withheld the ratification of the treaty, while Clay and his admirers here were snickering at the simplicity with which I had been bamboozled by the crafty Spaniard. The partisans of Crawford, and Crawford himself, were exulting in the same contemplation of a slur upon

my sagacity, and delighting in the supposed failure of the negotiation, because its failure brought unavoidable disgrace
upon me. By the goodness of that inscrutable Providence
which entraps dishonest artifice in its own snares, Onis divulged
his trick too soon for its success. Clay was the first to snuff
the fragrance of this hopeful blasting vapor, and to waft it as
his tribute of incense to the President. The demand of a formal declaration by Spain that the grants in question were by
the treaty null and void, completely and unequivocally obtained at last, has thoroughly disappointed all the calculators
of my downfall by the Spanish negotiation, and left me with
credit rather augmented than impaired by the result.

   Feb. 23. — The President read to me some detached paragraphs of the address which he proposes to deliver at his
second inauguration. Some question has been suggested to the
President whether he should deliver on that occasion any address; some of his Virginian friends having taken a fancy that
it is anti-republican and not authorized by the Constitution.
I entertained no such opinion, but told him that if he concluded
to omit the address, notice of his intention should be given
in the newspapers, as there would be a great concourse of people
to witness his taking the oath, and they would be much disappointed if there should be nothing but that naked ceremony.
He will refer the question to a Cabinet consultation.

   Feb. 25. — Hopkinson dined with us, and, according to his
engagement, came and sat with me an hour before dinner.
The object of his seeking this conversation with me was the
next Presidential election. He gave me to understand that he
was disposed to consider me as a candidate for that occasion;
that others were of similar disposition, but that it was necessary there should be a concert and understanding between
them, as there already was, and long had been between the
partisans of Mr. Crawford. He said that the extent and
activity of their intrigues was incredible, and unless systematically counteracted would infallibly be successful.

   I told Mr. Hopkinson that I was perfectly aware of the
exertions making by Mr. Crawford himself and his friends to
secure the Presidency at the next election. There were others
making exertions not less ardent and persevering for Mr.
Clinton, of New York. There was a third party, less apparent now, and the struggle of which was eventual, to depend

upon the conflict now raging in that State between Clinton and
Tompkins.   The State was now about equally divided, and,
as there is no marked difference of principle to contend for,
they are squabbling for men.   If either party should obtain
over the other such an ascendency as would carry a large majority of the State, its leader would be the candidate of New York
for the Presidency.   The only question between them will be
which shall be the man.   New York, at any rate, will have
a candidate of her own, and if both these rivals should be
out of the way she would sooner take up Mr. King than
resort to any other State.   The politics of Pennsylvania will
be greatly influenced by those of New York.   She too is a
divided State; but the scuffle for her Governor is between men
neither of whom has any prospects in the general government.   She will probably be an accessory to New York.
Whether any party or any one individual would support or
propose me as a candidate, I could not tell; but even in my
own native State of Massachusetts the predominating party,
the federalists, had a grudge against me, which they would not
lose the opportunity of indulging.   To one thing, however, I
had made up my mind: I would take no one step to advance or
promote pretensions to the Presidency.   If that office was to
be the prize of cabal and intrigue, of purchasing newspapers,
bribing by appointments, or bargaining for foreign missions, I
had no ticket in that lottery.   Whether I had the qualifications
necessary for a President of the United States, was, to say the
least, very doubtful to myself.   But that I had no talents for
obtaining the office by such means was perfectly clear.   I had
neither talent nor inclination for intrigue. . .

Hopkinson said that this very abstraction from all intrigues
would be my principal recommendation; that Crawford, having nothing but intrigue to support him, having manifested
utter incompetency to the very Department with which he is
charged, having never rendered one signal service to the country, and having a standing manifesto of charges affecting his
honor as a gentleman in the pamphlet of Governor Clarke
against him, would make no head, unless by mere want of
management in opposing him; that Clinton had embroiled
himself too much in the turmoil of his own passions, and in his
denunciation of the general government had completely failed
of substantiating his charges.   The prospects of Tompkins he

thought no better. He was deeply involved in debt, and stood equivocally before the public in relation to the settlement of his accounts.

March 1. — There was a Cabinet meeting at the President's, when he read the address which he had prepared to deliver at his second inauguration next Monday. But he proposed for regular consideration whether he should deliver any address at all. Mr. Thompson, the Secretary of the Navy, expressed again his doubts of the propriety of making any such speeches, which, he observed, were not required by the Constitution, and for which, he said, he did not see any adequate reason. The uniformity of the practice on former occasions might, he said, be a motive for continuing it, but if it were a new question he should be opposed to it.

My opinion was otherwise. Independent of the uniform usage, I thought there was a propriety in the thing itself. The inauguration was the only occasion presented by our institutions for direct intercourse between the Chief Magistrate and the nation. It was very proper at his first election to avail himself of it to declare succinctly the principles upon which he proposes to conduct his Administration; and when re-elected, there is equal propriety in reviewing before the world the progress of past events, as connected with the principles which have been pursued, and in announcing the perseverance with which they will be continued. There was nothing in the Constitution which required that the President should address Congress at the commencement of every session; but there was a manifest propriety that he should, and the practice was accordingly so. Mr. Thompson did not press the discussion, and the other members of the Administration agreed that there was no adequate reason for discontinuing the practice hitherto uniformly observed.

March 3. — Close of the Sixteenth Congress, and of the first term of the Administration of James Monroe. . . I walked home in company, as far as his house, with Mr. Calhoun. I found him in some degree dispirited by the results of the attacks systematically carried on through the whole Congress, but especially through the session just expired, against his management of the War Department. He thinks that the present embarrassments in the Administration all originated in two measures of the first session of Congress

under it — the repeal of the internal taxes, and the profuse
Pension Act. The present falling off in the revenue, he says,
ought to have been foreseen, and also that, on the failure of
revenue, the War Department would naturally be the first
upon which the scythe of retrenchment would fall. He observed also the coalition of Crawford's, Clinton's, and Clay's
partisans, though with views quite hostile to each other, in the
assaults of this session against the Administration; the vote of
thanks proposed by Clay to the Speaker, Taylor; the appointment by Taylor of the most violent opponents of the Administration upon committees; the combinations of the Georgia,
Tennessee, Kentucky, New York, and Vermont members, devoted to their respective leaders, and joining all their forces
against the Administration. All this is unquestionably true.
There have also been transactions in the War Department, in
the Post-Office, and in the Bank of the United States which
have unfortunately given handle to every class of disaffection.
Jackson's Seminole campaign, the Florida Treaty, and the
South American insurgents, have all been used in turn as
weapons of annoyance. By the practical operation of our
Government, the whole system of our politics is inseparably
linked with the views of aspirants to the Presidential succession; and by the peculiarity of our present position, the prospects of all the candidates in reserve for the next Presidency,
excepting the Vice-President, and setting aside the Secretary
of State, depend upon the failure of the present Administration for their success. The worst of it is that this applies more
forcibly to Crawford, a leading member of the Administration
himself, than to any other. Crawford has been a worm preying upon the vitals of the Administration within its own body.
He was the instigator and animating spirit of the whole movement, both in Congress and at Richmond, against Jackson and
the Administration. In all the vicissitudes of the Spanish negotiations, wherever there has been difficulty or prospect of
failure he has been felt when he could not be seen; and all the
attacks against the War Department during this Congress
have been stimulated by him and promoted by his partisans.
An essential impulse to this course on his part is the knowledge
he has obtained that Calhoun is not prepared to support him
for the next Presidency.

CHAPTER VIII

1821–1825

INTERNAL REVENUE — QUARREL WITH JONATHAN RUSSELL — THE HOLY ALLIANCE — THE MONROE DOCTRINE — ELECTION INTRIGUES — TOUR OF LAFAYETTE — ELECTION GOES TO THE HOUSE — CHOSEN PRESIDENT.

Washington, March 5, 1821. — Second inauguration of James Monroe as President of the United States. . . . A quarter before twelve I went to the President's house, and the other members of the Administration immediately afterwards came there. The Marshal and one of his deputies was there, but no assemblage of people. The President, attired in a full suit of black broadcloth of somewhat antiquated fashion, with shoe-and-knee buckles, rode in a plain carriage with four horses and a single colored footman. The Secretaries of State, the Treasury, War, and the Navy followed, each in a carriage-and-pair. There was no escort, nor any concourse of people on the way. But on alighting at the Capitol a great crowd of people were assembled and the avenues to the hall of the house were so choked up with persons pressing for admittance that it was with the utmost difficulty that the President made his way through them into the House. Mr. Canning and Mr. Antrobus, in full Court dress uniforms, were in the midst of this crowd, unable to obtain admission. We got in at last, after several minutes of severe pressure. There was not a soldier present, nor a constable distinguishable by any badge of office. The President took a seat on a platform just before the Speaker's chair. The Chief Justice was seated at his right hand, the other Judges of the Supreme Court in chairs fronting him; the President of the Senate and late Speaker of the House at his left hand; the heads of the Departments sidelong at the right; and the foreign Ministers in the seats of the members at the left. The House and galleries were as thronged as possible. There was much disorder of loud talking and agitation in the gallery, not altogether ceasing even while the President was reading his address, which he did immediately after taking the oath. At this ceremony the Chief Justice merely held the book, the President repeating the oath in the words prescribed by the Constitution. The address was delivered in a suitably grave and rather low tone of voice. After it was finished, several persons came up to the President and shook hands with him by way of congratulation. At his departure from the House there was a cheering shout from the people in the galleries, and the music of the Marine Band played both at his entrance and departure. I returned home with my family, and immediately afterwards went to the President's house, where there was a numerous circle for congratulation. I then passed a couple of hours at my office, and in the evening attended a ball at Brown's Hotel. The President and his family were there, but retired before supper. We came home immediately after, and finished a fatiguing and bustling day about midnight.

March 9. — Mr. Clay called at the office. He is pressing upon the President his claim for a half outfit for the negotiation of the Commercial Convention of 3d July, 1815, with Great Britain. I told him I thought it could not be allowed without a special appropriation for it by Congress, to which he said he did not know that he should have any objection; but he wants the money now. . . I had some conversation with him on political topics, and on his own present retirement from public life. I asked him if it would be consistent with his views, in case there should within two or three years be a vacancy in any of the missions abroad, to accept an appointment to it.

He said he was obliged to me for the question, but it would not. The state of his private affairs, and his duty to his family, had dictated to him the determination of a temporary retirement from the public service. But, by a liberal arrangement with him, the Bank of the United States had engaged him as their standing counsel in the States of Kentucky and Ohio. He expected that in the course of three or four years this would relieve him from all the engagements in which he had been involved, and enable him to return to the public service. In that case he should prefer over all others the station from which he had just retired, a seat in the House of Representatives, because that would be the place where he could hope to render the most useful service to the country. But, he said, he considered the situation of our public affairs now as very critical and dangerous to the Administration. Mr. Monroe had just been re-elected with apparent unanimity, but he had not the slightest influence in Congress. His career was considered as closed. There was nothing further to be expected by him or from him. Looking at Congress, they were a collection of materials, and how much good and how much evil might be done with them accordingly as they should be well or ill directed. But henceforth there was and would not be a man in the United States possessing less personal influence over them than the President.

I saw Mr. Clay's drift in these remarks, which was to magnify his own importance and to propitiate me in favor of his outfit claim. His total forbearance of attack upon me, either by himself or his underlings, in the late session of Congress, and his advance through Mr. Brush, I attribute to the same cause. I told him the President must rely, as he had done, upon the public sentiment and upright intention to support him, and with these his Administration must get along as well as it could. . . I said I also regretted the difference between his views and those of the Administration upon South American affairs. That the final issue of their present struggle would be their entire independence of Spain I had never doubted. That it was our true policy and duty to take no part in the contest I was equally clear. The principle of neutrality to all foreign wars was, in my opinion, fundamental to the continuance of our liberties and of our Union. So far as they were contending for independence, I wished well to their cause; but I had seen and yet see no prospect that they would establish free or liberal institutions of government. They are not likely to promote the spirit either of freedom or order by their example. They have not the first elements of good or free government. Arbitrary power, military and ecclesiastical, was stamped upon their education, upon their habits, and upon all their institutions. Civil dissension was infused into all their seminal principles. War and mutual destruction was in every member of their organization, moral, political, and physical. I had little expectation of any beneficial result to this country from any future connection with them, political or commercial. We should derive no improvement to our own institutions by any communion with theirs. Nor was there any appearance of a disposition in them to take any political lesson from us. . .

He did not pursue the discussion. Clay is an eloquent man, with very popular manners and great political management. He is, like almost all the eminent men of this country, only half educated. His school has been the world, and in that he is a proficient. His morals, public and private, are loose, but he has all the virtues indispensable to a popular man. As he is the first very distinguished man that the Western country has presented as a statesman to the Union, they are proportionably proud of him, and, being a native of Virginia, he has all the benefit of that clannish preference which Virginia has always given to her sons. Clay's temper is impetuous, and his ambition impatient. He has long since marked me as the principal rival in his way, and has taken no more pains to disguise his hostility than was necessary for decorum and to avoid shocking the public opinion. His future fortune, and mine, are in wiser hands than ours; I have never, even defensively, repelled his attacks. Clay has large and liberal views of public affairs, and that sort of generosity which attaches individuals to his person. As President of the Union, his administration would be a perpetual succession of intrigue and management with the legislature. It would also be sectional in its spirit, and sacrifice all other interests to those of the Western country and the slaveholders.

March 14. — The dinner was this day given to Mr. Clay at Brown's Hotel, at which he was toasted and made a speech. This is an English practice which has never been usual in this country. Clay seems to be desirous of introducing it here. It is a convenient practice for men who wish to keep themselves forever in the public eye. It is for such men a triple alliance of flattery, vanity, and egotism. The toast is always a fulsome compliment to the man, made to his face, and he makes it the occasion to manifest his rosy pudency in receiving it, and then delivering another semi-transparent panegyric upon himself, filled with professions of his gratitude and his patriotic prin-

ciples. Clay makes it also an occasion for doling out his
politics in driblets. It gives what they call in England a clever
man an opportunity of saying smart things and setting clap-
traps; but in England, when they have once begun, they go
round the table; everybody is toasted, and everybody makes a
speech of acknowledgment. It is a mixture of wit and dulness,
eloquence and nonsense, which I always found exceedingly
irksome and tedious.

March 19. — There was a Cabinet meeting at the President's, attended by all the members of the Administration
excepting Mr. Wirt, the Attorney-General, who is confined by
illness. The object of the meeting was to determine what
should be done with regard to the fortifications upon Dauphin
Island, at the mouth of the Mississippi River. They are part
of an extensive system for fortifying the whole coast of the
United States, for their protection, in the event of any future
war, against such invasions as we suffered in the last war with
England. The President, who formed this project, chiefly
from the experience of the defenceless state of the country in
that war, had set his heart upon its accomplishment, and looks
to it as one of the great objects by which his Administration
may be signalized in the view of posterity. Large appropriations have been made to effect it, for several successive years,
by Congress; but now, in the penury of the Treasury, and the
passion for retrenchment, they have not only reduced the
amount of appropriations, but withheld them for the fulfilment of contracts already made — for that of Dauphin Island
in particular.

March 22. — Mr. Calhoun called at my house, and I went
to the Navy Department to complete the arrangements for
taking possession of the Floridas. We have stipulated to
transport the Spanish officers and troops with their baggage
to the Havanna, and, by a liberal construction of the article,
have considered this engagement as including that of furnishing provision for them on the passage. We have also engaged
to provide an escort for them.

March 25. — I went with Dr. Thornton this morning to
the Quaker meeting. There were from forty to fifty men
present, and about as many females. We sat nearly two hours
in perfect silence — no moving of the spirit; and I seldom, in
the course of my life, passed two hours more wearily. Perhaps

from not having been inured to this form of public worship, I found myself quite unable to reduce my mind to that musing meditation which makes the essence of this form of devotion. It was rambling from this world to the next, and from the next back to this, chance-directed; and, curious to know what was really passing in the minds of those around me, I asked Dr. Thornton, after we came out, what he had been thinking of while we had been there. He said he did not know; he had been much inclined to sleep. Solitude and silence are natural allies, and social silence may be properly allied with social labor. But social meditation is an incongruity. I felt, on coming from this meeting, as if I had wasted precious time.

April 7. — Mr. T. P. Barton, came, a son of the late Dr. Barton, of Philadelphia, a young man who is going to spend four years in Europe for improvement — that is to say, to make himself good for nothing. He was with his father in London when I saw him there in 1815, and was then a boy. He is now a handsome young man, just fit to be ruined by a residence in Europe for improvement.

Oct. 15. — Mr. Calhoun came to mention the determination of the President upon some question relating to the barracks at St. Augustine. He also spoke of the altercations between General Jackson and Colonel Callava and Judge Fromentin, about which he is much concerned. He thinks that the President ought to come immediately to the city and determine upon the course to be pursued by the Administration in these cases. I concur in that opinion. Calhoun fears that a wrong direction may be given to public sentiment on these transactions by the spirit of faction and the crude precipitancy of newspaper commentaries. Calhoun is a man of fair and candid mind, of honorable principles, of clear and quick understanding, of cool self-possession, of enlarged philosophical views, and of ardent patriotism. He is above all sectional and factious prejudices more than any other statesman of this Union with whom I have ever acted. He is more sensitive to the transient manifestations of momentary public opinion, more afraid of the first impressions of the public opinion, than I am.

Oct. 20. — There were received this morning from the President a number of bundles of papers, forwarded by him from Oakhill, some of them public papers to be deposited at the Department, others which he had directed to be sent to his house. Among them was a letter from Spencer Roane, the Virginian Chief Justice, enclosing to him his lucubrations in the Richmond *Enquirer* against the Supreme Court of the United States. George Hay told me last summer that Roane was the author of the pieces signed " Algernon Sydney," against the Supreme Court, and that they had been excited by the words " we command you " in the mandamus in the case of Cohens vs. Virginia. Roane, in his letter to the President, glorifies himself as a very virtuous patriot, and holds himself out as a sort of Jefferson or Madison. All this is " close ambition varnished o'er with zeal." Jefferson and Madison did attain power by organizing and heading a system of attack upon the Washington Administration, chiefly under the banners of State rights and State sovereignty. They argued and scolded against all implied powers, and pretended that the Government of the Union had no powers but such as were expressly delegated by the Constitution. They succeeded. Mr. Jefferson was elected President of the United States, and the first thing he did was to purchase Louisiana — an assumption of implied power greater in itself and more comprehensive in its consequences than all the assumptions of implied powers in the twelve years of the Washington and Adams Administrations put together. Through the sixteen years of the Jefferson and Madison Administrations not the least regard was paid to the doctrines of rejecting implied powers, upon which those gentlemen had vaulted into the seat of government, with the single exception that Mr. Madison negatived a bill for applying public money to the public internal improvement of the country. But the same Mr. Madison signed a bill for incorporating the Bank of the United States, against which he and all the Virginian party had stubbornly contended as unconstitutional.

Nov. 4. — Mr. Crawford's character is fully developed in Governor Clarke's pamphlet, and, after reflecting upon the lineaments of that portrait, I cannot be surprised at anything bearing the mark of congenial features. A worthless and desperate man, against whom I have been compelled to testify in a Court of justice, attempts, in the face of his own conscience, to save himself from infamy by discrediting my testimony, and finds in Mr. Crawford a ready and willing auxiliary. To support him in this scandalous purpose, Crawford solemnly deposes in a court of justice that which is not true. I cannot yet bring myself to believe that it has been by wilful falsehood. Ambition debauches memory itself. Crawford has positively sworn to things as requested by me, which by his own showing he knew only by hearsay from the President. I never did request them. He has sworn to things as having been told him of my saying in February, 1818, bottomed upon facts which I did not know till the following March. In the fairest possible view that can be taken of his deposition, he began by a gross and total misconception, and has ended by a misrepresentation equally gross and total of the whole subject.

Nov. 23. — Cabinet meeting at the President's at noon — full.

Nov. 25. — The French Minister, Baron Hyde de Neuville, came, and had a long and somewhat angry conversation with me upon the state of our affairs, and especially upon the case of the *Apollon.* He said that he had informed me that he had been instructed by his Government to continue the discussion concerning that vessel, the *Neptune,* and the *Eugénie;* and he wished me to answer his last note upon that subject, upon which he should reply according to the instructions which he had received; that he was instructed to keep that affair distinct from all others, and that it must be settled the first of all. . . He intimated rather indistinctly that there ought to be an enquiry in Congress as to the legality of the Treasury Order of 6th May, 1818, and said that within two or three months American vessels would be arrested in the French ports for the affair of the *Apollon,* the *Neptune,* and the *Eugénie.* . . When he came to his declaration that American vessels would be arrested in the ports of France, I paused until he ran through his declamation about the honor of Captain Edou, and took no notice of his hint about an enquiry in Congress. As soon as he stopped, I said that I had understood him to say that, upon his word of honor, American vessels would within three months be arrested in the ports of France.

He said that the declaration upon his word of honor related not to that, but to something else. But as a private individual he had declared as his opinion that within three months American vessels would be detained in France unless satisfaction were given for the cases of the *Apollon,* the *Neptune,* and the

Eugénie, because they were considered, universally considered, as outrages upon the flag and national honor of France. They would be brought forward in the Chamber of Deputies, and measures of reprisal demanded and unanimously agreed to; for the Libéraux would be more ardent for them than any others.

I said I had understood him to say on his word of honor that American vessels would within three months be arrested in France; I was happy to hear his explanation that he only gave this as his private opinion, and should make report of the whole to-morrow to the President.

He seemed startled at this, but said I might report to the President what I pleased.

I said I should report exactly what has passed between us, and no more; as I had first understood him, and as he had afterwards explained.

He then, in a loud and peremptory tone, rising from his seat and with vehement gesture, said, "Well, sir, since you think proper to report to the President what I came here to say in confidential conversation with you, I desire you to tell him from me, as my individual opinion, that if satisfaction is not made to France in the affair of the *Apollon,* the *Neptune,* and the *Eugénie,* La France doit leur déclarer La Guerre."

These last words he spoke in a manner nearly frantic, dwelling upon the word *guerre* with a long and virulent emphasis and, without waiting for a reply, rushed out of the room, and through the inner and outer street doors into the street. I followed him composedly with a light. Antoine happened to be in the entry as he sallied forth, and followed him to the street door, calling out, " Monsieur! vous avez oublié votre surtout." He turned back and put on his great-coat, but said nothing further to me.

Nov. 26. — I told the President the substance of the conversation which I had last evening with the French Minister, at which he was much surprised and quite indignant. I told him I thought it would require a modification of his message to Congress, and that instead of saying, as he had proposed, that with the exception of the disagreement upon the commercial negotiation our relations with France are friendly, it would be necessary to refer immediately to the affair of the *Apollon,* and the claim under the Louisiana Treaty, and to communicate all the correspondence upon both. I considered this explosion of De Neuville's as offering a fair opportunity for both, and I thought it fortunate that it had happened before the message was delivered; for if that had spoken of friendly relations without communicating the papers on those two subjects, and immediately afterward this quarrel had burst upon the nation, the Administration would have been liable to the charge of having suppressed the real state of things.

Dec. 1. — Mr. Calhoun called this morning at my house, and I consulted him with regard to the election of a Speaker. Found him very decidedly against Taylor, but not decided whom to support in his stead. He did not expect Mr. Lowndes would be here, and, if here, did not believe he would consent to be a candidate: he had been too much mortified at his failure last year. Nelson would be friendly to the Administration, but the principal objection to him was his being a Virginian. There was already an inordinate proportion of citizens of that State in all the Departments of the Government.

Dec. 2. — I called on J. W. Taylor at his lodgings, and found him in his chamber, apparently under some agitation. After some conversation upon the census and the publication of the secret journals of the old Congress, and some accidents which have befallen some of the members of the New York delegation on their way, he asked me if I knew whether Mr. Rodney had arrived. I did not; but, perceiving the drift of the question, I told him that I understood Rodney was to be his competitor to-morrow. He said he had just now for the first time been so informed; and that he understood Mr. Rodney was the candidate favored at Washington. I said that if by Washington he meant the Administration of the general government, so far as I was personally concerned in it, Mr. Rodney was not my favored candidate. As far as I had a right to any preference, it had been in his favor, because he had been the Speaker before, and because a question of re-election was different from a question of election for the first time.

Dec. 3. — This day commenced the first session of the Seventeenth Congress; there was a quorum formed of both Houses; there were seven ballots for a Speaker in the House of Representatives without affecting a choice; about sixty votes for Taylor; upwards of a hundred against him — runing for Rodney, McLane, and others.

Dec. 4. — Mr. Canning, whom I had appointed to meet at one o'clock, came, and was with me nearly three hours, conversing on a great variety of subjects in a manner entirely desultory. . .

He spoke about the slave-trade, and asked me if I had seen a letter from Sir George Collier, recently published in the newspapers. I had, but made no remark upon it. He asked if we had any cruiser upon the African coast now. I said, the same Lieutenant Stockton who had captured the four French schooners. He asked if we could not so accommodate our naval arrangements as to increase our force there. I said I could not exactly say; but our force was sufficient to banish our flag from the whole coast. There had not been found for these two years a single slave-trader wearing the American flag. I asked him if he recollected the hint I had given him last spring to propose to his Government to advise their ally the King of Denmark to look a little at what was going on at his island of St. Thomas. He said certainly and he had availed himself of it. I said I had seen in our newspapers within these two days a notice from Copenhagen that the late Governor of St. Thomas, Bentzon, had been convicted of slave-trade participation and sentenced to pay a heavy fine. Canning said it might very probably be the result of our former conversation.

I told him we had almost got into a quarrel with France about these captures of Lieutenant Stockton. The French authorities in the West Indies, and the French Minister here, were all on fire about the outrage upon the French flag, and they had sent me volumes of testimony given by the slave-traders themselves, to prove Lieutenant Stockton was a pirate. Not only so, but the French Minister, with a lofty tone, maintained that these vessels were engaged in lawful trade — greatly injured persons. Three of four vessels were recaptured from their prize crews. Two of them went back, not to Guadaloupe, but to French Guiana, and there trumped up this story of interruption in their lawful trade by the pirate Stockton. The third is brought into Boston, and the French Minister peremptorily demands that she should be delivered up to the French Consul or to her owners, and in one of his notes to me says, "Le sort du quatrième n'est pas encore connu." I had told the Baron de Neuville that I could inform him what that "sort" was. She returned to the coast of Africa, took in her pre-engaged cargo of one hundred and fifty slaves, and carried them and landed them in the face of day at Guadaloupe, with Lieutenant Inman and the prize crew from whom the vessel had been recaptured all the time on board. Canning said he hoped these facts would be made known to the world. I assured him that indeed they should.

The President told me that the House of Representatives had chosen Mr. Philip P. Barbour, of Virginia, their Speaker. He was a new candidate, started this morning, and came in at the twelfth ballot, by a vote of eighty-eight upon one hundred and seventy-three.

Dec. 21. — Mr. Calhoun brought a letter from a person named Clarke, containing indications of suspicions against Hassler, the astronomer, who attended on the Commission under the fifth article of the Treaty of Ghent, as having been too intimate with the British astronomer, Tiarks. By their observations they have brought the forty-fifth degree of latitude nearly a mile further south, where it touches Lake Champlain, than it had been settled by former observations, by which a place called Rouse's Point, with costly fortifications erected upon it, will be thrown within the British line. This has given great uneasiness in this country, and especially in the State of New York, where Rouse's Point is situated. This Mr. Clarke tells a story of Dr. Tiarks, the British astronomer, having said to him in a steamboat, supposing him to be a Canadian, that Elliot, the first astronomer on the American side, had been a troublesome old fellow, but that Hassler was more accommodating, and then, pointing to the spot where they found the forty-fifth degree touch the lake, had said, "We shall run the line to end there." Upon this foundation Clarke built his surmise that Hassler had been corrupted. I told Mr. Calhoun that we had heard of this, and enquired into it more than two years ago, and found it was mere unwarranted suspicion.

Dec. 23. — Mr. Sparks, the Unitarian, preached for the first time at the Capitol, to a crowded auditory. His election as chaplain to the House of Representatives occasioned much surprise, and has been followed by unusual symptoms of intolerance. Mr. Hawley, the Episcopal preacher at St. John's Church, last Sunday preached a sermon of coarse invective upon the House, who, he said, by this act had voted Christ out-of-doors; and he enjoined upon all the people of his flock not to set their feet within the Capitol to hear Mr. Sparks.

Dec. 24. — I asked Stackelberg, the Swedish Chargé d'Affaires, whether he had seen the quarrel between Hyde de Neuville and Canning, in the entrance-hall at the President's.

He had seen it all; and twice interposed between them. I asked him what they had said. He answered he did not know; by which he merely meant to decline telling what they had said.

Poletica was a little more communicative. He said that the quarrel had long been brewing; that one of its principal recent causes was a letter of Sir George Collier's, lately published in all the newspapers, and containing severe reflections upon the French Government, as still suffering the slave-trade to be carried on under their flag. Mr. de Neuville had been much hurt at this letter, and Canning had indulged himself in some sarcastic remarks upon it. At the ball given by De Neuville last week in honor of the Duchess of Angoulême's birthday, Mr. Canning went away before supper. De Neuville spoke of this to Canning while sitting at table at the President's, and expressed his regret at the circumstance. Canning, it seems, answered that there were places where he took pleasure in staying, and others where attendance was mere compliance with forms. De Neuville was much offended at this, but said nothing more at table. They left the drawing-room after dinner nearly at the same time, and before the carriage of either of them had arrived. While in the entrance-hall, De Neuville took Canning aside, to ask explanation of what he had said at table, but, instead of being satisfied with his answer, was more incensed by it. The irritation increased on both sides, until De Neuville, raising his voice, said, " Oui, Monsieur, je vous le répète, en présence de tout le Corps Diplomatique, que la franchise et la politesse sont des qualités éminemment françaises."

Dec. 29. — Mr. Newton, Chairman of the Committee of Commerce, came this morning to the office in high spirits, saying he had brought me good news. He had in his hand a newspaper of the island of St. Christopher's with a letter from John Hollingsworth at St. Eustatius, enclosing it to Mr. Rodney, the member of the House who had given it to Mr. Newton. The newspaper contained a petition from the Legislative Assembly of the island of St. Kitts to the British House of Commons, imploring a relaxation of the restrictions upon the commerce between the West India Islands and the United States of America, and representing the islands as on the brink of ruin from perseverance in that system and from the counteracting navigation laws of the United States. Newton insisted upon reading to me the whole petition, which is long, and will serve as a full answer to the memorial which is coming on to Congress from his constituents of Norfolk.

Dec. 31. — Mr. Timothy Fuller of Massachusetts came. He spoke of the caucus in the South Carolina Legislature — one hundred and ten members, fifty-seven of whom had agreed to recommend Mr. William Lowndes as a candidate for the next Presidential election. He spoke also of the deputation of members of Congress from the North and the South who had waited upon Mr. Calhoun last Friday and invited him to stand a candidate also at the next election, to which he had, after some hesitation, assented; and since that time there had been an active canvass going on, and scarcely a member whose dispositions had not been sounded with a view to making partisans for him. Fuller said that he was afraid of appearing officious. I had appeared indisposed to making any exertions in my own favor; but if something should not be done to counteract the caballing, public opinion would be forestalled, and a party too strong to be broken would be formed. He had no interest of his own in view. He did not even intend to be a candidate for the next Congress. But he felt a pride in the honor of his country, and was unwilling to see its highest dignity thus disposed of. He should, therefore, on his return home suggest to some gentlemen the propriety of moving, to show at least that they are not disposed to abandon the claim to a candidate of their own.

Jan. 1, 1822. — This year began, as the last had commenced and closed, in solitary meditation. Mr. Bailey was here this morning on the subject concerning which Mr. Fuller spoke last evening. He was anxious that some answer to the slander in the Washington *City Gazette* of Saturday should be published; which I dissuaded. . . .

At noon we attended the drawing-room at the President's. The crowd of company was as great as I have ever known it on any similar occasion. We remained not long there. The Indians paid their visit after we came away.

Jan. 2. — I took over to the President a translation of the Spanish Minister Anduaga's letter of 27th December to me, and a copy of my answer. Mr. Thompson, the Secretary of the Navy, came in immediately afterwards. There was some conversation relating to the capture by Lieutenant Stockton, in the *Alligator,* of a Portuguese vessel which fired upon him, mistaking him for a South American Privateer. Stockton has sent her into Boston. The President read a letter which he had written to General Jackson, accepting his resignation as Governor of Florida. It was expressed in warm though general terms of regard, and Mr. Thompson objected that it would import the President's approbation of General Jackson's late transactions in Florida. This led to some discussion of them, in which Mr. Thompson admitted that he had a very imperfect knowledge of all the circumstances, not having seen a great portion of the papers, but upon the facts, as far as he was acquainted with them, his opinion was unfavorable to Jackson. The President asked him to read all the papers; which he promised to do. The President asked me if I thought the expressions in the letter were too strong. I said they were such that, after receiving the letter, General Jackson would naturally not expect that the President would at any future period express public disapprobation of anything done by him as Governor of Florida. But, in my opinion, there was not one word too much. General Jackson I thought had done nothing, with the exception of the papers seized at St. Augustine, but what he had a right to do. It was indeed impossible for me to scan the actions of General Jackson as I might those of an indifferent person. General Jackson had rendered such services to this nation that it was impossible for me to contemplate his character or conduct without veneration. But, setting this aside, in the whole of his transactions with Callava and Fromentin I saw nothing in what Jackson did which he had not the right, nay, more, which he was not bound in duty, to do.

Jan. 3. — W. Plumer, of New Hampshire, was at the office, and told me he had this morning seen and conversed with Mr.

Calhoun, who had assured him that his assent to stand as a candidate at the next election for the Presidency was qualified — a candidate against any Southern man. His own opinion had invariably been in favor of a Northern man for the next President, and personally for me. But the intimation given to him had been that I should have no support from the North; and in that case he had been willing to stand against any Southern man, and particularly against Mr. Crawford, whose principles and character he could not approve.

I asked Plumer if Calhoun had told him that he had spoken in the same manner to the deputation that went to his house and invited him to stand as a candidate. He had not. Plumer thought it would be advisable that some manifestation from the North should be made as evidence of opinions there. The Massachusetts and Maine Legislatures are now in session. Maine has been so canvassed against the current for three years as not to be yet prepared to act; and I told Plumer that if a legislative opinion should now be taken in Massachusetts, I should wish it might be confined to the Republican party, and with express assignment of the movements in South Carolina and here as the occasion of it. He said he would write to Fuller.

Jan. 6. — I had much conversation with Ninian Edwards, who told me much of Crawford's electioneering practices at the public expense. D. P. Cook has offered a resolution in the House of Representatives calling upon the Secretary of the Treasury for information, which will show the appointment of Jesse B. Thomas, a Senator from the State of Illinois, to examine land offices and banks in four or five of the Western States. And under this commission Thomas has been travelling from land office to land office, over all those States, everywhere canvassing for Crawford and reviling me. Edwards says that at Zanesville Thomas had a sharp quarrel with two men because they would not pledge themselves to support the election of Crawford. Edwards laughed at me, too, for having last winter appointed Radcliff to go for the votes of the State of Mississippi. He, too, took three months to perform his journey, which he ought to have completed in six weeks, and went electioneering for Crawford all the way. The poor creature died a few weeks after he came back. Now, Crawford has been seven years working himself up-hill in this manner, and has three years more to work himself up to the summit. What chance against him will a man have who neither can nor will use such means?

April 19. — Cabinet meeting of four hours, from one to five, at the President's, where the various questions which have already arisen from the recognition of the new Southern Governments were discussed. The first was, whether Ministers of Plenipotentiary rank should be immediately sent to them all, or whether we should wait first to receive Ministers from them and return Ministers of the same rank as they may send here. Mr. Crawford was for sending immediately four Ministers, without standing upon any point of etiquette.

I thought the best course would be to wait and reciprocate; to receive Mr. Torres as Chargé d'Affaires from the republic of Colombia; to receive the Minister from Mexico when he shall arrive, and immediately send one of the rank in return; to ascertain from the Governments of Colombia, Buenos Ayres, and Chili upon what footing they wish the political relations with us to be placed; and to send Ministers Plenipotentiary wherever they send Ministers of that rank to us.

April 21. — Besides the usual occupation of reading the letters and dispatches and newspapers that come by mail, I was involuntarily engaged in translating into verse a passage of seventeen lines in Horace's *Art of Poetry,* which diverted me from other objects of more importance.

April 22. — I found the President still undetermined whether to send a Minister immediately to the republic of Colombia or to send back Mr. Todd, or merely to receive Torres as Chargé d'Affaires and wait for further movements from thence. He concluded by merely directing me to write to Torres, informing him that whenever it shall suit him to come here I will present him, as Chargé d'Affaires of the republic of Colombia to the President. He said that from the letter which Mr. Clay had written to Woodson, to be shown to him, he had conjectured that Clay himself was disposed to accept one of these new missions. But Mr. Clay had pursued such a course of uniform hostility to this Administration that he had no pretension to notice from it, unless it should be to show that opposition was the way to favor.

I told the President of the conversation which I had with Mr. Clay before he left this last spring after the termination of his service in Congress, when I had asked if it would suit his convenience, in case a vacancy in any of the missions abroad should occur, to accept it; and he told me it would not, the state of his private affairs requiring all his attention, and the liberality of the Bank of the United States, in making him their agent-general for the States of Kentucky and Ohio, giving him the means of relieving himself from his embarrassments in the course of four years. I said now that my intention was, if Mr. Clay had answered that a mission abroad would be acceptable, to have named him for consideration to the President whenever a vacancy should occur. I added my belief, nevertheless, that Mr. Clay now wished for the offer of one of these missions and that he would accept that of Mexico, and perhaps that of Colombia, but not either of the others. But I distrusted so much Mr. Clay's views in relation to South American affairs, and was so apprehensive of their tendency to entangle us, that I doubted much the propriety of appointing him. I should have no objection to his going to Buenos Ayres or Chili, where he could do no harm. I esteemed the talents of Mr. Clay, and knew him to have some good qualities. But his ambition was too ardent to be very scrupulous or delicate, and he was too much addicted to intrigue.

The President concurred in these opinions, and said he had not determined upon any of the nominations to be made, but he had thought of selecting one from each of the four great sections of the Union. I said I had no favorites to recommend; but I told him what had passed between Mr. Sanford and me, and my opinion of Sanford's merits and pretensions, and I mentioned Mr. Russell, and also the applications of Colonel Wool and W. G. D. Worthington. The President spoke of General S. Smith and General Scott as having been recommended to him. I asked him if General Jackson had occurred to him. He said he had; but he was afraid of his getting us into a quarrel. . .

Mr. Russell left at the office with Mr. Brent a duplicate of his letter of 11th February, 1815, to Mr. Monroe, then Secretary, which has been called for by a resolution of the House of Representatives at the motion of Mr. Floyd. It is a letter of seven folio sheets of paper, and amounts to little less than a denunciation of the majority of the Ghent mission for proposing the article recognizing the fishery right and the British right to navigate the Mississippi, in the proposal of which he himself concurred. Russell wrote this letter at Paris, where we all were, without ever communicating it to me, or letting me know that he had any intention of writing such a letter. It is a most elaborate, disingenuous, and sophistical argument against principles in which he concurred, and the joint letter of 25th December, 1814, to which he signed his name. His motives for writing it then to a Virginian Secretary of State, under a Virginian President, were at once to recommend himself to their sectional prejudices about the Mississippi, and to give me a secret stab in their esteem and favor, for future effect. His motive now for abetting Floyd in his call of the paper, as a public document, is to decry my chances of popular favor in the Western country. It is, I doubt not, part of a system of measures concerted with others, the development of which is proceeding from day to day.

Calhoun called at the office with a letter recommending some person to an office. He spoke with great bitterness of Crawford, of whose manoeuvring and intrigues to secure the election to the next Presidency, and to blast the Administration of Mr. Monroe, of which he is a member, he (Calhoun) has a full and thorough knowledge. He said there had never been a man in our history, who had risen so high, of so corrupt a character or upon so slender a basis of service; and that he (Calhoun) had witnessed the whole series of Crawford's operations from the winter of 1816 to this time.

April 29. — Mr. Jonathan Russell came for the letter of the President to the Emperor of China, and mine to the Viceroy of Canton. He said he liked my substitute for the draft of the President's letter much better than the draft itself. Dropping this subject, I told Mr. Russell that I thought the letter he had left at the Department to be communicated to the House of Representatives in answer to Dr. Floyd's resolution was a very extraordinary paper, and his conduct in the whole transaction relating to it as equally extraordinary. He knew I had been at Paris, and that he was in habits of daily and professedly friendly intercourse with me when the original letter was written. That he should have written it without notice to his colleagues, whose conduct it so severely arraigned, was strange. That he should now have furnished a paper as the duplicate of that letter, but materially differing from it, was still more so. . . I then showed him on the book of records of the Department the letter from Mr. Monroe to the mission of 19th October, 1814, which was received on the 24th of November of that year, and also another letter of 6th October, 1814, containing the same authority, but which I told him had not been received by the mission. I further told him that President Madison by a message to Congress of 9th October, 1814, had communicated to Congress so much of our instruction as would show the terms upon which we were authorized to make peace. The instructions of 15th April, 1813, were included in that communication, but the passage cited in the duplicate in proof of violated instructions was omitted as having been subsequently cancelled.

During the whole of this exposition Russell's countenance gave the usual indications of detected imposture, alternately flushing and turning pale. He said he had no recollection of the receipt of this letter of 19th October, 1814; and asked if I thought the " status ante bellum " included necessarily the right of the British to navigate the Mississippi.

I said that was a matter upon which he was at liberty to make his argument; but when with the authority to conclude on the basis of the " status ante bellum " was connected the omission from the instruction communicated to Congress of the paragraph cited by him as having been violated; when copies of these instructions thus communicated were transmitted to us, as showing the terms on which we were authorized to conclude, it was impossible for me to doubt that the passage now cited by him had been cancelled. At all events it had been so considered at Ghent, for this instruction of 19th October had not only been received, but was actually produced in the course of the discussions of the mission.

He said, if I recollected that, there could be no question but it was so. But, he said, he could assure me he had not acted in this case in concert with my enemies, and had never written or published a word against me in the newspapers. He had acted from no motive of hostility to me.

I then said to him, " Mr. Russell, I wish not to enquire into your motives. Henceforth, as a public man, if, upon any occasion whatever, I can serve either you or your constituents, it will afford me as much pleasure as if nothing had ever occurred between us; but of private and individual intercourse, the less there is between us from this time forward the more agreeable it will be to me."

He only replied, " I wish you well," and left me.

April 30. — I called at the President's, who to my great surprise, read me a draft of a message to the House of Representatives, stating that on reference of their resolution to the Department of State, no such letter from Mr. Russell as that described in it had been found upon the files; then suppressing entirely the fact that Russell had delivered his duplicate there himself to be communicated to the House, and declining positively to send a copy of the original letter, as a private letter which could only occasion controversy to no useful purpose. I told the President that this message was totally different from anything I had heard him intimate his intention of sending before; that the resolution from the House had been officially referred by him to the Department of State, and I had officially reported to him upon that reference; that there was a letter there from Mr. Russell, delivered by himself, to be communicated as the letter called for by the resolution; that the letter itself was now of record in the Department; that my report to him upon it, and the remarks that I was preparing to him upon its contents, would also be of record in the Department. A message to the House, therefore, declaring that there was no such letter at the Department, would be liable to strong public animadversion, when it was impossible that the fact should not become notorious that there was such a letter, and when it could not but appear that the fact was known to him from my report.

"Your report!" said the President, in a tone of sharp anger. "'Tis my report. It is no report at all until I have accepted it." My feelings were wound up to a pitch at which it was with extreme difficulty that I preserved the control of my temper and the command of my expressions. I did so, however, and said, "Sir, it is your report, to do what you please with it, when received; but so far as I understand the Constitution of this country it is my report to make, and I am the responsible person in making it."

He said that he had always, when Secretary of State, considered the reports he had made to Mr. Madison as subject entirely to the control of the President, and had always felt himself bound to make any alteration in a report required by him.

I replied that I had invariably observed the same rule with him. I had never in a single instance written a public paper to be submitted to him without making every alteration in it suggested by him and insisted on. I was now willing to make any alteration that he would desire in this report, and had told him so when I had presented the report to him. But the report when made I considered as mine.

May 4. — I called at the President's, and Mr. Calhoun came in while I was there. He read to us a message which he had prepared to send to the House of Representatives with his negative upon a bill appropriating $9,000 for repairs upon the Cumberland road, and authorizing the erection of toll-gates upon it, and a toll for keeping it in repair. He said he had been suddenly called to take this measure, and had not time to consult the members of the Administration upon it. He promised with this message, and afterwards sent in the course of the day, his long dissertation against the constitutional power of Congress to make internal improvements. Mr. Floyd's recantation of the charge of forgery against General Scott was this day published in the newspapers.

Washington, June 2. — General D. Parker came in, and detained me at an interview of more than three hours. . . He said Mr. Calhoun was very sanguine in his expectations of succeeding to the Presidency, and believed he had a majority of Congress in his favor. And among the rest of his converts was General Scott, who was now gone to Richmond to ascertain whether by resigning his commission in the army he can obtain an immediate election to the Legislature of Virginia and then into the next Congress. He was in that case to be one of Mr. Calhoun's champions. And he was the author of a paper in the *National Intelligencer* attacking the majority of the Senate for their proceedings in the case of the rejected nominations. He said Scott had taken great pains to persuade him that Calhoun was friendly to him, and had several times repeated to him Mr. Calhoun had said to him how much he esteemed General Parker, and how fully satisfied he was with his conduct — all which, Parker said, he fully understood.

I said I believed that Mr. Calhoun was too sanguine in his calculations of success as a candidate for the next Presidency.

There were in Congress three parties — one for Mr. Crawford, one for Mr. Clay, and one for Mr. Calhoun. They
embraced indeed almost the whole. But the party for Mr.
Crawford was the strongest, and that of Mr. Calhoun the
weakest, of the three. And I had little doubt that the parties
of Crawford and Clay would finally coalesce together. Parker
said that he had heard Mr. Clay would come again, not only
into the next Congress, but probably even to the next session
of this Congress.

I said I doubted whether the Cabinet, as it is called, of Mr.
Monroe would continue entire through the next session of
Congress. Mr. Crawford or Mr. Calhoun, and most probably
the latter, would be compelled to resign. Very probably the
case might be my own. For the attacks upon me at the late
session of Congress had been from masked batteries, but they
had been of the most deadly character, and . . . I could not
possibly foresee what the next charge against me would be.
All I knew was, that it became me to be prepared for my
political decease at a moment's warning.

June 16. — General Scott told us that he had just returned
from Richmond, where he had been to ascertain whether he
could be returned to the next Congress. He had received all
possible encouragement, but he found that the county in which
his friend Archer lived would certainly be brought into the
district; and although there was probably no important public
question upon which Archer and he would vote on the same
side, yet he had been from college days his intimate friend,
and he could not possibly think of opposing him. He said
Archer was a Radical and inclined to be Jacobinical, and so,
he was sorry to say, was the State of Virginia, though nothing
could give him more pain than to differ in opinion upon any
subject from the people of Virginia.

We entered into a very earnest discussion upon the question
as to the power of Congress to make internal improvements
in the country by roads and canals. He avowed his concurrence with the opinion of the President, that Congress had
the power of appropriating money to make the roads, but not
to make them; which, I told him, was saying that they had the
right to use the means, but not to enjoy the end. I asked him
also several questions, till he said he did not like the Socratic
mode of reasoning.

June 20. — Cabinet meeting at one o'clock. Mr. Crawford, being indisposed, did not attend, and Mr. Wirt is absent
from the city. Mr. Calhoun and Mr. Thompson were present.
The President proposed again the question whether Ministers
should forthwith be sent to the Southern republics. The
opinions of Mr. Calhoun and Mr. Thompson were both
against the measure — Calhoun chiefly because there appeared
to be no urgent necessity for it, and because there was no strong
manifestation of public sentiment for it. He observed there
were only two or three newspapers, and those not leading
prints, that were clamorous for it, and in general the public
acquiesced in the course now pursued by the Executive. Mr.
Thompson's objection arose from a doubt of the power of
the President to appoint a Minister during the recess of the
Senate.

I observed that my opinion had been that we should receive
a Minister from the South American Governments before
sending one. As this opinion, however, had not been much
countenanced, I did not wish to hold it too pertinaciously and
with regard to the republic of Colombia there was less reason
to be punctilious, as, having received from them a Chargé
d'Affaires, the mere appointment of a person of higher rank
to go there would be less of a departure from the regular order
of establishing diplomatic intercourse than it would be to be
first in making any diplomatic appointment. . .

After Calhoun and Thompson were gone, I proposed to the
President that the mission to the republic of Colombia,
whether to be appointed now or at the meeting of Congress,
should be offered to Mr. Clay. I thought it doubtful whether
he would accept it — very probable that he would make no
delicate or generous use of it — and that the comments upon
the offer, both of his partisans and of others, would be various,
and in many cases invidious. But, upon the whole, the effect
upon the public would be favorable. He wanted the offer.
The Western country wished it might be made to him. His
talents were eminent; his claims from public service considerable. The republic of Colombia, and particularly Bolivar,
with whom he has been in correspondence, will be flattered by
his appointment, or even by information that he had the offer
of it. In the relations to be established between us and that
republic, Mr. Clay's talents might be highly useful; and I did

not apprehend any danger from them. The President appeared to be well disposed to take this course. He said that Mr. Clay's conduct towards him and his Administration had not been friendly or generous, but he was disposed entirely to overlook that.

June 29. — Mr. Canning had written me a note yesterday requesting to see me. I appointed this day at one, and he came. It was to take up the subject of the slave-trade. . . He took from his pocket some printed documents laid before Parliament — correspondence from British officers at Sierra Leone, containing lists of slave vessels examined on the coast of Africa, under French and Portuguese colors, and actively engaged in the slave-trade — and he launched into a strong and general invective against the trade.

I observed that in the lists contained in the papers there was not a single vessel under American colors, and alleged this circumstance as a proof of the efficacy of the measures adopted by us to suppress the use of our flag in the trade, which is all that could be accomplished by our agreeing to the right of search and the mixed courts. I remarked that it was evident from these papers that if we had, two years ago, signed treaties with Great Britain like those which she had obtained from Spain, Portugal, and the Netherlands, there would not have been one slave vessel the less upon these lists. Search and the mixed courts, therefore, would have effected nothing for the suppression of the trade, which has not been effected without them.

He said that a main purpose for which they wished to obtain our assent to the principle of search was, that it might be urged as an example to France. I said that we should rather wish France to adhere to her principles in this respect than to give them up. He asked if I could conceive of a greater and more atrocious evil than this slave-trade. I said, Yes: admitting the right of search by foreign officers of our vessels upon the seas in time of peace; for that would be making slaves of ourselves.

July 8. — In the evening Mr. Calhoun was here, and afterwards General Scott, with Mr. Dick, the District Judge of the United States in Louisiana. They came while Mr. Calhoun was with me, and interrupted our conversation. The relations in which I now stand with Calhoun are delicate and difficult.

At the last session of Congress he suffered a few members of Congress, with an Irishman named Rogers, editor of a newspaper at Easton, Pennsylvania, at their head, to set him up as a candidate for the succession to the Presidency. From that moment the caballing in Congress, in the State Legislatures, in the newspapers, and among the people, against me, has been multiplied tenfold. The *Franklin Gazette,* of Philadelphia, under the direction of Richard Bache, G. M. Dallas, T. Sergeant, and Ingham, in concert with Rogers, opened immediately upon me, and has kept up ever since an insidious fire against me. Calhoun's partisans have countenanced it, and have been as busy as those of Mr. Crawford in their efforts to degrade me in the public opinion. Meanwhile, Calhoun has always professed to be a friend and admirer of mine, and to persons whom he knows to be my friends has said that he did not mean to be a candidate against a Northern man, and that he himself was decidedly for a Northern President. There was a time during the last session of Congress when so large a proportion of members was enlisted for Calhoun that they had it in contemplation to hold a caucus formally to declare him a candidate. But this prospect of success roused all Crawford's and Clay's partisans against him. The administration of his Department was scrutinized with severity; sharpened by personal animosity and factious malice. Some abuses were discovered, and exposed with aggravations. Cavils were made against measures of that Department in the execution of the laws, and brought the President in collision with both Houses of Congress. Crawford's newspapers commenced and have kept up a course of the most violent abuse and ribaldry against him, and his projected nomination for the Presidency has met with scarcely any countenance throughout the Union.

July 26. — I have been this day married twenty-five years. It is what the Germans call the " Silberne Hochzeit " — the Silver Wedding. The happiest and most eventful portion of my life is past in the lapse of those twenty-five years. I finished the letter to my wife. Looking back — what numberless occasions of gratitude! How little room for self-gratification! Looking forward — what dependence upon the overruling Power! what frail support in myself! " Time and the hour wear through the roughest day." Let me have strength but to be true to myself, to my Maker, and to man — adding Christian meekness and charity to Stoic fortitude — and come what may.

July 28. — About two o'clock Mr. Calhoun called, and took us in his carriage to Mr. Daniel Brent's. The weather was intensely hot, and the sun beaming unclouded, so that we were about two hours on the road. We found there Colonel Freeman and Mr. Pleasanton, Gales and Seaton, Mr. Pearson and his daughter, and Miss Brent, a daughter of William Brent's. We had a pleasant dinner, and a little, not much, conversation. We returned early in the evening to the city. Mr. Calhoun said much to me, on the way, of the opposition to the Administration combined by Mr. Clay and Mr. Crawford, each having separate views of his own. He spoke also of the absolute necessity that there should be in this District an independent newspaper, to expose the intrigues of those gentlemen to the nation.

Aug. 3. — There is in the *Argus of Western America,* a newspaper published at Frankfort, Kentucky, under date of the 18th of July, an article, apparently editorial, headed " The Ghent Mission," which, both from its style and contents, I take to have been written by Mr. Clay; but, if not, certainly from him indirectly. It is bitter upon " the Secretary," and apologizes for Clay's having agreed to the Mississippi proposition upon the plea of the new instructions. It abandons all Russell's pretences, and says that Clay thought the Government ought not to have given the instructions. Clay's conduct throughout this affair towards me has been that of an envious rival — a fellow-servant whispering tales into the ear of the common master. He has been seven years circulating this poison against me in the West, and I have now no doubt that Russell's letter was brought forth upon suggestions originating with him. Russell has all along performed for him the part of a jackal. Clay seems to have fancied that I should have no means of self-vindication if Russell's letter should be brought before Congress, and this article in the *Argus* evidently betrays his vexation and disappointment at the result.

Aug. 10. — A woman by the name of Bridget Smith came to apply for a pardon for her brother, the man who is in prison at Boston for slave-trading. Miss Smith operated with the usual female weapon, a shower of tears. It seldom fails to disconcert my philosophy, especially when I see the spring is from the social affections. Here it was a brother, necessary for the comfort and subsistence of a mother. I promised to do my best to obtain his release, though in his own person he has very little claim to mercy or even to compassion.

Aug. 19. — Answered General Dearborn's letter, and received one from my wife, chiefly upon an attack against me in one of the Philadelphia newspapers on account of the negligence of my dress. It says that I wear neither waistcoat nor cravat, and sometimes go to church barefoot. My wife is much concerned at this, and several of my friends at Philadelphia have spoken to her of it as a serious affair. In the Washington *City Gazette,* some person unknown to me has taken the cudgels in my behalf, and answered the accusation gravely as if the charge were true. It is true only as regards the cravat, instead of which, in the extremity of the summer heat, I wear round my neck a black silk riband. But, even in the falsehoods of this charge, what I may profitably remember is the perpetual and malignant watchfulness with which I am observed in my open day and my secret night, with the deliberate purpose of exposing me to public obloquy or public ridicule.

Aug. 23. — Mr. Henry Johnson, the Senator from Louisiana, called upon me this morning, with Mr. Edward Livingston, of New Orleans. Livingston is elected a member of the next Congress from the State of Louisiana, and will probably be one of its most distinguished members. He is a man of very superior talents, whose career has been checkered with good and evil, with right and wrong, perhaps as much as that of any public man in this country. He is now going to Richmond, Virginia. He asked me whether I had received a copy of his report to the Legislature of Louisiana of a project for a criminal code, which he had sent me. I had, and was much pleased with it. I told him there were many of its opinions with which I fully concurred, and some upon which my mind was perhaps not so clearly made up.

Aug. 27. — Mr. Calhoun called to make enquiries. He noticed the decisive manner in which the Washington *City Gazette* came out yesterday in favor of Mr. Crawford, and against me. He has long considered the *Gazette* as edited from the Treasury Department, and all the articles in it against him as coming almost directly from Mr. Crawford himself. He says the course Crawford is now pursuing is precisely the same as he kept in 1815 and 1816, which he had great opportunities of then observing, as he was of the same mess with two or three of Crawford's managing partisans. He says that Crawford is a very singular instance of a man of such character rising to the eminence he now occupies; that there has not been in the history of the Union another man with abilities so ordinary, with services so slender, and so thoroughly corrupt, who has contrived to make himself a candidate for the Presidency. He thinks it, however, impossible that he should succeed.

Sept. 9. — Mr. Crawford's party was organized before the close of Mr. Madison's [term]. He was a caucus candidate in 1816 against Mr. Monroe, and had then the address ostensibly to decline opposing Mr. Monroe, seeming to sacrifice his own pretensions . . . so as to secure a seat in the Administration under him, during which he has been incessantly engaged in preparing the way to succeed him. Among the most powerful of his agents have been the editors of the leading newspapers. The *National Intelligencer* is secured to him by the belief of the editors that he will be the successful candidate and by their dependence upon the printing of Congress; the Richmond *Enquirer,* because he is a Virginian and a slave-holder; the *National Advocate* of New York, through Van Buren; the Boston *Statesman* and Portland *Argus* through William King; the *Democratic Press* of Philadelphia, because I transferred the printing of the laws from that paper to the *Franklin Gazette;* and several other presses in various parts of the Union upon principles alike selfish and sordid. Most of these papers have signals by which they understand one another, and the signal at Washington is given by the *City Gazette,* which has been re-secured since Irvine ceased to be its joint editor, and which from time to time gives notice of the newspapers which are successively induced to join in the train.

Sept. 21. — The President went to his seat at Oakhill, near Aldie, Loudoun County, Virginia. Mr. Force came and took the last sheet of my proposed pamphlet [against Russell], with the title-page, table of contents, and errata, all of which I have prepared, and which have occupied so fully since the

1st of July all the time that I could spare from the indispensable duties of my office, that my diary has in the interval been running into long arrears. Between the 26th and 29th of August, having finished the controversy with Russell, I resumed my diary, and brought it up to the 6th of July; but when Mr. Floyd took the field under a new mask, with a desperate lunge at me, under color of neutrality, I thought it necessary to strip the mask from him too. The editorial article of the Kentucky *Argus* is by or from Clay, and, as he fights under cover, I have adapted the defence to the attack. Force says the book will be published on Monday. I now dismiss it to its fate.

Sept. 27. — Attended at the President's at one o'clock. Mr. Calhoun only was there, Mr. Wirt being unwell and not able to attend. The proposition of Mr. Sanchez, as disclosed in Mr. Duponceau's letter to General Mason, was discussed. There was also a second letter, explanatory of the first, and more strictly confidential. The question was discussed what was to be done. Mr. Calhoun has a most ardent desire that the island of Cuba should become a part of the United States, and says that Mr. Jefferson has the same. There are two dangers to be averted by that event; one, that the island should fall into the hands of Great Britain; the other, that it should be revolutionized by the negroes. Calhoun says Mr. Jefferson told him two years ago that we ought, at the first possible opportunity, to take Cuba, though at the cost of a war with England; but as we are not now prepared for this, and as our great object must be to gain time, he thought we should answer this overture by dissuading them from their present purpose, and urging them to adhere at present to their connection with Spain.

I thought it advisable to take a different course; to give them no advice whatever; to say that the Executive of the United States is not competent to promise them admission as a State into the Union; and that if it were, the proposal is of a nature which our relations of amity with Spain would not permit us to countenance.

Oct. 5. — Mr. Calhoun brought me home from the funeral of Mr. Law. We had some conversation upon the quarrel between Colonel Cumming, of Georgia, and Mr. McDuffie, the member of Congress from South Carolina, Calhoun's protégé, friend, and partisan. This feud has become a sort of historical incident. It originated in the rivalry between Crawford and Calhoun for the Presidential succession; began by some vulgar abuse upon each other in newspapers, in consequence of which Cumming challenged McDuffie before the last session of Congress, and came here last winter during the session to fight him. The meeting was then postponed to thirty days after the close of the session of Congress, when they met, and McDuffie was shot in the back. They then returned to the war of newspaper ribaldry, till Cumming challenged him a second time. By double manoeuvring on both sides about the time, place, and circumstances of meeting, the second duel was avoided, and each party resorted again to hand-bills, posting, newspaper proclamations of imputed cowardice, and pamphleteering. The seconds, surgeons, and others have got involved in the dispute, and all have become the laughing-stock of the public throughout the Union, except in South Carolina and Georgia, where the parties are feasted and toasted " alive or dead." Never was such a burlesque upon duels since the practice existed.

Oct. 7. — Received a letter from George M. Dallas, of Philadelphia, enclosing a copy of the oration which I delivered on the 17th of July, 1787, at Commencement, upon taking my degree of Bachelor of Arts. He says he found it among some of his late father's papers, but does not know how it came there. Nor do I; but it is the copy which, at the request of the late Dr. Belknap, I furnished him for publication in a monthly magazine, then published at Philadelphia, and it was printed in the number for the month of September, 1787. I little thought of ever seeing the manuscript again; but the delivery of the oration was one of the most memorable events of my life. The incidents attending it were of a nature to make a deep impression upon my mind. The appointment to deliver it was itself a high distinction. Yet it was but the second honor of the class, and he who took the first, the preferred rival, sank at the age of thirty-five, to be forgotten. I re-perused this production now with humiliation; to think how proud of it I was then, and how much I must blush for it now!

Oct. 21. — Home between four and five o'clock to an early dinner, to attend the evening exhibition of *Mr. Mathews at Home.* The doors of the theatre were advertised to be opened

at a quarter before six, and the performance to begin at a
quarter before seven. We went near half an hour before the
doors opened, and were standing, ladies and gentlemen in a
crowd, waiting for admission to the audience of Mr. Mathews.
When the door was at length forced open, the house was
full to overflow in the space of time necessary for occupying all the seats. The performances were *The Trip to Paris*
and *The Diligence*. Mathews, the sole performer, personated
in the course of the evening ten or twelve characters, male
and female, with varieties of voice and countenance scarcely
credible.

Oct. 26. — Mr. Calhoun asked me if Mr. Early, of Georgia,
had called upon me. He had not. He had upon Calhoun,
and upon the President. His object was to represent that the
Marshal for the District of Georgia was now accumulating a
fortune of at least thirty thousand dollars a year by working
a number of African negroes who are in his possession as
Marshal of the District, while at the same time he is making
the most enormous charges against the public for the mainte-
nance of the very same negroes; that he makes it his open
boast that he holds the office of Marshal for no other purpose,
and that he intends to swamp the negroes — that is, to work
them to death — before they shall be finally adjudicated out
of his possession. Mr. Early adds that his cruelty to negroes
is universally notorious, and that it is equally well known that
he did commit the murder of the black man for which he was
tried and acquitted. The principal witnesses against him were
spirited away. Early declares himself to be of the same political party with the Marshal (Crawford's), but is so horror-
struck at the character and conduct of the man that he feels
it to be his duty to denounce him.

Nov. 2. — We had company to dinner — the Commissioners, White, King, and Tazewell, Major A. L. Austin, D.
Brent, J. A. Dix, F. C. Gray, H. Johnson, Mr. & Mrs. Orne,
T. Watkins, and Mr. & Mrs. Wirt. . . We were twenty at
table. The dinner was pleasant, with the exception of one
incident: in a desultory conversation upon wines, Mr. Tazewell asserted and perseveringly insisted, that Tokay was a
species of Rhenish wine. After insisting to the contrary for
some time in perfect good humor and civility, as he still persisted, in the warmth of the collision I said, " Why, you never

drank a drop of Tokay in your life." I set this down as a token of self-disapprobation for having said it. Tazewell made no reply, but looked hurt. The conversation turned upon other topics, and on leaving the table he went away without returning with the rest of the company to the drawing-room. I have no good apology to make to myself for this incivility; for that Tazewell himself is not sparing of feelings in the clash of conversation, and had been much otherwise even at this dinner, is no justification to me.

Nov. 7. — The day after I dismissed John B. Colvin from the Department of State I saw his hand in the Washington *City Gazette.* He has since commenced a series of numbers under the editorial part of that paper, headed " The Presidential Question," each of two or three columns. Five numbers have appeared, written in Colvin's best manner, professing to give a delineation of my character, and scanning my pretensions to the Presidency. They present me in caricature, and touch upon everything true, and everything false that can be made to resemble truth, which could degrade me in the popular opinion. They are written with just so much regard to truth as to seize on single facts to which a suspicious coloring may be given, from which a whole tale of falsehood is fabricated and asserted as fact, to exhibit me as a base and despicable character.

Nov. 9. — My short note to Gales and Seaton, exposing two of the many falsehoods in Colvin's abusive papers on the Presidential question, was published this morning in the *National Intelligencer,* as a communication, and a reply appeared in the Washington *Gazette* of this evening, re-asserting them, adding a number more of falsehoods, and redoubling scurrilous invectives.

Reading further in Walpole's *Memoirs,* or *Secret History of the British Administrations* from 1750 to 1760, I find in them many things that remind me of the present state of things here. The public history of all countries, and all ages, is but a sort of mask, richly colored. The interior working of the machinery must be foul. There is as much mining and countermining for power, as many fluctuations of friendship and enmity, as many attractions and repulsions, bargains and oppositions, narrated in these *Memoirs,* as might be told of our own times. Walpole witnessed it all as a sharer in the sport,

and now tells it to the world as a satirist.   And shall not I,
too, have a tale to tell?

Nov. 26. — Note from the President, directing a meeting
of the members of the Administration at one o'clock.   Present,
Mr. Crawford, Mr. Calhoun, and Mr. Thompson.   The
President read the draft prepared for his message to Congress
at the opening of the session of Congress.   It is very long,
and contains more of discussion than seemed to me suitable
for such a paper. . .

There was in the draft a very long paragraph upon the
Military Academy at West Point.   I thought it occupied too
large a space in the message.   I doubted whether any part of
it was necessary; and there were in it a number of remarks
upon the indocility and ardor of youthful minds, of a nature
too speculative and doctrinal for the occasion.   I started the
question first only upon these, and on the reperusal extended
it to the whole paragraph, with the exception of two or three
sentences, sufficient to declare explicitly the President's opinion
in favor of maintaining the institution, to check the disposition
to abolish it, should it reappear, which was manifested in
Congress at their last session.

Nov. 28. — Note from the President calling a Cabinet
meeting at half-past one.   The object was to consult upon the
expediency of sending the missions to South America, for
which appropriations were made at the last session of Congress.   There was much discussion upon this point, in the
course of which Mr. Crawford came out in character with his
opinion that the missions ought to be sent, but that there was
less reason for sending them now than there had been when the
appropriations were made last spring.   Mr. Calhoun and Mr.
Thompson gave no decisive opinions.   Mine has invariably
been that we ought to send none but in return for Ministers
sent by them here.   Mr. Crawford said he had understood it
was determined last spring to send none except in that manner.
The President said he had not so determined, but the appointments had been postponed on various considerations.   I observed that those countries were yet all in a convulsive and
revolutionary state.   Since the last session of Congress, Ytur-
bide had by the forms of election by a Congress, but in fact by
military usurpation, made himself Emperor of Mexico, but
without any of the necessary means for carrying on his Gov-

ernment. From the accounts we have, it is highly probable that his Government will be overthrown within a year. In the republic of Colombia, and in Peru, the Spanish party had rather gained ground this year.

Jan. 1, 1823. —

> All-gracious Parent! on my bended knee
> This dawning day I consecrate to Thee,
> With humble heart and fervent voice to raise
> The suppliant prayer and ever-grateful praise.
> To Thee the past its various blessings owes,
> Its soothing pleasures, its chastising woes;
> To Thee the future with imploring eye
> Looks up for health, for virtue, for the sky.
> Howe'er the tides of joy or sorrow roll,
> Still grant me, Lord, possession of my soul,
> Life's checkered scenes with steadfast mind to share,
> As thou shalt doom, to gladden or to bear.
> And oh, be mine, when closed this brief career,
> The crown of glory's everlasting year.

Jan. 10. — Just before breakfast I received a note from the President, desiring me to call upon Mr. Brown, of Louisiana, and propose to him the mission to Mexico. Immediately after breakfast I called at his house, but he was already gone to the Senate. I went to the Capitol, and saw him in the Senate-chamber, from which we retired into the committee-room. I told him I was charged by the President to enquire if the mission to Mexico would be agreeable to him. He expressed his acknowledgments for the confidence manifested in the offer, which he declined, the state of society and the condition of the country being such that he could not think of taking his wife there, and he could not think of going without her.

Jan. 12. — I went to Dowson's and saw Mr. Macon. In making the appointments to these South American missions, the President wishes to distribute them to citizens of the different parts of the Union. He wished particularly to take some distinguished notice of North Carolina. It happens that the weight of talents in that State is with the Federalists, so that the politics counteract the geography. . . I mentioned to him General Jackson for Mexico, and John Holmes, of Maine, for Chili. He received favorably the name of Jackson, but doubted whether he would accept, and made some question whether his quickness and violence of temper might not, in the opinion of a great part of the nation, make the expediency of his appointment questionable.

I said that although the language of General Jackson was sometimes too impassioned and violent, his conduct had always appeared to me calm and deliberate. Acting under responsibility, I did not apprehend he would do anything to the injury of his country, and even if he should commit any indiscretion, he would bear the penalty of it himself, for the nation would not support him in it.[1] There was another difficulty, which I thought more serious. He had been unanimously nominated by the members of the Legislature of Tennessee as a candidate for the Presidential election. To send him on a mission abroad would be attributed by some, perhaps, to a wish to get him out of the way. The President said there was something in that.

March 14. — Cabinet meeting. Calhoun and Thompson present; Crawford absent, unwell, and Wirt engaged in Supreme Court. War between France and Spain. What to be done? Agent in Cuba, Hernandez; P. U. S. to see him. Calhoun's anxiety. Information to be obtained. Consistency with what we have done to be observed. Fears of what England may do. Prospects of Spain. Danger of treachery.

March 15. — The Baron Maltitz was at my house, to announce the arrival of Baron Tuyl, the Russian Envoy at New York. Expects him here next week. Cabinet meeting at two; Calhoun and Thompson only present. Cuba. P. U. S. has seen Hernandez, who is going to the Havanna; not as Agent; what to do? Calhoun for war with England, if she means to take Cuba. Thompson for urging the Cubans to declare

---

[1] It is to be noted that Adams alone in the Monroe Administration stood staunchly by Jackson. As has been observed, there was something in Jackson's independence, vigor, and courage which touched a responsive chord in Adams, who had all these qualities. Jackson's duty had been to wage war against an Indian tribe. Actually he had hung two meddling British subjects after the most summary and inadequate trial; he had captured Spanish towns as if they were enemy fortresses; and when Florida had become American territory, he had thrown the Spanish commissioner into jail in defiance of all law, usage, and prudence. Clay denounced Jackson in the House of Representatives; Crawford was eager to make the most of these opportunities for destroying him as a dangerous political rival; President Monroe distrusted and disapproved of him and his rash measures. But Adams gallantly championed the military hero of the Southwest.

themselves independent, if they can maintain their independence. I assume for granted that they cannot maintain their independence, and that this nation will not, and could not, prevent by war the British from obtaining possession of Cuba, if they attempt to take it. The debate almost warm. Talk of calling Congress, which I thought absurd. Memorandum — to be cool on this subject.

March 27. — Canning read me three notes — Duke of Wellington to Montmorency, offering mediation of Great Britain between France and Spain; Montmorency's answer declining the mediation; and G. Canning's reply to it, addressed to the Chargé d'Affaires of France. Expressed my gratification at the substance of this correspondence. Spoke something of the slave-trade note, of the slave-indemnity note, and of the colonial trade navigation. Canning earnest about them all.

June 23. — Mr. Cutts came, and introduced to me Dr. Shaw, of Albany, formerly a member of Congress from Vermont, and father of Henry Shaw, some time member of Congress from Berkshire, Massachusetts. Dr. Shaw is a great canvasser with the Legislature of New York, at Albany, for the next Presidential election, and I suppose is now here upon that affair. He told me the Governor of New York had it in contemplation to recommend to the Legislature to pass a law authorizing the choice of electors for President and Vice-President to be made by the people by general ticket.

June 24. — Mr. Canning waived a further discussion of the subject, and took leave. He is to depart to-morrow. I shall probably see him no more. He is a proud, high-tempered Englishman, of good but not extraordinary parts; stubborn and punctilious, with a disposition to be overbearing, which I have often been compelled to check in its own way. He is, of all the foreign Ministers with whom I have had occasion to treat, the man who has most severely tried my temper. Yet he has been long in the diplomatic career, and treated with Governments of the most opposite characters. He has, however, a great respect for his word, and there is nothing false about him. This is an excellent quality for a negotiator. Mr. Canning is a man of forms, studious of courtesy, and tenacious of private morals. As a diplomatic man, his great want is suppleness, and his great virtue is sincerity. I finished the reply to his letter of 8th April last, on the slave-trade.

July 6. — Mr. Hay spoke in terms of great severity of Ritchie, the editor of the Richmond *Enquirer,* and said he was the most unprincipled fellow upon earth, whose whole efforts would be to work himself into the side of the majority. He was now endeavoring to buy up the newspaper lately estab-lished in Richmond against him, the Virginia *Times.* The Richmond *Enquirer* has been for several years the political barometer of the State of Virginia.

July 7. — Cabinet meeting at the President's; all there. The subject for consideration was, whether new and enlarged instructions should be given to our naval officers in the West Indies to protect our merchant vessels, and recapture them if they should be taken. The dispatch from T. Randall was read. It was finally concluded to do nothing at present.

July 8. — Swam with Antoine in the Potomac to the bridge — one hour in the water. While we were swimming, there sprang up a breeze, which made a surf, and much increased the difficulty of swimming, especially against it and the cur-rent. This is one of the varieties of instruction for the school. It sometimes occurs to me that this exercise and amusement, as I am now indulging myself in it, is with the constant risk of life. Perhaps that is the reason why so few persons ever learn to swim; and perhaps it should now teach me discretion.

July 10. — Swam with Antoine to and from the bridge, but, as the tide was strongly rising, we were full three-quarters of an hour in going to it, and not more than twenty minutes in returning. This was one of my swimming lessons, and a seri-ous admonition to caution.

July 11. — And I commence upon my fifty-seventh year. Swam with Antoine an hour in the Potomac. We started for the bridge, but after swimming about half an hour, I per-ceived by reference to a house upon the shore, beyond which we were to pass that we had ascended very little above where we had left our clothes, and that the current of the tide was insensibly carrying us into the middle of the river. We con-tinued struggling against the tide about twenty minutes longer, without apparently gaining a foot upon the tide. I then turned back, and in fifteen minutes landed at the rock where

I had left my clothes, upon which, in the interval, the tide had so much encroached that it began to wet them, and in another half-hour would have soaked them through or floated them away. We had been an hour and five minutes in the water, without touching ground, and before turning back I began to find myself weary.

July 17. — At the office, Baron Tuyl came, enquired if he might inform his government that instructions would be forwarded by Mr. Hughes to Mr. Middleton for negotiating on the Northwest Coast question. I said he might. He then manifested a desire to know as much as I was disposed to tell him as to the purport of those instructions. I told him as much as I thought prudent, as he observed that it was personally somewhat important to him to be so far confided in here as to know the general purport of what we intended to propose. I told him specially that we should contest the right of Russia to any territorial establishment on this continent, and that we should assume distinctly the principle that the American continents are no longer subjects for any new European colonial establishments.

July 28. — I called at the President's with the draft of instructions to Richard Rush, to accompany the project of a convention to regulate neutral and belligerent rights in time of war. The President had suggested a single alteration in the draft of a convention which I had sent him on Saturday.

Mr. Calhoun came in while I was reading to the President the draft of the instruction, and, after I had finished, started several doubts as to the propriety of proposing this project at all. He is confident it would not be accepted by Great Britain; and I have no expectation that it will at this time. But my object is to propose it to Russia and France, and to all the maritime powers of Europe, as well as to Great Britain. We discussed for some time its expediency. I appealed to the primitive policy of this country as exemplified in the first treaty with Prussia. I said the seed was then first sown, and had borne a single plant which the fury of the revolutionary tempest had since swept away. I thought the present a moment eminently auspicious for sowing the same seed a second time, and, although I had no hope it would now take root in England, I had the most cheering confidence that it would ultimately bear a harvest of happiness to mankind and of glory to this Union.

Aug. 2. — The President was suddenly seized this morning with cramps or convulsions, of such extreme violence that he was at one time believed dying, and he lay upwards of two hours in a state of insensibility. I did not hear of it till the fit was over. I called at his house, and saw Dr. Washington and Mr. Hay. The doctor said the President was disposed to sleep, and it would be best that no person should see him. Mr. Hay said Dr. Sim had pronounced the danger to be past, and did not apprehend a renewal of the attack. But, Hay added, he thought it would be some time before it would be prudent to lay before him business of any kind. Before returning home to dinner, I sent to enquire how he was, and the answer to the messenger was, " much better."

Aug. 9. — Swam in the Potomac to the bridge against the tide, and returned with it. One hour and fifty minutes in the water, Antoine being still at hand with the canoe. I was about an hour and a half in going, and not more than twenty minutes in returning. At the President's. He received me in his bed-chamber, which he was advised not to leave this day. He recommended to me to strike out from the instruction to Mr. Middleton upon the neutral and belligerent right project, all the reference to the Holy Alliance, because, that treaty being considered in this country as a mere hypocritical fraud, any reference to it whatever would have a turn given to it of odious misconstruction here against myself. . .

I accordingly struck it out, and thereby gave up what I considered the mainspring of the argument to the Emperor. I relied upon its operation incomparably more than upon anything else. The President is often afraid of the skittishness of mere popular prejudices, and I am always disposed to brave them. I have much more confidence in the calm and deliberate judgment of the people than he has. I have no doubt that the newspaper scavengers and scape-gibbets, whose republicanism runs in filthy streams from the press, would have attempted to exhibit this reference to the Holy Alliance in a false and odious point of view, but I would have trusted to the good sense of the people to see through their sophistry and their motives. They would have seen in it what was intended: a powerful engine of persuasion applied to the heart of him whom it was all-important to persuade; a bold and direct address to his intimate conscience, and a warning voice to check and control his acts bearing hard upon the liberties of nations. In this case, as in all others for which Mr. Monroe as the head of his Administration is responsible, I submit my own judgment to his.

Aug. 15. — Cabinet meeting at the President's at one. Mr. Wirt absent from indisposition. The subject first mentioned by the President for consideration was a letter to me from Andreas Luriottis at London, styling himself Envoy of the Provisional Government of the Greeks, a copy of which was sent me some months since by Richard Rush. This letter, recommending the cause of the Greeks, solicited of the United States recognition, alliance, and assistance. It was proper to give a distinct answer to this letter, and I had asked the President's directions what the answer should be.

The President now proposed the question. Mr. Gallatin had proposed in one of his last dispatches, as if he was serious, that we should assist the Greeks with our naval force in the Mediterranean — one frigate, one corvette, and one schooner. Mr. Crawford and Mr. Calhoun inclined to countenance this project. Crawford asked, hesitatingly, whether we were at peace with Turkey, and seemed only to wait for opposition to maintain that we were not. Calhoun descanted upon his great enthusiasm for the cause of the Greeks; he was for taking no heed of Turkey whatever. In this, as in many other cases, these gentlemen have two sources of eloquence at these Cabinet meetings — one with reference to sentiment, and the other to action. Their enthusiasm for the Greeks is all sentiment, and the standard of this is the prevailing popular feeling. As for action, they are seldom agreed; and after two hours of discussion this day the subject was dismissed, leaving it precisely where it was, nothing determined, and nothing practicable proposed by either of them. Seeing their drift, I did not think it necessary to discuss their doubts whether we were at peace with Turkey, their contempt for the Sublime Porte, or their enthusiasm for the cause of the Greeks. I have not much esteem for the enthusiasm which evaporates in words; and I told the President I thought not quite so lightly of a war with Turkey.

Quincy, Aug. 25. — Just at one we arrived at my father's house, and I was deeply affected at meeting him. Within the two last years since I had seen him, his eyesight has grown dim, and his limbs stiff and feeble. He is bowed with age, and scarcely can walk across a room without assistance.

Sept. 4. — Dined at General H. A. S. Dearborn's, at Brinley Place, Roxbury. There was a company of about thirty men, among whom Colonel Hayne, the Senator, and Mr. Archer — Crowninshield, Silsbee, and Sprague, of Salem. There was at table a conversation, chiefly between Colonel Hayne and George Blake, upon a decision of Judge Johnson's, of the United States Supreme Court, pronouncing an Act of the Legislature of South Carolina unconstitutional, in which Hayne discovered so much excitement and temper that it became painful, and necessary to change the topic. It was the Act prohibiting free persons of color from coming or being brought into the State as sailors, upon penalties, among which are their being sold as slaves.

Quincy, Sept. 11. — My father had been sitting to Stewart, the painter, and he told me that he would make a picture of it that should be admired as long as the materials should hold together.

Washington, Nov. 7. — Cabinet meeting at the President's from half-past one till four. Mr. Calhoun, Secretary of War, and Mr. Southard, Secretary of the Navy, present. The subject for consideration was, the confidential proposals of the British Secretary of State, George Canning, to R. Rush, and the correspondence between them relating to the projects of the Holy Alliance upon South America. There was much conversation, without coming to any definite point. The object of Canning appears to have been to obtain some public pledge from the Government of the United States, ostensibly against the forcible interference of the Holy Alliance between Spain and South America; but really or especially against the acquisition to the United States themselves of any part of the Spanish-American possessions.[2]

[2] The sequence of events which led up to the promulgation of the Monroe Doctrine, of which Adams was the principal author, was now fairly in train. President Monroe had decided in 1822 that the time had come for recognition of the South American republics, and had been supported by Congress, which appropriated $100,000 for Ministers to such of them as Monroe selected. In 1822 occurred the Congress of Verona, which resulted in the intervention of European Continental Powers to restore absolute government in Spain. There seemed reason to fear similar intervention in South America to restore Spanish sovereignty. England opposed any such action. In a confidential letter to the American Minister in London, Richard Rush, the British Foreign Minister, George Canning,

Mr. Calhoun inclined to giving a discretionary power to Mr. Rush to join in a declaration against the interference of the Holy Allies, if necessary, even if it should pledge us not to take Cuba or the province of Texas; because the power of Great Britain being greater than ours to seize upon them, we should get the advantage of obtaining from her the same declaration we should make ourselves.

I thought the case not parallel. We have no intention of seizing either Texas or Cuba. But the inhabitants of either or both may exercise their primitive rights, and solicit a union with us. They will certainly do no such thing to Great Britain. By joining with her, therefore, in her proposed declaration, we give her a substantial and perhaps inconvenient pledge against ourselves, and really obtain nothing in return. Without entering now into the enquiry of the expediency of our annexing Texas or Cuba to our Union, we should at least keep ourselves free to act as emergencies may arise, and not tie ourselves down to any principle which might immediately afterwards be brought to bear against ourselves.

Mr. Southard inclined much to the same opinion.

The President was averse to any course which should have the appearance of taking a position subordinate to that of Great Britain, and suggested the idea of sending a special Minister to protest against the interposition of the Holy Alliance.

I observed that it was a question for separate consideration, whether we ought in any event, if invited, to attend at a Congress of the allies on this subject.

Mr. Calhoun thought we ought in no case to attend.

The President, referring to instructions given before the Congress at Aix-la-Chapelle declaring that we would, if in-

suggested a joint Anglo-American declaration to the effect that the recovery of the South American colonies by Spain was hopeless; that neither England nor America aimed at the possession of any portion of them for herself; and they would not see the transfer of any portion of them to any other power with indifference. This unofficial note was dated Aug. 20, 1823.

President Monroe consulted Jefferson and Madison as to the advisability of accepting the British proposal for joint action, and both of them warmly approved it. Monroe seems himself to have favored such joint action. But Adams stoutly opposed any such movement in conjunction with the British Government, believing that the United States should act alone. He proposed an independent declaration against the interference by European Powers with South America by force. The succeeding pages of the Diary will show how his views were accepted and carried out.

vited, attend no meeting relative to South America of which less than its entire independence shall be the object, intimated that a similar limitation might be assumed now.

I remarked that we had then not recognized the South American independence ourselves. We would have been willing to recognize it in concert with the European allies, and therefore would have readily attended, if invited, a meeting of which that should have been the object. We could not now have the same motive. We have recognized them. We are very sure there will be now no meeting of the allies with that object. There would, therefore, be no use or propriety in resorting to the same limitation. Our refusal to attend should be less explicit and unqualified.

To this the President readily assented.

I remarked that the communications recently received from the Russian Minister, Baron Tuyl, afforded, as I thought, a very suitable and convenient opportunity for us to take our stand against the Holy Alliance, and at the same time to decline the overture of Great Britain. It would be more candid, as well as more dignified, to avow our principles explicitly to Russia and France, than to come in as a cock-boat in the wake of the British man-of-war.

This idea was acquiesced in on all sides, and my draft for an answer to Baron Tuyl's note announcing the Emperor's determination to refuse receiving any Minister from the South American Governments was read.

Nov. 13. — Morning occupied in making a draft of minutes for the message of the President upon subjects under the direction of the Department of State. I took to the President's my draft of minutes and copies of the instructions to Richard Rush dispatched last summer. I read and left my draft with him. I find him yet altogether unsettled in his own mind as to the answer to be given to Mr. Canning's proposals, and alarmed, far beyond anything that I could have conceived possible, with the fear that the Holy Alliance are about to restore immediately all South America to Spain. Calhoun stimulates the panic, and the news that Cadiz has surrendered to the French has so affected the President that he appeared entirely to despair of the cause of South America. He will recover from this in a few days; but I never saw more indecision in him. We discussed the proposals of Canning, and I told him if he would decide either to accept or decline them, I would draft a dispatch conformable to either decision for his consideration. He said he would talk further about it to-morrow.

Nov. 15. — I received a note from Mr. D. Brent, saying that the President wished to see me at the office at noon. I went, and found him there. He asked for the correspondence relating to the intercourse with the British American Colonies, with a view to the particular notice which he intends to take of it in the message; which I thought should have been only in general terms. He also showed me two letters which he had received — one from Mr. Jefferson, 23d October, and one from Mr. Madison of 30th October, giving their opinions on the proposals of Mr. Canning. The President had sent them the two dispatches from Richard Rush of 23d August, enclosing the correspondence between Canning and him, and requested their opinions on the proposals. Mr. Jefferson thinks them more important than anything that has happened since our Revolution. He is for acceding to the proposals, with a view to pledging Great Britain against the Holy Allies; though he thinks the island of Cuba would be a valuable and important acquisition to our Union. Mr. Madison's opinions are less decisively pronounced, and he thinks, as I do, that this movement on the part of Great Britain is impelled more by her interest than by a principle of general liberty.

At one I attended the Cabinet meeting at the President's. He read a note from Mr. Crawford saying he was not well enough to attend, but hoped to be out on Monday. Mr. Calhoun and Mr. Southard were there; Mr. Wirt absent at Baltimore. The subject of Mr. Canning's proposals was resumed, and I soon found the source of the President's despondency with regard to South American affairs. Calhoun is perfectly moon-struck by the surrender of Cadiz, and says the Holy Allies, with ten thousand men, will restore all Mexico and all South America to the Spanish dominion.

I did not deny that they might make a temporary impression for three, four, or five years, but I no more believe that the Holy Allies will restore the Spanish dominion upon the American continent than that the Chimborazo will sink beneath the ocean. But, I added, if the South Americans were really in a state to be so easily subdued, it would be but a more forcible motive for us to beware of involving ourselves in their fate. I set this down as one of Calhoun's extravagancies. He is for plunging into a war to prevent that which, if his opinion of it is correct, we are utterly unable to prevent. He is for embarking our lives and fortunes in a ship which he declares the very rats have abandoned. Calhoun reverts again to his idea of giving discretionary power to our Minister to accede to all Canning's proposals, if necessary, and not otherwise. After much discussion, I said I thought we should bring the whole answer to Mr. Canning's proposals to a test of right and wrong. Considering the South Americans as independent nations, they themselves, and no other nation, had the right to dispose of their condition. We have no right to dispose of them, either alone or in conjunction with other nations. Neither have any other nations the right of disposing of them without their consent. This principle will give us a clue to answer all Mr. Canning's questions with candor and confidence. And I am to draft a dispatch accordingly.

Nov. 20. — At the office I received a note from the President, proposing large alterations to my draft of instructions to Richard Rush upon Canning's proposals concerning South American affairs. Some of the alterations were unexceptionable; others I wished him further to consider. I called at his house, but he was out riding. He afterwards came to the office. I stated my objections to some of his proposed alterations of my draft, and suggested to him the substance of a substitute which I wished to offer to his projected paragraph. He agreed that I should draft a substitute, and proposed a meeting of the Administration to-morrow. He had adopted Mr. Calhoun's idea of giving Mr. Rush a discretionary power to act jointly with the British Government in case of any sudden emergency of danger, of which they and he should judge. I am utterly averse to this; and I told him that I thought the instructions should be explicit, authorizing him distinctly to act in specified contingencies, and requiring him in all others to refer for every important measure to his Government.

Nov. 21. — I had received a note from the President requesting me to attend a meeting of the members of the Administration at one. The meeting lasted till five. I took with me the draft of my dispatch to R. Rush in answer to Canning's proposals, with the President's projected amendments and my proposal of amendment upon amendment. We had a very long discussion upon one phrase, which seemed to me to require none at all. The sentiment expressed was, that although we should throw no impediment in the way of an arrangement between Spain and her ex-Colonies by amicable negotiation, we should claim to be treated by the South Americans upon the footing of equal favor with the most favored nation. The President had proposed a modifying amendment, which seemed to admit that we should not object to an arrangement by which special favors, or even a restoration of authority, might be conceded to Spain. To this I strenuously objected, as did Mr. Calhoun. . .

I mentioned also my wish to prepare a paper to be delivered confidentially to Baron Tuyl, and the substance of which I would in the first instance express to him in a verbal conference. It would refer to the verbal communications recently made by him, and to the sentiments and dispositions manifested in the extract of a dispatch relating to Spanish affairs which he lately put into my hands. My purpose would be in a moderate and conciliatory manner, but with a firm and determined spirit, to declare our dissent from the principles avowed in those communications, to assert those upon which our own Government is founded, and, while disclaiming all intention of attempting to propagate them by force, and all interference with the political affairs of Europe, to declare our expectation and hope that the European powers will equally abstain from the attempt to spread their principles in the American hemisphere, or to subjugate by force any part of these continents to their will.

The President approved of this idea; and then taking up the sketches that he had prepared for his message, read them to us. Its introduction was in a tone of deep solemnity and of high alarm, intimating that this country is menaced by imminent and formidable dangers, such as would probably soon call for their most vigorous energies and the closest union. It then proceeded to speak of the foreign affairs, chiefly according to the sketch I had given him some days since, but with occasional variations. It then alluded to the recent events in Spain and Portugal, speaking in terms of the most pointed reprobation of the late invasion of Spain by France, and of the principles upon which it was undertaken by the open avowal of the King of France. It also contained a broad acknowledgment to the Greeks as an independent nation, and a recommendation to Congress to make an appropriation for sending a Minister to them.

Of all this Mr. Calhoun declared his approbation. I expressed as freely my wish that the President would reconsider the whole subject before he should determine to take that course. I said the tone of the introduction I apprehended would take the nation by surprise and greatly alarm them. It would come upon them like a clap of thunder. There had never been in the history of this nation a period of so deep calm and tranquillity as we now enjoyed. We never were, upon the whole, in a state of peace so profound and secure with all foreign nations as at this time. This message would be a summons to arms — to arms against all Europe, and for objects of policy exclusively European — Greece and Spain. It would be as new, too, in our policy as it would be surprising.

Nov. 22. — Mr. Gallatin was with the President, but withdrew on my going in. I left with the President my draft for a second dispatch to R. Rush on South American affairs. And I spoke to him again urging him to abstain from everything in his message which the Holy Allies could make a pretext for construing into aggression upon them. I said there were considerations of weight which I could not even easily mention at a Cabinet meeting. If he had determined to retire from the public service at the end of his present term, it was now drawing to a close. It was to be considered now as a whole, and a system of administration for a definite term of years. It would hereafter, I believed, be looked back to as the golden age of this republic, and I felt an extreme solicitude that its end might correspond with the character of its progress; that the Administration might be delivered into the hands of the successor, whoever he might be, at peace and in amity with all the world. If this could not be, if the Holy Alliance were determined to make up an issue with us, it was our policy to meet, and not to make it. We should retreat to the wall before taking to arms, and be sure at every step to put them as much as possible in the wrong.

Nov. 24. — I called at the President's, and found Mr. Gallatin with him. He still adhered to his idea of sending a naval force and a loan of money to the Greeks; and as he is neither an enthusiast nor a fool, and knows perfectly well that no such thing will be done, I look for the motives of this strange proposal, and find them not very deeply laid. Mr. Gallatin still builds castles in the air of popularity, and, being under no responsibility for consequences, patronizes the Greek cause for the sake of raising his own reputation. His measure will not succeed, and, even if it should, all the burden and danger of it will bear not upon him, but upon the Administration, and he will be the great champion of Grecian liberty. 'Tis the part of Mr. Clay towards South America acted over again. After he withdrew, the President read me his paragraphs respecting the Greeks, Spain, Portugal, and South America. I thought them quite unexceptionable and drawn up altogether in the spirit that I had so urgently pressed on Friday and Saturday.

Nov. 25. — I made a draft of observations upon the communications recently received from the Baron de Tuyl, the Russian Minister. Took the paper, together with the statement I had prepared of what has passed between him and me, and all the papers received from him, to the President. I found General Swartwout of New York, with him, but he immediately withdrew. Mr. Southard just then came in, and the President sent for the other members of the Administration, Mr. Calhoun and Mr. Wirt. Mr. Crawford continues convalescent, but was not well enough to attend. My proposal was that a paper like that which I had prepared, modified as the President should finally direct, be delivered by me to the Baron de Tuyl in the form of an inofficial verbal note; that I should invite him to a conference, then read the paper to him, deliver him a copy of it, and tell him that I was willing to converse with him concerning it if he thought proper. The paper itself was drawn to correspond exactly with a paragraph of the President's message which he had read me yesterday and which was entirely conformable to the system of policy which I have earnestly recommended for this emergency. It was also intended as a firm, spirited, and yet conciliatory answer to all the communications lately received from the Russian Government, and at the same time an unequivocal answer to the proposals made by Canning to Mr. Rush. It was meant also to be eventually an exposition of the principles of this Government, and a brief development of its political system as henceforth to be maintained: essentially republican — maintaining its own independence, and respecting that of others; essentially pacific — studiously avoiding all involvement in the combinations of European politics, cultivating peace and friendship with the most absolute monarchies, highly appreciating and anxiously desirous of retaining that of the Emperor Alexander, but declaring that, having recognized the independence of the South American States, we could not see with indifference any attempt by European powers by forcible interposition either to restore the Spanish dominion on the American Continents or to introduce monarchical principles into those countries, or to transfer any portion of the ancient or present American possessions of Spain to any other European power.

This paper was read, and thereupon ensued a desultory discussion till near five o'clock, when the President adjourned the meeting till twelve o'clock to-morrow. Calhoun, with many professions of diffidence and doubt, but only to prompt discussion, questioned whether it would be proper to deliver any such paper to the Russian Minister. The paper contained rather an ostentatious display of republican principles; it was making up an issue, perhaps too soon, with the Holy Alliance. It would perhaps be offensive to the Emperor of Russia, and perhaps even to the British Government, which would by no means relish so much republicanism. . .

Calhoun's objections were not supported; but Mr. Wirt made a question far more important, and which I had made at a much earlier stage of these deliberations. It was, whether we shall be warranted in taking so broadly the ground of resistance to the interposition of the Holy Alliance by force to restore the Spanish dominion in South America. It is, and has been, to me a fearful question. It was not now discussed; but Mr. Wirt remarked upon the danger of assuming the attitude of menace without meaning to strike, and asked, if the Holy Allies should act in direct hostility against South America, whether this country would oppose them by war? My paper and the paragraph would certainly commit us as far as the Executive constitutionally could act on this point; and if we take this course, I should wish that a joint resolution of the two Houses of Congress should be proposed and adopted to the same purport. But this would render it necessary to communicate to them, at least confidentially, the existing state of things.

Nov. 26. — I attended the adjourned Cabinet meeting at the President's, from half-past twelve — four hours.   At the President's request, I read the statement of what has passed between Baron Tuyl and me since the 16th of last month, and then my proposed draft of observations upon the communications recently received from him.   The President then read the draft of the corresponding paragraph for his message to Congress, and asked whether it should form part of the message.   I took a review of the preceding transactions of the Cabinet meetings; remarking that the present questions had originated in a draft which he had presented merely for consideration, of an introduction to the message, of unusual solemnity, indicating extraordinary concern, and even alarm, at the existing state of things, coupled with two paragraphs, one containing strong and pointed censure upon France and the Holy Allies for the invasion of Spain, and the other recommending an appropriation for a Minister to send to the Greeks, and in substance recognizing them as independent; that the course now proposed is a substitute for that, and that it is founded upon the idea that if an issue must be made up between us and the Holy Alliance it ought to be upon grounds exclusively American; that we should separate it from all European concerns, disclaim all intention of interfering with these, and make the stand altogether for an American cause; that at the same time the answer to be given to the Russian communications should be used as the means of answering also the proposals of Mr. George Canning, and of assuming the attitude to be maintained by the United States with reference to the designs of the Holy Alliance upon South America.   This being premised, I observed that the whole of the papers now drawn up were but various parts of one system under consideration, and the only really important question to be determined, as it appeared to me, was that yesterday made by Mr. Wirt, and which had been incidentally discussed before, namely, whether we ought at all to take this attitude as regards South America, whether we get any advantage by committing ourselves to a course of opposition against the Holy Alliance. . .

I said, with regard to the objections of Mr. Wirt, that I considered them of the deepest moment.   I was glad they had been made, and trusted the President would give them full consideration before coming to his definitive decision. If they prevailed, neither the paragraph in the message nor my draft would be proper. The draft was prepared precisely to correspond with the paragraph in the message. I did believe, however, that both would be proper and necessary. Not that I supposed that the Holy Alliance had any intention of ultimately attacking us, or meant to establish monarchy among us. But if they should really invade South America, and especially Mexico, it was impossible, in the nature of things, that they should do it to restore the old exclusive dominion of Spain. Spain had not, and never could again have, the physical force to maintain that dominion; and if the countries should be kept in subjugation by the armies of the Allies, was it in human absurdity to imagine that they should waste their blood and treasure to prohibit their own subjects upon pain of death to set foot upon those territories? Surely not. If then the Holy Allies should subdue Spanish America, however they might at first set up the standard of Spain, the ultimate result of their undertaking would be to recolonize them, partitioned out among themselves. Russia might take California, Peru, Chili; France, Mexico — where we know she has been intriguing to get a monarch under a Prince of the House of Bourbon, as well as at Buenos Ayres. And Great Britain, as her last resort, if she could not resist this course of things, would take at least the island of Cuba for her share of the scramble. Then what would be our situation — England holding Cuba, France Mexico? And Mr. Gallatin had told me within these four days that Hyde de Neuville had said to him, in the presence and hearing of ten or twelve persons, that if we did not yield to the claim of France under the eighth article of the Louisiana Convention, she ought to go and take the country, and that she had a strong party there. The danger, therefore, was brought to our own doors, and I thought we could not too soon take our stand to repel it.

There was another point of view, which the President had in part suggested, and which I thought highly important. Suppose the Holy Allies should attack South America, and Great Britain should resist them alone and without our coöperation. I thought this not an improbable contingency, and I believed in such a struggle the allies would be defeated and Great Britain would be victorious, by her command of the sea. But, as the independence of the South Americans would then be only protected by the guarantee of Great Britain, it would throw them completely into her arms, and in the result make them her colonies instead of those of Spain. My opinion was, therefore, that we must act promptly and decisively. . .

The President retained the paper, to determine finally upon it to-morrow morning.

Nov. 28. — J. W. Taylor was here part of the evening, just arrived from New York. He says there were this afternoon one hundred and twenty seats of members of the House already taken, and he had no doubt there were one hundred and fifty members in the city. This is earlier than usual. We had about two hours of conversation upon various political topics — the recent election in the State of New York, the impending election of Speaker of the House of Representatives, and the more distant Presidential election. He spoke especially of the election of a Vice-President, and intimated that Mr. Crawford's friends had in view for that office Governor Yates, of New York, who desired it.

Dec. 2. — In the evening I called again upon Mr. Clay, and afterwards upon Mr. Gaillard, to inform them of the arrangements made for the funeral of Mr. Greuhm. They said it was probable the two Houses would adjourn over the day without public assignment of the reason. But Clay said he did not know but there might be a debate in the House upon it. He entered also into conversation upon the message, which, he said, seemed to be the work of several hands, and that the War and Navy Departments made a magnificent figure in it, as well as the Post Office. I said there was an account of a full treasury; and much concerning foreign affairs, which was within the business of the Department of State.

He said, yes, and the part relating to foreign affairs was, he thought, the best part of the message. He thought the Government had weakened itself and the tone of the country by withholding so long the acknowledgment of the South American independence, and he believed even a war for it against all Europe, including even England, would be advantageous to us.

I told him I believed a war for South American independence might be inevitable, and, under certain circumstances, might be expedient, but that I viewed war in a very different light from him — as necessarily placing high interests of different portions of the Union in conflict with each other, and thereby endangering the Union itself.

Dec. 4. — I went to the President's, and found Gales, the half-editor of the *National Intelligencer,* there. He said the message was called a war message; and spoke of newspaper paragraphs from Europe announcing that an army of twelve thousand Spaniards was to embark immediately to subdue South America.[3]

I told him there was absurdity on the face of these paragraphs, as the same newspapers announced with more authenticity the disbanding of the Spanish army. The President himself is singularly disturbed with these rumors of invasion by the Holy Alliance.

Jan. 6, 1824. — I called at the President's, and asked him if it would be agreeable to him to attend at the party we propose to give the day after to-morrow to General Jackson, it being the anniversary of his victory at New Orleans. We have invited all the members of both Houses of Congress excepting Alexander Smyth and John Floyd. Their personal deportment to me has been such that I could not include them in the invitation. To avoid inviting the President I thought might be taken as a failure of attention to him; though I did not expect he would come. He said he would think of it and give me an answer.

Jan. 8. — I called at the President's, and while I was there Mr. Calhoun came, with a deputation of five Cherokee Indians. This is the most civilized of the tribes of North American Indians. They have abandoned altogether the life of hunters, and betaken themselves to tillage. These men were dressed entirely according to our manner. Two of them spoke English with good pronunciation, and one with grammatical accuracy. This was a young man of twenty-three, who has passed three or four years at a missionary school in Connecticut.

This being the anniversary of the victory at New Orleans, we gave an evening party or ball to General Jackson at which about one thousand persons attended. General Jackson came about eight o'clock, and retired after supper. The dancing

---

[3] The Monroe Doctrine was enunciated in President Monroe's message to Congress of Dec. 2, 1823.

continued till near one in the morning. The crowd was great, and the house could scarcely contain the company. But it all went off in good order, and without accident. The President this morning excused himself from attending, as I had expected he would. He said that when Mr. Crawford went into Virginia last summer he (the President) had pointedly avoided meeting him — even when he was sick at Governor Barbour's; and at the present moment, if he should depart from his rule of not visiting at private houses, it might be thought he was countenancing one of the candidates for the Presidency, while he had so cautiously abstained from giving even seeming countenance to another.

Jan. 12. — Captain O'Brien came, and talked much upon his own affairs and upon general politics. He gave me a copy of the printed circular from thirteen members of the House of Representatives and one Senator from Pennsylvania, assigning their reasons for declining to attend a partial Congressional caucus. This is apparently maturing into a great party question. The Legislatures of New York and Virginia have declared in favor of a caucus nomination; Tennessee, South Carolina, Alabama, and Maryland against one. The movement of Pennsylvania is even now not absolute and decisive; it declares only against a partial caucus; but it has the aspect of an effort in Pennsylvania to take the lead of the affairs of the Union out of the hands of Virginia. There is yet room for much development of policy between those States.

Jan. 25. — I visited Vice-President Tompkins, who arrived in the city and took the chair of the Senate last Tuesday. He told me that he had recovered his health, with the exception of sleepless nights, and that he was relieved from all his embarrassments; that he had no intention of being a candidate either for election to the Presidency or for re-election as Vice-President. All he wanted was justice. He could speak with a voice of thunder to the Legislature of New York; but he had determined to take no part in the approaching election, and wished for nothing hereafter but quiet and retirement.

I next called upon John W. Taylor, and had with him a conversation of nearly three hours. He and Mr. Livermore had called at my house last evening. The Presidential canvassing proceeds with increasing heat. The prospects in the

Legislature of New York are at present highly favorable to
Mr. Crawford and his party; and the prospect that he will obtain the whole electoral vote of that State has suggested to the
friends of the other candidates here the necessity of *concert*
among them in opposing him, and the first measure upon which
this concert was sought was in the opposition to a Congressional
caucus nomination.

I told Taylor that my mind was made up. I was satisfied
there was at this time a majority of the whole people of the
United States, and a majority of the States, utterly averse
to a nomination by Congressional caucus, thinking it adverse to
the spirit of the Constitution, and tending to corruption. I
thought it so myself; and therefore would not now accept
a Congressional caucus nomination, even for the Presidency.
And of course a nomination for the Vice-Presidency, in co-
operation with one for Mr. Crawford as President, could
have no charms for me. Not that I despised the Vice-
Presidency, or wished peevishly to reject the second place because I could not obtain the first; but because the people disapproved of this mode of nomination, and I disapproved of it
myself.

Feb. 4. — S. D. Ingham called again, and I had a full and
explicit conversation with him respecting G. M. Dallas,
and generally respecting the treatment of me by Mr. Calhoun
and his friends; the professions of friendship and the acts of
insidious hostility; the requisitions upon me to dismiss the
Democratic Press and appoint the *Franklin Gazette* to publish
the laws in Philadelphia; the vindictive malice of Binns, which
they thereby excited against me; the flaunting declaration
in the *Franklin Gazette* immediately afterwards, that they
were under no obligation to me for the appointment; the
decided part taken against me by that paper in the controversy
with Jonathan Russell, and its frequent ill-disguised attacks
upon me since; the courtship of the New England federalists
for Mr. Calhoun; the toast to the memory of Fisher Ames,
at the Edgefield dinner to McDuffie; the newspapers set up
in Massachusetts to support Mr. Calhoun; the smuggled
paragraphs, asserting that my friends in New England had
abandoned me for him; and the panegyric of the Washington
Republican upon the Boston *Galaxy,* a paper for years advertised for sale to the highest bidder of the Presidential

candidates, and which has at last opened a battery of scurrilous abuse upon me, and in ;avowed support of Mr. Calhoun. I mentioned all these things to him in frankness, but told him they had not the slightest effect upon my opinion with regard to the appointment of Mr. Dallas. . .

I attended in the evening the drawing-room at the President's. On returning home, I found J. W. Taylor at my house, and had a long conversation with him. He told me that Jesse B. Thomas, a Senator from Illinois, had strongly urged upon him the expediency of my acquiescing in the nomination as Vice-President, with Mr. Crawford for the Presidency. He said that Mr. Crawford would certainly be elected, and he spoke of certain members of Congress as ultimately to vote for him who appear to be far otherwise disposed at this time; that it was, however, very desirable that he should carry with him the strength which he would derive from the coöperation of my friends; that from the state of Mr. Crawford's [4] health it was highly probable the duties of the Presidency would devolve upon the Vice-President, which had made it necessary to select with peculiar anxiety a person qualified for the contingency which was to be anticipated; that a compliance with the views of Mr. Crawford's friends on this occasion would be rendering them a service which would recommend me to their future favor, and would doubtless secure my election hereafter to the Presidency. Taylor said he had answered that admitting even the certainty that Mr. Crawford should be elected, that was no sufficient reason for the acquiescence of my friends in the proposed arrangement.

March 10. — Mr. Southard, Secretary of the Navy, came to ask for a letter from Commodore Stewart which he had sent me and which I had just sent back to the Navy Department. Southard talked with me largely upon election prospects and was apparently desirous of ascertaining my sentiments concerning Calhoun and Jackson. I gave them to him without reserve. The Pennsylvania Convention at Harrisburg have nominated Jackson for President, and Calhoun Vice-President. Southard thought the Vice-Presidency was not the place for Calhoun, but yet seemed inclined that he should be voted for

[4] In the early stages of the four-cornered contest for the Presidency, with Adams, Clay, Crawford, and Jackson as the aspirants, Crawford had easily held the lead. But he was now in chronic bad health, having been bled until he was quite devitalized. There hung over his head a heavy blow of fate.

to it. He asked me who my friends would vote for. I told
him, probably Jackson. He asked if that would not strengthen
Jackson's chance of success for the Presidency. I had no doubt
it would. But what then? My friends would vote for him on
correct principle — his fitness for the place, the fitness of the
place for him, and the peculiar advantage of the geographical
association. If by voting for him as Vice-President my friends
should induce others to vote for him as President, they and I
must abide by the issue.

March 15. — I dined at General Jackson's, with a company
of about twenty-five — heads of Departments, members of
Congress, and officers of the army and navy. Clay and Calhoun were there. It was the General's birthday, and apparently the occasion upon which he gave the dinner. Clay
had been arguing in the Supreme Court this morning the case
of the *Apollon* against the Government, and had taken the
opportunity of being, as he professed, very severe upon me.
At the dinner he became warm, vehement, and absurd upon the
tariff, and persisted in discussing it, against two or three attempts of Eaton to change the subject of the conversation. He
is so ardent, dogmatical, and overbearing that it is extremely
difficult to preserve the temper of friendly society with him.

March 19. — Johnson says Mr. Crawford's friends, particularly Governor Barbour, are very sanguine of his election,
and entirely sure of the vote of New York. They consider
all prospect of my being supported as having vanished, and that
all New England will abandon me and vote for Crawford. I
believe Mr. Crawford's prospects and mine equally unpromising. Intrigue against the voice of the people will probably
give him New York. Virginia, Georgia, North Carolina, and
Delaware will also probably be for him; but no others; and if
New York fails him he will decline and withdraw. Whether
all New England will support me is yet problematical, and the
rest is yet more uncertain. The issue must be where it ought
to be and my duty is cheerful acquiescence in the event.

March 21. — I called at the beginning of the evening upon
Colonel John Taylor, the Senator from Virginia, and R. P.
Garnett, the member of the House, who has just returned from
a visit home. Taylor continues low in health and feeble. He repeated to me the anecdote concerning Patrick Henry which he
had related some weeks since at my house; that in the campaign

of 1781 Henry actually proposed in a secret session of the Legislature of Virginia that she should be the first to submit to Great Britain, in order that she might obtain the most favorable terms. Taylor was himself a member of the Legislature, and heard him move to go into secret session, there make the proposition, and support it by an eloquent speech. It met with such immediate, indignant, and universal opposition that when the debate closed he had changed his side, and was among the most ardent and sanguine for perseverance in the war. Taylor thinks there is great exaggeration in the panegyric upon Henry by Mr. Wirt, and says that Henry had much less efficient agency in the Revolution than many others.

He spoke also of the debates in the Senate on Thursday and Friday last, which he said would continue, and intimated his intention to take further part in them. He told me that the alteration of the Constitution in 1803, of the mode of electing the President and Vice-President, had been determined upon in a caucus, and the introduction of the amendment had been assigned to him. He had introduced it, and it was carried, but he now repented of it, and would be in favor of Mr. Mill's amendment, to repeal that amendment and restore the Constitution as it originally was.

March 24. — On the Georgian compact and Indian land rights the President read a new draft of a message, different from that of the last meeting. In this he very distinctly declared his opinion that the Indians cannot, with justice, be removed from their lands within the State of Georgia by force. But, after setting forth all that has been done by the Government of the Union in fulfilment of the compact, the positive refusal of the Cherokees to cede any more of their lands upon any terms whatever, and the impossibility of devising any other means short of force to prevail upon them to go, there was a new and rather elaborate argument introduced, of the absolute necessity that the Indians should remove west of the Mississippi; and, after concluding that nothing further could be done by the Executive, there were direct intimations that something should be done by Congress. . . The President spoke of the compact as a very unfavorable bargain to the United States — as it certainly was. Mr. Calhoun thinks that the great difficulty arises from the progress of the Cherokees in civilization. They are now, within the limits of Georgia, about fifteen thousand, and increasing in equal proportion with the whites; all cultivators, with a representative government, judicial courts, Lancaster schools, and permanent property. Ridge, Hicks, and Lowry, now here, are principal chiefs, and Ross. They write their own State papers, and reason as logically as most white diplomatists. Each of the chiefs here named possesses from fifty to a hundred thousand dollars property.

March 31. — I attended alone the drawing-room at the President's. Thinner than usual. Conversations with W. Plumer, Crowninshield, J. W. Taylor, and Burton. All accounts from Albany unfavorable to the Crawford interest, but otherwise uncertain and contradictory. Taylor's letter from Stewart holds up Clay as predominant. His conversations with Moore, a Calhounite transferred to Jackson. Calhoun's game now is to unite Jackson's supporters and mine upon him for Vice-President. Look out for breakers!

Day. I have received in the course of this month two hundred and thirty-five visitors, which is an average of about eight a day. A half an hour to each visitor occupies four hours a day; but that is short of the average. The interruption to business thus incessantly repeated is distressing, but unavoidable.

April 2. — I walked with Plumer to the Capitol, to hear the close of Mr. Webster's speech upon the tariff — which I did. He spoke about an hour; but the principal part of his speech was delivered yesterday. It was universally admitted to be an able and powerful speech.

April 10. — The President adverted to another subject, of which he had never before spoken to me, but which for years has given him trouble. On the 3d of March, 1817, there was appropriated twenty thousand dollars, and on the 20th of April, 1818, thirty thousand dollars, for furnishing the President's house, to be expended under his direction. He charged Colonel Lane, Commissioner of the Public Buildings, chiefly with it. Lane died about a year and a half ago, a defaulter for several thousand dollars, and rumors have since been in obscure circulation that the President himself had used large sums of the money and thereby occasioned the defalcation. At the last session of Congress, John Cocke, member of the House from Tennessee, instituted in the House an enquiry concerning the state of Lane's accounts after his decease, and, finding upon examination that the President had received a part of the money, sent him a message to enquire if he would appear before the committee, to answer interrogatories or give explanations concerning these expenditures.

He desired the person who brought him the message to tell Cocke that he was a scoundrel, and that that was the only answer he would give him. Cocke had then intended to make a report, but the committee which had been raised at his instance would not agree to it. At the present session of Congress, Cocke had again raised a committee on the subject, and is pushing the investigation to a report.

April 11. — I read this day the President's memoir upon the transactions relating to the appropriations for furnishing the President's house. It enters into details of a very humiliating character, and which ought never to have been, or to be, required of him. The principal difficulty appears to have sprung from his having used his own furniture until that provided for by the appropriations could be procured, and having received for it six thousand dollars, to be repaid upon the redelivery of his furniture to him. This produced an intermingling of Lane's public and private accounts with him, which, by Lane's sickness and death, remained unsettled at his decease. There arises from all this an exposure of domestic and household concerns almost as incongruous to the station of a President of the United States as it would be to a blooming virgin to exhibit herself naked before a multitude. The malignity of political opposition has no feeling of delicacy. There appears to be nothing really censurable in all these transactions, but Lane was an unfortunate selection as an agent, and his final insolvency has produced all these awkward consequences.

April 17. — At the office, Albert H. Tracy came, and had a conversation with me of nearly two hours, chiefly on the prospects of the Presidential election. He said there was a great and powerful party getting up for General Jackson as President in New York; that it could not possibly succeed, but that its probable effect would be to secure the electoral vote of the State to Mr. Crawford. He said that the Legislature, having retained the choice of the electoral ticket to themselves, and thereby incurred some unpopularity, would be careful to choose a ticket the vote of which would be decisive of the election, and thereby endeavor to justify themselves before the people. Tracy has more than once expressed to me the opinion that among the people as well as in the Legislature of New York the political impulse to action was founded upon the doctrine of equivalents.

April 19. — A much graver affair has this day broken out afresh in the House of Representatives. An address to the House was read from N. Edwards, lately a Senator from Illinois, now appointed Minister to Mexico, defensive of himself against a charge contained in a report to the House, made by Mr. Crawford since Edwards left this place, that Edwards had made false statements against Crawford before a committee of the House at the last session. Edwards retaliates by six direct allegations of official misconduct in Crawford, closing with a broad insinuation against him of perjury.

This paper came upon the House by surprise, and they showed titubation as to what they should do with it. They fianally referred it to a select committee, with power to send for persons and papers. Edwards avows himself the author of the A. B. papers of last winter, and challenges a charge against himself, of having falsely inculpated Mr. Crawford, admitting that, if he has, it is a misdemeanor which renders him unworthy of the office that he holds. In this affair Edwards is under great disadvantages, by his absence; by the want of any person here daring enough to sustain his cause against the browbeating temper of Crawford's partisans, and by the dastardly spirit of the rest. Crawford will be sustained against demonstration itself. But they will only substitute invective against Edwards for impeachment.

April 28. — Richard M. Johnson, Senator from Kentucky, called to renew recommendations of a person named Steele, as Consul at Acapulco, in Mexico. He talked also upon general politics, and told me, as an illustration of the extent to which the system of "espionage" of Crawford's partisans is now carried, that he had lately been to Philadelphia, where he passed two or three days. While there, he occasionally conversed with persons whom he met on the prospects of the Presidential election. Yesterday Van Buren accosted him with, "So, you have been electioneering at Philadelphia!" and, upon being asked what he meant took out a letter and gave it him to read folding down the page so that he could not see the name of the writer; and this letter spoke of, and gave a false coloring to, his conversations at Philadelphia.

Mr. John Reed, member from Massachusetts, came for a further conversation upon the subject on which we had spoken last Saturday. He had since then seen and talked with Webster; and had asked him to see and talk with me; which he had declined. He said that Webster had expressed apprehensions that in the event of my election there would be a general proscription of federalists from office, and intimated that he could not favor a system by which such men as Jeremiah Mason, of New Hampshire, and Joseph Hopkinson, of Pennsylvania, should be excluded from the public service. Reed said he did not believe that I should act upon any such principle, but did not tell Webster that he had conversed with me. I told Reed that with regard to individuals it was impossible for me to give any pledge whatever. I had no personal acquaintance with Mr. Mason, but knew him by reputation as a man of fine talents and highly respectable character. Mr. Hopkinson was, and had been for many years, my personal friend. I consider them both as well qualified for the public service, and never, under any circumstances, would I be made the instrument of a systematic exclusion of such men from it.

May 8. — Mr. McLean, the Postmaster-General, called. He wrote me, some days since, a letter asking my opinion upon the subject of internal improvement, and a copy of the resolution offered by me to the Senate on the 23d of February, 1807. I answered his letter, and he now came to ask my leave to send a copy of my answer to his brother, in the State of Ohio. I told him I had no objection, but wished him only not to suffer it to get into the newspapers, as that would look too much like advertising my opinions. He said he would take care of that. His brother is one of the names on the proposed electoral ticket of Ohio, and writes that he is sanguine of success. We know so little of that in futurity which is best for ourselves, that whether I ought to wish for success is among the greatest uncertainties of the election. Were it possible to look with philosophical indifference to the event, that is the temper of mind to which I should aspire; but

Who can hold a fire in his hand
By thinking on the frosty Caucasus?

To suffer without feeling is not in human nature; and when I consider that to me alone, of all the candidates before the nation, failure of success would be equivalent to a vote of censure by the nation upon my past service, I cannot dissemble to myself that I have more at stake upon the result than any other individual in the Union. Yet a man qualified for the elective Chief Magistracy of ten millions of people should be a man proof alike to prosperous and to adverse fortune. If I am able to bear success, I must be tempered to endure defeat.

May 10. — Dr. Thornton called upon me this morning, to say that he had prepared a book to be deposited in the Congress library at the Capitol, to contain the subscriptions of all persons in the service of the United States, at Washington, for the Greeks. His project was that every individual would subscribe one day's pay. He had requested the subscription of the President, who told him he would consult the members of his Administration upon the propriety of his subscribing. The Doctor hoped I should advise him to do it. The Secretaries of War and the Navy had said they would subscribe if the President and I did. Lord Eldon, the English Chancellor, had subscribed a hundred pounds sterling, and even the Quakers in England had subscribed upwards of seven thousand pounds. The Greeks were in great want of it, and in deep distress. . . I told him I should not subscribe for the Greeks, nor advise the President to subscribe. We had objects of distress to relieve at home more than sufficient to absorb all my capacities of contribution; and a subscription for the Greeks would, in my view of things, be a breach of neutrality, and therefore improper.

May 19. — Mr. Mower, of New York, was here, as I inferred from his conversation, to renew in behalf of De Witt Clinton the attempt to obtain for General Jackson the electoral vote of New York for the Presidency. He told me that he had seen Mr. Clinton, and a particular and intimate friend of his (Ambrose Spencer), who thoroughly approved of all the arrangements of Mower here, and were decidedly of opinion that there was in the Legislature no chance for any person against Mr. Crawford but me. Mr. Clinton was, however, doubtful whether by the purchase of Young, of Peter B. Porter, and with them of Clay's party, Mr. Crawford would not ultimately prevail in the Legislature. But Mr. Crary and

Solomon Van Rensselaer were confident that Crawford could under no circumstances whatever obtain the vote of New York. But Governor Yates had determined to call the Legislature together and recommend to them the passage of an Act giving the choice of electors to the people. The proclamation was already prepared, and would issue immediately after the adjournment of Congress. It would instantly kill two men — William H. Crawford and Henry Clay; and if the election went before the people, no man could stand in competition with General Jackson. The 8th of January and the battle of New Orleans was a thing that every man would understand, and Mr. Clinton had told him that General Jackson would beat him (Clinton himself) before the people of New York by thirty-three and one-third per cent.

May. 23. — Mr. Hay spoke, as he always does, with extreme bitterness of Mr. Jefferson, whom he declares to be one of the most insincere men in the world. He reminded me of a letter written by Mr. Jefferson to Mr. Monroe in 1818–19, upon my controversial papers with Spain, and relating to the Seminole War. They were in a style even of extravagant encomium. Precisely at the same time, Hay says, Ritchie, of Richmond, told him that Mr. Jefferson had spoken of the same papers in terms of severe reprobation to a gentleman from whom he had it. Hay said he told Ritchie that that gentleman lied; but he knew better: the gentleman was Edward Coles, and he had told the truth. Mr. Jefferson! — his enmity to Mr. Monroe was inveterate, though disguised, and he was at the bottom of all the opposition to Mr. Monroe in Virginia.

May 26. — Colonel Taylor told me he should leave the city, to return home, to-morrow. He spoke, therefore, freely upon the Presidential election. The Legislature of Virginia, he said, had been managed into a declaration in support of Mr. Crawford as the caucus candidate; and the State would support him if he continued on the list of candidates. But he was again ill: rumors were afloat that he had suffered a paralytic affection of the tongue, and since Sunday had been quite or nearly speechless.[5] It was doubtful whether he would recover, at least so as to be sustainable for a Presidential candidate. The State of Virginia would be compelled to look

[5] Crawford had in fact suffered a stroke of paralysis, brought on by a physician's unskilful administration of lobelia.

elsewhere, and he felt perfectly sure that neither Mr. Clay not General Jackson could obtain the vote of the State. The Richmond junto would attempt to bring up Clay; but they could not succeed, and if the choice should come to the House of Representatives, I might take it for a certainty that the vote of the Virginia delegation would be neither for Jackson nor Clay. He thought everything depended upon the State of New York, and had not a doubt that Virginia would declare for me if New York should do so.

May 27. — Before leaving the Capitol, the President in close confidence told Mr. Calhoun, Mr. Southard, and me that a friend of his had informed him confidentially, and that he might be prepared to act upon such an event, that Mr. Webster had assured him that unless Edwards upon his examination should furnish more satisfactory grounds for his inculpation of Mr. Crawford, the final report of the committee would be decisive against him; and the President strongly intimated that he would in that case remove Edwards. I expressed a doubt whether the committee would thus decide; Calhoun said it was impossible. With the exception of the indefinite charge of having mismanaged the finances, they had found all the facts as charged by Edwards. They had made at least two glaring misstatements to operate against him, and had credited Mr. Crawford for all the bad money that he had passed off upon public creditors as if he had never received it. I asked the President who it was that had given him this hint, but he declined telling. He took me home in his carriage.

May 31. — *Day*. Rise between six and seven. Breakfast between nine and ten. With this interval, I write and receive visitors till between one and two. Then at the office and the President's till between five and six. Home to dine. Walk after dinner. Write or receive visitors till near midnight. This is the very regular course of my occupations. My time is chiefly worn out with visitors, of whom the number personally received in the course of the month has been two hundred and sixty-four. I never exclude any one. But necessary and important business suffers by the unavoidable waste of time.

June 3. — The President this day gave me two sheets of paper, dated 20th and 21st January, 1823, being confirmations by the Senate of nominations to office at the session of Congress before the last. These papers had been loosely

mixed among others now nearly eighteen months, and for want
of these confirmations new nominations, in several instances,
have been made, at this last session, of persons whose appointments were already complete — among them, that of Mr.
Woodbridge as Secretary of the Michigan Territory, who I
feared had been in the same predicament with Governor
Miller, of Arkansas — acting upwards of a year without any
appointment.   These irregularities happen for want of system
. . . and of an efficient private secretary.

July 7. — Correspondence with the committee of arrangements in the *National Journal*.   Writing a statement of facts
relating to the debate on the Embargo.   Note from P. U. S.
Cabinet meeting at noon.   Only Calhoun and myself present.
Salazar's note.   How to be answered.   The Colombian republic to maintain its own independence.   Hope that France
and the Holy Allies will not resort to force against it.   If they
should, the power to determine our resistance is in Congress.
The movements of the Executive will be as heretofore expressed.   I am to draft an answer.   State of Mr. Crawford's
health.   Attorney-General's opinion; use of a facsimile lawful; conditionally, if the mind and sight are competent to the
transaction of business.   Otherwise P. U. S. ought to make a
temporary appointment.   Calhoun differed from Wirt's opinion; thought the practice was eminently dangerous.   Case of
Governor McKean in Pennsylvania.   Papers relating to it
sent by N. Biddle to Crawford.   P. U. S. will refer to the
Comptroller Anderson, to see Mr. Crawford, ascertain his
own opinion, and report.

July 10. — At the President's, with letters from the Slave
Indemnity Commissioners.   Draft of answer to them.   Mr.
Crawford's health and facsimile.   Anderson's report; speaks
strongly of Mr. Crawford's rapid convalescence; refers the
main question to the President's own observation upon any
interview promised by Mr. Crawford on the 8th, but did not
come.   Many warrants were paid without any signature by
Mr. Crawford; but after payment, the facsimile was applied
to them.   P. U. S. said he would call upon Anderson for a
more specific report.

July 29. — I went out after dinner with Mr. Everett, and
paid a visit to Mr. Crawford at his residence in the country.
We found him convalescent, in cheerful spirits, and intending

to go next week upon his excursion to Pennsylvania and New York. His articulation is still affected by a salivation not entirely passed off, but he appears otherwise quite well.

July 31. — *Day.* I rise between five and six, and, when the tide serves, swim between one and two hours in the Potomac. Breakfast about nine, then write or meditate or receive visitors till one or two. Attend at my office till six, then home to dine. Take an evening walk of half an hour, and from ten to eleven retire to bed. There are eight or ten newspapers of extensive circulation published in various parts of the Union acting in close concert with each other and pouring forth continual streams of slander upon my character and reputation, public and private. No falsehood is too broad, and no insinuation too base, for them, and a great portion of their calumnies are of a nature that no person could show or even assert their falsehood but myself. As the Presidential election approaches, numerous correspondents from every quarter write me letters professing good will, or enquiring of my opinions, from men most of them entirely unknown to me. I answer very few, and perhaps ought to answer none of them Particular friends write to me by way of consultation and of anxiety; and they can seldom be answered with entire freedom. The result is a great waste of time and of mental occupation upon subjects personal to myself, to the necessary neglect of public business and detriment to the public service. I have no reason to hope to be released from this state of trial for many months to come. To pass through it with a pure heart and a firm spirit is my duty and my prayer.

Aug. 5. — Swam an hour in the Potomac alone; but the morning was cool, and the remonstrances of my friends against the continuance of this practice will induce me to abandon it perhaps altogether. Mr. Lemuel Sawyer, formerly a member of Congress, called upon me with a subscription-book for the publication of a tragedy in five acts, entitled *The Wreck of Honor*, by him.

Aug. 12. — Walk with G. Hay, who afterwards passed an hour with me. He told me that the President had lately received an anonymous letter, in a disguised hand, and affecting false spelling, but undoubtedly from an able hand, advising him to dismiss all the members of his Administration except Mr. Crawford: Calhoun, because he is presumptuous and extravagant; Southard, to go and keep school in New Jersey; Wirt because he is treacherous, and no real friend to Mr. Monroe; and me, because I despise his abilities. Hay said he did not consider Mr. Crawford a member of the Administration at all, and he persists in thinking his state of health desperate. This is prejudice.

Aug. 27. — Swam with Antoine to and from the bridge — the same as I had done yesterday; but this morning I was an hour and twenty-five minutes in going through the distance I had yesterday traversed in fifty minutes. This difference was owing to the different state of the tide, which was running this morning so much more rapidly than yesterday. Last summer, when the tides were so strong, I desisted from the attempt to reach the bridge, which I now find I can accomplish; but it takes as much time as crossing the river at full tide, and is more fatiguing.

Mr. McLean, the Postmaster-General, called at my house. I gave him a copy of my speech on the Louisiana Appropriation bill, 3d November, 1803. Dr. Watkins showed me a letter from a Mr. Brawner, one of the candidates as an elector of President and Vice-President in Maryland, which gives a particular account of the exertions making by the partisans, both of Mr. Crawford and of General Jackson, to slander me and run down my reputation. There is a common chime to the same purpose in all the presses devoted to Crawford, and in several devoted to Jackson. About fifteen newspapers in various parts of the United States, several of them daily papers, others printed two or three times a week, are, and for the ensuing four or five months at least will be, filled column upon column with everything that truth, misrepresentation, or falsehood can supply to defame or disgrace me. In passing through this ordeal, may the Spirit which has hitherto sustained me still be my staff and guide!

Boston, Sept. 6. — At about eleven we took a hack, and came out to my father's house at Quincy. The infirmities of age have much increased upon my father since I was here last year. His sight is so dim that he can neither write nor read. He cannot walk without aid, and his hearing is partially affected. His memory yet remains strong, his judgment sound, and his interest in conversation considerable.

Quincy, Sept. 8. — The remainder of this day I passed in

conversation with my father. He bears his condition with
fortitude, but is sensible to all its helplessness. His mind is
still vigorous, but cannot dwell long upon any one subject.
Articles of news and of political speculation in the newspapers
are read to him, on which he remarks with sound discernment.
He receives some letters, and dictates answers to them. In
general the most remarkable circumstance of his present state
is the total prostration of his physical powers, leaving his mental faculties scarcely impaired at all.

Sept. 19. — I had a long conversation with Sprague on the
subject of the Vice-Presidency. With regard to General Jackson as the prospect now is that he will stand the highest on the
list of candidates for the Presidency, it appears useless to sustain him for the second office. But as the Pennsylvania nomination, Jackson and Calhoun, is absolute proscription of New
England, I advised Sprague that my friends here should be-
think themselves twice before they lend their aid to any part
of this inveterate exclusion of themselves.

Sept. 20. — I walked in the burying-yard, and viewed the
granite tombstones erected over the graves of my ancestors
by my father. Henry Adams, the first of the family, who
came from England; Joseph Adams, Sr., and Abigail Baxter,
his wife; Joseph Adams, Jr., and Hannah Bass, his second
wife; John Adams, Sr., my father's father, and Susannah
Boylston, his wife. Four generations, of whom very little more
is known than is recorded upon these stones. There are three
succeeding generations of us now living. Pass another century, and we shall all be mouldering in the same dust, or resolved into the same elements. Who then of our posterity
shall visit this yard? And what shall he read engraved upon
the stones? This is known only to the Creator of all. The
record may be longer. May it be of as blameless lives!

Sept. 24. — This day we took our departure to return to
Washington. I took leave of my father with a heavy and
foreboding heart. Told him I should see him again next
year.

Philadelphia, Oct. 2. — Called this morning before breakfast again upon General La Fayette. He had not risen; but
a few minutes after sent me word he was rising, and wished
to see me. I went immediately, and found him in his bed-
chamber, dressing. In his breakfast-chamber I met also his

son George Washington, and his Secretary, Mr. Le Vasseur. After breakfast, I went to Mr. Joseph R. Ingersoll's. . . I went with Ingersoll and Chapman to the theatre, which is fitting up for the great ball to be given to General La Fayette next Monday. Met there G. M. Dallas; Strickland, the architect; Wood, the manager of the theatre; and some others. They have inscriptions and portraits and mottoes and painted scenery, and columns with the names of distinguished military officers of the Revolutionary War. I observed to Dallas that they had no naval names, and, as Philadelphians, ought not to have forgotten that of Biddle. I next went to Mr. Hopkinson's again, and there met Mrs. Chapman, with whom I walked to General Cadwalader's. An evening party, at which General La Fayette, with his son, and Mr. Le Vasseur, attended. The two Misses Wright, maiden ladies, who have followed General La Fayette to this country, were also there. Mrs. Morris, widow of the late Robert Morris, Bishop White, the two daughters of the late Dr. Bollman, and many others, were of the company.

Oct. 5. — Mr. John Vaughan called upon me, and I went with him to the Academy of the Fine Arts. Mr. Hopkinson, the President, delivered diplomas to General La Fayette and his son as honorary members. I met there Mrs. Meredith, and part of her family; thence went with Mr. Vaughan to the Athenaeum, and thence to the State-House. General La Fayette was received in the Hall of Independence, so called from being that where the Congress of the Confederation used to meet, and whence the Declaration of Independence issued. Its interior has, however, since been entirely altered. From the Hall, General La Fayette went upon the steps of the south front door of the State-House, where the children of the schools passed in review before him, two thousand two hundred and fifty girls and one thousand eight hundred boys — chiefly from seven to fourteen years of age. There were several addresses — numerous emblematic and mottoed banners — one song — and a speech in French, by General Cadwalader's son, a lad of about fourteen.

Oct. 7. — The night was fine, and we rose this morning in sight of North Point. We had barely time to breakfast when four steamboats crowded with passengers came down from the city to meet and escort the General. There was great

shouting and cheering at the meeting, and we proceeded up
the river with four boats, two in front and two in rear of
ours, and at equal distances. We landed in barges at Fort
McHenry. The barge in which the General went, and in
which I accompanied him, was rowed by six captains of mer-
chant-vessels. At the fort, the General was received by Colonel Hindman, the commandant, in handsome military style.
Colonel Jones, General Macomb, and Major Vandeventer
were present. The tent used by General Washington during
the Revolutionary War, borrowed from Mr. Custis, of Ar-
lington, was spread there, and beneath it the General was met
by Governor Stevens, of Maryland, who addressed him in
a respectable speech, which he answered with his customary
felicity. Mr. Charles Carroll of Carrollton, one of the three
surviving signers of the Declaration of Independence, Colonel
John E. Howard, one of the highly distinguished officers of
the Revolutionary War, and several other veterans of the
same class, were there — all deeply affected by the scene,
which was purely pathetic.

Washington, Nov. 10. — Cabinet meeting. Present W. H.
Crawford, J. C. Calhoun, Samuel L. Southard, and J. Q.
Adams. . . Mr. Crawford told twice over the story of
President Washington's having at an early period of his Administration gone to the Senate with a project of a treaty to
be negotiated, and been present at their deliberations upon it.
They debated it and proposed alterations, so that when Washington left the Senate-chamber he said he would be damned if
he ever went there again. And ever since that time treaties
have been negotiated by the Executive before submitting them
to the consideration of the Senate.

The President said he had come into the Senate about eighteen months after the first organization of the present Government, and then heard that something like this had occurred. . .

This was the first Cabinet meeting at which Mr. Crawford
had attended since last April. His articulation is yet much
affected, and his eyesight impaired. But his understanding
remains, except with some deficiencies of memory and ignorance
of very notorious facts, probably because he was many months
unable to read with his own eyes. Mr. Rush's advice to send
a frigate to the Columbia River was mentioned by the President. Mr. Crawford thought a military post there would

be proper and sufficient. He was not for sending a colony or establishing a Territory there. He said he had last winter advised Dr. Floyd to change his plan from a Territory to a military post, and the Doctor had told him he would.

Nov. 30. — Tuesday — Cabinet meeting. Present W. H. Crawford, J. C. Calhoun, Samuel L. Southard, and J. Q. Adams. Draft of the message read by the President. His method of writing it is upon loose sheets of paper like Sibylline leaves — a separate sheet for each subject distinctly noticed in it. He receives minutes for it from each of the heads of Departments, but that from the Treasury has not yet been furnished him. Mr. Crawford intimated that it was because Mr. Calhoun had sent for his estimates back, to make some change in them, and that they had not been returned; but Mr. Calhoun said the alteration had been trifling, and that they had been returned the same day that he had sent for them. The message is very long.

Dec. 3. — R. M. Johnson here. Presidential speculations; Clay or Crawford in the House; resentments against the caucus; thinks the dismission of Crawford from the Treasury will be made a test of voting with many members; Crawford's health; Scott, of Missouri's, remark, that he was more infirm than he had expected to find him. Preparing papers for Congress.

Dec. 10. — Visits from members of Congress — Mangum, of N. C., Letcher, of Kentucky, Wright and McLean, of Ohio, and Wood and Craig of New York. With the ladies to the Capitol, and witnessed the public reception of General La Fayette by the House of Representatives. Mr. Clay, the Speaker's, address, and his answer. G. W. La Fayette's observation to me — what a glorious day for his father! . . At. P. U. S. He spoke of Mr. Crawford's health with concern; of his annual Treasury report with anxiety, that it might contain views of fiscal concerns different from those of the message; said he had not obtained the Treasury returns till the Friday before the message was to be delivered; interviews between S. L. Gouverneur and A. Dickens. The President had also urged Anderson, the Comptroller, to hasten the Treasury returns, to avert surmises as to Mr. Crawford's health.

Dec. 12. — Mr. Clay came in, and spoke of the projected grant to General La Fayette; said the President had spoken of two hundred thousand dollars. His own minimum was one hundred thousand; his maximum, a hundred and fifty thousand and a township of land. Letcher said it would be hard for him to vote even for one hundred thousand dollars.

Dec. 17. — At the office. Visits from W. Kelly, Senator from Louisiana, Letcher, member of H. R. from Kentucky, and G. B. English. Letcher came ostensibly with a claim of an assistant to the Marshal of Kentucky for additional compensation for his service in taking the census of 1820. But his apparent main object was to talk about the Presidential election. The account was yesterday received of the choice of electors in Louisiana by the Legislature, from which it is rendered almost certain that three of the votes have been for General Jackson, probably four, and perhaps all five — but certainly none for Mr. Clay. This leaves Mr. Crawford with forty-one, and Mr. Clay with thirty-seven, electoral votes. Mr. Crawford, therefore, will, and Mr. Clay will not, be one of the three persons from whom the House of Representatives, voting by States, will be called to choose a President. Mr. Letcher is an intimate friend of Mr. Clay's, and lodges at the same house with him. He expects that after the result is known, that Mr. Clay cannot be voted for in the House, there will be meetings of the people in the several counties instructing their members to vote for Jackson, and perhaps that similar instructions will be sent on by their Legislature. These, he supposes, will be gotten up by what they call the Relief party in the politics of the State, and by men like Rowan, Barry, and Bibb, secondary leaders of the State, not daring to oppose Clay openly, on account of his own popularity in the State, but seizing upon the first opportunity afforded them indirectly, to put him down.

Letcher wished to know what my sentiments towards Clay were, and I told him without disguise that I harbored no hostility against him; that whatever of difference there had been between us had arisen altogether from him, and not from me. I adverted to Jonathan Russell's attack upon me, which, I said, I believed Mr. Clay had been privy to and countenanced. But having completely repelled that attack I felt no amimosity against any person concerned in it.

Letcher said Clay's friends thought he had been wrong in his letter concerning that affair. It was written in a moment of excitement. He was sure Clay felt now no hostility to me. He had spoken respectfully of me, and was a man of sincerity. Of the fourteen electors of Kentucky, seven voted for Calhoun as Vice-President; and this vote I thought and Letcher fully concurred in the opinion, was more hostile to Clay than any vote for Jackson as President could be. It held up Calhoun as a future competitor against Clay, and thereby postponed all his prospects indefinitely. The drift of all Letcher's discourse was much the same as Wyer had told me, that Clay would willingly support me if he could thereby serve himself, and the substance of his meaning was, that if Clay's friends could know that he would have a prominent share in the Administration, that might induce them to vote for me, even in the face of instructions.

Dec. 22. — Visit from Mr. James Barbour, Senator from Virginia, with whom I had a confidential conversation of more than two hours upon the prospects of the Presidential election. He spoke at first of papers relating to the piracies, which I had sent him as Chairman of the Committee on Foreign Relations of the Senate, and for copies of which there is now a call by resolution of that body. He soon, however, introduced the other topic, and freely stated to me his own impressions, and what he believed to be those of a majority of the Virginia delegation in the House of Representatives. Their first choice had been Mr. Crawford. The electors of the State had voted for him, and a majority of the people of the State were favorable to him. The representation of the State in the House would vote for success; but, if they should find that impracticable their next preference would be for me. He had no doubt this was the feeling of the people of the State; that I was much more popular there then General Jackson, or even than Mr. Clay, though he was one of their own natives.

Jan. 1, 1825. — . . . I attended the dinner given by the members of both Houses of Congress to General La Fayette, as Williamson's Hotel. It was attended also by the President. About one hundred and fifty members of the two Houses were present, and about thirty officers of the Government — civil and military. There were sixteen regular toasts, after which the President, General La Fayette, and most of the invited guests retired to the rooms of Colonel Hayne and Mr. Livingston, where they took coffee with Mrs. Hayne, Mrs. Livingston, Mrs. Ticknor, and Miss Gardner. I came home about nine in the evening, and our family party soon after retired. A storm of rain, afterwards turning to snow, continued through the day. The President's Administration was toasted, to which he answered by a short address of thanks. General La Fayette answered also very briefly the toast to himself. Mr. Clay made a speech about Bolivar and the cause of South America, and seemed very desirous of eliciting speeches from me and Mr. Calhoun. He told me that he should be glad to have with me soon some confidential conversation upon public affairs. I said I should be happy to have it whenever it might suit his convenience. At the beginning of this year there is in my prospects and anticipations a solemnity and moment never before experienced, and to which unaided nature is inadequate.

Jan. 9. — Mr. Clay came at six, and spent the evening with me in a long conversation explanatory of the past and prospective of the future. He said that the time was drawing near when the choice must be made in the House of Representatives of a President from the three candidates presented by the electoral colleges; that he had been much urged and solicited with regard to the part in that transaction that he should take, and had not been five minutes landed at his lodgings before he had been applied to by a friend of Mr. Crawford's, in a manner so gross that it had disgusted him; that some of my friends also, disclaiming, indeed, to have any authority from me, had repeatedly applied to him, directly or indirectly, urging considerations personal to himself as motives to his cause. He had thought it best to reserve for some time his determination to himself: first, to give a decent time for his own funeral solemnities as a candidate; and, secondly, to prepare and predispose all his friends to a state of neutrality between the three candidates who would be before the House, so that they might be free ultimately to take that course which might be most conducive to the public interest. The time had now come at which he might be explicit in his communication with me, and he had for that purpose asked this confidential interview. He wished me, as fast as I might think proper, to satisfy him with regard to some principles of great public importance, but without any personal considerations for himself. In the question to come before the House between General Jackson, Mr. Crawford, and myself, he had no hesitation in saying that his preference would be for me.[6]

Jan. 13.— I called this morning on James Barbour, S. U. S., and asked him to return the long report of Richard Rush's negotiation and then move a call for it, and for the instructions under which the negotiation was conducted, in Senate upon executive business. He agreed to take this course. I spoke to him confidentially with regard to the approaching election, and told him the present condition of things, at which he appeared surprised. He repeated the unalterable determination of Virginia to vote in the first instance for Mr. Crawford, but her determination at all events to vote for another than a mere military leader.

Jan. 15. — Horatio Seymour, S. U. S., from Vermont, in great concern about the instructions, from the Kentucky House of Representatives to the members of that delegation here, to vote for General Jackson as President. He is alarmed for its probable effect on the votes of all the Western States. I advised him to see and converse with Mr. Clay.

Jan. 17. — W. C. Bradley, member from Vermont, was here, and afterwards W. Plumer, Jr. of New Hampshire, much concerned about these instructions from the legislature of Kentucky. Bradley said he had seen Clay this morning, who told him the resolutions would confirm the majority of the delegation in their determination to vote otherwise, but who spoke of the event of the election as exceedingly uncertain — of Missouri and Illinois particularly, the votes of both the States being in single persons. Bradley said he had urged Clay to see me, but Clay had told him it was altogether unnecessary — that his course was fixed, and he should consider the elevation of the Hero as the greatest calamity which could befall the country.

Plumer spoke again about Webster, and his ambition to go as Minister to England, which I thought might be gratified hereafter, but not immediately.

Jan. 18. — Mr. S. L. Southard came, to ask for the papers he had left with me yesterday, of which Mr. Kirkpatrick wishes to take copies. I gave them to him. He then asked me some question respecting the election, upon which I spoke to him

---

[6] Of this momentous interview, and of what assurances he gave Clay in return for his support, Adams cautiously says nothing more.

with entire confidence. I asked him if he wished me so to speak to him, and he said he did. I told him of the present state of things, so far as it is known to myself, of the present prospect, that a majority of the friends of Mr. Clay and Mr. Crawford would finally vote for me, but that the whole of the aspect may be changed from day to day. I mentioned the doubtful situation both of the New York and Virginia delegations, and how they will be liable to be swayed by the slightest incident which may occur between this and the day of election. And I informed him of the exertions made and making by De Witt Clinton, both in the State of New York and with its delegation here, to secure the election of General Jackson — particularly that he had written to General Van Rensselaer, and spoken to Mr. Hayden, to prevail on them to vote for him. I observed that he had an agent here, acting for him as far as he could, and through whom I believed he had influenced the election in New Jersey.

Jan. 25. — There is at this moment a very high state of excitement in the House, Mr. Clay and the majority of the Ohio and Kentucky delegations having yesterday unequivocally avowed their determination to vote for me. This immediately produced an approximation of the Calhoun, Crawford, and Jackson partisans, and will effectually knit the coalition of the South with Pennsylvania.[7]

W. Plumer, Jr., and A. H. Tracy were here, and both spoke of this incident as having produced a great sensation in the House. It appears that General Jackson has not visited Mr. Crawford, but that the ladies have interchanged visits, and that Mr. Samuel Swartwout, of New Jersey, has mediated a peace between the General and the Secretary of the Treasury. Plumer had yesterday a conversation with Louis McLane of Delaware, who told him they would overthrow the Capitol sooner than he would vote for Jackson, but who professed an intention almost as decided not to vote for me. The impression almost universal, made yesterday, was that the election was settled in my favor; but the result of the counter-movement will be the real crisis, and I have little doubt that will be decisive the other way. My situation will be difficult and try-

---

[7] Clay's course was actually never in doubt after he found that Crawford's health was for at least a long time to come utterly wrecked. He had long disliked General Jackson and had expressed a decisively unfavorable opinion of him. He believed " the hero " an entirely unsafe man. Clay had no great love for J. Q. Adams, but he much preferred him to the Tennesseean.

ing beyond my powers of expression.   May but my strength be proportioned to my trial!

Jan. 27. — General Brown came, and told me that he had had a long and grave conversation this morning with Mr. Calhoun, who, with the most solemn asseverations, had declared himself neutral between General Jackson and me, and that his personal wish was for my election.   This contrasts singularly with the conduct of all his electioneering partisans.

Jan. 29. — On my return home, Mr. Clay came in, and sat with me a couple of hours, discussing all the prospects and probabilities of the Presidential election.   He spoke to me with the utmost freedom of men and things; intimated doubts and prepossessions concerning individual friends of mine, to all which I listened with due consideration.   He was anxious for the conciliation of Webster and Louis McLane, and expressed some jealousy as from Webster of the persons by whom he supposed me to be surrounded.

I told him the sources of Webster's anxieties, and my own earnest desire to conciliate him; the manner in which my overtures had been received by him, and my own high opinion of his talents and capacities for service.

Jan. 30. — I called at the President's, and found Messrs. Calhoun and Southard with him, but they immediately withdrew.   I delivered to him two or three dispatches received from R. Rush, and the letter last received from S. Mullowny. . .   We had much more conversation, in which the President appeared to be greatly shocked at the idea of a coalition between General Jackson and Mr. Crawford.   He said it was horrible to think of.   He said Elliott was the only man of the Georgian delegation who saw him in a friendly manner, that Elliott at the last session of Congress, had spoken to him with the deepest distrust of Calhoun, and when I told him that I knew Elliott had said the Georgia delegation would in the last resort vote for Jackson, he seemed scarcely to credit his own ears.   He spoke of Mr. Crawford's conduct respecting his Administration as he had done before.   He thought that when two or three years since, the violent opposition against the Administration was roused by Crawford's friends, and apparently under his countenance, in disavowing that opposition he ought to have done some act publicly to separate himself from them.

I thought so too.

But he said that in consequence of his former relations with Mr. Crawford, he had treated him with uniform and unqualified kindness — instancing his permitting him the use of a facsimile signature, and forbearing to appoint a temporary acting Secretary of the Treasury, upon the certificate of Mr. Crawford's physicians that he was competent to discharge the duties of his office.

I said I approved this, and thought that as there had not been sufficient cause for him to remove Mr. Crawford, so there would not be sufficient cause for his successor to remove him.

Feb. 3. — The flood of visitors is unceasing. Mr. Webster called and spent the evening with me. The excitement of electioneering is kindling into fury. George Kremer's " Another Card," an answer to that of Henry Clay on Monday, appeared in the *Intelligencer* this morning. Mr. Clay called upon the House to institute an investigation. Kremer did the same, and a debate ensued upon it in the House, which is postponed till to-morrow.[8]

Webster's talk was about the election. He read to me a letter from Warfield, of Maryland, to him, concerning the election, and asking advice of him with regard to his vote; and the draft of an answer which he had prepared; and said he would send it or not, as I should think proper. He said that J. Lee, also of Maryland, had consulted him too, and was under impressions similar to those of Warfield. Their concern was lest, in the event of my election, the federalists should be treated as a prescribed party. Webster's answer to Warfield expressed entire confidence that I should be governed by no such considerations, and said that he should show this confidence by his vote. It intimated a hope that the object of the Administration would be to promote harmony among the people, and that the disposition would be marked by conferring some one prominent appointment upon a person of that party.

---

[8] Representative Kremer of Pennsylvania, doubtless acting for acuter men behind the scenes, accused Henry Clay of having corruptly or at least improperly sold his support to Adams. It was generally believed that the great influence of Clay in Congress would suffice to carry the election in the House in favor of the candidate whom he favored. On its face the charge by Kremer was fatuous, yet silly as it was, it found believers — among them in time Andrew Jackson.

I observed that if that referred to the formation of an Administration, it would imply more than I could confirm.

He said it did not — but to an appointment perhaps of a Judge.

I said I approved altogether of the general spirit of his answer, and should consider it as one of the objects nearest to my heart to bring the whole people of the Union to harmonize together. I must, however, candidly tell him that I believed either General Jackson or Mr. Crawford would pursue precisely the same principle, and that no Administration could possibly succeed upon any other.

He said that General Van Rensselaer entertained similar sentiments to his own, and by his advice would call on me at eleven o'clock to-morrow morning.

Feb. 4. — General Stephen Van Rensselaer came at eleven o'clock, and spoke to me much in the same manner as Webster had done. I answered him in the same manner, and, as he said, entirely to his satisfaction. He spoke of Mr. Van Buren, with whom he lodges, somewhat doubtfully — and also of Louis McLane. He says they have not yet abandoned all hope of the success of Mr. Crawford; that A. Dickins is the messenger between them; that Mr. Crawford will not release them from the obligation of voting for him, though he thinks some of the caucus men will vote for me at once. He mentioned Solomon Van Rensselaer, of Albany, as a very ardent supporter of mine; and I told him I thought Mr. Van Buren had been wrong in the measures he took to prevent his appointment as postmaster at Albany. I said Mr. Van Buren was a man of great talents and of good principles, but he had suffered them to be too much warped by party spirit. At other times he had followed a much more generous and wiser policy, and I hoped he would ultimately return to it.

Feb. 7. — The city swarms with strangers, and the succession of visitors this morning was so numerous that the names of several of them escaped my recollection. General Brown told me he had yesterday morning had a long conversation with the President, and had distinctly told him his impressions of the present and recent conduct of Calhoun. He said the President had heard it with surprise. Brown himself is deeply affected by it. At the office, he showed me a letter from Ambrose Spencer, at Albany, whose election to the Senate hitches be-

tween the two Houses of the Legislature. He was nominated
without formal opposition by the House of Assembly, having,
however, only seventy-seven votes. In the Senate he had
from ten to twelve votes, with at least twenty against him.
These so scattered their votes that no nomination was made
by the Senate, and they could not go into joint ballot. The day
passed without completing the election, and now they must
pass a law to fix another day for the choice. Spencer writes
Brown that my friends in the Senate concurred in this postponement, from an opinion that he was hostile to me, which
he solemnly protests he is not. . .

Mr. Warfield came, upon the notice given him, as I had
yesterday requested, by Mr. Webster. He said that he had
not expressed his determination for whom he should vote in
the House on Wednesday. His friends, Mr. Charles Carroll,
of Carrollton, and Mr. Taney, of Baltimore, had urged him to
vote for General Jackson, under an impression that if I should
be elected, the Administration would be conducted on the
principle of proscribing the federal party.

I said I regretted much that Mr. Carroll, for whose character I entertained a profound veneration, and Mr. Taney, of
whose talents I had heard high encomium, should harbor such
opinions of me. I could assure him that I never would be at
the head of any Administration of proscription to any party —
political or geographical. I had differed from the federal
party on many important occasions, but I had always done
justice to the talents and services of the individuals composing it, and to their merits as members of this Union. I
had been discarded by the federal party upon differences of
principle, and I had not separated from one party to make myself the slave of another.

Feb. 9. — May the blessing of God rest upon the event of
this day! — the second Wednesday in February, when the
election of a President of the United States for the term
of four years, from the 4th of March next, was consummated. Of the votes in the electoral colleges, there were
ninety-nine for Andrew Jackson, of Tennessee; eighty-four for
John Quincy Adams, of Massachusetts; forty-one for William
Harris Crawford, of Georgia; and thirty-seven for Henry
Clay, of Kentucky: in all, two hundred and sixty-one. This
result having been announced, on opening and counting the

votes in joint meeting of the two Houses, the House of Representatives immediately proceeded to the vote by ballot from the three highest candidates, when John Quincy Adams received the votes of thirteen, Andrew Jackson of seven, and William H. Crawford of four States. The election was thus completed, very unexpectedly, by a single ballot.[9] Alexander H. Everett gave me the first notice, both of the issue of the votes of the electoral colleges as announced in the joint meeting, and of the final vote as declared. Wyer followed him a few minutes afterwards. Mr. Bolton and Mr. Thomas, the Naval Architect, succeeded; and B. W. Crowninshield, calling, on his return from the House to his lodgings, at my house, confirmed the report. Congratulations from several of the officers of the Department of State ensued — from D. Brent, G. Ironside, W. Slade, and Joseas W. King. Those of my wife, children, and family were cordial and affecting, and I received an affectionate note from Mr. Rufus King, of New York, written in the Senate-chamber after the event. . .

After dinner, the Russian Minister, Baron Tuyl, called to congratulate me upon the issue of the election. I attended, with Mrs. Adams, the drawing-room at the President's. It was crowded to overflowing. General Jackson was there, and we shook hands. He was altogether placid and courteous. I received numerous friendly salutations. D. Webster asked me when I could receive the committee of the House to announce to me my election. I appointed to-morrow noon, at my own house.

[9] The fact that the first ballot was decisive was due to the action of Representative Stephen Van Rensselaer of New York, who took Henry Clay's advice, and threw that State into the Adams column instead of into Crawford's. Martin Van Buren relates in his autobiography the story of how Van Rensselaer happened to take this unexpected course. " He took his seat fully resolved to vote for Mr. Crawford, but before the box reached him, he dropped his head upon the edge of his desk and made a brief appeal to his Maker for his guidance in the matter — a practise he frequently observed on great emergencies — and when he removed his hand from his eyes he saw on the floor directly below him a ticket bearing the name of John Quincy Adams. This occurrence, at a moment of great excitement and anxiety, he was led to regard as an answer to his appeal, and taking up the ticket he put it in the box."

CHAPTER IX

1825–1829

LABOR AS PRESIDENT — DEATH OF JOHN ADAMS — JACKSON'S ENMITY
— CHESAPEAKE AND OHIO CANAL OPENED — RELATIONS WITH
HENRY CLAY — JACKSON CHOSEN PRESIDENT.

Washington, March 4, 1825. — After two successive sleepless nights, I entered upon this day with a supplication to
Heaven, first, for my country; secondly, for myself and for
those connected with my good name and fortunes, that the
last results of its events may be auspicious and blessed. About
half-past eleven o'clock I left my house with an escort of several
companies of militia and a cavalcade of citizens, accompanied
in my carriage by Samuel L. Southard, Secretary of the Navy,
and William Wirt, Attorney-General, and followed by James
Monroe, late President of the United States, in his own carriage. We proceeded to the Capitol, and to the Senate-
chamber. The Senate were in session, and John C. Calhoun
presiding in the chair, having been previously sworn into office
as Vice-President of the United States and President of the
Senate. The Senate adjourned, and from the Senate-chamber,
accompanied by the members of that body and by the judges of
the Supreme Court, I repaired to the hall of the House of
Representatives, and after delivering from the Speaker's chair
my inaugural address to a crowded auditory, I pronounced
from a volume of the laws held up to me by John Marshall,
Chief Justice of the United States, the oath faithfully to
execute the office of President of the United States, and, to the
best of my ability, to preserve, protect, and defend the Con-
situation of the United States. After exchanging salutations
from the late President, and many other persons present, I
retired from the hall, passed in review the military companies
drawn up in front of the Capitol, and returned to my house

with the same procession which accompanied me from it. I found at my house a crowd of visitors, which continued about two hours, and received their felicitations. Before the throng had subsided, I went myself to the President's house, and joined with the multitude of visitors to Mr. Monroe there. I then returned home to dine, and in the evening attended the ball, which was also crowded, at Carusi's Hall. Immediately after supper I withdrew, and came home. I closed the day as it had begun, with thanksgiving to God for all His mercies and favors past, and with prayers for the continuance of them to my country, and to myself and mine.[1]

March 5. — An Administration was to be formed. Soon after noon, James Lloyd and Nathaniel Macon came as a committee from the Senate to notify me that they were in session, ready to receive any communication from me; to which I answered that I should make them a communication at an early hour this day. On the evening of the 3d I had, at about nine o'clock, received a note from Mr. Monroe informing me that he had shortly before received a letter from Mr. Crawford resigning the office of Secretary of the Treasury. I now sent by Daniel Brent, chief clerk of the Department of State, a message to the Senate nominating —

Henry Clay, of Kentucky, to be Secretary of State.

Richard Rush, of Pennsylvania, to be Secretary of the Treasury.

James Barbour, of Virginia, Secretary for the Department of War.[2] . .

I concluded, after much deliberation, to offer to Joel Roberts Poinsett, of South Carolina, the nomination of Minister to

[1] As Charles Francis Adams states in his twelve-volume edition of the Diary, the materials bearing upon the Presidency are not continuous. Adams did not keep up his entries. "The overwhelming pressure occasioned by the constant interruption of visitors, as well as the performance of imperative official duties, evidently disabled him from persevering in this minor duty, and caused gaps in the record which he never afterwards found time to fill."

[2] Adams nominated at the same time a great number of minor officers, and renominated many of Mr. Monroe's appointees. He had no sympathy with the struggle for spoils. "Efforts," he writes, "had been made by some of the Senators to obtain different nominations, and to introduce a principle of change or rotation in office at the expiration of these commissions; which would make the government a perpetual and unintermitting scramble for office. A more pernicious expedient could scarcely have been devised." It was left for Adams's successor, Jackson, to bring in the spoils system in its full scope. "I determined," Adams states, "to renominate every person against whom there was no complaint which would have warranted his removal."

Mexico. I accordingly sent for him this morning and made him the offer. It had been made to him by Mr. Monroe early during the late session of Congress, and declined upon considerations most of which do not now apply. He made, however, now, two objections: one that upon vacating his seat in Congress, a very troublesome and unprincipled man would probably be chosen in his place; the other, that he had recommended to Mr. Monroe another person for the mission to Mexico. I knew who this person was. It was Thomas H. Benton, a Senator from Missouri, who from being a furious personal and political enemy of General Jackson, became, about the time of this recommendation, a partisan not less ardent in his favor. I now told Poinsett that with regard to the consequences of his vacating his seat in Congress, I could form no judgment, having little knowledge of the state of politics of Charleston, and no acquaintance with the person who might be his successor; but that if he should decline, I should not offer the mission to the person whom he had recommended to Mr. Monroe. He asked time for consideration, and promised to give me a definitive answer tomorrow.

March 6. — Mr. Poinsett called, and accepted the mission to Mexico.

March 9. — The special session of the Senate, which met as called on the 4th of March, was this day closed. . . French and Russian Ministers came in full costume, for the purpose of congratulation.

April 7. — Henry Clay reported the substance of his conversations with Obregon, the Mexican, and Salazar, the Colombian Minister, upon the proposal of a Congress of American Ministers to be held at Panama next October. Mr. Clay continues earnest in the desire that a Minister should be appointed to attend this Congress.

April 30. — *Day.* Since my removal to the Presidential mansion I rise about five; read two chapters of Scott's Bible and Commentary, and the corresponding Commentary of Hewlett; then the morning newspapers, and public papers from the several departments; write seldom, and not enough; breakfast an hour, from nine to ten; then have a succession of visitors, upon business, in search of place, solicitors for donations, or from mere curiosity, from eleven till between four and five o'clock. The heads of departments of course occupy much of this time. Between four and six I take a walk of three or four miles. Dine from about half past five to seven, and from dark till about eleven I generally pass the evening in my chamber, signing land-grants or blank patents, in the interval of which, for the last ten days, I have brought up three months of arrears in my diary index. About eleven I retire to bed. My evenings are not so free from interruption as I had hoped and expected they would be.

May 15, 1825. — Chilly Mackintosh, Colonel Mackintosh, Jim Tallazan, Ben Tallazan. These four Creek Indians called on me this morning before breakfast with a letter from Governor Troup, of Georgia, and a talk sent by him to certain other Creek chiefs. The letter, which is in a style similar to that which the same personage used with Mr. Monroe, announced to me the murder of the chief called General Mackintosh, which was confirmed by Chilly, who narrowly escaped himself with his life. It was on Saturday, the 30th of last month, that a party of about four hundred surrounded and set fire to his house, and killed him and another chief, his next-door neighbor. Troup charges Crowell, the Agent, with having instigated this massacre, and vows revenge with a spirit as ferocious as ever inspired any Creek Indian. I told Chilly that I was deeply distressed at these melancholy tidings, and would do all that would be in my power for him; advising him to call upon the Secretary of War tomorrow.

May 18. — G. Sullivan came and took leave. Spoke of his visits to Mr. Jefferson and Mr. Madison, the latter of whom, he said, appeared cordially disposed to this Administration; Mr. Jefferson less so, and particularly with regard to Mr. Clay. Sullivan said he should pass through Worcester on his way home, and asked what he should say for me to the Governor, Lincoln. I said he should give my compliments to him, and congratulations upon his election, with my hopes that he would find the Chair of Massachusetts a bed of roses, which I could assure him the Presidential Chair was not.

May 19. — With General Brown, I had a long conversation upon the prospects of a war with the Creek Indians. He remarked upon the extreme violence of Govenor Troup, but observed that an Indian war might be an object of profitable interest to the State of Georgia. He spoke of Gaines as a very fair, honorable, and virtuous man, but somewhat excitable, entertaining sentiments of strong aversion to the Indians, and perhaps liable to be influenced by some indiscreet persons connected with him.

May 31. — Bulfinch and Persico came at one o'clock, and we discussed the new design [for the tympanum of the Capitol], which was a personification of the United States standing on a throne, leaning upon the Roman fasces, surmounted with the cap of liberty, with Justice at her right hand, blindfolded, holding the suspended balance, and in the other hand an open scroll, and Hercules at her left, seated on a corner of the throne, embracing the fasces, and emblematical of strength; to which were added, separately drawn, and to fill up the space, Plenty seated with her cornucopia, in one corner, and Peace, a flying angel, extending a garland of victory towards America with one hand, and bearing a palm in the other.[3]

These two last figures I advised should be discarded, as well as the Roman fasces and the cap of liberty. The Hercules had also too much of the heathen mythology for my taste, and I proposed to substitute in his place a figure of Hope, with an anchor — a Scriptural image, indicating that this Hope relies upon a Supreme Disposer of events; " which hope we have as an anchor to the soul, sure and steadfast." Instead of the fasces I proposed a pedestal, with 4th July, 1776, inscribed on its base, and 4th March, 1789, upon its upper cornice. The whole design then would represent the American Union founded on the Declaration of Independence and consummated by the organization of the general government under the Federal Constitution, supported by Justice in the past, and relying upon Hope in Providence for the future.

Day. — Entering upon a new course of life, momentous not alone to myself, and specially responsible to God, to my

---

[3] The Capitol of the United States was still decidedly unfinished. The two wings had been completed, but the rotunda, the cornerstone of which had been laid in 1818, was yet in progress. At this time some two hundred workmen were busy amid a chaos of massive stone blocks. John Trumbull had been commissioned to paint several historic canvases for the walls of the chamber below the rotunda; Luigi Persico, an Italian sculptor, had been set to work on the pediment of the east portico; and the architect Charles Bulfinch was helping direct the whole. On the occasion here described by Adams the models had been set up in the East Room of the White House, and were inspected by the President, Bulfinch, and " several distinguished gentlemen of science and taste " named by Adams. They were not quite satisfactory. Adams therefore stepped in determinedly, and told Persico just what to do with his figure of " the Genius of the United States."

country, and to mankind, I have intensely felt my obligation to devote all my time and all my faculties to the discharge of my duties. To this end I have endeavored to make a regular distribution of time — which I have been, however, enabled but very imperfectly to execute. The ordinary day during the month has been generally like that of April. My rising hour is between four and six. But the bathing season has come, and the heat of summer, which renders it necessary to transpose my hours of exercise from the afternoon, before dinner, to the morning, before breakfast. This I have done for the last three days, taking two morning hours for bathing and swimming in the Potomac. My diary has been more steadily kept up, yet not without negligent interruption. Incessant and distractingly various occupation continues to fill the space between breakfast and dinner, and most of the evenings are wasted in idleness or at the billiard-table, a resource both for exercise and amusement.

June 8. — After dinner I heard Dr. Caldwell's lecture upon the organ of amativeness, which I thought more indelicate than philosophical. The weather was intensely warm, and I had no temptation to learn more either of phrenology or of craniology.

June 13. — I attempted to cross the river with Antoine in a small canoe, with a view to swim across it to come back. He took a boat in which we had crossed it last summer without accident. The boat was at the shore near Van Ness's poplars; but in crossing the Tiber to the point, my son John, who was with us, thought the boat dangerous, and, instead of going with us, went and undressed at the rock, to swim and meet us in midway of the river as we should be returning. I thought the boat safe enough, or rather persisted carelessly in going without paying due attention to its condition; gave my watch to my son; made a bundle of my coat and waist-coat to take in the boat with me; put off my shoes, and was paddled by Antoine, who had stripped himself entirely naked. Before we had got half across the river, the boat had leaked itself half full, and then we found there was nothing on board to scoop up the water and throw it over. Just at that critical moment a fresh breeze from the northwest blew down the river as from the nose of a bellows. In five minutes' time it made a little tempest, and set the boat to dancing till the river came in at the sides. I jumped overboard, and Antoine did the same, and lost hold of the boat, which filled with water and drifted away. We were as near as possible to the middle of the river, and swam to the opposite shore. Antoine, who was naked, reached it with little difficulty. I had much more, and, while struggling for life and gasping for breath, had ample leisure to reflect upon my own indiscretion. My principal difficulty was in the loose sleeves of my shirt, which filled with water and hung like two fifty-six pound weights upon my arms. I had also my hat, which I soon gave, however, to Antoine. After reaching the shore, I took off my shirt and pantaloons, wrung them out, and gave them to Antoine to go and look out for our clothes, or for a person to send to the house for others, and for the carriage to come and fetch me. Soon after he had gone, my son John joined me, having swum wholly across the river, expecting to meet us returning with the boat. Antoine crossed the bridge, sent a man to my house for the carriage, made some search for the drifted boat and bundles, and found his own hat with his shirt and braces in it, and one of my shoes. He also brought over the bridge my son's clothes with my watch and umbrella, which I had left with him.

While Antoine was gone, John and I were wading and swimming up and down on the other shore, or sitting naked basking on the bank at the margin of the river. John walked over the bridge home. The carriage came, and took me and Antoine home, half dressed. I lost an old summer coat, white waistcoat, two napkins, two white handkerchiefs, and one shoe. Antoine lost his watch, jacket, waistcoat, pantaloons, and shoes. The boat was also lost. By the mercy of God our lives were spared, and no injury befell our persons.

July 13. — Brown, General Jacob, just returned from his visit to Mr. Monroe, at Oakhill. Message from Mr. Monroe, repeating the invitation to me to visit him with General La Fayette.

July 22. — I walked as usual to my ordinary bathing-place, and came to the rock where I leave my clothes a few minutes before sunrise. I found several persons there, besides three or four who were bathing; and at the shore under the tree a boat with four men in it, and a drag-net. There was a large two-mast boat in the channel oposite the rock, at anchor, and a man on the shore, who requested those in the two-mast boat to raise their anchor and drop thirty or forty yards down the stream, as they were in the way of the boat with the drag-net, which was going in search of a dead body. I enquired if any one had been drowned, and the man told me it was old Mr. Shoemaker, a clerk in the post-office, a man upwards of sixty years of age, who last evening, between five and six o'clock, went in to bathe with four other persons; that he was drowned in full sight of them, and without a suspicion by them that he was even in any danger. They had observed him struggling in the water, but, as he was an excellent swimmer, had supposed he was merely diving, until after coming out they found he was missing. They then commenced an ineffectual search for him, which was continued late into the night. The man said to me that he had never seen a more distressed person than Mrs. Shoemaker last evening. While the two-mast boat was dropping down the stream, and the other boat was preparing to go out with the drag, I stripped and went into the river. I had not been more than ten minutes swimming, when the drag-boat started, and they were not five minutes from the shore when the body floated immediately opposite the rock, less than one hundred yards from the shore, at the very edge of the channel, and where there could not be seven feet deep of water. I returned immediately to the shore and dressed. A rope was tied round one of the arms, and the boat remained at the spot till a blanket had been sent for, which was spread under the tree. The boat then returned to the shore, drawing the body through the water, and it was lifted from the water, and brought and laid upon the blanket, and covered up. The only part of the body which had the appearance of stiffness was the arms, both of which were raised at the shoulder-joints and crooked towards each other at the elbows, as if they had been fixed by a spasm at the very moment when they were to expand to keep the head above water. There was a dark flush of settled blood over the face, like one excessively heated, and a few drops of thin blood and water issued from one ear. There was nothing terrible or offensive in the sight, but I returned home musing in sympathy with the distressed lady, and enquiring uncertainly whether I ought to renounce altogether my practice of swimming in the river.

Aug. 6. — At four, General La Fayette, his son G. W., Mr. Ringgold, and I departed on a visit to Mr. Monroe at Oak-

hill.[4] My son John and Mr. Le Vasseur went with us; and
the General's valet-de-chambre, Bastien, and Antoine Michel
Giusta, in a carryall with one horse, took the baggage. William, the groom, followed us on horseback. We crossed the
Potomac bridge and rode sixteen miles to Fairfax Court-House.
Arrived there just after sunset, at seven in the evening, and
lodged at Bronaugh's Hotel.

Aug. 10. — The night was oppressively hot, and this day
still more so. The General was detained in writing for the
press his answers to the addresses of yesterday, and his toasts,
so that it was between nine and ten when we took our leave of
Mr. Ludwell Lee, and of Mr. Monroe, who returned home to
Oakhill. We had a blazing and suffocating day; and a choice
of roads most unfit to be travelled by light carriages and pampered horses. We stopped for an hour, after riding about
eight miles; than proceeded about a mile on an old road which
had been recommended as not so bad as the others, but upon
which we found we could scarcely fail of oversetting if we
proceeded. We returned, and took the turnpike road, hilly and
excessively rough, nine miles to Drane's. On ascending the hill
called the Bull's Neck, within a hundred yards of the house,
the most spirited of my four horses fell, never again to rise.
He was bled in the neck and leg, but died in about three-
quarters of an hour. We had sent word this morning to Mrs.
Adams to expect us home to dinner at five o'clock, which this
accident rendered impossible. We stopped to dine, and give
rest to the surviving horses, at the inn. After dinner, between
five and six, we proceeded, taking the thill-horse of my son's
gig for our fourth in the carriage. We came to the Little
Falls bridge soon after sunset. The road from the bridge
to Georgetown is very bad — but we reached home safely,
about nine in the evening.

Aug. 23. — Clay, Henry, Secretary of State. His daughter
died two days after he left Lebanon. Conversation upon pub-

[4] Monroe now divided his time between his residence at Oakhill in Loudoun
County, Virginia, just west of Washington, and the home of his son-in-law
Samuel Gouverneur in New York City. After a breakdown on the road, Adams
and La Fayette arrived about noon on Aug. 7. The next two days were extremely
hot and dull. The whole party on the ninth went to the home of Ludwell Lee,
near Leesburg, where " a chamber with two beds was allotted to Mr. Monroe and
me." At Leesburg there was a reception, an awkward little military parade, and
an open-air dinner with toasts. "I have no pleasure in such scenes," Adams
sententiously records.

lic affairs. I sent Mr. Clay Governor Troup's last letters, requesting him to read them, and pass them to the other members of the Administration for a subsequent consultation. General La Fayette; the frigate *Brandywine;* W. C. Somerville; Sweden and Greece; State of Kentucky, good principles prevailing there.

Aug. 28. — Conversation with General La Fayette after breakfast. I take every opportunity to dissuade him from having any participation in revolutionary projects in France. He says he will go quietly to La Grange; that he is sixty-eight years old, and must leave revolutions to younger men. But there is fire beneath the cinders.

Aug. 29. — Major Vandeventer brought a letter of the 15th of August from Governor Troup, of Georgia, to the Secretary of War, full as usual of " guns, drums, trumpets, blunderbuss, and thunder," but declaring that he will not make the threatened survey of the Creek Indian lands. Mr. Southard came to recommend a chaplain for the frigate *Brandywine.*

Oct. 27. — My time was absorbed from breakfast till dinner with the visitors — the Secretaries all conversing upon public affairs, and bringing me multitudes of papers, which I had not time to assort, and still less to dispose of in a satisfactory manner. Mr. Clay is in deep affliction, having lost two daughters in the course of a month. The last was married at New Orleans, and he has received within a few days the account of her death. His own health is so infirm that he told me he feared he should be obliged to resign his office; but said he would try to retain it through the winter, and declared himself entirely satisfied with my conduct towards him, and with the course of the Administration hitherto.

Nov. 26. — Calhoun, John C., Vice-President, called to visit me; conversed upon some topics of interest, and others indifferent. Generally of the prosperous state of the country.

Dec 2. — Peter Force called here before breakfast, and I gave him a copy of the message to be printed, under injunctions to guard against the disclosure of it before its time. He said he had been applied to from Cincinnati, and also from Alexandria, to print several hundred copies to be forwarded the moment it is delivered. I mentioned to Force Mr. Walsh's request to have a copy mailed the morning of the day when it will be delivered, and assented to it.

Dec. 3. — Mr. Southard and Mr. Clay had conversation upon the prospects of election of the Speaker. They think Taylor will be chosen without difficulty, perhaps at the first ballot. Mr. Clay expressed some doubt whether he ought to visit the Vice-President; thought he had used him ill; and intrigued particularly to obtain votes against him upon his nomination as Secretary of State. He believed he had specially prevailed upon Mr. McIlvaine, of New Jersey, to vote against him.

Dec. 5. — This day commenced the first session of the Nineteenth Congress. Mr. John W. Taylor was chosen Speaker of the House of Representatives at the second ballot. His competitors were Mr. Campbell, of Ohio, Mr. McLane, of Delaware, and Mr. Stevenson, of Virginia, neither of whom had more than forty votes at the first ballot. Taylor had eighty-nine, and at the second ballot ninety-nine.

Dec. 10. — Mr. Edward Livingston came, apparently for the purpose of saying to me that he approved my message to Congress in every part. He said there was not a line of it in which he did not heartily concur. We had some conversation also upon his code for Louisiana, and his proposal to abolish capital punishments.

Dec. 14. — Dickins said that a few weeks before the close of the Administration, some words used by Mr. Monroe to Mr. Crawford had induced the latter to abstain thenceforward from coming to this house, or ever seeing Mr. Monroe again.

When Mr. Southard came in, I asked him if this fact had been known to him. He said, yes; that one day last winter, on coming here on business, he found Mr. Monroe walking to and fro across the room in great agitation; that he told him Crawford had just left him; he had come to him concerning the nomination of certain officers of the Customs in the Northern ports; that Crawford recommended the nomination of several persons, against whom Mr. Monroe expressed several objections; that Mr. Crawford at last rose in much irritation, gathered the papers together, and said, petulantly, " Well if you will not appoint the persons well qualified for the places, tell me whom you will appoint, that I may get rid of their importunities." Mr. Monroe replied with great warmth, saying that he considered Crawford's language as extremely improper and unsuitable to the relations between them; when

Crawford, turning to him, raised his cane, as in the attitude to strike, and said, " You damned infernal old scoundrel! " Mr. Monroe seized the tongs at the fireplace for self-defence, applied a retaliatory epithet to Crawford, and told him he would immediately ring for servants himself and turn him out of the house; upon which Crawford, beginning to recover himself, said he did not intend, and had not intended, to insult him, and left the house. They never met afterwards.

Mr. Southard does not recollect the precise day on which this happened. I told him that if I had known it at the time, I should not have invited Mr. Crawford to remain in the Treasury Department. It resembles the scene between Boling-broke and Oxford in the last days of Queen Anne.

Dec. 31. — The life that I lead is more regular than it has perhaps been at any other period. It is established by custom that the President of the United States goes not abroad into any private companies; and to this usage I conform. I am, therefore, compelled to take my exercise, if at all, in the morning before breakfast. I rise usually between five and six — that is, at this time of the year, from an hour and a half to two hours before the sun. I walk by the light of moon or stars, or none, about four miles, usually returning home in time to see the sun rise from the eastern chamber of the House. I then make my fire, and read three chapters of the Bible, with Scott's and Hewlett's Commentaries. Read papers till nine. Breakfast, and from ten till five P.M. receive a succession of visitors, sometimes without intermission — very seldom with an interval of half an hour — never such as to enable me to undertake any business requiring attention. From five to half-past six we dine; after which I pass about four hours in my chamber alone, writing in this diary, or reading papers upon some public business — excepting when occasionally inter-rupted by a visitor. Between eleven and twelve I retire to bed, to rise again at five or six the next morning.

The year has been the most momentous of those that have passed over my head, inasmuch as it has witnessed my eleva-tion at the age of fifty-eight to the Chief Magistracy of my country; to the summit of laudable, or at least blameless, worldly ambition; not, however, in a manner satisfactory to pride or to just desire; not by the unequivocal suffrages of a majority of the people; with perhaps two-thirds of the whole people adverse to the actual result. Nearly one year of this service has already passed, with little change of the public opinions or feelings; without disaster to the country; with an unusual degree of prosperity, public and private.

January 2, 1826. — The usual visitation of the New Year's day was made at this house from noon till three o'clock, and the crowd of company was said to have been greater than ever had been known before, amounting to from two to three thousand persons. The greater portion of the members of both Houses of Congress were here; and formed only a small part of the company. The British and Mexican Ministers came, and the Brazilian Chargé d'Affaires; but neither the Russian nor French Ministers, nor any persons of their Legations. They had applied last week to Mr. Clay, the Secretary of State, suggesting their old objection to coming with the crowd, and proposed to come in state another day — say to-morrow; which I explicitly declined, being unwilling to make two days of ceremony instead of one, and still more so to yield to their pretensions, which I think quite unreasonable. I desired Mr. Clay to inform them that if they were desirous of avoiding a crowd they might do so by coming before half-past twelve, or about three.

Feb. 7. — Messrs. Rush, Barbour, Southard, and Wirt were here in Cabinet meeting upon Mr. Barbour's letter to the Chairman of the Committee on Indian Affairs of the House of Representatives. The letter was read, and variously commented upon by the other members of the Administration. Mr. Clay was absent, confined to his house by a relapse of influenza. Mr. Barbour's plan is differently modified from that which he had at first prepared. He has given up the idea of incorporating the Indians into the several States where they reside. He has now substituted that of forming them all into a great territorial Government west of the Mississippi. There are many very excellent observations in the paper, which is full of benevolence and humanity. I fear there is no practicable plan by which they can be organized into one civilized, or half-civilized, Government.

Feb. 16. — Mr. Lowrie brought me this morning the two resolutions of the Senate adopted in executive session. The first declares that the question of the expediency of the Panama mission ought to be debated in Senate with open doors, unless the publication of the documents to which it would be necessary to refer in debate would prejudice existing negotiations. The second is a respectful request to the President of the United States to inform the Senate whether such objection exists to the publication of all or any part of those documents, and, if so, to specify to what part it applies.

These resolutions are the fruit of the ingenuity of Martin Van Buren, and bear the impress of his character. The resolution to debate an executive nomination with open doors is without example, and the thirty-sixth rule of the Senate is explicit and unqualified that all documents communicated in confidence by the President to the Senate shall be kept secret by the members. The request to me to specify the particular documents the publication of which would affect existing negotiations, was delicate and ensnaring . . . ; and this being necessarily a matter of opinion, if I should specify passages in the documents as of such a character, any Senator might make it a question for discussion in the Senate, and they might finally publish the whole, under the color of entertaining an opinion different from mine upon the probable effect of the publication. Besides, should the precedent once be established of opening the doors of the Senate in the midst of a debate upon Executive business, there could be no prospect of ever keeping them shut again.

I answered the resolutions of the Senate by a message, stating that all the communications I had made to the Senate on this subject had been confidential; and that, believing it important for the public interest that the confidence between the Executive and the Senate should continue unimpaired, I should leave to themselves the determination of a question upon the motives for which, not being informed of them, I was not competent to decide.

July 1. — Governor Barbour proposes that on the 4th instant, after the usual ceremonies at the Capitol, he should address the audience, and invite an immediate subscription for the benefit of Mr. Jefferson. Says he proposes to give a hundred dollars himself. Mr. Rush came in while we were speaking of it. I doubted the expediency of the measure, and its success; and thought it would be more likely to succeed if a meeting should be called and a subscription raised as elsewhere. Governor Barbour says the late rains have done immense and irreparable damage to his estate — his loss many thousands.

July 3. — Dr. Watkins called to say that he and Mr. Asbury Dickins, two members of the Committee of Arrangements, would attend me to the Capitol to-morrow. He also showed me the answers from the surviving signers of the Declaration of Independence and ex-Presidents, declining the invitations to attend the celebration here. Mr. Jefferson's is in the freest style; my father's is signed with his own hand; Mr. Carroll's apparently written with his own hand, as are Mr. Madison's and Mr. Monroe's. T. Ringgold, the Marshal, came to take directions for the arrangements of police to-morrow.

July 4. — Mr. Rush and Governor Barbour came about nine in the morning. Mr. McLean, the Postmaster-General, and the Reverend Messieurs Baker and Hawley. The volunteer companies assembled on the square fronting the house, and paid the passing salute by marching through the yard. I then joined in the procession, Mr. Ringgold, the Marshal, and Messrs. Watkins and Dickins, two of the members of the Committee of Arrangements, riding in the carriage with me. General Philip Stuart, with Commodore Bainbridge on his right, and General Jessup on his left, immediately preceded, on horseback my carriage, bearing the standard of the United States. Vice-President Calhoun, in his carriage, followed mine. Arriving at the door of the Capitol, I was there met by Mr. Anderson, the Comptroller, with whom we entered the hall of the House of Representatives. The Reverend Mr. Ryland made an introductory prayer. Joseph Anderson, the Comptroller, read the Declaration of Independence; Walter Jones delivered an oration commemorative of the fiftieth anniversary; the Reverend Mr. Post, Chaplain of H. R. U. S., made a concluding prayer.

After which, Governor Barbour delivered an address to the citizens assembled, soliciting subscriptions for the relief of Mr. Jefferson. Mr. Rush also, upon the floor of the House, made a short address to the same purpose. Not more than four or five subscribers were obtained, and notice was given by Governor Barbour that others would have the opportunity to subscribe afterwards. The procession, with the exception of the military companies, returned to the President's house, where we received visitors till about three o'clock, when I withdrew to my cabinet.

July 6. — Governor Barbour brought information of the decease of Mr. Jefferson at Monticello on the 4th inst., at ten minutes past one in the afternoon — a strange and very striking coincidence. It became a question whether the event should not be noticed by some act of the Administration. Several measures suggested themselves, and were taken for further consideration. The precedent in the case of General Washington's decease was adverted to and examined. But the Congress were then in session, and, excepting the orders for military honors, all was done at the recommendation and by resolutions of that body. We now concluded that general orders to the army and navy would be proper and indispensable, and would reflect till to-morrow on the expediency of issuing a proclamation to the people. Governor Barbour will prepare the order to the army, and Mr. Rush, in the absence of Mr. Southard, that to the navy, and I prepared this evening the draft of a proclamation, but after writing it became convinced in my own mind that no such paper should issue.

July 7. — Henry Lee called, and told me that he had been last week to Monticello to consult some papers relating to the Revolutionary War in Mr. Jefferson's possession, and of which he had promised Mr. Lee the perusal. He was there last week, on Thursday, when Mr. Jefferson was, though ill, yet able to converse with him on the subject, and hoped to be able to examine the papers with him in a few days. But from that time Mr. Jefferson grew worse, and on Sunday Lee gave up all expectation of seeing the papers, and left Monticello and Charlottesville, and returned.

July 8. — The mail this morning brought me three letters. One, dated the 3d, from my brother Charles's daughter, Mrs. Susan B. Clark, informing me that my father's end was approaching; that she wrote me because my brother was absent in Boston; that Dr. Holbrook, who was attending as his physician, thought he would probably not survive two days, and certainly not more than a fortnight. The second was from my brother, written on the morning of the 4th, announcing that, in the opinion of those who surrounded my father's couch, he was rapidly sinking; that they were sending an express for my son in Boston, who might perhaps arrive in time to receive his last breath. The third was from my brother's wife to her daughter Elizabeth to the same purport, and written in much distress.

I immediately took the determination to proceed as speedily as possible to Quincy; and the remainder of the day was occupied in making preparations for my departure to-morrow morning. Mr. Southard, Mr. Rush, and Mr. Barbour were here separately in the course of the day, and together in the evening; as was Mr. Brent, of the Department of State. I left the affairs of each Department in charge of the officer at its head; and had not even time to give directions with regard to any special business of either Department. . . I was up, in anxiety and apprehension, till near midnight. The suddenness of the notice of my father's danger was quite unexpected. Some weeks since, my brother had written to me that he was declining, though not so as to occasion immediate alarm; and my intention had been to visit him about the beginning of the next month. I had flattered myself that he would survive this summer, and even other years.

July 9. — Sun rose 4.39. Washington; Baltimore; Frenchtown. At five this morning I left Washington, with my son John, in my own carriage with four horses. Yesterday had been one of the hottest days of the summer, and there was every prospect that this day would be not less so. A light easterly breeze, however, came up as the sun rose, and continued through the day. The heat of the sun was, however, intense. My servant, William Pote, was sent with our trunks of heavy baggage in the stage. We stopped half an hour, between seven and eight, at Ross's Tavern, and reached Merrill's, at Waterloo, where we breakfasted, before eleven. Mr. Merrill told me that he had come this morning out from Baltimore, and was informed there that my father died on the 4th of this month about five o'clock in the afternoon. From the letters which I had yesterday received, this event was so much expected by me that it had no sudden and violent effect on my feelings.

My father had nearly closed the ninety-first year of his life — a life illustrious in the annals of his country and of the world. He had served to great and useful purpose his nation, his age, and his God. He is gone, and may the blessing of Almighty Grace have attended him to his account! I say not,

"May my last end be like his!"—it were presumptuous. The time, the manner, the coincidence with the decease of Jefferson, are visible and palpable marks of Divine favor, for which I would humble myself in grateful and silent adoration before the Ruler of the Universe. For myself, all that I dare to ask is, that I may live the remnant of my days in a manner worthy of him from whom I came, and, at the appointed hour of my Maker, die as my father has died, in peace with God and man, sped to the regions of futurity with the blessings of my fellow-men.

We proceeded on to Baltimore, and dined at Barnum's Tavern. I wrote a short letter to my wife, to be taken by the coachman, who returns with the carriage and horses to Washington.

Boston, July 12.—The day was fine, and on rising this morning the steamboat was off the Gull Island Light. We touched at Newport at half-past ten. Mr. Dutee J. Pearce came on board, and gave me a pressing invitation to stop there on my return. At half-past one we arrived at Providence, and I took immediately a carriage to proceed to Boston. I invited Mr. Davis, a son of Jonathan Davis, of Boston, and his cousin, Miss Deblois, to ride with me. Mr. Wheaton and his children went no farther than Providence. At Attleborough we saw Colonel Hatch. Dined at Fuller's, at Waltham, and at half-past nine in the evening alighted at Hamilton's Exchange Hotel at Boston. Four days from Washington. The weather all the time fine, but the heat intense. Fahrenheit's thermometer this day at ninety-six.

My son George came in shortly after, and was with me till near one in the morning. He informed me of the circumstances of my father's last moments, and of those attending the funeral. George himself was on the 4th in Boston, expecting to attend with his company at the celebration of the day. An express was sent for him, and he came out about noon. My father recognized him, looked upon him, and made an effort to speak, but without success. George was with him at the moment when he expired, a few minutes before six in the evening. Mr. Quincy, who, on the 4th, delivered an oration at Boston, came out the next morning. The arrangements for the funeral were made with his concurrence. It took place on Friday, the 7th. There was a great concourse of people from this and the neighboring towns. Mr. Whitney delivered a sermon from 1 Chronicles xxix. 28: "He died in a good old age, full of days and honor." About two thousand persons took a last look at his lifeless face, and all that was mortal of John Adams was deposited in the tomb.

July 13. — Boston; Quincy. Night of intense heat. I know not that I ever experienced at Washington a warmer night. The morning, however was cooler. Mr. Edward Cruft, Dr. T. Welsh, Mr. D. Webster, Judge Joseph Hall, and Mr. F. C. Gray called upon me this morning. After breakfast I came out with my two sons, George and John, to Quincy. I found at my father's house my brother with his family. Everything about the house is the same. I was not fully sensible of the change till I entered his bed-chamber, the place where I had last taken leave of him, and where I had most sat with him at my two last yearly visits to him at this place. That moment was inexpressible painful, and struck me as if it had been an arrow to the heart. My father and my mother have departed. The charm which has always made this house to me an abode of enchantment is dissolved; and yet my attachment to it, and to the whole region round, is stronger than I ever felt it before. I feel it is time for me to begin to set my house in order, and to prepare for the church-yard myself.

July 14. — Company occupied most of the day. My reflections upon my own situation and duties engrossed the remainder, so that I found barely time for writing to my wife. My father, by his will, has given me the option of taking this house and about ninety-three acres of land round it, upon securing the payment of ten thousand dollars, with interest, in three years from the time of his decease. After making this request, he made a donation to the town of part of the lands, detaching eight acres on the road, of the grounds opposite to the house, but leaving the condition unaltered. It is repugnant to my feelings to abandon this place, where for near forty years he has resided, and where I have passed many of the happiest days of my life. I shall within two or three years, if indulged with life and health, need a place of retirement. Where else should I go? This will be a safe and pleasant retreat, where I may pursue literary occupations as long and as much as I can take pleasure in them.

July 16. — Heard Mr. Whitney from 1 Corinthians xv. 19: "If in this life only we have hope in Christ, we are of all men most miserable." A discourse somewhat occasional upon the decease of my father. But he preached a sermon at the funeral. I have at no time felt more deeply affected by that event than on entering the meeting-house and taking in his pew the seat which he used to occupy, having directly before me the pew at the left of the pulpit, which was his father's, and where the earliest devotions of my childhood were performed. The memory of my father and mother, of their tender and affectionate care, of the times of peril in which we then lived, and of the hopes and fears which left their impressions upon my mind, came over me, till involuntary tears started from my eyes. I looked around the house with enquiring thoughts. Where were those whom I was then wont to meet in this house? The aged of that time, the pastor by whom I had been baptized, the deacons who sat before the communion-table, have all long since departed. Those then in the meridian of life have all followed them. Five or six persons, then children like myself, under the period of youth, were all that I could discern, with gray hairs and furrowed cheeks, two or three of them with families of a succeeding generation around them. The house was not crowded, but well filled, though with almost another race of men and women. It was a comforting reflection that they had the external marks of a condition much improved upon that of the former age.

July 21. — Dr. Holbrook, who as a physician attended my father, gave me some particulars of his last days. He retained his faculties till life itself failed. . . On Tuesday morning an express was sent for my son George, who was at Boston attending the celebration of the day. He came out immediately; was here between noon and one. He was recognized by my father, who made an effort to speak to him, but without success. George received his expiring breath between five and six in the afternoon. He had in the morning been removed from one bed to another, and then back. Mrs. Clark said to him that it was the 4th of July, the fiftieth anniversary of independence. He answered, "It is a great day. It is a good day." About one in the afternoon he said, "Thomas Jefferson survives," but the last word was indistinctly and imperfectly uttered. He spoke no more. He had sent as a toast to the celebration at Quincy, " Independence forever." Dr. Holbrook said his death was the mere cessation of the functions of nature, by old age, without disease.

July 26. — Mrs. Cushing entertained us with many anecdotes of ancient days, from the time of my father's law-studies with Mr. Putnam, at Worcester, down to the decease of her husband in 1811. Among the rest, she says that on the day when my father argued his first cause in the Superior Court, some of the Judges were afterwards enquiring at dinner who he was, and Governor Hutchinson, then Chief Justice, said that whoever should live to see it would find in him a great man. She also told of the last meeting of the Judges of the Superior Court under the King's Government, in 1774, to which her husband had then just been appointed in the place of her father — when, at the dinners given to the Judges by Sheriff Greenfeal and others, she heard much political conversation, and Mr. Putnam said that five hundred redcoats would set all the minute-men throughout the Colony, a-scampering.

July 31. — I read to the family Mr. Edward Everett's oration delivered at Cambridge on the 4th of this month. It is like all his writings — full of thought, of argument, and eloquence, intermixed with a little humorous levity and a few paradoxical fancies. There is at this time in this Commonwealth a practical school of popular oratory, of which I believe myself to be the principal founder by my own orations and lectures, and which, with the blessing of Him who reigns, will redound to the honor and advantage of this nation and to the benefit of mankind.

Aug. 2. — At eleven I went to the Senate-chamber in the State House, where the Governor and Lieutenant-Governor, Thomas L. Winthrop, with the Mayor and authorities of the city, were assembled, and when we went in procession to Faneuil Hall, and heard a eulogy upon John Adams and Thomas Jefferson by Mr. Daniel Webster. The prayers were performed by Mr. Charles Lowell. There was a funeral symphony, anthem, and dirge. The streets from the State House to the hall were thronged with a greater concourse of people than I ever witnessed in Boston. The hall itself was crowded to the utmost of its capacity. Mr. Webster was about two hours and a half in delivering his discourse, during which attention held the whole assembly mute. He returned with us to the hotel, and thence to his own home.

Aug. 26. — Dr. Kirkland and Mr. Gray came as a committee from the Corporation of the University to request my attendance next Wednesday at Commencement. . . Mrs. Willard, my next visitant, is the keeper of a female seminary of education at Troy, in New York. About a week since I received a letter from her, urging the expediency that Congress should patronize an institution for female education, with a small pamphlet published by her, recommending the same subject to the Legislature of New York. Mrs. Willard is a sensible and spirited woman, and I told her that her purpose of improving female education had my approbation and hearty good wishes; and, with regard to any assistance from Congress, I was sorry she must expect nothing more. Congress, I was convinced, would now do nothing. They will do nothing for the education of boys, excepting to make soldiers. They will not endow a university. I hoped this disposition would change, but, while it continues, any application to Congress for female education must be fruitless.

Washington, Oct. 20. — Rain. After a night of sound repose, I rose this morning entirely refreshed and well — rose to the cares and trials, anxieties and dangers, which surround the station assigned me, and from which I have been for about a hundred days partially released. As my day shall be, so may be my strength for action in the performance of duty, and for submission to the will of Heaven. The visitors of this day came chiefly to welcome my return. The Secretaries of State, the Treasury, and War, spoke of business in general terms. Mr. Barbour, after consultation with Mr. Clay, had written, about ten days since, to Mr. Monroe, enquiring if he would accept an appointment as Minister to the Congress of American nations, transferred from Panama to Mexico. He had received no answer, and now proposed that he and Mr. Southard should go on Sunday to Mr. Monroe's, in Loudoun, and converse with him upon the proposal — to which I readily agreed.

Oct. 22. — Governor Barbour and Mr. Southard called this morning, the former having received an answer from Mr. Monroe, declining the mission to the Congress of American nations on two grounds — the state of Mrs. Monroe's health, which he thinks will not admit of his leaving her, and the necessity of his remaining at home to retrieve, if possible, his private affairs.

Oct. 31. — I am resuming my habits of the last winter. Since my return, rising irregularly from four to seven; walking four miles, to return and see the sun rise from my northeastern window. Breakfast at nine, dine at five P.M., and in the intervals receive visitors, write letters or drafts of official papers, and read dispatches, proceedings of Courts-martial, and newspapers till ten in the evening, when I retire to bed.

Nov. 17. — Henry Lee came to ask me to return some manuscript letters of General Washington which he had lent me, I believe, a year ago. I could not immediately recollect where they were, but promised to look them up and return them soon. I returned to him another bundle of letters, which the Postmaster-General had given me concerning Lee himself. Lee's reputation is bad with regard to private morals, and his political course is unprincipled; but he writes with great force and elegance, and Mr. Calhoun has used him for that purpose. Through Calhoun's influence, the Postmaster-General gave Lee some small office in that Department, where it is said he has used the advantages of the situation against the Administration, and to promote the purposes of his patron, while he has at the same time been constantly writing abusive pieces for the newspaper called the *Telegraph,* the Phoenix from the ashes of the Washington *City Gazette.*

Nov. 22. — Round Capitol Square, one hour five minutes. Sun rose vii. 12.

Mrs. Weeden was a solicitor for charity. She said she had rent to pay, and if she could not obtain money to pay it this day, her landlord threatened to distrain upon her furniture. Of such visitors I have many.

Nov. 27. — In the evening I had a visit from Mr. D. P. Cook, Representative from Illinois. He has been much out of health, and has lost his election for the next Congress. Among the causes of his failure is said to have been his resistance to projects for altering the system of the land laws, and for distributing all the lands in the Western country among the people there for little or nothing. Benton has been the first broacher of this system, and he relies upon it to support his popularity in the Western country. He made a proposal in the Senate last winter for this graduation of the prices of public lands, and supported it by a speech, the whole drift of which was to excite and encourage hopes among the Western people that they can extort the lands from the Government for nothing. He printed an edition of this speech in a pamphlet, and Cook says he scattered copies of it all over the country as he went home; and now he is returning to Congress. Cook says that the minds of the people upon this subject are all debauched; that they say they must have the lands for nothing, and that the debt they owe for those they have bought must be spunged. He adds that Benton made himself amazingly popular by the resolution he offered for graduating and reducing the price of the lands, though his popularity has been somewhat shaken by a powerful exposure of him in the newspapers in the course of the summer.

Nov. 28. — At noon I rode up to the Capitol, and met Colonel Trumbell in the rotunda. His four pictures are placed, and in such a favorable light that they appear far better than they had ever done before. There are four other spaces to be filled with pictures of the same size, for which the Colonel is very desirous of being employed. He had therefore placed under them his small pictures of the deaths of Warren and Montgomery, and two others, bare sketches, one, of the death of Mercer at Princeton, and the fourth, another battle; and with them he had brought two small pictures for churches, religious subjects, which, he said, he had painted this present year, and had taken here with him to show that he was not too old to paint yet.

A French workman in sculpture, engaged upon a bas-relief of Penn's Treaty, came and asked me to go up on his scaffolding and view his work; which I did. But all the bas-reliefs in the rotunda are execrably bad. I went up likewise within the scaffolding to the pediment, where Persico was at work. One of his three figures is nearly finished, and I think the design when completed will be good.

Nov. 29. — Cabinet meeting; at which I read the first draft of the annual message to Congress, upon which not much of observation was made. Mr. Wirt said he did not see what there was for the Richmond *Enquirer* to take hold of. The Richmond *Enquirer* will find or make enough. But there are several supplementary paragraphs yet to be added.

Nov. 30. — I rise irregularly from half-past four to half-past seven but, with very few exceptions, between five and six. Walk round the Capitol Square, four and a half miles, returning in time to see the sun rise from my northeast window. Make my own fire, then my toilet, and read papers till nine. Breakfast from nine to ten. Receive the heads of departments, and all visitors, from ten till five in the afternoon. Dine, and sit at table, or in Mrs. Adams's chamber, from five till seven; and then till eleven at night in my own chamber, writing the draft of the message, this diary, and letters. I have this month not been interrupted by evening visitors more than two or three times, nor detained by dinner company more than as often. The ensuing months will not be so much disengaged. The days of trial are coming again.

Dec. 1. — This was a harassing day, as well with visitors as with business. Mr. Edward Everett called, and spent part of the evening with me, conversing upon various topics. He spoke of a letter from Mr. Jefferson to Mr. Van Buren, of several sheets, which he had seen, explanatory of his letter to Mazzei. It disclaims many of the inferences which were drawn from it at the time, and questions the right of the federal party to claim President Washington as having been of their side. Everett said he thought he could obtain this letter for my perusal.

Dec. 2. — I went out to walk this morning after sunrise, and, having a sprain on one foot, was an hour and a half walking round the Capitol Square. I met and spoke to Mr. Hayne, the Senator from South Carolina. And Mr. Clay overtook me near the Capitol. He walked round the Square with me, and left me at the central market.

Dec. 4. — The nineteenth Congress, second session, commenced this day. Mr. Southard called twice, with his report at length prepared, and the papers to be communicated to Congress with it. The two Houses met, and the House of Representatives proceeded to business with about a hundred and seventy members; the Senate with about forty. The Vice-President, Calhoun, took the Chair of the Senate.

Dec. 5. — [Twenty-four names in the margin.] Mrs. West is the sister of a man named Hare, who in 1818 was convicted at Baltimore of robbing the mail, and sentenced to ten years' imprisonment. His brother was capitally convicted for the same crime, and executed. This man has repeatedly petitioned to be released, and now his sister came with a recommendation signed by many respectable persons, recommending that the remaining time of his imprisonment might be remitted. It is difficult to resist the solicitation of a woman, particularly for mercy to her brother. I told her that I would reflect upon the subject, and, if I could find it consistent with my own sense of duty, would comply with the petition; but that the case was of such a nature that I could not give her encouragement to expect this result.

Governor Barbour came in soon after, and, in consulting him, I found him more disposed to relenting than I could be myself. Mail-robbery is one of those offences the full punishment of which in this country ought perhaps never to be remitted, and the sentence of ten years' imprisonment was, in this case, itself a very mitigated penalty.

Dec. 7. — I wrote very little this evening, and my diary now runs again in arrear day after day, till I shall lose irretrievably the chain of events, and then comes another chasm in the record of my life. The succession of visitors from my breakfasting to my dining hour, with their variety of objects and purposes, is inexpressibly distressing, and now that members of Congress come and absorb my evening hours, it induces a physical impossibility that I should keep up with the stream of time in my record. An hour's walk before daylight is my only exercise for the day. Then to dress and breakfast I have scarce an hour. Then five-and-twenty visitors, or more, from ten of the morning till five in the afternoon, leave me not a moment of leisure for reflection or for writing. By the time evening approaches, my strength and spirits are both exhausted. Such has been the course of this day. Such will be that of how many more?

Dec. 12. — T. Jefferson Randolph is the grandson of the deceased ex-President, and had brought me last spring a letter of introduction from him. I asked him what had been the success of the lottery granted by the legislature of Virginia last winter for the sale of his grandfather's estate.

He said it had totally failed; but that the contractors for the lottery, Yates and McIntire, thought it might succeed if, by an Act of Congress, it could be connected with a city corporation lottery. I asked if there were any constitutional difficulties in the way of such an arrangement. He said yes; that the Virginia delegation had it now before them for consideration. He knew not how they would decide upon it. I told him I should be happy to give him any assistance in my power and consistent with my duty.

Dec. 16. — John A. King, late secretary to the legation to Great Britain, arrived, bringing with him a convention concluded on the 13th of last month by Mr. Gallatin, with the British plenipotentiaries Huskisson and Addington, by which, if it please God, the long controversy respecting slaves carried away from this country in violation of the first stipulation of the Treaty of Ghent will be closed by a payment on the part of Great Britain of a sum a little exceeding twelve hundred thousand dollars, to be distributed by the American Government among the claimants. I receive this intelligence with the most fervent gratitude and joy.

Dec. 21. — Mr. Clay spoke of the ensuing Presidential election, and intimated that some of his friends, Eastern and Western, had expressed a wish that he should be supported as the candidate for the Vice-Presidency. He said he thought the selection ought to be made exclusively with reference to its influence upon the issue of the election of President; that for himself, he had no wish either to be a candidate for the Vice-Presidency or to withhold himself from it, if it should be thought useful to the cause that he should be run for that office.

I told him that I had hitherto heard very little said upon the subject; that if the failure of his health should render the duties of the Department of State too oppressive for his continuance in it, I should be satisfied if he should be transferred to the Vice-Presidency; but otherwise I should think it more advantageous both for the public and personally for him that he should continue in the far more arduous and important office of Secretary of State; which, in the event of his retiring from it, I should find it extremely difficult to fill. I said it was not my intention to compliment him, but I must say it would be no easy matter to supply his place in that Department. He said he was entirely satisfied with it; that, without complimenting me, he should say that he had found every facility in transacting business under me; and he should be equally well pleased to continue in the Department of State or to pass to the Vice-Presidency, according as the general cause of the Administration might be promoted by either event.

Feb. 3, 1827. — Southard, S. L.   Letter from General Jackson; not that heretofore threatened, but another, brought by General Houston.   The letter asks explanations of matters alleged to have been spoken last summer by Mr. Southard at a dinner-table at Mr. Welford's, at Petersburg, in Virginia. The Genèral affects to consider this conversation as in the nature of charges against him by a member of the Government.

Feb. 5. — Southard said Houston asked him on Saturday night to deliver his answer to General Jackson's letter to him open, and not to send it through the post-office.   I suggested to Mr. Southard the propriety of his answering the letter by a cool denial of the imputations upon General Jackson which imported a departure on his part from public duty, without indicating any sensibility to the violation of the confidence of social intercourse or to the tale-bearing misrepresentations which had called forth the General's letter, and without noticing the insidious allegation of the General, imputing to the Government of the United States the sentiments expressed on a casual topic of conversation at a dinner-table.

Feb. 14. — Mr. Clay spoke of the instructions to be given to Mr. Gallatin.   I agreed that he should be authorized to renew the Convention of October, 1818, without alteration, for ten years, preferring that term to the one proposed by the British Government, of twenty or fifteen years.   I would leave the North-western boundary in statu quo rather than accept anything proposed by the British, or concede anything to them. A statement must be made to present to the umpire in relation to the Northeastern boundary.   The prospects of our relations with Great Britain are dark.

Feb. 25. — I was engaged till near midnight in tracing through the second volume of United States Laws, the journals of the old Congress, and the speeches of President Washington, the history of our relations with the Indian tribes since the Revolution, and the origin of the army, with its progressive increase.[5]   This examination, like many others,

---

[5] The Cherokees of western Georgia and eastern Alabama, a peacable and largely civilized people, occupied lands which the white Georgians coveted for the cultivation of cotton.   During Monroe's Administration Gov. Troup of

leads me deeper and deeper in research, till I am compelled to stay my enquiries for want of time to pursue them. In the controversy with Georgia, the powers of the general government and those of the Government of Georgia are in conflict, and it is indispensable to know the whole history of our Indian relations of peace and war, to understand the ground upon which we stand. It was debatable ground far more under the Confederation than now, but Georgia and some other States are disposed to revert to the State claims under the Confederation.

March 3. — At the Capitol — where I continued until the adjournment of Congress. I had only five or six bills, of little importance, to sign. The Colonial Trade bill was lost by a disagreement between the two Houses. The House of Representatives having last evening adhered to an amendment, the Senate this morning adhered to their non-concurrence with it. The Loan and Woollen bills were left among the unfinished business. The current Appropriation bills for all the Departments have been liberal enough; but the only bill which I consider as a permanent benefit to the nation and creditable to the Congress just expired is the bill for the gradual improvement of the navy — stripped as it was of half its worth by the exclusion from it of a Naval Academy, which the bill from the Senate had provided for.

March 5. — Of the forty visitors whose names are in the margin, about one-half are members of Congress, who came to take leave before their departure homeward. . .

I was from ten this morning till ten at night never five minutes without one or more of these marginal notes. And I can scarcely conceive a more harassing, wearying, teasing condition of existence. It literally renders life burdensome. What retirement will be I cannot realize, but have formed no favorable anticipation. It cannot be worse than this perpetual motion and crazing cares. The weight grows heavier from day to day. Mr. Clay says that these times of trouble are the

---

Georgia had manifested constant hostility toward the Indians, and toward the Federal Indian Agent who strove to protect them. Believing the Administration of Adams to be weak, the Georgians now decided that the time had come to dispossess the Indians. Despite all that the national government could do, they marched into the reservation — guaranteed to the Indians by a Federal treaty which Washington had drafted in 1791 — and seized the desired area. It was an unhappy event in the career of Adams and in the history of the Presidency.

times which try the spirits of men. Even so. And may our strength be proportioned to the ordeal through which we must pass!

March 15. — Varied my morning walk from the Capitol Square to the College Hill, the distance being the same. Mr. Anderson, the Comptroller, called this morning, to converse with me upon the circular instruction to the Collectors, to be sent with the proclamation. He spoke also of other subjects, and particularly of the bitter and rancorous spirit of the opposition. It has produced during the late session of Congress four or five challenges to duels, all of which, however, happily ended in smoke; and at a public dinner given last week to John Randolph of Roanoke, a toast was given directly instigating assassination. Mr. Anderson remarked to me that General Jackson was deeply indebted to me for his character before the nation, and thought I had been ill requited for kindness and service to him.

March 18. — There came on this morning a heavy storm of rain, which detained me from attendance at church. I finished a long letter to Albert Gallatin. I write few private letters, and those under irksome restraints. I can never be sure of writing a line that will not some day be published by friend or foe. Nor can I write a sentence susceptible of an odious misconstruction but it will be seized upon and bandied about like a watch-word for hatred and derision. This condition of things gives style the cramp. I wrote also the weekly letter to my son. These at least will escape the torture of the press.

March 20. — E. Wyer brought me last evening the signet-ring which I had requested him to procure for me in London — the device a very simple one, of which a sixpenny seal had been given me — a cock, with the motto, "Watch." I wished it in better garb and execution. But the precept of Jesus is to pray as well as watch, and he used the cock as a monitor to recall to duty the faithful disciple who denied him at the crisis of his fate. To fix the fleeting solemnity of these thoughts, I threw them this morning, before breakfast, into a sonnet to Chanticleer, which is here in the margin, and of which, when I come to be ashamed of the poetry, I may still adhere to the morality. . .

WATCH AND PRAY

SONNET TO CHANTICLEER

Minstrel of morn, whose eager ken descries
  The ray first beaming from night's regions drear;
  Herald of light, whose clarion sharp and clear
Proclaims the dawning day-star to the skies.

Bird of the brave, whose valiant heart supplies
  The beak of eagles and the falcon's spear;
  Bird of the lofty port, disdaining fear,
Unvanquish'd spirit, which o'ercomes or dies.

Bird of the faithful, thy resounding horn
To thee was given the child of man to warn
  Of sinking virtue and of rising day.
Oh, while from morn to morn I hear thy strain,
Let the shrill summons call me not in vain
  With fervor from on high to Watch and Pray.

March 29. — Hearing the clock strike at the half-hour, I rose, believing it between four and five. After rising, I found it was an hour earlier; but I beguiled the tediousness of time with occupation. Wheaton came to expose to me his penury and distress. He told me he was seventy-three years of age; that he began with the American Revolution; that he received in the course of it many dangerous wounds. He was one of the clerks in the Land Office, and is among those recently dismissed from it, to starve with a daughter who has a worthless husband — worse than dead — and four small children, all destitute even of bread. He has almost totally lost his memory, and has long been unable to perform any duty at the Land Office; but his removal from it has placed him in a pitiable condition, and his appeal to me was pathetic, not without tears.

March 30. — Governor Barbour called with a pamphlet published by General Scott, apparently being a letter from him to the Secretary of War upon the subject of the contest for rank between Scott and Gaines, and a pamphlet previously published, no doubt by Gaines. Scott had already sent his letter in manuscript to the Secretary of War, and it is not only full of coarse invective upon Gaines, but offensive in several passages to the Secretary of War himself. Governor Barbour thinks that some notice of censure should be taken of it, and proposed a meeting of the members of the Administration to consider of it to-morrow; to which I assented.

April 2. — Mr. Southard called twice in the course of the morning — first, to mention letters received from Commodore Hull in the Pacific, and from Rodgers at Malta, in December; and afterwards, to read me a reply from General Jackson to the answer Southard had sent him to the letter which Jackson had written to him about the after-dinner conversation last summer at Fredericksburg. This reply is in two or three sheets of paper, written in a coarse and insulting style, somewhat verbose, and with passion partly suppressed; alleging that he had received the statement of Mr. Southard's remarks from Dr. Wallace and a Mr. Johnson in writing; these were two of the guests at table.

Dec. 1. — The names in the margin . . . are those of members of Congress who called in the course of this day and evening. They occupied so large a portion of the time that little was left me for writing. . . At the first session of the last Congress there was only one Senator, and not more than three members of the House, who declined coming to the house. The besotted violence of John Randolph at that session excluded him thenceforward from all right of personal civility from me.

May 22, 1828. — The Senate this day passed the Chesapeake and Ohio Canal bill, with two subsidiary bills for giving it effect, to the great joy of the people of the District. A cannonading salute was fired at Georgetown, and another in the city, upon this occasion. The confinement of these two days, with the continual rain of yesterday and this day till noon, affected my health; the distraction of business and of visitors gave me a headache, which disqualified me for writing.

May 23. — I rose before daylight, and wrote two hours; then rode two hours with John. My pony, dull and vicious, stumbled and threw me from my saddle on his neck, not without some hurt. Before dinner, I visited the nursery, where I now found fifty Spanish cork-oaks up, or appearing at the surface. I discovered also several black walnuts, planted the 22d of March; several almond-trees, the kernels of which were also then planted; ash and ash-leaved maples, planted last

November by Mr. Foy. The black walnut, therefore, and the almond, planted in spring, vegetate to the surface in precisely two months.

May 24. — Mr. Rush, Mr. Southard, and Mr. Everett dined with us, and went with me at seven in the evening to the Capitol. My son John followed, and Mr. Clay joined us at the Capitol. I remained there till midnight, reading and signing bills brought me successively by the Senators Ellis and Bateman, and the members of the House of Representatives Forward and Maxwell, the joint Committee of Enrolled Bills. Among them was the bill authorizing a treaty to be held with the Winnebago and other Indians; immediately after signing which I sent in to the Senate message No. 41, nominating Lewis Cass and Pierre Menard as the Commissioners. They were immediately confirmed.

May 26. — Mr. Mercer, the member of the House from Virginia, called on me a second time this evening, to speak upon the subject of General Scott and General Macomb. Mercer is a Virginian, and a friend of Scott's. He is also very unfriendly to Macomb, of whose character he spoke in very disparaging terms; said that his courage was very doubtful; that Colonel Snelling averred that his conduct at Plattsburg had been contemptible; that his pretence of being a citizen of New York was false, because he was born in the Territory of Michigan; that as Chief Engineer his conduct had occasioned all the difficulties in the surveys for internal improvements; that he had degraded himself by accepting the office of Chief Engineer with the rank of colonel; and that the nomination of him had turned twenty-five votes in the House of Representatives in favor of abolishing the office. He proposed, therefore, that, at the demand of General Scott, a Court-martial should be assembled, and that General Macomb and General Scott should engage to abide by their decision. . .

This has been a harassing day; but I perceived a tamarind heaving up the earth in the centre of tumbler No. 2; and I planted in tumbler No. 1 three whole Hautboy strawberries.

May 27. — I rode the Governor's horse the long or twelve-mile tour. He is very spirited, but easily managed; paces, trots, canters, and never needs whip or spur. But he trips in pacing, and has a weakness in the left hind ankle, which is dangerous. I despair of procuring a safe horse, and must make my option between renouncing this mode of exercise and taking its chances. . .

General Macomb came, and made his acknowledgments to me for the appointment of Major-General, and said he had sent in his resignation to the War Department as Chief Engineer, and had received his new commission. He said he had twice met accidentally General Scott, who had omitted to return the usual salutations of civility.

May 28. — General Harrison called to express his satisfaction at receiving the appointment of Envoy Extraordinary and Minister Plenipotentiary to the republic of Colombia, and to take leave, being on the point of departure for Cincinnati. He proposes to embark for his destination in the autumn, when the unhealthy season of that region will be over.

May 31. — I rise generally before five — frequently before four. Write from one to two hours in this diary. Ride about twelve miles in two hours, on horseback, with my son John. Return home about nine; breakfast; and from that time till dinner, between five and six, afternoon, am occupied incessantly with visitors, business, and reading letters, dispatches, and newspapers. I spend an hour, sometimes before and sometimes after dinner, in the garden and nursery; and hour of drowsiness on a sofa, and two hours of writing, in the evening. Retire usually between eleven and midnight. My riding on horseback is a dangerous and desperate resort for the recovery of my health.

June 6. — Mr. Clay was twice here. First with a draft of his answer to a letter from the Central Administration Committee, in Kentucky, respecting a letter from him to a Mr. Blair of that State, and to testimony of Amos Kendall, given before the Senate of Kentucky, intended to support charges against Mr. Clay of corrupt bargaining with me; and even of his having tempted Kendall himself with a bribe. Mr. Clay declines publishing the letter to Blair, but authorizes the committee to exhibit a copy of it to any person wishing to see it. He sends also three original letters from Kendall to him — one dated in January and one in February, 1825, and one in October, 1826 — which will prove Kendall, what he is already well known to be, a liar. Kendall is one of those authors to be let, whose profligacy is the child of his poverty. Mr.

Clay's second call was with a dispatch from Count Nesselrode, the Russian Minister of Foreign Affairs, to Baron Krudener, informing him that the Emperor Nicholas had reviewed the claim for indemnity in the long-standing cases of the *Hector* and the *Commerce,* and that by his orders it had been granted, and a settlement effected satisfactory to the agents of Colonel Thorndike and of Mr. Loud. Mr. Clay proposed that some public notice should be taken in the newspapers of this act of justice in the Emperor Nicholas; to which I readily agreed, and requested him also to give notice of this settlement to Colonel Thorndike and Mr. Loud.

Mr. R. H. Lee called again, and mentioned that he was making progress in his Memoir of the Life of Arthur Lee. I read to him a passage concerning Arthur Lee in the third volume of Hutchinson's History.

June 9. — The morning was cool. I bathed in the river, from the boat, but in fifteen minutes' swimming found myself so much fatigued that I was obliged to return to the boat before reaching the shore. Visited the garden, and afterwards the nursery. In the southern seedling-bed a few black walnuts and shagbarks are still coming up — scarcely enough to replace those that die. In the eastern seedling-bed there has been for weeks no new vegetation, except of weeds and a few straggling self-planted lilacs.

June 10. — From breakfast I was called by Judge Thurston, who, in his peculiar way, came to scold because his son had not been appointed a lieutenant in the Marine Corps, and to supplicate some appointment for him to save him from desperation. The Judge met Mr. Southard in the antechamber, and was scarcely civil to him. I have now been so long acquainted with Judge Thurston, and have witnessed so many of his sensitive paroxysms, that they produce little impression upon me. I told the Judge that I could do no more for his son than was compatible with my duties to others, and, if the occasion should occur, I should readily do that. The Judge is partially insane, and knows and avows it, but retains intelligence enough to make his insanity a plea for his title to compassion.

June 12. — Mr. Clay was here, and submitted a letter to W. P. Preble authorizing the employment of a Mr. Deane as an Assistant Agent upon the Northeastern Boundary arbitration. Mr. Clay expressed some apprehension that Mr. Gallatin would be somewhat intolerant of an associate Agent. He thinks Mr. Gallatin's conduct towards the Administration unfriendly and unfair, and he says Mr. Gallatin's discourse is neither generous nor just. He also repeated severe animadversions upon the circumstances showing great abuses in the post-offices, intended to operate against the Administration. He said he had asked Judge Brook to speak to me on the subject. He complained of being again severely unwell, excused himself from dining with us next Saturday, and said he wished to leave the city upon his summer excursion next Wednesday.

June 16. — Mr. Wirt, the Attorney-General, spent an hour with me; spoke of the unlucky controversy that has arisen between the Chesapeake and Ohio Canal and the Baltimore Railroad Companies, which must terminate in a lawsuit. He intimated that the Railroad Company had applied to him for his professional services, and asked if this would interfere with his official duty as Attorney-General.

I said I thought it would, the United States being interested in the stock of the Canal Company by their subscription of one million of dollars.

June 19. — The wife of Willis Anderson came again to petition for his pardon. All importunities are trials of temper. The importunities of women are double trials. I had refused this woman three times, and she had now nothing new to allege. I now desired her not to come to me again. She hinted that her husband did not wish to be discharged from prison himself, and that it would be no relaxation of his punishment to turn him over to her. It reminded me of the old song about Orpheus and Eurydice.

June 21. — Mr. Clay called to take leave, intending to take his departure upon his summer excursion to-morrow. He said he hoped to be back here in August. . .

We rode this morning by the race-ground to Rock Creek, before which I read Evelyn and visited the garden. After dinner I walked round the nursery.

June 22. — [Sunday: A sermon at the Unitarian church contrasting the careers of Napoleon and Washington]. When Bonaparte was at the pinnacle of his power, in the summer of 1810, I told poor Six d'Oterbeck, then Minister of Louis

Bonaparte at St. Petersburg, that Napoleon knew nothing but how to win battles, and that after all, standing by itself, it was but a precarious kind of knowledge. Six then all but worshipped him; but he told me that Napoleon had conceived the opinion that he was possessed of supernatural power; that he was more than a human being; and that this phantasy had taken possession of all his family. Six believed that he would finish by establishing a Western empire embracing the whole continent of Europe, and that he would claim to be the prophet of God, and enact over again the tragedy of Mahomet. He also believed that he would succeed in carrying that plan into effect. Bonaparte was a man of great genius for military combinations and operations, whose head was turned by success, who had magnificent imaginations and some generous purposes, but was under no control of moral principle. Very shortly after my conversation with Six, here referred to, Napoleon drove his brother Louis from the throne of Holland, which he annexed to the French Empire. Six d'Oterbeck was recalled, and not long afterwards drowned in one of the canals of Amsterdam. Napoleon and his preternatural power have crumbled into dust, and now he becomes the moral of a sermon against selfishness.

June 23. — For the benefit of my health I began this day to combine the river bath and the ride. Rode to the rock near the bridge. Swam about ten minutes, and then rode again around the Capitol Square home. Labor in the garden is a third expedient of exercise to which I shall perhaps hereafter resort. I have not yet ventured to undertake it. My complaints result from sedentary habits, for which laborious and hardy exercise is the best remedy. I visited this morning the garden. . .

General Porter brought me a fresh letter from General Scott. He says he is distressed and embarrassed by my reiterated decisions against him; that he cannot obey the commands of his junior and inferior officer; that he intends to apply for redress in some form to Congress, and he asks a furlough of six or nine months for that purpose.

As this is an affair in which I deem it necessary to take every step with deliberation, I desired General Porter to give notice to the other members of the Administration of a meeting on the subject at one o'clock to-morrow, and in the mean time to communicate General Scott's letter to Mr. Rush and Mr. Southard. . .

Mrs. Adams is winding silk from several hundred silkworms that she has been rearing, and I am engaged in a long correspondence with my son Charles, and now much involved in giving him an analysis of Cicero's *Oration for Roscius of Ameria*.

June 24. — Cabinet meeting at one. Mr. Rush, General Porter, and Mr. Southard present. I stated to them that in every step of these proceedings with General Winfield Scott I wished to act with the benefit of their advice; that the conduct of General Scott was insubordinate and disrespectful to a degree that, were it not for the gallant services which he has rendered to the country, I should some time since have dismissed him from the army; that on the rigorous principle of military subordination it was perhaps my duty so to have done. But it was entirely in the nature of our principles and institutions to temper with kindness and indulgence even the rigidity of military discipline. And I thought it particularly proper so to do in the case of an officer who stood so high in the estimation of his country, and towards whom personally I had no other than friendly feelings.

He had three times successively manifested a disposition of disobedience to lawful commands, and now asked for a furlough till next April, avowedly to make an application in some form to Congress, against the order and decisions of the President. This allegation was itself an insult; for in what manner could Congress control these orders and decisions? Certainly by no other mode than by impeachment of the President, or by an ex post facto law to annul a purely executive act. I should, therefore, on no consideration grant him a furlough. It had occurred to me that in giving him this answer it would be proper to order him peremptorily to his post, and to fix a day when his present leave of absence from it should cease.

General Porter thought an intimation ought to be given in the answer not only that the furlough could not be granted, but that the request was not admissible, even as a subject of consideration; which was approved.

June 30. — The eighth day in succession of my river-baths. I rode to the rock, swam fifteen minutes, and then rode to the navy-yard. Overtaken by a shower, near the Capitol, and took shelter under one of the arches. Found Mr. Persico, the Italian sculptor, there, and went up to view his work at the pediment, of which I furnished him the design. He is now upon the last figure, Hope; and thus far his execution is very satisfactory. His eagle had been indifferent in the drawing; better, but not good, in the model. In the work itself it is the pouncing bird. He called my attention to the anchor, and said I had told him the anchor of his model was a Dutch anchor: he had, therefore, gone to Commodore Tingey and taken for his model a true anchor of a ship of war. "And now," said he, "whenever a sailor looks at this pediment he will say, How exact the anchor is!" . .

Day. I rise at the average of a quarter-past four. Sometimes write an hour or two, but more frequently devote the morning to exercise and idle occupation — watching the plants in my pots and boxes; visiting the garden; reading Evelyn's *Sylva;* riding from eight to fourteen miles on horseback, or swimming from a quarter to half an hour in the Potomac. Breakfast between nine and ten. Receive visitors, transact business, and write at intervals, and read newspapers, public documents, and dispatches, till between five and six, when we dine. Visit my nursery, and make trivial observations upon the vegetation of trees till dark. Repose in torpid inaction from one to two hours. Write from one to two more, and between eleven and midnight retire to bed.

July 4. — Independence Day. Chesapeake and Ohio Canal commenced. Between seven and eight this morning I went with my son John to the Union Hotel, at Georgetown, where were assembling the President and Directors of the Chesapeake and Ohio Canal Company; the Mayors and Committees of the corporations of Washington, Georgetown, and Alexandria; the heads of Departments, foreign Ministers, and a few other invited persons. About eight o'clock a procession was formed, preceded by a band of music, to the wharf, where we embarked in the steamboat *Surprise;* followed by two others, we proceeded to the entrance of the Potomac Canal, and up that in canal-boats to its head — near which, just within the bounds of the State of Maryland, was the spot selected for breaking the ground. The President of the Chesapeake and Ohio Canal Company, with a very short address, delivered to me the spade, with which I broke the ground, addressing the surrounding auditory, consisting perhaps of two thousand persons. It happened that at the first stroke of the spade it met immediately under the surface a large stump of a tree; after repeating the stroke three or four times without making any impression, I threw off my coat, and, resuming the spade, raised a shovelful of the earth, at which a general shout burst forth from the surrounding multitude, and I completed my address, which occupied about fifteen minutes. . .

The marshals of the day escorted me home on horseback, came in and took a glass of wine, and took leave with my thanks for their attentions. The day was uncommonly cool for the season, with a fresh breeze, and towards evening there was a gentle shower. The exertion of speaking in the open air made me hoarse, and with the anxiety, more oppressive than it should have been, to get well through the day, exhausted and fatigued me, so that I was disqualified for thought or action the remainder of the day. As has happened to me whenever I have had a part to perform in the presence of multitudes, I got through awkwardly, but without gross and palpable failure. The incident that chiefly relieved me was the obstacle of the stump, which met and resisted the spade, and my casting off my coat to overcome the resistance. It struck the eye and fancy of the spectators more than all the flowers of rhetoric in my speech, and diverted their attention from the stammering and hesitation of a deficient memory.

July 7. — Took the morning bath from the boat in the river, and the day was absorbed by a succession, almost uninterrupted, of visitors, from the breakfast to the dining hour. First, from Mr. Mercer. Next, from a man who said his name was Arnold; that he belonged to the county of Middlesex, Massachusetts; that he had been travelling, and found himself here without money; he would be much obliged to me for a loan to bear his expenses in returning home; which I declined. Colonel Thomas followed, going shortly for New York, and his suttling expedition to Bangor, Maine. He spoke very favorably of the new Treasurer, Mr. Clark, and mentioned to me some new indications of the political treachery of the Postmaster-General, McLean. Of this I can no longer entertain a doubt. He has been all along a supple tool of the Vice-President, Calhoun, but plays his game with so much cunning and duplicity that I can fix upon no positive act that would justify the removal of him.

July 25. — General Porter had an insolent letter from Duff Green, one of the editors of the *Telegraph,* demanding inspection and copies of documents in the War Department for the defence of General Jackson against charges contained in publications of C. S. Todd and T. H. Shelby, republished from Kentucky papers in the *National Journal* of yesterday. This demand was made in minatory language, and with a lying charge of partiality in the late Secretary of War in cases of similar demands made upon him. General Porter expressed a doubt whether he should answer this letter at all, but showed me a draft of an answer which he had written. It declared a readiness to furnish inspection or copies of any documents to persons having any right to claim them, but declined granting them in this instance on account of the reflections in Green's letter upon Governor Barbour, with some argument to justify this course. I thought it would be better after the first sentence to say that the tenor of Green's letter was such as forbade the compliance with his request and the holding any further communication with him.

July 26. — Dr. Watkins called, and returned a volume of the Journals of the Senate that he had borrowed. He spoke of a long article in the *National Journal* of this morning against John Randolph of Roanoke, which, he said, was written by Mr. Rush. Randolph is the image and superscription of a great man stamped upon base metal. His mind is a jumble of sense, wit, and absurdity. His heart is a compound of egotism, inflated vanity, and envy. In his drunken speeches in the Senate in the spring of 1826, with the brutality incident to the condition in which he was when he delivered them, he assailed not only the character of Mr. Rush, but the memory of his deceased father. And last spring, after repeating his attack on Mr. Rush in a speech in the House of Representatives, he published the speech in a pamphlet, with notes, and a second edition, with additional notes, and full of slander upon Mr. Rush, whose publication in the *Journal* this day, under the signature of " Julius," is only severe retaliation.

July 27. — With my son John, my nephew, and Antoine, I crossed the river in our canoe, and swam a quarter of an hour on the other side; but the shore is so deceptive that after diving from the boat, as I supposed, within a ten minutes' swim of the shore, before reaching half the distance I found myself so fatigued that I called the boat to me, and clung to her till she was rowed to the shore. We had crossed nearly opposite the Tiber point, and were annoyed with leeches and ticks at the landing. The decline of my health is in nothing so closely brought to my conviction as in my inability to swim more than fifteen or twenty minutes without tiring. This was the day of most overpowering heat that we have had this season.

Baltimore, Aug. 5. — We left Rossburg at five A.M. and arrived at Merrill's Tavern, at Waterloo, fifteen miles, at eight; there breakfasted, rested our horses till half-past eleven, and then rode to Baltimore, and at fifteen minutes past two alighted at Barnum's Tavern. The morning was cloudy, with a succession of light drizzling showers, by which, being on horseback I was not a little annoyed; and, having been so long disused to this exercise, the ride of twenty-seven miles this day, following that of nine last evening, was very fatiguing. I found myself also somewhat sore from excoriation. We dined immediately after our arrival at Baltimore, and from four in the afternoon till near eleven at night had a continual stream of visitors, almost all strangers, but who came to shake hands with the President. In the evening there was a Jackson-party popular meeting in the square adjoining to Barnum's House, at which a young man named McMahon, a member of the State Legislature, harangued the multitude for about three hours upon the unpardonable sins of the Administration and the transcendent virtues of Andrew Jackson. He was still speaking when I retired to bed, and I heard his voice, like the beating of a mill-clapper, but nothing that he said. The meeting dispersed about eleven at night. There was a similar meeting of the friends of the Administration a few nights since, and there are ward meetings or committee meetings of both parties every day of the week. It is so in every part of the Union. A stranger would think that the people of the United States have no other occupation than electioneering.

Philadelphia, Aug. 6. — At seven in the evening we arrived at Philadelphia. There was a large concourse of people assembled on the wharf, who gave three cheers at my landing, and a multitude of whom followed me as I walked from the wharf to Head's Mansion House, in South Third Street.

They shouted continually as I went, and crowded round me so that I had barely room to pass along. With their shouts occasionally two or three voices among them cried, " Huzza for Jackson! "

Washington, Dec. 1. — R. M. Johnson, Senator from Kentucky, quite shocked at the virulence of newspaper slanders against the Administration.

Dec. 3. — A continual stream of visitors, members of Congress, and a few others, from breakfast till near four P.M., when I took my ride of an hour and a half on horseback. Most of the members of Congress who came were friends, and they had but one topic of conversation — the loss of this day's election. I have only to submit to it with resignation, and to ask that I and those who are dear to me may be sustained under it. The sun of my political life sets in the deepest gloom. But that of my country shines unclouded.[6]

Dec. 4. — The visits of members of Congress continue, and absorbed all the morning, and unseated my tranquillity of mind. This day several members of the Senate, of my inveterate opponents, came to pay visits of form. Mr. Everett called to recommend the appointment of Mr. Davis, of New York, as a bank director. I invited him to dine with us, and he promised he would, but afterwards sent a note of excuse, saying he would call in the evening; which he did.

Dec. 9. — Mr. Bailey spent the evening with me. He enquired if I would accept a seat in the Senate from Massachusetts if it should be offered me. I answered that the first objection would be that I would on no consideration displace any other man. He said he believed Mr. Silsbee was very

[6] Adams's Diary, which contains a complete hiatus from Aug. 6 to Dec. 1, 1828, says nothing of the progress of Andrew Jackson's successful campaign to wrest the Presidency from him. No mention is made of the false accusations against Adams — that he had made a fraudulent bargain with Clay; that he was an aristocrat of European training and predilections; that he had received enormous sums of public money; that his purchase of a billiard table for the White House showed his dissipated tastes. Adams's own position was above criticism in the campaign. He refused to do anything to prevent holders of Federal offices from taking part in the effort to defeat him. He had no lieutenants who were able to cope with the two chief Jackson managers in the North, Van Buren of New York and James Buchanan of Pennsylvania. The result of the election was that Jackson won 178 electoral votes, and Adams only 83. But as Edward Channing states, " Jackson was raised to the Presidency by the over-representation of the South combined with the employment of most unjustifiable methods by his partisans in Pennsylvania and New York. On the whole, possibly it was more honorable to have been defeated in 1828 than to have been elected."

averse to coming again to the Senate, and would be glad to decline if I would accept. I said there were other objections, my intention being to go into the deepest retirement, and withdraw from all connection with public affairs. He said Dr. Condict, of New Jersey, had expressed to him the hope that I should not thus withdraw.

Dec. 17. — Mr. Mitchell, a member of the House of Representatives from South Carolina, called to visit me. I spoke to him of the controversy in which he has been engaged, the last autumn, with the rest of the South Carolina delegation at the last session of Congress, there having been meetings at Mr. Hayne's lodgings of a violent character as threatening disunion. Mitchell has all the delegation against him excepting W. Smith, the Senator; but his testimony overbalances all theirs.

Dec. 25. — I was engaged all the leisure time of this day in reading over the observations upon the claim of General Scott to command Generals Macomb and Gaines, the second draft of which is now finished, forming a manuscript of a hundred and twenty pages. It would require a third writing over, for which I shall not have the time. Its great fault now is its length, and the numerous repetitions contained in it. There is also perilous matter for myself. But I have written it under a deep sense of duty.

Dec. 31. — Mr. Clay spoke to me with great concern of the prospects of the country — the threats of disunion from the South, and the graspings after all the public lands, which are disclosing themselves in the Western States. He spoke of a long message from Ninian Edwards, Governor of Illinois, to the Legislature of that State, who, he said, wished to take the lead from Thomas Hart Benton, Senator from Missouri, who commenced this inroad upon the public lands. I told Mr. Clay that it would be impossible for me to divest myself of a deep interest in whatever should affect the welfare of the country, but that after the 3d of March I should consider my public life as closed, and take from that time as little part in public concerns as possible. I shall have enough to do to defend and vindicate my own reputation from the double persecution under which I have fallen.

Jan. 1, 1829. — The year begins in gloom. My wife had a sleepless and painful night. The dawn was overcast, and, as

I began to write, my shaded lamp went out, self-extinguished. It was only for lack of oil; and the notice of so trivial an incident may serve but to mark the present temper of my mind. But in every situation in which mortal man can be placed there is a line of conduct before him which it is his duty to pursue; and the season of adversity, though depriving him of the means which in prosperity he may possess of doing good to his fellow-men, is perhaps not less adapted to the exercise of virtues equally conducive to the dignity of human nature. But, in good or in evil fortune, " It is not in man that walketh to direct his steps." Let him look to the Fountain of all good; let him consult the oracles of God. I began the year with prayer, and then, turning to my Bible, read the first Psalm.

Jan. 20. — Mr. Force brought back the part of my manuscript upon the brevet which I had given him, and showed me the pamphlet sent him by General Jackson, with the passionate and illiterate writing of his own upon a blank page of it.

Jan. 21. — Mr. Crowninshield called, to say that his son Benjamin had been taken dangerously ill with a fever, at Salem, and he feared he should be obliged to go home. He spoke to me of the deportment that I should hold towards my successor, which I told him would depend upon his towards me. I should treat him with respect to his station, but should make no advance to conciliation with him, as I had never wronged him, but much the reverse; but he had slandered me. He spoke also of the new federal struggle in Massachusetts, and the prospects of its success.

Feb. 11. — This day the votes for the election of President and Vice-President of the United States for four years from the 4th of March next were opened, and Andrew Jackson, of Tennessee, declared President, and John C. Calhoun Vice-President. The President-elect came into the city.

Feb. 21. — The Seneca Indian chief, Red Jacket, called upon me with his interpreter, Henry Johnson, to take leave of me and to ask some assistance for him to return home, for which I referred him to the Secretary of War. He has been exhibiting himself for some time past, upon theatres in several of our cities, for money. He carries with him a small silver-mounted emblematic tomahawk. He told me that he came to take leave of me, for that he and I were of the past age, and should soon be called for by the Great Spirit. I answered him that was true, and I hoped it would be to a better world than this.

Feb. 23. — Mr. Ringgold, the Marshal, called this morning and offered to attend me this evening to the ball. I desired him to come in the course of the week, and, with Mr. Elgar, to take an inventory of the furniture in the house belonging to the public and to be delivered up; and to inform General Jackson that the house would be ready to receive him and his family by the 4th of next month. Mr. Bell, the Senator from New Hampshire, called, and had some conversation with me; but we were interrupted.

Feb. 28. — Mr. Hoffman had a long conversation with me, advising me to attend the inauguration next Wednesday, and afterwards to visit the President; which, I told him, I would consider. Mr. Jackson and Colonel Taylor were visitors. Colonel Bomford told me that he and Commodore Patterson had been deputed by the subscribers to the inauguration ball to invite my attendance; but he had called upon me to enquire if it would be agreeable to me to receive such invitation. I told him that under present circumstances it would be as agreeable to me not to receive it, as I should be obliged to decline it if I did. . .

The month has been remarkable, as the last of my public service; and the preceding pages will show that the business of my office crowds upon me with accumulation as it draws near its end. Three days more, and I shall be restored to private life and left to an old age of retirement, though certainly not of repose. I go into it with a combination of parties and of public men against my character and reputation such as I believe never before was exhibited against any man since this Union existed. Posterity will scarcely believe it, but so it is, that this combination against me has been formed, and is now exulting in triumph over me, for the devotion of my life and of all the faculties of my soul to the Union, and to the improvement, physical, moral, and intellectual, of my country. The North assails me for my fidelity to the Union; the South, for my ardent aspirations of improvement. Yet " bate I not a jot of heart and hope." Passion, prejudice, envy, and jealousy will pass. The cause of Union and of improvement will remain, and I have duties to it and to my country yet to discharge.

On the 11th of this month Andrew Jackson, of Tennessee, was declared to be elected President, and John C. Calhoun, Vice-President, of the United States for four years from the 4th of March next. On the same day the President-elect arrived in this city, and took lodgings at Gadsby's Hotel. A self-constituted Central Committee, of persons pretending to be his exclusive friends and partisans, with John P. Van Ness at their head, undertook to usher him into the city, to order the firing of guns and manifestations of public rejoicing in his honor, and to assume the office of Masters of Ceremonies, to introduce to him all his visitors. They continued to exercise these functions till the public disgust became audible. They even published a regulation of the ceremony of his inauguration, and proclaimed Colonel Towson, the Paymaster-General, and one of their own number, Marshal for arranging the procession to the Capitol. This, however, has since been given up. The President-elect, a few days since, sent for Colonel Towson and requested him to resign his office of Marshal for the Central Committee; which he did, and the Marshal of the District of Columbia is to have the ordering of the Commission, as has been customary heretofore. Mrs. Jackson having died in December, the General has signified his wish to avoid all displays of festivity or rejoicing, and all magnificent parade. He has not thought proper to hold any personal communication with me since his arrival.[7] I sent him word by Marshal Ringgold that I should remove with my family from the house, so that he may, if he thinks proper, receive his visits of congratulation here on the 4th of March. He desired Ringgold to thank me for this information; spoke uncertainly whether he would come into the house on the 4th or not, but said if it would be in any manner inconvenient to my family to remove, he wished us not to hurry ourselves at all, but to stay in the house as long as it should suit our convenience, were it even a month. He has with him his nephew,

[7] John P. Van Ness, whom Adams mentions in these disdainful terms, was mayor of Washington, and had been head of a Jackson campaign committee. Jackson ignored etiquette and refused to call on the President on the ground that he could have nothing to do with a man who had gained office by a corrupt bargain with Clay. The Jacksonians were noisily triumphant in these closing days of the Adams Administration. But the designation of Postmaster-General Towson as marshal of the day offended public sentiment, for Tench Ringgold had officiated at so many inaugurations that he was regarded as having the honor by vested right.

Andrew Jackson Donelson, with his wife, a Miss Easten, an adopted son named Jackson and perhaps some others. His avoidance of me has been noticed in the newspapers. The *Telegraph* newspaper has assigned for the reason of this incivility that he knows I have been personally concerned in the publications against his wife in the *National Journal*. This is not true. I have not been privy to any publication in any newspaper against either himself or his wife.

March 2. — At seven in the evening I went with my son John and T. B. Adams, Jr., to the Capitol. Mr. Clay, Mr. Rush, and General Porter were there. I signed in the course of the evening about thirty bills. Several of the members of both Houses of Congress came and took leave. I returned to the President's house.

March 3. — Close of the Twentieth Congress, and of my public life. General Porter brought me the papers relating to a claim of Captain Campbell's company of Ohio Volunteers in the year 1812. I wrote a decision that they should be allowed pay for twelve months, at the foot of Mr. Whittlesey's letter. Mr. Johnston, the Indian Agent, came for a decision upon the sale of an Indian reservation; but I was compelled to decline it. He said he should be removed, for there were at least four here after his place. . .

About noon I rode with my son John and T. B. Adams, Jr., to the Capitol, and sent to both Houses of Congress message No. 8 with the Panama instructions. I signed fifteen bills, and between two and three o'clock a joint committee, S. Smith and Burnet, of the Senate, Ward and Bates of Massachusetts, announced to me that the Houses were ready to adjourn. I told them that I had no further communication to make to the Houses, and wished every individual member health and happiness. I walked back to the President's house. Concluded the contract with Persico. Consulted the members of the Administration whether I should attend the inauguration tomorrow. All were against it except Mr. Rush. About nine in the evening I left the President's house, and, with my son John and T. B. Adams, Jr., came out and joined my family at Meridian Hill. Dined. Received and accepted the resignations of Richard Rush, P. B. Porter, E. L. Southard, and William Wirt.

CHAPTER X

1829–1831

RETIREMENT AND STUDY — JEFFERSON'S MEMOIRS — QUARRELS OF
THE JACKSON ADMINISTRATION — DEATH OF MONROE — ELECTION
TO CONGRESS.

Meridian Hill, March 4, 1829. — This day Andrew Jackson, of Tennessee, was inaugurated as President of the United States. I had caused a notification to be published in the *National Intelligencer,* and *Journal,* requesting the citizens of the District and others, my friends, who might be disposed to visit me, according to the usage heretofore, to dispense with that formality. Very few, therefore, came out. Mr. Williams, of North Carolina, and Mr. Bartlett, of New Hampshire, came with Mr. Gales, who brought the inaugural address of the President. It is short, written with some eloquence, and remarkable chiefly for a significant threat of reform. Dr. Huntt was here, and Lloyd Rodgers, with Charles Carroll, a grandson of the patriarch of that name. Colonel Mercer came with Miss Hay and R. Peters. Sergeant, Silsbee, Crowninshield, Chambers, and Blake came together, and Dr. Watkins rode out alone. The day was warm and spring-like, and I rode on my horse, with Watkins, into the city, and thence through F Street to the Rockville Turnpike, and over that till I came to the turn of the road, by which I returned, over College Hill, back to the house. Near the postoffice I was overtaken by a man named Dulaney, who first inquired whether I could inform him how he could see John Quincy Adams, and when I gave him my name told me his, and that he came from Waterford, in Virginia, and was charged to ask of me a return of papers sent to me last summer and relating to the postoffice at that place. He came with me to my house, and I gave him the papers, which he took away. I resumed drowsily this evening the writing of my reply to the appeal of the confederates.

I can yet scarcely realize my situation. Hitherto I have prayed for direction from above in concerns of my country and of mankind. I need it not less, and pray for it with equal fervor, now, for those of myself, my family, and of all whose dependence is upon me. From indolence and despondency and indiscretion may I specially be preserved!

March 9. — My old servant Antoine came out this morning and took leave of me. I settled with him his last account for expenses at the President's house. He and his wife remain in the service of President Jackson. I took him at Amsterdam, in June, 1814, as a valet. Since my return to this country he has acted as my steward and butler.

March 12. — Mr. Clay came out this morning and took leave of us. He goes with his family by the way of Baltimore, to-morrow. Last Saturday his friends, and those of the Administration, gave him a dinner, at which he made a speech. He told me some time since that he had received invitations at several places on his way to Lexington to public dinners, and should attend them, and that he intended freely to express his opinions. I mentioned to him the letter from Rahway, New Jersey, and the answer I had given to it. He expressed himself much gratified with what I told him I had said in it of him, and told me he had written a very short answer to the letter which he had received. He manifested some sensibility at parting, and expressed a wish occasionally to hear from me.

March 14. — I walked before dinner to Mr. Southard's. Found him again convalescent. He told me some anecdotes of the manner in which the new Administration is commencing its operations, and which portend no good. To feed the cormorant appetite for place, and to reward the prostitution of canvassing defamers, are the only principles yet discernible in the conduct of the President, and indecision and instability are already strongly marked in his movements. He dropped from my naval nominations Stockton and McKeever, for masters-commandant, then, at the remonstrance of McKeever, sent them in by themselves. The Senate rejected them, and this morning he sent them in again.

March 17. — I began reading the third Philippic of Cicero, and consulted in Plutarch the lives of Cicero, of Antony, and of Brutus for the co-temporary facts. Looked likewise into Shakspeare's *Antony and Cleopatra*. There is something strange, and which would now be thought very affected, in the language of Shakspeare, whose most common thoughts are expressed in uncommon words.

March 19. — There was a fall of snow that entirely covered the ground. It confined me all day to the house. I walked an hour on the porch before dinner. . . Horatio Seymour says there is already a great bitterness between the partisans of Van Buren and those of Calhoun. Yesterday, the day after the adjournment of the Senate, William Lee, Second Auditor, Tobias Watkins, Fourth Auditor, and Richard Cutts, Second Comptroller of the Treasury, were removed from office, and Amos Kendall, a Major Lewis, who came with the President from Tennessee, and Isaac Hill, of New Hampshire, are appointed in their places.

March 23. — I rode my horse to the Capitol Hill and back before dinner; suffered much with the cold. In my conversation with Mr. Webster on Saturday he said that he was in the winter of 1803 and 1804 reading law in the office of Thomas W. Thompson, and then read several letters from William Plumer to him, very violent against Mr. Jefferson, and full of all sorts of wild projects; that Plumer was a very weak man, without any steadiness of principle or solidity of judgment. I saw from this the soreness of Mr. Webster's feelings. His character of Mr. Plumer is altogether incorrect. His feelings with regard to Harrison Gray Otis are not more favorable. He described him as a man altogether selfish, without principle, and of very slender abilities; though he admitted that he had a certain kind of talent. He said that his great object was to tack the Hartford Convention upon the whole federal party, so that he might make them all responsible for his own acts.

March 26. — Mr. Persico came, and took a sitting of three hours, but during the greater part of which time I was reading the first volume of *Pelham, or the Adventures of a Gentleman.*[1] The most prolific school of literature at present is novel-writing. The marvellous of character and manners is substituted in the place of the marvellous in narrative. Pelham, the Gentleman, is a compound of dandy, statesman, and

---

[1] This novel, by Bulwer-Lytton, was published in 1828, and contained many sketches of well-known English people then living.

philosopher, epicurean, coxcomb, duellist, courtier, patriot, satirist, demagogue, and political Vicar of Bray; who begins by presenting his father and mother as odious and ridiculous characters, and speaks of his own vices, and what he means to pass off for good deeds, with equal indifference. The book is, nevertheless, interesting, and abounds with keen observations and ingenious reflections.

March 31. — Commodore and Mrs. Rodgers called to pay us a morning visit, but Mrs. Adams was gone into the city when they were here. The morning was clear summer sunshine, but the weather clouded up towards evening. I rode my horse from three to five, and was musing, as I rode, upon the construction of half a dozen elegiac stanzas to versify a similitude upon Corinthian brass. I accomplished it in part, and very much to my dissatisfaction. It is with poetry as with chess and billiards: there is certain degree of attainment which labor and practice will reach, and beyond which no vigils and no vows will go. . .

Day. The greatest change in my condition occurred at the beginning of this month which has ever befallen me — dismission from the public service and retirement to private life. After fourteen years of incessant and unremitted employment, I have passed to a life of total leisure; and from living in a constant crowd, to a life of almost total solitude. I have continued as yet, however, to be much engaged with writing. Some letters, and my reply to the appeal of the confederates, absorb my time. I rise between five and six; write till nine; breakfast; read the newspapers, the Philippics, Pelham, Senate journals, documents, and my own diary, and write alternately till three or four; walk or ride from one to two hours; dine between five and six ; read, write, or doze from seven to eleven, and then to bed.

April 4. — Mr. Van Buren, the new Secretary of State, paid me a morning visit with Mr. Hamilton. Of the new Administration he is the only person who has shown me this mark of common civility. General Jackson had received from me attentions of more than a common character, besides obligations of a much higher order, which at the time when they were rendered he had expressly acknowledged and declared he would remember. All the members of his Administration have been with me upon terms of friendly acquaintance, and have repeatedly shared the hospitalities of my house. I never was indebted for a cup of cold water to any one of them, nor have I ever given to any one of them the slightest cause of offence. They have all gradually withdrawn from all social intercourse with me — from the old impulse, " odisse quem læseris: " they hate the man they have wronged. Ingham is among the basest of my slanderers, Branch and Berrien have been among the meanest of my persecutors in the Senate. . . Van Buren, by far the ablest man of them all, but wasting most of his ability upon mere personal intrigues, retains the forms of civility, and pursues enmity as if he thought it might be one day his interest to seek friendship. His principles are all subordinate to his ambition, and he will always be of that doctrine upon which he shall see his way clear to rise.

April 16. — Dr. Huntt came out this morning and vaccinated my son's infant daughter. He sat and talked with me perhaps an hour upon the only subject which now furnishes materials for conversation at Washington, which is the removals and new appointments to office. They are effected a few at a time, and in such a manner as to keep up a constant agitation and alarm among the office-holders. Multitudes of applicants are kept in suspense, and now and then one goes off gratified. The appointments, almost without exception, are conferred upon the vilest purveyors of slander during the late electioneering campaign, and an excessive disproportion of places is given to editors of the foulest presses. Very few reputable appointments have been made, and those confined to persons who were indispensably necessary to the office, such as Asbury Dickins to the place of Chief Clerk in the Treasury Department.

April 18. — The newspapers announce this morning the appointment of Louis McLane, of Delaware, as Envoy Extraordinary and Minister Plenipotentiary to Great Britain, in the place of James Barbour, removed. This is the most painful incident to me which has occurred since the change of the Administration, and it proves the utter heartlessness of Van Buren. He and McLane and Governor Barbour were all partisans of Crawford in 1825. McLane voted for him in the House, and thereby gave him the State of Delaware. McLane is utterly incompetent to the mission to London, and if he does not disgrace the country, will effect nothing for her interest. His only merit is the sale of himself and his Crawford stock to Jackson.

April 23. — The day was sultry and at summer heat. I rode only about an hour before dinner, and composed the fable of *The Lion and the Gnat,* and one stanza more of the *Ode to Licinius.* One stanza of Horace costs me more thought than five fables of La Fontaine. The thoughts of La Fontaine are more manageable. His versification differs so little from prose that it is much easier for me to compose while riding than it would be to compose the same fables in prose itself; the rhymes at the ends of the lines, and the measure of the lines, affording aids to the memory, which sometimes enable me to retain a whole fable of fifty lines.

April 27. — The removals from office are continuing with great perseverance. The custom-houses in Boston, New York, and Philadelphia have been swept clear, also at Portsmouth, New Hampshire, and New Orleans. The appointments are exclusively of violent partisans; and every editor of a scurrilous and slanderous newspaper is provided for. My next visitor was James A. Hamilton, who began by telling me that he totally disapproved of a publication of his brother, Alexander Hamilton, in the New York *Evening Post.* I had not seen this publication. James A. did not particularly describe the purport, but his object was to entreat me, if I should think it necessary to reply to his brother, not to refer to anything that he has said to me in his conversations with me.

June 8. — Rode the ten-mile round before breakfast. Met Mr. Van Buren riding also his horse, and we stopped and exchanged salutations. Van Buren is now Secretary of State. He is the manager by whom the present Administration has been brought into power. He has played over again the game of Aaron Burr in 1800, with the addition of political inconsistency, in transferring his allegiance from Crawford to Jackson. He sold the State of New York to them both. His first bargain failed, by the turn of the choice of Electors in the Legislature. The second was barely accomplished by the system of party management established in that State; and Van Buren is now enjoying his reward. His pale and haggard looks show that it is already a reward of mortification. If it should prove, as there is every probability that it will, a reward of treachery, it will be but his desert.

Aug. 5. — I began upon the collection of minutes and memoranda preparatory to the biographical memoir of my father. I propose to devote henceforth three hours a day to that portion of my business. My brother reminded me that it is this day twenty years since I embarked at Charlestown for Russia. I embark this day upon a more perilous, perhaps a more difficult, expedition.

Sept. 24. — In the evening I read several of Madame du Deffand's letters. It belongs probably to the effect of age upon the taste and judgment that these letters are more interesting to me than any novel. They are records of realities. In youth it was directly the reverse — fairy-tales, the *Arabian Nights,* fictitious adventures of every kind, delighted me. And the more there was in them of invention, the more pleasing they were. My imagination pictured them all as realities, and I dreamed of enchantments as if there was a world in which they existed. At ten years of age I read Shakspeare's *Tempest, As You Like It, Merry Wives of Windsor, Much Ado About Nothing,* and *King Lear.* The humors of Falstaff scarcely affected me at all. Bardolph and Pistol and Nym were personages quite unintelligible to me; and the lesson of Sir Hugh Evans to the boy William was too serious an affair. But the incantations of Prospero, the loves of Ferdinand and Miranda, the more than ethereal brightness of Ariel, and the worse than beastly grossness of Caliban, made for me a world of revels, and lapped me in Elysium. With these books, in a closet of my mother's bed-chamber, there was also a small edition, in two volumes, of Milton's *Paradise Lost,* which, I believe, I attempted ten times to read, and never could get through half a book. I might as well have attempted to read Homer before I had learnt the Greek alphabet. I was mortified, even to the shedding of solitary tears, that I could not even conceive what it was that my father and mother admired so much in that book, and yet I was ashamed to ask them an explanation. I smoked tobacco and read Milton at the same time, and from the same motive — to find out what was the recondite charm in them which gave my father so much pleasure. After making myself four or five times sick with smoking, I mastered that accomplishment, and acquired a habit which, thirty years afterwards, I had much more difficulty in breaking off. But I did not master Milton. I was nearly thirty when I first read the *Paradise Lost* with delight and astonishment. But of late years I have lost the relish for fiction. I see nothing with sympathy but men, women, and children of flesh and blood.

Washington, Dec. 30. — Mrs. Rush spoke about the paragraph in the President's message against the bank, and about Mrs. Eaton, wife of the Secretary of War, now the centre of much political intrigue and controversy. Mrs. Eaton is the daughter of a man named O'Neal, who some years since kept a tavern and failed, so that his house was sold to pay his debts. Mrs. Eaton was wife of a purser in the navy, named Timberlake, who being on service in the Mediterranean squadron, his wife lived at her father's, where Mr. Eaton and General Jackson, when a Senator, were lodgers. When O'Neal's house was sold, it was purchased by Mr. Eaton. About a year and a half since, Timberlake died, and very shortly after Eaton married his widow. Her reputation was not in good odor; and last spring, when Eaton was appointed Secretary of War, a grave question arose among the dignitaries, high and low, of the Administration, whether Mrs. Eaton was to associate with their wives. This question has occasioned a schism in the party, some of whom have more, and some less, of moral scruple; the Vice-President's wife, Mrs. Calhoun, being of the virtuous, and having then declared that rather than endure the contamination of Mrs. Eaton's company she would not come to Washington this winter; and accordingly she remains in the untainted atmosphere of South Carolina. I told Mrs. Rush that this struggle was likely to terminate in a party division of Caps and Hats.

Jan. 3, 1830. — William Lee came about nine in the evening, and spent two hours with me. He arrived last evening from New York, and told me he saw Mr. Gallatin the evening before last at Baltimore. He says Gallatin spoke to him slightingly of the President and members of the Administration, commented upon the President's obstinacy and ignorance, and said if Jefferson had treated him as Jackson treats all the members of his Cabinet, he would immediately have resigned his office. Lee told me also that Mrs. Huygens had told him of her refusal at Baron Krudener's party to go to the supper-room with Mr. Eaton, the Secretary of War, and of the Baron's expostulation with her upon her refusal. She has now sent out cards for an evening party herself, to which Mr. and Mrs. Eaton are not invited.

Jan. 5. — While we were at dinner, Mr. Gerry came in, and in great agitation told us that the President had yesterday sent to the Senate a nomination of General McNeill as Surveyor of the port of Boston in his place; and that when he went to him this day and reminded him of his promise, he flew into a passion, denied that he had made him any promise, and ordered him out of his house for his impertinence in circulating a report that he had. General Hayne, the senator from South Carolina, was present, and advised Gerry to take this answer as conclusive. Gerry went to Ingham, who at first refused to see him, and, when he did receive him, sullenly refused to give him any reason but that offices were not hereditary. Gerry supported from the emoluments of his office his mother and four unmarried sisters. His father was a signer of the Declaration of Independence, and died Vice-President of the United States. His distress was great, and affected me deeply. He said he should go for Boston to-morrow morning.

Jan. 27. — This day I received the English *Quarterly Review* for November, 1829, which contains cheek-by-jowl two articles of villification — one upon America and one upon Russia; one a review of the Duke of Saxe-Weimar and Captain Hall's travels, and the other of several recent publications upon Turkey. They are both full of rancorous English passions; but I had not time to read them through.

Feb. 6. — All the members of Congress are full of rumors respecting the volcanic state of the Administration. A busybody Presbyterian clergyman of Philadelphia, named Ezra Styles Ely, is the principal mischief-maker in the affairs of Mr. and Mrs. Eaton. He has been called here for the third time to pacify internal commotions. He was here several days, but went away without accomplishing anything. The President had determined to remove Branch, the Secretary of the Navy; but H. L. White, the Senator from Tennessee, and, it is said, Edward Livingston, went in deputation to the President, and informed him that if Mr. Branch should be dismissed the Senators from North Carolina would join the opposition, and all the dubious nominations now before the Senate would be rejected. He was also given to understand that Ingham, the Secretary of the Treasury, and Berrien, the Attorney-General, would resign. He concluded, therefore, to retain Mr. Branch, and became a mediator between him and Eaton, to bring them to speaking terms together. Such is their present state. Ingham, Branch, Berrien, Towson, have given large evening parties, to which Mrs. Eaton is not invited. On the other hand, the President makes her doubly conspicuous by an over-display of notice. At the last drawing-room, the night before last, she had a crowd gathered round her, and was made the public gaze. But Mrs. Donelson, wife to the President's private secretary, and who lives at the President's house, held no conversation with her. The Administration party is split up into a blue and a green faction upon this point of morals; but the explosion has been hitherto deferred. Calhoun heads the moral party, Van Buren that of the frail sisterhood; and he is notoriously engaged in canvassing for the Presidency by paying his court to Mrs. Eaton. He uses personal influence with the wives of his partisans to prevail upon them to countenance this woman by visiting her. There is a story current here, which whether true or false, is significant of the general estimate of Van Buren's character. It is, that he asked for a private conversation with Mrs. Donelson, and for three-quarters of an hour urged her with pathetic eloquence to visit Mrs. Eaton; that she defended as well as she could her own course, but, being no match for him at sophisticating, she at last said, " Mr. Van Buren, I have always been taught that ' honesty is the best policy.' " Upon which he immediately started up, took his hat, and departed.

Feb. 10. — Mr. Holmes, member of the Senate from Maine, called, and mentioned that he intended to speak again upon this resolution of S. A. Foote's upon the public lands. Thomas Hart Benton, a liar of magnitude beyond the reach of Ferdinand Mendez Pinto, among his other proofs that Eastern men have always had a settled policy of hostility to the West, alleged in the Senate, as he has been all last summer publishing in the Missouri newspapers, that I, in this spirit of hostility to the West, had given up to Spain the boundary of the Rio del Norte in the Florida Treaty. Holmes and S. Smith both, in replying to Benton, said that this treaty was made by Mr. Monroe and his Cabinet, and that they knew I was the last person who had consented to take the boundary of the Sabine.

Feb. 11. — In my walk this morning I met Chief-Justice Marshall near the head of the Avenue, and he walked down with me to its termination, opposite the yard of the Treasury Building. I asked him who, since the decease of the late Judge Washington, was the owner of President Washington's papers. He said he did not know, but that they were now in the possession of Mr. Sparks, who was to publish his letters, and some of the letters to him. I asked the Judge if there had ever been an adjudication in England of the property of epistolary correspondence. He knew of none. I mentioned the opinion or statement in a late number of the *North American Review,* that the property is in the writer of the letter, to whom, or to whose representatives, it ought to be returned after the decease of the receiver. He said he had formed no deliberate opinion upon the question, but that his first-made impression was that the property was in the receiver; a property qualified by the confidence of the writer.

Feb. 19. — The debate in the Senate upon Foote's resolution, concerning the public lands, continues, and has elicited a number of able and animated speeches. Benton and Hayne, by a joint and concerted attack upon the Eastern portion of the Union proposed to break down the union of the Eastern and Western sections, and of restoring the old joint operation of the West and the South against New England. Benton's objection is personal advancement and plunder; Hayne's, personal advancement, by the triumph of South Carolina over the tariff and internal improvement, and Calhoun's succession to the Presidency. The assault was so vehement and rancorous and desperate that it roused the spirit of the East, and Webster and Sprague have made eloquent speeches in its defence.

Feb. 23. — The *National Intelligencer* had this day half a recent speech of Mr. Webster, which has been much celebrated, in reply to a violent invective against him of Robert Y. Hayne. It fills almost two sides of the paper, and the other half is to come on Thursday. It is defensive of himself and of New England, but carries the war effectually into the enemy's territory. It is a remarkable instance of readiness in debate — a reply of at least four hours to a speech of equal length. It demolishes the whole fabric of Hayne's speech, so that it leaves scarcely the wreck to be seen.

March 3. — Dr. Huntt had some new gossiping tales of

scandal, which constitute the history of the present Administration. President Jackson has forced Mrs. Donelson, his wife's niece, who lives in the house with him, to visit Mrs. Eaton, and to invite her to the christening of her child, to which Mr. Van Buren stood sponsor and Miss Cora Livingston godmother. And now the rumor is that Mrs. Donelson is to go in the spring to Tennessee. Mr. Vaughan, the British Minister, gave a ball last Monday night, which was opened by Mr. Bankhead, the Secretary of the British Legation, and Mrs. Eaton; and Mr. Van Buren has issued cards also for a ball, which is to be in honor of the same lady.

March 22. — Mr. Sparks told me he had sold the *North American Review* to Alexander H. Everett. Edward Everett was here this evening, and told me that his brother had given fifteen thousand dollars for three-fourths of the *Review* — one-fourth being the property of the publishers. He said his brother had written him to ask him to write for the July number of the *Review* an article on the debate still pending in the Senate upon Mr. Foote's resolution concerning the public lands.

March 27. — Mr. Bell, the Senator from New Hampshire, passed two hours with me. He was enquiring who had been the former Comptrollers of the Treasury. He entertains a feeble hope that some of the most profligate publishers of scurrilous newspapers, now in nomination before the Senate for offices, will be rejected; but he will be disappointed. . . The movements upon these nominations pending in the Senate are intimately connected with a controversy between the *Telegraph,* Calhoun's newspaper here, and the New York *Courier,* Van Buren's paper, upon the question whether Jackson is or is not a candidate for re-election as President — the *Courier* insisting that he is, and the *Telegraph* declaring it premature to ask the question. Mr. Van Buren has got the start of Calhoun, in the merit of convincing General Jackson that the salvation of the country depends upon his re-election. This establishes the ascendency of Van Buren in the Cabinet, and reduces Calhoun to the alternative of joining in the shout of hurrah for Jackson's re-election or of being counted in opposition. Tun' contra Caesaris nutum?

April 15. — As I was walking out, I met Mr. Sparks, who was coming to see me, and walked with him round the Capitol

Hill. He said he had just returned from a visit to Pittsburgh, where he had been to inspect the spot of Braddock's defeat in 1775, which he had done much to his satisfaction. There was no person left there who had any recollection of the event, but there were many traditions, from which he had collected valuable information. I asked him when he expected to publish his correspondence of Washington. He thought there would be a volume out before the end of this year.

May 13. — Mr. Poinsett, our late Minister to Mexico, called to visit me. He has been at Philadelphia and Baltimore, where they have given him public dinners, where speeches were made and toasts given. He told me he was going immediately home to South Carolina, even at this season of the year to see if he could, by good advice, calm the excitement which he does not share. He spoke of a toast recently given by the Governor of the State — "The right to fight" — and said it was unfortunate that the most violent man they had was to be their next Governor — James Hamilton. South Carolina has been potioned and philtered and back-scourged, like an old lecher, into a frenzy of excitement, and has now a prospect of coming into physical collision with the Government of the Union. As the Government is now administered, there is every prospect that her bullies will succeed, to the sacrifice of the interest of all the rest of the Union, as the bullies of Georgia have succeeded in the project of extirpating the Indians, by the sacrifice of the public faith of the Union and of all our treaties with them.

May 22. — I called and spent an hour of the evening with Mr. Rush. He told me some particulars of the Jefferson birthday dinner, lately got up by Benton and Calhoun, to proclaim anti-tariff and nullification doctrine under the shelter of Jefferson's name. The ostensible purpose was to honor Jefferson's birthday by an assemblage of members of Congress dining together upon Republican principles. The real object was to trick the Pennsylvania members into the drinking of anti-tariff and nullification toasts. Eight members of the Pennsylvania delegation, Jefferson Republicans dyed in the wool, agreed to go. The company were assembled. The President was there by invitation. George R. Leiper, one of the Pennsylvania members, told Miller, his colleague, one of the toast-making committee, that he should like to see the toasts, and read them, till he came to the thirteenth, when Leiper told him he had enough; he need not read any more. He then collected the whole eight together, and told them he should not sit down at the table where these toasts were to be drunk; and they all agreed to withdraw together, which they accordingly did. The obnoxious toasts were drunk. But President Jackson, being called upon for his toast, gave, "The Union: it must be preserved." — Aio te, Æacida, Romanos vincere posse; and from that day the two sides of the faction have been each claiming the Presidential toast to itself.[2]

Quincy, Aug. 15. — I finished reading the first Tusculan, upon the contempt of death, and the argument in it is admirable. Philosophy had undoubtedly great influence upon the conduct of individuals in the age of Cicero, and upon his own particularly. The question whether death was an evil was perhaps an idle one. Nature has implanted in all animated beings a horror of death, and has made it doubly terrible to man by the agonies and convulsions which usually precede and attend it, as well as by that interest in the future which Cicero considers as an argument in favor of the immortality of the soul. . . I have read this dissertation at the most favorable moment of my life for giving it all its weight, when I have no plausible motive for wishing to live, when everything that I foresee and believe of futurity makes death desirable, and when I have the clearest indications that it is near at hand. I should belie my conscience should I not acknowledge that the love of life and the horror of dissolution is as strong in me as it ever was at any period of my existence, and that I deeply feel the hollowness of the whole argument of Cicero. It is utterly delusive. Yet I do not believe my hold upon life more tenacious than that of most other human beings, especially of those who have great enjoyment of life.

Aug. 18. — I this day finished the reading of the Bible, which I began about the 1st of May last year. This reading has not been so profitable to me as it ought to have been. Among the decays of age which I cannot dissemble to myself is a falling off of the discipline of the mind. The operation of the mind in reading should be like that of the leech upon the body; but the leech sometimes wanders over the veins without

[2] But Jackson's toast was unmistakably a defiance of Calhoun and Nullification.

taking hold of any one; and so it is in the dissipation of spirits which comes on with the lassitude of years.

Sept. 18. — I was called into the house to Mr. John B. Davis. While Davis was here, Mr. Richardson came, and Davis said he had seen in the newspaper that he declined a re-election to the next Congress. He said it was a determination long since taken by him; that he thought it due to the people of his congregation at Hingham, who had been exceedingly reluctant at his going even to the present Congress; and he came purposely to enquire of me if I would serve, if elected, as member for the district. . . Mr. Richardson said that if I would serve he believed the election could be carried by a large majority, as the *Old Colony Memorial,* and the Hingham *Gazette,* the only newspapers printed in the district, and another paper published in the adjoining district, and taken by some of his constituents, would support the nomination; but if I should decline, it was not probable that the district would unite upon any other person, and there would be no election. He then said that he thought that the service in the House of Representatives of an ex-President of the United States, instead of degrading the individual, would elevate the Representative character.

I said I had in that respect no scruple whatever. No person could be degraded by serving the people as a Representative in Congress. Nor, in my opinion, would an ex-President of the United States be degraded by serving as a selectman of his town, if elected thereto by the people. But age and infirmity had their privileges and their disqualifications. I had not the slightest desire to be elected to Congress, and could not consent to be a candidate for election. I knew not how the election would turn, and if chosen, it might depend upon circumstances whether I should deem it my duty to serve or to decline. The state of my health, the degree of opposition to the choice, the character of the candidate in opposition, might each or all contribute to my determination.

Mr. Richardson said this was sufficient, and he would go to work. He desired Mr. Davis to consider as secret and confidential what had passed here; which he promised.

Nov. 6. — The newspaper of this evening brought the last returns of the Congressional election for the district of Plymouth. Twenty-two towns gave 2565 votes, of which 1817

were for John Quincy Adams, 373 for Arad Thompson
(Jacksonite), 279 for William Baylies (federal), and 96
scattering votes. The authentic returns will perhaps make
some slight difference in the number of votes, but can make
none in the result. I am a member elect of the Twenty-Second
Congress.

Nov. 7. — No one knows, and few conceive, the agony of
mind that I have suffered from the time that I was made by
circumstances, and not by my volition, a candidate for the
Presidency till I was dismissed from that station by the failure
of my re-election. They were feelings to be suppressed; and
they were suppressed. No human being has ever heard me
complain. Domestic calamity, far heavier than political disappointment or disaster can possibly be, overtook me immediately after my fall from power, and the moment of my distress
was seized by an old antagonist to indulge a hatred overflowing with the concentrated rancor of forty years, and who could
not resist the pleasure of giving me what he thought the finishing blow at the moment when he saw me down. . . In the
French opera of *Richard Cœur-de-Lion,* the minstrel, Blondel,
sings under the walls of his prison a song, beginning:

> O, Richard! O, mon Roi!
> L'univers t'abandonne.

When I first heard this song, forty-five years ago, at one of
the first representations of that delightful play, it made an indelible impression upon my memory, without imagining that I
should ever feel its force so much closer home. In the year
1829 scarce a day passed that did not bring it to my thoughts.
In the course of last winter a vacancy occurred in the Board of
Overseers of Harvard University. Absent, I was very unexpectedly elected to fill that vacancy. I attributed this to the
personal friendship and influence of President Quincy. But
this call upon me by the people of the district in which I reside, to represent them in Congress, has been spontaneous
and, although counteracted by a double opposition, federalist
and Jacksonite, I have received nearly three votes in four
throughout the district. My election as President of the
United States was not half so gratifying to my inmost soul.
No election or appointment conferred upon me ever gave me
so much pleasure. I say this to record my sentiments; but no

stranger intermeddleth with my joys, and the dearest of my friends have no sympathy with my sensations.

Nov. 14. — In the evening I finished reading to my wife Galt's *Life of Lord Byron*. This person has now been seven years dead, and the public interest in him has not abated. He was one of the wonders of his age, and was, like Napoleon Bonaparte, the torso of a Hercules. A " grand homme manqué " — a club-footed Apollo — in mind as in person. There are sublime and beautiful passages of detail in his poetry; and if he had finished his *Don Juan* it would have been a worthy companion to Voltaire's *Pucelle,* in the Temple of Cloacina upon the summit of Parnassus. Galt had a slight acquaintance with him, having been for some time a fellow-passenger with him on his first voyage to Greece, and feels kind to his memory. He publishes this life of him because, he says, Moore's has not been satisfactory to the public. This book is very amusing, seldom tedious, and has passages of fine writing.

New York, Dec. 12. — After dinner, I visited Mr. Monroe at his son-in-law's, Samuel L. Gouverneur's.

Dec. 13. — David Williams, the only surviving captor of Major André, with one of the Aldermen and another young man, came to visit me. He had the silver medal given him by Congress hung over his neck by a three-colored silk ribbon. He said he was seventy-seven years of age; and he related to me all the circumstances of the taking of Andre. He was anxious to obtain an increase of his pension of two hundred dollars a year, and was warmly second by the Alderman.

Dec. 24. — Our house is a hospital of invalids. My cough continues, varying in its symptoms, but no better. A hoarse sore throat every night. Lungs loaded with phlegm every morning. I consulted Huntt, and he advised trash which will tease me and leave me just where I am — rye mush and milk for breakfast, a plaster on the breast, Seidlitz powders, and no suppers. I do not sup. The rest is about as effective as the bread and cheese of Molière's *Médecin Malgré Lui.*

Jan. 7, 1831. — When we suffer the shame and mortification of defeat, there is some consolation in saying, " Thou, by some other, shalt by laid as low." Canning and Huskisson, the two British statesmen from whose bitter hatred and jealousy towards this country the last British interdict to the trade between the United States and British West Indies in American vessels arose — where are they? Cut short in their career by the hand of death — Canning in the midst of Quixotic projects of pride and ambition for himself and his country, now crumbling into ruin; Huskisson by a melancholy accident after having been screwed out of office as scornfully by the Duke of Wellington as he and his colleagues had treated us in Parliament and in negotiation. And where is the Duke of Wellington? Pelted with stones by the rabble of London; frightened — the vainqueur du vainqueur de la terre — frightened from attendance at the Lord Mayor's feast by the threat of popular violence upon his person; outvoted in the House of Commons and compelled with all his Ministry to resign; cowering before a Whig Administration who are pledged to bring forward and carry through a reform in Parliament.

Washington, Jan. 11. — I . . . read about fifty pages of the first volume of Jefferson's *Memoirs*. He states that he began his autobiography on the 6th of January, 1821, in the seventy-seventh year of his age. . . The account of his childhood and youth is short, and not boastful; but there are no confessions. He tells nothing but what redounds to his own credit. He is like the French lady who told her sister she did not know how it happened, "mais il n'y a que moi au monde qui a toujours raison." Jefferson, by his own narrative, is always in the right. This is not uncommon to writers of their own lives. Dr. Franklin was more candid. Mr. Jefferson names the teachers from whom he learnt Greek, Latin, and French, and speaks gratefully of William Small, a Scotchman, professor of mathematics at William and Mary College, who became attached to him, and probably fixed the destinies of his life. It is rather intimated than expressly told that Small initiated him in the mysteries of free-thinking and irreligion, which did fix the destinies of his life. Loose morals necessarily followed. If not an absolute atheist, he had no belief in a future existence. All his ideas of obligation or retribution were bounded by the present life. His duties to his neighbor were under no stronger guarantee than the laws of the land and the opinions of the world. The tendency of this condition upon a mind of great compass and powerful resources is to produce insincerity and duplicity, which were his besetting sins through life.

Jan. 12. — I finished the memoir of Jefferson's life, which terminates on the 21st of March, 1790, when he arrived at New York to take upon him the office of Secretary of State. There it ends; and there, as a work of much interest to the present and future ages, it should have begun. It is much to be regretted that he did not tell his own story from that time until his retirement from the office of President of the United States in 1809. It was then that all the good and all the evil parts of his character were brought into action. His ardent passion for liberty and the rights of man; his patriotism; the depth and compass of his understanding; the extent and variety of his knowledge, and the enviable faculty of applying it to his own purposes; the perpetual watchfulness of public opinion, and the pliability of principle and temper with which he accommodated to it his own designs and opinions; — all these were in ceaseless operation during those twenty years; and with them were combined a rare mixture of infidel philosophy and epicurean morals, of burning ambition and of stoical self-control, of deep duplicity and of generous sensibility, between which two qualities, and a treacherous and inventive memory, his conduct towards his rivals and opponents appears one tissue of inconsistency. His treatment of Washington, of Knox, of my father, of Hamilton, of Bayard, who made him President of the United States, and, lastly, of me, is marked with features of perfidy worthy of Tiberius Caesar or Louis the Eleventh of France. This double-dealing character was often imputed to him during his life, and was sometimes exposed. His letter to Mazzei, and the agonizing efforts which he afterwards made to explain it away; his most insidious attack upon my father with his never-ceasing professions of respect and affection for his person and character; and his letter to Giles concerning me, in which there is scarcely a single word of truth — indicate a memory so pandering to the will that in deceiving others he seems to have begun by deceiving himself.

Jan. 14. — I received a letter from John C. Calhoun, now Vice-President of the United States, relating to his present controversy with President Jackson and William H. Crawford. He questions me concerning the letter of General Jackson to Mr. Monroe which Crawford alleges to have been produced at the Cabinet meetings on the Seminole War, and asks

for copies, if I think proper to give them, of Crawford's letter to me which I received last summer, and of my answer. I
answered Mr. Calhoun's letter immediately, rigorously con-
fining myself to the direct object of his enquiries. This is a
new bursting out of the old and rancorous feud between Crawford and Calhoun, both parties to which, after suspending
their animosities and combining together to effect my ruin, are
appealing to me for testimony to sustain themselves each
against the other. . . The bitter enmity of all three of the
parties — Jackson, Calhoun, and Crawford — against me, an
enmity the more virulent because kindled by their own ingratitude and injustice to me; the interest which every one of them,
and all their partisans, have in keeping up that load of obloquy and public odium which their foul calumnies have brought
down upon me; and the disfavor in which I stand before a
majority of the people, excited against me by their artifices; —
their demerits to me are proportioned to the obligations to me
— Jackson's the greatest, Crawford the next, Calhoun's the
least of positive obligation, but darkened by his double-
faced setting himself up as a candidate for the Presidency
against me in 1821, his prevarications between Jackson and
me in 1824, and his icy-hearted dereliction of all the de-
cencies of social intercourse with me, solely from the terror
of Jackson, since the 4th of March, 1829. I walk between
burning ploughshares; let me be mindful where I place my
foot.

Jan. 21. — Leslie Combs, whom I had seen at New York,
called, and told me he was going this evening or to-morrow on
his return to Kentucky. He spoke of some public controversy
with General Jackson, which I had forgotten; and he told me
two anecdotes, which, whether verities or investions, are characteristic. One, that Jackson, upon his last summer's tour to
Tennessee, was earnestly urged by a clergyman to stand a
candidate for re-election, upon which he said, " Well, if my
fellow-citizens insist upon my serving them another term, I
hope they will give me a Vice-President in whom I can have
some confidence." The other, that Calhoun, within a very few
days, has said that if Jackson had followed his advice the Administration would have been approved by the people; but, as
it was, it had lost all its popularity.

Jan. 25. — Read a few stanzas of *Childe Harold,* and fur-

ther in the correspondence of Jefferson, till the letter of 28th
of May, 1781, to General Washington, announcing his long-
declared resolution of retiring from the oppression of his office
as Governor of Virginia to private life. . .   Where was he
from June, 1781, to the close of the war?   No mortal can tell
from the memoir or the correspondence.   In that very June,
1781, at the moment when he resigned his office as Governor
of Virginia, he was appointed one of the Ministers for negotiating peace with Great Britain, then, he says, expected to be
effected through the mediation of the Empress of Russia.
He declined this appointment, he says, for the same reasons
for which he had declined in 1776.   And what were they?
Take his words: "such was the state of my family that I
could not leave it, nor could I expose it to the dangers of the
sea, and of capture by the British ships, then covering the
ocean.   I saw, too, that the laboring oar was really at home,
where much was to be done of the most permanent interest, in
new-modelling our Governments, and much to defend our
fanes and firesides from the desolations of an invading enemy,
pressing on our country on every point."   The first of these
reasons are mere private considerations.   He could not leave
his family, and would not expose his family to capture by
British ships.   John Adams three times exposed himself and
two boys to capture by British ships during the war.   He left
his wife, daughter, and one infant son to the protection of his
country.   John Jay's wife and children went with him.   Dr.
Franklin went safe in 1776, as Jefferson would have gone if
he had been with him.   Henry Laurens was taken and sent to
the Tower, and harshly treated; but his son was not even imprisoned, and was allowed to visit him; and so might it have
been with Mr. Jefferson if he had gone, with or without his
family, and been taken.   There are dangers which a high-
souled man engaged in a sacred cause must encounter and not
flinch from.   To assign them as reasons for declining the post
of honor savors more of the Sybarite than of the Spartan.
They remind one of the certain lord, neat, trimly dressed, who
but for those vile guns would himself have been a soldier.   As
to the other reason, of staying at home to defend our fanes
and firesides, it certainly did not apply to Mr. Jefferson either
in 1776, when there was neither actual nor threatened invasion of Virginia, or in June, 1781, when Mr. Jefferson had

slunk from that very defence into the inactive safety of a private citizen. Perhaps Mr. Jefferson was sufficiently punished for his dereliction of the cause by the humiliating necessity under which he has been of drawing a veil over this portion of his life. "Pends-toi, brave Crillon," wrote Henry of Navarre to one of his heroic followers, "nous avons vaincu, et tu n'y etois pas."

Jan. 27 — In the evening I read a few pages of Jefferson's correspondence . . . Mr. Jefferson's love of liberty was sincere and ardent — not confined to himself, like that of most of his fellow slave-holders. He was above that execrable sophistry of the South Carolinian nullifiers, which would make of slavery the corner-stone to the temple of liberty. He saw the gross inconsistency between the principles of the Declaration of Independence and the fact of negro slavery, and he could not, or would not, prostitute the faculties of his mind to the vindication of that slavery which from his soul he abhorred. Mr. Jefferson had not the spirit of martyrdom. He would have introduced a flaming denunciation of slavery into the Declarationn of Independence, but the discretion of his colleagues struck it out. He did insert a most eloquent and impassioned argument against it in his Notes upon Virginia; but on that very account the book was published almost against his will. He projected a plan of general emancipation in his revision of the Virginian laws, but finally presented a plan of leaving slavery precisely where it was. And in his memoirs he leaves a posthumous warning to the planters, that they must at no distant day emancipate their slaves, or that worse will follow; but he withheld the publication of his prophecy till he should himself be in the grave.

Jan. 31. — The Senate this day, by a vote of twenty-two to twenty-one, acquitted Judge Peck of the misdemeanor charged against him by the House of Representatives. . . . It is highly probable that Jackson did not wish to see an impeachment of a Judge, commenced by Buchanan, successfully carried through. The same motive contributed to save Judge Chase in 1805. Jefferson saw that the conviction of Chase would have riveted the power of John Randolph over both Houses of Congress, and he dreaded the consequences to himself and his own Administration. They would have been formidable and mischievous. Jackson's aversion to Buchanan is more immediately personal and vindictive. It arises from the disclosure by Buchanan of his dirty intrigue with Jackson in December, 1824, to authorize him to purchase Clay by the promise of sacrificing me — which authority Jackson gave him, and Buchanan made an abortive attempt to carry into effect. Buchanan afterwards revealed the whole transaction, with an obtuseness of moral feeling, seemingly unconscious of moral turpitude in the avowal, and with a dulness of intellect, equally unconscious of the javelin he was thrusting into the side of Jackson, who never will forgive him nor miss any opportunity of inflicting punishment upon him. This I take to be the secret of the votes of Hugh Lawson White and Felix Grundy upon this trial. . .

The hours of rising and retiring to rest, of breakfast and dinner, are as at the close of the last month. I frequent no society, and, with the exception of my daily walks, we are confined within the walls of our house as if it were a ship at sea. I spend about six hours of the day in writing — diary, arrears of index, and letters. I have given up entirely my classical reading, and almost all other, excepting the daily newspapers and, interruptedly, a few pages of Jefferson's writings. My reflections upon these as I proceed I now introduce into this journal, and it swells the record of almost every day. I enjoy a degree of tranquillity such as I never before experienced; interrupted only by the idea that by my own as yet insuperable indolence it is a time of faineantise, and by the consciousness that it must be speedily changed for a return to all the caress, mortifications, and perplexities of ungracious public life.

Feb. 13. — Wirt spoke to me also in deep concern and alarm at the state of Chief-Justice Marshall's health. He is seventy-five years of age, and has until lately enjoyed fine health, exercised great bodily activity, and sustained an immense mass of bodily labor. His mind remains unimpaired, but his body is breaking down. He has been thirty years Chief Justice of the Supreme Court, and has done more to establish the Constitution of the United States on sound construction than any other man living. The terror is, that if he should be now withdrawn some shallow-pated wild-cat like Phillip P. Barbour, fit for nothing but to tear the Union to rags and tatters, would be appointed in his place. Mr. Wirt's anticipations are gloomy and I see no reasonable prospect of improvement.

On returning home, I found the young Quaker to whom Gales and Seaton had given a letter of introduction, Lindley, and another by the name of Benjamin Lundy, editor of a weekly paper called *The Genius of Universal Emancipation.* It was first published in Tennessee, afterwards in Baltimore, and now comes out in this city. Its object is to promote the abolition of slavery — of which Lundy freely expressed his confidence and hopes.

Feb. 15. — I met in walking Captain Morgan of the navy, with a young man, one of the sons of Mr. Middleton, our late Minister at St. Petersburg — quite a young man, and almost feminine in his appearance, except that he had a complete beard, about three inches long. I suppose this is the dandy costume at present in Europe, and have been expecting it these two years. The beard has been creeping down the cheeks from the ears till the two sides have met at the chin. The same fashion prevailed about twenty-five years since; but the tip of the chin was then respected.

Feb. 16. — Dr. Huntt was here, more full of politics and personalities than of physic. He says Mr. Calhoun's pamphlet is to be published to-morrow morning. Duff Green, editor of the *Telegraph,* has been elected by both Houses public printer for the next Congress. Green is understood to be in the interest of Mr. Calhoun. A new paper, published twice a week, and called the *Globe,* has been established, supposed to be under the auspices of Mr. Van Buren, Secretary of State. These are the two candidates in embryo for the succession to the Presidency. Each of them must have his newspaper, and in our Presidential canvassing an editor has become as essential an appendage to a candidate as in the days of chivalry a squire was a knight. Dr. Huntt is grievously annoyed by the appointment of H. Ashton as Marshal of the District, in the place of his father-in-law, Tench Ringgold. . . . When Mr. Monroe was here last winter, he dined with President Jackson, who affected to treat him with affectionate respect and kindness; and on taking leave of him Mr. Monroe said to him that he might probably never see him again; that he would venture to ask of him only one favor, and that was, to recommend Marshal Ringgold to his kindness; and then he spoke

with much feeling of the causes of his own attachment to Ringgold; upon which Jackson took Monroe's hand, pressed it between both his own, and said, " Say not one word more, Mr.
Monroe," which Ringgold took for an inviolable promise
that he should be continued in his place.   Jackson now denies
that he meant it as a promise, or even as encouragement to
Mr. Monroe to expect that his wish would be gratified.

Feb. 20 — After church I paid two visits.   The first at
L'Etourno's, to Mr. White, the delegate from Florida.
While I was with him, Judge Breckenridge, District Judge of
West Florida, came in.   Mr. White continues to be deeply
concerned at the determination of the present Secretary of
the Navy to break up the plantation of live-oaks which I had
taken so much pains, and incurred so much public expense, to
commence. . .   The malicious pleasure of destroying everything of which I had planted the germ, and the base purpose
of representing as wasteful prodigality the most useful and
most economical expenditures, are the motives that act upon
the Secretary of the Navy and the present Administration.
It happened that for the live-oak plantation purchases were
made of about sixteen hundred acres of land from White and
Breckenridge; and, although the timber upon them was worth
more than they cost, this circumstance was seized upon to
represent the transaction as a fraudulent job and squandering
of public money.   Judge Breckenridge, when this was suggested, immediately petitioned Congress to be permitted to
take back his land at the same price which he had received for
it; and that petition was rejected.   The plantation, both of
young trees growing when I commenced it and of those from
the acorn which I had caused to be planted, is now in a condition as flourishing as possible, and more than a hundred
thousand live-oaks are growing upon it.   All is to be abandoned by the stolid ignorance and stupid malignity of John
Branch and of his filthy subaltern, Amos Kendall.

Feb. 26. — I had visits in the morning from Mr. Middleton, recently returned from his mission of ten years in Russia,
and in the evening from Mr. Lawrence.   Mr. Middleton was
recalled last summer, and John Randolph of Roanoke was
appointed in his place.   Randolph, who turns his diseases to
commodity, stipulated before he went that if his health should
require it he should have permission to pass the winter in a

more genial climate; went to Russia in a frigate, behaved for a few weeks at St. Petersburg like a crazy man, then sent home a servant with his baggage, and went to spend his winter in London, where he is figuring in speeches at the turtle-feasts of the Lord Mayor, and he is now announced as a candidate in his district for election to the next Congress, where there is no doubt he will be chosen; for the people of his district are as much enamored with him as the Queen of the Fairies was with the ass's head of Bottom after the drop of juice from love-in-idleness had been squeezed upon her eyelids in her sleep.   Mr. Middleton told me numerous anecdotes of his eccentricities at St. Petersburg.

March 2. — Morning visit from Mr. Williams, of North Carolina, who introduced me to his friend Manning, from Tennessee; also from Dr. Kent, the former Governor of Maryland, and member of Congress, and afterwards from Mr. Calhoun, the Vice-President.   This is the first time he has called upon me since the last Administration closed.   He said something about political considerations, as he had done in one of his letters, to which I made no reply then or now. Explanation can do nothing.   I meet Mr. Calhoun's advances to a renewal of the intercourse of common civility because I cannot reject them.   But I once had confidence in the qualities of his heart.   It is not totally destroyed, but so impaired that it can never be fully restored.   Mr. Calhoun's friendships and enmities are regulated exclusively by his interests.   His opinions are the sport of every popular blast, and his career as a statesman has been marked by a series of the most flagrant inconsistencies.   Crawford is more desperately reckless in his changes, and capable of more wilful perfidy.   Calhoun veers round in his politics, to be always before the wind, and makes his intellect the pander to his will.

[*March* 4, 1831. — On this day the writer must be regarded as commencing a new term of official service, although he did not enter upon the duties until the ensuing month of December.

This term embraces the sixteen remaining years of his life.[3]]

March 8. — It is a doctrine of the medical faculty that bodily exercise to be salutary should be taken with a vacant

---

[3] From C. F. Adams's edition of the Diary.

mind; such is the precept of Mr. Jefferson. . . At certain seasons, however, the propensity becomes too strong for me. I walk and muse and pour forth premeditated verse, which it takes me six or nine months to lay by and resume to find it good for nothing. It never appears so to me when I compose it. In a few instances I have suffered the publication of my effusions, and I am accredited as one of the smallest poets of my country. Very short fugitive pieces and translations are the only rhymes I have ever committed to the press; one short poem, the lines to Mrs. Hellen on the death of her two children, and one translation, the thirteenth satire of Juvenal, have been favorably noticed.

April 16. — I finished this morning the fair copy of my poem of *Dermot MacMorrogh,* and have now the measure of my own poetical power. Beyond this I shall never attain; and now it is an important question whether I should throw this, and almost all the other verses I have ever written, into the fire. Hitherto I have confined myself to translations and fugitive pieces of a very few lines or stanzas — a small portion of which have been published in newspapers and magazines. I have now completed an historical tale of upwards of two thousand lines; the subject of my own selection; the moral clear and palpable; the characters and incidents strictly historical; the story complete and entire. It has amused and occupied two months of my life, and leaves me now, like a pleasant dream, to dull and distressing realities, to a sense of wasted time, and to the humiliation of enterprise ashamed of performance; yet, at the same time, with an insatiate thirst for undertaking again higher and better things.

April 18. — Edward Wyer called. . . He said much of the editor of the *Telegraph,* Duff Green, who in two successive papers of the 14th and 15th has been giving a history of the internal convulsions of the present Administration, which he represents as having arisen from the appointment of John H. Eaton as Secretary of War, and from the influence of his domestic concerns upon the Government. Green details his own conversations with the President, with Eaton himself, and with Mr. Van Buren, in all which he appears to be a primary personage. He alludes in a manner affectedly respectful to the similarity of Jackson's own case with his wife with that of Eaton and his. Jackson lived some time in adultery with his wife, for which her prior husband obtained a regular divorce; but this was nearly forty years ago, and she had lived as Jackson's wife an inoffensive, amiable, and charitable life, and had become quite a pious old woman. In the Presidential canvass her character and history have been very freely handled, and she died in the very month of his election to the Presidency. Eaton was married to his wife about the same time; he had lived very openly with her during the life of her former husband, Timberlake, who was a purser in the Navy — who did not indeed obtain a divorce from his wife, but whose death has been generally attributed to his dishonor. Calhoun, and three members of Jackson's Administration — Ingham, Branch, and Berrien — would not permit the females of their families to associate with Eaton's wife; and even Mrs. Donelson, wife to Jackson's private Secretary, and living in the President's house, did the same. This state of things produced during the first year of the Administration scenes equally disgusting and ludicrous — Jackson having, with all the violence of his temper, taken up the cause of Eaton and his wife as his own. Green now, with all his respect for Jackson, and with equally affected veneration for Mrs. Jackson, says it was from sympathy, and that Van Buren became the champion and negotiator for Eaton's wife because he was a widower.

April 20. — The *Globe* newspaper of this morning contains a letter from Martin Van Buren, Secretary of State, to the President, dated the 11th of this month, tendering the resignation of his office, and assigning at some length his reasons for this step; and the answer of the President, dated the 12th, accepting his resignation. The *Globe* further states that the Secretary of War, John H. Eaton, tendered his resignation on the 7th, which was accepted, and that Samuel D. Ingham, Secretary of the Treasury, and John Branch resigned yesterday; from which it infers that there will be a new organization of the Cabinet. The *Telegraph* of this evening says that Ingham and Branch resigned at the request of the President.

Philadelphia, April 25. — There is scarcely any other topic of conversation than the recent breaking up of the President's Cabinet at Washington. His correspondence with each of the ex-Secretaries on this occasion has been given one by one —

each day one. Those of the Secretaries of State and of War were published before I left the city; that with Ingham on Friday, and that with Branch on Saturday. The letters to the two last were apparently written by Jackson himself; and they afford matter for much amusement. Ingham and Branch were not inclined to resign, and he was not willing to pass for having requested them to resign. He puts it upon the ground that his Cabinet proper was a unit, which had come together in great harmony, and, as two individuals of the unit had voluntarily withdrawn, he thought it necessary to reorganize the whole Cabinet. There was a caricature published here on Saturday upon this incident, called " the rats leaving a falling house." Four sleek rats, with faces of recognizable likeness to the four Secretaries, are scampering away upon the floor. Jackson is struggling to sustain himself in a chair that is breaking under him; and his right foot is pressing upon Van Buren's tail, as if to detain him. An altar of reform is falling over, with an imp having the head of an ass, the body of a monkey, and the wings of a bat, armed with a broom. The room is hung round with papers, on each of which is inscribed " Resignation; " and the President's spitting-box and broken tobacco-pipe are on the floor. Two thousand copies of this print have been sold in Philadelphia this day. Ten thousand copies were struck off, and will all be disposed of within a fortnight. This is an indication of the estimation in which Jackson and his Administration are held. Not a human being of any party regrets the loss of the services of any of the Secretaries withdrawn.

New York, April 27. — I paid a visit to the ex-President, Monroe, at the house of his son-in-law, Samuel L. Gouverneur. He was confined to his chamber, and extremely feeble and emaciated. Congress passed at their last session an Act making a further allowance to him, to his claims, of thirty thousand dollars, which have been paid him. He has advertised for sale his estate in Loudoun County, Virginia, and proposes to go there in a few weeks; but it is doubtful whether he will ever be able to leave his chamber. Mr. Monroe is a very remarkable instance of a man whose life has been a continued series of the most extraordinary good fortune, who has never met with any known disaster, has gone through a splendid career of public service, has received more pecuniary reward from the public than any other man since the existence of the nation, and is now dying, at the age of seventy-two, in wretchedness and beggary. I sat with him perhaps half an hour. He spoke of the commotions now disturbing Europe, and of the recent quasi-revolution at Washington; but his voice was so feeble that he seemed exhausted by the exertion of speaking.

Quincy, June 7. — I am writing a third discourse upon the Declaration of Independence, to be delivered on the next Fourth of July to the inhabitants of Quincy, if they should hold the proposed celebration, and, if not, for use hereafter. To avoid repetition of what I have said before upon the same subject is one of the difficulties of my present task. As I proceed, I perceive the effect of age upon the style of composition. I know not that the influence of age upon style has ever been observed by critics; yet it must be discernible. Voltaire wrote his *Œdipé* at eighteen, his *Agathocle* at eighty; compare them together.

June 19. — The intervals of the day were occupied with the revisal of my discourse for the Fourth of July. Why is it that I feel more anxiety and more apprehension of failure on this occasion than I ever did in youth, when success was important to my standing in the world and to my hopes of a long-anticipated futurity upon earth? Success or failure is now of little consequence to me, who have, and can have, but a few days to live. I fear the exhibition of faculties in decay. I fear a severity of judgment of the hearers, and yet more of the readers. I experienced this on my second Fourth of July oration, delivered at Washington ten years since, at the meridian of my life. I shall now assail passions and prejudices as earnestly as then, deeming it now, as I deemed it then, my duty.

July 4. — My discourse occupied an hour and twenty-five minutes in the delivery, and I omitted about one-third of what I had written. It was well received, frequently interrupted by applause, and closed with plaudits long continued. The procession then moved to the town-hall, where was a dinner of about one hundred and twenty persons. Mr. Thomas Greenleaf presided.

July 7. — Received this morning a letter from Samuel L. Gouverneur of the 4th, and one from George Sullivan of the 5th, at New York, announcing the decease, at three o'clock in the afternoon of the 4th, of the ex-President of the United States, James Monroe, a man whose life has been marked with vicissitudes as great as have befallen any citizen of the United States since the beginning of our national existence. . . His life for the last six years has been one of abject penury and distress, and they have brought him to a premature grave, though in the seventy-third year of his age. His Administration, happening precisely at the moment of the breaking up of old party divisions, was the period of the greatest tranquillity which has ever been enjoyed by this country; it was a time of great prosperity, and his personal popularity was unrivalled. Yet no one regretted the termination of his Administration, and less of popular veneration followed him into retirement than had accompanied all his predecessors. His last days have been much afflicted, contrasting deeply with the triumphal procession which he made through the Union in the years 1817 and 1819.[4]

Boston, July 21. — Attended a meeting of the Phi Beta Kappa Society, which had been called by Edward Everett, their President, by an advertisement in the newspapers. I was surprised to find assembled at the hall of the American Academy of Arts and Sciences between fifty and sixty members. The President, soon after I entered, called the meeting to order, and stated his object in calling it; which was to consider the propriety of revising the charter and fundamental laws of the Society, which he read.

July 28. — I had not even completed the revisal of my Fourth of July oration for the press when the application came from the Corporation of Boston to deliver an eulogy upon Mr. Monroe, which I had scarcely the right, and could

---

[4] The chief event of the summer for Adams was the delivery of a eulogy upon James Monroe at the Old South Church in Boston on Aug. 25. He labored upon this paper with characteristic diligence. For example, on July 18 he writes that he was "occupied from breakfast to dinner-time almost entirely in refreshing my memory upon the important military events of our Revolutionary War." He had found that Monroe was wounded at the battle of Princeton, and had thought it necessary to study the campaigns in Pitkin's and Belsham's histories, Almon's *Remembrancer*, and Washington's letters. His notes of the summer also contain frequent mention of the growing Anti-Masonic movement. He attended an Anti-Masonic oration at Faneuil Hall, and regretted that there seemed little enthusiasm. "The application of a blister upon the bosom of the public is wanting," he wrote. On returning through New York City Adams had a conversation of three hours with William H. Seward, chiefly upon the progress of the Anti-Masonic Party. Many of the Anti-Masons, said Seward, were desirous of nominating Adams for the Presidency. Adams declared he had no wish for a nomination.

not have the inclination, to decline. But it has from that time oppressed me with reading and writing almost night and day, in the heart of a summer damp and sultry beyond example. And I have been not less oppressed with anxiety than with labor. The oration succeeded far beyond expectation, and has been hitherto spared very generally by malignant criticism. "Non nobis, Domine, sed nomini tuo sit gloria." It touched upon popular topics, and presented them under new views. This I cannot again do, nor can I do justice to the subject without coming in collision with passions and resentments which will not sleep.

Aug. 6. — I am still toiling upon the eulogy on Mr. Monroe, my plan of which forms itself as I proceed. It has assumed the shape of a memoir upon his life. It was long, eventful, and connected with the principal events of our history, from the Declaration of Independence, for a full half-century. The fragment of autobiography sent me by Mr. Gouverneur comes down only to the close of Mr. Monroe's first mission to France. For the narrative during the War of the Revolution I have been obliged to recur to the published collection of General Washington's letters, to Marshall's Life of him, to Gordon's and Stedman's histories of the war, to possess myself fully of the chain of facts; and it absorbs half my time. It also convinces me that my plan is not a good one — that my narrative will be long, tedious, and dull, and that I shall be compelled to abridge without knowing exactly where.

Aug. 11. — I met Alderman R. D. Harris, whom I informed that I should be ready to deliver the eulogy on Mr. Monroe either the 24th or 25th of this month. He said the examination of the public schools would be on the 24th; that my day might be either the 23d or the 25th. I told him either would suit me. He promised to consult the Council and let me know the result. I asked him where they proposed it should be. He said they had first thought of Faneuil Hall, but, as that place was not favorable for the voice, they now probably would choose the Old South Church, which I told him would suit me better than Faneuil Hall.

Aug. 25. — The procession moved from the State-House at the appointed time, and came through a pouring rain — entering the church about a quarter-past four. A voluntary on the organ, and the prayers of the Episcopal service, with a long occasional one, composed by Mr. Doane, made it full five before I began. The house was crowded to suffocation; the heat excessive; crowds of people at the church-door, wrangling and fighting to get in; trucks, wagons, and carriages rolling over the pavement in the streets adjoining the church all the time I was speaking; and, as the sun went down, it grew so dark that it was becoming impossible for me to read my manuscript. I was forced to read so rapidly that my articulation became indistinct, and my voice and my eyes, both affected by the state of the atmosphere, were constantly threatening to fail me. My situation was distressing; but I pushed on. I shortened the discourse much more than I had intended, and finally over-leaped ten or twelve pages at once. They lighted at last the two lamps at the sides of the pulpit, and I got through in an hour and a half, omitting more than half of what I had written. There was constant attention in the auditory — occasional applause, in one or two instances long-continued and repeated.

Oct. 10. — This evening we read a number of passages of poetry by American poets — Percival, Halleck, Dana, Bryant, Peabody, Willis — and a review of their compositions,[5] gravely settling the pretensions to precedence among them, and placing Dana at their head. Halleck has poetical powers, smothered by a burden of burlesque; Percival has half the property of a poet — wild and fanciful conceptions; Peabody has tenderness and pathos, for copies of verses; and Bryant has some talent at description. With the exception of Halleck, it would take nine such poets to make a Tate. There was an ode of Percival's called *Genius Waking,* which has acquired some reputation. 'Tis Pindar's *Eagle,* stolen from Gray, and scourged round the welkin, through every medium of passage, and, among the rest, through rocks.

New York, Oct. 31. — I received two successive invitations from Mr. Hamblin, the manager of the Bowery Theatre, to attend a representation there, with offers to select for performance any one of several plays which I should prefer. After once declining, I finally consented to go this evening, the performance to be without alteration for me, and no notice to be publicly given of my attendance. I received also a written invitation, signed by William Wilkins, President of the Tariff Convention, to attend at their meeting within the bar. I went

[5] See the *North American Review,* vol. 33, p. 297 ff.

accordingly about eleven o'clock; but, being alone, and having some difficulty in finding the hall where they were in session, I finally went in among the spectators below the bar; and being seen there by Mr. James Tallmadge, one of the Vice-Presidents, he came to me and introduced me to a seat immediately behind the President, within the bar. As I passed through the hall, the members all rose, and, on my taking the seat offered me, gave a general manifestation of applause.

Nov. 5. — From dinner I went and spent part of the evening with ex-Chancellor Kent, talking of his Commentaries, of Blackstone and Wooddeson, Mansfield, Pothier, Emerigon, and Valin, common law and civil law, Littleton's Tenures, and Justinian. I read to him my stanzas on the foot of Penn's Hill, which he approved, but which reminded him too much of both Gray's *Elegy* and of Goldsmith's *Deserted Village*. I also talked with him and his son of Shakspeare's *Othello* and Desdemona, Juliet, Imogen, and Miranda. I observed to him how much of the charm and interest of the tragedy of *Romeo and Juliet* depended upon the age of Juliet — a child in her fourteenth year; how emphatically the poet had marked that age; and how stupidly the stage-men had changed the age from fourteen to nineteen. I said I took little interest in the character of Desdemona, whose sensual passions I thought over-ardent, so as to reconcile her to a passion for a black man; and although faithful to him, I thought the poet had painted her as a lady of rather easy virtue — very different from the innocence of Miranda or the rosy pudency of Imogen.

Philadelphia, Nov. 9. — I called upon Nicholas Biddle at the United States Bank, and received two dividends of my bank stock, by an order upon the branch bank at Washington. I left with Mr. Biddle my certificate of stock to be sold, and the proceeds to be remitted according to such directions as I may give. I told him that, as I might be called to take part in public measures concerning the bank, and was favorable to it, I wished to divest myself of all personal interest in it. I endorsed my name in blank on the certificate.

Nov. 11. — I met J. Sergeant, and went with him to dine at Nicholas Biddle's. A large party. I met there Messrs. De Tocqueville and De Beaumont, the commissioners of the French Government, with whom I had dined at Alexander H. Everett's, in Boston.

CHAPTER XI

1831–1835

SERVICE IN THE TWENTY-SECOND CONGRESS — NULLIFICATION —
JACKSON'S STAND APPROBATED — FRANCES KEMBLE — TWENTY-
THIRD CONGRESS — DEATH OF WILLIAM WIRT — HARVARD AFFAIRS.

Washington, Nov. 13, 1831. — I return to Washington with
less tranquillity of mind than at the last and the preceding
winter. That before me is of an aspect to which I look with
an aching heart. One experiment which I have made upon
this journey has been successful, as far as it could succeed —
I mean that of employing my time. I have lost none. Since
I left Quincy I have composed twenty-three stanzas of versions of the Psalms — all bad, but as good as I could make
them.

Nov. 18. — I walked round the Capitol this morning.
There was a double attack upon me this morning in the *National Journal,* which I take for the Clay declaration of war.

Nov. 21. — Finished my letter on imprisonment for debt,
in which, without opposing the project of those who are
pressing for the total abolition of it, I have endeavored to
impress them with the necessity of providing some other substitute for the security which it gives to credit. In this light
it has not been viewed by these gentlemen. They consider
nothing but the popularity of relieving prisoners from jail.
I shall surely get no thanks from anyone for pointing to
the consequences of this innovation upon the security of
property and upon fidelity to contracts, as well as upon
credit.

Nov. 25. — Mr. Edward Everett is much concerned about
Mr. Clay's prospects for the Presidency, but much gratified
at his election to the Senate of the United States by the legislature of Kentucky. He spoke with much reserve upon the

Masonic and Anti-Masonic controversy; and more freely about the election of a Speaker to the House of Representatives. He has an extreme aversion to Andrew Stevenson, the Speaker of the last two Congresses.

Dec. 5. — The first session of the Twenty-second Congress of the United States commenced. Half an hour before noon, I attended in the hall of the House of Representatives, and took the seat No. 203. At noon, the members were called to order by Matthew St. Claire Clarke, the clerk of the House in the last Congress. The members were called alphabetically by States, and two hundred answered to their names; one or two more afterwards came in. The clerk sent round the ballot-boxes to collect the votes for Speaker, and when the boxes were returned to his table, asked Messrs. Bates of Maine, Crawford of Pennsylvania, and McCoy of Virginia to act as tellers. There were only 195 votes returned, of which 98 were necessary to a choice. Andrew Stevenson, of Virginia, had ninety-eight votes, and was declared to be chosen. Eleutheros Cooke, a member from Ohio, brought up his vote to the table after the other votes had been given in. The tellers refused to receive it. His vote was for Joel B. Sutherland, of Philadelphia, the principal competitor of Mr. Stevenson, who had fifty-four votes. If Cooke's vote had been received, Stevenson would not have been chosen at that ballot, and probably not at all. There were votes for John W. Taylor, eighteen; Wickliffe, fifteen, and some others would have rallied, after two or three ballots, upon Sutherland. The two candidates are both men of principle according to their interest, and there is not the worth of a wisp of straw between their value.

Dec. 12. — Attended the House of Representatives. The appointment of the standing committees was announced, and I am Chairman of the Committee of Manufactures — a station of high responsibility, and, perhaps, of labor more burdensome than any other in the House; far from the line of occupation in which all my life has been passed, and for which I feel myself not to be well qualified. I know not even enough of it to form an estimate of its difficulties. The petitions were called for by States, commencing with Maine and proceeding southward. I presented fifteen petitions, signed numerously by citizens of Pennsylvania, praying for the abolition of slavery and the slave-trade in the District of Columbia. I moved that they should be referred to the Committee on the District of Columbia.

The practice is for the member presenting the petition to move that the reading of it be dispensed with, and that it be referred to the appropriate, or to a select, committee; but I moved that one of the petitions presented by me should be read, they being all of the same tenor and very short. It was accordingly read. I made a very few remarks, chiefly to declare that I should not support that part of the petition which prayed for the abolition of slavery in the District of Columbia. It is so long since I was in the habit of speaking to a popular assembly, the assemblies in which I had ever spoken extemporaneously have been, comparatively speaking, so little popular, and I am so little qualified by nature for an extemporaneous orator, that I was at this time not a little agitated by the sound of my own voice. I was not more than five minutes upon my feet; but I was listened to with great attention, and, when I sat down, it seemed to myself as if I had performed an achievement.

Dec. 14. — I sent round a notification to all the members of the Committee of Manufactures, requesting their attendance at the room of the Committee immediately after the adjournment of the House. I called at the seat of Dr. Condict, who had been a member of the same committee at the last session, to show me the way to the committee-room. At Dr. Condict's seat I met Mr. Clay, who appears to be in fine health. He said he would call and see me some evening. He was nominated by the National Republican Convention at Baltimore yesterday for the Presidency of the United States at the next election — one hundred and sixty-five votes out of one hundred and sixty-six present naming him successively as their choice; and a committee of thirteen came last evening to inform him of his nomination.

Dec. 18. — Between the services I had a visit from Mr. Webster, who has very recently arrived. I asked him his views with regard to the diminution of duties in the tariff; but he appeared to have formed no fixed opinion. I asked him if he thought a remission of six or seven millions of duties, and a reservation of five millions a year for purposes of internal improvement, would be supported by the National

Republicans; he thought they would, but said he would enquire and ascertain.

Dec. 28. — Dr. Condict gave me notice to attend a committee meeting this evening at Edward Everett's. . . Mr. Clay
was Chairman of the committee, and the report was the draft
of a bill, to be presented forthwith to the Senate, for the
immediate and total repeal of all the duties upon tea, coffee,
spices, indigo, and many other articles, almost the whole duty
upon wines, and effecting a diminution of revenue for the
coming year, 1832, of upwards of seven millions of dollars.

This is Mr. Clay's scheme, which he has already attempted
in the Senate, as General Dearborn attempted it in the House.
It is now to be attempted in this form. Mr. Clay laid down
the law of his system. He said the policy of our adversaries
was obvious — to break down the American system by accumulation of the revenue. Ours, therefore, should be specially
adapted to counteract it, by reducing immediately the revenue
to the amount of seven or eight millions this very coming
year. He would hardly wait for the 1st of January to take
off the duties; and he would adhere to the protective system,
even to the extent of increasing the duties on some of the
protected articles.

Mr. Clay's manner, with many courtesies of personal
politeness, was exceedingly peremptory and dogmatical. There
was some discussion of his statements, but nothing said in
opposition to them. . . I observed that an immediate
remission of duties, with a declared disposition to increase the
duties upon the protected articles, would be a defiance not only
in the South, as had been observed by Mr. Everett, but defiance also of the President, and of the whole Administration
party; and against them combined I thought it not possible
that this bill should pass. Mr. Clay said he did not care
who it defied. To preserve, maintain, and strengthen the
American system he would defy the South, the President, and
the devil; that if the Committee of Manufactures had committed themselves as I had stated, they had given a very
foolish and improvident pledge; there was no necessity for the
payment of the debt on the 4th of March, 1833; and much
more of like import. To which I made a respectful, but very
warm, reply. I said that without determining whether the
President's passion to pay off the whole of the public debt by

the 4th of March, 1833, was the wisest idea that ever entered into the heart of man, it was one in which I thought he ought to be indulged, and not opposed. It was an idea which would take greatly with the people; to oppose it would be invidious, and there was justice in it, too. It was true the three per cents. must be paid off dollar for dollar, while the use of the money might be worth double the interest they were paying for it. But this was only justice to the original holders of the three per cents., which ought, like the rest of the debt, to have been paid off at six per cent. It would be a great and glorious day when the United States shall be able to say that they owe not a dollar in the world; and this payment of the debt would obviate another difficulty suggested by Mr. Clay. There would certainly be no accumulation of revenue within that time. As to the bill, I thought it would be well to watch its progress with a vigilant eye; for, if I mistook not, it would produce remarkable political disclosures. I was much surprised to hear that the Chairman of the Committee on Finance would report such a bill. Mr. Clay said he would report it. He perhaps would not vote for it, but the Senate would pass it.

Jan. 2, 1832. — Began the version of the 62d Psalm. The Presidential mansion was open this day at noon, and some of its overflowings came over the Square. From noon till three there was a succession of visitors — foreign Legations, members of Congress, citizens, Shawanese Indians, and Quakers, officers of the army and navy, and some strangers. Among the company was Mr. Smith, the Registrar of the Treasury, and Major Lewis, the Second Auditor of the Treasury, whom I did not know. In a casual conversation with them, I adverted to the remark of Gibbon, that the courage of a soldier is the cheapest quality in human nature. By the looks of some persons present, I saw it was thought I had a special meaning in what I said — when in truth it was a mere thoughtless indiscretion.

Jan. 10. — Mr. Lewis is a member of the Society of Friends, and has taken much part for the last twenty years in the measures leading to the abolition of slavery. He came to have some conversation with me upon the subject of slavery in the District of Columbia. I asked him if he had seen the remarks that I made on presenting the petitions from Pennsylvania.

He said he had — but wished to know my sentiments upon slavery. I told him I thought they did not materially differ from his own; I abhorred slavery, did not suffer it in my family, and felt proud of belonging to the only State in the Union which at the very first census of population in 1790 had returned in the column of slaves — none; that in presenting the petition I had expressed the wish that the subject might not be discussed in the House, because I believed discussion would lead to ill will, to heart-burnings, to mutual hatred, where the first of wants was harmony; and without accomplishing anything else.

Jan. 29. — Chief-Justice Marshall and Judge Story visited me before dinner. The Chief Justice told me that the debate in the Legislature of Virginia upon the proposal for a gradual emancipation of the slaves in the State was closed by a majority of about twenty for postponement of the question, though in the form of rejecting the resolution — several of the members who voted against it declaring that they were individually in favor of it, but wished time and opportunity to ascertain the sentiments of the people concerning it.

Feb. 20. — This was a heavily rainy, gloomy day. I rode to the Capitol. Being Monday, the States were successively called for presentation of petitions; a most tedious operation in the practice, though to a reflecting mind a very striking exemplification of the magnificent grandeur of this nation and of the sublime principles upon which our Government is founded. The forms and proceedings of the House, this calling over of States for petitions, the colossal emblem of the union over the Speaker's chair, the historic Muse at the clock, the echoing pillars of the hall, the tripping Mercuries who bear the resolutions and amendments between the members and the chair, the calls of ayes and noes, with the different intonations of the answers from the different voices, the gobbling manner of the clerk in reading over the names, the tone of the Speaker in announcing the vote, and the varied shades of pleasure and pain in the countenances of the members on hearing it, would form a fine subject for a descriptive poem. There was little done in the House after receiving the petitions.

Feb. 21. — Mr. Blair, of South Carolina, gave Mr. Webster and me a letter from a Mr. Witherspoon to read. It proposes, in the event of Congress's doing nothing satisfactory to them about the tariff, to secede from the Union. They make a great distinction between this and nullification. I told Blair I had heard the nullifiers would oppose them in the project of seceding. He said he supposed they would. They did not want to have the tariff repealed. The House adjourned, soon after two o'clock, over till Wednesday.

Feb. 22. — Centennial birthday of Washington. The solemnities intended for this day at this place lost all their interest for me by the refusal of John A. Washington to permit the remains of George Washington to be transferred to be entombed under the Capitol — a refusal to which I believe he was not competent, and into the real operative motives to which I wish not to enquire. I did wish that this resolution might have been carried into execution, but this wish was connected with an imagination that this federative Union was to last for ages. I now disbelieve its duration for twenty years, and doubt its continuance for five. It is falling into the sere and yellow leaf. For this, among other reasons, I determined that my celebration of this day should only be by sharing in its devotions. I attended the performance of divine service at the Capitol, where a very ordinary prayer was made by M. Post, the Chaplain to the House of Representatives, and a singular, though not ineloquent, sermon was delivered by Mr. Durbin, Chaplain to the Senate.

March 2. — Colonel Richard M. Johnson asked me to walk with him, and said he wished to speak with me of the state of the personal relations between the President, Jackson, and me; that he (Johnson) wished the relations of friendly personal intercourse between us to be restored, and that he thought the first advances to it should be made by him. He had also spoken of it to Mr. Cass, the Secretary of War, who agreed with him on this point.

I said that the personal intercourse between General Jackson and me had been suspended by himself, without informing me of the reason why. I had never known his reason. I had seen at the time in the *Telegraph* an anonymous statement that it was because he knew that I had caused or countenanced abusive charges against Mrs. Jackson in the newspapers. The fact was not so. I never had caused or countenanced, directly or indirectly, any such publication.

But General Jackson had never asked of me the question, and I did not deem it necessary to notice anonymous charges in the *Telegraph*.

Colonel Johnson said he had always been sure it was so; that General Jackson had come here with dispositions entirely friendly to me, and intending to call upon me; that his mind had been poisoned here by scoundrel office-seekers; that he was a warm-tempered, passionate man, and had been led to believe that I was the cause of those publications against his wife; but that he (Johnson) knew that the President's feelings were now as friendly to me as they had ever been. He had told him that at the time of the debate in the House of Representatives on the Seminole War questions he had received more assistance from me, in drawing up the minority report of the military committee, than from all the world beside. He did not now speak by the authority of General Jackson, but he knew that his disposition towards me was friendly, and had no doubt, if a friendly advance from him would be accepted by me, that he would make it.

I said I had no desire that the interruption of social intercourse between us should continue, and was disposed to receive any friendly advance from General Jackson with kindness.

March 3. — I received from Colonel Richard M. Johnson a note without date or signature, which I copy for curiosity: " General Jackson expressed great satisfaction that I had the conversation with you which I detailed to him, and expressed a wish that I should assure you of his personal regard and friendship, and was anxious to have a social and friendly intercourse restored between you. There I left it, and have satisfied my own mind. I shall communicate to Governor Cass the same; and there it rests with me, having done what my heart suggested. The President expresses himself as perfectly satisfied now that you never did countenance the publications to which I alluded, and entertains for you the highest opinion as a man of honor, etc. Please destroy this when you read it."

So far so good. . . A restoration of friendly, social, and personal intercourse between President Jackson and me at this time would attract much public notice, and could not fail to expose me to obloquy. The old federal party, now devoted

to Mr. Clay, have already more than once tried their hands
at slandering me. They have drawn the sword and brandished
it over my head. If I set my foot in the President's house,
they will throw away the scabbard. I must, therefore, walk
with extreme circumspection; even that will not protect me
from their malignity. Something is due to myself; and the
path is narrow to avoid on the one hand the charge of an
implacable temper, and on the other of eagerness to propitiate
the dispenser of power.

Washington, Dec. 1. — Walking round the Capitol Hill
this morning, I met and spoke to Andrew Stevenson, Speaker
of the House of Representatives, also C. A. Wickliffe, a member of the House from Kentucky, and several other members
of Congress. Mr. Featherstonhaugh paid me a morning
visit. He had a small book in his hand, which he said was the
Journal of a Nullifier, a political satire, published at Charleston, South Carolina, and the scene of which is appropriately
laid in hell.

Dec. 5. — The message of the President gives great dissatisfaction to those with whom I converse, and will be received with rapture by his partisans. He has cast away all the
neutrality which he had heretofore maintained upon the conflicting interests and opinions of the different sections of the
country, and surrenders the whole Union to the nullifiers of
the South and the land-robbers of the West. I confess this is
neither more nor less than I expected, and no more than I
predicted nearly two years since, in a letter, I think, to Peter
B. Porter. This message already puts my temper and my
discretion upon a trial equally severe. Dissimulation I cannot practice. Passion can do nothing but mischief. I walk
between burning plough-shares, and have no support upon
earth, with a fearful foreboding that every effort I could
make for the good of my country would recoil in evil upon
myself and my family.

Dec. 10. — The House adjourned at three P.M., and walking home with J. W. Taylor we met Major Hamilton, who
gave him, and he to me, the President's proclamation to and
against the South Carolina nullifieres.

Dec. 13. — I had a friendly and jocular conversation with
McDuffie, who told me they had nullified in South Carolina
our Tariff Act of last summer. I said we must leave the

ordinance and the proclamation to fight it out. He said Hamilton would issue a counter-proclamation.

Dec. 24. — I met a man in the street who accosted me and said there had been a battle; that General James Blair, a member of the House of Representatives, had knocked down and very severely beaten Duff Green, editor of the *Telegraph* and printer to Congress. What changes in the affairs and passions of men! Duff Green and his *Telegraph* were set up here against my Administration, and for its overthrow, by Calhoun, Hayne, Hamilton, Eaton of Tennessee, Drayton, and the united gang of Calhoun and Jackson conspirators against me. They sent a man by the name of Berryman to Charleston to obtain subscriptions for the *Telegraph;* and I have among my papers Drayton's recommendation of him to some of the men of his party. They made Green printer to the Senate, and he became the prince of slanderers against me. When Jackson came in, they rewarded Green by making him the printer to the Houses of Congress, which he still is. But he attached himself to the fortunes of Calhoun. Men baser than himself have supplanted him in the favor of Jackson. He has plunged into the maelstrom of nullification, and it is dashing him and his instigators to destruction. His *Telegraph* has lately had some violent publications against the Union men in South Carolina, of whom Blair is one. To make them odious, it designates them as Tories — a name of special abhorrence there, from remembrances of the Revolution. This was the immediate provocation to Blair, who is of the race of the giants — a man of fifteen stone, and who has nearly killed Green.

Dec. 25. — The conversation with the members of Congress was chiefly upon the effect of the President's proclamation upon the Legislature of South Carolina, the news of which has just come. It was a blister-plaster.

Jan. 4. 1833. — John C. Calhoun took this morning his seat as a Senator from South Carolina, having resigned his office as Vice-President of the United States. W. C. Rives had also taken his seat as a Senator from Virginia. I spoke with Mr. Calhoun and Mr. Clay. When I returned to the House they were just about adjourning; Mr. Everett asked me to attend a meeting of the Massachusetts delegation at his lodgings this evening; which I did. The two Senators, D.

Webster and N. Silsbee, and the members of the House, Bates, Briggs, Choate, Dearborn, Everett, Grennell Hodges, Kendall, Nelson and Reed, were present; Appleton and Davis absent. The object was a consultation upon the course to be pursued with regard to the tariff bill reported by the Committee of Ways and Means. The opinion was unanimous that its passage should be opposed, but no hope could be entertained by anyone that the passage of it in the House could be prevented. There were some feeble hopes expressed that it might be defeated in the Senate. It was remarked that the protective system would be abandoned by the Kentucky delegation. Everett asked me if I thought Mr. Clay would be again a candidate for the Presidency. I said, no doubt, if he could with any prospect of success, of which there was at present none.

Feb. 13. — At one o'clock the Senate came in. Hugh Lawson White, President pro tempore of the Senate, presided. The electoral votes for President and Vice-President of the United States were opened, counted, and announced. Of two hundred and eighty-eight votes, Andrew Jackson had two hundred and nineteen for President; Henry Clay, forty-nine; John Floyd, eleven; William Wirt, seven.

Feb. 15. — At noon the balloting for printer to the House of Representatives for the next Congress recommenced. At the first ballot there were ninety votes for Blair and ninety-one for Gales and Seaton. There were still votes for Condy Raguet and Duff Green, and blanks. At the third ballot, Gales and Seaton had ninety-three and Blair ninety. . . At the next, fourth ballot, the votes were one hundred and ninety-seven. Gales and Seaton had ninety-nine, and were chosen. A buzz of satisfaction went round the hall, outside of the bar. I secured this election to Gales and Seaton by prevailing upon the Anti-Masons, twelve of whom had at the first ballot voted for Thurlow Weed, to vote finally for them.

Feb. 21. — At the House, the bill for enforcing the collection for the revenue came from the Senate; passed at ten o'clock last evening — thirty-two to one, all the other members opposed to it having seceded. Long debate in the House whether it should be printed, and order taken to dispose of it. Final refusal to take it up in preference to the Tariff bill.

Feb. 23. — I went into the Senate-chamber and heard a

debate upon Mr. Clay's Compromise bill, at the second reading — a debate brisk, animated, and somewhat acrimonious.

Feb. 25. — In the House, the Clay Tariff bill was passed by previous question — one hundred and nineteen to eighty-five. I desired to ask a question with regard to the construction of the first section of the bill, but was not permitted. The Revenue Collection bill, otherwise called the Force bill, or, as the nullifiers, call it, the Bloody bill, was then taken up, and a very disorderly struggle to put it off continued till four o'clock, when the House took a recess till six.

March 2. — About two o'clock in the morning, Chittenden Lyon, of Kentucky, drunk as a lord, presented resolutions of the Legislature of Kentucky, which he said he had just received, and which he moved to be laid on the table and printed. On being asked what was the subject of the resolutions, he drivelled out, "Nullification." Almost every quarter of an hour, after midnight, business was suspended for want of a quorum. . . Finally, Stevenson, the Speaker, made a silly speech in return for the vote of thanks, and adjourned the House without day. The hands of the clock were pointing at five as we passed under them out of the hall. I took Edward Everett home, and we were in imminent danger of oversetting in the midst of Pennsylvania Avenue, nearly opposite to Gadsby's. We got out of the carriage. Kirk was asleep, and the horses had stopped. I ordered Ball to take the reins; we re-entered the carriage, and got into the macadamized part of the Avenue. On reaching Mr. Everett's lodgings, I alighted with him, and thence walked home, with Fahrenheit's thermometer at 6° — the extremest cold of the winter, and the ground covered with snow. The day was dawning, and I retired to bed, exhausted and dejected, but with blessings of gratitude to the Supreme Disposer of events for the merciful dispensations of His providence in bringing the affairs of the country to a condition more favorable to peace and union than it has been of late, and though still surrounded with dangers.

March 4. — Andrew Jackson was this day inaugurated for a second term of four years as President of the United States, and Martin Van Buren was sworn into office as Vice-President. Mr. John Sergeant called here; he had attended the ceremony at the Capitol. The inaugural speech was brief, and full of smooth professions.

March 7. — Mr. Calhoun's speech of 15th February, upon the Enforcement bill, is published in the *Telegraph.* It contains his system of nullification. His learning is shallow, his mind argumentative, and his assumption of principle destitute of discernment. His insanity begins with his principles, from which his deductions are ingeniously drawn.

March 9. — I walked to the Capitol, where, in the Supreme Court, I found Mr. Clay and Mr. Webster arguing the two sides of a writ of error from a Court in Louisiana — dry as dust, and the eloquence of the champions would not make it otherwise.

March 29. — As I was returning home I met at the door of Mrs. Strother's house a man named Andrew Wallace, who was coming to see me, and came. He said he was one hundred and three years of age the 26th of this month. A Scot born, descended from Robert, a brother of Sir William Wallace. He was at the battles of Preston-Pans and Culloden, a soldier of Prince Charles Edward, whom, as well as the Duke of Cumberland, he well remembers. After the battle of Culloden, he fled first to Scotland, and thence, in 1752, to this country; served in our army from 1776 till it was disbanded; re-enlisted in 1786; and continued as a sergeant-major in the army till 1813; then discharged at the age of eighty-three; has since been a teacher till his strength failed; lives at West Chester, Pennsylvania, and comes here now to solicit an increase of pension. His eye-sight, hearing, and memory seem unimpaired. What a life and survival of chances!

Baltimore, April 12. — We loosed from the wharf five minutes after six. The boat was full of passengers — I suppose at least one hundred and fifty. Among them, besides Mr. Bradley and his family, and Colonel Worth, were Mr. John H. Eaton and his wife, Mr. Duff Green, and, I believe, his daughter, Andrew Wallace, the centenarian Scot, Professor Henry Ware and his wife, Dr. Waterhouse's daughters, returning from a sanatory excursion to Alexandria, and an Englishman named Messenger, now residing at New York; also a little band of Italian musicians, with two harps, one violin, a clarionet, and a flute, who enlivened the passage with much discourse of sweet music. I got into a discussion with Duff Green, upon the tariff, domestic manufactures and protection, slave labor, and consolidation, which attracted round us a circle of listeners, to my great annoyance. . . We landed at Frenchtown at eleven o'clock, and crossed the Peninsula to New Castle in the railway cars, impelled by the locomotive-engine in fifty minutes — sixteen miles. But we had flakes of fire floating about us in the cars the whole time. With the allowance of two minutes for the slackening of speed at the departure and arrival, we travelled at the rate of a mile every three minutes, and were precisely one hour from landing at Frenchtown from one steamer to leaving the wharf at New Castle in the other. We landed at four o'clock at Philadelphia, and I took my lodgings at the United States Hotel.

Quincy, May 10. — The newspapers contain accounts of a personal assault by the late Lieutenant Randolph, of the navy, upon President Jackson, on board a steamboat, at Alexandria. He simply tweaked him by the nose and went away. Jackson was much disposed to chastise him with his cane; but Randolph got away without even being arrested by the President's retinue.

May 11. — I went into Boston, and dined at Dr. George Parkman's with Mr. Charles Kemble and his daughter, Frances Ann. . . I had much conversation with Miss Kemble, chiefly upon dramatic literature, but it differed not from what it might have been with any well-educated and intelligent young woman of her age. I spoke to her of some of her own poetical productions, but she did not appear inclined to talk of them. What she appeared chiefly to pride herself upon was the feats of horsemanship. She said she had rode this morning about thirty miles, and leaped over many fences and stone walls. She said they expected to remain in this country till about this time next year. I asked her if she had ever seen her aunt, Mrs. Siddons, upon the stage. She had not, but had heard her read Shakspeare. She had known her only as a very good woman. She observed that she herself had been chiefly educated, and spent the greater part of her life, in France, and until a very few years since had no idea of going upon the stage.

June 17. — Anniversary of the battle of Bunker's Hill and the burning of Charlestown — one of the first events of which I have a personal recollection. Fifty-eight years have since then elapsed; about one person in ten then living yet exists. I was reminded of this anniversary upon hearing, with the rising sun, a salute of thirteen guns from Fort Independence, but passed the day in profound tranquillity, contrasting with the deep and awful agitation of that day in 1775. I am reading and making petty annotations upon the Book of Leviticus, strolling about my garden and nursery, hoeing and plucking up weeds — a never-ceasing occupation.

June 18. — Called from my nursery and garden by a visit from Mr. Quincy, President of Harvard University. . . He told me also that as President Jackson is about visiting Boston, the Corporation of the university had thought it necessary to invite him to visit the colleges; that he (Mr. Quincy) should address him in a Latin discourse, and confer upon him the degree of Doctor of Laws; and he intimated that I should receive an invitation to be present at these ceremonies.

I said that the personal relations in which President Jackson had chosen to place himself with me were such that I could hold no intercourse of a friendly character with him. I could therefore not accept an invitation to attend upon this occasion. And, independent of that, as myself an affectionate child of our Alma Mater, I would not be present to witness her disgrace in conferring her highest literary honors upon a barbarian who could not write a sentence of grammar and hardly could spell his own name. Mr. Quincy said he was sensible how utterly unworthy of literary honors Jackson was, but the Corporation thought it was necessary to follow the precedent, and treat him precisely as Mr. Monroe, his predecessor, had been treated. As the people of the United States had seen fit to make him their President, the Corporation thought the honors which they conferred upon him were compliments due to the station, by whomsoever it was occupied. Mr. Quincy said it was thought also that the omission to show the same respect to President Jackson which had been shown to Mr. Monroe would be imputed to party spirit — which they were anxious to avoid. . . I adhered to my determination to stay at home.

June 22. — There was much cannonading this afternoon at the President's reviewing of the military companies in Boston. The distant report of them gave me a double relish for the solitary tranquillity of my own occupations. No period of life has ever yielded me so much quite contentment as that which I enjoy with my family in health about me, totally uninterupted by visitors, and cultivating, in such health as I have, my seedling plants and trees; laboring bodily from three to four hours a day upon horticultural experiments, all hitherto fruitless, but some few of them beginning to promise fruit. " Alteri Seculo " is the motto of all my plantations; but I am yet sensible and conscious that this life of pleasure is not a life of profit.

June 27. — Dr. Waterhouse came and dined with us. . . He was present yesterday at the ceremony of conferring the degree of Doctor of Laws upon President Jackson, and was much captivated by the ease and gracefulness of his manners. He shook hands with him twice, and told him he had heard of him many years ago, and was very glad to take him by the hand now. But he says Jackson is so excessively debilitated that he should not be surprised if he should never reach Washington again. I believe much of his debility is politic — part his own policy, to suit his returns of civility to his own convenience and pleasure, and part the policy of his physician, pour se faire valoir. He is one of our tribe of great men who turn disease to commodity, like John Randolph, who for forty years was always dying. Jackson, ever since he became a mark of public attention, has been doing the same thing. He is so ravenous of notoriety that he craves the sympathy for sickness as a portion of his glory. He is now alternately giving out his chronic diarrhoea and making Warren bleed him for a pleurisy, and posting to Cambridge for a Doctorate of Laws; mounting the monument of Bunker's Hill to hear a fulsome address and receive two cannon-balls from Edward Everett, and riding post to Lynn, Marblehead, and Salem, receiving collations, deputations, and addresses at them all, in one and the same day. Four-fifths of his sickness is trickery, and the other fifth mere fatigue.

July 2. — President Jackson has been obliged by the feeble state of his health to give up the remainder of his tour, and from Concord, in New Hampshire, yesterday, returned through Lowell to Roxbury without passing through Boston. He lodged last night at the house of Mr. Bradford, one of his partisans in Roxbury, to proceed this day to Providence, thence in the steamboat to New York, and intending to reach Washington on Thursday. And so ends this magnificent tour; but whether from real disease, crafty sickness, or the collisions of rival servility between the two parties in New Hampshire, is yet uncertain; perhaps a little of all three.

Aug. 5. — Another painful day, with a gathering eruption on my right hand. It suspends most of my labors of the hand in the garden and nursery, and of the head in my chamber. Mrs. Adams sent for Dr. Woodward to whom I gave a history of my complaints, my constitution, and almost of my life. He prescribed sundry remedies, some of which I shall perhaps try, but with a strong conviction that my only effectual remedies are patience and resignation, and, above all, preparation for my last change.

Aug. 9. — Cold and cloudy day, clearing off towards evening. In the multitudinous whimseys of a disabled mind and body, the thick-coming fancies often occur to me that the events which affect my life and adventures are specially shaped to disappoint my purposes. My whole life has been a succession of disappointments. I can scarcely recollect a single instance of success to anything that I ever undertook. Yet, with fervent gratitude to God, I confess that my life has been equally marked by great and signal successes which I neither aimed at nor anticipated.

Aug. 14. — Mr. Alexander H. Everett had requested a conversation with me, and it was to urge me to consent to be nominated for election as Governor of the Commonwealth; which I persisted in declining. He thought they could not agree upon his brother Edward, but gave me no substantial reason for changing my determination.

Sept. 17. — Teaching also my granddaughter to read — a trying school of patience to myself. In the evening we played a rubber of whist. A late Scottish traveller in this country, named Hamilton, who visited me at Washington, introduced by Mr. B. O. Tayloe, has published a book entitled *Men and Manners in America*. He announces that the standard of morality in the United States is low; that the Scot is a much more honest man than the Yankee; that there are no Jews in New England; and that from their Puritan descent the New Englanders have a double portion of intellect and only half a heart. There are certainly no Sir Archy McSarcasms or Sir Pertinax McSycophants in New England. They are all of Scottish breed, and well suited to travel in America and furnish books of men and manners for the London market.

Sept. 28. — There is much agitation in the public mind about an order from President Jackson to withdraw the deposits of public moneys from the Bank of the United States and to place them in sundry State banks, and about a paper read by him to the members of his Cabinet on the 18th of this month, followed by the dismission of William J. Duane, and the appointment of Roger B. Taney, as Secretary of the Treasury. Upon all which I take time for reflection.

Oct. 7. — The state of my health, I fear, is irretrievable. The summer is gone, and I have done nothing of what I had intended. My time is now absorbed — 1. In the mornings, minutes of Thomson's translation of the Septuagint Bible. 2. In teaching my granddaughter to read; a task to which I devote from two to three hours of every day. 3. In the exercise of my garden and nursery, an average of two hours more. 4. My diary, one hour. 5. Correspondence, two hours. 6. Miscellaneous reading, two hours. There are twelve: seven in bed, three at and after meals, and two wasted, I know not how. This wasted time I have found by constant experience to be as indispensable as sleep. It cannot be employed in reading, nor even in thinking upon any serious subject. It must be wasted upon trifles — doing nothing. The string of the bow must be slackened, and the bow itself laid aside.

Oct. 13. — I heard my granddaughter read twice, and in the evening waded through thirty pages of Professor Dew's review of the debate on the project for slave emancipation.[1] It is a monument of the intellectual perversion produced by the existence of slavery in a free community. To the mind of Mr. Dew, slavery is the source of all virtue in the heart of the master. His argument against the practicability of abolishing slavery by means of colonization appears to me conclusive; nor do I believe that emancipation is the object of the Colonization Society, though it may be the day-dream of some of its members. Mr. Dew's argument, that the danger of insurrection among the slaves is diminished in proportion as their relative numbers increase over those of the white masters, is an ingenious paradox in which I have no faith.

Oct. 22. — Mr. Clay came out from Boston this morning

[1] This was Professor Thomas R. Dew of William and Mary College, whose *Essay in Favor of Slavery* had great influence in turning the South against emancipation or the limitation of the slavery area.

and paid me a visit, with Messrs. Lawrence, Gorham, and
Appleton. Mr. Clay arrived in Boston yesterday. He is
making a tour, and since he reached the Atlantic border has
been received at Baltimore, Philadelphia, New York, Providence, and Boston with great demonstrations of respect. This
fashion of peddling for popularity by travelling round the
country gathering crowds together, hawking for public dinners, and spouting empty speeches, is growing into high fashion. It was formerly confined to the Presidents, but DeWitt
Clinton made some unsuccessful experiments of it. Mr. Clay
has mounted that hobby often, and rides him very hard.
President Jackson made an awkward figure at it last summer,
having upon one of his excursions got his nose pulled, and
being in his procession here *tres-pressé* with a dysentery. Mr.
Clay had two deputations sent to him at Boston from Providence — one, of the tough seignors, to invite him to a public
dinner, and one, of the tender juveniles, to escort him into the
city. He entered Boston yesterday in a procession, and was
paraded round the streets in the midst of all the rain. He
appears to be in good health, though he said he was not so.

Providence, Nov. 7. — We came to Providence without
stopping to breakfast, and embarked in the steamboat *Boston,*
Captain William Comstock, at noon.

New York, Nov. 8. — Blessed, ever blessed be the name of
God, that I am alive and have escaped unhurt from the most
dreadful catastrophe that ever my eyes beheld! We arrived
at New York at half-past six this morning. I took leave of
Mr. Harrod, his daughter, my niece Elizabeth, took a hack
with Mr. Potter, and crossed from the East to the North
River, put my baggage into the steamboat *Independence,* Captain Douglas, and walked to the City Hotel. . . I then returned to the steamboat, which left the wharf at eight, and
landed the passengers at Amboy about twenty minutes past
ten. . . There were upwards of two hundred passengers in
the Amboy railroad cars. There were two locomotive-engines,
A and B, each drawing an accommodation car, a sort of moving stage, in a square, with open railing, a platform, and a row
of benches holding forty or fifty persons; then four or five
cars in the form of large stage-coaches, each in three compartments, with doors of entrance on both sides, and two opposite
benches, on each of which sat four passengers. Each train

was closed with a high, quadrangular, open-railed baggage-wagon, in which the baggage of all the passengers in the train was heaped up, the whole covered with an oil-cloth. I was in car B, No. 1, and of course in the second train. Of the first ten miles, two were run in four minutes, marked by a watch of a Mr. De Yong, in the same car and division with me. They stopped, oiled the wheels, and proceeded. We had gone about five miles further, and had traversed one mile in one minute and thirty-six seconds, when the front left wheel of the car in which I was, having taken fire and burned for several minutes, slipped off the rail. The pressure on the right side of the car, then meeting resistance, raised it with both wheels from the rail, and it was oversetting on the left side, but the same pressure on the car immediately behind raised its left side from the rail till it actually overset to the right, and, in oversetting, brought back the car in which I was, to stand on the four wheels, and saved from injury all the passengers in it. The train was stopped, I suppose, within five seconds of the time when our wheel slipped off the rail, but it was then going at the rate of sixty feet in a second, and was dragged nearly two hundred feet before it could stop. Of sixteen persons in two of the three compartments of the car that overset, one only escaped unhurt — a Dr. Cuyler. One side of the car was stove in, and almost demolished. One man, John C. Stedman, of Raleigh, North Carolina, was so dreadfully mangled that he died within ten minutes; another, named, I believe, Welles, of Pennsylvania, can probably not survive the day.

Washington, Nov. 11. — In the evening I had a visit from General Macomb, one of the few men in this world who have uniformly shown me that he forgets not a benefit conferred.

Nov. 26. — This evening I was with a lamp in my hand reading a prosy article in the *Telegraph,* when it lulled me to a doze, and my lamp set fire to the newspaper, which it took some expense of breath to extinguish. I made several efforts to write, but was obliged to give it up. I had a morning visit from Dr. Sewall, and before dinner walked to the Capitol. There I met Chilton Allen of Kentucky, Mr. Foster of Georgia, and Mr. Potts of Pennsylvania. On coming out, I met in the Avenue Heman Allen of Vermont and afterwards Colonel David Crockett of Tennessee. I did not recognize him till he came up and accosted me and named himself. I congratulated him upon his return here, and he said, yes, it had cost him two years to convince the people of his district that he was the fittest man to represent them; that he had just been to Mr. Gales and requested him to announce his arrival and inform the public that he had taken for lodgings two rooms on the first floor of a boarding-house, where he expected to pass the winter and to have for a fellow-lodger Major Jack Downing, the only person in whom he had any confidence for information of what the Government was doing. This Major Jack Downing is the fictitious signature of a writer in some of the newspapers, assuming the character of a shrewd, trickish, half-educated Yankee major of militia; writes letters from the President's house as entirely in his confidence, and telling all the petty intrigues of the Cabinet and favorites by whom he is surrounded.

Dec. 3. — At the House, Mr. Ward, of New York, offered a joint resolution to wait on the President to notify him of the meeting of Congress. Mr. Ward reported from the committee to wait upon the President that he would make a communication to Congress at one o'clock, and at that hour the message came. Its most peculiar characteristic is a bitter invective upon the Bank of the United States. Not a word about Alabama. It was laid on the table, and ten thousand copies of it ordered to be printed.

Dec. 22. — I dispatched a letter for my son Charles, enclosing one to the Speaker of the House of Representatives of the Commonwealth of Massachusetts, withdrawing my name from the canvass of candidates to be sent from the House to the Senate for the election of a Governor. I have determined upon taking this step against the earnest inclination and advice of the Anti-Masonic party by which I was nominated, and at the risk of making myself as unpopular with them as I am with the two other parties in Massachusetts. To be forsaken by all mankind seems to be the destiny that awaits my last days. In such cases a man can be sustained only by an overruling consciousness of rectitude.

Dec. 26. — On the Capitol Hill I left the carriage, and went to the Senate-chamber, into which I penetrated with difficulty, it was so crowded, and particularly by ladies. Mr. Clay was speaking upon two resolutions which he had offered to the Senate — the first, declaring that " by dismissing the late Secretary of the Treasury because he would not, contrary to his sense of his own duty, remove the money of the United States in deposit with the Bank of the United States and its branches, in conformity with the President's opinions, and by appointing his successor to effect such removal, which has been done, the President has assumed the exercise of a power over the Treasury of the United States not granted to him by the Constitution and laws, and dangerous to the liberties of the people;" and the second, "that the reasons assigned by the Secretary of the Treasury for the removal of the money of the United States deposited in the Bank of the United States and its branches, communicated to Congress on the 3d day of December, 1833, are unsatisfactory and insufficient." Mr. Clay was going over the same ground occupied by Mr. McDuffie in the House of Representatives.

Jan. 2, 1834. — Polk took the floor nearly half an hour before the usual time for proceeding to the orders of the day. He spoke nearly three hours, and his speech is said to have given entire satisfaction to his party. It consisted of a repetition of all the matter which has been gathering for years against the bank, sufficiently methodized, and delivered with fluency. But the galleries were empty, and there was scarcely a quorum in the House. Polk is the leader of the Administration in the House, and is just qualified for an eminent County Court lawyer — " par negotiis, neque supra." He has no wit, no literature, no point of argument, no gracefulness of delivery, no elegance of language, no philosophy, no pathos, no felicitous impromptus; nothing that can constitute an orator, but confidence, fluency, and labor.

Jan. 23. — After the House adjourned, I went into the Senate-chamber where Mr. Preston, of South Carolina, was in the midst of a very eloquent speech on Mr. Clay's resolutions. I heard him only three or four minutes, for, without finishing, he gave way for a motion to adjourn. The Senate-chamber was crowded, and Mr. Preston, a new member, coming in the place of Governor Miller, has produced a strong sensation by this speech. Warren R. Davis was there, and, as the hall was emptying, after the adjournment, said to some one, " I trained that colt."

Feb. 6. — George Chambers, of Pennsylvania, made a very earnest speech against Chilton's resolution for extending the

pension system. . . He was followed by Henry A. Wise, a
new and young member from Virginia, who made a very keen,
satirical speech in favor of the restoration of the deposits and
of a National bank, and against all those who are of the same
opinions. He is coming forward as a successor of John Randolph, with his tartness, his bitterness, his malignity, and his
inconsistencies.

Feb. 18. — Passing in my way to the Capitol this morning
by the house where Mr. William Wirt had lodged, a crape
tied to the knocker of the door announced his decease. And
thus pass away in succession the glories of this world. He has
not left a wiser or better behind. At the last election of
President of the United States, he was one of the candidates
who received the suffrages of the people, and a very little
difference in the state of the public mind at that time would
have effected his election. He had never been in public life,
excepting in connection with his profession, which was the law;
but for twelve years, during the Administration of James
Monroe and mine, he was Attorney-General of the United
States.

Feb. 21. — Before the House met, I asked the Speaker if
the journal of the House would notice the decease of Mr. Wirt
as being the occasion of adjournment yesterday. He said, no.
I asked him if he could not have it so entered upon the journal.
He said, no. This I expected; and I asked him if he would
object to my asking the unanimous consent of the House that
the entry should be so made. He said, certainly not. Accordingly, when the House met, I made my proposal, and delivered
my short address of five minutes. It concluded with saying
that, as my proposal was not a fit subject for debate, if there
should be an objection made to it I wished him to consider it
as withdrawn. The Speaker said he could not have the entry
made without the authority of the House, and he should consider it as granted if he should hear no objection made to it.
Joel K. Mann, precisely the rankest Jackson man in the House,
said, no. There was a general call upon him from all quarters of the House to withdraw his objection, but he refused.
Blair, of South Carolina, rose, and asked if the manifest sense
of the House could be defeated by one objection. The
Speaker said I had requested that my proposal should be considered as withdrawn if objection should be made, but that the

House was competent to give the instruction upon motion made. I was then called upon perhaps by two-thirds of the voices in the House, — " Move! Move! Move! " — and said I had hoped the proposal I made would have obtained the unanimous assent of the House; and as only one objection had been heard, which did not appear to be sustained by the general sense of the House, I would make the motion that the addition should be made which I had proposed in the journal. The Speaker took the question, and nine-tenths at least of the members present answered aye.

Feb. 28. — Mr. Edward Everett brought me a letter from Caleb Cushing, a Royal Arch Mason, and member of the Massachusetts legislature, to Mr. Webster. This gentleman had written to enquire what was the reason of their delay to act upon the resolutions respecting the distress and removal of deposits and recharter of the Bank of the United States.

Cushing answers, bitterly complaining that they are paralyzed by the Anti-Masons, who upon all occasions vote with the Jackson party, and enquired if I could not do something to heal this breach. I said I had done everything in my power, and if anything had been done to conciliate the Anti-Masons they would have met every advance in the same spirit. But Mr. Cushing must look to himself and his party for the failure of all my endeavors to conciliate. I had given fair notice and warning both to Governor Davis and Mr. Webster, from both of whom I had received encouraging assurances of conciliation to the Anti-Masons, instead of which every possible thing had been done to fret and exasperate them: all their candidates for the Senate had been swept off the board; not one Anti-Mason had been elected to the Council; a fraudulent law against unlawful oaths was now in connection to baffle and deceive them; and just now the Senate had refused to grant to the joint investigating committee the power to send for persons and papers; and now their aid was implored to pass National Republican resolutions in favor of the bank. It was impossible for me to do anything more with them, and I did believe they would go over to Jacksonism. I had done all I could to prevent it, but in vain.

March 10. — This was the regular day for the reception of memorials and petitions, but the Speaker gave the floor to James H. Gholson, of Virginia, to make a speech in opposition to that of John M. Patton, made last Monday. . . Then succeeded H. L. Pinckney, of South Carolina, in defence of his State against Patton's charge of rashness in her recent councils and measures. Pinckney talks much nullification, and indulges himself in bitter invective against Andrew Jackson. All the members of the House from South Carolina, excepting one, are of the nullification school, and so fanatical in their devotion to it that they cannot resist the temptation to introduce it into all their speeches, the consequence of which has been the forfeiture of every particle of their influence in the House. Pinckney, who is a very able and eloquent and pious man, raved till half-past three o'clock, when the House adjourned, leaving his speech unfinished.

March 17. — When Massachusetts was called, I presented the resolutions of the Legislature upon the currency and the removal of the public deposits from the Bank of the United States, with a very few remarks, touching somewhat personally upon the President; and I moved that they should be read, printed, and laid on the table, to be referred to a select committee, with instructions to report a plan for continuing to the people the advantages resulting from a National bank. Polk started up and fell into an idolizing and mawkish glorification of Doctor Andrew Jackson, with some coarse and equally dull invective against me. I rose, and said I should not reply to his speech, and gave notice once for all that whenever any admirer of the President of the United States should think fit to pay his court to him in the House, either by a flaming panegyric upon him or by a rancorous invective upon me, he should never elicit one word of reply from me.

> No! let the candied tongue lick absurd pomp,
> And crook the pregnant hinges of the knee,
> Where THRIFT may follow fawning.

Polk shrunk back abashed into his shell, and said not a word. The lines from Hamlet struck the House like a spark of electricity.

March 27. — At seven in the evening I attended the meeting of the Anti-Masonic members of the House of Representatives. . . The occasion of the meeting was the presence of Mr. Granger, of New York, in the city; and he was present at the meeting. Nothing special was proposed, but Mr. Granger was requested to give a statement of the condition of Anti-Masonry in the State of New York, and especially in that part of it where he resides. He said that in all the western counties of New York Masonry was extinct; the lodges and chapters were all abandoned, and almost all of them formally dissolved; that the spirit of Anti-Masonry had consequently subsided — there was no adversary left to contend with, and as a distinctive party there could scarcely be said to be any Anti-Masonry left. If the Freemasons should attempt to revive their institutions in those counties, he had no doubt the Anti-Masonic spirit would instantly revive with as much zeal and ardor as it had ever manifested.

March 28. — On Wilde's amendment, Rufus Choate spoke an hour and a half, arguing to the majority, friends and supporters of the Administration, that the restoration of the deposits is a measure of high interest and true policy *to them*. It was the most eloquent speech of the session, and in a course of reasoning altogether impressive and original; but seed sown at broadcast, which will take no root in the soil. Choate is a young man of great power and promise, whose political career has been short but brilliant. His health is indifferent, and he has a cadaverous look. He proposes to resign his seat in Congress, which interferes too much with the profits of his practice at the bar.

April 2. — James Blair, a member of the House of Representatives from South Carolina, shot himself last evening at his lodgings at Dowson's, No. 1, after reading part of an affectionate letter from his wife, to Governor Murphy, of Alabama, who was alone in the chamber with him, and a fellow-lodger with him at the same house. . . Poor Blair! Blair was a man of amiable natural disposition, of excellent feelings, of sterling good sense, and of brilliant parts, irredeemably ruined by the single vice of intemperance, which had crept upon him insensibly to himself till it had bloated his body to a mountain, prostrated his intellect, and vitiated his temper to madness. He had paid three hundred dollars fine for beating and breaking the bones of Duff Green because he had charged the Union party of South Carolina with being Tories; he had discharged a pistol at an actress in the theatre at Washington, from one of the boxes; he had within the last ten days given the lie to Henry L. Pinckney while speaking in his place in the House of Representatives; and he was in the constant habit of bringing a loaded pistol with him to the House. The chances were quite equal that he should have shot almost any other man than himself.

April 7. — Uriah Tracy, thirty years ago, used to say that the soldiers of the Revolution claimants never died — that they were immortal. Had he lived to this time, he would have seen that they multiply with the lapse of time. As petitioners they are more numerous at every session of Congress than before. And of late, as some of them have died, their widows have begun to petition; and this day there was a petition from the son of a deceased pensioner praying that the pension may be continued to him.

April 17. — The President of the United States this day sent to the Senate a protest against their resolution of censure upon him for his recent interferences with the public revenues, and he calls upon them to enter his protest upon their journals. Great excitement. Poindexter moved that it should not be received. Clay, Webster, and Preston are absent.

May 9. — Immediately after the reading of the journal, it appeared there was no quorum in the House, and a motion was made to adjourn. The yeas and nays were called. The object was to attend the race-grounds, where numbers of the members were in actual attendance. The motion was rejected — twelve to one hundred and eighteen.

May 10. — A session of nearly fifteen hours, without intermission and without refreshment, exhausted me so much that on returning home I merely took a plate of soup, a small piece of bread, and half a glass of water, upon which I went immediately to bed, and slept soundly till seven.

May 23. — I was up this morning before five o'clock, and my son John went with me over to Georgetown, to the landing-place of the Chesapeake and Ohio Canal. There we found two canal-boats, one of them of cast-iron. They were filled with a company chiefly of members of Congress, and a few of them had their families with them; all invited by the President and Directors of the Chesapeake and Ohio Canal Company to make an excursion to Harper's Ferry. My son left me at the landing-place and returned home. I entered the largest of the two boats, which was full of company, among whom a small number of ladies. The band of music of the Marine

Corps were also there, distributed in the two boats. Mr.
Charles F. Mercer, late President of the Corporation, and
the real founder of the whole undertaking, was of the company. John P. Van Ness, Mayor of Washington, Mr. Coxe,
of Georgetown, and Colonel Abert, a Director on the part of
the Government, did the honors of the party. The passage
on the canal was very slow, and continually obstructed by
stoppage of the locks. Of these there are thirty-four between
Georgetown and Harper's Ferry. There was a light collation
and dinner, and, after it, some drinking of strong wine, which
made some of the company loquacious and some drowsy. The
band gave occasional reports of animating instrumental music.
The canal almost the whole way follows close upon the course
of the Potomac River; the country along the margin of which
is generally beautiful, sometimes wild, and in other parts
variously cultivated, but seemingly little inhabited. There is
not a luxuriously comfortable country-seat on the whole way,
nor one that bespeaks affluence and taste.

Harper's Ferry, May 24. — At one o'clock we all dined
together at the inn, and after dinner first visited the armory,
where the rifles are made; but the works are not comparable
to those at Springfield. We then ascended the hill which over-
looks the college, and rested at the residence of Captain John
P. Hall. There we saw the junction of the Potomac and
Shenandoah Rivers, described somewhat enthusiastically by
Mr. Jefferson. I went to the hanging rock, that bears his
name, and observed the double range of precipitous rocky hills
between which the river flows. It has some resemblance, on a
much smaller scale, to the course of the Elbe between Dresden
and the borders of Bohemia. There is not much of the sublime in the scene, and those who first see it after reading Mr.
Jefferson's description are usually disappointed.

June 2. — At the House, immediately after the reading of
the journal, Andrew Stevenson, the Speaker, addressed the
House, and resigned his office, stating that he had this day
addressed a letter to the Executive of Virginia resigning his
seat as a member of the House. He then took leave of the
House, in a speech of fifteen minutes, full of good principles
and good feelings, in elegant language very handsomely delivered. The House immediately proceeded to ballot for
Speaker. There were ten ballots taken, at the last of which

John Bell, of Tennessee, was chosen by one hundred and fourteen of two hundred and fifteen votes.   He was conducted by
me and Richard M. Johnson to the chair.

  June 4. — I dined with Mr. Webster upon salmon sent him
from New York.

  June 21. — Wasted the morning of the summer solstice.
Just before going to the House I heard that intelligence had
been received of the death of General La Fayette.   At the
meeting of the House, I moved a joint resolution for the appointment of a committee to consider and report what measures it may be proper for Congress to adopt, honorary to the
memory of General La Fayette.   The resolution was unanimously adopted, and a committee of one member from each
State on the part of the House was appointed.

  Quincy, July 16. — That which absorbed the largest portion of the day was a research respecting the origin of committees of correspondence in the approach of our war for
independence.   George Tucker, Professor of Moral Philosophy at the University of Virginia, recently wrote me a letter
of enquiry upon this subject.   He is writing the life of Thomas
Jefferson, and enquires whether any committees of correspondence were appointed by the Legislature of the Colony of
Massachusetts Bay before 1773.   Jefferson claims the invention of committees of correspondence for Virginia, and it has
become a controverted point of history.

  Boston, July 17. — Went to the State-House, and in the
Secretary's office I saw Mr. Bangs, and extracted from the
journal of the House of Representatives of the Province of
Massachusetts Bay, of the 6th of November, 1770, the entry
of an order for the appointment of a committee of correspondence to correspond with the Agent of the Province and others
in England, with the Speakers of the several Assemblies, and
with committees of correspondence appointed, or who might
be appointed, by them.

  July 30. — Rode over and visited Mr. John Bailey, at
Dorchester, and had with him two hours of conversation.
There is at present a great calm in the political world, and no
prospects upon which I can dwell with satisfaction.   The
system of administration for the government of the Union is
radically and, I believe, irretrievably vitiated — vitiated at the
fountain.   The succession to the Presidency absorbs all the

national interests, and the electioneering contests are becoming merely venal. My hopes of the long continuance of this Union are extinct. The people must go the way of all the world, and split up into an uncertain number of rival communities, enemies in war, in peace friends. Were it otherwise, and were the future destinies of the nation to be as prosperous and as glorious as they have been hitherto, my lease of life is so near its close that I should live to witness little of it. My own system of administration, which was to make the national domain the inexhaustible fund for progressive and unceasing internal improvement, has failed. Systematically renounced and denounced by the present Administration, it has been undisguisedly abandoned by H. Clay, ingloriously deserted by J. C. Calhoun, and silently given up by D. Webster.

Sept. 6. — Early this morning I went into Boston. At ten o'clock I went to the Council-chamber, in the State-House, where I met a few acquaintances and many strangers. It was the anniversary of La Fayette's birthday and the day fixed for the commemoration of his life and character by the young men of Boston. A large procession, civil and military, was formed which went from the State-House to Faneuil Hall, where a splendid oration of an hour and fifty minutes was delivered by Edward Everett. He commenced precisely at two o'clock, and for lack of time abridged his discourse perhaps nearly an hour. It was received with universal applause, and in the delivery was often interrupted by long-protracted shouts and hand-clappings of exulting approbation. It was delivered every word from memory; his manuscript lying on the table, and he never once recurred to it.

Oct. 9. — The prosperity of the country, independent of all agency of the Government, is so great that the people have nothing to disturb them but their own waywardness and corruption. They quarrel upon dissensions of a doit, and split up into gangs of partisans of A, B, C, and D, without knowing why they prefer one to another. Caucuses, County, State, and National Conventions, public dinners, and dinner-table speeches two or three hours long, constitute the operative power of electioneering; and the parties are working-men, temperance reformers, Anti-Masons, Union and States-Rights men, Nullifiers, and, above all, Jackson men, Van Buren men, Clay men, Calhoun men, Webster men, and McLean men,

Whigs and Tories, Republicans and Democrats, without one ounce of honest principle to choose between them. New Hampshire is governed by a knave of the name of Isaac Hill, editor of a newspaper, mail contractor, and now a Senator of the United States — just cunning enough to grow rich by railing against the rich, and to fatten upon the public spoils, bawling Democracy. This is the besetting sin of popular governments, and it is now as it always has been. Van Buren is a demagogue of the same school, with a tincture of aristocracy — an amalgamated metal of lead and copper. There are five or six candidates for the succession to the Presidency, all of them demagogues, and not one of them having any consistency of system for the government of the Union.

Washington, Dec. 24. — I had hoped to finish by this day my second and abridged oration upon the life and character of La Fayette, but am disappointed, and have yet work for three or four days.

Dec. 31. — The House was called to order, as usual, at twelve o'clock. The journal of yesterday was read. At a quarter-past twelve I accompanied the members of the joint committee of arrangements on the part of the House . . . to the Senate-chamber, where seats had been assigned to us at the right hand of the Vice-President's chair. The President of the United States, with the Secretaries of State, Treasury, War, and Navy, the Postmaster-General, and Attorney-General, came in and took seats in front of the Secretary's table. At half-past twelve we proceeded to the House of Representatives: first the committee of arrangements of both Houses, whom I followed; then the Senate, preceded by their President; then the President of the United States and heads of Departments.

I took the Speaker's chair, which he left for the purpose, and I delivered an oration upon the life and character of La Fayette, which occupied two hours and fifty minutes. The House and galleries were crowded; many ladies in the seats of the members upon the floor. Immediately after closing, I left the Speaker's chair, which he resumed, and the House adjourned over to Friday. The President and the heads of Departments and the members of the Senate immediately withdrew. My voice held out far beyond my expectation. Many of the members greeted me with congratulation. I came home, relieved from great anxiety.

Jan. 18, 1835. — I paid a morning visit to Miss Harriet Martineau and Miss Jeffrey, her companion. She had brought me letters of introduction from Mr. Furness, of Philadelphia, and Mr. Charles Brooks, of Hingham, in company with whom Miss Martineau came from England. She is the author of *Conversations upon Political Economy,* which I have not read or seen. She is a young woman — I suppose about thirty; deaf, and hearing only through an ear-trumpet. Her conversation, however, is lively and easy, and she talks politics, English or American. I met there Mr., Mrs. and Miss Webster, and Mr. I. C. Bates.

Jan. 30. — Rode to the Capitol and attended the funeral of Warren Ransom Davis, a member of the House of Representatives from South Carolina. . . I rode to the grave-yard with Charles G. Ferris, from New York. As we were descending the broad flight of steps from the rotunda, on the eastern front of the Capitol, I heard the snap of a pistol, sounding like a squib. It was aimed at the President of the United States by an insane man named Lawrence, and it was said he snapped a second pistol; but I heard only one report. They both missed fire. The incident occasioned some commotion, but the funeral procession was not delayed.

Feb. 22. — The remainder of this day was absorbed in writing upon the present state of our dispute with France — a subject upon which my anxious feelings have outstripped the necessity of the case. My apprehension is not of war, but that the rights of the claimants under the treaty, and the honor of the country, will on this subject be ultimately sacrificed and abandoned.[2]

[2] In the matter of the French claims Adams magnanimously stood by President Jackson. By the treaty of 1831 France engaged to pay the United States an indemnity of $5,000,000, but this sum it proved impossible to collect. Jackson in irritation resolved either to have the money or a fight, and sent a message to Congress recommending that if France did not promptly pay her debt, letters of marque and reprisal should be issued against her commerce. The American Minister was at the same time ordered from Paris. Though many timid Americans denounced and opposed this vigorous course, Adams championed it with great gallantry and effectiveness.

CHAPTER XII

1835–1838

TWENTY-FOURTH AND TWENTY-FIFTH CONGRESSES — DEATH OF
MARSHALL — BENJAMIN LUNDY — THE SLAVERY QUESTION — ELEC-
TION OF VAN BUREN — THE STORM OVER ANTI-SLAVERY PETITIONS.

Washington, March 4, 1835. — Rose much exhausted, and
disqualified for all occupation. About the middle of the day
I rode to the Capitol, and spoke at the Clerk's office for the
documents and papers to be sent me during my stay here from
the postoffice of the House.

March 18. — In the evening Mr. Lyon called, and spent
an hour with me. The legislature of the State of Ohio have
passed an act directing their Governor to take possession of
the disputed territory by force; and the legislative council of
Michigan have resolved to make resistance also by force. . .
He said I had been the only cause of the failure of the bill in
the last House, and that the people in the Territory of Michigan were grateful to me for it.

Yes, grateful. I know what that means. Never in my life
have I taken in public controversies a part more suicidal to
my own popularity than on the present occasion. The people
of Ohio, Indiana, and Illinois will hate me with perfect hatred
for crossing their interests. The people of Michigan, while
the question is at issue, may pass cold resolutions of approbation or of thanks to me for espousing their cause, and then
forget me. I place in perpetual opposition to me, and to
everything that I propose or support, twenty-nine members of
the House and six of the Senate; and for all this and its consequences I have no compensation in prospect but the bare
consciousness of having done my duty.

March 26. — I finished this morning the draught of a
speech upon J. C. Calhoun's Patronage bill, which would fill
eleven columns of the *National Intelligencer,* and would take

between three and four hours to deliver. Upon reading it over, I find it is without method, and, in a great measure, without point — a desultory discussion upon the debate in the First Congress on the President's power of removal from Executive offices, with a severe and cutting review of Daniel Webster's speech in the Senate in favor of the bill. That speech is indeed so shallow, so unprincipled, and so subversive of all constitutional doctrine, that I could not possibly treat it with respect; but this is not wise. Some time past noon I walked to the Capitol, and looked into two volumes of Swift's Works, Scott's edition, for the passage cited in Johnson's Dictionary under the word " executive," but could not find it. I found, however, several references to Hobbes's opinions, and examined the folio volume of Hobbes's Works till three o'clock, when I was obliged to leave the library, which is closed at that hour. I did not find the word " executive " in his book. He speaks of legislative power, but scouts all ideas of mixed monarchy, and rejects with the utmost disdain all ideas of a division of powers. His *Leviathan* was published in Paris in 1751, three years after the execution of Charles the First. His book was exceedingly obnoxious — more, however, for its anti-religious than for its monarchical principles. He insists upon the sovereign's power to levy soldiers and taxes as he may need them. It seems to me there is nothing in the book worth retaining.

April 3. — The Whigs of Philadelphia have made a magnificent banquet at the Arch Street Theatre in honor of Mr. Poindexter, against whom the basest conspiracy ever witnessed in this country has been defeated and exposed, growing out of the attempt of Richard Lawrence to assassinate the President at the Capitol, on the 29th of January, the day of Warren R. Davis's funeral. Immediately after Lawrence's two pistols missed fire, the President said it was a Poindexter affair. Soon after, a man named Coltman, a member of the Common Council, suborned two men, named Fay and Stewart, to make affidavits that they had seen Lawrence go to Poindexter's house, and talking with him, a day or two before the attempted assassination. The President was treasuring up these affidavits, when they were communicated to Dutee J. Pearce when visiting at the house, and by him to Southworth, a newspaper correspondent and reporter. The facts got thus into the newspapers. Poindexter wrote to the President demanding an

explanation, but received no answer. Poindexter demanded
an investigating committee of the Senate; and there was one
appointed, who detected and exposed the conspiracy, so far at
least as to fasten the subordination by Coltman and the falsehood of the two affidavits. They reported a triumphant vindication of Poindexter's innocence, and the report was unanimously accepted by the Senate. The public indignation is thus
transferred from the assassin of the person to the assassin of
character, and Jackson himself bears no small portion of the
public odium. The Philadelphia Whigs turn it to political
account, and give a great festival to Poindexter, to celebrate
his escape from the conspiracy. Poindexter avails himself of
the occasion to make a flaming opposition speech, which may
be excusable in him, but which seems to me not well judged.
The whole affair is sickening to me, and looks too much as if
we were running into the manners of the Italian republics.

April 10. — My own time is swallowed up in seeking information upon subjects which there is reason to apprehend
will come up for consideration at the next session of Congress.
The further I press my enquiries into the Patronage bill, the
more occasion I find to reflect, to pause, and to prepare. The
reasoning of Mr. Clay, of Mr. Calhoun, and of Mr. Webster
appears to me all shallow and sophistical; but they speak to
popular prejudices, and it is true of great masses of men
as it is of individuals — he who is convinced against his will
is of the same opinion still. The task of eradicating prejudices seems to be desperate.

April 20. — I read over most of the debates in the Senate
through the memorable session of 1829–30, and made out a
list of all the speakers on the numerous questions involving
this constitutional principle. I perused also the Executive
Journal of that session, published as an appendix to the Legislative journal of the same session. It was Webster's speeches
and replies to Hayne in that session, in the debates on Foote's
resolution, which raised his reputation to the highest pitch,
and not without reason. They are monuments of eloquence
and debatable power. Neither he nor Hayne, in their speeches
on that resolution, introduced the patronage question; but
Foote himself and others did, particularly Clayton, Johnson,
Grundy, Livingston, and Bibb. The great effort of every
member was to show that he could make a tiresome, long
speech. Webster, however, putting his whole stake upon the

answer to Hayne, rather affectedly avoided noticing Benton, who was the great and real assailant. The policy of this is extremely doubtful. It seems to me, upon a review of the whole debate, that Webster should have answered Benton as well as Hayne; that he should have assumed the offensive against both, and exposed the profligate combination between nullification and the robbery of the public lands, which urged the joint attack of Benton and Hayne upon the East. This he did not do. He kept wholly on the defensive as to the East, and suffered Hayne to sacrifice all the rights of the old States to their portions of the public lands with impunity. This was the deadly poison of that league which brought in the Jackson Administration, and it has never yet been exposed. The failure of its consummation hitherto has been owing to the breach between Jackson and Calhoun, brought about by Van Buren; to the consequent precipitation of the nullification rebellion of South Carolina; to the compromise between Clay and Calhoun; and to Clay's Land bills, which, though defeated by Jackson's veto, have yet defeated, or rather delayed, the total sacrifice of the public lands, which yet Jackson openly recommended in his message of December, 1832.

April 24. — Mr. Van Buren, the Vice-President, paid me a morning visit. Our conversation was upon the surprising growth and increase of the city and State of New York in the half-century since I landed there from France, in July, 1785, when the population of the city was less than twenty thousand souls. It is now little short of two hundred and forty thousand, and still increasing with unexampled rapidity. He remarked that very few persons had made fortunes by this course of events, although the rise in the price of lands had kept full pace with the growth of population; that John Jacob Astor had systematically invested his property in lands, and had now an estate worth thirteen or fourteen, some said fifteen, millions of dollars. He said he himself had foolishly, two or three years since, sold the greater part of his own estate in lands, and that now the same lands were worth at least forty per cent. more than he sold them for.

July 10. — John Marshall, Chief Justice of the United States, died at Philadelphia last Monday, the 4th instant. He was one of the most eminent men that this country has ever

produced.   He has held this appointment thirty-five years.
It was the last act of my father's Administration, and one
of the most important services rendered by him to his country.
All constitutional governments are flexible things; and as the
Supreme Judicial Court is the tribunal of last resort for the
construction of the Constitution and the laws, the office of
Chief Justice of that Court is a station of the highest trust,
of the deepest responsibility, and of influence far more extensive than that of the President of the United States.   John
Marshall was a federalist of the Washington school.   The
associate judges from the time of his appointment have generally been taken from the Democratic, or Jeffersonian party.
Not one of them, excepting Story, has been a man of great
ability.   Several of them have been men of strong prejudices,
warm passions, and contracted minds; one of them, occasionally insane.   Marshall by the ascendency of his genius, by the
amenity of his deportment, and by the imperturbable command of his temper, has given a permanent and systematic
character to the decisions of the Court, and settled many great
constitutional questions favorably to the continuance of the
Union.   Marshall has cemented the Union which the crafty
and quixotic democracy of Jefferson had a perpetual tendency
to dissolve.   Jefferson hated and dreaded him.   Marshall
kept Jefferson much under the curb — sometimes, as perhaps
in the case of Aaron Burr's conspiracy, too much so; but Marshall's mind was far better regulated than that of Jefferson.
It is much to be feared that a successor will be appointed of
a very different character. . .

The death of Judge Marshall has occurred under circumstances of deep melancholy.   His disease was the stone.   He
had been saved and relieved about three years since by the
operation of lithotomy, performed with consummate skill by
Dr. Physick.   He had now been brought a few days before
his death to Philadelphia, for a further and last resource to
save him.   His eldest son, a man of more than forty years of
age, having a wife and family of six children, was at Baltimore, on his way to Philadelphia, to soothe with filial affection and tenderness the last moments of his father's life,
when, by the falling of the timber of a house, in a tornado,
upon his head, he was mortally wounded, and died, after being
trepanned, three or four days before his father.   Oh, how

much suffering is in the best and happiest condition of human existence!

Aug. 11. — There is a great fermentation upon this subject of slavery at this time in all parts of the Union. The emancipation of the slaves in the British West India Colonies; the Colonization Society here; the current of public opinion running everywhere stronger and stronger into democracy and popular supremacy contribute all to shake the fetters of servitude. The theory of the rights of man has taken deep root in the soil of civil society. It has allied itself with the feelings of humanity and the precepts of Christian benevolence. It has armed itself with the strength of organized association. It has linked itself with religious doctrines and religious fervor. Anti-slavery associations are formed in this country and in England, and they are already coöperating in concerted agency together. They have raised funds to support and circulate inflammatory newspapers and pamphlets gratuitously, and they send multitudes of them into the Southern country, into the midst of the swarms of slaves. There is an Englishman by the name of Thompson, lately come over from England, who is travelling about the country, holding meetings and making eloquent inflammatory harangues, preaching the immediate abolition of slavery. The general disposition of the people here is averse to these movements, and Thompson has several times been routed by popular tumults. But in some places he meets favorable reception and makes converts. There has been recently an alarm of slave insurrection in the State of Mississippi, and several white persons have been hung by a summary process of what they call Lynch's law; that is, mob-law. Add to all this the approach of the Presidential election, and the question whether the President of the United States shall be a slave-holder or not. They never fail to touch upon this key in the South, and it has never yet failed of success. Rouse in the heart of the slave-holder the terror of his slave, and it will be a motive with him paramount to all others never to vote for any man not a slave-holder like himself. There are now calls in the *Atlas,* the Webster paper, and the *Morning Post,* the Jackson and Van Buren paper, at Boston, for a town-meeting to put down the abolitionists; but the disease is deeper than can be healed by town-meeting resolutions.

Aug. 14. — The accounts of the riots in Baltimore continue. In the State of Mississippi mobs are hanging up blacks suspected of insurgency, and whites suspected of abetting them. At Charleston, South Carolina, mobs of slave-holding gentlemen intercept the mails and take out from them all the inflammatory pamphlets circulated by the abolitionists, who, in their turn, are making every possible exertion to kindle the flame of insurrection among the slaves. We are in a state of profound peace and over-pampered with prosperity; yet the elements of exterminating war seem to be in vehement fermentation, and one can scarcely forsee to what it will lead.

Nov. 23. — After dinner I had a visit from Mr. Fendall, and had much conversation with him respecting Jonathan Russell's Ghent conspiracy against me; a full account of which I gave him, from his private letter of 24th December, 1814, to Mr. Monroe, to his triplicate letter in *Walsh's Gazette* of May, 1822. Among the dark spots in human nature which, in the course of my life, I have observed, the devices of rivals to ruin me have been sorry pictures of the heart of man. They first exhibited themselves at college, but in the short time that I was there their operation could not be of much effect. But from the day that I quitted the walls of Harvard, Harrison Gray Otis, Theophilus Parsons, Timothy Pickering, James A. Bayard, Henry Clay, Jonathan Russell, William H. Crawford, John C. Calhoun, Andrew Jackson, Daniel Webster, and John Davis, W. B. Giles, and John Randolph, have used up their faculties in base and dirty tricks to thwart my progress in life and destroy my character. Others have acted as instruments to these, and among these Russell was the most contemptible, because he was the mere jackal of Clay. He is also the only one of the list whom I have signally punished.

Jan. 4, 1836. — I attended the House with feelings of no small anxiety. After the reading of the journal, the Speaker called the States for petitions, beginning with Maine.[1] When he came to Massachusetts, I presented the memorial of F. C. Gray, and others, praying for an Act similar to that which passed the Senate at the last session of Congress to indemnify them for French spoliations prior to the year 1800. The memorial was, at my motion, without reading, referred to the

---

[1] From this day dates the great struggle which J. Q. Adams waged to maintain the right of petition in the House of Representatives.

Committee of Foreign Affairs. I next presented the petition of Albert Pabodie and one hundred and fifty-three inhabitants of Millbury, in the county of Worcester and Commonwealth of Massachusetts, praying for the abolition of slavery and the slave-trade in the District of Columbia. The petition was couched in the same language with that which Briggs had presented last week, and which, after it had been referred to the Committee of the District of Columbia, was by a reconsidered vote laid on the table, together with the motion that it should be printed. I therefore now, after stating the contents of the petition from Millbury, said it was my intention to move that, without reading, it should be laid on the table.

I was instantly interrupted by my next neighbor, John M. Patton, who enquired whether the petition had been received; to which the Speaker answered that it had not; whereupon Thomas Glascock, a new member from Georgia, moved that it be not received, and was proceeding to make a speech, when I called him to order; and, appealing to the forty-fifth rule of the House, which prescribes that there shall be no debate upon petitions on the day when they are presented, I demanded that the debate should now be postponed to a day certain; that this day might be free for the receipt of petitions from all the States. The Speaker decided that as the petition had not been received, it was not in possession of the House, and that the fortieth rule of the House, interdicting debate, did not apply. From this decision I appealed, and asked for the yeas and nays; which were ordered, and a debate arose upon the appeal, which consumed the day. I spoke twice, the second time after a clamorous call for the question; but after I had spoken, Vinton, of Ohio, moved an adjournment; which was carried, leaving the question undecided.

Jan. 17. — I was writing an answer to a letter from Thaddeus Stevens, a member of the Pennsylvania Legislature, in which he asked my opinion of General William H. Harrison's Anti-Masonry. Stevens is the great Anti-Masonic leader in Pennsylvania at this time; he is also a partisan of Mr. Webster for the succession to the Presidency. He had a correspondence with Harrison upon Masonry, and was not satisfied with his answers.

Jan. 18. — Petition day at the House. My appeal from the decision of the Speaker had been postponed to this day, and was now, at the motion of Hawes, postponed again till Thursday next.[2]

[Here occurs a gap of nearly three months in the diary.]

Apr. 13. — Finished reading Holland's *Life of Martin Van Buren,* a partisan electioneering work, written with much of that fraudulent democracy by the profession of which Thomas Jefferson rose to power in this country, and of which he set the first successful example. Van Buren's personal character bears, however, a stronger resemblance to that of Mr. Madison than to Jefferson's. These are both remarkable for their extreme caution in avoiding and averting personal collisions. Van Buren, like the Sosie of Molière's *Amphitryon,* is " l'ami de tout le monde." This is perhaps the great secret of his success in public life, and especially against the competitors with whom he is now struggling for the last step on the ladder of his ambition — Henry Clay and John C. Calhoun. They indeed are left upon the field for dead; and men of straw, Hugh L. White, William H. Harrison, and Daniel Webster, are thrust forward in their places.

May 18. — Immediately after the reading of the journal, H. L. Pinckney presented the report of the select committee to whom all the abolition petitions were referred, and said that the report had the unanimous assent of the committee. He moved that five thousand copies of the report should be printed for the use of the House. It was immediately attacked with extreme violence, and a fiery debate arose, which continued until one o'clock, and then, by a suspension of the rules, for another half-hour. Motion was made to print ten thousand and twenty thousand copies, and Waddy Thompson said he would commit it to the flames or to the hangman.[3]

[2] Adams on this day renewed the struggle over abolition petitions. He presented several, including one signed by 148 Massachusetts ladies; " for, I said, I had not yet brought myself to doubt whether females were citizens." Hammond made the usual motion not to receive; and then a New York Democrat, Gideon Lee, offered a new device for choking off anti-slavery petitions in the shape of a motion that the motion not to receive be laid on the table. On Feb. 8 this new scheme was referred to a select committee under H. L. Pinckney as chairman.

[3] Adams does not describe or summarize the report of Pinckney's committee. This report declared, first, that Congress had no power to interfere with slavery in any State; second, that Congress ought not to interfere with slavery in the District of Columbia; and third, that since the agitation of the topic was disquieting, all petitions or papers relating to slavery " shall, without being either printed or referred, be laid upon the table, and that no further action whatever

Philadelphia, July 9. — Atlee, Edwin B.; Barton, Isaac; Semple, Matthew; Buffum, Arnold. The four persons named came this morning as committees — 1. Of the Pennsylvania Society for Promoting the Abolition of Slavery; 2. Of the Philadelphia Anti-Slavery Society, with votes of thanks to me and to the other members of Congress who, at the late sessions of Congress, opposed the influence of the slavery predominant party in that body. . . I declined attendance at any public meeting of the societies, and said I believed the cause itself would be more benefited by such service as I could render to it in the discharge of my duty in Congress than by giving notoriety to any action on my part in support of the societies or in connection with them. They acquiesced in these determinations, and declared themselves well satisfied with the result of this interview.

July 11. — With praise and prayer to God, and a solemn sense of my earthly condition, and hopes of a better world, I enter upon the seventieth year of my pilgrimage. Benjamin Lundy came this morning, and, in a conversation of about two hours, made me acquainted with his principles, prospects, and purposes relating to slavery. He was heretofore the editor of the *Genius of Universal Emancipation,* and has now the intention of commencing the publication of a newspaper devoted, like that, to the extinguishment of slavery — a cause which, within the last two or three years, has fallen into great discouragement. He solicited assistance from me for the matter of his exposed publication, but I thought best not to give him any expectation of it.

After dinner, Mr. William B. Reed came in, but I had not time to converse with him. Benjamin Lundy came at six, and I walked with him to the house of his friend James Mott, No. 136 North Ninth Street, where there was a large tea and evening party of men and women — all of the Society of Friends. I had free conversation with them till between ten and eleven o'clock, upon slavery, the abolition of slavery, and other topics; of all which the only exceptionable part was the undue proportion of talking assumed by me, and the indiscretion and vanity in which I indulged myself. Lucretia Mott, the mistress of the house, wife of James Mott, is a native of

---

shall be had thereon." All three resolutions were passed over Adams's protest; the third by the vote of 117 to 68. Such was the origin of the famous gag-rule.

the island of Nantucket, and had heard of my visit there last September. She is sensible and lively, and an abolitionist of the most intrepid school. Benjamin Lundy and another friend came home with me to Mr. Biddle's, and Lundy came in, and conversed with me nearly another hour.

Quincy, July 22. — This afternoon Alderman Greeley and Hunting, and the members of the Common Council of the city of Boston, came out as a committee and invited me, in the name of the city government, to deliver before them an eulogy upon the life and character of the late James Madison.

Aug. 8. — Mr. Edward Everett, now Governor of the Commonwealth, and Mrs. Everett, paid us a morning visit; and he gave me a volume of his orations and speeches recently published. They are among the best ever delivered in this country, and, I think, will stand the test of time. The custom of delivering orations on public occasions was introduced into this country by the Boston massacre of 5th March, 1770, of which there were thirteen delivered successively till 1783, in Boston town-meeting. The 4th of July was then substituted for the yearly town oration, and these have been continued till the present time. Other towns and cities have followed the example, and other occasions have been taken for the delivery of similar discourses, till they have multiplied so that they now outnumber the days of the year. Of the thousands and tens of thousands of these orations, which teem in every part of this country, there are, perhaps, not one hundred that will be remembered " alteri seculo; " and of them, at least one-half have been, or will be, furnished by Edward Everett. He has largely contributed to raise the standard of this class of compositions, and his eloquence has been the basement story of his political fortune — as yet, one of the most brilliant ever made in this Union.

July 29. — Mr. Greenleaf brought me a message from Mr. Armstrong, the Mayor, requesting me to fix a day for the delivery of the eulogy on Mr. Madison. This is rather embarrassing, as I do not see the end of my work, and have yet much to write, and more to revise. I have come now to Mr. Madison's course of conduct relating to the Alien and Sedition Acts, a subject of extreme difficulty to manage, inasmuch as it forms, in the opinion of his party friends, perhaps the greatest of his merits and services, while I myself believe him to have been in error throughout the whole of those transactions. To refresh my memory on these subjects, and to retrace the history of those controversies more accurately, I read over the portion of Jefferson's correspondence during that period, published by his grandson. It shows his craft and duplicity in very glaring colors. I incline to the opinion that he was not altogether conscious of his own insincerity, and deceived himself as well as others. His success through a long life, and especially from his entrance upon the office of Secretary of State under Washington until he reached the Presidential chair, seems, to my imperfect vision, a slur upon the moral government of the world. His rivalry with Hamilton was unprincipled on both sides. His treatment of my father was double-dealing, treacherous, and false beyond all toleration. His letter to Mazzei, and his subsequent explanations of it, and apologies for it, show that he treated Washington, as far as he dared, no better than he did my father; but it was Washington's popularity that he never dared to encounter. His correspondence now published proves how he dreaded and detested it. His letter to my father, at the first competition between them for the Presidency, the fawning dissimulation of his first address as Vice-President to the Senate, with his secret machinations against him from that day forth, show a character in no wise amiable or fair; but his attachment to those of his friends whom he could make useful to himself was thoroughgoing and exemplary. Madison moderated some of his excesses, and refrained from following others. He was in truth a greater and a far more estimable man.

Aug. 30. — I wrote little, and continued reading the letters of Jefferson from 1793 till August, 1803, published by his grandson. His duplicity sinks deeper and deeper into my mind. His hatred of Hamilton was unbounded; of John Marshall, most intense; of my father, tempered with compunctious visitings, always controlled by his ambition. They had been cordial friends and coöperators in the great cause of independence, and as joint Commissioners abroad after the Peace of 1783; there had then been a warm and confidential intimacy between them, which he never entirely shook off, but which he sacrificed always to his ambition, and, at the last stage of his life, to his envy and his poverty; for he died insolvent, and on the very day of his death received eleemosynary donations from the charity of some of those whom he had most deeply injured.   This circumstance is not creditable to his country.   She ought not to have suffered a man, who had served her as he had, to die with his household wanting the necessaries of life.   But it was the natural consequence of the niggardly doctrines which his political system had imposed upon him, and which he had passed off upon the country for patriotism.   Among his slanders upon the Administration of my father was the charge of extravagance in diplomatic expenditure; and when he sent Mr. Monroe on the Louisiana mission to France, he wrote to him that he could not have an outfit, and that the refusal of outfits was one of his reforms upon extraordinary missions.   The end of all which was, that Mr. Monroe obtained not only the outfit, but gratuities and allowances more than any other Minister abroad has ever had, and dies leaving still unsatisfied claims.   I am compelled to draw many other harsh conclusions against this great man from his now published letters.

Sept. 2. — I looked this day into Mr. Wirt's life of Patrick Henry, to see his account of the debates in the Virginia Convention upon the Constitution of the United States, and of Henry's opinion and conduct on the occasion of the Alien and Sedition laws.   It seems difficult to reconcile them together. His opposition to the Constitution was founded perhaps on the peculiarity of his situation.   His opinions then were in the highest tone of republican doctrine, and his aversion to the consolidation of the Union deeply rooted.   This makes his approbation of the Alien and Sedition laws the more extraordinary.   But in truth the opposition to those laws was merely factious.   The main argument of Mr. Madison's report against the Alien law was, that it applied to alien friends when such measures should be applied only to alien enemies. But there was a fallacy in it.   The foreign emissaries against whom the Alien Act was pointed were in no wise friends of this country.   They were chiefly Frenchmen.   Jefferson, in his Correspondence, says its principal object was Volney.   The relative situation of the United States and France at that time was . . . such that measures of defence against French secret emissaries were more necessary than they would have been in avowed and open war.   The Sedition Act was an ineffectual attempt to extinguish the fire of defamation; but it operated like oil upon the flames.

Sept. 27. — Tuesday; Boston; eulogy on James Madison. . . Two hours and a half were occupied in the delivery, and yet I omitted much of the abridgment of my discourse in the copy made chiefly by my son. The house was crowded to the utmost of its capacity. I had undertaken this task with a most painful anxiety and fear that I might be disabled from performing it altogether — an anxiety much sharpened by the illness which for the last three days had almost extinguished my voice. I did get through, but with extreme difficulty, with frequent imperfections of delivery, without being able to raise my voice to be heard throughout the house, and with entire conviction that I must never again engage to address such an auditory on a day fixed beforehand, or, indeed, upon any day, or any occasion. Forty-three years and more have passed away since I first spoke to a crowded audience in Boston. My voice is now gone; my eyes are in no better condition. The day was uncommonly darkened with clouds, and threatened rain the whole morning; there was a heavy shower while I was speaking, and, the house being lighted only by skylights from above, there were parts of the time when I found it impossible to read, and was obliged to pass over towards the end, or repeat from memory. The delivery was accordingly bad, and I was under much agitation, with the fear that I should be forced to break off in the midst of my address and declare my inability to proceed. There was, however, an uninterrupted and fixed attention of the auditory throughout the whole time, occasional slight cheerings of applause, and at the close a full and long-continued manifestation of satisfaction. Mr. Abbott Lawrence and Mr. Stephen C. Phillips were the first to greet me with their hands, and the expression of warm and entire approbation.

Sept. 28. — I read the article from the *North American Review* upon nullification, sent to me by Mr. Edward Everett, and written by him in 1830. I read also the letters from Mr. Madison to him upon the subject, of the same date. I have undertaken to mark, in very explicit terms, the difference between the opinions, the purposes, and the conduct of Mr. Madison and Mr. Jefferson with reference to the Alien and the Sedition Acts. They were very remarkably different. I

foresee that this may engage me in a controversy with the
Jeffersonian school of the South, and that it will be specially
unpalatable in Virginia.   There are many considerations
which make this exceedingly hazardous at my time of life, but
after long deliberation I have concluded that there is a duty
for me to perform — a duty to the memory of my father; a
duty to the character of the people of New England; a duty
to truth and justice. If controversy is made, I shall have an
arduous and probably a very unthankful task to perform, and
may sink under it; but I will defend my father's fame. I will
vindicate the New England character, and I will expose some
of the fraudulent pretences of slave-holding democracy.   I
pray for temper, moderation, firmness, and self-control; and,
above all, for a pure and honest purpose; and, if it so please
Heaven, for success.

Nov. 3. — I received a letter from S. S. Southworth expressing in terms of extravagant applause his opinion of the
eulogy, and requesting a copy of it. Quite probably he may
publish a bitter and sneering critical review of it. Jefferson
paid Callender for reviling and slandering my father, and
called it charity. Webster paid Southworth, or at least promised to pay him, for reviling and slandering me, and may call
it charity, if he has paid. Southworth is one of the best representatives of the class of political writers for hire in this
country. He has been one of the most virulent lampooners
upon me of the whole tribe, and has written me many letters
full of kindness and veneration.

Washington, Nov. 11. — The excitement of the Presidential election is here as we have found it all along on the road.
The remarkable character of this election is, that all the candidates are at most third-rate men whose pretensions rest
neither upon high attainments nor upon eminent services, but
upon intrigue and political speculation. The Presidency has
fallen into a joint-stock company. Jackson came in upon the
trumpet tongue of military achievement. His Presidency has
been the reign of subaltern knaves, fattening upon land jobs
and money jobs, who have made him believe that it was a
heroic conception of his own to destroy the Bank of the United
States, and who, under color of this, have got into their own
hands the use of the public moneys, at a time when there is a
surplus of forty millions of dollars in the Treasury.   Two

political swindlers, Amos Kendall and Reuben M. Whitney, were the Empson and Dudley of our Solomon, and, by playing upon his vanity and his thirst of petty revenge, have got into their own hands the overflowing revenue of the country; with the temporary and illegal use of which they are replenishing their own coffers and making princely fortunes. Jackson has wearied out the sordid subserviency of his supporters, and Van Buren has had the address to persuade him that he is the only man who can preserve and perpetuate the principles of his Administration. And as his term of eight years has run through, and his gang are weary of his sway, he has set his heart upon bringing in Van Buren as his successor, and has successfully exercised all his influence to promote that result.

The opposition, divided between three talented aspirants to the Presidency, neither of whom would yield subordination to either of the others, have been driven in mere desperation to set up men of straw in their places, and they have taken up Hugh Lawson White and William Henry Harrison, as the Israelites set up a calf, and as the Egyptians worshipped oxen and monkeys. White and Harrison are men of moderate capacity, but of varied public service, and of long experience in the affairs of the nation. They are as competent for the Presidency at least as Jackson, and, like him, if elected to his station would rule by the proxy of subalterns — by party management and political love-potions. White and Harrison are now the golden calves of the people, and their dull sayings are repeated for wit, and their grave inanity is passed off for wisdom. This bolstering up of mediocrity would seem not suited to sustain much enthusiasm; but a practice has crept in of betting largely upon the issue of elections, and that adds a spur of private, personal, and pecuniary interest to the impulse of patriotism. This is the exciting cause of all the ardor which we have met with throughout this journey.

Nov. 25. — I wrote a few lines to Governor Edward Everett, and to John H. Eastburn, of whom I have asked another hundred copies of the eulogy on James Madison. This is occasioned by a number of applications which I have received from various persons, strangers to me, and who have just curiosity enough to see the work, without being at the cost of a quarter of a dollar to pay for it. There are in the eastern, central, and western parts of the country multitudes of collectors of pamphlets of this description, who bedaub me with flattery for gratuitous copies of my speeches and orations, while others do them about equal honor by malicious and caustic reviews. There is in the Boston *Courier,* which Gales this day sent me, such a review of the eulogy on Madison, by a blue-light federalist of the Hartford Convention school, while in the *Telegraph* newspaper of this day there is a deadly onset upon me from the clanking chains of a Southern slave-holder for my speech upon the Texan imposture last June.

Dec. 5. — Precisely at noon, James K. Polk, Speaker of the House of Representatives of the United States, took the chair of the House, and announced that this was the day fixed by the Constitution of the United States for the annual meeting of Congress. The names of the members were called over alphabetically by States, beginning with Maine, and one hundred and fifty-four members answered at the first call.

Dec. 6. — At the meeting of the House, Dutee J. Pearce, chairman of the committee on the part of the House to notify the President that the two Houses were ready to receive any communication from him, said they had performed the service, and that he was requested by the President to inform the House that he would make a written communication to both Houses at twelve o'clock this day. The message was accordingly brought in immediately afterwards, and took the Clerk nearly an hour and a half to read. The message repeatedly alludes to the fact of its being the last annual message that will ever be addressed to Congress by him. It teems with glorification upon the prosperous condition of the country, with a considerable spice of piety; a hasty and not very satisfactory view of the state of our foreign relations; an unsettled boundary question with Great Britain; long-standing claims of indemnity upon the Belgian Government; no reference to the quarrel with Buenos Ayres, but a boastful notice of a commercial treaty with Siam; a very lame account of the wanton disregard of the rights of nations in the invasion of the Mexican territories; there is excuse, apology, extenuation, and a flimsy argument to justify the invasion; a recommendation to pass the Act for settling the boundary between the United States and Mexico, and earnest caution to preserve a strict and faithful neutrality between Texas and Mexico, with expressions of much regret that Gorostiza, the Mexican Minister, had returned home.

But three-fourths of the message consisted of a dissertation upon banks, banking, and the currency, with a new tribunitian invective against the Bank of the United States; a lamentation over the excesses of money in the public treasury; a direct thrust at the compromise tariff, and abundance of verbiage about gold and silver and the injustice of bank paper to the laboring poor.

Dec. 7. — This is the day of the meeting of the Electoral Colleges for the choice of a President and Vice-President of the United States for four years from the 4th of March next. It is already well ascertained that a majority of the whole number of the votes will be for Martin Van Buren, of New York, as President, and almost certain that Richard M. Johnson, of Kentucky, will be the Vice-President.

Dec. 22. — A message was received from the President concerning the new republic of Texas — the recognition of her independence, and her application to be annexed to the United States. This message was in a tone and spirit quite unexpected to me, and certainly to a large portion of the House — a total reverse of the spirit which almost universally prevailed at the close of the last session of Congress, and in which the President notoriously shared. This message discourages any precipitate recognition of Texas, and speaks with due caution and reserve of its annexation to the United States.

Dec. 24. — A succession of visitors from almost immediately after breakfast till past three o'clock kept me at home. . . I asked Cushing if there would be a report from the Committee of Foreign Affairs on the President's message concerning Texas. He had some doubts.

Cushing, as a member of that committee, concurred in their excellent senseless report of the 4th of July last, on Texas, screwed through the House by the previous question, without allowing one word of discussion. The tone is now totally changed. Waddy Thompson told me yesterday that he would give me the report of General James Hamilton to the Senate of South Carolina upon the subject, which spoke the sentiments of the people of that State; the message of the Governor, McDuffie, did not. Hamilton's report was published in the *Telegraph* of last evening. It represents the Texans as a people struggling for their liberty, and therefore entitled to our sympathy. The fact is directly the reverse — they are fighting for the establishment and perpetuation of slavery, and that is the cause of the South Carolinian sympathy with them. Can this fact be demonstrated to the understanding, and duly exhibited to the sentiment, of my countrymen? with candor, with calmness, with moderation, and with a pencil of phosphoric light? Alas, no!

Dec. 26. — At the House, W. C. Dawson, a member from Georgia, who comes in the place of Coffee, deceased since the close of the last session, was qualified, and took his seat. Petitions called for by States. I presented the petition of Joseph Page and twenty-six citizens of the town of Silverlake, Susquehanna County, Commonwealth of Pennsylvania, praying for the abolition of slavery and the slave-trade in the District of Columbia.

Pickens, of South Carolina, attempted to raise a question upon the reception of the petition, and appealed to the resolutions of the last session.

The Speaker said it was too late, the petition being already in possession of the House; and he considered the resolutions of the last session as expired with the session itself.

Davis, of Indiana, called up the resolution that he had offered, and which was on the Speaker's table, that all petitions which may be offered praying for the abolition of slavery in the District of Columbia, or in the Territories, shall be laid on the table without reading or being printed, and without debate.

Davis had not the wit to see that his resolution instigated the very debate that he wanted to suppress.

I said the resolution deserved a full and thorough consideration, and I hoped would have it. But I suggested to him the expediency of moving to postpone, and make it the special order of some future day, to avoid interrupting the presentation of petitions.

Davis's friends moved to lay his resolution and the whole subject on the table; which was done, by yeas and nays — one hundred and sixteen to thirty-six.

Dec. 31. — The year 1836 has been a year of some vicissitude in my public life and in my private concerns — strewed with roses and beset with thorns; for the results of which I bow in grateful homage to the Disposer of all events. A year of severe trials, which I have sustained without sinking, by the aid of a merciful protector, but which, in the course of nature, I cannot expect to sustain me much longer. The year began by a desperate and furious, yet insidious and crafty, onset upon my character by Daniel Webster, in the form of a speech in the Senate on the 14th of January, published with great flourishes of trumpets in the *National Intelligencer* of the 18th. I answered by the offer of a resolution of enquiry and a speech on the 22d of the same month; it demolished the speech of Webster, drove him from the field, and whipped him and his party into the rank and file of the nation in the quarrel with the French King. But it opened upon me the whole pack of the Presidential opposition candidates, and their abettors in and out of Congress, who would have sunk me into perdition temporal and eternal if they had had the power. I weathered this storm, and was re-elected to the next Congress without formal opposition, but almost without Whig votes. The delivery of the eulogy upon President Madison was the principal incident of the year; and was successful. I have to bless the giver of all good for improved health — not only my own, but that of my dearest friend.

Jan. 2, 1837. — Intense cold, with a strong gale from the northwest, and a clear sky. The visitors were fewer than they have ever been upon a New Year's day since we have resided in this house. The cause of this, besides the severity of the weather, was, that for the first time for many years the President's house was not opened to visitors. Many of them, before or after going there, were accustomed to come here. But the President had some weeks since a bleeding of the lungs, from which, though much recovered, he remains yet too feeble to receive multitudes of visitors. In addition to which, it is but three days since he received the tidings of the death of Mrs. Donelson, the wife of his Secretary, and who has always lived with him at the President's house.

[Here is a blank in the record, extending beyond the remainder of the Twenty-Fourth Congress. This is to be regretted the more that it passes over in silence the memorable attempt to censure Mr. Adams on the 23d of January, in the House of Representatives, consequent upon the presentation by him of twenty-one petitions, some of them purporting to come from slaves. This was the first of his great struggles in that cause. The history of this proceeding was, however, very fully given by himself in another form, printed soon after the close of the session. The pamphlet has the following title: Letters from John Quincy Adams to his Constituents of the Twelfth Congressional District in Massachusetts; to which is added his Speech in Congress delivered February 9th, 1837. Boston, published by Isaac Knapp, No. 25 Cornhill, 1837. The introductory remarks bear the initials of John G. Whittier.]

April 2. — I wrote to Mr. Biddle, and read the printed letter of Gerrit Smith to the Rev. James Smylie, late state clerk of the Presbytery of Mississippi, author of a book in defence of slavery, to which this letter is an answer. I have read scarcely anything upon this controversy, and am quite incompetent to discuss it myself. I come to the conclusion without examining the premises. I have an abhorrence of slavery, but how bad it is no one can imagine without understanding the details. Smylie defends slavery as an institution sanctioned by the Scriptures. The punishment of death was prescribed for a multitude of what we should consider very trivial offences. The theory of the rights of man was then utterly unknown; and Mr. G. Smith shows that the servitude of that time was a milder condition than the slavery of the present age and of this country. This subject of slavery, to my great sorrow and mortification, is absorbing all my faculties.

April 8. — I read this morning in the manuscripts of Mr. Madison the report of the speech of Alexander Hamilton in the Convention of 1787, upon presenting his plan for a Constitution of the United States. The speech occupied a whole day, and was of great ability. The plan was theoretically better than that which was adopted, but energetic, and approaching the British Constitution far closer, and such as the public opinions of that day never would have tolerated. Still less would it be endured by the democratic spirit of the present age — far more democratic than that; for, after half a century of inextinguishable wars between the democracy of the European race and its monarchy and aristocracy, the democracy is yet in the ascendant, and gaining victory after victory over the porcelain of the race. If Hamilton were now living, he would not dare, in an assembly of Americans, even with closed doors, to avow the opinions of this speech, or to present such a plan even as a speculation.

April 13. — There was a gathering this morning of perhaps a hundred laborers in the front yard of the President's house. It was said their object was to remonstrate against working more than ten hours a day. It was said the President sent them word that he could not parley with them so long as they should present themselves in that manner.

April 15. — In the library, I took up the second volume of Matthias's edition of Gray's Works, and wandered over it till the clock struck three and warned me to depart. I found in it the analysis of the writings of Plato, which I had no time to examine, but which I hope to find time to look into hereafter. I read some of his letters to his mother, to his father, and to his friend West, and mused over that affecting incident, that Gray's *Ode to Spring* was sent by him when first written in a letter to West, who died just before he should have received it. I have literary tastes peculiar to myself, and the correctness of which I distrust, because they differ from the general voice. There is no lyric poet of ancient or modern times who so deeply affects my feelings as Gray. Every one of his odes is to me an inestimable jewel, and nothing in all Dr. Johnson's writings is so disgusting to me as his criticisms upon them. *The Progress of Poesy* and *The Bard* are the first and second odes that ever were written; Dryden's *Alexander's Feast,* Horace's *Carmen Saeculare,* and Collins's *Passions,* pari passu, come after; Pindar's *Pythics* are admirable, and Anacreon is charming as a songster; but the *Progress of Poesy* is the point of the pyramid — the first of odes — as the *Churchyard* is the first of elegies. Yet I have read scarcely anything of Gray except the very small collection of his poems; and these two thick quartos of his works are almost all new to me. Why is it that I must reproach myself for an hour given to them as wasted time?

April 19. — I answered a letter from John G. Whittier, inviting me, on the part of the managers of the Massachusetts Anti-Slavery Society, to attend the meeting of the New England Anti-Slavery Convention at Boston, to be held on the last

Tuesday of May. I have not absolutely declined to attend, but have assigned reasons for not attending, which will probably be decisive to my own mind. Upon this subject of anti-slavery my principles and my position make it necessary for me to be more circumspect in my conduct than belongs to my nature. I have, therefore, already committed indiscretions, of which all the political parties avail themselves to proscribe me in the public opinion. The most insignificant error of conduct in me at this time would be my irredeemable ruin in this world, and both the ruling political parties are watching with intense anxiety for some overt act by me to set the whole pack of their hireling presses upon me.

It is also to be considered that at this time the most dangerous of all the subjects for public contention is the slavery question. In the South, it is a perpetual agony of conscious guilt and terror attempting to disguise itself under sophistical argumentation and braggart menaces. In the North, the people favor the whites and fear the blacks of the South. The politicians court the South because they want their votes. The abolitionists are gathering themselves into societies, increasing their numbers, and in zeal they kindle the opposition against themselves into a flame; and the passions of the populace are all engaged against them. The exposure through which I passed at the late session of Congress was greater than I could have imagined possible; and, having escaped from that fiery furnace, it behooves me well to consider my ways before I put myself in the way of being cast into it again.

April 25. — Walked to the Capitol, and visited the library of Congress. I examined the second volume of Gales and Seaton's collection of American State papers on their foreign relations. I found among them many valuable public documents which I had not before seen, or had very slightly perused — among the rest, several memoirs of Robert R. Livingston, addressed to Napoleon, dissuading him from the settlement of his colony in Louisiana, and then to cede it to the United States. It seems as if there was something providential in the turn of all those transactions. The Spanish monarchy was an old, worn-out, rotten Government, dropping to pieces by the weight of its own corruptions — Napoleon shaking it almost to atoms, first by war, then stripping it of its European possessions, encroaching upon it over the Pyrenees to the Ebro; forcing its pusillanimous Bourbons to abdicate, and the father and mother, with her despicable paramour, Godoy, to go and die in ignominious obscurity at Rome, and the son Ferdinand — ame lache et pusillanime, as General Pardo characterized him to me — to abdicate and pine in prison at Bayonne.

In the preliminary steps to all this process, because Louisiana had once been a French colony, Napoleon undertakes to recover it, and to settle there a *military* colony of his veteran soldiers — having a triangular view for futurity upon Mexico, upon Canada and the British northern Colonies, and upon the United States. R. R. Livingston was then Minister from the United States at his Court, and ingratiated himself by falling in without scruple into the ultra-royal etiquette of the Imperial upstart; and, coming from the stern Republican Government of the United States, this species of adulation was more flattering than it could be from the representatives of monarchs. Mr. Livingston thus obtained access to the ear of Napoleon, who received and read his papers. They had no effect until the war with Great Britain came on; but then they found the mind prepared for the reception of argument, and when the war was once resolved on, Louisiana became a burden, which it was the clear interest of France to get rid of as soon as possible, and upon as good terms as she could obtain. The finger of Heaven appears in all this; and when we think of Mr. Jay's proposing, in 1786, to renounce the navigation of the Mississippi for twenty-five years, and, in 1794, negotiating for the delivery of the posts on the Canadian Lakes, and observe the condition of things now, when the city of Mexico can scarcely be kept out of our clutches, we can but contemplate with wonder the ways of God to man. But upon looking at our two frontiers, north and south, it is no pleasing consideration to find that while our boundary has been constantly advancing on the south it has been receding at the north.

April 27. — I have cleared off the arrears of my correspondence, with the exception of several letters from strangers asking for autographs — a recent fashion, like that of keeping albums. The album is, I believe, a German invention, never introduced till of late years into this country, and now perverted by its multiplication and its degeneracy into a mere

catalogue of insignificant names. Those in which sentiments
are added are records of human imbecility, bushels of chaff
without the two grains of wheat. Ashamed to write my bare
name in answer to a request for an autograph, I have usually
added a few lines of rhyme, without reason.

For the last two months there have been a succession of
enormous failures in New Orleans and New York, extending
to Philadelphia, Boston, and partially to other cities. The
blowing-up has been the most extensive in New York where,
after various other abortive expedients, a great Whig meeting
was held, and a committee of fifty persons appointed to come
to Washington to remonstrate with him (the President)
against the Administration, and to demand — 1, that he
should rescind the Treasury circular forbidding the Western
land offices to receive anything but gold and silver in payment
for the public lands; 2, that he would order a suspension of
the collection of the custom-house bonds till next January; 3,
that he would convoke Congress at an early day. A sub-
committee of fifteen members are said to have been here yesterday and this day. At their first interview with President
Van Buren he required that whatever proposition they had to
offer should be made in writing. This was accordingly done,
and the general rumor is that the answer was negative upon
all the demands.

May 6. — Before leaving the city I thought it a decent
mark of courtesy to visit Mr. Van Buren at the President's
house. I went accordingly, and was received by him in his
cabinet alone. I had not before set my foot in the house since
I left it on the evening of the 3d of March, 1829. The conversation with Mr. Van Buren was upon subjects of a general
nature, and not at all upon the public affairs of the country —
upon the inconvenience of a summer residence in this city, and
on my custom heretofore, when under that necessity, of bathing and swimming every morning in the Potomac; then upon
the general state of European politics.

Quincy, June 1. — These gentlemen came as a committee
of the delegation in the House of Representatives of the Commonwealth from the towns composing the Twelfth Congressional District of Massachusetts. Mr. Thayer, on their
part, read to me an address, and left it with me, expressing
their approbation of my conduct as their Representative in

Congress, especially at the last session, and presented me a cane made of the timber of the frigate *Constitution*.

Aug. 23. — The District Convention of delegates from the towns of the Twelfth Congressional District of Massachusetts convened to pass resolutions approving of my conduct at the last session of Congress, in the discussions upon the right of petition and against the annexation of Texas to the United States, was held this day at the Town Hall. . . I addressed them for about an hour and a half on their resolutions. I was frequently interrupted by cheering applause, and, although my speech was far below mediocrity, it was very favorably received. Mr. May then moved that some poetical lines which he had read, written by Mr. Pierpont, of Boston, should be published with the proceedings of the meeting; which was agreed to without opposition. The meeting was then dissolved, and notice was given that at half-past seven o'clock this evening the Rev. Samuel J. May would deliver a lecture on the right of petition. A number of copies of the pamphlet edition of my letters to the inhabitants of the Twelfth Congressional District were gratuitously distributed.

Aug. 29. — In Boston, I was going to call on Dr. George Parkman, when I met Mr. Abbott Lawrence in the street, and he took me with him to his house, where I had with him a conversation of nearly two hours. He has just returned from an excursion to New York and Philadelphia. Three of the deposit banks at New York have issued a circular inviting a convention of all the banks, to consult about a simultaneous resumption of specie payments. Mr. Lawrence told me that neither the Philadelphia nor the Boston banks would comply with the invitation of the New York banks. He also told me that Mr. Nicholas Biddle was under the impression, which he did not share, that the Executive Government of the United States would be compelled, and were already disposed, to return to the Bank of the United States for the collection and disbursement of the revenue.

Philadelphia, Sept. 1. — I went to the Anti-Slavery office, 223 Arch Street; thence to Samuel Webb's house, and afterwards to Benjamin Lundy's office. I saw and had long conversations with them both, and with two or three others whom I found with them, of whom was Mr. Buffum, who told me he was a hatter. Lundy returned with me to my lodgings. He and the abolitionists generally are constantly urging me to indiscreet movements, which would ruin me and weaken and not strengthen their cause.   My own family, on the other hand — that is, my wife and son and Mary — exercise all the influence they possess to restrain and divert me from all connection with the abolitionists and with their cause.   Between these adverse impulses my mind is agitated almost to distraction.   The public mind in my own district and State is convulsed between the slavery and abolition questions, and I walk on the edge of a precipice in every step that I take.

Washington, Sept. 9. — I called at the President's house, and spent half an hour in conversation with him respecting the weather, the climate, and Queen Victoria, the girl of eighteen, sovercign of all the British dominions — " Youth at the prow, and Pleasure at the helm."   I had been told that in these troublous times Mr. Van Buren was so deeply affected by them that he looked extremely wretched; but I found no such thing.   He had every appearance of composure and tranquillity.   He spoke, indeed, of the cares and afflictions of the station which he now occupies, and said it was surprising how universal the delusion was that anyone could be happy in it; and he spoke of the calm, philosophical spirit of Dr. Franklin, and of Mr. Madison, who, he said, had expressed to him a very high esteem for me.

There are many features in the character of Mr. Van Buren strongly resembling that of Mr. Madison — his calmness, his gentleness of manner, his discretion, his easy and conciliatory temper.   But Madison had none of his obsequiousness, his sycophancy, his profound dissimulation and duplicity.   In the last of these he much more resembles Jefferson, though with very little of his genius.   The most disgusting part of his character, his fawning servility, belonged neither to Jefferson nor to Madison.

Sept. 16. — I called at the office of the Secretary of State, and saw Mr. Forsyth.   He told me that the correspondence with Mexico, with Texas, and with Great Britain concerning the Northeastern boundary, would be sent in next week.   He said that no proposition for the cession of Texas had ever been made to the Mexican Government; that when Butler had been Chargé d'Affaires there, he came back here once all of a sudden, and made the old General believe that if he would give him sufficient authority he would not only make the proposition, but would accomplish the object. He was furnished with the authority, sent back, and never made the proposition. His reliance had been upon what he believed was the disposition of Santa Anna.

From the Department of State I went to the office of Mr. Peter Force, the Mayor of the city. He is preparing a vast collection of ancient documents relating to the history of this country, and has a very great and curious collection of his own.

Sept. 20. — H. R. U. S. I presented twelve petitions and remonstrances against the admission of Texas into the Union. Many others were presented by other members.

Sept. 28. — H. R. U. S. I presented petitions for the abolition of slavery in the Territories; for refusing the admission of any new slave-holding State into the Union; and for the prohibition of the inter-State slave-trade.

With the last I asked leave to offer a resolution calling upon the Secretary of the Treasury to report at the next session of Congress the number of slaves exported from, and imported into, the several ports of the United States by the coasting trade. There was what Napoleon would have called a superb "No!" returned to my request from the servile side of the House.

Sept. 29. — H. R. U. S. I reached the House at the instant of time to present fifty-one petitions and remonstrances against the order of the House of Representatives of the 18th of January, 1837; which was to lay on the table, without printing, or further action of the House upon them, all petitions, resolutions, and papers in any manner relating to slavery. Most of these were received by me during the last session; but the majority of the House, by evading after the 6th of February the reception of all petitions, excluded the reception of these, and of one hundred and fifty others all of which I have now presented, and they have all been received and laid on the table.

Oct. 3. — This being the last of the thirty days from the commencement of the session for the presentation of petitions, I presented two against the annexation of Texas; but I reserve a considerable number for the winter session. F. O. J. Smith obtained leave of absence for his colleague, George Evans, from next Monday for the remainder of the session. Evans is one of the ablest men and most eloquent orators in Congress.

His powers of reasoning and of pathos, his command of language, and his elocution, are not exceeded by any member of this Congress; much superior to the last. The last effort that he made was in January, 1836, and was the most furious personal philippic against me that ever was delivered; afterwards printed in a pamphlet and circulated by thousands in my own district. I never answered him, though I wrote a full and complete answer, which I was prepared to deliver had the occasion presented itself. I have not spoken to him since his outrageous and unprovoked attack upon me, with whom he had always before been upon terms of professed friendship. But the other day he silently rose and offered me a chair on which he was sitting; and I can hardly forgive myself for not offering him, as I had a strong impulse to do, my hand.

Oct. 10. — Committee of the whole on the state of the Union. The Divorce or Sub-Treasury bill from the Senate was called up — not by Cambreleng, but by Pickens, of South Carolina, who made in support of it a prepared speech of two hours, with which he has been swelling like a cock turkey ever since Calhoun's bargain and sale of himself to Van Buren, at the commencement of this session. Pickens is a fixture to the house of Calhoun, and Van Buren bought him with Calhoun. Cambreleng tickles his vanity by pushing him forward as the champion of this bill, and saving himself the trouble and the odium of this task, which indeed he could not have performed himself. Pickens is a coarse sample of the South Carolina school of orator statesmen — pompous, flashy, and shallow. Legaré is another, much more polished, better educated, and better disciplined; a fine speaker, a brilliant scholar, but yet a shallow bottom. He opposed the taking up of this bill; but it was carried against him. Pickens's speech was a jumble of indigested political economy, of abuse upon Jackson for his war against the bank, of abuse, repeated from Calhoun, upon banks, banking, and the bank, of South Carolina nullification, of slave-driving autocracy, and of ranting radicalism. He said, if the abolitionists of the North would preach insurrection to the Southern slaves, he would retort upon them by preaching insurrection to the laborers against the capitalists of the North.

Oct. 13. — Committee of the whole on the State of the Union, Smith in the chair. Sub-Treasury or Bank Divorce bill;

Dawson's substitute the question. Legaré, of Charleston, South Carolina, delivered one of the most eloquent speeches, of two hours, ever pronounced in that hall; against the bill, asking for time; dealing altogether in generalities; descanting upon the march of intellect, the progressive improvement in the condition of mankind, the wonders effected by the modern system of credit, and the steam-engine. He glanced obscurely at the subject of slavery, and dashed away from it as if between fear and shame to speak about it at all. He contrasted the condition of this country with that of Europe with regard to the progress of improvement, quoted a number of recent English writers on political economy, and referred to his own observations during his late residence and travels in Europe.

Legaré has not the ideal form of an orator — short, thick, with a head disproportioned in size to his body; a fattish, ugly, but intelligent face, dark complexion, and slightly limping left foot; but his voice is strong; his enunciation distinct, though rapid; his action not graceful, but energetic; his intonations alternately high and low; and his command of language copious and ornamental. He is, like Hoffman, rather of the English than the American school, and will surely rank among the distinguished orators of the nation. . .

Oct. 14. — I retired to the chamber of the Committee on Manufactures, and wrote a letter to my wife. I have found this so agreeable and so useful a manner of transacting the business in the House, and disposing of the time in the recess, that I regretted the single exception of the day, when, by the invitation of Elisha Whittlesey, I went and dined with him at his lodgings. Five or six small crackers and a glass of water give me a sumptuous dinner. I consume an hour and a quarter in writing a letter, and the time passes like a flash of lightning. I am calm and composed for the evening session, and far better prepared for taking part in any debate than after the most temperate dinner at home or abroad.

Oct. 24. — This morning I visited Mrs. Madison, who has come to take up her residence in this city. I had not seen her since March, 1809. The depredations of time are not so perceptible in her personal appearance as might be expected. She is a woman of placid, equable temperament, and less susceptible of laceration by the scourges of the world abroad than most others. The term of her husband's Presidency was tem-

pestuous and turbulent; but he weathered the storm by that
equanimity which carried him also through an eventful period
and a boisterous age. The two closing years of his Presidency
terminated his political life with honor and tranquillity, eminently successful in its general result and glorious individuality
to him. The succeeding twenty years she has passed in retirement — so long as he lived, with him, and now upwards of a
year since his decease. She intended to have removed to this
place last autumn, but was prevented by an inflammatory disease in her eyes, from which she has almost wholly recovered.
There is no trace of it in her appearance now.

Nov. 1. — Nathan Allen, the husband of the woman and
father of the children sold last week, came this evening with
the subscription paper to pay Birch for them. They are now
in jail, waiting for this money to be raised to have them delivered over to the husband and father. I subscribed fifty dollars, to be paid if the sum be made up to complete the purchase.

Nov. 9. — The black man Nathan Allen came again about
the contribution to purchase his wife and children, which he
finds it very difficult to accomplish. He said General Smith,
of Georgetown, had agreed to endorse the balance of the sum
which was to be paid for the redemption of his wife and children; but the doubt remains whether they will be emancipated.

Nov. 16. — In the evening I read to the ladies three chapters of the *Life of Aaron Burr,* by Matthew L. Davis — two
extraordinary men, perhaps such as no other part of this
Union could have produced. Burr's life, take it all together,
was such as in any country of sound morals his friends would
be desirous of burying in profound oblivion. The son and
grandson of two able and eminent Calvinistic divines, he had
no religious principle, and little, if any, sense of responsibility
to a moral Governor of the universe. He lost both his father
and mother before he was three years old, and with them appears to have lost all religious education. He lived and died
as a man of the world — brave, generous, hospitable, and
courteous, but ambitious, rapacious, faithless, and intriguing.
This character raised him within a hair's breadth of the Presidency of the United States, sunk him within a hair's breadth
of a gibbet and a halter for treason, and left him, for the last
thirty years of his life, a blasted monument of Shakespeare's
vaulting ambition. There are in the chapters that I read this

evening three of his collegiate essays; something above mediocrity, but not much. His principle for style was simplicity.

Nov. 17. — Dr. Mayo paid me a morning visit, with a
prospectus of a book which he proposes to publish under the
title of *Eight Years' Residence in Washington* — that is, a
secret history of the Kitchen Cabinet, the Hickory Club, and
the Administration of Andrew Jackson. . . In his pamphlet
already published, called " A Chapter of Sketches on Finance,"
Dr. Mayo has disclosed a curious history of the transactions
of this Hickory Club; but of the whole pamphlet the most
curious part is a letter to President Jackson from himself, under the secret of the Masonic cipher, dated 2d December,
1830, containing a detailed account of Samuel Houston's
conspiracy against Texas at that time. And Dr. Mayo showed
me this morning a confidential letter from President Jackson,
in his own handwriting, to Mr. Fulton, then Secretary of the
Territory of Arkansas, and now a Senator from that State,
dated 10th December, 1830, sternly denouncing this project
against Texas, and instructing him by all the means in his
power to defeat and break it up. These papers, the Doctor
told me, were all returned to him from President Jackson in
1836 at his own request, and among them was, he supposed
by mistake, this original letter from Jackson; but whether it
had ever been sent to Fulton he did not know, and doubted;
but he referred to it as a demonstration of the duplicity of
Jackson's Administration with regard to the relations of the
country with Mexico and Texas.

It is so, and proves that Jackson's bold and dashing character was nevertheless capable of double-dealing worthy of
Ferdinand the Catholic or of Tiberius Cæsar. All the proceedings relating to Texas and Mexico have been in the same
style.

Nov. 22. — There was a riotous assemblage of people,
perhaps three hundred in number, with a cannon, who went
round last night to the President's house and the houses of
some of the heads of Departments, discharged their cannon,
and made much disturbance, in celebration of the Whig victories in the late elections, especially in the State of New York.
I heard little of it myself, though it once awoke me out of
sleep, and I knew not what it was. This effervescence of
popular feeling is too common and too little discountenanced

by any of the predominant parties; both of them use the populace to glorify their triumphs and to depress their enemies, and both of them suffer for it in turn. The most atrocious case of rioting which ever disgraced this country happened on the night of the 7th of this month at Alton, in the State of Illinois, where a man by the name of Lovejoy, one of the leading abolitionists of the time, has been striving to establish a newspaper. Three times he had imported printing-presses in the place, and three times they had been destroyed by mobs, and once or twice the offices in which they were placed. The fourth time the press was imported and deposited in a merchant's warehouse. The mob assembled in the night, surrounded the warehouse, and demanded that the press should be delivered up to them. It was refused. They assailed the house with musketry, forced their way into it, set fire to the roof of the building, shot Lovejoy dead, wounded several others, till the press was delivered up to them, which they broke in pieces and threw into the river. One of the assailants also, by the name of Bishop, was killed in the affray.

This Lovejoy wrote me a letter last January, which I answered in April. He was a man of strong religious, conscientious feeling, deeply indignant at what he deemed the vices and crimes of the age. Such men are often fated to be martyrs; and he has fallen a martyr to the cause of human freedom.

Dec. 5. — The House at noon was called to order. . . Van Buren's message gave me a fit of melancholy for the future fortunes of the republic. Cunning and duplicity pervade every line of it. The sacrifice of the rights of Northern freedom to slavery and the South, and the purchase of the West by the plunder of the public lands, is the combined system which it discloses. It is the system of Jackson's message of December, 1832, covered with a new coat of varnish.

Dec. 6. — In the evening I wrote to Mr. Philip Ammidon, and read in the second volume of Burr's *Life*. Matthew L. Davis, its author, is here, as he has been during several late sessions, as a correspondent of the New York *Courier and Enquirer*. He writes under the signature of "The Spy in Washington." He came to my seat this morning, and I told him I was reading his book. His account of the origin of the political parties in New York during the Revolutionary War, and of their subsequent bearing on the fortunes of Burr, throws some light upon the history of the time. The failure of my father's re-election in 1801 was the joint work of Burr and Alexander Hamilton; and it is among the most remarkable examples of Divine retributive justice, that the result to them was the murder of one of them in a duel, and the irretrievable ruin of the murderer by the very accomplishment of his intrigues. Even-handed justice never held a better balance scale. Between my father and Jefferson the final decision of that same justice was reserved for a higher state of being. The double-dealer succeeded in this world; yet his death-bed was less tranquil and composed than that of him whom he had wronged.

Dec. 12. — As soon as the journal was read, the Speaker called the States for petitions, beginning with Maine. When the turn of Massachusetts came, I waited till all the other members from the State had presented their petitions, and then offered first, all the petitions and memorials which I had presented at former sessions, and which had not been finally acted upon, and had them referred to the appropriate committees. I then called up the memorial of Feuchtwanger, and a memorial from Vermont, praying for retrenchment and reform, and had them referred to the Committee on Ways and Means. . .

I next presented a petition for the abolition of slavery and the slave-trade in the District of Columbia, and moved its reference, with all petitions on the same subject presented at the special session, to the committee on the District of Columbia. Wise moved to lay all these on the table; which was carried, by yeas and nays — 135 to 73. I offered several others, with the same result, till Lawler objected to receiving one; but upon the yeas and nays the vote was 144 to 60 to receive, but it was immediately laid on the table. Then I presented a petition for the abolition of slavery in the Territories; which again was laid on the table, by a vote of 127 to 73. I then left the remaining anti-slavery petitions to be presented hereafter.

Dec. 20. — Slade's motion of Monday, to refer a petition for the abolition of slavery and the slave-trade in the District of Columbia to a select committee, came up.

Polk, the Speaker, by some blunder had allowed Slade's motion for leave to address the House in support of the peti-

tion without putting the question of laying on the table. So
Slade today got the floor, and in a speech of two hours on
slavery, shook the very hall into convulsions. Wise, Legaré,
Rhett, Dawson, Robertson, and the whole herd were in com-
bustion. Polk stopped him half a dozen times, and was forced
to let him go on. The slavers were at their wits' ends. At
last one of them *objected* to his proceeding, on the pretence
that he was discussing slavery in Virginia, and on this pretence,
which was not true, Polk ordered him to take his seat. A
motion to adjourn, made half a dozen times before out of
order, was now started and carried by yeas and nays.

Formal notice was immediately given by a member of a
meeting of all the slave-holding members in the chamber of
the Committee on the District of Columbia. Most if not all
of the South Carolina members had left the hall.

Dec. 21. — H. R. U. S. The journal had disfigured and
falsified the transactions. Slade moved to amend the journal
so as to state the facts correctly; but his motion was rejected.
Patton had a resolution ready drawn, agreed upon at the
slavery meeting of yesterday — a resolution like that of the
16th of January last — that no petitions relating to slavery
or the trade in slaves in any State, district, or Territory of
the United States shall be read, printed, committed, or in any
manner acted upon by the House.

I objected to the reception of the resolution, and Patton
moved to suspend the rules; which was carried — 136 to 65;
and after a speech, he moved the previous question; which
was carried, as was the resolution.

When my name was called, I answered, " I hold the resolution to be a violation of the Constitution, of the right of petition of my constituents, and of the people of the United States,
and of my right to freedom of speech as a member of this
House."

I said this amidst a perfect war-whoop of " Order! " In
reading over the names of the members, the clerk omitted
mine. I then mentioned it, and the Speaker ordered the clerk
to call my name again. I did not answer, but moved that my
answer when first called should be entered on the journal.
The Speaker said the motion was not in order; that the only
answer that could be given was aye or no. I moved that my
motion might be entered on the journal, with the decision of

the Speaker that it was not in order; to which he made no answer.

Dec. 22. — H. R. U. S. On the reading of the journal, I found my motion, yesterday made, to insert on the journal my answer to the gag resolution. I moved to amend the journal by inserting that when my name was called, I rose and said, "I hold the resolution to be a violation of the Constitution of the United States, of the right of petition, of my constituents, and of the people of the United States, and of my rights to freedom of speech as a member of this House."

Boon asked if my motion was debatable. I said I hoped it was, and that the House would allow me to debate it. Boon moved to lay my motion on the table. I asked for the yeas and nays, but they were refused, and the motion was laid on the table; but my answer was entered on the journal. Patton had come charged with a speech to prevent the entry upon the journal. Boon's motion to lay mine on the table balked him, and I bantered him upon his resolution, till he said that if the question ever came to the issue of war, the Southern people would march into New England and conquer it. I said I had no doubt they would if they could, and that it was what they were now struggling for with all their might. I told him that I entered my resolution on the journal because I meant his name should go down to posterity damned to everlasting fame.

Jan. 1, 1838. — The new year began with one of the most beautiful days that the course of the seasons ever brought round — a clear sky, a bright sun, a calm atmosphere, and all physical nature moving in harmony and peace. The President's house was open, as usual, from eleven in the morning to eight in the afternoon, and was crowded with visitors innumerable. I was not among them. I have found it necessary to assume a position in public towards him and his Administration which forbids me from any public exhibition of personal courtesy which would import a friendly feeling. Mr. Clay, whose public position, not precisely the same as mine, differs little from it, went and escorted Mrs. Bell of Tennessee, wife of the late Speaker of the House. They afterwards came here, as did about three hundred ladies and gentlemen of those who had been at the President's house. Mr. Clay told me that he had twice during his visit spoken to Mr. Van Buren, and the second time congratulated him upon his happiness in being surrounded by *so many of his friends;* to which Mr. Van

Buren answered, "The weather is very fine." No insignificant answer, for it implied his conscious assent to the satirical reflection implied in Clay's remark — fair-weather friends.

Jan. 15. — H. R. U. S. Petitions, beginning with Virginia, going south and west, and then back from Wisconsin through to Maine. There were a great multitude of abolition and anti-Texas petitions from all the free States; all laid on the table. I presented nearly fifty myself.

Jan. 28. — I received this day thirty-one petitions, and consumed the whole evening in assorting, filing, endorsing, and entering them on my list, without completing the work. With these petitions I receive many letters, which I have not time to answer. Most of them are so flattering, and expressed in terms of such deep sensibility, that I am in imminent danger of being led by them into presumption and puffed up with vanity. The abolition newspapers — the *Liberator, Emancipator, Philanthropist, National Enquirer,* and New York *Evangelist,* all of which are regularly sent to me, contribute to generate and nourish this delusion, which the treacherous, furious, filthy, and threatening letters from the South on the same subject cannot sufficiently counteract. My duty to defend the free principles and institutions is clear; but the measures by which they are to be defended are involved in thick darkness. The path of right is narrow, and I have need of a perpetual control over passion.

Feb. 14. — Henry, of Pennsylvania, moved and carried a suspension of the rules, that the States might be called for the presentation of petitions. The call commenced with me, and I presented three hundred and fifty petitions; of which one hundred and fifty-eight were for the rescinding of the Patton gag, or resolution of 21st December; sixty-five for the abolition of slavery and the slave-trade in the District of Columbia; four in the Territories; seventeen for the prohibition of the internal slave-trade; two against the admission of any new State whose constitution tolerates slavery; and fifty-four against the annexation of Texas to the Union. . .

There was one, praying that Congress would take measures to protect citizens of the North going to the South from danger to their lives. When the motion to lay that on the table was made, I said that "in another part of the Capitol it had been threatened that if a Northern abolitionist should go to North Carolina and utter a principle of the Declaration of

Independence — " Here a loud cry of " Order! Order "
burst forth, in which the Speaker yelled among the loudest.
I waited till it subsided, and then resumed, " that if they could
catch him they would hang him." I said this so as to be
distinctly heard throughout the hall; the renewed deafening
shout of " Order! Order! " notwithstanding. The Speaker
then said, " The gentleman from Massachusetts will take his
seat; " which I did, and immediately rose again, and presented
another petition. He did not dare to tell me that I could not
proceed without permission of the House; and I proceeded.
The threat to hang Northern abolitionists was uttered by
Preston, of the Senate, within the last fortnight.

March 10. — I went into the Senate chamber, where I
found John C. Calhoun discoursing to his own honor and
glory, and vituperating Henry Clay — upon which delicious
topics he had already been two hours occupied, and used up
another hour after I went in. It was the settlement of accounts
which Calhoun had threatened when Clay attacked him a fortnight or three weeks ago. Clay replied instantly, saying that,
though much indisposed, he would not take three weeks to
concoct a retort upon the Senator from South Carolina. He
was from a half to three quarters of an hour, and had manifestly the advantage in the debate. Calhoun had affected to
consider himself as on the defensive in this contest. But between the special and the present session of Congress he had
written a letter at Fort Hill, his residence, to vindicate himself
for his change of party, in which he declared that he had no
reason to confide in the firmness or patriotism of the Whigs,
and that if he continued to act with them the fruits of victory
would all go to them, and not to him and his friends. Clay
took his text from that letter, and drove him from his defensive ground irrecoverably. There was rejoinder, surre-
joinder, rebutter, and surrebutter. The truth and the victory
were with Clay, who closed with a taunting hope that the
settlement of accounts was as satisfactory to the Senator from
South Carolina as it was to him. Clay spoke of the South
Carolina nullification with such insulting contempt that it
brought out Preston, who complained of it bitterly. These
personal oratorical encounters between Clay and Calhoun are
Lilliputian mimicry of the orations against Ctesiphon and for
the crown, or the debate of the second Philippic.

May 27. — After dinner at St. John's Church. . . There were scarcely thirty persons in the House. The neglect of public worship in this city is an increasing evil, and the indifference to all religion throughout the whole country portends no good. There is in the clergy of all the Christian denominations a time-serving, cringing, subservient morality, as wide from the spirit of the Gospel as it is from the intrepid assertion and vindication of truth. The counterfeit character of a very large portion of the Christian ministry of this country is disclosed in the dissensions growing up in all the Protestant churches on the subject of slavery. The abolitionists assume as the first principle of all their movements that slavery is sin. Their opponents, halting between the alternative of denying directly this position and of admitting the duty binding upon them to bear their own testimony against it, are prevaricating with their own consciences, and taxing their learning and ingenuity to prove that the Bible sanctions slavery; that Abraham, Isaac, and Paul were slaveholders; and that St. Paul is the apostle of man-stealers, because he sent Onesimus back to his master Philemon. These preachers of the Gospel might just as well call our extermination of the Indians an obedience to Divine commands because Jehovah commanded the children of Israel to exterminate the Canaanitish nations. This question of slavery is convulsing the Congregational Churches in Massachusetts; it is deeply agitating the Methodists; it has already completed a schism in the Presbyterian Church.

June 23. — Morning hour. Texas. On the system of suppression. I alluded to the transactions in the House from the 6th to the 11th of February, 1837. Slave petitioning. I was called to order by Legaré, and peremptorily stopped by the Speaker. I called on the Speaker to have the disorderly words taken down. He refuses. I appeal from his decision. He is sustained, by the yeas and nays — 115 to 36; 205 members in the House. I resumed speaking for one minute. . .

Saw Shakespeare's *As You Like It*. Ellen Tree for Rosalind; all the other parts wretchedly performed. — Jaques by Fredericks, who had no conception of the part, left out some of the finest passages, spoke some set down for others, and delivered with lifeless insipidity the " Seven Ages."

June 24. — Attended at St. John's Church. I spoke to President Van Buren, and asked half an hour's conversation with him at six o'clock this evening; to which he acceded. I went to the President's, and putting into his hand the letter which I have received in duplicate from R. Rush of 15th May, requested him to read it. I then had a conversation with him of two hours upon the Smithsonian bequest, referring to my report, and entreating him to have a plan prepared to recommend to Congress for the foundation of the Institution at the commencement of the next session of Congress. I suggested to him the establishment of an astronomical observatory, with a salary for an astronomer and assistant, for nightly observations and periodical publications; then annual courses of lectures upon the natural, moral, and political sciences; and above all, no jobbing — no sinecures — no monkish stalls for lazy idlers.

Dec. 14. — W. B. Calhoun presented several slavery abolition petitions, all at once; upon which Mr. Wise objected to their being received. The Speaker said that, under the resolutions which had been adopted by the House, the question of reception could not be made. From this decision Wise took an appeal. . . At last Taylor, of New York, called for the previous question; which was carried — the main question being, whether the decision of the Speaker should stand. When my name was called by the clerk, I rose and said, " Mr. Speaker, considering all the resolutions introduced by the gentleman from New Hampshire as — " The Speaker roared out, " The gentleman from Massachusetts must answer aye or no, and nothing else. Order ! "

With a reinforced voice — " I refuse to answer because I consider all the proceedings of the House as unconstitutional." While in a firm and swelling voice I pronounced distinctly these words, the Speaker and about two-thirds of the House cried, " Order ! Order ! " till it became a perfect yell. I paused a moment for it to cease, and then said, " A direct violation of the Constitution of the United States." While speaking these words with loud, distinct, and slow articulation, the bawl of " Order ! Order ! " resounded again from two-thirds of the House. The Speaker, with agonizing lungs, screamed, " I call upon the House to support me in the execution of my duty ! " I then coolly resumed my seat.

CHAPTER XIII
1839–1841

THE TWENTY-SIXTH CONGRESS — WEBSTER AND WHITTIER — SHOULDER DISLOCATED — WILLIAM HENRY HARRISON ELECTED — HIS INAUGURATION AND DEATH — ACCESSION OF TYLER.

Washington, March 23, 1839. — I have determined to accept the invitation of the New York Historical Society to deliver, if I possibly can, an address before them on the 30th of next month, the fiftieth anniversary of the inauguration of George Washington as first President of the United States. I have brought myself to this conclusion with extreme repugnance, and under a sense of obligation to that Society which I cannot suppress. The subject is rugged with insurmountable difficulties. My reputation, my age, my decaying faculties, have all warned me to decline the task. Yet I cannot resist the pressing and repeated invitations of the Society.

April 18. — I took up this day and read some pages of a small volume — *Narrative and Correspondence concerning the Removal of the Deposits and Occurrences Connected Therewith, by William J. Duane.* There is a meekness of manner in this narrative, and in the correspondence on the part of the author, which excites compassion, and contrasts with the crafty and scratching style of the papers written by Amos Kendall and signed by Andrew Jackson.

April 27. — *Saturday.* Cars from Washington to Baltimore from six to eight. T. H. Benton; stopped at the Relay House for Western Railroad to Missouri. Call at R. Gilmer's in the country. Cars from Baltimore to Philadelphia. Gunpowder seventeen miles, Bush River twenty-four, Havre de Grace, Susquehanna, thirty-five miles from Baltimore. Five miles further, axle-tree of our locomotive broke; sent back for another engine; detained more than two hours. Mr. Newkirk a fellow-passenger. Go ahead. Take steamboat *Robert Morris* at Wilmington. Land at new wharf, Philadelphia, at seven — sunset.

New York, April 30, v 30. — *Tuesday.* Jubilee of the inauguration of George Washington as first President of the United States. . . At eleven a.m., meeting of the Historical Society at the City Hotel. At noon, short procession to Middle Dutch Church, corner of Nassau Street. Prayer by the pastor; ode by the choir. I delivered an address of two hours; well received. Crowded church. Mr. D. Duer, president of the Columbia College, accompanied me to my lodgings. I then went with him and Charles to the college; saw the library, and portraits of presidents and professors. Return to my lodgings; two hours' repose. At five p.m., dinner at the City Hotel of three hundred persons.

May 24. — Foul weather. A cold northeast storm confined me to the house almost the whole day. I ought to have done much; mais helas! il n'en est rien. There is such seduction in a library of good books that I cannot resist the temptation to luxuriate in reading; and, because I have so much to write, I count all time lost that is not spent in writing.

I finished reading Dr. Channing's letter to Jonathan Phillips upon slavery. He demolishes all the argument of Clay's speech — which is, indeed, nothing at all. The remark of Junius, that the arguments of tyranny are as despicable as its power is dreadful, applies especially to all arguments in behalf of slavery.

June 13. — Miss Cutts has a small album with engraved devices at the top of some of the pages. There are some pretty lines of Edward Everett's upon a cottage, and two lines, equally ingenious and delicate, from Mr. Madison signed J. M.:

> Errors, like straws, upon the surface flow;
> He who would search for pearls must look below.

And *below* are verses of Mrs. Madison. There is a flat complimentary prosaic of Mr. Clay. Miss Martineau says that Watts is laid under contribution for all the album poetry in the country. I have seen very little in any album so good as the worst verses of Watts. I have kept copies of all my contributions to albums, and I sicken at the sight of them.

Oct. 6. — I have heretofore held a correspondence with

Mr. James H. Hackett upon Shakespeare's tragedy of *Hamlet*. I this day received a letter from him, dated London, August, 1839; on opening of which, the first thing that met my eye was, as I thought, my own letter to him of 19th February last from Washington, but which on examination I found was a lithographic copy of mine, which he says he had taken because he had lent the original to so many of his numerous friends and acquaintances that it had been nearly used up. The lithographic copy of my letter is so perfect a facsimile that, if it had been presented to me as the original, I should have acknowledged it without an instant of hesitation as my own, but for a notification at the bottom of the fourth page, in characters so small as to be scarcely legible with the naked eye, that it was lithographed for Mr. Hackett. And with this letter there was a packet containing three lithographic portraits of himself . . . one in his own person, engraved for the New York *Mirror* in 1833, one in the character of Monsieur Mallet, and one in the character of Falstaff in *Henry the Fourth*. . . Mr. Hackett in his letter mentions also that he has very recently heard of an analysis by me of the tragedy of *Othello,* and enquires where he can procure it. This extension of my fame is more tickling to my vanity than it was to be elected President of the United States.

Dec. 2. — About eleven o'clock I walked to the Capitol, and found the hall of the House of Representatives swarming with members, new and old. After half an hour of mutual greetings, precisely at noon the clerk of the last House of Representatives called the meeting to order, and said that, according to the established rule of usage, he should call over the roll of members, of whom he had formed a list, by States. He then began with Maine, called over the six New England States and New York, and Joseph M. Randolph, of New Jersey. He then said there were five other seats from the State of New Jersey, which were contested; and, not feeling himself authorized to decide the question between the contesting parties, he would, if it were the pleasure of the House, pass over the names of those members and proceed with the call till a House shall be formed, who will then decide the question.[1]

---

[1] The obstacles to the organization of the Twenty-sixth Congress were formidable. The seats of five claimants from New Jersey, who brought the regular gubernatorial certificate of election, were contested by five other claimants. The holders of the certificates were all Whigs; their opponents were all Democrats.

This gave rise to a debate which continued till past four o'clock, when a motion was made to adjourn. The Clerk said he could put no question, not even for an adjournment, until the House itself should be formed. There could nothing be done but by general consent. There was then a general call to adjourn; and, although one voice cried " No! " and others called out to adjourn till eleven o'clock, the Clerk declared the House adjourned till twelve.

This movement has been evidently prepared to exclude the five members from New Jersey from voting for Speaker; and the Clerk had his lesson prepared for him. Under color of a modest disclaimer of the right to decide between the conflicting claimants, he sets aside the five members from their seats, and excludes them from voting at the organization of the House. It seems to have been supposed that this course would be acquiesced in by the whole House, for the Clerk was unprepared to meet the objection to it. His two decisions form together an insurmountable objection to the transaction of any business and an impossibility of organizing the House. He stops the call before a quorum of the House is formed, and then refuses to put any question until there shall be a quorum formed. The most curious part of the case is that his own election as Clerk depends upon the exclusion of the New Jersey members.

Dec. 3. — Vanderpoel, Rhett, Cave Johnson and Bynum made party speeches, frothy with the rights of the people, technicalities, and frauds, till after four o'clock, when a motion was made to adjourn — the clerk still persisting in his refusal to put any question until the House should be organized, and Cushing telling him that he should not consider the House adjourned unless by a vote. The Clerk said he would judge upon inspection around him whether a majority of the members were in favor of adjourning; and then he declared the House adjourned, Cushing and others calling out, " A count! a count! " and Wise, as the members were rushing out of the hall, saying " Now we are a mob."

So evenly were the two parties divided in the House that the admission or exclusion of the Whigs would determine the political character of the body. The clerk wished to keep them out until the organization of the House could be determined; and his effort to do so raised a terrific storm. The story of Adams's intervention in this struggle is one of the dramatic chapters of his career

Dec. 5. — This day Randolph got the floor. . . Immediately on his taking his seat, I rose and said, " Mr. Clerk," and obtained the floor. I then turned to the House, and said, " Fellow citizens, members-elect of the Twenty-sixth Congress of the United States." I showed them the necessity I was under of addressing them directly, the two decisions of the Clerk having rendered it impossible for the House to proceed at all unless by an appeal from the Clerk to them. I then called upon them in the name of the people, of their country, and of mankind, to organize themselves. I offered, finally, the resolution yesterday presented by Graves, ordering the Clerk to call the members from New Jersey possessing credentials from the Governor of the State; and I declared my determination to put the question to the meeting myself. I said any member might offer an amendment to my resolution, which would bring the question before the meeting to an immediate issue. . . Two members of the House conducted me to the chair.

Dec. 12. — Randolph, of New Jersey, presented a protest of the five commissioned members from that State who were yesterday refused the right to vote, which he demanded should be inserted on the journal of the House. Thereupon a petulant debate, in which Bynum said that Randolph ought to be expelled for offering the protest. A great struggle against the reading of it; but it was read. Then another struggle to escape the question whether it should be inserted on the journal; finally decided by yeas and nays — 114 to 117 — that it should not. In the meantime the roll had been called, according to the first part of Rhett's resolution, excluding the members from New Jersey, and the House was constituted.

Dec. 16. — When I went to the House this morning, it was with a firm conviction that Dixon H. Lewis, the Silenus of the House — a Falstaff without his wit or good humor — would be chosen Speaker, probably at the first trial. . . At the eleventh trial of 232 votes Robert M. T. Hunter of Virginia had 119, and was chosen. He finally united all the Whig votes, and all the malcontents of the Administration. I then, upon receiving the report of the tellers, read it, and announced that Robert M. T. Hunter, having received a majority of all the votes given, was elected Speaker of the House. I requested Mr. Banks and Mr. Lawrence to conduct the Speaker to the chair, and Lewis Williams, the oldest member of the House, to administer to him the oath. My functions were at an end. I resigned to him the Speaker's chair, and retired to my seat, with an ejaculation of gratitude to God for my deliverance. At the motion of Wise, the House immediately adjourned; and I walked home with a lightened heart.

Dec. 25. — I received this afternoon from James F. Otis a newspaper published at New York, called *Brother Jonathan,* in which is printed, announced as from the original manuscript, a poem by me, called *The Vision,* written in 1789 or 1790, while I was a student at law in the office of Theophilus Parsons, at Newburyport. It is nearly fifty years since I had seen this effusion of my early love, and on reading it now the first impression on my mind is that I have never since written anything equal to it. But I had no copy of it myself and knew not that a copy existed in the world.

Dec. 26. — Before dinner I visited President Van Buren, and while I was there the Vice President, Richard M. Johnson, came in, with another Kentuckian whom I did not know. Colonel Richard M., whose Vice-Presidential chair, it is said, is to be gently drawn from under him at the next Presidential election, appeared much elated in effecting his passage over the snow-choked mountains, so as to reach this city the evening before last. He thought it a fair parallel to Napoleon's passage over the Alps. It cost him fifty dollars for extra carriage hire, an inflexible determination to achieve what all the stage-drivers and inn-keepers pronounced impossible, and sundry bumps on the head, having been twice overset.

Mr. Van Buren is growing inordinately fat. His son Abraham, lately returned from England, was with him.

Jan. 1, 1840. — From eleven in the morning till four p.m. there was a succession of friendly visitors, as has been usual on the New Year's day since we left the President's house. Neither my wife nor Mary received visitors, and I was left to entertain the ladies as I could. This ceremony grows more and more irksome to me every year. The young and the prosperous may take pleasure in the recollections of the past and the anticipations of the future which associate themselves with the commencement of the year; but the idea which ought first and last to present itself to the mind of one who has already passed through so many New Year's days as I have, is the great probability that it will be the last.

Among the visitors of this day was General Scott, who has been recently talked of as a Whig candidate for the office of President of the United States. William H. Harrison was however, preferred both to him and to Henry Clay. A very curious philosophical history of parties might be made by giving a catalogue raisonné of the candidates for the Presidency voted for in the Electoral Colleges since the establishment of the Constitution of the United States. . . Would not the retrospect furnish as practical principles in the operation of the Constitution — 1, that the direct and infallible path to the Presidency is military service coupled with demagogue policy; 2, that in the absence of military service, demagogue policy is the first and most indispensable element of success, and the art of party drilling is the second; 3, that the drill consists in combining the Southern interest in domestic slavery with the Northern riotous Democracy; 4, that this policy and drill, first organized by Thomas Jefferson, first accomplished his election, and established the Virginia dynasty of twenty-four years, a perpetual political contradiction of his own principles; 5, that the same policy and drill, invigorated by success and fortified by experience, has now placed Martin Van Buren in the Presidential chair, and disclosed to the unprincipled ambition of the North the art of rising upon the principles of the South? . . Meanwhile, the consummation of the peace and alliance between Van Buren and Calhoun was manifested by the appearance of Calhoun this day at the New Year's gathering at the President's house.

Jan. 20. — On entering the House, I found Mr. Slade on the floor upon Waddy Thompson's resolution for a rule to exclude abolition petitions; into the vortex of which he had drawn the whole subject of slavery, slave-trade, and abolition. He took nearly three hours to conclude the speech that he had commenced on Saturday, and delivered himself of the burden that has been four years swelling in his bosom. The House was nearly deserted before he finished. Garland, of Virginia, took the floor to answer him.

Jan. 22. — At the meeting of the House this morning, I had the floor upon my amendment to Waddy Thompson's resolution, which I have had such extreme difficulty in getting before the House.

Jan. 28. — Going to the House, I met in the Capitol yard Daniel Webster, and greeted him upon his recent return from his visit to England. I found the House in session, and W. Cost Johnson upon the floor, concluding his anti-abolition speech, which took him between two and three hours. He was about half-tipsy, and in his merriest and wittiest mood. In undertaking to answer my last speech, he took the course, under the form of nauseous and fetid flattery, to make me as ridiculous before the House and the country as he possibly could. He closed with offering a resolution, as an amendment to mine, providing that no petition, resolution, or paper relating to slavery or the abolition of slavery, or the slave trade, in any State, District, or Territory, should be received or in any manner entertained by the House.

I objected to this as not in order, my own resolution being an amendment to an amendment, beyond which, in the uniform practise of the House, such motions are inadmissible. But (Waddy) Thompson accepted Johnson's resolution as an addition to his own; and Linn Banks, who had been put by the Speaker into his chair expressly for the occasion, declared the combined resolutions in order. Vanderpoel made a short and furious speech, which he closed by calling the previous question. The main question was on the combined resolutions, carried, by yeas and nays — 116 to 106; and then carried as amended, 114 to 108. And thus it is made a rule of the House that no abolition petition shall be received.

Jan. 29. — Morning visits from John G. Whittier, Isaac Winslow, and Samuel Mifflin, all of the Society of Friends, and all abolitionists. Whittier is now the editor of the *Pennsylvania Freeman* newspaper, published weekly at Philadelphia. Whittier said he thought this last outrage upon the right of petition, the establishment of a rule refusing to receive or entertain any abolition petition, might perhaps be the best thing that could have been done to promote the cause of abolition. It was, at least, casting off all disguise.

I said it would depend on the impression which it would make on the people; and I had little expectation from that. They had been familiarized to the privation of the right, and could not be roused to take an interest in it. The difference between the resolution of the four preceding sessions of Congress and the new rule of the House is the difference between petty larceny and highway robbery. I had much conversation with these men upon the dissensions between the anti-slavery men and abolitionists, and concerning the late Benjamin Lundy.

Jan. 30. — Commodore Isaac Chauncey, president of the Board of Naval Commissioners, died last Monday, and his funeral was announced for this morning at eleven o'clock. . . President Van Buren offered me a seat in his chariot, which I accepted.

Feb. 16. — Mr. Meehan, the Librarian of Congress, yesterday told me that in the violent storm of the night before last one arm of the emblematical statue of America in the pediment over the entrance-door of the hall of the House of Representatives — my design, so beautifully executed by Persico — had been blown away, and came down with a tremendous crash. He said the group was of freestone. I said it was ominous. He said he hoped not. But he was mistaken as to the statue mutilated. It is not the figure of America, but that of Justice, which has lost her right arm nearly to the elbow — still more ominous, and painfully significant of the condition of the Hall within, where Justice has emphatically lost her right arm.

Feb. 26. — In the House, the New Jersey election case was brought up at once. Johnson, of New York, moved a resolution for an investigation into the dirty bargain by the Clerk of the House, given to Langtree.

March 6. — I went this morning to the Capitol with a heavy heart, expecting that Petriken's resolution to swear in the five false claimants to their seats would be forced through by the previous question, without waiting for the evidence to come, reading that which has been received, or hearing the commissioned members on their claim. I had resolved, if thus called, not to answer to my name. Many other members had determined to do the same; and if all the minority would do so, the majority could not form a quorum of the House, and therefore could not perpetrate this outrage upon all justice and all law. I found there were so many Southern members afraid to hazard this experiment that it cannot be carried effectively into execution. I resolved, however, at all events, to practise it myself, and await the consequences. I found, soon after the reading of the journal, that there was some flinching also on the Administration side. The whole party could not be brought to the point of taking the question now without a word of discussion upon the report of the committee.

March 16. — In the House, the pretenders from New Jersey, Dickerson, Vroom, Cooper, Ryall, and Kille, appeared, were sworn in by the Speaker, and took seats.

March 24. — "Nuit blanche." At the House, after an ineffectual motion of Rariden to suspend the rules to conclude the call of the States for resolutions, the New Jersey election report came up for the morning hour, which was consumed without his concluding. Jones, of the Ways and Means, called for the orders of the day. Committee of the whole on the state of the Union, Dawson in the chair. Trumbull made a speech against the Treasury Note bill. . . About sunset, Mr. Barnard rose, and said that he wished to present his views at large upon the bill, but being somewhat indisposed, and much exhausted, he asked the indulgence of the House to postpone hearing him until tomorrow, and moved the committee should rise, with a view to the adjournment of the House. The men of Kinderhook had decided that they would force the bill through, without answering any of the opposition speeches, this night. They refused to rise, by a vote of tellers — 53 to 90. Mr. Barnard, after a few remarks, reasserting his inability from physical weakness to do justice to himself or to his constituents, indisposed and exhausted as he was at that time, moved again the committee to rise. The count was again taken by tellers, and was 10 ayes, 85 noes — all the opposition members forbearing to vote, and thus leaving the majority without a quorum. The committee were thus compelled to rise and report this fact to the House; and this first disclosed to both parties of the House the secret of the defensive strength of the minority — a strength the more impregnable as it consists in silence and precludes all disorder. The rage of the majority at this discovery was unbounded; but it was impotent.

March 25. — A quorum voting [temporarily, just after midnight]. Thirty-four Whigs afraid to abstain from voting on a call of the yeas and nays. If only five of them had had the firmness to abstain from voting, the majority would even then have been compelled to adjourn from want of a quorum. But, a present quorum being ascertained, the Speaker called the chairman of the committee of the whole again to the chair. Barnard immediately renewed the motion that the committee should rise and the vote was 10 to 85; no quorum. The majority finding themselves impotent for business, resorted to expedients. The first was a call to *count* the members present, to prove a quorum present, which Dawson, the chairman, at first decided he had no right to do, but for which he afterward said he had found a precedent, and did. A number of the opposition members then left their seats and went outside the bar. Dawson counted, and announced 107 members present. I never left my seat, but did not vote. . . At the second call of the names, 149 answered, 15 were excused, 62 were not excused. The doors were closed and the sergeant-at-arms was dispatched for the absentees. Taylor moved that I should be compelled to vote. Not in order. Beatty moved a resolution of censure upon me for not voting. Not in order. Motions to suspend the call, and to adjourn, were multiplied, and failed. . . The call was suspended, and about 11 a.m. Mr. Barnard began his speech against the bill, and kept the floor, with some interruptions, till near two p.m. . . At five o'clock a motion to adjourn was carried by yeas and nays — 73 to 34.

I walked home and found my family at dinner. From my breakfast yesterday morning till one this afternoon, twenty-eight hours, I had fasted. My carriage had been waiting for me four or five hours last evening, till Thomas, the coachman, could hold out no longer, and came home sick and faint. Jerry Leary remained at the Capitol nearly the whole night, and brought me this morning a couple of small sandwiches, which I ate. But I felt during the whole process neither hunger, thirst, nor drowsiness.

April 6. — This morning was devoted principally to the perusal of the dispatches from N. P. Trist, consul of the United States at the Havanna, concerning the fraudulent use of the flag of the United States for carrying on the African slave-trade. They are voluminous, and manifest either the vilest treachery or the most culpable indifference to his duties. For the last three years it is apparent there has been the most shameful prostitution of the American flag to carry on that traffic; that it has been openly notoriously practised before his face; that as consul of the United States, and at the same time acting-consul for Portugal, he has actively lent his aid to it, and when detected in malpractises by the members of the British and Spanish mixed commission, held a most grossly insulting and insolent correspondence with them, and then, in a long series of letters to the Secretary of State, charges all this unlawful and unhallowed trade to defects in the laws.

April 17. — A dark-colored mulatto man, named Joseph Cartwright, a preacher of a colored Methodist church, came this morning with a subscription book to raise $450 to purchase the freedom of his three grandchildren — two girls and one boy, all under three or four years of age. He told me that he had been upwards of twenty years in purchasing his own freedom and that of his three sons; that after this, Henry Johnson, late a member of the House of Representatives from Louisiana, had bought his son's wife and her three children, with many other slaves, to carry them away to Louisiana; that after the purchase he had been prevailed upon to consent to leave them here for a short time in the charge of a man to whom he had ostensibly sold them, but with the consent that this Joseph Cartwright should purchase them for $1,025. He had actually purchased and paid for the mother, and was now endeavoring to raise $450 for the three children. There were in the subscription book certificates of two white Methodist ministers, Hamilton and Cookman, to the respectability of this man — a preacher of the gospel! What a horrible exemplification of slavery!

April 23. — In the House, I had the floor from yesterday, on the resolution for abolishing the Committee on the Public Expenditures. I had intended to speak not more than five minutes, but actually spoke till near the expiration of the hour. . . The House then went into committee of the whole on the state of the Union upon the Appropriation bill; and McKay, who had taken the floor last evening, made one of his insidious, snake-like speeches, interweaving with an ostensible defence of the present Administration venomous insinuations against me and mine. McKay is a political Mrs. Candour, smooth as oil in outward form and fetid as a polecat in inward savor. He damned with faint praise my report of the minority of the Committee on Manufactures in February, 1833. I made no answer; but Evans, of Maine, gave him an instantaneous

and most effectual threshing, which left his argument not a
whole bone.

May 6. — The members of the Baltimore Whig Convention
of young men are flocking to this city by hundreds. The Convention itself consisted of thousands; an immense unwieldy
mass of political machinery to accomplish nothing — to form
a procession polluted by a foul and unpunished murder of one
of their own marshals, and by the loss of several other lives.
I am assured that the number of delegates in attendance from
the single State of Massachusetts was not less than twelve
hundred. And in the midst of this throng, Henry Clay, Daniel
Webster, William C. Preston, Senators of the United States,
and four times the number of members of the House of Representatives, have been two days straining their lungs and
cracking their voices, to fill this multitude with windy sound
for the glorification of William Henry Harrison and the
vituperation of Martin Van Buren.

May 18. — Mr. Silas Wright, chairman of the committee on
finance, took me into the committee room, where I had a long
conversation with him on the Revenue bill. . . Between six
and seven, returning to the hall, I found the House had adjourned, and, walking over the floor, was tripped up by the
new-laid matting, pitched forward, prostrated, and dislocated
my right shoulder. Several of the members who remained in
the House came immediately to my assistance, and attempted
to set the bone, without success. I was taken to Mr. Monroe's
lodgings, where, in about half an hour, the bone was set by
Drs. Thomas and May, jr.

May 19. — I had rather an uneasy night, and my right arm
all this day in a sling. I write against the kindest remonstrances of my family, and attended the morning sitting of the
House against those of both my doctors. I rode to the Capitol,
and stopped on my way at the office of the *National Intelligencer* and enquired of Mr. Gales, who came out to the carriage, for Wheeler's notes of my speech of Saturday, the 9th
instant, on the Revenue bill.

May 20. — I had a night of quiet repose, but the soreness
and pain in my shoulder were more troublesome this day than
yesterday. This was a day of constant rain, and although convinced that I should have suffered less by attending at the
House upon my duty than by staying at home, I yielded to the

entreaties of my wife and confined myself at home. . . One of the first questions asked me by Dr. May was, whether my shoulder had ever been dislocated before. I had no recollection of any such event, but remembered having been told by my mother that, when a child two or three years old, I was straying out into the street, when the nursery-maid ran out after me, and seizing me by the right hand, gave it an involuntary sudden jerk, and dislocated the shoulder. My right hand has consequently, I suppose, upon this early disability, been weaker than the left all my days — always unable to write fast, and for the last twenty-five years unable to write at all, as other men do, with the forefinger and thumb.

June 19. — After a good night's rest, this was the first day since my disaster that the pain in my shoulder and arm is sensibly diminished. It has constantly been affected by the atmosphere. Yesterday was a sultry day, and my walk home from the Capitol Hill, under the burning sun and without an umbrella, was a heedless experiment.

July 25. — I finished the day in drudgery to assort and file my papers. . . At least forty-nine fiftieths of my unanswered letters are from total strangers, and utterly worthless — multitudes of applications to attend public meetings, and to deliver orations, addresses, lectures to lyceums, literary societies, and political gatherings of the people. Household cares are superadded, more and more burdensome with the advance of years. Anxieties for the journey, for the return home, and for those I am to leave behind, an hourly-reminded and daily-deepening consciousness of decay in body and mind, an unquenchable thirst for repose, yet a motive for clinging to public life till the last of my political friends shall cast me off — all this constitutes my present condition. These are my cares and sorrows; but with them I have numberless blessings, for which I cease not to be grateful to the Author of all good, and I have the cheering hope of a better world beyond the grave.

July 26. — I . . . went to the Methodist Foundry Chapel, where the pews were all as crowded as they could hold, with decent, respectable, well-dressed men, women, and children, not one of whom I personally knew. . . Mr. Thornton is not very eloquent; but he drew from me many tears.

Quincy, Aug. 2. — The sentiment of religion is at this time, perhaps, more potent and prevailing in New England than in any other portion of the Christian world. For many years since the establishment of the theological school at Andover, the Calvinists and Unitarians have been battling with each other upon the atonement, the divinity of Jesus Christ and the Trinity. This has now very much subsided; but other wandering of mind takes the place of that, and equally lets the wolf into the fold. A young man, named Ralph Waldo Emerson, and a classmate of my lamented son George, after failing in the everyday avocations of a Unitarian preacher and schoolmaster, starts a new doctrine of transcendentalism, declares all the old revelations superannuated and worn out, and announces the approach of new revelations and prophecies. Garrison and the non-resistant abolitionists, Brownson and the Marat democrats, phrenology and animal magnetism, all come in, furnishing each some plausible rascality as an ingredient for the bubbling cauldron of religion and politics. Pearce Cranch, ex ephebis, preached here last week, and gave out quite a stream of transcendentalism, most unexpectedly. Mr. Lunt's discourse this morning was intended to counteract the effect of these wild and visionary phantasies, and he spoke with just severity of the application of this spirit of hurly-burly innovation to the most important and solemn duties of the Christian faith.

Aug. 13. — The Boston papers, *Courier, Daily Advertiser,* and *Atlas,* are now filled with election returns from North Carolina, Kentucky, Indiana, and Alabama — all for the State governments, and all hitherto more or less favorable to the Whigs, as the opposition to the present Administration call themselves. The imposture of Jackson and Van Buren Democracy would seem to be drawing to its catastrophe.

Aug. 29.— Mr. Thomas P. Beal alighted from the Plymouth stage, and spent an hour with me under great political excitement. The whole country throughout the Union is in a state of political agitation upon the approaching Presidential election such as was never before witnessed. From the organization of the government under the present Constitution of the United States, the nomination of candidates for the office of President were made in caucus conventions by members of Congress, and by the members of the State legislatures. The Congressional caucus nomination of 1824 was in favor of William H. Crawford, and signally failed. The State Legislature nominations produced only cross purposes, and have been superseded by party popular conventions, increasing in numbers, till that of last May, at Baltimore, of the young men to confirm the nomination of W. H. Harrison, made before by a select caucus convention at Harrisburg, Pa., last December, amounted, it is said, to 20,000 delegates. This has been followed by numerous assemblages in all the States where the opposition is in any strength, and not a week has passed within the last four months without a convocation of thousands of people to hear inflammatory harangues against Martin Van Buren and his Administration, by Henry Clay, Daniel Webster, and all the principal opposition orators in or out of Congress. I received earnest invitations to attend these meetings, and address the people, at Nashville, Tenn., Chillicothe, O., Wheeling, Va., Baltimore, Alexandria, Georgetown, and many other places, all of which I declined, both from general principles and from considerations specially and peculiarly applicable to myself. One of these assemblies was held yesterday by a public dinner given to Caleb Cushing by some of his constituents at Newburyport, and a ball in the evening by him to them. I was invited also there but did not attend. Mr. Webster and Mr. Saltonstall were there, and a stump-speech scaffold, and, it is said, a procession of 6,000 people or more, and a dinner of 1800. Here is a revolution in the habits and manners of the people. Where will it end? These are party movements, and must in the natural progress of things become antagonistical. These meetings cannot be multiplied in numbers and frequency without resulting in yet deeper tragedies. Their manifest tendency is to civil war.

Sept. 24. — Charles attended a meeting of the Democratic party this evening, at which George Bancroft . . . delivered an electioneering Democratic address. This practise of itinerant speechmaking has suddenly broken forth in this country to a fearful extent. Electioneering for the Presidency has spread its contagion to the President himself, to his now only competitor, to his immediate predecessor, to one at least of his Cabinet councillors, the Secretary of War, to the ex-candidates Henry Clay and Daniel Webster, and to many of the most distinguished members of both houses of Congress. Immense assemblages of the people are held — of twenty, thirty, fifty thousand souls — where the first orators of the nation address the multitude, not one in ten of whom can hear them, on the most exciting topics of the day.

Sept. 27. — Read the sixth chapter of the first volume of Bancroft's *History of the United States*. This chapter is entitled " Restrictions on Colonial Commerce." It is a very lame account of the English Navigation Act, and a florid panegyric upon the first settlers of Virginia, upon the soil and climate of that country, upon the Indian monarchs Powhatan and Opecancanough, in equal measure. With all this he has transcendent talents and indefatigable industry. Every page of his history teems with evidences of profound research, quick perception, and brilliant imagination. It is extremely entertaining; the style diffuse and declamatory, far less chaste, though more fascinating, than that of Irving or of Prescott; the morality ostentatious, but very defective.

Philadelphia, Nov. 22. — I dined with Mr. Nicholas Biddle *en famille,* with no other addition save Judge Hopkinson. We sat after dinner settling the nation till near eight in the evening, little satisfied with the result. Hopkinson is snug in port, content with his office of district judge, undisturbed by ambition or fear. Biddle broods with smiling face and stifled groans over the wreck of splendid blasted expectations and ruined hopes. A fair mind, a brilliant genius, a generous temper, an honest heart, waylaid and led astray by prosperity, suffering the penalty of scarcely voluntary error — 'tis piteous to behold.

Dec. 1. — [At Barnum's Hotel in Baltimore for a lecture]. I would have dined at the ordinary, but Mr. Barnum insisted on having my dinner served in my parlor. Mr. Harris dined with me. It so happened that I was quite unwell, suddenly taken in the cars soon after leaving Washington, and had so totally lost my appetite that I could scarcely swallow anything of the sumptuous dinner which was served. The day was frosty and raw, and I had taken a chill in the cars. I was fearful I should not be able to perform my engagement of the evening, and had the utmost difficulty to conceal from Mr. Harris my discomposure. I received and answered a second note of invitation to dine tomorrow from Mr. Robert Gilmor. I had numerous visitors, among whom several old acquaintances, whose names and persons, to my great mortification, had alike vanished from my memory. I remembered Isaac

Munroe, editor of the Baltimore *Patriot*. Mr. Barnum sat and chatted with me for an hour after dinner, and Mr. Findley, heretofore Marshal of the district, another. The lecture had been fixed for eight o'clock. At half-past seven Mr. Harris and another gentleman came and took me to Dr. Duncan's church, which was so crowded that I had no small difficulty to get in. My chill had passed off, but left me with a hoarse and broken voice. . . I spoke from a platform fronting the pulpit and delivered the lecture on Society and Civilization. It was well received — the stanzas and the close applauded.

Washington, Dec. 4. — Morning visits from Col. Henderson of the Marine Corps and Mr. Cazenove of Alexandria. Mutual gratulation at the downfall of the Jackson-Van Buren Administration is the universal theme of conversation. One can scarcely imagine the degree of detestation in which they are both held. No one knows what is to come. In four years from this time the successor may be equally detested. He is not the choice of three fourths of those who have elected him. His present popularity is all artificial. There is little confidence in his talents or his firmness. If he is not found time-serving, demagogical, unsteady, and Western-sectional, he will more than satisfy my present expectations. Jackson's Administration commenced with fairer prospects and an easier career before him than had ever before been presented to any President of the United States. His personal popularity, founded exclusively upon the battle of New Orleans, drove him through his double term, and enabled him to palm upon this nation the sycophant who declared it glory enough to have served under such a chief for his successor. Both the men have been for twelve years the tool of Amos Kendall, the ruling mind of their dominion. Their edifice has crumbled into ruin by the mere force of gravitation and the wretchedness of their cement. But what is to come? No halcyon days. One set of unsound principles for another; one man in leading-strings for another. Harrison comes in upon a hurricane; God grant he may not go out upon a wreck.

Dec. 7. — This day commenced the second session of the Twenty-sixth Congress. The heavy fall of snow compelled me to ride to the Capitol.

Dec. 8. — Of the members who came in this day, John

Sergeant, W. B. Calhoun, Millard Fillmore, and Daniel D. Bernard, who travelled with his wife and two children, left Philadelphia on Saturday morning in the cars, and at nine o'clock that evening found themselves twenty-three miles from Baltimore in the middle of the road, with the snow falling and the storm howling around them, and unable equally to proceed or recede.   There of 80 passengers in the train, 30 of whom were women, the greater number remained the whole night of Saturday, the whole day and night of Sunday, and Monday till near noon, when fresh engines came and took them up and brought them last night into Baltimore.   A small part of their company found a refuge in two or three hovels near the place where they were arrested, but fared worse than those who adhered to the cars.   These made themselves comfortable by shutting out the tempest, keeping up good fires, and foraging successfully round the neighborhood for a supply of provisions.

Dec. 11. — I paid morning visits to Mr. Henry Clay, lodging at Mrs. Arguelles's, and to Mr. Solomon Lincoln at Brown's Hotel.   While I was at Mr. Clay's numerous other visitors came in, among whom the Russian Minister Bodisco, who Mr. Clay bantered coarsely about his marriage last spring with a young girl at Georgetown, daughter of a clerk in one of the public offices, named Williams.   Bodisco took Clay's greasy jokes very good-humoredly, and with no small complacency assured him that all was right.   Clay said he had visited Mr. Van Buren yesterday, and had an hour's conversation with him on the issue of the Presidential election.   Mr. Clay further told us that before leaving home he had seen the President-elect, Harrison, and that he looked well, though somewhat shattered.

Dec. 12. — I thought it necessary to look into the case of the *Amistad* captives, to prepare for the argument before the Supreme Court in January — of which I dare scarcely to think.

Jan. 2, 1841. — Governor Lincoln came alone, and I had a long conversation with him on the present state and prospective movements of parties.   The Governor gave me to understand that he knew Webster was to be Mr. Harrison's Secretary of State, but left it rather uncertain whether he had it from himself or from good authority.

Jan. 20. — The correspondence between the Governors of New York and Virginia has absorbed two of my evenings, and is of awful import. Its most alarming feature is the tameness of tone on the part of W. H. Seward, the Governor of New York, and the insolence of Hopkins, the Lieutenant-Governor, and of Gilmer, the Governor of Virginia, throughout the whole correspondence.

Jan. 29. — Wise held the floor for three hours in conclud-ing his speech [on the Treasury Note bill] — a motley com-pound of eloquence and folly, of braggart impudence and childish vanity, of self-laudation and Virginian narrow-mindedness. Wise is the personified caricature of Virginia — great conception, wild but energetic elocution, bathos of con-clusion, small and pitiful result. He was followed by Hubbard, of Alabama, who began grunting against the tariff for about half an hour, and then gave way to a motion to rise.

Jan. 30. — An inflammation in my left eye threatens me with complete disability to perform my final duty before the Supreme Court in the case of the *Amistad* captives; while the daily and hourly increasing weight of the pressure of prepara-tion aggravates that disability.

Feb. 4. — On my return to the House, I found Charles Shepard on the floor, discussing the topics of the Treasury Note bill as a Southern planter, for an hour; followed by James Garland of the same interest. I then took my turn for an hour, and arraigned before the committee, the nation, and the world the principles avowed by Henry A. Wise, and his three-colored standard of overseer, black; duelling, blood-red; and dirty, cadaverous nullification, white. Of its effect I will not now speak. At the close of his reply, his gang of duellists clapped their hands, and the gallery hissed. William Cost Johnson began his usual rhodomontade, but the whole committee was in fermentation; they rose, and the House ad-journed at half-past four.

Feb. 5. — Sleepless night. The step that I have taken yesterday absorbs all the faculties of my soul. Deliberately taken, to have any useful effect it must be calmly, firmly, ju-diciously, perseveringly, alas! skilfully pursued. I fear I have estimated too highly its importance. I fear my own incompe-tence to sustain it effectively and successfully. I know not what support I shall receive in or out of the House; I stand alone in this undertaking. Few, if any, of my colleagues appear to understand my purpose, and from their deportment yesterday, I should conclude that they thought it one of my eccentric, wild, extravagant freaks of passion. . .

Mr. Merrick, Senator from Maryland, and David Hoffman of Baltimore visited here this day, and told my wife that Mr. Webster had been highly delighted at hearing of my speech; but all around me is cold and discouraging, and my own feelings are wound up to a pitch that my reason can scarcely endure. I trust in God to control me.

Feb. 18. — A severe visitation of Providence. There was an exhibition at a quarter past eleven, in the front yard of the Capitol, of firing with Colt's repeating firearm — a new-invented instrument of destruction, for discharging twelve times a musket in as many seconds. I rode to the Capitol with Mr. Smith. We had alighted from the carriage from five to ten minutes, when the firing commenced. My carriage was then going out of the yard; the horses took fright, the carriage was jammed against a messenger's wagon, overset, the pole and a whippletree broken, the harness nearly demolished; the coachman, Jeremy Leary, and the footman, John Causten, precipitated from the box, and Jerry nearly killed on the spot. He was taken into one of the lower rooms of the Capitol, where, as soon as I heard of the disaster, I found him, in excruciating torture.

Feb. 19. — I walked home; and about half-past six, Jeremy Leary died, almost without a groan.

Feb. 20. — The arrangements had been made for the funeral of my poor, humble, but excellent friend Jeremy Leary, at three o'clock this afternoon. I walked to the Capitol this morning, with a spirit humbled to the dust, with a heart melted in sorrow, and a mind agitated and confused. The case of the *Amistad* captives had been fixed to commence in the Supreme Court this morning.[2] . . I therefore, as soon as the Court was opened and the case was called, requested as

[2] The case of the *Amistad* negroes enlisted Adams's emotions powerfully. A number of Cuban slaves, being transported from Havana to Principe on the schooner *Amistad*, rose, took possession of the craft, and compelled the survivors of the crew to steer for Africa. The helmsman took the ship instead into Long Island Sound. Here the negroes were seized. The Secretary of State and the Attorney-General both tried to uphold the claim of the Spanish Minister to the negroes; but the friends of emancipation took the case through the courts, and thanks in large part to Adams's activities, the blacks were ultimately freed.

a personal favor of the Court to suspend the proceedings in this case from 2 o'clock p.m. today till Monday; to which Chief Justice Taney answered, " Certainly."

Feb. 24. — I was busied in preparation in the Clerk of the Supreme Court's room nearly an hour — to the moment of the meeting of the Court. When that was opened, Josiah Randall and Mr. Polk, now a clerk in the Department of War, were admitted as attorneys and counsellors of the Court; and Chief-Justice Taney announced to me that the Court were ready to hear me. The judges present were Taney, Story, Thompson, McLean, Baldwin, Wayne, Barbour, and Catron. Judge Mc-Kinley has not been present during any part of the trial. The courtroom was full, but not crowded, and there were not many ladies. I had been deeply distressed and agitated till the moment when I rose; and then my spirit did not sink within me. With grateful heart for aid from above, though in humiliation for the weakness incident to the limits of my powers, I spoke four hours and a half, with sufficient method and order to witness little flagging of attention by the Judges or the auditory — till half-past three o'clock, when the Chief Justice said the court would hear me further tomorrow.

March 4, 1841. — The inauguration of William Henry Harrison as President of the United States was celebrated with demonstrations of popular feeling unexampled since that of Washington in 1789, and at the same time with so much order and tranquillity that not the slightest symptom of conflicting passions occurred to disturb the enjoyments of the day. Many thousands of the people from the adjoining and considerable numbers from distant States had come to witness the ceremony. The procession, consisting of a mixed military and civil cavalcade, and platoons of voluntary militia companies, Tippecanoe clubs, students of colleges, and schoolboys, with about half a dozen veterans who had fought under the hero in the war of 1812, with sundry awkward and ungainly painted banners, and log cabins, without any carriages or showy dresses, was characteristic of the democracy of our institution while the perfect order with which the whole scene was performed, and the absence of all pageantry, was highly creditable to them. The numbers were not complimentary to those of the military assemblage at Baltimore upon the reception of La Fayette in 1824; nor was there anything now of the pride, pomp, and circumstance of that day. The *coup-d'œil* of this day was showy-shabby. The procession passed before the windows of my house. General Harrison was on a mean-looking white horse, in the centre of seven others, in a plain frock-coat or surtout, undistinguishable from any of those before, behind, or around him. He proceeded thus to the Capitol, where, from the top of the flight of steps at the eastern front, he read his inaugural address, occupying about an hour in the delivery, and before pronouncing the last paragraph of which, the oath of office was administered to him by Chief-Justice Taney.

The procession then returned to the President's house, and he retired to his chamber, while an immense crowd filled for an hour or more all the lower rooms of the house.

March 29. — I am yet to revise for publication my argument in the case of the *Amistad* Africans; and, in merely glancing over the slave-trade papers lent me by Mr. Fox, I find impulses of duty upon my own conscience which I cannot resist, while on the other hand are the magnitude, the danger, the insurmountable burden of labor to be encountered in the undertaking to touch upon the slave-trade. No one else will undertake it; no one but a spirit unconquerable by man, woman or fiend can undertake it but with the heart of martyrdom. The world, the flesh, and all the devils in hell are arrayed against any man who now in this North American Union shall dare to join the standard of Almighty God to put down the African slave-trade; and what can I, upon the verge of my seventy-fourth birthday, with a shaking hand, a darkening eye, a drowsy brain, and with all my faculties dropping from me one by one, as the teeth are dropping from my head — what can I do for the cause of God and man, for the progress of human emancipation, for the suppression of the African slave-trade? Yet my conscience presses me on; let me but die upon the breach.

April 2. — The condition of the President's health is alarming. He was seized last Saturday with a severe chill, and the next day with what his physicians called a bilious pleurisy. Since that time he has been very ill, with symptoms varying from day to day, and almost from hour to hour. The porter at the door answers all enquirers, that he is better; while Mr. Chambers and Mr. Todd report that there is no change, and the physicians agree to answer all alike. Yesterday, during the daytime, the answer was, much better; last evening, not so well; this morning, quite out of danger.

April 3. — The President's illness returned shortly after noon with extreme violence. Expresses had already been sent to Baltimore for Dr. Alexander, who came, and for Dr. Chapman to Philadelphia. The reports from the house were more and more desponding the whole evening, and the physicians pronounced that he could not survive the night.

April 4. — At thirty minutes past midnight, this morning of Palm Sunday, the 4th of April, 1841, died William Henry Harrison, precisely one calendar month President of the United States after his inauguration. The first impression of this event here where it occurred is of the frailty of all human enjoyments and the awful vicissitudes woven into the lot of mortal man. He had reached, but one short month since, the pinnacle of honor and power in his own country. He lies a lifeless corpse in the palace provided by his country for his abode. He was amiable and benevolent. Sympathy for his sufferings and his fate is the prevailing sentiment of his fellow-citizens. The bereavement and distress of his family are felt intensely, albeit they are strangers here and known to scarcely anyone. His wife had not even left his residence at North Bend, Ohio, to join him here. An express was sent for her two or three days since; but the tidings of death must meet her before she can reach this city.

The influence of this event upon the condition and history of the country can scarcely be seen. It makes the Vice-President of the United States, John Tyler of Virginia, Acting President of the Union for four years less one month. Tyler is a political sectarian, of the slave-driving, Virginian, Jeffersonian school, principled against all improvement, with all the interests and passions and vices of slavery rooted in his moral and political constitution — with talents not above mediocrity, and a spirit incapable of expansion to the dimensions of the station upon which he has been cast by the hand of Providence, unseen through the apparent agency of chance. To that benign and healing hand of Providence I trust, in humble hope of the good which it always brings forth out of evil. In upwards of half a century, this is the first instance of a Vice-President's being called to act as President of the

United States, and brings to the test that provision of the Constitution which places in the Executive chair a man never thought of for it by anybody.   This day was in every sense gloomy — rain the whole day.

April 5. — The corpse of the late President Harrison was laid out, in a plain coffin covered with black velvet, on a table in the middle of the entrance hall at the President's house. At two p.m., I went, with my wife and Mrs. Smith, and took a last look at the face of the patriot warrior, taken away thus providentially from the evil to come.

April 6. — The Vice-President, John Tyler of Virginia, arrived here at five o'clock this morning, and took lodgings at Brown's Hotel.   At noon, the heads of departments waited upon him.   He requested them all to continue in their offices, and took the official oath of President of the United States, which was administered to him by William Cranch, Chief Justice of the Circuit Court of the District of Columbia.   The Judge certifies that although Mr. Tyler deems himself qualified to perform the duties and exercise the powers and office of President, on the death of President Harrison, without any other oath than that which he had taken as Vice-President, yet as doubts might arise, and for greater caution, he had taken and subscribed the present oath.

April 7. — Funeral of W. H. Harrison, President of the United States.   This ceremony was performed in a decent and unostentatious manner, with proper religious solemnity, and with the simplicity congenial to our republican institutions.   A quarter before twelve, noon, I attended at the President's house, where, in the centre of the East Room, the coffin, covered with a black velvet pall, was placed on a plain table, by the side and crosswise of which was another, at which the Rev. Mr. Hawley, rector of St. John's Church, read the Episcopal funeral service, with a very brief additional statement of two facts.   The first, that the day after General Harrison entered the President's house, he walked out into the city and purchased a Bible and Prayer-book, both of which were on the table, and were exhibited to the assembled auditory by the officiating divine, who said that it had been the daily habit of the late President to commence the day by reading in that Bible.   The other fact was, that he had expressed his regret at not having joined in full communion with the Church, and that it was his intention to have done so on the ensuing Easter-day — next Sunday.

After the reading of the Church service, the order of procession was formed, Mr. Carroll, the Clerk of the Supreme Court of the United States, officiating as one of the marshals. . . Mr. Semmes, the chief clerk of the Navy Department, rode with me in my carriage. The corps diplomatique were in full costume, but Mr. Fox, the British Minister, was not present, nor, I believe, any member of the British Legation. Vast crowds of people followed in the procession, and the avenue from the palace to the Capitol was equally thronged. The city bells were tolled, and minute-guns were fired from the western terrace of the Capitol. A floating multitude, male and female, of all ages and colors, followed the procession to the Navy Burying ground, where the corpse was deposited in the receiving-vault — with some difficulty from the excessive crowd, but not the slightest disorder. On the return, only the military escort continued in procession. I took up Mr. William Brent, who had lost his carriage, and left him on Capitol Hill. I reached home at half-past four, and idled off the remainder of the day.

April 16. — I paid a visit this morning to Mr. Tyler, who styles himself President of the United States, and not Vice-President acting as President, which would be the correct style. But it is a construction in direct violation both of the grammar and context of the Constitution, which confers upon the Vice-President, on the decease of the President, not the office, but the powers and duties of the said office. There is a dogmatical article in the *National Intelligencer* asserting this false construction; which is not worth contesting, but which to a strict constructionist would warrant more than a doubt whether the Vice-President has the right to occupy the President's house, or to claim his salary, without an Act of Congress. He moved into the house two days ago, and received me in the old southeast Cabinet chamber. He received me very kindly, and apologized for not having visited me without waiting for this call. To this I had no claim or pretension. My visit was very short, as there were several persons in attendance, and among them Mr. Southard, now president of the Senate.

CHAPTER XIV

1841–1843

QUARRELS OF THE TYLER ADMINISTRATION — RESIGNATION OF THE
CABINET — THE BUNKER HILL CELEBRATION — TOUR IN THE WEST
— OVATIONS IN NEW YORK AND OHIO — RETURN TO WASHINGTON.

Washington, April 20, 1841. — In my conversation with
Mr. Bell last evening, I had reason to conclude that the policy
of Mr. Tyler will look exclusively to his own election for the
next four years' term as President, and that of Webster will
be to secure it for him; that Mr. Clay will be left to fight
his own battles with the Land bill, without aid or support
from the Administration; and that between Tyler and Webster
there will be a concert of mutual concession between the North
and the South. Clay will soon be in unequivocal opposition,
and the Administration will waddle along, living from hand to
mouth; for as to any great commanding and compact system,
Webster is a " great baby " and Ewing is another. Of course
this Administration will be a failure, and a general bankruptcy
is impending.

Quincy, May 21. — Immediately after dinner I had visits
from Mr. Stone and Mr. Sayles, persons connected with the
manufactures at Lowell, and much concerned for the prospects of that interest under the present Administration. I
feel an utter distrust of the principles of John Tyler, a Virginia
nullifier now acting as President of the United States, and no
confidence in the principles or belief in the sincerity of the
Secretary of State. Between them and the manufacturing interest my position is so perilous that I am strongly inclined to
refuse the office of chairman of the Committee on Manufactures, and to propose to the Speaker, whoever he may be, to
place me on the Naval Committee. The confidence of these
gentlemen in the present Administration is not more sanguine

than my own. They are very anxious for the passage of my
bill of the last Congress for the suppression of frauds on the
revenue; for which there is now little chance.

Washington, May 31. — Twenty-seventh Congress, first session, commences. . . At the roll call by the clerk of the late
House, Hugh A. Garland, two hundred and twenty-seven members answered to their names. John White, of Kentucky, was
chosen Speaker at the first viva voce vote.

June 3. — At the House, the discussion upon the adoption of
the rules of the House in the last Congress was resumed, on my
amendment to Underwood's amendment to Wise's motion.

June 4. — I paid a visit to the Acting President, John Tyler,
and had a conversation with him upon the condition and prospects of the Smithsonian Fund. The Secretary of the Treasury, Ewing, has not communicated to him my letter of 19th
April last, nor the report, nor any of the documents which I
sent him with it. When I went into the room where Mr. Tyler
received me, I saw H. A. Wise in the back portico facing the
Potomac; but he did not come in while I was there.

June 7. — At eleven o'clock the House met. Wise came
over to my seat and asked me to yield him the floor on the
question about the rules to read a precedent exactly in point in
the year 1800. I said, certainly. The Speaker announced my
amendment to the motion for adopting the rules of the last
House of Representatives as the subject under consideration.
I yielded the floor to Wise, who with a great bustle of pomposity, read his precedent of 1800, with all the yeas and nays;
and it was in truth a precedent as strong as possible against
him. As soon as he sat down, I rose and said, " And the
mountain is delivered of its mouse;" and in a speech of about
three hours I replied to the speeches of Wise and W. C. Johnson in opposition to mine, supporting my amendment — but as
much as one third of the time in interruptions by Wise and
Johnson with fresh speeches, under color of explanations.
Thomas Butler King of Georgia replied to me with great bitterness and virulence. Millard Fillmore then moved the
previous question, which the Speaker stated would be first on
my amendment . . . and then upon the resolution to adopt the
rules. After much chicanery, the previous question was carried; and the vote, by yeas and nays, on my amendment was
carried — 112 to 104; almost exclusively bond and free.

June 11. — At the House . . . Wise began in a tone which I saw would break him down — loud, vociferous, declamatory, furibund; he raved about the hell-hounds of abolition, and at me, as the leader of the abolitionists throughout the Union, for a full hour — till his voice had broken into a childish treble two or three times.   Arnold, of Tennessee, came to my seat and with deep earnestness entreated me not to reply to him; and I promised that I would not.   Without abatement of his vehemence, Wise came to speak of the controversy between the States of Virginia and New York; and then his tone suddenly fell, he became bewildered in his argument, his voice failed him, he became ghastly pale, said he felt himself unwell, sank into his chair, and fainted.   Several of his friends flew to his assistance, led him out of the hall, and took him to his lodgings. The House postponed the further consideration of the subject till tomorrow.   Then, after a sufficient dose of Kinderhook chicanery and an appeal by Atherton from a decision by the Speaker, confirmed by a vote of nearly two to one, Gales and Seaton were elected printers to the House, by 134 viva voce votes.   Blair and Rives had 75 votes, and Peter Force 6.

June 14. — At the House, immediately after the reading of the Journal, Mr. Wise resumed his speech in support of Fornance's motion to reconsider the vote adopting the old rules except the 21st, and spoke for upwards of six hours, a continual invective upon me.   He was apparently recovered from his fainting-fit of last Friday, and he had sufficient self-control to avoid the bawling, brawling tone with which he then broke himself down; but, beginning every successive sentence with a loud and vehement clatter, he immediately bowed down over his desk till his head and chest became horizontal, his mouth pouring out all the time his words in a whisper.   Abolition, abolition, abolition, was the unvarying cry; and he represented me as a fiend, the inspirer and leader of all abolition.   He gave a history in his own way, full of misrepresentations, of all the gag motions, orders, and resolutions, down to the rule of 28th January, 1840, from Pinckney's gag in 1835.

June 16. — At the House, Stuart, of Virginia, offered a resolution of compromise to hang up all petitions for this session, and put off the debate on the rule till the winter session, and moved the previous question, which was at last carried — 113 to 101; and Stuart's motion was carried — 119 to 103.

June 26. — At nine this morning the committees of the Senate and House of Representatives, appointed to superintend the removal of the remains of the late President of the United States, William H. Harrison, met in the committee-room of the Committee on Post-offices and Post-roads, together with the committee from the inhabitants of Cincinnati, consisting of Jacob Burnet, John C. Wright, and sundry others, and all proceeded in hackney coaches to the receiving vault in the Congressional burying-ground, where the corpse had been deposited. I rode with Richard H. Bayard . . . Thomas Hart Benton . . . and William S. Archer. Colonel Henderson, commander of the Marine Corps, attended with a detachment of eight athletic marines, who drew out from the vault the oaken chest in which the coffin was enclosed, and placed it upon the hearse, which was then followed in somewhat irregular procession to the railway depot at the foot of Capitol Hill. There the chest enclosing the coffin was transferred from the hearse to one of the railway cars, and precisely at noon they departed for Baltimore. President Tyler, accompanied by the heads of departments, was present to witness the scene. There was a great concourse of people at the depot, but no disorder, and no manifestation of sensibility of any kind.

June 30. — Morning visit from John Ross, chief of the Cherokee Nation, with Vann and Benn, two others of the delegation. Ross had written to request an interview for me with them on my appointment as chairman of the committee on Indian affairs. I was excused from that service at my own request, from a full conviction that its only result would be to keep a perpetual harrow upon my feelings, with a total impotence to render any useful service. The policy, from Washington to myself, of all the Presidents of the United States had been justice and kindness to the Indian tribes — to civilize and preserve them. With the Creeks and Cherokees it had been eminently successful. Its success was their misfortune. The States within whose borders their settlements were took the alarm, broke down all the treaties which had pledged the faith of the nation. Georgia extended her jurisdiction over them, took possession of their lands, houses, cattle, furniture, negroes, and drove them out of their own dwellings. All the Southern States supported Georgia in this utter prostration of faith and justice; and Andrew Jackson, by the simultaneous operation of fraudulent treaties and brutal force, completed the work. The Florida War is one of the fruits of this policy, the conduct of which exhibits one uninterrupted scene of the most profligate corruption. All resistance against this abomination is vain. It is among the heinous sins of this nation, for which I believe God will one day bring them to judgment — but at His own time and by His own means. I turned my eyes away from this sickening mass of putrefaction, and asked to be excused from serving as chairman of the committee. Ross and his colleagues are here, claiming indemnity for the household furniture, goods, and cattle stolen from their people when they were expelled from their dwellings, and a new treaty, to give them some shadow of security for the permanent possession of the lands to which they have been driven. They complain of delays and neglect by the new Secretary of War, Mr. Bell; and I promised to speak to him in their behalf; and I told them to call upon me freely, if upon any occasion I could be serviceable to them.

July 5. — The celebration of the anniversary of Independence was more signalized on this day than it has been for several years, and in a manner hitherto unusual. . . There was a procession of the temperance societies, very numerous, but which I did not see. . . The Senate had adjourned over from Saturday till tomorrow. The weather was intensely warm, and the sky bright with a blazing sun. I came home, and at five o'clock went and dined with President Tyler, and a company chiefly of members of the House of Representatives. . . There was turtle soup from a turtle weighing three hundred pounds, a present from Key West. The President drank wine with every person at table, by squads. He gave two toasts, and called on me for one. I gave, " The application to our political institutions of that principle of the law of nature, by which all nature's difference keeps all nature's peace."

July 11. — My birthday happens this day upon the Sabbath. Every return of the day comes with a weight of solemnity more and more awful. How peculiarly impressive ought it then to be when the annual warning of the shortening thread sounds in tones deepened by the churchbell of the Lord's Day! The question comes with yearly aggravation upon my conscience. What have I done with the seventy-four years that I have been indulged with the blessing of life?

July 24. — Edward Southwick, the man who visited me

yesterday, told me that he was a native of Massachusetts, but now resided in the western part of New York; that he was an abolitionist, but was now going South to discuss the matter with them there. He asked me what I thought of it. I said the best thing he could do was to turn round and go home. He asked if I thought there would be danger of harm to him. I said the least he could expect to get was a ducking.

Aug. 14. — The President of the United States, the members of his Cabinet, and all the members of both houses of Congress had received invitations to visit the line-of-battleship *Delaware,* lying off Annapolis, this day. Commodore Morris, who is going out in command of her, had given me an additional verbal invitation; and I had concluded to go, until the feud between the President and the two houses of Congress, festering ever since a special Providence placed John Tyler in the Presidential chair, came to an issue by the passage of the Bank law, which it is known he intends to negative. The excitement in both houses and in public is so great that I thought it no time for festivity or hollow-hearted pageantry. The President himself appears to have become sensible that this exhibition of himself to public gaze and outward display of adulation was ill-suited to the real feelings of the time, and did not go. The House yesterday adjourned over Monday, for this frolic; but the Senate refused to adjourn, and sat this day as usual.

Aug. 16. — The House adjourned shortly after two. When the veto message [of the bill for a virtual recharter of the United States Bank] was read in the Senate, there was some slight disorder in the galleries; whereupon T. H. Benton made a ridiculous scene, till a man was taken into custody, and the doughty knight of the stuffed cravat abated his manly wrath. The veto message and its inevitable consequences will utterly prostrate the Administration and the party by which it was brought in. It surrenders the country to the profligate political swindlers so recently driven from power. There is a Providence in the fall of a sparrow!

Aug. 28. — After the adjournment, and some casual conversation, I went into the Senate-chamber, where they were debating amendments to the Revenue bill, from the House. Upon a question of exempting sumac from duty there was a sparring of a full half an hour, with sharp personalities, between Henry Clay and John C. Calhoun, about protective

duties and free trade.   I attended an evening promiscuous
party of Whigs of all shades, at Mr. Crittenden the Attorney-
General's.   Mrs. Crittenden there — sola.   Sideboard supper — madeira and champagne.

Aug. 30. — Robert C. Winthrop told me in the House that,
after I came away from Mr. Crittenden's Saturday evening, a
regular deputation was sent over to the President's house to
constrain him to join the party, to which he had been invited
but had sent an excuse.   On this deputation were Dawson and
Triplett.   They went over, roused him, if not from bed, after
the house had been closed for the night, obtained access to
him, took him by storm after the Kentucky fashion, led him
over to Crittenden's in triumph, where Clay received him at the
door with, " Well, Mr. President, what are you for, Kentucky
whiskey or champagne? "   He chose champagne, and entered
into the spirit of this frolicsome agony as if it were congenial
to his own temper.   But all this was as false and hollow as it
was blustering and rowdyish.

Sept. 3. — Colonel Hayne, of South Carolina, came to my
seat to request a conversation with me at some convenient
time about a plan which he has formed for settling by compromise the great slavery question, and which he wishes me
to undertake.   His views are pure and benevolent.   I promised
cheerfully to see and hear him on the subject, without fixing the
time.

The Senate this day passed the Fiscal Corporation bill —
27 to 22 — with a certainty that it will be vetoed by President
Tyler.

Sept. 6. — There are numerous nominations pending before
the Senate, made at the commencement of or very early in
the session, and upon which the action of the Senate has been
and is yet suspended.   Among them is that of Edward Everett,
upon the charge of his being an abolitionist.

Sept. 8. — My poem on the *Wants of Man* is published
in the *National Intelligencer* this morning, from the Albany
Evening Journal, from a copy taken from Christopher Morgan
and sent to Mrs. Seward, wife of the Governor of New York.

Sept. 10. — Meeting at Mr. Webster's of the Massachusetts delegation.

Sept. 11. — The meeting at Mr. Webster's last evening was
at his request.   He stated that the Secretary of the Treasury,

Thomas Ewing, the Secretary of the Navy, George E. Badger
of North Carolina, and the Attorney-General, John J. Crittenden of Kentucky, had called on him this day and informed
him that they and John Bell of Tennessee had determined to
send in their resignations to their respective offices (the latter,
of Secretary of War) to President Tyler at eleven o'clock
tomorrow morning.

Mr. Webster then, addressing me, said that, being thus
placed in a peculiar position, and seeing no sufficient cause for
resigning his office, he had requested this meeting to consult
with the members of the delegation and to have the benefit
of their opinions, assuring them that as to the office itself
it was a matter of the most perfect indifference to him whether
he retained or resigned it — a declaration which it is possible
he believed when he made it. But he had prefaced it by
saying that he saw no cause sufficient to justify his resignation.
It was like Falstaff's recruit " Bullcalf." " In very truth, sir,
I had as lief be hanged, sir, as go; and yet, for mine own part,
sir, I do not care; but rather because I am unwilling, and for
my own part have a desire to stay with my friends; else, sir,
I did not care for mine own part so much." . . For himself,
Mr. Webster said, Mr. Tyler had never treated him with disrespect, and he had no doubt it was his desire that he should
remain in the Department of State. He gave a very brief
narrative of the progress of the two Bank bills, and intimated
his own belief that Mr. Tyler would have signed the second
bill but for the publication of Botts's letter to the " Richmond
Coffee House." . .

We all agreed that Mr. Webster would not be justified in
resigning at this time; but we all felt that the hour for the
requiem of the Whig Party was at hand.[1]

Sept. 12. — Mr. Webster told us last evening that the

---

[1] President Tyler was by this time completely estranged from the Whig
Party which had elevated him to the Vice-Presidency. His opposition to the bill
which contemplated the virtual reëstablishment of the United States Bank would
alone have effected this end; but to his offense of opposition to it he added, as
most of his Cabinet and most of the Whigs in Congress believed, the crime of
treachery. That is, he told Cabinet members that he would support legislative
measures of the Whigs which he later vetoed. It was on this ground of treachery
that the Cabinet resigned, leaving the entire Whig Party with the bitterest animosity
toward the accidental President. Webster remained for a time, believing that his
services as Secretary of State were needed to carry through the settlement with
England which was soon afterward embodied in the Webster-Ashburton Treaty.

Postmaster-General, Francis Granger, desired and intended to remain in office; but he resigned this morning together with the four other heads of departments, leaving Daniel Webster, Secretary of State, the sole remnant of the Harrison Administration, alone in his glory.

Sept. 14. — I met Mr. Henry A. Wise, who spoke to me and offered me his hand — civilities which I accepted and returned; though I should not have offered them after his openly pointing to me in the House as the only man there unfit to be his judge, by supposed personal hostility to him, at the very moment when I was toiling to save him from all censure, and others were offering repeated motions for his expulsion.

Sept. 17. — After a long spell of dry weather, we had a moderate cool rain nearly all this day, and the setting in of autumn. I revised the proof-slips of my speech delivered on the 4th instant on the McLeod resolution, the language of which, wholly extemporaneous, is mean and tautological, full of repetitions, and desultory, but has the mérite de l'apropos. The speech has for the time saved Webster from the catastrophe which has befallen his colleagues. It has given him the means of saving himself from ruin, and his country from a most disastrous war. My reward from him will be professions of respect and esteem, speeches of approbation and regard for me to my friends, knowing that they will be reported to me, secret and deep-laid intrigues against me, and still more venomous against my son. Such is human nature, in the gigantic intellect, the envious temper, the ravenous ambition, and the rotten heart of Daniel Webster. His treatment of me has been, is, and will be an improved edition of Andrew Jackson's gratitude.

Boston, Nov. 5. — After breakfast, I called upon Mr. Abbott Lawrence, and had an hour of conversation with him upon the electioneering politics of the day. The Whig party, as they call themselves, is splitting up into a thousand fragments. Mr. Lawrence is struggling to sustain it, and Rufus Choate and Robert C. Winthrop and Leverett Saltonstall are haranguing Whig caucus meetings throughout the State, in vain, to support it. The general expectation is that Marcus Morton will be again elected governor of the Commonwealth, and that Democracy will ride roughshod over the entire country. Webster has been spending several weeks at Marshfield,

fishing, shooting, ut olim, leaving his son Fletcher to act the
Secretary of State, and affecting the Stoic to the still-recurring
rumors that he is to be discarded or hoisted out of his Department into some foreign mission. He has avoided or evaded
all conversation with Mr. Lawrence upon the thorny questions
of bank, tariff, and negotiations with England, and Lawrence
has lost all confidence in him. Caleb Cushing has taken a
lover's leap over to the Tyler territory, and makes his court
to the Lady Elizabeth.

Nov. 20. — I walked out before dinner and called at the
office of Mr. Ellis Gray Loring, with whom I had about an
hour's conversation. He is under no small concern from apprehension upon two points at the approaching session of Congress; one, the rule excluding the reception of all petitions,
resolutions, and papers relating to slavery; and the other, upon
a revived project of annexing Texas to the United States — a
project of which formal notice has been given in newspapers
devoted to the interests and aspirations of President Tyler. I
look forward to both these designs with alarm and anguish —
not from the power of the South, which can effect nothing by
itself, but from experience of the treachery of the Northern
representation, both to Northern interests and principles.

Washington, January 1, 1842. — This was the thirtieth
New Year's Day that, in the course of my life, I have passed at
the city of Washington, and the twenty-fifth in succession, and
the physical atmosphere was, without exception, the finest of
all those days. One of the consequences of which was, that the
President's house was thronged with visitors beyond all former
example — so thronged, as we heard from many of those
that were there, that the crowd in the house was so great
that, to avert the danger of suffocation, the porter at the outer
door was obliged to lock out hundreds who were rushing to it
for admission, and that among the excluded were both the
Generals Scott and Gaines. I say visitors to the house; for it
is the house and not the President who is visited. From the
first establishment of the government of the United States to
this day, there never has been a time when the personal
sympathies of the people of all parties were so utterly indifferent as they are this day to John Tyler. Our own visitors this
day were not less than five hundred, more than double the
number we have ever had before.

Jan. 18. — At the House, the day was occupied in calling the States for petitions. The progress made was northward from Kentucky to New York. The delay was chiefly caused by the presentation of petitions, abolition, anti-slavery, and for and against the repeal of the Bankrupt law. After much desultory discussion, these last were all referred to the Committee on the Judiciary. The abolition petitions which came within the gag-rule were all quietly excluded; and for every anti-slavery petition which could not be disposed of thus, when presented, Wise, Hopkins, and Campbell of South Carolina interchangeably moved the question of reception, and then moved to lay that question of reception on the table. The yeas and nays were taken several times, and the vote to lay on the table always prevailed.

Jan. 21. — A resolution of a Pennsylvania anti-slavery society against a war with England to hold native Americans in slavery. Wise objected to this as *not presentable,* because it was not a petition, but the Speaker overruled that. He then attempted to prevent me from reading it, but did not succeed in that; but it was laid on the table.

I finally presented the petition from Georgia for my own removal from the office of chairman of the committee of foreign relations, and demanded to be heard in my own defence; which produced a fractious debate, cut off, after four o'clock, by the adjournment of the House. Marshall of Kentucky had moved that I should have leave to be heard in my own defence. Wise moved to lay the motion on the table; rejected — 82 to 84; whole subject laid on the table — 94 to 92.

Jan. 24. — I renewed the motion to refer the petition to the committee, with instructions to choose a chairman if they think proper. Debate arising thereon, it was laid over, and I presented sundry other petitions.

One from Benjamin Emerson and 45 others of Haverhill, Mass., praying Congress to take measures for peaceably dissolving the Union, with an assignment of three reasons. I moved its reference to a select committee, with instructions to report an answer assigning the reason why the prayer of the petition ought not to be granted. Then came another explosion, and after a snarling debate, a resolution offered by Thomas W. Gilmer, that I deserved the censure of the House for presenting a petition praying for the dissolution of

the Union.   Hot debate arose upon this, in the midst of which
the House adjourned.   Evening in meditation.

Jan. 25. — At one, Gilmer's resolution of censure upon me
was taken up.   Thomas F. Marshall offered a much more violent one, with a flaming preamble charging me in substance with
subornation of perjury and high treason, and resolutions that
the House might well expel me, but would only pass upon me
the sentence of their highest indignation, and turn me over,
for the rest, to my own conscience and the contempt of the
world.

The Speaker received this resolution, and when Marshall
finished his speech in support of it he called upon me for my
answer to it, and said the question would be on the adoption
of the resolution.   I said I thought it impossible the House
should entertain the resolution, and after a few remarks, post-
poning my defence till it should be ascertained that I stand
accused, I finished, and was followed by Henry A. Wise, who in
a speech of personal invective upon me, took nearly two hours,
and then, at the motion of his colleague Hopkins, the House
adjourned.

Jan. 26. — Wise resumed his philippic against me, and kept
it up about three hours before he finished.   I then said that I
had determined not to interrupt him till he had disgorged his
whole cargo of filthy invective, but I thought it impossible that
the House should entertain the resolution which charged me
with subornation of perjury, and consequential high treason
— crimes for which I could only be tried by a regular Circuit
Court, by an impartial jury; and I claimed the benefit of the
sixth article amendatory to the Constitution of the United
States.

The Speaker required me to reduce my point of order to
writing; which I did, and congratulated the Speaker upon his
discovery of the expediency of having points of order reduced
to writing — a favor which he had repeatedly denied to me.
He said it was a power exclusively possessed by the Speaker;
but that my demand was a question not for him to decide, but
for the House.

I then addressed the House, and denied their power to try
me for the crimes with which I was charged, and that they had
no right to assume the guilt without allowing me the privilege
of a trial.   And as to the resolution itself, I denied the right

of at least one hundred members of the House to sit in judgment upon me, their personal and pecuniary interest in the question carrying such a bias against me as would make them challengeable as jurors in a court of law. . . Fillmore finally moved to lay the whole subject on the table — which was rejected, by a vote of 90 to 100, and the House adjourned. . .

My dear wife, in her kind and affectionate assiduity and in her anxious and faithful solicitude for me, overplied the energies of her nature, so that she suffered this day a fainting fit; but it was transient, and she soon recovered, and was up again when I returned this evening from the House.

Jan. 27. — Underwood took the floor in a speech of an hour and a half against the resolution; he was followed by Botts, and he by Arnold of Tennessee, and he by Saltonstall. The effect of these speeches against the resolution was so powerful that Richard W. Thompson of Belford, Lawrence County, Indiana, immediately moved to lay the whole subject on the table. That motion would unquestionably have prevailed if taken then.

Jan. 28. — Marshall . . . commenced a violent, declamatory, and most eloquent philippic of nearly two hours against me. He labored with agonizing energy to answer the speeches of Underwood and of Botts delivered yesterday, and was particularly resentful against Underwood. I interrupted him occasionally, to rectify gross misrepresentations of facts, and sometimes to provoke him into absurdity; as, for example, at one part of his speech, that the Northern abolitionists knew nothing about the condition of the slaves. He assumed a courteous tone, and invited me to visit the Western country. " To be lynched," said I. " Very likely," said he; and proceeded.

Jan. 29. — Mr. Rufus Choate, one of the Senators from Massachusetts, came this morning and offered me any assistance that it might be in his power to render me in my present strait; for which I thanked him, and may perhaps avail myself of his offer, my means of defence requiring searches of books and documents, multiplying upon me as I proceed.

Jan. 31. — *Day.* My occupations during the month have been confined entirely to the business of the House, and for the last ten days to the defence of myself against an extensive combination and conspiracy, in and out of Congress, to crush the liberties of the free people of this Union by disgracing me with a brand of censure and displacing me from the chair of the Committee on Foreign Affairs for my perseverance in presenting abolition petitions. I am in the midst of that fiery ordeal, and day and night are absorbed in the struggle to avert my ruin. God send me a good deliverance!

Feb. 3. — Gilmer consumed nearly two hours in his long-meditated and bitterly rancorous speech against me. When he closed, Cushing started up; but the Speaker said I was entitled to the floor in my own defence. I spoke accordingly about an hour and a half, and brought to light the conspiracy among the Southern members of the Committee on Foreign Affairs to displace me as chairman and to elect Cushing in my stead. I produced the anonymous letter from Jackson, N. C., 20th January, 1842, threatening me with assassination, and the engraved portrait of me with the mark of a rifle-ball on the forehead, with the motto, ". To stop the music of John Quincy Adams, sixth President of the United States,

> Who, in the space of one revolving moon,
> Is statesman, poet, babbler, and buffoon."

These were Gilmer's own words, excepting the word fiddler, which his echo changed to babbler. I produced also and read the minutes of the proceedings in the Committee on Foreign Affairs. I reviewed my relations with the Virginian Presidents of the United States heretofore — Washington, Jefferson, Madison, Monroe — and contrasted them with this base conspiracy of three Virginians, banded here, together with numerous accomplices in and out of the House, for my destruction. Near four o'clock I closed for the day, with an apt quotation from Moore's *Loves of the Angels,* and came home very much exhausted.

Feb. 4. — I occupied the whole of this day in continuing my defence before the House. I began by renewing the charge upon Gilmer of having tampered with my colleague, Cushing, by the offer to choose him chairman of the Committee on Foreign Relations in my place. . . I charged the newspapers of this city and District with injustice to me, the *Globe* being daily filled with abuse and invective upon me while I am here on my trial, and the reporters of the *Intelligencer* suppressing the most essential parts of my defence. I specially refuted the pretence that the Union could be dissolved only by force, and cited the example of the peaceable dissolution of the Confederation Union by the present Constitution of the United States. Adjourned after three.

Feb. 5. — No report of my yesterday's speech in the *National Intelligencer,* but a blustering notification that, as I have chosen to complain of their reporters, they will report no more without my own authority. This is a mere subterfuge to suppress the publication of my defence and the exposure which I made of the conspiracy in and out of the House against me. . . I . . . proceeded. I was not well prepared, having expected that there would be no opposition to my motion for postponement; but I found no lack of matter for discourse, till the motion between three and four for adjournment, which was carried. My last missile upon Marshall was an exquisite blast upon slavery by himself in his pamphlet letters to the *Commonwealth* newspaper. He writhed under it in agony. Before I had read half the extract through, Romulus M. Saunders started up on a point of order on the old pretence — that I had no right to discuss the subject of slavery. The Speaker ruled the point against him. He appealed, and demanded the yeas and nays, which were refused, and the decision of the Speaker sustained — 97 to 25. I saw my cause was gained, and Marshall was sprawling in his own compost. I came home scarcely able to crawl up to my chamber, but with the sound of " Io triumphe " ringing in my ear.

Feb. 6. — At St. John's Church. . . My attention, morning and afternoon, involuntarily wandered from the preachers and their discourses to the critical nature of my own position; confident of deliverance from this particular assault upon me, so senseless that its malignity merges, by its stupidity, not into innocence, but into harmlessness; but always distrustful of my own control over my own spirit. One hundred members of the House represent slaves; four fifths of whom would crucify me if their votes could erect the cross; forty members, representatives of the free, in the league of slavery and mock Democracy, would break me on the wheel, if their votes or wishes could turn it round; and four fifths of the other hundred and twenty are either so cold or so lukewarm that they are ready to desert me at the very first scintillation of indiscretion on my part. The only formidable danger with which I am beset is that of my own temper.

Feb. 7. — Mr. Weld was here this morning, with a cheering report of the impression of my defence of Thursday, Friday, and Saturday upon the current of popular opinion. . .

I prepared a minute of the outlines of the continuance and conclusion of my defence, which would have occupied at least a week. But I saw on Saturday that the House was tired of the whole subject, and that to close it now would afford relief to all parties. I went to the House, therefore, prepared to proceed, but willing to stop short and dismiss the subject from the consideration of the House forever. I was belated, and the House had been about ten minutes in session when I entered and took my seat. Other business was under consideration, but the question of privilege, or my trial, was soon called up. I then observed that, having perceived on Saturday some impatience on the part of the House to get rid of this subject, and persevering in the determination not to be responsible for one hour of time unnecessarily consumed on this subject, if the House was ready to lay it on the table forever, I would acquiesce in that decision without requiring further time for my defence; of which I should need much if required to proceed.

Botts then moved to lay the whole subject on the table forever; carried, by yeas and nays — 106 to 93. Meriwether of Georgia asked to be excused from voting, because he hotly lusted for a vote of the severest censure upon me, but despaired of obtaining it. The House refused to excuse him, and he voted to lay on the table the whole subject. They then took in hand the Haverhill petition, and refused to receive it — 166 to 40, Briggs, Baker, Cushing, and Hudson voting with the majority.

March 10. — Mr. Nathaniel Tallmadge, one of the Senators from New York, came into the House with Charles Dickens, and called me out from my seat and introduced him to me. I dined with Robert C. Winthrop and John P. Kennedy. They went expressly to Dickens's lodgings at Fuller's to prevail on him to come and dine with them; but he was at dinner, and they did not see him.

March 14. — Dinner at Boulanger's to Charles Dickens;

to which I was invited by Aaron Ward. G. M. Keim presided. Mr. St. Clair Clarke, Vice-President. J. E. Holmes; Sutton, a reporter; Roosevelt; French; Robert Tyler. Toasts; speeches; songs. It was near midnight when I came home.

March 21. — [Joshua] Giddings, of Ohio, offered a series of resolutions relating to slavery and the *Creole* case. Ward moved the previous question. Everett moved to lay them on the table; lost by yeas and nays — 53 to 125. Everett moved a call of the House; refused. After much turbulence and confusion, Giddings withdrew the resolutions. Botts then moved a suspension of the rules to offer a preamble and resolution of censure upon Giddings; yeas 128, nays 68, not two-thirds.

March 22. — In the House, the resolution of censure upon Giddings, with a preamble first moved yesterday by Botts, then moved by Weller, moving at the same time the previous question, was taken up, and after two full hours of twistings, decisions by the Speaker reversed by the House, motions that he should have permission to be heard in his defence, by reconsideration, by suspension of the rules, by general consent, the resolution of censure was actually passed by yeas and nays — 125 to 69; and then the preamble was adopted — 119 to 66.

I can find no language to express my feelings at the consummation of this act. Immediately after the second vote, Giddings rose from his seat, came over to mine, shook cordially my hand, and took leave. I had a voice only to say, " I hope we shall soon have you back again." He made no reply, but passed to the seats of other members, his friends, and took leave of them as he had done of me. I saw him shake hands with Arnold, who had voted against him. He then left the House, and this evening the city.

March 23. — The Speaker presented a letter from Joshua R. Giddings, resigning his seat in the House.

April 3. — As we were returning home [from church], we met a carriage laden with two travelling trunks, part of the baggage of Lord Ashburton, once Alexander Baring, who arrived last evening in the *Warspite* from England, whence he now comes as Envoy Extraordinary and Minister Plenipotentiary, upon a special mission.

April 21. — I dined at Mr. Webster's. Lord Ashburton,

with his secretaries, Mildmay, Bruce, and Spedding, were there. . . Mrs. Webster was very amiable.

May 5. — Morning visit from Mr. Lay. . . Next came Mr. Joshua Leavitt, with the gratifying intelligence that Joshua R. Giddings was here, reëlected by a majority of upwards of 3,000 of his old constituents of the Sixteenth Congressional District of Ohio.

May 7. — Henry A. Wise assaulted and caned Edward Stanly this day on the race-course.

May 21. — The chill northeastern continues, but this day without rain. I wrote lines in the album of Mrs. Payne, Mrs. Madison's niece; and in the Boston *Mercantile Journal,* edited by a man characteristically called Sleeper, Mr. G. Brown has published, with a puff, my paraphrase of the first and second verses of the 61st chapter of Isaiah, written at his request. Not a day passes but I receive letters from the North, and sometimes the West, asking for an autograph and a scrap of poetry or of prose, and from the South almost daily letters of insult, profane obscenity, and filth. These are indices to the various estimation in which I am held in the free and the servile sections of this Union; indices to the moral sensibilities of free and of slavery-tainted communities. Threats of lynching and of assassination are the natural offspring of slave-breeders and slave-traders; profanity and obscenity are their natural associates. Such dross the fire must purge.

June 10. — There was a large wedding-party last evening at the house of Mr. Samuel L. Gouverneur, to witness the nuptials of his daughter with Dr. Heiskell, and a much more numerous company after the ceremony was over. President Tyler, the Secretaries of War and the Navy, Spencer and Upshur, with their families, Mrs. Madison, Lord Ashburton, with his secretaries, Mr. Bodisco, sundry members of both houses of Congress, General Scott, and several officers of the army and navy, were present at the solemnity, performed by Mr. Hawley, rector of St. John's, according to the rites of the Protestant Episcopal Church. We came home soon after ten; but the dissipation of the evening infected this morning with idleness.

June 12. — The party at the President's house last evening consisted of about a hundred persons, invited by Mrs. Tyler. Mrs. Madison, with her niece Anna Payne, my family and myself, and all the remnants of President Monroe's family — the bride, Mrs. Heiskell, being the only surviving grand child of Mr. Monroe.   There was dancing in the now gorgeously furnished East Room, and an elegant supper.   The courtesies of the President and of Mr. R. Tyler to the guests were all that the most accomplished European court could have displayed.   The President led the bride in to the supper-table, and requested me to escort Mrs. Robert Tyler.   Lord Ashburton followed with Mrs. Madison, and Mr. Webster, the Secretary of State, with my wife.   After supper I had a long conversation with Lord Ashburton, and went into the room where Mr. Healy is copying the full-length portrait of President Washington, and where the portrait of Mr. Guizot, painted by him, is deposited.   He has also the President's daughter Alice, painted by him.   It was within five minutes of midnight when we came home.

June 15. — Lieutenant Wilkes, in his conversation with me last evening, complained bitterly of the reception which he had met from the President of the United States and the Secretary of the Navy.   He said that his name had been omitted from the list of nominations for promotion in the navy, recently submitted by the President to the Senate; while the name of an officer whom he had been obliged to send home under arrest had been included in it.   That officer, while under arrest, had been permitted to make charges utterly frivolous and futile against him; and contrary to the first principles of justice, and what he believed the universal usage, those charges had been entertained.   All the other officers and men, returned from the expedition after three years of hardships, toils, and dangers, had naturally expected to be welcomed home with some cheering smile and some kind word from the government of their country.   They had found, instead of this, a cold, insulting silence.   Had this ungenerous treatment been confined to himself, he would have borne it with patience; but extended as it was to all the gallant and meritorious men, and to the accomplished officers and artists and men of science, whose labors had achieved results of which they might well be proud, it had overpowered him; and all the anxieties and cares and sufferings of the whole three years were as nothing to the anguish he had endured within the last five days.

July 24. — On my return homeward I stopped at Lord

Ashburton's and spent an hour with him. I understood from him that all the sharp points of his negotiation are adjusted and settled, though the treaty is not yet drawn up and executed in form. The Oregon Territory and Columbia River question remains open.

Aug. 19. — I was roused twice in the night by severe cramp in the legs, and feel that my body and mind are rapidly falling into decay. The position that I have taken is arduous enough to crush any man in the vigor of youth; but at seventy-five, with failing senses and blunted instruments, surrounded by remorseless enemies and false and scary and treacherous friends, how can it end but in my ruin? But I must meet the shock.

Sept. 1. — I called at the Treasury Department. The Secretary, Mr. Walter Forward has been for several weeks absent at the Bedford Springs, convalescent from a bilious fever. I read from the *National Intelligencer* and the *Globe* the reports of the passage through the House of the joint resolution from the Senate appropriating $6,000 for the expense of liberating citizens of the United States from Mexican captivity, taken as Texan prisoners of war in the expedition against Santa Fe last summer, and desired him particularly to mark my earnest and repeated remonstrances against it as unconstitutional. I said I knew not whether the President had signed the resolution or not, but I objected to the drawing of any money from the Treasury under its authority.

Sept. 5. — I received this day an impertinent letter from Fletcher Webster, bloated with self-sufficiency as an executive officer, maintaining that an appropriation by resolution is quite as proper and valid as if made by law, and that he has already made the requisition at the Department of the Treasury for the $6,000 appropriated by the resolution. He says in his letter that there are numerous precedents of this course. I answered him this evening, and called for a specification of his numerous precedents.

I went also to the Capitol, and examined the journal of the Senate, and traced up the fraud to the South Carolina Senator W. C. Preston, connived at by George Evans, chairman of their Committee on Finance — as arrant a piece of sheer knavery as ever was perpetrated at Eastcheap or found its reward at Tyburn. And Preston and Evans are two of the ablest men and most efficient Whigs in Congress.

Sept. 6. — I received this day from Fletcher Webster a reply to my answer, as impertinent, as ignorant, and as insolent as the former. Into what hands have the Presidency, the Departments of State and of the Treasury, fallen! Daniel Webster, his father, Secretary of State, has gone to Marshfield to shoot snipes and fish for trout, and to patch up some shameful rents in his private finances.

Sept. 7. — At precisely six took seats in the railroad cars for Baltimore. The weather warm but pleasant. Among our fellow travellers, not more than thirty, was Robert Tyler, the President's son, who spoke coldly to the ladies with me, but on inquiry of someone whether he had spoken to me, answered no, because I had abused his father. Captain Tyler's two sons are to him what nephews have usually been to the Pope, and among his minor vices is nepotism. He has quartered both of them upon the public for salaries, and made old Cooper, the broken-down stage player, father of his son Robert's wife, a military storekeeper. The son John was so distended with his dignity as secretary that he had engraved on his visiting cards, "John Tyler, jr., Private and Confidential Secretary of his Excellency John Tyler, President of the United States." Robert is as confidential as John, and both of them divulged all his cabinet secrets to a man named Parmalee and John Howard Payne, hired reporters for Bennett's *Herald* newspaper in New York, who by their intimacy with these upstart princes, crept into the familiarity of domestic inmates at the President's house.

Washington, Dec. 5. — Third session of the Twenty-seventh Congress commences. I was absorbed in reading the letters and papers received by the mail this morning, till I was belated in reaching the House of Representatives. The House had been in session ten minutes when I took my seat, and they were occupied in calling the roll of members by States when I entered.

Dec. 9. — The four members of the House who were overset in the stage coming from Zanesville — Caruthers, Gentry, Wallace, and Lane — arrived here this day, not wholly recovered from their wounds. Smith, the Senator from Indiana, still remains behind.

January 2, 1843. — Morning absorbed in reading the newspapers of the last night's mail and the *Globe* of Saturday evening upon my table. It contains the speeches of John C. Calhoun in the Senate of the United States last August, in favor of advising and consenting to the ratification of the Webster and Ashburton Treaty. Calhoun is the high-priest of Moloch — the embodied spirit of slavery. He has resigned his seat in the Senate of the United States, to take effect from the close of the present Congress, the 3d of March next, and immediately upon the acceptance of his resignation by the legislature of South Carolina they unanimously nominated him as a candidate for election as President of the United States for four years from the 4th of March, 1845. His speech is remarkable for one of those glaring, unblushing, dare-devil inconsistencies which, as far as I know, are peculiar to the doctrinal school of slavery. He begins by a broad, explicit, and unqualified declaration that he has always believed the claim of Maine upon the Northeastern boundary question just, and then proceeds with an elaborate argument to prove that on the same identical boundary question the title of Great Britain is clear to more than she has ever claimed. On the subject of slavery and the slave-trade the negotiation itself was a Scapinade, a struggle between the plenipotentiaries to outwit each other and to circumvent both countries by a slippery compromise between freedom and slavery. Calhoun crows about his success in imposing his own bastard law of nations upon the Senate by his preposterous resolutions, and chuckles at Webster's appealing to those resolutions now, after dodging from the duty of refuting and confounding them then. Calhoun concludes, upon the whole, to put up with the ticklish truce patched up between the treaty and the correspondence; and this was what, in fact, reconciled him to the ratification. There is a temperance in his manner obviously aiming to conciliate the Northern political sopranos, who abhor slavery and help to forge fetters for the slave.

Jan. 7. — I sit up so late at night, reading the newspapers and letters which come by the mail from nine to ten in the evening, that I seldom reach my bed before midnight — which necessarily delays for two hours at least that of my rising. "Sex horas somno," says Lord Coke, quoting from I know not whom; and that has been for more than forty years the rule of my life; and the six hours are from ten at night to four in the morning. But the rule of life must be modified by external causes, and by social relations with others. If I sit up till midnight, I cannot rise before six, and that irregularity leads to the laxity of the rule itself, to indulging in morning laziness, encroaching upon the best hours of the day.

Jan. 12. — General Cass came in last evening after dinner at Mr. Webster's, and told me what he had spoken of at my house on the 2d of this month. General Cass said that shortly after he left France, the King, Louis Philippe, asked him what in nature had got into Mr. Adams, with whom he recollected to have formed a very pleasing acquaintance in England, and whom he had ever since considered as a friend. Mr. Cass said he was surprised, and asked the King to what he alluded. " Why," says Louis Philippe, " he denies my title." The general said he did not know what to say in reply.

I told him that in a lecture delivered before a literary society, speaking of the dangerous and convulsed condition of Europe, and referring to France, I said that its king held his crown neither by the monarchical title of hereditary succession, nor by the republican title of popular election; but I spoke of it as an historical fact, without evil intention to him, and without imagining that it would have been remembered by anyone the next day.

" Well," said Mr. Cass, " but it was true."

Jan. 25. — John Davies, a colored man, came this morning with a letter from himself to me, asking my advice in behalf of his wife's son, named Joseph Clark, sold some years since . . . to a Colonel Curry, an agent or sub-agent employed in the removal of the Cherokee Indians. Curry took him to the State of Arkansas, employed him as an interpreter, and promised him his freedom. Curry afterwards died, and by his will declared Clark *free* after three years' service to his brother. The rascal brother sold him for $900, and he is now in irredeemable slavery for life. The mother of this poor man, " Jenny," lived some time with us, and at her instance her husband, Davies, came to ask my advice what can be done for him. But he has neither means to sue for his freedom nor evidence to prove the will. He is now living with a Dr. Davis Flint, Cherokee Nation, and acting as interpreter. Can I not possibly do something for this man?

Feb. 15. — Before going to the House, I had a quarter of an hour's conversation with Cushing, and told him there was a war now in parturition between Freedom and Slavery throughout the globe; that it would be a war for the abolition of slavery, at the head of which would be Great Britain; that in this war I could take no part — I was going off the stage; but he was coming on to it; and I conjured him, as he cherished his own and his country's honor, not to commit himself in this great controversy to the side of slavery; and to return to the cause of liberty, from which he had not yet irrevocably strayed.

He heard me without taking offence, but apparently without conviction.

Feb. 28. — Meeting of the Committee on Foreign Affairs at nine this morning. . . I . . . presented two resolutions to be reported to the House, on the reference of the resolution from the legislature of Alabama in favor of the annexation of Texas to this Union, and of sundry petitions against that measure — my first resolution denying the constitutional power of Congress or of any Department or Departments of the government of the United States to annex any foreign state or people to this Union, and the second that any attempt by act of Congress or by treaty to annex the republic of Texas to this Union would be a violation of the Constitution, null and void, and to which the free States of the Union, and their people ought not to submit. . . [Defeated, 6 to 3.] The vote was partisan sectional, except Cushing's, which was Northern servile, or dough-face.

March 2. — At the House, Reynolds, of Illinois, presented several impertinent resolutions of the Legislature of that State. Illinois is one of the bilking States, and Reynolds is one of her accredited cheats; and these States, just as they grow bold in sponging their debts, become profuse of their advice to Congress.

March 3. — In the House, the chaos of a closing Congress was more than usually magnificent. . . Adjourned, without day, at half-past one a.m., leaving the Senate in session upon executive business. They sat till half-past two, and thrice rejected Wise and Cushing.

March 21. — The controversy between Lewis Cass and Daniel Webster about the Ashburton Treaty, the rights of visitation and search, and the Quintuple Treaty, still, with the comet, the zodiacal light, and the Millerite prediction of the second advent of Christ and the end of the world within five weeks from this day, continue to absorb much of the public and of my attention. The *Intelligencer* of this day announces another letter from Cass to Webster, who in his last letter declares the correspondence closed.

March 23. — Another letter from Lewis Cass to Daniel Webster about the Ashburton Treaty, the right of visitation and search, and the offended dignity of the aforesaid Lewis Cass at the lordly tone assumed by the Secretary of State in the previous part of this correspondence.

I am thinking if there is anything parallel to this correspondence in our diplomatic history. Silas Deane came home from France and made a " rumpus " (that word is not in Webster's Dictionary — what a pity!) for several years, blew up a flame which kept this Union long in a " phease " (another Websterless word), and has left a large claim of his heirs and legal representatives against the United States, of which not a dollar is due, but which on some lucky day they will recover. Mr. James Monroe was recalled by President Washington through Timothy Pickering, wireworked by Alexander Hamilton. Mr. Monroe published a volume of his correspondence against the Administration of Washington, by whom he had been appointed and recalled; which book largely contributed to the fall of Washington's Administration as continued by his successor. It helped to bring in the Jefferson Administration, which laid the foundation for the dissolution of the Union.

March 29. — The day was fair and the temperature mild, but my *vis inertiae* so insuperable that it was near one when I got to Mr. Hunter's chamber at the Department of State. I took up again the volume of Anthony Butler's dispatches to the Department of State and to President Jackson during his mission to Mexico. . .

The appetite for Texas was from the first a Western passion, stimulated by no one more greedily than by Henry Clay. He had denounced the Florida Treaty for fixing the boundary at the Sabine, and held and preached the doctrine that we should have insisted upon our shadow of a claim to the Rio del Norte. President Monroe actually preferred the line of the Sabine, thinking that the extension of the boundary would weaken us for defence; and Jackson expressly approved the line of the Sabine. The first act of the Mexican Government, after declaring their independence, was to claim the boundary as settled by the Florida Treaty; and we had consented to it. But with the commencement of my Administration I appointed Poinsett Minister to Mexico, and Mr. Clay instructed him to propose the purchase of Texas. This they declined; but two years after the proposition was renewed. They then rejected it resentfully. But Jackson was so sharpset for Texas that from the first year of his Administration he set double engines to work, of negotiating to buy Texas with one hand, and instigating the people of that province to revolt against Mexico with the other. Houston was his agent for the rebellion, and Anthony Butler, a Mississippi land-jobber in Texas, for the purchase. Butler kept him five years on the tenterhooks of expectation, negotiating, wheedling, promising, and finally boasting that he had secured the bargain by bribing a priest with half a million of dollars. Jackson at last found him out and dimissed him rather abruptly. But he carried off some of the most important documents of the negotiation.

April 1. — I finished the extracts from Anthony Butler's letter to the Secretary of State, Forsyth, of 17th June, 1835. Neither this letter nor that of W. A. Slocum of 1st August, 1835, was ever communicated to Congress; but in them originated the project of enlarging the encroachment upon Mexico, from the mere acquisition of Texas, to embrace all New Mexico to the thirty-seventh parallel of latitude, and thence across the continent to the South Sea. Butler's letter connects with it a project for a commercial line of communication between the Arkansas River and the Colorado of California, uniting the Atlantic and Pacific Oceans. The Texan expedition of last year from Santa Fe must have been a sucker from the same root. Ap Catesby Jones's occupation of Monterey, Dr. Linn's bill for the organization of Oregon Territory, and above all, the tampering of Webster with the Mexican Minister here, Almonte, by a proposition that Mexico should cede to the United States the port of San Francisco and the parallel thirty-six of north latitude across the continent, to buy the consent of Great Britain with a cession to her from forty-nine to the Columbia River, present altogether a spectacle and prospect truly appalling. The root of the danger is the convulsive impotence of Mexico to maintain her own integrity, geographical, political, or moral, and the inflexible perseverance of rapacity of our South and West, under the spur of slavery, to plunder and dismember her.

April 3. — Morning call from Mr. Heman Lincoln. He is connected with the Baptist missions, and has been on an excursion to Virginia. He was inquisitive upon the prospects of the approaching Presidential election. He asked my opinion of the chances, and agreed with me that the prospects were in favor of Martin Van Buren. He thought the prospects of Henry Clay irretrievably gone; as I have no doubt they are. Those of Tyler, Calhoun, Cass, are equally desperate. Buchanan is the shadow of a shade, and General Scott is a daguerreotype likeness of a candidate — all sunshine, through a camera obscura. Mr. Lincoln's partiality was for Theodore Frelinghuysen or Judge John McLean. I had never heard the name of Frelinghuysen as a candidate before, and McLean is but a second edition of John Tyler — vitally Democratic, double-dealing, and hypocritical. They will all go into the Democratic convention, and all melt into the Corinthian brass of Kinderhook.

April 25. — Dr. Heap was here again this morning, very anxious about the prospect of his obtaining some appointment for subsistence in his old age. He has been shabbily treated — removed from his quiet sinecure at Tunis. . . I told him I had spoken of him and recommended his case to Mr. Webster, though I know not with what success. He said Mr. Webster had received him with coldness, and Mr. Tyler with much more; and upon his representing the unceremonious manner in which he had been displaced from office at Tunis, Mr. Tyler, in a tone of fretful uneasiness, had said, "I cannot remove my friend Payne" — meaning John Howard Payne, the histrionic parasite, who was here all the summer of 1841, currying favor by writing niminy-piminy meretricious letters of courtly adulation to John Tyler, to be published in the New York *Herald*. This was the sycophant, and this the service for which "my friend Payne" was appointed consul at Tunis, instead of an old public servant of forty years, with a large family, to linger about the world for a beggarly subsistence.

Quincy, June 16. — This was the day of the reception of the President of the United States, by the city of Boston. He comes with his Cabinet, and a ridiculous parade of ostentation, to attend the celebration of the completion of the Bunker Hill Monument — a costly pageant, first got up by Joseph Tinker Buckingham, president of the Bunker Hill Monument Association, and editor of the Boston *Courier,* the most respectable of Webster's trumpeters. The cornerstone of the monument was laid by La Fayette, on the 17th of June, 1825, on which occasion Webster delivered an eloquent discourse. He is to deliver another. The object now is to glorify him. A formal invitation was sent to him last fall, immediately after the completion of the monument, inviting him to the performance of this service, which he then accepted, and the invitation and acceptance were published in newspapers all over the country. The invitation to the President and his Cabinet to attend is a political device of Webster's own — a gull-trap for popularity, both for himself and for Tyler, by which he hopes to whistle back his Whig friends, whom he had cast off as a huntsman his pack, and who now threaten to hunt him, like the hounds of Actaeon. The reception of the President this day had all the appearances of cordiality, notwithstanding a drenching rain to cool it. He is lodged at the Tremont House, at an enormous expense to the city, was entertained there with a sumptuous dinner by the city council, and went to the theatre, and to an evening party at the postmaster, Gordon's, house. I was invited to the dinner, but sent an excuse.

June 17. — This was the day of the great celebration of the completion of the monument on Bunker Hill; and never since the existence of the three hills was there such a concourse of strangers upon their sides as has been assembled on the banks of " majestic Charles " this day. What a name in the annals of mankind is Bunker Hill! what a day was the 17th of June, 1775! and what a burlesque upon them both is an oration upon them by Daniel Webster, and a pilgrimage by John Tyler and his Cabinet of slave-drivers, to desecrate the solemnity by their presence! And then a dinner at Faneuil Hall in honor of a President of the United States, hated and despised by those who invited him to it, themselves as cordially hated and despised by him.

I have throughout my life had an utter aversion to all pageants and public dinners, and never attended one when I could decently avoid it. I was a student at Cambridge when, on the 17th of June, 1786, Charles River Bridge was opened. The colleges were emptied on that day of the students, who flocked to witness the procession and the pageant. I passed the day in the solitude of my study, and dined almost alone in the hall. I had then no special motive for my absence. But now, with the ideal associations of the thundering cannon, which I heard, and the smoke of burning Charlestown, which I saw, on that awful day, combined with this pyramid of Quincy granite, and Daniel Webster spouting, and John Tyler's nose, with a shadow outstretching that of the monumental column — how could I have witnessed all this at once, without an unbecoming burst of indignation, or of laughter? Daniel Webster is a heartless traitor to the cause of human freedom; John Tyler is a slave-monger. What have these to do with the Quincy granite pyramid on the brow of Bunker Hill? What have these to do with a dinner in Faneuil Hall, but to swill like swine, and grunt about the rights of man?

I stayed at home, and visited my seedling trees, and heard the cannonades of the rising, the meridian, and the setting sun, and answered a letter from the Rev. Joseph Emerson. . .

Boston, July 4. — My only surviving son, Charles Francis, delivered the annual Boston City Oration on the anniversary of independence, an incident of the most intense interest to me, it being this day fifty years since I performed the same service to the town. At half past eight this morning we left my gate, and went into Boston. . . About a quarter past one the ceremonies were all over. The last time I had been in Boston on the 4th of July was in 1809. I went up the hill at sunset, and witnessed the fireworks on the Common of Boston. No language can express the agitation of my feelings and the remembrances of this day.

July 6. — At ten o'clock I left home, with my son's wife and her son John Quincy. We went into Boston and dined at Dr. Frothingham's, meeting there her father, Mr. Peter Chardon Brooks. Immediately after dinner we proceeded to the depot of the Western Railroad, where after taking leave of Charles, who had just come in from Cambridge, we started in the cars at half past three. The weather was fine clear sunshine, yet comfortably cool.[2]

Springfield, July 7. — After breakfast, Colonel Howard and Mr. Ashmun called to see us, and accompanied Mr. Brooks and myself, with John Quincy, to the arsenal and the armory. At the arsenal we saw thirty thousand stand of arms, and were told that there were 150,000 ready for use in case of need. At the armory Major Ripley went round with us, and we saw the various processes of making the gun-barrels and the black walnut gun-stocks. I had seen these processes in 1828, but they are constantly making improvements in the manipulation of the musketry. They are now substituting the percussion lock and cap for the flint-lock and pan.

Niagara, July 25. — Mr. Millard Fillmore and Mr. Love, heretofore members of Congress, came this day, deputed from the city of Buffalo to invite me to visit that place, and Mr. Fillmore delivered to me a similar written invitation signed by thirteen citizens of Syracuse. I went this morning with General Porter to Goat Island, to bespeak a warm bath at the bathing-house just above the single-sheeted fall from which it borrows the stream that supplies the bath. They had then no heated water, but promised to have some ready for me this evening. I then walked about an hour before breakfast with the General, to reinspect all the points from which the cascades and the rapids are seen to the best advantage. The sky was unusually clear, the sun shining in cloudless splendor, and the snowy foam of the spray reflected the burning beams in a constantly-shifting rainbow, adding exquisite beauty to the awful grandeur of the falling flood.

Buffalo, July 26. — The passage from Schlosser to Buffalo occupied four hours, the banks of the river on both sides presenting a succession of beautiful landscapes. Some of us landed on Grand Island and inspected the pyramid announcing in Hebrew and in English the city of Ararat, founded by Mordecai M. Noah. We dined in the steamer, a cold-water dinner, and at four o'clock entered in beautiful style the harbor

---

[2] Adams began his trip into western New York for the health of his daughter-in-law, Mrs. Charles Francis Adams. He had no suspicion that it would develop into the tremendous ovation which it immediately became. He followed it with a trip to Cincinnati to dedicate a new astronomical observatory there, and found this expedition also seized upon for enthusiastic popular tributes to him and his services.

of Buffalo, at the entrance of Lake Erie. We were received
by shouting multitudes at the landing. I was conducted in an
open barouche to a stage at the park, received a complimentary
address from Mr. Fillmore, which was answered by me, addressing the people. After this I rode round the city with
Mr. Fillmore and the Mayor, then to the American Hotel,
and shook hands with some hundreds of men and women.
Firemen's torchlight procession. Thunder-shower, and evening party.

Rochester, July 27. — At half-past eight a.m. we left
Buffalo in the cars, thirty-five miles to Batavia. Here they
stopped to take in wood and water. Here a crowd was assembled, with Phineas L. Tracy, heretofore a member of Congress, who introduced me to them. A platform in front of
the door broke down from the weight of the pressure upon
it, and one gentleman, who had accompanied us from Buffalo,
was so much hurt that he was obliged to leave us. I was step-
ping from the platform into the house when the crash happened, and just escaped falling through. From Batavia to
Rochester is thirty-two miles. We arrived at Rochester between two and three, and found guns firing, bells ringing, and
an immense crowd of people shouting. The first person whom
I saw before alighting from the cars was Francis Granger. . .
We dined at the Eagle Hotel. After dinner, rode round the
city and to the cemetery of Mount Hope — a copy of that of
Mount Auburn, superior to the original. At six p.m. was the
public meeting. The mayor, Isaac Mills, addressed me from
a stage in front of a public building. I answered him by a
speech, and Granger, being called out, made a short one.
Then came the shaking of hands. In the evening I received
the ladies at the Eagle Hotel, and made them a short speech.
The firemen's torchlight procession closed the day.

Rochester, July 28. — We breakfasted at the hotel, and as
we were passing into the cars, Mr. Isaac Mills, the mayor of
Rochester, sent to our ladies a basket of delicious black-heart
and white-heart cherries, perfectly ripe, and of a size such as
I have not seen for many years. Mr. Granger and Mr. Jared
Wilson accompanied us to Canandaigua, whence they had been
sent as a deputation to meet us. At the entrance of the town
we met a cavalcade in military uniform, with a band of music,
and numerous carriages, all of which united in a procession of

a full mile, with bells ringing and a firing of cannon, which left me in amazement to enquire of myself what all this was for. The procession, however, led me to the Brick Church, where Mr. Francis Granger introduced me to all the beauty and fashion of Canandaigua, in a highly complimentary address, which I answered as best I could, in a speech full of inanity and gratitude, shamefaced and awkward, as I must always be in answering compliments to myself. After the speeches and shaking hands with all the men and women introduced to me in the church, I rode with Mr. Francis Granger, whose brother John A. Granger was the marshal of the day, to the house of his mother, with whom he resides and where I found his daughter. Thence I went to the splendid residence of Mr. John Greig — a princely palace — where I dined with a select party of his friends. . . We proceeded in the cars to Auburn, accompanied by the ex-Governor William H. Seward, and another deputy from Auburn, with an invitation to me to stop there. At Geneva and several other places on the road crowds were collected to shake hands with me, to hear me speak a few words, and to shout me onward. We arrived at Auburn between nine and ten at night, and by the torchlight procession of the firemen I was transported to Governor W. H. Seward's house for the night.

Auburn, July 29. — At nine o'clock we went to the Presbyterian church, where Mr. Seward addressed and introduced me to the people; and I answered in a speech of about half an hour. Christopher Morgan, a member of the 26th and 27th Congresses, had come from Aurora to meet me and invite me there; but I could not go. He came on with me to Syracuse, as did Mr. Seward and others of the Auburn committee, and the whole military company of the Auburn Guards. The distance from Auburn to Syracuse is twenty-six miles, which we traversed in one hour and five minutes. Repetition of address, answer, and shaking of hands, a public dinner with cold water, and a speech and toast from Governor Seward, briefly answered by me.

Utica, July 30. — Mr. Ezekiel Bacon called on me early this morning. Though chairman of the committee of arrangements for my reception at Utica, such was the confusion in the crowd and darkness of last evening that he missed meeting me. I was taken to a carriage and brought to Mr.

Johnson's house through a dense mass of population, I know not how or by whom. They brought me by the torchlight procession of firemen. From the porch of Mr. Johnson's house I thanked them for their kindness, and said I hoped and trusted that we should all devote this day to the worship and service of Almighty God, and that tomorrow I should have the happiness of meeting again my fellow-citizens face to face, when I should endeavor to find words to thank them for their kindness.

Aug. 1. — My first visit this morning, immediately after breakfast, was to the Female Seminary, where I was introduced to the assembled teachers and pupils, and addressed in behalf of the trustees of that institution by Mr. Spencer in a manner so affecting that it made a child of me. It consisted chiefly of extracts which he read from my mother's published letters of 19th August, 1774, to my father, and of June, 1778, to me. I actually sobbed as he read, utterly unable to suppress my emotion. Oh, my mother! Is there anything on earth so affecting to me as thy name? so precious as thy instructions to my childhood, so dear as the memory of thy life? I answered I know not what.

Aug. 2. — From Utica to Schenectady the distance is seventy-seven miles, and from Schenectady to Albany sixteen. At Herkimer, fourteen miles, at Little Falls, twenty-two, from Utica, and at every place in the valley of the Mohawk where the cars stopped five minutes for wood and water, crowds of people were assembled, received me with three cheers, and manifested a desire to see and hear me — with which I complied by descending from the cars, shaking hands with as many of them as could reach me, and addressing them till the passing bell called me back to my seat.

Aug. 3. — At ten o'clock this morning I met again the people of Albany, in company with Mr. Barnard, who addressed and welcomed me in their name from the stoop of Mr. Gregory's house facing the Capitol Park. There was no public building in the city capable of containing a tithe of the assembled multitude. I answered Mr. Barnard's address by a speech of about half an hour, well received. . . When the shouts that followed its close had subsided, notice was given to the citizens that I would repair to the Governor's chamber in the Capitol and there shake hands with anyone who would desire it. About five hundred of them, perhaps one-tenth of the whole number, went through this ceremony.

Buffalo, Oct. 30. — We embarked this morning before eight in the steamer *General Wayne,* with falling snow, which began about five. We had many opinions of the great imprudence of going out in that state of the weather; but the deputation from Erie were impatient to get home, and I was not the less impatient to reach as soon as possible the point of my destination, Cincinnati.

Cleveland, Nov. 1. — We landed at Cleveland at seven this morning, and here parted from Mr. Standart, one of our fellow-passengers from Buffalo, by whose advice we had come on without stopping from Ashtabula. From this place there are two modes of proceeding to Columbus, distant 232 miles — one by land stages travelling night and day, with excessively bad and very dangerous roads; the other by canal-boat on the Ohio Canal, which will take us four days to reach Columbus. We were advised by all means to take the latter mode, which we concluded to do, and took passage in the packet canal-boat *Rob Roy,* Captain Phillips. She was to depart at two o'clock p.m., and in the meantime I was to undergo a reception. I was first recognized at the barber's shop, while being shaved before breakfast. Immediately after breakfast a crowd of people thronged my chamber at the American Hotel, to be introduced and to shake hands with me.

Akron, Nov. 2. — I came on board of the canal packet-boat *Rob Roy* yesterday very unwell with my catarrh, hoarseness, and sore throat, and some fever. This boat is eighty-three feet long, fifteen wide, and had, besides the persons I have named, about twenty other passengers. It is divided into six compartments, the first in the bow, with two settee beds, for the ladies, separated by a curtain from a parlor bed-chamber, with an iron stove in the centre, and side settees, on which four of us slept, feet to feet; then a bulging stable for four horses, two and two by turns, and a narrow passage, with a side settee for one passenger to sleep on, leading to the third compartment, a dining-hall and dormitory for thirty persons; and lastly, a kitchen and cooking apparatus, with sleeping-room for cook, steward, and crew, and necessary conveniences. So much humanity crowded into such a compass was a trial such as I had never before experienced, and my heart sunk

within me when, squeezing into this pillory, I reflected that
I am to pass three nights and four days in it.   We came on
board the boat at two o'clock, the time when she was to depart,
but it was four before she left the wharf.   We were obliged
to keep the windows of the cabins closed against the driving
snow, and the stoves, heated with billets of wood, made the
rooms uncomfortably warm. . .

After a restless, sleepless night I rose twice, first at four and
again at half-past six.   As soon as daylight came, I was taken
in a carriage to a hotel, where we had a plentiful breakfast.
I was then taken again in a carriage to the Town Hall,
where I was addressed, and answered by a short speech, after
which I shook hands with the men, women, and children.
Among the women, a very pretty one, as I took her hand,
kissed me on the cheek.   I returned the salute on the lip,
and kissed every woman that followed, at which some made
faces, but none refused.   We returned to the boat and continued all day our progress through the canal, at the rate of
about two and a half miles an hour. . . There was snow great
part of the day — no encouragement to open the windows, or
to view the country through which we pass.

Columbus, Nov. 6. — We were to have left Columbus at
eight this morning, but there we were two military companies
of Germans from whom I had received a message requesting
leave to escort me out of the city, which I cannot resist.   It
delayed our departure about an hour, during which numerous
visitors thronged the house, among whom was the Governor
of the State, Shannon.   The German companies, with a band
of martial music, escorted us to the Scioto River and over it,
and Mr. Neil accompanied us in person.

Cincinnati, Nov. 8. — We breakfasted at Lebanon, and
proceeded twenty-two miles to Cincinnati.   We had now with
us a numerous committee from the Astronomical Society, and
on approaching the city, met a large cavalcade, with several
carriages, the mayor of Cincinnati, and Professor O. M.
Mitchel.   I descended from the stage and was conducted to an
elegant open barouche with four horses, in which I took a seat
with Judge Burnet, the mayor of the city, and Professor
Mitchel.   The day was fine and the sun shone bright; but
Cincinnati is embosomed in a circle of steep and lofty hills —
at the turn of a corner in descending one of which the pole of

our carriage snapped short off, and we were obliged to pass into an ordinary barouche and pair. An immense crowd of people followed us to the Henry House, in Third Street, kept by Major Henry, where lodgings were provided for us. In front of this house there is a large balcony overlooking the street, upon which Mr. Spencer, the mayor, delivered a complimentary address, welcomed me to the city, and introduced me to the assembled multitude, who answered by deafening shouts of applause. My answer was flat, stale, and unprofitable, without a spark of eloquence or a flash of oratory, confused, incoherent, muddy, and yet received with new shouts of welcome. The crowd then dispersed; but a continual succession of visitors beset my chamber till late in the evening, leaving scarcely an interval for dinner and tea.

The arrangements for laying the cornerstone of the Observatory, and for the delivery of my oration tomorrow, were concerted with Professor Mitchel, Judge Burnet, and Mr. Greene; but the address on the spot, in the act of laying the cornerstone, was not yet prepared. Worn down with fatigue, anxiety, and shame, as I was, and with the oppression of a catarrhal load upon my lungs, I sat up till one in the morning, writing the address, which, from utter exhaustion, I left unfinished, and retired to a sleepless bed.

Nov. 9. — I rose again at four, and before breakfast finished the address to be delivered at the laying of the cornerstone. A succession of visitors, invitations, and deputations ensued till ten o'clock, when a dense crowd of people gathered in the street fronting the Henry House, and the procession of the members of the Astronomical Society was formed. . . As we entered the carriage it began to rain, and we were obliged to raise the sides over our heads for shelter, and exclude the sight of me from the people, and the people from me. The procession marched round sundry streets, the rain increasing till it poured down in torrents; yet the throng in the streets seemed not at all to diminish. It looked like a sea of mud. The ascent of the hill was steep and slippery for the horses, and not without difficulty attained. The summit of the hill was a circular plain, of which the cornerstone was the centre. At the circumference a stage was erected, from which my discourse was to have been delivered; but the whole plain was covered with an auditory of umbrellas, instead of faces. It was then deter-

mined that the discourse should be delivered tomorrow morning in the Wesleyan Chapel, and the cornerstone now laid —
which ceremony I performed, and read the address which I
had written last evening and this morning, to which the circle
of hearers gathered around responded by three hearty cheers.

Washington, Nov. 24. — I have performed my task, I have
executed my undertaking, and am returned safe to my family
and my home. It is not much in itself. It is nothing in the
estimation of the world. In my motives and my hopes, it is
considerable. The people of this country do not sufficiently
estimate the importance of patronizing and promoting science as a principle of political action; and the slave oligarchy
systematically struggle to suppress all public patronage or
countenance to the progress of the mind. Astronomy has been
specially neglected and scornfully treated. This invitation had
a gloss of showy representation about it that wrought more on
the public mind than many volumes of dissertation or argument.

CHAPTER XV

1843—1845

THE JACKSON FINE BILL — STEPHEN A. DOUGLAS — EXPLOSION ON
THE "PRINCETON" — THE PETITION FIGHT RENEWED — VICTORY
WON AT LAST — DEATH.

Washington, December 15, 1843. — At the House, immediately after the reading of the journal, Dromgoole called up the question about the rules. . . The previous question was carried, and the rules, with the exception of two struck out on Wise's motion, with my amendment for going into and coming out of committee of the whole by mere majority votes, were adopted, including the hour rule and the gag. Dromgoole then moved his rule for excluding from the journal any paper which the House refuses to receive; and it was carried without even taking the yeas and nays.

Mr. John J. Crittenden, one of the senators from the State of Kentucky, left with me for my perusal a private and confidential letter from Henry Clay to him, on the subject of Texas, dated the 5th of this month. He thinks Texas in Tyler's hands is a mere firebrand, to be noticed as little as possible. Mr. Crittenden concurs with him.

Dec. 16. — I expended all the leisure of this morning in copying a list of the yeas and nays on my motion to except the twenty-third or anti-petition rule from the adoption of the House by the last Congress. . . The Democratic majority may be set down as two-thirds; yet on my motion the vote stood 91 to 94 — a majority of only three to retain the gag rule. Twenty-seven members from New York voted for my motion — only five against it; twelve from Pennsylvania for, and eight against; Ohio, thirteen for and five against it.

Dec. 17. — The explosion which took place in the House on my presenting yesterday the anti-slavery petition of citizens

of Western New York, is a premonitory symptom of the desperation with which the slave-power will be exercised in the
present Congress.   The Latimer petition, signed by upwards
of 50,000 names, was received at the last session of Congress
and referred to the Judiciary Committee.   The petition from
New York, which I presented yesterday, contains the same
prayer in the same identical words.   The Speaker instantly
decided that it was excluded from reception by the gag rule,
now the twenty-third.

I remonstrated that on the journals of the last session it was
recorded that petitions in the same words were received and
referred to the Judiciary Committee.   Half a dozen slave-
breeders were already on their feet.   The Speaker coolly said,
" Does the gentleman appeal from the decision of the Chair? "

I said I had already had too much experience not to be
aware of the fate of any appeal from the decision of the Chair,
but that I entreated the Speaker to revise his own decision
so far as to look at the precedent on the journal of the last
session.   The Speaker said he considered the petition excluded
by the rule.   I then said that if the Speaker refused to look at
the precedent I had no other alternative, and *must* take an
appeal from his decision.   At this instant F. W. Gilmer started
up in a panic and moved to adjourn.

Dec. 20 — Petitions.   The Speaker reversed his decision
of Saturday, and declared the petition of James B. Cooper and
525 citizens of New York State not excluded by the rule; but
the question of reception was made and laid on the table —
97 to 80 — and the new vital struggle for the right of petition
commenced, in the midst of which the House adjourned.

Dec. 21. — In the House, the life-and-death struggle for
the right of petition was resumed.   The question of reception
of the petition from Illinois was laid on the table — 98 to 80
— after a long and memorable debate.   I then presented the
resolves of the Massachusetts Legislature of the 23d of
March, 1843, proposing an amendment to the Constitution of
the United States, making the representation of the people in
the House proportioned to the numbers of free persons, and
moved it should be read, printed, and referred to a select committee of nine.   And now sprung up the most memorable debate ever entertained in the House, in the midst of which the
House, at half-past three, adjourned.   I can give no account of

it. Wise formally surrendered at discretion his citadel rule to
the right of petition. Then came a cross-fire between Holmes,
Beardsley, Weller, and French, till at the motion of Belser, of
Alabama, the House adjourned. R. D. Davis of New York
had taken the floor.

The crisis now requires of me coolness, firmness, prudence,
moderation, and for attitude beyond all former example. I
came home in such a state of agitation that I could do nothing
but pace my chamber.

Dec. 22. — Pilgrim anniversary. The agony continues.
Meeting of the committee on the revisal of the rules. Wise,
the chairman, came in reasonable time, but Vinton was very
late. I had moved to strike out the twenty-fifth rule. . . Wise
had prepared a substitute ten times worse than the rule to be
rescinded — the same that was palmed upon the committee to
revise the rules at the first session of the last Congress —
that, on the presentation of any petition, memorial, or paper
relating in any manner to slavery, the question of consideration
shall always be considered as raised, and they shall be laid
on the table. Wise now declined to offer it, but Chapman did,
and the vote upon it was — ayes, Chapman, Ingersoll, Wise;
nays, Adams, Beardsley, Davis, Vinton, and White. . .

The occurrences in the House yesterday and this day have
been so extraordinary that they would require a narrative,
which it is impossible for me to write out, but a brief summary
of which I must borrow a supernumary page to record.

Yesterday, after a long snarling debate to suppress the
enthusiastical petition from the State of Illinois, finally read,
and, upon question of its reception, laid on the table, when I
presented the resolves of the legislature of Massachusetts
and moved the reference of them to a select committee of
nine, Jameson moved the Committee on the Judiciary, Cave
Johnson a committee of one member from each State. Wise
rose, called upon the reporters to take note of what he was
about to say, asked the particular attention of the House, and
declared once for all, and forever, that he renounced this
WAR against Southern rights which had been for several years
waged in the hall. He would vote for my motion to refer these
resolves to a select committee, and hoped I should be chairman
of it, that the whole committee should be of the same complexion, and that the whole mass of abolition petitions should

be referred to the same committee, that we might make a report in our own way, and the House and the country might see what we were after. Whereupon Holmes, Beardsley, Weller, and French made frothy and foaming speeches about abolition. . .

This day . . . Belser moved to lay the resolves of the legislature of Massachusetts on the table. Lost — 64 to 104. Jameson withdrew his motion to refer them to the Committee on the Judiciary, and my motion to refer them to a select committee of nine was carried without a division.

Dec. 26. — The Speaker called for petitions. I presented one from Connecticut, containing four prayers — the first of which was for the abolition of slavery and the slave-trade in the District of Columbia; the other three prayers were not within the rule, and I moved the reference of the fourth — intercourse with Hayti — to the Committee on Foreign Affairs. The Speaker decided that the whole petition was excluded. This was contrary to the precedents. I appealed from the decision; but it was sustained by the House — 105 to 40.

Dec. 28. — The States were called through for petitions. Giddings presented one from a negro claiming to be free, a citizen of Virginia named William Jones, but now in jail here, and advertised to be sold for jail-fees. Giddings moved its reference to a select committee of five, with power to send for persons and papers. Another explosion, and the subject laid over because it gave rise to debate.

Dec. 29. — The record of yesterday must overflow upon this day. When Giddings presented the petition from the negro William Jones, now in jail and advertised to be sold for jail-fees, the whole slave-representation was up in arms. Fifty-five names are recorded in favor of a motion to lay the petition on the table. The Speaker ordered the whole subject to lie over, because it raised debate.

January 1, 1844. — From ten to three o'clock, an uninterrupted stream of visitors absorbed the time and exhausted my patience. It is generally meant in kindness — always in civility — and for a succession of fifteen years, since I left the President's house, has greeted me in still increasing numbers. Among the visitors of this day were some of the bitterest political enemies, North and South, that I have in the world.

Holmes and Campbell, of South Carolina, Burke and Hale, of New Hampshire, were of the number, and Charles Jared Ingersoll, the cunningest and most treacherous cat of them all. . . Immediately after I got disengaged from the throng, about three, I walked to Mrs. Madison's house and paid her a visit.

Jan. 8. — The Jackson fine bill. . . Pratt, of New York, moved . . . a resolution to stop debate and take the bill out of committee in two hours, with a long preamble stating that the legislatures of seventeen States, representing a population of fifteen out of seventeen millions of the people of the United States, had demanded the restoration of this fine. . . Schenck, of Ohio, had the floor from Saturday and made an hour speech of unrivalled eloquence in that department of debate which one of the Athenian orators called the Shears — cutting up the arguments of the adversary. Schenck said little about the first principles involved in this case, and not much about the facts, but he did cut up the malignant sycophantic declamations of Kennedy, Weller, Dean, and Douglas, so that there was scarcely a shred of them left. His manner is cool, firm, unhesitating, with conscious mastery of his subject; his voice clear and strong, his elocution neat and elegant, with a swelling vein of sarcastic humor, which more than once made the hall ring with shouts of laughter. He had got hold of Douglas, and was shaking him as a bulldog shakes between his teeth a dead rat, when his hour expired, and A. V. Brown took the floor, and from that time, with the exception of a short quarter of an hour for Severance, the Jackson trumpeters blew till they brayed like jackasses. At four they passed the bill, and closed the day with a triumphal drunken bout at the Apollo Hall, toasting and crepitating with a cannon in the street till long after midnight.

Jan. 21. — The question about keeping the Sabbath holy as a day of rest is one of the numerous religious and political excitements which keep the free people of this Union in perpetual agitation. They seem to be generated by the condition of the country — in a state of profound peace. There are in this country, as in all others, a certain proportion of restless and turbulent spirits — poor, unoccupied, ambitious — who must always have something to quarrel about with their neighbors. These people are the authors of religious revivals.

They formed, in the days of Washington's Administration, the germ of Jacobin clubs. During the last war with Great Britain, they generated the Washington benevolent societies and peace societies. In later times they have bred the Masonic and anti-Masonic Societies, the temperance societies, the colonization, abolition, and anti-slavery societies; and they are now beating the drum and blowing the trumpet for a holy Sabbath society. A numerous convention is already advertised to promote the cause, and Mr. Edwards has come to preach for it in the Representative Hall.

Jan. 23. — A poor negro came almost in a state of distraction, to implore me to save his wife from being sold away. I asked him, how I could do that? He said, by purchasing her myself for $400. I told him that was impossible. The poor fellow went away in despair.

Jan. 30. — Between the preparation of my report on the Massachusetts resolves, and keeping time with my daily record, the labor is more than Herculean, and my correspondence is almost entirely suspended. Five days in the week, the report of the Committee on the Rules is the first business in order to be transacted in the House; and if I were to be absent one day, when it would be called up, it would be laid upon the table without redemption. When I call it up, scarcely a day passes but some dirty trick is devised to postpone the taking of the question. This day Stiles, of Georgia, finished his hour speech, and twenty-three minutes were lost of the morning hour. Andrew Johnson, of Tennessee, another slave-holder, obtained the floor and said he wished to deliver his whole speech at once, and so he moved to postpone the further consideration of the subject till tomorrow; against which I remonstrated in vain.

Jan. 31. — I hurried up to the Capitol, to be there at the meeting of the House. The report on the rules was immediately taken up, and Andrew Johnson, a new member from Tennessee, made an hour's speech in support of the gag-rule, and especially abusive upon me. So they all are. I am compelled not only to endure it with seeming insensibility, but to forbear, so far as I can restrain myself, from all reply.

Feb. 13. — . . . To escape an hour or two of soporifics, I left the hall and went into that where the Supreme Court were in session, to see what had become of Stephen Girard's will,

and the scramble of lawyers and collaterals for the fragments
of his colossal and misshapen endowment of an infidel charity-
school for orphan boys. Webster had just closed his argument, for which, it is said, if he succeeds, he is to have fifty
thousand dollars for his share of the plunder. The courtroom was nearly deserted.

Feb. 14. — At the House, Stephen A. Douglas, of Illinois,
the author of the majority report from the Committee on
elections, had taken the floor last evening, and now raved out
his hour in abusive invectives upon the members who had
pointed out its slanders, and upon the Whig party. His face
was convulsed, his gesticulation frantic, and he lashed himself
into such a heat that if his body had been made of combustible
matter it would have been burnt out. In the midst of his
roaring, to save himself from choking, he stripped and cast
away his cravat, unbuttoned his waistcoat, and had the air and
aspect of a half-naked pugilist. And this man comes from a
judicial bench, and passes for an eloquent orator!

Feb. 28. — Dies irae. I had received an invitation from
Captain Robert F. Stockton, to another party of pleasure,
with the ladies of my family, on board the war steamer
Princeton. We declined the invitation, as I could not intermit
my attendance at the House, and my wife and daughters were
expecting the arrival of our friends Mr. and Mrs. F. B. Stockton, who came to spend a few days with us. Isaac Hull Adams
had a separate invitation, and went to the ill-fated party. I
had engaged also to dine at six o'clock this evening with Mr.
Grinnell and Mr. Winthrop, in company with Mr. Pakenham,
the new British Minister. . .

While we were at dinner, John Barney burst into the chamber, rushed up to General Scott, and told him, with groans, that
the President wished to see him; that the great gun on board
the *Princeton,* the "Peacemaker," had burst, and killed the
Secretary of State, Upshur, the Secretary of the Navy, T. W.
Gilmer, Captain Beverley Kennon, Virgil Maxcy, a Colonel
Gardiner of New York, and a colored servant of the President, and had desperately wounded several of the crew.
General Scott soon left the table; Mr. Webster shortly after;
also Senator Bayard. I came home before ten in the evening.

March 2. — I had met yesterday at the Capitol Mr. Rives,
the chairman of the Senate's committee of arrangements for

the funeral, who told me that the members of the two houses
were to assemble at their respective halls this morning at half-
past ten, and thence to proceed in a body to the President's
house, where the corpses were deposited, and where, in the
East Room, the religious services were to be performed.   I
went, accordingly, to the House this morning.   A large portion of the members of both Houses assembled, and hack carriages were provided for them.   I stepped into one of them
with the Speaker, John W. Jones. . .

At the President's the Speaker parted from me to resume
his place at the head of the House — a special place having
been assigned in the procession, immediately after the President and his Cabinet, to the ex-Presidents of the United
States, of whom I was the only one present.   There were four
corpses in plain coffins — those of the three public officers,
with the Union flag stretched over them, and Colonel Gardiner's covered with a black pall.   The East Room was
crowded with the President, his Cabinet and sons, and women
of his family, the two Houses of Congress, foreign Ministers,
the mayors of Washington, Georgetown, and Alexandria,
municipal officers and of the departments, army, and navy,
and the relatives of the deceased.   Mr. Hawley read a part
of the Episcopal funeral service . . . after which the long funeral blackened all the way from the East Room to the Congressional burial-ground, near the eastern branch of the
Potomac.   At the common depository vault I heard the
remainder of the Episcopal funeral service recited, and
then came home alone.   It was four in the afternoon; and I
mused.

March 6. — Miss Thompson is a young woman of South
Carolina, much in want of money to enable her to go to her
brother in Beaufort in that State.   She came here yesterday
to solicit charity of my wife, and repeated her visit this morning to me.   I did not think her a very piteous claimant of alms,
for she was apparently healthy, and somewhat ambitiously
dressed; but she reminded me so much of her State that I gave
her a five dollar bill.

March 13. — At the House, R. C. Winthrop came to
my seat and said he proposed to move tomorrow morning a
suspension of the rules to offer a resolution against the annexation of Texas.   He read the resolution that I had prepared

yesterday of a call on the President to inform the House whether he was negotiating for the annexation of Texas, and said the answer to that call would be of deeper import than perhaps I imagined. He said he believed it necessary to make an explosion on the subject. The explosion will come too late.

March 25. — I approach the term when my daily journal must cease from physical disability to keep it up. I have now struggled nearly five years, without the interval of a day while mind and body have been wearing away under the daily, silent, but unremitting erosion of time. I rose this morning at four, and with smarting, bloodshot eye and shivering hand, still sat down and wrote to fill up the chasm of the closing days of the last week; but my stern chase after Time is, to borrow a simile from Tom Paine, like the race of a man with a wooden leg after a horse.

March 26. — The Commissioner of Patents, H. L. Ellsworth, came with Jeremiah E. Cary of Cherry Valley, member of the twenty-first Congressionial district of New York, and delivered a letter to me from himself, with one from Julius Pratt & Co., manufacturers of Meriden, Conn., and a present of a milk-white ivory cane, one yard long, made of one elephant's tooth, tipped with silver and steel, and the American eagle inlaid with gold on its top, and a ring under the pommel, inscribed with my name, and the words, " Justum et tenacem propositi virum." The letter requests that on the day when the gag rule shall be finally abolished I will insert the date after the inscription on the ring.

After expressing my deep sensibility to this testimonial of kindness and approbation of my public conduct, I promised a written answer to Mr. Pratt's letter, and alluding to my custom of declining valuable presents from individuals for public service, I accepted the cane as a trust to be returned when the date of the extinction of the gag rule shall be accomplished.

April 20. — At the House, John Wentworth, of Illinois, made a personal explanation assuring the House that he did not use the words " By God! " yesterday, as reported in the *Intelligencer,* but only exclaimed " My God! " — an exclamation of deep sensibility, but in no sense or intention of using profane language.

April 22. — This was a memorable day in the annals of the world. The treaty for the annexation of Texas to this Union was this day sent into the Senate; and with it went the freedom of the human race.

May 1. — A copy of the treaty for the annexation of Texas, with all the correspondence communicated with it, printed in confidential secrecy for the use of the Senate, by some treachery was conveyed to the table of the editor of the New York *Evening Post,* and they have been all published. Letters from Henry Clay, Martin Van Buren, and Thomas H. Benton, all concurring in the injustice and impolicy of annexing Texas at this time to the United States, have been published within the last five days, and the reading them has consumed so much time that my diary runs again into arrears, and my head into confusion.

This was the first day of the Whig Convention at Baltimore, to nominate Henry Clay as their candidate for the office of President of the United States for four years from the 4th of March next, and to agree upon a candidate for the office of Vice-President. They met accordingly, 275 in number, from the twenty-six States, equal to the constitutional number of the two Houses of Congress.

May 4. — The stream of visitors, returning delegates from the Baltimore Convention, is yet copious and unabated. Many of my old acquaintances come to shake hands with me as they pass, and many others ask to be introduced to me for the same purpose. Their names are seldom pronounced by their introducers so that I distinctly hear them, and their names and their persons slip alike from my memory the moment they part from me. But they consume time, and multiply subjects of excitement tending to distraction.

At the same time the treaty for the annexation of Texas to the United States, with the President's message transmitting it to the Senate, and the accompanying documents, and the conflicting opinions of the leading men of the Union, disclosed in letters and speeches at public meetings, all indicate the immediate crisis of a great struggle between slavery and freedom throughout the world. I must retire from this contest, or perish under it, probably before the close of the present year, or even of the present session of Congress. The issue is precipitated by its bearing on the approaching Presidential election. It is John Tyler's last card for a popular whirlwind to carry him through; and he has played it with equal intrepidity and address.

May 9. — A new subject of political excitement is opening upon this country, the extent and duration of which it is impossible for me to foresee, but which must have great influence for good or evil (God grant it may be for good) upon the future history and fortunes of this Union. It is a deadly feud between the native American poor population and the Roman Catholic Irish multitudes gathered in the city of Philadelphia. The animosities betweeen these two classes of people have been fermenting in all our Atlantic cities for several years, and hence been much aggravated by the pernicious factious influence of these Irish Catholics over the elections in all the populous cities. The reaction of the native American population effected a total revolution in the recent election of the city government of New York. They have now broken out in furious riots at Philadelphia, where from the first of this week, a succession of bitterly exasperated mobs have destroyed multitudes of human lives, dwelling houses, schools, and churches, unrestrained by the governments of the city or the State.

May 24. — This was the day on which the two Democratic conventions to nominate candidates for the offices of President and Vice-President of the United States for four years from the 4th of March next were held at Baltimore, and also a convention to nominate a candidate for the office of Governor of Maryland. By the new invention of the electro-magnetic telegraph of Professor Morse, the proceedings of these bodies throughout the day were made known here at the Capitol, and announced as soon as received, in manuscript bulletins suspended to the wall in the rotunda.

June 10. — The vote in the United States Senate on the question of advising and consenting to the Texan Treaty was, yeas, 16; nays, 35. I record this vote as a deliverance, I trust, by the special interposition of Almighty God, of my country and of human liberty from a conspiracy comparable to that of Lucous Sergius Catalina. May it prove not a mere temporary deliverance, like that, only preliminary to the equally fatal conspiracy of Julius Cæsar! The annexation of Texas to this Union is the first step to the conquest of all

Mexico, of the West India islands, of a maritime, colonizing, slave-tainted monarchy, and of extinguished freedom.

June 17. — The first shock of slave Democracy is over. Moloch and Mammon have sunk into momentary slumber. The Texas treason is blasted for the hour, and the first session of the most perverse and worthless Congress that ever disgraced this Confederacy has closed. This last day, from ten in the morning till noon, was a continuation of tumult from the adjournment of yesterday morning. The joint resolution of the two houses had fixed the adjournment, by their respective presiding officers, at twelve o'clock meridian this day.

June 27. — This day set in the extreme heat of summer the trial of climate to my constitution. A burning sun; the thermometers in my chamber at ninety, and a light breeze from the southwest — a fan delicious to the face, but parching instead of cooling the skin. I have been a full month longing for a river bath without daring to take it. This morning at five I went in the barouche to my old favorite spot, found the tide unusually high; all my station rocks occupied by young men except one, and that surrounded by the tide, already upon the ebb. I had some difficulty to dress and undress, but got my bath, swam about five minutes, and came out washed and refreshed. It was my exercise for the day. After returning home I did not not again pass the sill of the street door.

July 4. — One of my reasons for remaining in this city after the close of the session of Congress till this day shall be past, was to escape from all the celebrations to which I was or might be invited, the noise and bustle and excitement and ranting of this day having become irksome to me. I intended, nevertheless, to attend this oration and entertainment at the Georgetown College; but my driver took a holiday for himself and disappointed me. I was, however, well pleased with my disappointment; passed the day very quietly at home till close upon sunset, when I strolled out for an hour, and on returning, stopped at Mrs. Madison's and took leave of her for the summer. Morning and evening visitors as by the margin, chiefly military officers who had been in grand costume to pay their devoirs to the President. The wedding visit last Saturday and that of Independence Day came so close together that the attendance this day was thin. Captain Tyler and his bride are the laughing stock of the city. It seems as if he was racing for a prize-banner to the nuptials of the mock-heroic — the sublime and the ridiculous. He has assumed the war power as a prerogative, the veto power as a caprice, the appointing and dismissing power as a fund for bribery; and now, under circumstances of revolting indecency, is performing with a young girl from New York the old fable of January and May.

Quincy, Nov. 8. — I understood the meaning of the guns fired last night on receipt of the election returns from the western counties of New York by the train of cars from Albany. They settle the Presidential election, and James K. Polk of Tennessee is to be President of the United States for four years from the 4th of March, 1845. What the further events of this issue may be is not clear, but it will be the signal for my retirement from public life. It is the victory of the slavery element in the constitution of the United States. Providence, I trust, intends it for wise purposes and will direct it to good ends. From the sphere of public action I must, at all events, very soon be removed. My removal now is but a few days in advance of the doom of nature, and gives me time, if I have energy to improve it, which will not be lost.

Nov. 9. — There was an immense meeting of Whigs last evening in Faneuil Hall, in Boston. Daniel Webster was there, and made a speech commencing, with " What though the field is lost; all is not lost," etc. The depression and despondency of the Whig Party at the issue of the Presidential election in the State of New York is beyond all example or precedent. I spent the evening in folding up copies of my two addresses to my constituents at Braintree and North Bridgewater, and in reflecting upon the duty that will now devolve upon me, to retire for the short remainder of my days from public life altogether.

Washington, Nov. 25. — I arrived here on Saturday evening, with a clear sky, bright moonlight, and the atmosphere of May rather than of November. Yesterday morning it was yet warm, but the wind came round to the northeast, and it was all day growing cold. . . I walked out for exercise, and at the *National Intelligencer* office saw Mr. Gales in deep distress at the issue, totally unexpected, of the Presidential election. He is in despair, and foresees that it must prove his irretrievable ruin. It has been accomplished by fraud through the slave representation. The partial associations of Native Americans, Irish Catholics, abolition societies, Liberty party, the Pope of

Rome, the Democracy of the sword, and the dotage of a ruffian, are sealing the fate of this nation, which nothing less than the interposition of Omnipotence can save.

Dec. 2. — Precisely at noon, John W. Jones, Speaker . . . took the chair and called the House to order. The roll was then called, and 175 members answered to their names.

Dec. 3. — At the meeting of the House this day . . . R. M. Saunders moved the appointment of the standing committees; which was agreed to. In pursuance of the notice I had given yesterday, I moved the following resolution: " Resolved, that the twenty-fifth standing rule for conducting business in this House, in the following words, ' No petition, memorial, resolution, or other paper praying the abolition of slavery in the District of Columbia or any State or Territory, or the slave trade between the States or Territories in which it now exists, shall be received by this House, or entertained in any way whatever,' be, and the same is, hereby rescinded." I called for the yeas and nays. Jacob Thompson of Mississippi, moved to lay the resolution on the table. I called for the yeas and nays on that motion. As the clerk was about to begin the call, the President's message was announced and received. A member called for the reading of the message. I said I hoped the question upon my resolution would be taken. The clerk called the roll, and the motion to lay on the table was rejected — 81 to 104. The question was then put on the resolution; and it was carried — 108 to 80. Blessed, forever blessed, be the name of God! [1]

February 27, 1845. — The Senate this evening, by a vote of 27 to 25, adopted the resolutions of the House of Representatives for admitting Texas as a state into this Union, with two additional resolutions giving the President an alternative as to the manner of consummating this transaction. This addition was proposed by Robert J. Walker, Senator from Mississippi, and is in substance the plan of Thomas H. Benton. It is a signal triumph of the slave representation in the constitution of the United States.

[1] The majorities which upheld the gag rule had been steadily declining. In 1842 the slaveholders' margin was only four votes; in 1843, it was only three. Now at last the victory was won. Adams conquered in his fight by the splendid margin of twenty-eight votes, and might well rejoice that his last great goal had been so triumphantly attained. In the very next week anti-slavery petitions were received and referred to the Committee on the District of Columbia.

Feb. 28. — The day passes, and leaves scarcely a distinct trace upon the memory of anything, and precisely because, among numberless other objects of comparative insignificance, the heaviest calamity that ever befell myself and my country was this day consummated. Immediately after the meeting of the House, the joint resolutions of the House for the admission of Texas as a State into this Union were returned from the Senate, with an amendment consisting of two additional resolutions. . . Then, after another struggle to go into committee of the whole on the state of the Union, which the majority inflexibly refused until the Texas resolutions were referred to that committee, they were referred, and after many fruitless efforts to delay their passage, were forced through without the allowance of any debate, and with stubborn rejection of every proposed amendment.

I took in this transaction no part save that of silent voting. I regard it as the apoplexy of the Constitution. The final vote of concurrence with the amendment of the Senate was 132 to 76.

March 4. — There was an unusual degree of pomposity paraded in the inauguration of James Knox Polk as President of the United States by the Democracy; but I witnessed nothing of it. . . There was a procession of ten or eleven military companies, who escorted Mr. Polk and Mr. Tyler, who rode together in an open carriage from Coleman's National Hotel to the Capitol. They first assembled in the Senate-chamber, where George Mifflin Dallas, as Vice-President, was qualified as president of the Senate, and whence they proceeded to a platform protruding from the portico at the top of the flight of stairs ascending the eastern front to the entrance of the rotunda. There Mr. Polk delivered his inaugural address, half an hour long, to a large assemblage of umbrellas, for it was raining hard all the time. The official oath was then administered to him by Chief Justice Taney, and the draggle-tail procession, thinned in numbers, escorted him back to the President's house.

March 13. — At the Patent Office, I applied to the Commissioner, Henry L. Ellsworth, for the ivory cane made from a single tooth, presented to me by Julius Pratt & Co. of Meriden, Conn., and which on the 23d of April last I deposited in the Patent Office. There is in the top of the cane a golden

eagle inlaid, bearing a scroll with the motto " Right of Petition Triumphant " engraved upon it. The donors requested
of me that when the gag-rule should be rescinded I would cause
the date to be added to this motto; which I promised to do,
if the event should happen in my lifetime. Mr. Ellsworth
sent the cane to my house. There is a gold ring immediately
below the pommel of the cane, thus engraved:

TO JOHN QUINCY ADAMS
JUSTUM ET TENACEM PROPOSITI VIRUM

I crave pardon for the vanity of this memorial.[2]

[2] Scattering and increasingly feeble entries continue the Diary, as we have it
in printed form, till November, 1846; and Adams served in the House till Feb.
21, 1848, when he was fatally stricken there. He was seated working at his desk,
when a neighboring member saw suddenly that he was in a state of convulsion;
and, removed to a committee room, he died on Feb. 23. This record may fittingly
terminate with his victory in rescinding the gag-rule.

INDEX

A

Abolition, petitions on, 427, 429, 430; agitation of, 462, 466; press, 493; petitions, 533 ff.

Adams, Abigail, death of, 202.

Adams, Brooks, ix.

Adams, Charles Francis, 113; 247, 248; 445; delivers oration, 551.

Adams, George, 360–362.

Adams, John, ix ff.; 1, 2; inaugurated President, 15; and the Revolution, 172; in Boston, 185, 186; 233; feebleness, 300, 301; death, 358, 359; funeral, 360 ff.

Adams, John Quincy, career of, ix ff.; as minister of Holland, 1–16; special envoy to Prussia, 16; elected Senator, 16, 17; service as Senator, 17–57; as professor of oratory at Harvard, 36; on British outrages, 40; installed as professor, 41, 42; and the *Chesapeake-Leopard* affair, 46; beaten for reëlection, 57; resigns, 57*n*; minister to Russia, 58, 59; sails for Russia, 60, 61; service in Russia, 63 ff.; household, 68; peace negotiations, 101 ff.; leaves Russia, 118, 119; reaches Ghent, 119; negotiations, 121–155; reaches Paris, 156; visit there, 157–163; in England, 163–183; appointed Secretary of State, 180; assumes duties, 186; defends Jackson, 198 ff.; on Missouri, 225 ff.; on slavery, 245–247; quarrel with Canning, 249–252; report on weights and measures, 254, 255; quarrel with De Neuville, 267, 268; on South America, 276, 277; clash with Monroe, 280; swims in Potomac, 297 ff.; on Greece, 300; and the Monroe Doctrine, 301 ff.; suggested for Vice-President, 316; ambition for Presidency, 322; routine, 327; attacks on, 328; Presidential prospects, 333 ff.; elected President, 341, 342; inaugurated, 343; as President, 343–391; defeated for reëlection, 387; attacks on, 388; leaves White House, 390; versification, 396; reading, 404; elected to Congress, 405, 406; begins Congressional service, 416; eulogy on Monroe, 421, 422; raises abolition question, 429; overtures from Jackson, 431, 432; railway accident, 443, 444; speaks on Lafayette, 455; begins petition struggle, 464; eulogy on Madison, 468–470; fight for petitions, 475–500; oration on Washington, 497, 498; struggle to organize House, 499 ff.; and quorum issue, 507 ff.; shoulder dislocated, 509; calls on Tyler, 522; renews battle on petitions, 533 ff.; tour to Buffalo, 551 ff.; tour to the West, 555 ff.; battle over gag-rule, 506 ff.; the fight won, 573 ff.; exhaustion, 568; death, 575.

Adams, Louisa Johnson, marriage, 16; silver wedding, 285, 286.

Adams, William, British peace commissioner, 122, 125 ff., 164.

Akron, O., 556.

Alexander I, Czar, Adams meets, 63–65, attentions of, 71; conversation with, 76, 77, 78, 79, 83, 87, 88, 89, 90; war with France, 92, 93; joins army, 102; in Ghent, 119, 120.

Alien and Sedition Acts, 470.

Ambrister, execution of, 221.

Amelia Island affair, 190 ff.

Amistad case, 516, 517, 519.

Antoine, swim with, 348, 349; leaves Adams, 392.

Arbuthnot, execution of, 197, 202, 221.

Armstrong, Minister to France, 41.

Ashburton, Lord, in Washington, 539–542.

Ashburton Treaty, 544, 546, 547.

Astor, J. J., and treaty of Ghent, 147; in New York, 184; on Gallatin, 242.

Astronomy, Adams on, 558, 559.

B

Bagot, Charles, British minister, 200 ff.; takes leave, 218.

Baltimore Convention, 509; in 1844, 569.

Bancroft, George, 512, 513.

Bank of the United States, 222.

Barbour, James, on slavery, 233; on the Presidency, 334; as Secretary of War, 344; on Indian affairs, 355; on Jefferson's poverty, 356.

Barbour, Philip, as Speaker, 271.

Baring, Alexander, 169.

Barnum's Hotel, 513.

Barron, Commodore James, in duel, 234, 235.

Bautzen, battle of, 107.

Bayard, James A., as Senator, 29; as peace commissioner, 107; in St. Petersburg, 108, 109; 111, 112; his unfriendliness, 113–115; 116; at Ghent, 120 ff.

Bell, John, 523, 527.

Bennett, James Gordon, 543.

Bentham, Jeremy, Adams dines with, 181.

Benton, Thomas Hart, 345, 365, 366, 386; mendacity of, 400; 460; 528, 573.

Bentzon, at Ghent, 147.

Berlin decree, 85.

Biddle, Nicholas, 217, 253, 424, 477; his ruin, 513.

Binns, John, 240, 241, 315.

Blair, James, suicide of, 450.

Bodisco, Count, 515, 540.

Bolivar, 335.

Bonaparte, Jerome, his marriage, 21, 22.

Boyd, George, 137.

Boylston, Nicholas, professorship of oratory, 36.

Bryant, William Cullen, 423.

Buckingham, J. T., 550.

Buffalo, N. Y., 552.

Bulfinch, Charles, 347.

Bunker's Hill celebration, 438; in 1843, 550, 551.

Burr, Aaron, as Vice-President, 20; duel with Hamilton, 24; in Chase trial, 32; takes leave of Senate, 34; in Paris, 69, 70; life of, 487 ff.

Burwell, W. A., 254.

Butler, Anthony, 548.

Byron, Lord, Adams on, 407.

C

Calhoun, John C., 46; as Secretary of War, 188, 189; character, 191; condemns Jackson, 199 ff.; offered mission to France, 208, 209; on slavery question, 228 ff., 231 ff.; on the future of the Union, 241, 242; on Missouri, 245; on political outlook, 258, 259; fairness of, 265; altercation with De Neuville, 272; and the Presidency, 275, 281, 282; relations with Adams, 285, 286; on Cuba, 289; on Monroe Doctrine, 301 ff.; 304; as Vice-President, 352; quarrel with Van Buren, 393, 402; quarrel with Jackson, 409 ff.; calls on Adams, 416; resigns Vice-Presidency, 434; on nullification, 437; his patronage bill, 457; clash with Clay, 494; reconciled with Van Buren, 503; 528; high-priest of slavery, 544.

Canada, security of, 130 ff.; cession of, 138 ff.

Canning, George, 170; Adams meets, 175; and Monroe Doctrine, 301 ff., 303 ff.; ruin of, 407, 408.

Canning, Stratford, as Minister from England, 244; Adams quarrels with, 249–252; on slave trade, 270 ff.; 296; character, 296, 297.

Carroll, Charles, 233, 331, 341.

Cass, Lewis, 375, 545; and Ashburton Treaty, 546, 547.

Castlereagh, Lord, 112, 116, 144n.; Adams dines with, 163, 164; 165, 166; interviews with, 177 ff., 182.

Cathcart, Lord, 98.

Caucus, Presidential, in 1808, 51, 52; in 1820, 238 ff.; in 1824, 314; history of, 511, 512.

Channing, Ellery, 498.

Chase, Samuel, impeachment of, 26–33; Adams reviews trial, 35, 36; character of, 247.

Chateaubriand, his works, 88.
Chauncey, Isaac, 505.
Cherokee Indians, 313, 318, 319, 346, 370, 526.
Chesapeake-Leopard outrage, 46.
Chesapeake and Ohio Canal, 381, 452.
Chesapeake, capture of, 110.
Cheves, Langdon, 219.
Choate, Rufus, 450, 531; offers aid, 535.
Cincinnati., O., 557 ff.
Clay, Henry, as peace commissioner, 116; reaches Ghent, 120; in deliberations, 121 ff.; objects to Adams draft, 129; at cards, 133 ff.; and American reverses, 139; quarrels with Adams, 141 ff.; dispute over papers, 152, 153–155; in Paris, 156; in London, 164; signing of treaty, 167, 168; and Walter Scott, 172; on South America, 190; ambitions of, 194; opposition to Monroe, 207 ff.; and Florida treaty, 216; at Monroe's table, 223; his desperate affairs, 237, 238; resigns, 239, 240; on South America, 253 ff.; claims, 261, 262; character, 263; South American recognition, 276, 277; on Ghent negotiations, 286; receives Lafayette, 332; Presidential chance lost, 333; relations with Adams, 334, 336; becomes Secretary of State, 344; domestic losses, 352; and the Vice-Presidency, 369, 370; on the state of the country, 386; leaves Washington, 392; and the tariff, 428 ff.; Jackson defeats for Presidency, 435; tour of the North, 443; attacks Jackson, 445, 446; congratulates Van Buren, 492, 493; clash with Calhoun, 494; Harrison defeats, 503; 512, 515; 528; and Texas, 547 ff., 560.
Cleveland, O., 556.
Clinton, DeWitt, 20, 185, 193; his career, 219; desire for Presidency, 256, 257.
Clinton, George, as Vice-President, 36, 44; renominated, 52; burial, 248.
Colonization Society, activities of, 208.
Columbus, O., 557.
Congress of Vienna, 144n.
Constant, Benjamin, 157.
Constitution, frigate, 106.
Constitutional Convention, 203.

Conventions, party, 512, 569, 570.
Cook, D. P., 365, 366.
Copley, John S., 6, 7.
Crabbe's Poems, 115, 116.
Crawford, W. H., as Minister to France, 109, 156; as Secretary of the Treasury, 187, 188; jealousy of Adams, 193; Adams's contacts with, 204 ff.; his talents, 214, 215; ambitions, 239, 240; intrigues, 256, 257; 259; 266, 267; 275, 276; newspaper support, 287, 288; on South America, 293; illness of, 304, 310; bad health, 316; and Ninian Edwards, 321; paralysis, 324; convalescence, 326, 327; in Cabinet, 331 ff.; Presidential prospects, 333 ff.; defeated, 342; clash with Monroe; 353, 354; feud with Calhoun, 409, 410.
Crittenden, J. J., 529, 560.
Crockett, David, 444.
Cuba, annexation discussed, 289; 295; 302.
Cushing, Caleb, on the Bank, 448; on Texas, 474 ff.; 512, 536; and slavery, 546.

D

Dallas, George M., 290, 313; as Vice-President, 574.
Dana, R. H., 423.
Davis, M. L., 487–489.
Decatur, Stephen, killed in duel, 234, 235.
Detroit, capture of, 100.
Dew, Thomas R., 442.
Dickens, Charles, visits Washington, 538, 539.
Douglas, Stephen A., 566.
"Downing, Major Jack," 445.
Dresden, Napoleon at, 104; battle of, 111.
Duane, William, supports Madison, 54; his demands, 224, 225; 240, 241.
Duane, William J., 442.
Dumouriez, Gen. Charles, 168.

E

Eaton, John H., 418.
Eaton, Peggy, affair of, 398–400; 402.

Edwards, Senator Ninian, on Jackson, 217; on Clay, 241; on Crawford, 275, 276; attack on, 321, 325; as Governor of Illinois, 386.

Ellsworth, H. L., 574.

Embargo, the, 49 ff., 51, 57.

Emerson, R. W., 511.

Empress-mother of Russia, 65, 66.

Enghien, Duc d', 73.

Erskine, Lord, 45, 48, 170, 175, 176.

Erving, G. W., Minister to Spain, 194, 202, 212 ff.

Everett, Alexander H., 441.

Everett, Edward, 226, 227, 326, 363, 367, 421, 425; on Lafayette, 454; oratory, 467; 529.

Exmouth, Lord, at Algiers, 176.

F

Fauchet, French minister, 3; and Edmund Randolph, 11, 12.

Fillmore, Millard, 515, 524; welcomes Adams, 552.

Fisheries, in Treaty of Ghent, 148 ff.

Florida, war in, 196 ff., 202, 210 ff.; acquisition of, 216; Clay on, 237, 238; ratified, 254; reviewed, 255, 256; possession taken, 264, 265; 527.

Floyd, William, 233.

Foote, S. A., on public lands, 400.

Force, Peter, 352, 484.

Forsyth, Secretary, 483, 548.

Fouché, 161.

Fox, Charles James, 8.

Franklin, Benjamin, and the Revolution, 172.

Franklin, William Temple, 173, 203.

French claims, 456.

Fuller, Timothy, 273.

G

Gag-rule, 465 ff.; destroyed, 575; see Petition.

Gales, Joseph, 218, 313, 509, 572.

Gales and Seaton, 292, 479, 525.

Galitzin, Princess Woldemar, 72, 117.

Gallatin, Albert, appointed peace commissioner, 107; in St. Petersburg, 108, 109; 111, 112; 116; reaches Ghent, 120; part in negotiations, 124 ff.; good-nature, 135; in London, 164; quarrel over treaty form,

167, 168; minister to France, 242, 243; on aid to Greeks, 300 ff.; diplomatic work, 369, 372; Clay on, 378; on Jackson, 398.

Gambier, Lord, as British peace commissioner, 122 ff.; in Boston, 125; dinner with, 140.

Genet affair, 2, 9.

George III, Adams's interview with, 12; madness of, 233.

George IV, Adams sees (Prince Regent), 165; opens Parliament, 179 ff.; character of, 181, 182.

Georgia, and the Cherokees, 318, 319, 346, 526.

Gerry, Elbridge, 248.

Gerry, Elbridge, Jr., 399.

Ghent, 107n; American commissioners reach, 119, 120; negotiations at, 121–150; peace signed, 150, 151.

Giddings, Joshua, 539, 563.

Giles, James Branch, and the Chase impeachment, 26 ff.; on Georgia land claims, 30.

Gilmer, Thomas W., angry at Monroe, 531; 533 ff., 536 ff., 561; death, 566.

Girard, Stephen, his will, 565.

Goulburn, Henry, as British peace commissioner, 122 ff.; in London, 164.

Gouverneur, Samuel, 540.

Granger, Francis, 449, 450, 531, 554.

Great Britain, war with, 101 ff.; peace negotiations with, 120 ff.

Greek Rebellion, and American policy, 300 ff.; 323.

Green, Duff, 383, 414, 434, 450.

Guerrière, capture of, 100.

H

Hackett, James H., 499 ff.

Halleck, Fitz-Greene, 423.

Hamburg, capture of, 105, 107.

Hamilton, Alexander, political views, 477, 478.

Hammond, George, 3; Adams's conversations with, 10, 11.

Harris, chargé at St. Petersburg, 63, 65, 71, 100, 104; and Bayard, 113–115.

Harrison, W. H., 376, 464; nomination of, 503; campaign, 509; 512 ff.; election, 514; 515; inauguration, 518 ff.; death, 520; funeral, 521, 522; body removed, 526.

Harper, Robert Goodloe, 30.

Harvard College, Adams urged for presidency of, 23; Adams professor of oratory in, 36.

Hayne, Robert Y., 301; debate with Webster, 401; 529.

Henry, Patrick, 318, 469.

Henry IV, 116.

Hill, Isaac, 455.

Hobbes, John, 458.

Holland, Lord, Adams dines with, 171, 172.

Holy Alliance, 299, 300; and Monroe Doctrine, 301 ff.; menace of, 311 ff.; 326.

Hopkinson, Joseph, 256–258, 322, 330, 513.

Houston, Samuel, 488, 548 ff.

Howard, John E., 331.

Hull, Commodore Isaac, 374.

Hull, General William, surrender of, 100.

Hunter, R. M. T., chosen Speaker, 501.

Hutchinson, Gov. Thomas, 363.

I

Illinois, default of, 546.

Indian affairs, see Cherokees; 355.

Indian question, in Treaty of Ghent, 126 ff., 142, 143.

Ingersoll, C. J., 253, 564.

Internal improvements, Monroe on, 206, 207.

Ireland, William Henry, his Shakespearean forgeries, 8, 9.

J

Jackson, Andrew, IX; and Monroe, 195; in Florida, 196–198; Adams defends, 199 ff., 202 ff.; agitation against, 210; Crawford attacks, 212; in Washington, 212 ff.; Adams again defends, 274, 294, 295; at ball, 313, 314; dinner with, 317; his Presidential prospects, 320, 321; 323, 329; Presidential chances, 333 ff.; defeated, 342; enmity to Adams, 370, 374; movement for, 384; his campaigning, 385; elected President, 387; in Washington, 389 ff.; inauguration, 391; ignores Adams, 394, 395; his appointments, 393–400; and the Union toast, 403, 404; overtures to Adams, 431, 432;

reëlection, 435; reception in Boston, 439 ff.; attempt at assassination, 456; political character, 471, 472; last message, 473, 474; duplicity, 488; work reviewed, 514; and Texas, 548 ff.; and the fine bill, 564.

Jackson, William, 202, 203, 222.

Java, capture of frigate, 106.

Jay, John, Adams confers with, 5, 6, 7; on the Mississippi, 480.

Jefferson, Thomas, ix; and Ledyard, 15, 16; Adams dines with, 19, 24, 25, 28; and the Chase impeachment, 28; on French privateering, 37; dinner with, 38; on non-importation, 40; dinner with, 46, 47; on Andrew Jackson, 195, 233; on Cuba, 289; 324; attitude toward Adams, 346; financial difficulties, 356, 357; death, 358 ff.; his Memoirs, 408 ff., 411 ff.; on committees of correspondence, 453; letters of, 468 ff.

Johnson, Andrew, attacks Adams, 565.

Johnson, Cave, 562.

Johnson, Cost, 504, 516, 524.

Johnson, Joshua, 8, 16.

Johnson, R. M., 224, 225; 321, 322; as Vice-President, 502.

Jones, J. W., as Speaker, 573.

K

Kean, Charles, Adams sees, 180, 253.

Kemble, Charles, 438.

Kemble, Frances, 438.

Kemble, John Philip, 9.

Kendall, Amos, 376; appointed to office, 393; his power, 514.

Kennedy, John P., 538.

Kent, Chancellor James, 424.

King, Rufus, as Senator, 23; opposes Missouri Compromise, 225 ff., 229, 232.

Koutouz of, Prince, 100, 101; funeral, 108.

Kremer, George, as Jackson partisan, 339.

L

Lafayette, in Paris, 157–163; visit to America, 329 ff.; dinner to, 334, 335; visit to Monroe, 350, 351; death, 453; oration on, 455.

Lake of the Woods, as boundary mark, 150.
Lamb, Lady Caroline, 173.
Lawrence, Abbott, 482, 531.
Leary, Jerry, 507; death, 517.
Ledyard, John, his travels, 15, 16.
Lee, Henry, 358, 365.
Lee, R. H., 377.
Legaré, Hugh, 486, 491.
Leopard, outrage of, 46.
Liverpool, Lord, 144n, 175.
Livingston, Edward, 287; 353.
Livingston, Robert, 479, 480.
Logan, Dr., 39.
Loring, E. S., 532.
Louis Philippe, on Adams, 545.
Lovejoy, Elijah, 489.
Lowndes, William, 273.
Lundy, Benjamin, 414, 466, 482.
Lützen, battle of, 106.

M

Macomb, Gen. Alexander, 375, 376.
Macon, Nathaniel, as Speaker, 19.
Madison, Dolly, 486, 487, 498, 540.
Madison, James, 37; as farmer, 47; nominated for President, 52; as President, 58; and war on England, 96; and Adams, 346; eulogy on, 468–470.
Marie Antoinette, 1.
Marshall, John, 31, 227, 251; on Washington's papers, 401; health, 413; visit from, 430; death, 460 ff.
Marshall, Thomas F., 534 ff., 536 ff.
Martin, Luther, 30, 32.
Martineau, Harriet, 456, 498.
Mason, A. T., death in duel, 215.
Mason, Jeremiah, 322.
Massachusetts Historical Society, 46.
Matthews, Charles, 291.
McDuffie, George, duel of, 289, 290; on nullification, 434; 446.
McLane, Louis, 395.
McLean, John, 322, 328; treachery, 382, 383; 549.
Mexico, and the Holy Alliance, 311 ff.
Milan decree, 85.
Mississippi, navigation of, 141 ff., 145 ff.; fortification of, 264.
Missouri Compromise, 225 ff., 230 ff., 245–247.
Mitchel, Ormsby M., 557 ff.
Monroe, James, as Minister to England,

39; in Washington, 51; as Secretary of State, 116, 117; as President, 175, 178, 179; appoints Adams Secretary of State, 180; gives Adams directions, 186; as President, 216–341 *passim*; Adams dines with, 223; his difficulties, 223, 224; or Missouri question, 230 ff.; reëlection, 238, 249; indulgent temper, 243; second inauguration, 260; on South America, 276, 277; clash with Adams, 280; sudden illness, 299; on belligerent rights, 299, 300; and the Monroe Doctrine, 301 ff.; neutrality among Presidential candidates, 313, 314; his financial troubles, 319, 320; on Crawford, 338, 339; at Oakhill, 350, 351; clash with Crawford, 353, 354; declines South American mission, 364, 365; Adams visits, 419.
Monroe Doctrine, origin of, 301; development of idea, 302 ff.
Moose Island, in Treaty of Ghent, 128 ff., 148 ff.
Morris, Gouverneur, on French politics, 9, 10; in New York, 184.
Moscow, capture of, 99, 100.
Mott, James, 466.
Mott, Lucretia, 466.

N

Napoleon, Russian gossip on, 69 ff.; 73; and Russia, 82; invades Russia, 94, 95; in Moscow, 99, 100; retreat, 101 ff.; at Dresden, 104; defeat, 111, 112; return from Elba, 158 ff.
Native American agitation, 570.
Nesselrode, 94.
Neuville, Hyde de, French Minister, 198; his ball, 209, 210; and Florida, 216; and slave trade, 267, 268; fight with Canning, 272; threat by, 311.
New York, growth of, 460.
Noah, M. M., 244, 552.
Nullification, 403, 434, 437, 449.

O

O'Neal, Peggy, 398 ff.
Onis, the Spanish Minister, 192; 212 ff., 216, 254–256.
Orders in Council, 105; 170.
Oregon question, 542.
Otis, G. A., 234.

Otis, Harrison Gray, 17, 46, 55, 393.

P

Panama Congress, 345, 356.
Panic of 1837, 481.
Passamaquoddy Bay, 139.
Payne, John Howard, 543, 549.
Pearce, Dutee J., 458, 473.
Perceval, Spencer, 105.
Persico, Luigi, 347, 366, 381.
Petition, right of, 464 ff., 475 ff., 484 ff., 490 ff., 496 ff., 532; battle renewed, 533 ff., 560 ff.; the fight won, 573.
Pichegru, in Holland, 7, 8.
Pichon, M., French Minister, 22.
Pickens, Francis W., 485.
Pickering, Timothy, as Senator, 18 ff., 22.
Pinckney, Charles, 6.
Pinckney, H. L., 449; and the right of petition, 465 ff.
Pinkney, William, 225.
Pioming, Washington receives, 2.
Pitt, William, 112.
Plattsburg, capture of, 139.
Plumer, William, 227, 253, 254, 274, 393.
Poindexter, Senator, 458, 459.
Poinsett, Joel R., 76; Minister to Mexico, 344, 345, 403.
Pole, Mrs. Wellesley, 173, 174.
Polk, James K., 446; as Speaker, 473, 491; elected President, 572; inauguration, 574.
Porter, Peter B., as Secretary of War, 379 ff., 383 ff.; at Niagara, 522.
Preston, Senator William, 446.
Prince Regent, see George IV.
Princess Charlotte, marriage of, 170, 171.
Princeton, explosion on, 566.

Q

Quincy, residence at, 1 ff., 27.
Quincy, Josiah, 23, 46, 48, 439.
Quorum, question in House, 506, 507.

R

Randolph, Edmund, 1, 2; and the Fauchet scandal, 11, 12.
Randolph, John, 17; and the Chase impeachment, 26–33; as a speaker, 229; at Decatur's funeral, 235; 372; as Minister to Russia, 415, 416.
Randolph, T. J., 368, 369.
Red Jacket, 387.
Ritchie, Thomas, 297.
Roane, Spencer, 266.
Rochester, N. Y., 553, 554.
Romanzoff, Russian Chancellor, 64 ff.; interview with, 67; conference with, 84, 85; 90, 91; 98, 99; on Napoleon, 103, 104; 106; and peace with England, 107 ff.
Ross, John, 526.
Rush, Richard, 186, 187, 298, 301 ff., 336; Secretary of the Treasury, 344.
Russell, Jonathan, as peace commissioner, 116, 117; at Ghent, 119 ff.; in deliberations, 129; as Minister to Sweden, 220; attack on Adams, 277, 278; quarrel with, 279, 280; 286; 463.

S

Schlegel, August, 105, 106.
Scott, Walter, 172; his novels, 176.
Scott, Winfield, 218, 281; and Congress, 282; controversy with Gaines, 373, 374; difficulties with Adams, 379 ff., 386; Harrison defeats, 503; 540.
Seminole War, 196 ff., 202, 210 ff., 214.
Seward, W. H., 516, 554.
Shakespeare, Adams on, 424, 498 ff.
Siddons, Sarah, 6, 9.
Slave Trade, 177, 178; 267, 268; 270 ff.
Slavery question, 225 ff, 228 ff., 230 ff., 245–247; ferment on, 462; Adams's views, 477; and Christianity, 495; Hayne on, 529; and petitions, 533 ff.; and Calhoun, 544; 546; and petitions, 561 ff.
Smith, Gerrit, 477.
Smith, Gen. Samuel, 238.
Smithsonian Fund, 524.
Smolensk, 95; battle of, 97.
Southard, Samuel L., 316, 336, 343, 353, 354; on Jackson, 392.
South America, recognition of governments, 190, 253 ff., 276, 277, 283,

284, 293, 294; and the Monroe Doctrine, 302 ff.

South Carolina, 403.

Spain, see Florida; and the Holy Alliance, 309 ff.

Sparks, Jared, 271, 402.

Speculation, in 1820, 242.

Spencer, Ambrose, 340.

Staël, Mme. de, in Russia, 97, 98, 105, 106; in Paris, 157.

Stevens, Thaddeus, 464.

Stevenson, Andrew, as Speaker, 426; resigns, 452.

Sully's *Memoirs*, 115, 116.

T

Tariff, question of, 319, 427; Clay's system, 428 ff.; 435; passed, 436; debate, 528, 529.

Talleyrand, 2.

Tallmade, Nathaniel, 538.

Taney, Roger, 341, 442; as Chief Justice, 516, 574.

Taylor, J. W., 312, 314, 316; as Speaker, 353.

Taylor, John, 317, 324.

Tazewell, Senator Littleton W., 291, 292.

Telfair, Gov., 204.

Temperance, 527.

Texas, Jackson on, 474; question of, 495 ff., 532; reviewed, 547–549; Clay on, 560; the treaty rejected, 570; annexation of, 573, 574.

Thomas, Jesse B., 316.

Thompson, Smith, as Secretary of the Navy, 186 ff.

Tocqueville, Alexis De., 424.

Tolstoy, Count, 79.

Tompkins, D. D., 257, 314.

Torres, Manuel, 236, 276.

Tracy, A. H., 320.

Tracy, Uriah, 451.

Trumbull, John, 185, 201, 347.

Tucker, St. George, 453.

Turreau, General, 159.

Tuyl, Baron, 298; and Monroe Doctrine, 306; 342.

Tyler, John, becomes President, 520, 521; Adams calls on, 522; distrust of, 523; 528; dinner with, 527; Cabinet troubles, 529–531; 532, 540, 541, 549; at Bunker Hill, 550;

551; 556, 567; marriage of, 571, 572.

Tyler, John jr., 543.

Tyler, Robert, 543.

U

Upshur, Abel P., death of, 566.

V

Van Buren, Martin, 340; on Panama Congress, 356; a Jackson partisan, 385; quarrel with Calhoun, 393; visits Adams, 394, 395; Adams on, 395, 396; and Peggy Eaton affair, 400, 402; clash with Calhoun, 402 ff.; and journalism, 414; resignation, 418; becomes Vice-President, 436; visits Adams, 460; character of, 465; campaign of 1836, 472; elected, 474; visit to, 481, 483; message of, 490; grows fat, 501; reconciled with Calhoun, 503; defeat, 511, 514; Presidential prospects, 549.

Van Rensselaer, Solomon, 324, 337, 340.

Van Rensselaer, Stephen, 340, 342.

Vaughan, William, 6, 8.

W

Walker, Robert J., 573.

Walpole, Horace, 292, 293.

Walpole, Lord Spencer, 112, 117.

Washington, Bushrod, 31.

Washington, George, appoints Adams minister, 1; receives Indians, 2, 3; letters, 365; remains of, 431; oration, 497, 498.

Waterloo, battle of, 166.

Watts, Isaac, on education, 93.

Webster, Daniel, on the tariff, 319; and the Presidency, 322; 325; 338; visits Adams, 339; 341; 361; eulogy on Adams and Jefferson, 363; on Plumer, 393; reply to Hayne, 401; on tariff, 428; 457; eloquence of, 459, 460; attacks Adams, 476; return from England, 504; 512; and Tyler, 529 ff.; ingratitude, 531; at Marshfield, 543; and Ashburton Treaty, 546, 547; at Bunker Hill, 550, 551; on Whig defeat, 572.

Webster, Fletcher, 542, 543.

Weights and measures, report on, 254, 255.

Wellington, Duke of, 166; at dinner, 173-175; calls on Adams, 180; 296; later career, 408.

Wentworth, John, 568.

West Point Military Academy, 293.

Whig National Convention, 509, 569.

White, John, as Speaker, 524.

Whittier, John G., 478, 504.

Wilberforce, William, 168.

Wilkes, Lieut. Charles, 541.

Wilkinson, Gen. James, 51.

Williams, David, 407.

Willis, N. P., 423.

Winthrop, R. C., 529, 531, 538, 566, 568.

Wirt, William, as Attorney-General, 188, 196; Adams's contacts with, 204 ff.; on the Holy Alliance, 309 ff.; 344; and private practise, 378; death, 447; life of Henry, 469.

Wise, Henry A., 491, 496, 500; characterized, 516; 524, 525, 531; and petitions, 533 ff.; canes Stanly, 540.

Wittgenstein, Count, 101.

Wolcott, Oliver, as Senator, 23.

Wright, Fanny, 330.

Wright, Silas, 509.

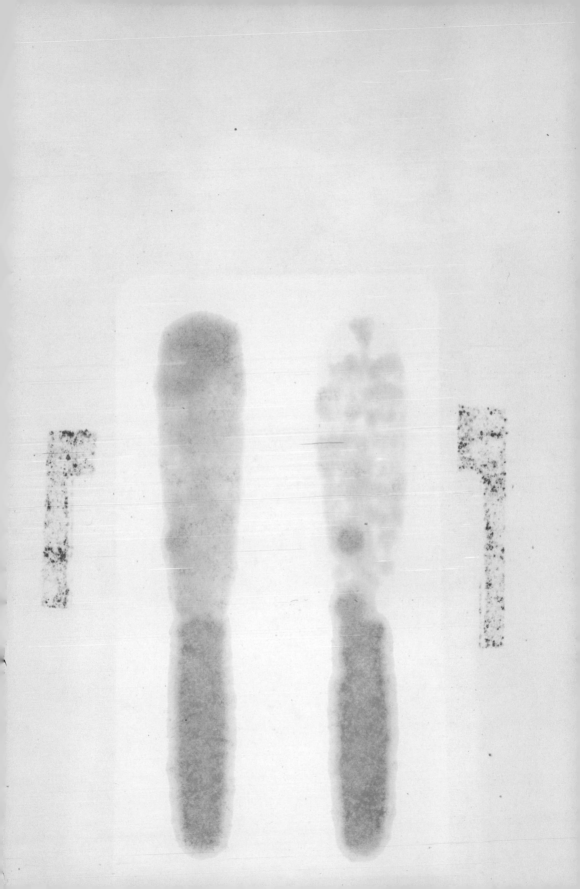

DATE DUE	